PRESENT DAY
POLITICAL ORGANIZATION
OF CHINA

BY

H. S. Brunnert and V. V. Hagelstrom

STUDENT-INTERPRETERS OF THE
IMPERIAL RUSSIAN LEGATION, PEIPING

REVISED BY

N. Th. KOLESSOFF

CHINESE SECRETARY OF THE
IMPERIAL RUSSIAN LEGATION, PEIPING

TRANSLATED FROM THE RUSSIAN
WITH THE AUTHORS' SANCTION

BY

A. BELTCHENKO

H.I.R.M. CONSUL AT FOOCHOW; AND

E. E. MORAN, Ph. B. (YALE)

OF THE CHIN. E IMPERIAL MARITIME CUSTOMS SERVICE

First published 1912

Transferred to digital printing 2007
by Routledge
2 Park Square, Milton Park, Abingdon, Oxon OX14 4RN

Simultaneously published in the USA and Canada
by Routledge

711 Third Avenue, New York, NY 10017

© H.S. Brunnert and V.V. Hagelstrom

Routledge is an imprint of the Taylor and Francis group an informa business

First issued in paperback 2013

Publisher's Note

The publisher has gone to great lengths to ensure
the quality of this reprint but points out that some
imperfections in the original may be apparent

ISBN 13:978-0-700-71469-8 (hbk)
ISBN 13:978-0-415-84950-0 (pbk)

TRANSLATORS' NOTE.

Since the issue of the original edition of the "Present Day Political Organization of China," in May, 1910, numerous and varied changes have been effected in China's government system. Many establishments and posts have been abolished, such as the Grand Secretariat and the Ministry of Civil Appointments ; others have been re-organized, while some have been newly-instituted, for instance, the Cabinet and the Privy Council.

These changes and modifications, thanks to the untiring energy of Messrs. Brunnert and Hagelstrom, the joint-authors of the "Present Day Political Organization of China," have been incorporated in the text of this translation or are separately treated in the Supplement.

The translators tender their heartiest thanks to Mr. H. S. Brunnert, who kindly checked the translation with the original text, and to Mr. E. T. C. Werner, H. B. M. Consul at Foochow, for his kindly interest in re-reading the manuscript.

A. BELTCHENKO.

E. MORAN.

Foochow, 15th August, 1911.

PREFACE

" The activity for reform in China has of late become so intense that it has affected various branches of the Government, and the old organization of the State—an inheritance of grey antiquity—is gradually making way for another, based, for the most part, on principles brought to China from other countries.

" An Imperial Edict stated that it was necessary for China to become a Constitutional State and, conforming to this, there began a radical demolition of existing institutions or their adjustment to a new government organization. The system of competitive examinations for literary degrees, held periodically, existing long since, was abolished, and the Government is now occupied in the organization of a net of schools, where the younger generation may study sciences as in Europe, America and Japan.

" There is being gradually introduced the principle of separation of judicial and administrative authorities and throughout the whole of China new judicial establishments are making their appearance, organized on the European model.

" The Police have been organized on new lines and the prisons reformed.

" With the object of strengthening the national power there is being carried out a scheme for the organization of an army, and measures are being taken to re-create a navy.

" The Bannermen, up to now a favoured class, are being gradually placed on an equal footing with the mass of the population and are, bit by bit, losing the privileges obtained three centuries ago.

" In the various towns and villages the Government is striving by every means to inculcate the principles of local self-government.

"The population is acquainted with the principles of representative government and an assembly of the people has been called, in the beginning to be a deliberative organization, for the discussion of government affairs.

"The whole country watches with strained attention the activity of the Government in its efforts for the enlargement and improvement of means of communication, the fostering of industry and commerce, the reinforcement of the colonization on the borders, and, finally, its measures looking towards the placing of the control of the finances of the Empire in the hands of one responsible establishment—the Ministry of Finance.

"In connection with general reforms the Government is materializing a practice of centralization of power and abolition of that abnormal phenomenon, historically formed, by which the highest provincial official was its full and irresponsible master and ruler, to the Central Government appertaining a general supervision and the right of appointment of provincial officials only. At the same time there is observed on the part of the Chinese Government a policy of entire re-organization of the government of the dependencies, looking towards their gradual conversion into actual provinces of China.

"Although all the proposed reforms are, so far, not completed, nevertheless, the achievement in this direction has greatly altered the political organization of the country. Many institutions have been entirely abolished, others have been re-organized on new lines, while some have just been called into existence.

"For everyone interested in the life of China, and following attentively all the reforms in progress, it is, of course, very interesting and important to know, at least in general, the internal organization of the old, the reformed, and the newly-organized institutions.

"Until lately there was no dearth of works in European languages furnishing copious information in this direction.

"Every student of Chinese is acquainted, of course, with the well-known work of W. F. Mayers, "The Chinese Government," a work enjoying a well-deserved reputation in the sinological world and, as a classic, unique in its genre, which, notwithstanding its small size, gives in a very concise form a mass of information and acquaints the reader with the government organization of China as it existed, with no substantial changes, for a long period.

"A good sequel to the work of W. F. Mayers is "Melanges sur l'Administration," by P. Hoang (from series "Varietés Sinologiques,") which, though not a systematic exposition, gives much information concerning the political organization of China, gathered from Chinese sources chiefly.

"It is to be regretted that both works mentioned above, edited, the first in 1896 (3rd edition) and the second in 1902, are now largely obsolete and hence their use by persons unable to follow the reforms in China presents great inconvenience.

"The Trade and Administration of the Chinese Empire," by H. B. Morse, issued in 1908, a masterpiece in all other respects, where the present government organization of China is treated, does nothing, we regret to say, but disseminate the information already compiled by W. F. Mayers, presenting nothing new in the literature on this subject.

"The articles "Pekinger Zentralregierung," by Dr. Hauer, and " Die Provianzial behörden," by Dr. Betz, in " Mittheilungen des Seminars für Orientalische Sprachen an der Königlichen Friedrich-Wilhelms-Universität zu Berlin, Jahrgang XII," are, so far as we are aware, the first and only attempts to draw a general picture of the administrative organization of China from the latest sources of information.

"In Russia our venerable and respected sinologue, Professor P. S. Popoff. following attentively all movements in China, did not permit that part of which we are speaking to escape him and in his work "Government Organization of China and Branches of Administration," St. Petersburg, 1903, Supplement, St. Petersburg, 1909, in a compact form but, nevertheless, of sufficient fullness, the ordinary reader (the book was chiefly intended for the use of the students of the Professor—students of 廿 Oriental Languages Section of the St. Petersburg University) is made acquainted with the government organization, as well as with the latest reforms affecting it.

"On the one hand, the obsoleteness of some works, on the other, the insufficiency of the information supplied (for those who are constrained to a close acquaintance of the complicated mechanism of the government establishments of China), encouraged us to devote part of our leisure to the study, from Chinese sources, of the reforms undertaken by China during the past ten years.

"As a result of our labours we now present this book to the judgment of Russian students of Chinese, whose remarks as to mistakes, inexactitudes and imperfections in general will be gratefully received and, should a subsequent edition be needed, taken into consideration.

"Invaluable assistance was rendered us by Mr. N. Th. Kolessoff, Chinese Secretary of the Imperial Russian Legation, who not only placed at our disposal his numerous manuscripts but, also, undertook the heavy task of scrutinizing the text from beginning to end and corrected numerous errors therein, for which we express our sincere and grateful thanks.

"In conclusion we consider it our duty to express our gratitude to His Excellency J. J. Korostovetz, Imperial Russian Envoy Extra-ordinary and Minister Plenipotentiary, to whose keen interest and moral support the issue of this volume is greatly due."

H. BRUNNERT.
V. HAGELSTROM.

PEKING, 28th March, 1910.

TABLE OF CONTENTS.

TABLE OF CONTENTS.

TABLE OF CONTENTS.

TABLE OF CONTENTS.

[iv]

PART I.

THE EMPEROR AND THE IMPERIAL COURT

METROPOLITAN GOVERNMENT ESTABLISHMENTS
(MINISTRIES EXCEPTED)

THE
EMPEROR AND THE IMPERIAL COURT.

1. 皇帝 Huang² Ti⁴, The Emperor. Ordinary designation, 皇上 Huang² Shang⁴; 上 Shang¹. Title of respect, 天子 T'ien¹ Tzu³, the Son of Heaven. Popular appellation, 當今佛爺 Tang¹ Chin¹ Fo² Yeh², the Buddha of the present day. Also 主子 Chu³ Tzu², the Master, Lord; 聖主 Shêng¹ Chu³, the August Master, or Lord. In addresses, 萬歲爺 Wan⁴ Sui⁴ Yeh², Lord of Ten Thousand Years; 陛下 Pi⁴ Hsia⁴, Your Majesty (literally, beneath the footstool). The Emperor usually designates himself by the term 朕 Chên⁴, I, We.

1 to 1ᴀ

A symbol of the Emperor's dignity in China is a mythological animal, the Dragon. Therefore, everything appertaining to the Emperor is styled 龍 Lung², Dragon; for instance, 龍座 Lung² Tso⁴, the Emperor's (Dragon) Throne, etc.

Since 1644 the 大清朝 Ta⁴ Ch'ing¹ Ch'ao² or Manchu dynasty has reigned in China; the present Emperor, the tenth of this House, has reigned since the 22nd January, 1909. He is known from his reign as 宣統 Hsüan¹ T'ung³ and is the nephew of the late Emperor 光緒 Kuang¹ Hsü⁴. His real name, 溥儀 P'u³ I², ceased to exist for his subjects on the day he ascended the throne.

1ᴀ. 在毓慶宮行走 Tsai⁴ Yü⁴ Ch'ing⁴ Kung¹ Hsing² Tsou³. Performing duties at the Yü Ch'ing Palace (Palace of the Heir Apparent; *see* No. 104ᴀ). This expression refers to the instruction of the Emperor (授皇帝讀 Shou⁴ Huang² Ti⁴

1

Tu²), for which duty it is customary to appoint the most worthy and most learned officials of the Empire. Thus, as tutors of the late Emperor 光緒 Kuang Hsü there were appointed the late Assistant Grand Secretary 翁同龢 Wêng¹ T'ung²-ho² (deceased in 1904), and the late Grand Secretary 孫家鼐 Sun¹ Chia¹-nai⁴ (deceased in November, 1909).

The instruction of the reigning Emperor has been entrusted, by Edict of the Empress Dowager, 隆裕 Lung² Yü⁴, dated the 10th July, 1911, to the Chancellor of the National Academy, Grand Secretary 陸潤庠 Lu⁴ Jun⁴-hsiang², Vice-President (of a Ministry) 陳寶琛 Ch'ên¹ Pao³-ch'ên¹, and Deputy Lieutenant-General 伊克坦 I¹ K'o⁴-t'an³. The latter is specially entrusted with the instruction of the Emperor in the Manchu language and literature (國語清文 Kuo² Yü³ Ch'ing¹ Wên²).

2. 皇后 Huang² Hou⁴, The Empress. Literary designation, 中宮 Chung¹ Kung¹, the Central Palace (from her place of residence). Title of respect, 國母 Kuo² Mu³, Mother of the State.

When there are two Empresses they are distinguished by their places of residence ; one is styled 東宮 Tung¹ Kung¹, and the other 西宮 Hsi¹ Kung¹ (the Empress occupying the East Palace and the Empress occupying the West Palace).

3. 太上皇帝 T'ai⁴ Shang⁴ Huang² Ti⁴, the Father of the Emperor. Also 太上皇 T'ai⁴ Shang⁴ Huang². These titles are used only when the Emperor's father is alive during his son's reign.

4. 皇太后 Huang² T'ai⁴ Hou⁴, the Empress Dowager; the Empress of a deceased Emperor.

The Empress Consort of the late Emperor 光緒 Kuang¹ Hsü⁴ is now known, from her title of respect, as 隆裕 Lung² Yü⁴.

5. 太皇太后 T'ai⁴ Huang² T'ai⁴ Hou⁴, the Great Empress Dowager. This title was bestowed after the death of

the Emperor 光緒 Kuang¹ Hsü⁴, which took place on the 14th November, 1908, on the Empress 慈禧 Tzu² Hsi³, in order that she might be distinguished from the Empress of the preceding Emperor (*see* No. 4).

t
12

6. 皇貴妃 Huang² Kuei⁴ Fei¹, Imperial Concubine of the First Rank. A concubine of the second rank (*see* No. 7) may be advanced by imperial favour to this rank and, especially in the event of giving birth to a son, the Empress Consort having borne none, a concubine of the first rank may be raised to the position of Empress Consort.

7. 貴妃 Kuei⁴ Fei¹, Imperial Concubine of the Second Rank.

8. 妃 Fei⁴, Imperial Concubine of the Third Rank.

9. 嬪 Pin¹, Imperial Concubine of the Fourth Rank.

10. 貴人 Kuei⁴ Jên², Imperial Concubine of the Fifth Rank.

11. 答應 Ta² Ying² and 帝在 Ch'ang² Tsai⁴, Female Attendants of the Emperor. These may be elevated to the rank of concubine.

In addition there are 使女 Shih³ Nü³, Serving Women of the Imperial Family.

12. 太子 T'ai⁴ Tzu³ or 皇太子 Huang² T'ai⁴ Tzu³, the Heir Apparent. Also called 世子 Shih⁴ Tzu³, literary designation, 皇儲 Huang² Ch'u³, 儲君 Ch'u³ Chün¹, and 東宮 Tung¹ Kung¹.

Emperors of the reigning dynasty, presumably fearing the organisation of parties and intrigues for the succession, have not, as a rule, appointed the Heir Apparent during their lifetime. As a general rule the Heir Apparent must be of the generation following that of the Emperor. Exceptions to this may be noticed, however, as the Emperor 穆宗 Mu⁴ Tsung¹ (1862-

**18
to

16**

1875) and the Emperor 德宗 Tê² Tsung¹ (1875-1908) were of the same generation (of 載 Tsai³).

13. 皇子 Huang² Tzu³, Prince, Son of an Emperor (in conversation 阿格 A⁴ Ko⁴; further distinguished by 大 Ta⁴, great, eldest, and by numerals). This title is applied to the sons of an Emperor until such time as they receive princely rank, *i.e.* 親王 Ch'in¹ Wang², literary designation, 王邸 Wang² Ti³ or 邸 Ti³.

14. 公主 Kung¹ Chu³, Imperial Princess; Daughter of an Emperor. This is the general designation.

Princesses born to an Empress are called 固倫公主 Ku¹ Lun² Kung¹ Chu³ (from the Manchu word Gurun, the equivalent of the Chinese Kuo, meaning State); those born to Imperial Concubines are called 和碩公主 Ho² Shê⁴ Kung¹ Chu³ (from the Manchu word Hoshê, meaning appanage). Imperial Princesses retain these titles after marriage.

15. 額駙 Ê¹ Fu⁴, Husband of an Imperial Princess (in former dynasties the designation was 駙馬 Fu⁴ Ma³).

Conforming to the rank of the Imperial Princesses, their husbands are styled :—

1. 固倫額駙 Ku¹ Lun² Ê⁴ Fu⁴,
2. 和碩額駙 Ho² Shê⁴ Ê⁴ Fu⁴,
3. 多羅額駙 To¹ Lo² Ê⁴ Fu⁴,
4. 固山額駙 Ku¹ Shan¹ Ê⁴ Fu⁴,
5. 郡主額駙 Chün⁴ Chu³ Ê⁴ Fu⁴,
6. 縣主額駙 Hsien⁴ Chu³ Ê⁴ Fu⁴,
7. 郡君額駙 Chün⁴ Chün¹ Ê⁴ Fu⁴,
8. 縣君額駙 Hsien⁴ Chün¹ Ê⁴ Fu⁴, and
9. 鄉君額駙 Hsiang¹ Chün¹ Ê⁴ Fu⁴.

1o. 和碩親王 Ho² Shê⁴ Ch'in¹ Wang², Prince of the Blood of the first degree.

[4]

This title, as well as the eleven following, are conferred on Manchus and Mongols only, *i.e.* on kinsmen of the Imperial House.

17. 多羅郡王 To¹ Lo² Chün⁴ Wang², Prince of the Blood of the second degree.

18. 多羅貝勒 To¹ Lo² Pei¹ Lê⁴, Prince of the Blood of the third degree.

19. 固山貝子 Ku¹ Shan¹ Pei¹ Tzu³, Prince of the Blood of the fourth degree.

20. 奉恩鎭國公 Fêng⁴ Ên¹ Chên⁴ Kuo² Kung¹, Prince of the Blood of the fifth degree.

21. 奉恩輔國公 Fêng⁴ Ên¹ Fu³ Kuo² Kung¹, Prince of the Blood of the sixth degree.

22. 不入八分鎭國公 Pu⁴ Ju⁴ Pa⁴ Fên² Chên⁴ Kuo² Kung¹, Prince of the Blood of the seventh degree.

23. 不入八分輔國公 Pu⁴ Ju⁴ Pa⁴ Fên² Fu³ Kuo² Kung¹, Prince of the Blood of the eighth degree.

24. 鎭國將軍 Chên⁴ Kuo² Chiang¹ Chün¹, Noble of the Imperial lineage of the ninth rank. This title is of three classes, 等 Têng³.

25. 輔國將軍 Fu³ Kuo² Chiang¹ Chün¹, Noble of the Imperial lineage of the tenth rank. This title is of three classes, 等 Têng³.

26. 奉國將軍 Fêng⁴ Kuo² Chiang¹ Chün¹, Noble of the Imperial lineage of the eleventh rank. This title is of three classes, 等 Têng³.

27. 奉恩將軍 Fêng⁴ Ên¹ Chiang¹ Chün¹, Noble of the Imperial lineage of the twelfth rank.

27A. 公 Kung¹, Princes of the Blood of the fifth and sixth degree bear the titles 鎭國 Chên⁴ Kuo², Guarding the Dynasty (State), and 輔國 Fu³ Kuo², Assisting the Dynasty (State).

27B   The distinction 不入八分 Pu⁴ Ju⁴ Pa⁴ Fên² in the title of Princes of the Blood of the seventh and eighth degrees signifies that eight special privileges, allowed the Princes of the Blood of the first six degrees, are denied them.   These privileges are :—

1.   The wearing of a purple button,

2.   The wearing of the three-eyed peacock feather,

3.   The wearing of dragon embroidered plaques on official dress,

4.   The presence of red-painted spears at the entrances of their residences,

5.   The attachment of tassels at the breasts of their horses,

6.   The using of purple bridle reins,

7.   The using of a certain tea-pot (carried by a special servant when going abroad),

8.   The right to a small carpet of yellow or red colour for seating themselves.

將軍 Chiang¹ Chün¹, Nobles of the Imperial lineage, are distinguished in the several grades by the titles 鎭國 Chên⁴ Kuo², Guarding the Dynasty (State), 輔國 Fu² Kuo² Assisting the Dynasty (State) 奉國 Fêng⁴ Kuo², Serving the Dynasty (State), and 奉恩 Fêng⁴ Ên¹, By Imperial Favour.

The above-mentioned· titles (*see* Nos. 16 to 27) are transmitted in a descending scale.   For instance, a 貝勒 Pei¹ Lê⁴'s eldest son becomes a 貝子 Pei¹ Tzu³.

An exception to this rule appears, however, in those cases in which the titles are conferred 世襲罔替 Shih⁴ Hsi² Wang³ T'i⁴, with Right of Perpetual Inheritance (for instance, the eldest son of the Princes 醇 Ch'un², 恭 Kung¹ and 慶 Ch'ing⁴ succeeds to father's rank).

27B.   The following table shows the method in which Imperial titles of nobility are transmitted to following generations:

ORDER OF RANK.	ELDEST SON INHERITS RANK OF	YOUNGER SONS INHERIT RANK OF	SONS BY CONCUBINES INHERIT RANK OF	ADOPTED SONS INHERIT RANK OF
Prince of First Degree	Prince of First Degree	Prince of Seventh or Eighth Degree	Noble of Imperial lineage of 9th rank, 2nd class	Noble of Imperial lineage of 9th rank, 3rd class
Prince of Second Degree	Prince of Second Degree	Noble of Imperial lineage, 9th rank, 1st class	Noble of Imperial lineage of 9th rank, 3rd class	Noble of Imperial lineage of 11th rank, 3rd class
Prince of Third Degree	Prince of Fourth Degree	Noble of Imperial lineage, 9—2	Noble of Imperial lineage, 10—1	Noble of Imperial lineage, 12
Prince of Fourth Degree	Prince of Fifth Degree	Noble of Imperial lineage, 9—2	Noble of Imperial lineage, 10—2	Noble of Imperial lineage, 12
Prince of Fifth Degree	Prince of Sixth Degree	Noble of Imperial lineage, 10—1	Noble of Imperial lineage, 10—2	—
Prince of Sixth Degree	Prince of Seventh Degree	Noble of Imperial lineage, 10—2	Noble of Imperial lineage, 11—1	—
Prince of Seventh Degree	Prince of Eighth Degree	Noble of Imperial lineage, 10—3	—	—
Prince of Eighth Degree	Noble of Imperial lineage, 9—3	Noble of Imperial lineage, 10—3	—	—
Nobles of Imperial lineage, 9th rank, 1st, 2nd and 3rd classes	Nobles of Imperial lineage, 10—1 2 and 3	Nobles of Imperial lineage, 10—3	—	—
Nobles of Imperial lineage, 10th rank, 1st, 2nd and 3rd classes	Nobles of Imperial lineage, 11—1 2 and 3	Nobles of Imperial lineage, 11—3	—	—
Nobles of Imperial lineage, 11th rank, 1st, 2nd and 3rd classes	Nobles of Imperial lineage, 12	Nobles of Imperial lineage, 12	—	—
Nobles of Imperial lineage of 12th rank	Nobles of Imperial lineage, 12	Imperial Clansmen (wearing "yellow girdle")		—

Note.—By Imperial favour the rank of anyone of Princely origin may be raised above inherited rank.

[7]

28
to
37

28. 世子 Shih[4] Tzu[3], Son of a Prince of the Blood of the first degree (*see* No. 16). Designated thus until the title of Prince is attained. The colloquial designation is 阿格 A[4] Ko[4].

29. 長子 Chang[3] Tzu[3], Son of a Prince of the Blood of the second degree (*see* No. 17). Designated thus until the title of Prince is attained. The colloquial designation is 阿格 A[4] Ko[4].

30. 郡主 Chün[4] Chu[3], Daughter of a Prince of the Blood of the first degree (*see* No. 16).

31. 縣主 Hsien[4] Chu[3], Daughter of a Prince of the Blood of the second degree (*see* No. 17).

32. 郡君 Chün[4] Chün[1], Daughter of a Prince of the Blood of the third degree (*see* No. 18).

33. 縣君 Hsien[4] Chün[1], Daughter of a Prince of the Blood of the fourth degree (*see* No. 19).

34. 鄉君 Hsiang[1] Chün[1], Daughter of a Prince of the Blood of the fifth (or sixth) degree (*see* Nos. 20 to 22).

35. 格格 Ko[4] Ko[4], thus are designated, in colloquial usage, the daughters of Princes of the Blood of the first six degrees (*see* Nos. 30 to 34). They are further distinguished as follows :

和碩格格 Ho[2] Shê[4] Ko[4] Ko[4], Daughter of a Prince of the Blood of the first degree,

多羅格格 To[1] Lo[2] Ko[4] Ko[4], Daughter of a Prince of the Blood of the second (or third) degree, and

固山格格 Ku[1] Shan[1] Ko[4] Ko[4], Daughter of a Prince of the Blood of the fourth degree.

35A. 宗女 Tsung[1] Nü[3], Daughter of a Prince of the Blood of lower rank (below the sixth).

36. 福晉 Fu[2] Chin[4], Princess Consort of a Prince of the Blood of the first (or second) degree.

37. 側福晉 Ts'ê[4] Fu[2] Chin[4], Concubine of a Prince of the Blood of the first (or second) degree.

[8]

38. 夫人 Fu[1] Jên[2], Princess Consort of a Prince of the Blood of the third (or fourth) degree.

39. 宗室 Tsung[1] Shih[4], Imperial Clansmen. (Also called 黃帶子 Huang[2] Tai[4] Tzu[3], wearing a yellow girdle). They are the descendants of the acknowledged founder of the reigning Manchu dynasty, 顯祖 Hsien[3] Tsu,[3] A.D. 1583-1615.

40. 覺羅 Chio[1] (Chüeh[1]) Lo[2], Collateral relatives of the Imperial House. Also called 紅帶子 Hung[2] Tai[4] Tzu[3] (wearing a red girdle). They are the descendants from the collateral line of the Emperor Hsien Tsu (*see* No. 39).

41. 鐵帽子王 T'ieh[3] Mao[4] Tzu[3] Wang[2], The Iron-capped Princes or Princes of the Iron Cap (Crown) (also called 八大家 Pa[1] Ta[4] Chia,[1] Eight Great or Princely Houses). Thus are designated the descendants of certain of the supporters of the Manchu Emperors in their conquest of China. These Princes, by right of perpetual inheritance, are Princes of the first or second degree, as shown below :

1. 禮親王 Li[3] Ch'in[1] Wang[2], Li (family name), Prince of the first degree,

2. 睿親王 Jui[4] Ch'in[1] Wang[2], Jui (family name), Prince of the first degree,

3. 豫親王 Yü[4] Ch'in[1] Wang[2], Yü (family name), Prince of the first degree,

4. 肅親王 Su[4] Ch'in[1] Wang[2], Su (family name), Prince of the first degree,

5. 鄭親王 Chêng[1] Ch'in[1] Wang[2], Chêng (family name), Prince of the first degree,

6. 莊親王 Chuang[1] Ch'in[1] Wang[2], Chuang (family name), Prince of the first degree,

7. 順承郡王 Shun[4] Ch'êng[2] Chün[4] Wang[2], Shun Ch'êng (family name), Prince of the second degree,

8. 克勤郡王 K'o[4] Ch'in[2] Chün[4] Wang[2], K'o Ch'in (family name), Prince of the second degree.

41A
to
50

All the above Princes are descended in a direct line from the sons and grandsons of the Emperors 太祖 Tai⁴ Tzu³ and 太宗 Tai⁴ Tsung.[1]

41A. 怡親王 I² Ch'in¹ Wang², I (family name), Prince of the first degree. The holder of this title of perpetual inheritance is descended from the Prince of Hsien, thirteenth son of the Emperor 康熙 K'ang Hsi, A.D. 1662-1722.

ESTABLISHMENT (PALACE) OF PRINCES OF THE BLOOD.

42. 王府 Wang² Fu³, Establishments (palaces) of Princes of the Blood. The management of these establishments is vested in the following officials :

43. 長史 Chang³ Shih³, Commandant of a Prince's Palace ; 3A.*

44. 司儀長 Ssu¹ I² Chang³, Major-domo of a Prince's Palace ; 4A.

45. 護衛 Hu⁴ Wei⁴, Officers of a Prince's Bodyguard ; from 3B to 5B.

46. 典儀 Tien³ I², Assistant Major-domo of a Prince's Palace (*see* No. 44) ; from 4B to 8B.

47. 包衣 Pao¹ I¹, Bondservants (*see* No. 97 for details).

48. 包衣參領 Pao¹ I¹ Ts'an¹ Ling³, Chief Controller of Bondservants ; 3B.

49. 包衣佐領 Pao¹ I¹ Tso³ Ling³, Department Controller of Bondservants ; 4B.

EUNUCHS.

50. 總管太監銜宮殿監督領侍 Tsung³ Kuan³ T'ai⁴ Chien⁴ Hsien² Kung¹ Tien⁴ Chien⁴ Tu¹ Ling³ Shih⁴, Chief Eunuch.

* Here, and in pages following, the numeral and letter signify official grade (*see* No. 965).

51. 總管太監銜宮殿監正侍 Tsung³ Kuan³ T'ai⁴ Chien⁴ Hsien² Kung¹ Tien⁴ Chien⁴ Chêng⁴ Shih⁴, Senior Assistant Chief Eunuch.

52. 總管太監銜宮殿監副侍 Tsung³ Kuan³ T'ai⁴ Chien⁴ Hsien² Kung¹ Tien⁴ Chien⁴ Fu⁴ Shih⁴, Junior Assistant Chief Eunuch.

53. 首領太監銜執守侍 Shou³ Ling³ T'ai⁴ Chien⁴ Hsien² Chih² Shou³ Shih⁴, Chief of Office of Eunuch Affairs.

54. 首領太監銜侍監 Shou³ Ling³ T'ai⁴ Chien⁴ Hsien² Shih⁴ Chien⁴, Senior Assistant Chief of Office of Eunuch Affairs.

54A. 副首領太監銜侍監 Fu⁴ Shou³ Ling³ T'ai⁴ Chien⁴ Hsien² Shih⁴ Chien⁴, Junior Assistant Chief of Office of Eunuch Affairs.

55. 太監 T'ai⁴ Chien⁴, Eunuch (or 宦官 Huan⁴ Kuan¹, 璫 Tang¹, 中傅 Chung¹ Fu⁴; colloquially called 老公 Lao³ Kung¹; 閹割 Yen³ Ko¹).

THE IMPERIAL CLAN COURT.

56. 宗人府 Tsung¹ Jên² Fu³, The Imperial Clan Court. This department controls all affairs relating to the Imperial Kindred (*see* Nos. 39 and 40), has judicial and disciplinary authority over them, and preserves the Family Roll or Genealogical Record, 玉牒 Yü⁴ Tieh.²

57. 宗令 Tsung¹ Ling⁴ (literary designation, 宗卿 Tsung¹ Ch'ing¹), Presiding Controller of the Imperial Clan Court. This official is appointed from the ranks of the Senior Princes of the Blood.

58. 左宗正 Tso³ Tsung¹ Chêng⁴, Senior Assistant Controller of the Imperial Clan Court.

59. 右宗正 Yu⁴ Tsung¹ Chêng⁴, Junior Assistant Controller of the Imperial Clan Court.

60. 左宗人 Tso³ Tsung¹ Jên², Senior Director of the Imperial Clan Court.

[11]

61. 右宗人 Yu⁴ Tsung¹ Jên², Junior Director of the Imperial Clan Court.

61ᴀ. The positions aforementioned (*see* Nos. 58 to 61) are all filled by Princes of the Blood.

62. 府丞 Fu³ Ch'êng², Vice-directo of the Imperial Clan Court (appointed from the ranks of Chinese) ; 3ᴀ.

63. 經歷司 Ching¹ Li⁴ Ssu¹, Registry Office of the Imperial Clan Court. This office is supervised by :

64. Two 經歷 Ching¹ Li⁴, Registrars ;. 6ᴀ.

65. 左司 Tso³ Ssu¹, First Department.

66. 右司 Yu¹ Ssu¹, Second Department.

66ᴀ. Only Clansmen of the Imperial House (*see* No. 39) are eligible for office in the two departments mentioned above (*see* Nos. 65 and 66).

67. 理事官 Li³ Shih⁴ Kuan¹, Administrators ; 5ᴀ. There are two at the Registry Office (*see* No. 63), three in the First Department (*see* No. 65), one in the Second Department (*see* No. 66), and one at the Bullion Vaults (*see* No. 71).

68. 副理事官 Fu⁴ Li³ Shih⁴ Kuan¹, Assistant Administrators ; 5ʙ. There are two at the Registry Office (*see* No. 63), one in the First Department (*see* No. 65), and three in the Second Department (*see* No. 66).

69. 堂主事 T'ang² Chu³ Shih⁴, Senior Secretaries ; 6ᴀ. Four are stationed at the Registry Office (*see* No. 63), two of whom are Chinese.

69ᴀ. 主事 Chu³ Shih⁴, Secretaries ; 6ᴀ. There are two Secretaries in both the First and Second Departments (*see* Nos. 65 and 66) and one at the Bullion Vaults (*see* No. 71).

70. 筆帖式 Pi³ T'ieh³ Shih⁴, Clerks. The number of these officials to be employed at the Registry Office (*see* No. 63), in the First and Second Departments (*see* Nos. 65 and 66), and at the Bullion Vaults (*see* No. 71), is not fixed.

71. 銀庫 Yin² K'u⁴, Bullion Vaults.

[12]

72. 管理銀庫事務 -Kuan³ Li³ Yin² K'u⁴ Shih⁴ Wu⁴, 72 Treasurers-in-chief. Two of these officials are in charge of the to Bullion Vaults.

73. 空房 K'ung¹ Fang², Prison of the Imperial Clan Court (prison; lit. empty room).

74. 黃檔房 Huang² Tang⁴ Fang², Genealogical Record Office of the Imperial Clan Court (see No. 56).

THE IMPERIAL HOUSEHOLD.

75. 內務府 Nei⁴ Wu⁴ Fu³, The Imperial Household. his department serves numerous and varied needs of the nperial Court. Being in character more private than governmental, however, it is not included in the list of Ministries or " Boards."

76. 總管內務府大臣 Tsung³ Kuan³ Nei⁴ Wu⁴ Fu³ Ta⁴ Ch'ên², Ministers of the Household (their number is not fixed; at present there are four). To the Ministers of the Household are directly subordinated :

One 堂郎中 T'ang² Lang² Chung¹, Department Director (attached to the Ministers),

Two 堂主事 T'ang² Chu³ Shih⁴, Secretaries of the Ministers, and

Numerous 堂筆帖式 T'ang² Pi³ T'ieh³ Shih⁴, Clerks.

The establishment of the Imperial Household is divided into 7 departments (see below) and special bureaux and offices; the officials employed therein are as follows :

郎中 Lang² Chung¹, Department Directors (1 to 4; at the Bullion Vaults, although having the same rights as other Department Directors, they are called 總辦郎中 Tsung³ Pan⁴ Lang² Chung¹),

員外郎 Yüan² Wai⁴ Lang², Assistant Department Directors (from one to twelve),

[13]

主事 Chu³ Shih⁴, and 事主署委 Wei³ Shu⁴ Chu³ Shih⁴, Secretaries (from one to three), and

筆帖式 Pi³ T'ieh³ Shih⁴, Clerks (number not fixed).

Distinctive officials in the various departments, bureaux and offices of the Imperial Household will be treated later.

77. 廣儲司 Kuang³ Ch'u³ Ssu¹, Department of the Privy Purse (Iakhinf, in his "Description of Peking," No. 16, styles this department "Department of Supplies.")

This department supervises six storehouses or vaults, *i.e.*

1. 銀庫 Yin² K'u⁴, Bullion Vaults,
2. 皮庫 P'i² K'u⁴, Fur Store,
3. 磁庫 Tz'u² K'u⁴, Porcelain Store,
4. 緞庫 Tuan⁴ K'u⁴, Silk Store,
5. 衣庫 I¹ K'u⁴, Imperial Wardrobe, and
6. 茶庫 Ch'a² K'u⁴, Tea Store.

The administration of these stores is vested in four Department Directors, two of whom are designated 總管六庫事務 Tsung³ Kuan³ Liu⁴ K'u⁴ Shih⁴ Wu⁴, Superintendents of the Six Imperial Storehouses, and the others 兼攝六庫事務 Chien¹ Shê⁴ Liu⁴ K'u⁴ Shih⁴ Wu⁴, Assistant Superintendents of the Six Imperial Storehouses.

In addition to the officials mentioned in No. 76 there is, for each of the Imperial Storehouses, an Assistant Department Director, appointed from one of the Ministries ("Boards"), styled (taking the Bullion Vaults for an example) 兼攝銀庫事務 Chien¹ Shê⁴ Yin² K'u⁴ Shih⁴ Wu⁴, Assistant Superintendent of the Bullion Vaults. Further, there are 六品司庫 Liu⁴ P'in³ Ssu¹ K'u⁴, Controllers of the Sixth Class (one or two), 無品級司庫 Wu² P'in³ Chi⁴ Ssu¹ K'u⁴, Controllers of Unclassed Rank, 副司庫 Fu⁴ Ssu¹ K'u⁴, Assistant Controllers, 庫使 K'u⁴ Shih³, Inspectors, and 八品司匠 Pa¹ P'in³ Ssu¹ Chiang⁴, Overseers of the Eighth Class. Of the last mentioned there are two at the Bullion Vaults, Porcelain Store and Imperial Wardrobe.

[14]

78. 會計司 Hui⁴ Chi⁴ Ssu¹, Accounts Department. This department collects rent of Banner property.

78ᴀ. 三旗銀糧莊頭處 San¹ Ch'i² Yin² Liang² Chuang¹ T'ou² Ch'u⁴, Office for collecting rents of Imperial lands (lands given on lease to the three Household Banners, *see* No. 97).

79. 掌禮司 Chang³ Li³ Ssu¹, Department of Ceremonial (by Imperial edict of the 12th April, 1909, changed from 掌儀司 Chang³ I² Ssu¹). This department regulates sacrificial and ceremonial observances of the Court and has control over the Eunuchs (*see* Nos. 50 to 55).

Officials attached to the Department of Ceremonial, in addition to those mentioned in No. 76, are :

讀祝官 Tu² Chu⁴ Kuan¹, Readers of Prayers at Sacrifices,

贊禮郎 Tsan⁴ Li³ Lang², Heralds,

司俎官 Ssu¹ Tsu³ Kuan¹, Supervisors of Sacrificial Attributes,

司稅 Ssu¹ Shui⁴, Rent Collectors (for lands of the department),

司香 Ssu¹ Hsiang¹, Acolytes,

司碓 Ssu¹ Tui⁴, Supervisors of Preparation of Incense (supervise the powdering of bark used in the manufacture of incense), and

司爨 Ssu¹ Ts'uan⁴, Supervisors of Preparation of Eatables for Sacrifices.

Also included in the department are :—

79ᴀ. 果房 Kuo³ Fang², Fruit Office, which supplies the fruit used in sacrifices. Its staff comprises :

果房掌果 Kuo³ Fang² Chang³ Kuo³, Controllers of the Fruit Office, and

副掌果 Fu⁴ Chang³ Kuo³, Assistant Controllers of the Fruit Office.

79ʙ. 昇平署 Shêng¹ P'ing² Shu³. The Court Theatrical Bureau (or 南府 Nan² Fu³), which arranges theatricals in which

Eunuchs are the performers. It has at its head two Department Directors (or their Assistants), designated 兼理昇平署事務 Chien[1] Li[3] Shêng[1] P'ing[2] Shu[3] Shih[4] Wu[4], Chiefs of the Court Theatrical Bureau.

79ᴀ. 神房 Shên[2] Fang[2], Office of Shamanism. This is attached to the 坤寧宮 K'un[1] Ning[2] Kung[1], the Shamanic Chapel (*see* No. 104ᴀ), where Eunuchs or 薩嬤太太 Sa[1] Mo[2] T'ai[4] T'ai[4] (*idem* 薩摩太太 Sa[1] Mo[2] T'ai[4] T'ai[4] or 薩滿太太 Sa[1] Man[2] T'ai[4] T'ai[4]), Shamanic Priestesses, daily offer sacrifices to the spirits of the ancestors of the Emperors of the reigning dynasty (compare No. 573ʙ).

These Priestesses and Eunuchs are under the control of the Office of Shamanism.

80. 都虞司 Tu[1] Yu[2] Ssu[1], Department of the Household Guard and the Imperial Hunt. This department has charge of the Imperial hunts and of a staff of huntsmen, divided into three detachments.

In this department are found :

1. 狗房 Kou[3] Fang[2], The Imperial Kennels,

2. 鷹房 Ying[1] Fang[2], The Imperial Gerfalcon Aviary, and

3. 鶻房 Hu[4] Fang[2], The Imperial Hawk Aviary.

81. 愼刑司 Shên[4] Hsing[2] Ssu[1], Judicial Department. This department takes cognisance of all cases relating to members of the Imperial Clan Court and determines the punishment.

To the department there is attached the 番役處 Fan[1] I[4] Ch'u[4], Police Bureau, which has, amongst other duties, control of the Eunuchs of the Court.

The officials at the head of the Police Bureau (Department Directors, Assistant Department Directors or officials of lower rank) are styled 管轄番役 Kuan[3] Hsia[2] Fan[1] Yi[4], Controllers of the Police Bureau.

82. 營造司 Ying² Tsao⁴ Ssu¹, Department of Works. This department is responsible for the supplies of the Court and also for the repairing of streets, buildings and walls of the Forbidden City.

At the head of the department there is a 值年大臣 Chih² Nien² Ta⁴ Ch'ên², Chief of the Department of Works, to whom, in addition to those mentioned in No. 76, are subordinated

1. 掌庫 Chang³ K'u⁴, Storehouse Overseers,
2. 副掌庫 Fu⁴ Chang² K'u⁴, Assistant Storehouse Overseers,
3. 庫守 K'u⁴ Shou³, Storehouse Keepers,
4. 司匠 Ssu¹ Chiang⁴, Inspectors of Works, and
5. 委署司匠 Wei³ Shu⁴ Ssu¹ Chiang⁴, Assistant Inspectors of Works.

Under the Department of Works is the 官房租庫 Kuan¹ Fang² Tsu¹ K'u⁴, Office for Collecting Rent of Confiscated Property. The heads of this office (Department Director, Assistant Department Director, etc.) are designated 兼理官房租庫事務 Chien¹ Li³ Kuan¹ Fang² Tsu¹ K'u⁴ Shih⁴ Wu⁴, Superintendents of the Office for Collecting Rent of Confiscated Property.

83. 慶豐司 Ch'ing⁴ Fêng¹ Ssu¹, Pasturage Department, which manages the flocks and herds maintained for Palace use, both near the capital and in the provinces. At its head is a 值年大臣 Chih² Nien² Ta⁴ Ch'ên², Chief of the Pasturage Department.

84. 錢糧衙門 Ch'ien² Liang² Ya² Mên², Pay Office (pays the wages of the Household Banners).

85. 掌關防管理內管領事務處 Chang³ Kuan¹ Fang² Kuan³ Li³ Nei⁴ Kuan³ Ling³ Shih⁴ Wu⁴ Ch'u⁴, 關防事務處 Kuan¹ Fang² Shih⁴ Wu⁴ Ch'u⁴, or 掌關防處 Chang³ Kuan¹ Fang² Ch'u⁴, Chancery of the Imperial Household. At its head there is a Department Director, styled 掌關防事務 Chang³

2   [17]

**86
to
87A**

Kuan¹ Fang² Shih⁴ Wu⁴, Chancellor of the Imperial Household. In addition there are two Assistant Department Directors, called 協理關防事務 Hsieh² Li³ Kuan¹ Fang² Shih⁴ Wu⁴, Assistant Chancellors of the Imperial Household, thirty 內管領 Nei⁴ Kuan³ Ling³, Chancery Overseers, and thirty 副內管領 Fu⁴ Nei⁴ Kuan³ Ling³, Assistant Chancery Overseers (compare No. 104 D).

86. 造辨處 Tsao⁴ Pan⁴ Ch'u⁴, Workshops of the Imperial Household (Iakhinf, in his "Description of Peking," No. 14, styles these workshops the "Office of Arts and Crafts.") These workshops are attached to the 養心殿 Yang³ Hsin¹ Tien⁴ (*see* No. 104B).

At the head of the Workshops of the Imperial Household are Ministers of the Household, styled 管理造辨處事務 Kuan³ Li³ Tsao⁴ Pan⁴ Ch'u⁴ Shih⁴ Wu⁴, Superintendents of the Imperial Workshops. In addition, there are two Department Directors, two Assistant Department Directors, two Secretaries and numerous Clerks (*see* No. 76). Also, there are 六品庫掌 Liu⁴ P'in³ K'u⁴ Chang³, Overseers of the Sixth Class, and 八品催長 Pa¹ P'in³ Ts'ui¹ Chang³, Overseers of the Eighth Class (from five to seven of each).

87. 官學 Küan¹ Hsüeh², Schools of the Imperial Household (Government Schools); three in all.

87A. 咸安宮官學 Hsien² An¹ Kung¹ Kuan¹ Hsüeh², School at the Palace of Universal Peace; maintained for the children of the high officials of the eight Banners (compare Iakhinf's "Description of Peking," No. 14). In charge of this school are Ministers of the Household, styled 管理咸安宮官學事務 Kuan³ Li³ Hsien² An¹ Kung¹ Kuan¹ Hsüeh² Shih⁴ Wu⁴, Curators of the School at the Palace of Universal Peace. To these are subordinated Department Directors, called 總管官學事務 Tsung³ Kuan³ Kuan¹ Hsüeh² Shih⁴ Wu⁴, Superintendents of Government (Imperial Household) Schools.

[18]

87B. 景山官學 Ching³ Shan¹ Kuan¹ Hsüeh², School at the Red Hill (close to 景 山 Ching³ Shan¹, Red Hill—or 煤山 Mei² Shan¹, Coal Hill). This school is for the children of the three Superior Banners. For its administration *see* No. 87A.

87C. 南府官學 Nan² Fu³ Kuan¹ Hsüeh², Court Theatrical School (attached to the Court Theatrical Office; *see* No. 79B). This school prepares actors for the Court Theatre. For its administration *see* No. 87A.

88. 上駟院 Shang⁴ Ssu⁴ Yüan⁴, The Palace Stud. At its head is a Minister of the Household, styled 管理上駟院事務 Kuan³ Li³ Shang⁴ Ssu⁴ Yüan⁴ Shih¹ Wu⁴, Superintendent of the Palace Stud, and two 上駟院卿 Shang⁴ Ssu⁴ Yuan⁴ Ch'ing¹, Directors of the Palace Stud.

The Palace Stud is divided into two departments, *i.e.* 左 司 Tso³ Ssu¹, the First Department, and 右 司 Yu⁴ Ssu¹, the Second Department, and, in addition to the officials mentioned in No. 76, furnishes employment for the following :—

21 阿敦侍衛 A⁴ Tun¹ Shih⁴ Wei⁴, Supervisors of Droves, 3 司鞍長 Ssu¹ An¹ Chang³, Saddlery Inspectors, 2 副司鞍長 Fu⁴ Ssu¹ An¹ Chang³, Assistant Saddlery Inspectors, 3 醫師長 I¹ Shih¹ Chang³, Veterinary Surgeons, and 2 副醫師長 Fu⁴ I¹ Shih¹ Chang³, Assistant Veterinary Surgeons.

The Stables are distinguished as (1). 內廐 Nei⁴ Chiu⁴, Stables at the Capital, and (2). 外廐 Wai⁴ Chiu⁴, Provincial Stables, and are directed by 廐長 Chiu⁴ Chang³, Inspectors of the Stables, and 廐副 Chiu⁴ Fu⁴, Assistant Inspectors of the Stables. Besides there are 牧長 Mu⁴ Chang³, Inspectors of Droves, and 牧副 Mu⁴ Fu⁴, Assistant Inspectors of Droves.

89. 武備院 Wu³ Pei⁴ Yüan⁴, The Imperial Armoury (in Iakhinf's "Description of Peking," under No. 68, styled "War Depôt"). This establishment supervises the arsenal, fullery, harness shop, saddle shop, etc., where arrows, bows,

90 armour, helmets, saddles, tents, etc., are manufactured for the Emperor's use and for the army.

In charge of the Armoury is a Prince or Minister of the Household, called 管理武備院事務 Kuan³ Li³ Wu³ Pei⁴ Yüan Shih⁴ Wu⁴, Superintendent of the Imperial Armoury, and two 武備院卿 Wu³ Pei⁴ Yüan⁴ Ch'ing¹, Directors of the Imperial Armoury. In addition, besides the officials mentioned in No. 76, there are 六品庫掌 Liu⁴ P'in³ K'u⁴ Chang³. Overseers of the Sixth Class (six), 委署六品庫掌 Wei³ Shu⁴ Liu⁴ P'in³ K'u⁴ Chang³, Assistant Overseers of the Sixth Class (three), 無品級庫掌 Wu² P'in³ Chi⁴ K'u⁴ Chang³, Unclassed Overseers (six) 庫守 K'u⁴ Shou³, Storehouse Keepers (42), 司函 Ssu¹ Han² Supervisors of Armour-making, 司幄 Ssu¹ Wo⁴, Supervisors of Tent-making, 副司幄 Fu⁴ Ssu¹ Wo⁴, Assistant Supervisors of Tent-making, 司弓 Ssu¹ Kung¹, Supervisors of Bow-making, 司矢 Ssu¹ Shih³, Supervisors of Arrow-making, 掌傘總領 Chang³ San³ Tsung³ Ling³, also 委署掌傘總領 Wei³ Shu⁴ Chang³ San³ Tsung³ Ling³, Supervisors of Umbrella-making, their Assistants and 八品催長 Pa¹ P'in³ Ts'ui¹ Chang³, Overseers of the Eighth Class, as well as others.

90. 奉宸苑 Fêng⁴ Ch'ên² Yüan⁴, Bureau of Imperial Gardens and Hunting Parks; controlling the Imperial Gardens and Hunting Parks and the growing of rice for the Court.

The chief of this bureau is a Prince or a Minister of the Household, styled 管理奉宸苑事務 Kuan³ Li³ Fêng⁴ Ch'ên² Yüan⁴ Shih⁴ Wu⁴, Superintendent of the Imperial Gardens and Hunting Parks. He is assisted by two 奉宸苑卿 Fêng⁴ Ch'ên² Yüan⁴ Ch'ing¹, Directors of the Imperial Gardens and Hunting Parks, to whom are subordinated Department Directors, Assistant Department Directors, Secretaries, Clerks, etc. (compare No. 76).

Under the bureau's administration are the following estates, situated in or near Peking :—

1. 南苑 Nan³ Yüan⁴ (commonly called 海子 Hai³ Tzu³). 90ᴀ
2. 圓明園 Yüan² Ming² Yüan². to
3. 暢春園 Ch'ang⁴ Ch'un¹ Yüan² (also called 長春園 91
Ch'ang² Ch'un¹ Yüan²), and

4. 靜宜園 Ching⁴ I² Yüan² (also called 清漪園 Ch'ing¹
I³ Yüan² or 靜明園 Ching⁴ Ming² Yüan²). At the head of
these are Ministers of the Household, styled 管理圓明園暢春
園事務 Kuan³ Li³ Yüan² Ming² Yüan² Ch'ang⁴ Ch'un¹ Yüan²
Shih⁴ Wu⁴, Superintendents of the Yüan Ming and Ch'ang Ch'un
Gardens (*i.e.* Palace of Eternal Spring) or 管理清漪園等處
事務 Kuan³ Li³ Ch'ing¹ I³ Yüan² Têng³ Ch'u⁴ Shih⁴ Wu⁴, Superintendents of the Ch'ing I and other Gardens.

The actual management of the various gardens is vested in
苑丞 Yüan⁴ Ch'êng², Inspectors (nine at each garden or park)
of the sixth class (六品苑丞 Liu⁴ P'in³ Yüan⁴ Ch'êng²) and
seventh class (七品苑丞 Ch'i¹ P'in³ Yüan⁴ Ch'êng²), assisted by
苑副 Yüan⁴ Fu⁴, Deputy Inspectors (not exceeding 21 at each
garden) of the seventh and eighth classes (七品苑副 Ch'i¹
P'in³ Yüan⁴ Fu⁴ and 八品苑副 Pa¹ P'in³ Yüan⁴ Fu⁴), and
委署苑副 Wei³ Shu⁴ Yüan⁴ Fu⁴, Assistant Deputy Inspectors
(not exceeding 11).

Also under the supervision of the Bureau of Imperial
Gardens and Hunting Parks is the :

90ᴀ. 稻田塲 Tao⁴ T'ien² Ch'ang³, Imperial Agriculture
Office ; controlling the sowing of rice and gardening for the
Court.

91. 御茶膳房 Yü⁴ Ch'a² Shan⁴ Fang², Imperial Buttery
(also 御茶膳處 Yü⁴ Ch'a² Shan⁴ Ch'u⁴).

In charge of the Imperial Buttery are Ministers of the
Household, called 管理御茶膳房事務 Kuan³ Li³ Yü⁴ Ch'a²
Shan⁴ Fang² Shih⁴ Wu⁴, Superintendents of the Imperial
Buttery ; there are also three 尙膳正 Shang⁴ Shan⁴ Chêng⁴,
Chief Trencher-Knights, one 尙膳副 Shang⁴ Shan⁴ Fu⁴, Assistant

[21]

Chief Trencher-Knight, twelve 尚膳 Shang⁴ Shan⁴, Serving-men, three 尚茶正 Shang⁴ Ch'a² Chêng⁴, Chief Cup-bearers, one 尚茶副 Shang⁴ Ch'a² Fu⁴, Assistant Chief Cup-bearer, and six 尚茶 Shang⁴ Ch'a², Cup-bearers (compare No. 570).

92. 御藥房 Yü⁴ Yao⁴ Fang², The Imperial Dispensary. At its head is a Minister of the Household, styled 管理御藥房 事務 Kuan³ Li³ Yü⁴ Yao⁴ Fang² Shih⁴ Wu⁴, Superintendent of the Imperial Dispensary ; the subordinate officials (compare No. 76) are styled 兼理御藥房事務 Chien¹ Li³ Yü⁴ Yao⁴ Fang² Shih⁴ Wu⁴, to show that their duties at the Dispensary are in addition to those of whatever substantive post they may hold.

93. 御船處 Yü⁴ Ch'uan² Ch'u⁴, Imperial Boats Office. Its chief is a Minister of the Household having the title of 管理御船處事務 Kuan³ Li³ Yü⁴ Ch'uan² Ch'u⁴ Shih⁴ Wu⁴, Superintendent of the Imperial Boats Office. The subordinate officials (compare No. 76) bear the title 兼理御船處事務 Chien¹ Li³ Yü⁴ Ch'uan² Ch'u⁴ Shih⁴ Wu .

93ᴀ. 御鳥槍處 Yü⁴ Niao³ Ch'iang¹ Ch'u⁴, Imperial Game Preserve. One of the Princes or Ministers of the Household is at its head and is styled 管理御鳥槍處事務 Kuan³ Li³ Yü⁴ Niao³ Ch'iang¹ Ch'u⁴ Shih⁴ Wu⁴, Superintendent of the Imperial Game Preserve. He has assisting him :

2 藍翎總承 Lan² Ling² Tsung³ Ch'êng², Senior Game-keepers (Subalterns of the Guards, No. 99), 2 副總承 Fu⁴ Tsung³ Ch'êng², Junior Gamekeepers, 5 鳥槍長 Niao³ Ch'iang¹ Chang³, Keepers of the Gunroom, and 2 內火藥庫庫掌 Nei⁴ Huo³ Yao⁴ K'u⁴ K'u⁴ Chang³, Keepers of the Ammunition-store.

94. 武英殿脩書處 Wu³ Ying¹ Tien⁴ Hsiu¹ Shu¹ Ch'u⁴, Printing Office and Bookbindery at the Throne Hall (see No. 104ʙ). This office prepares books for the Court use.

In the above-mentioned Throne Hall were stored, from times long past, stereotype plates, many of which have, unfortunately, been destroyed by fires that have taken place there.

94A
to
95

In charge of the Printing Office is a Prince or Minister of the Household, styled 管理武英殿脩書處事務 Kuan³ Li³ Wu³ Ying¹ Tien⁴ Hsiu¹ Shu¹ Ch'u⁴ Shih⁴ Wu⁴, Superintendent of the Printing Office and Bookbindery at the Throne Hall, and subordinated to him, in addition to the usual officials (*see* No. 76), are 1 Assistant Department Director, styled 正監造 Chêng⁴ Chien¹ Tsao⁴, Overseer of Works, 1 Assistant Chancellor of the Imperial Household, (*see* No. 85) styled 副監造 Fu⁴ Chien¹ Tsao⁴, Assistant Overseer of Works, 4 庫掌 K'u⁴ Chang³, Inspectors, 6 委署庫掌 Wei³ Shu⁴ K'u⁴ Chang³, Deputy Inspectors, 2 總裁 Tsung³ Ts'ai², Revisers (1 Chinese and 1 Manchu), 2 提調 T'i² Tiao⁴, Assistant Revisers, 12 纂脩 Tsuan³ Hsiu¹, Proof Readers, and 10 協脩 Hsieh² Hsiu¹, Assistant Proof Readers.

94A. 御書處 Yü⁴ Shu¹ Ch'u⁴, The Imperial Library (also the private library of the Emperor).

At the head of the Imperial Library is a Prince or Minister of the Household, styled 管理御書處事務 Kuan³ Li³ Yü⁴ Shu¹ Ch'u⁴ Shih⁴ Wu⁴, Curator of the Imperial Library, subordinated to him, in addition to the officials mentioned in No. 76, designated 兼理御書處事務 Chien¹ Li³ Yü⁴ Shu¹ Ch'u⁴ Shih⁴ Wu⁴, are 1 正監造司庫 Chêng⁴ Chien¹ Tsao⁴ Ssu¹ K'u⁴ Librarian-in-Chief (Overseer of Works), 1 副監造庫掌 Fu⁴ Chien¹ Tsao⁴ K'u⁴ Chang³, Deputy Librarian-in-Chief (Assistant Overseer of Works), 2 庫掌 K'u⁴ Chang³, Librarians, and 6 委署庫掌 Wei³ Shu⁴ K'u⁴ Chang³, Deputy Librarians.

95. 總理工程處 Tsung³ Li³ Kung¹ Ch'êng² Ch'u⁴, Imperial Construction Office; as opposed to the 造辦處 Tsao⁴ Pan⁴ Ch'u⁴ (*see* No. 86), this office has to do with large Palace buildings only.

At the head of the Imperial Construction Office is a Prince or Minister of the Household, bearing the title 管理工程處事務

96 to 97

Kuan³ Li³ Kung¹ Ch'êng² Ch'u⁴ Shih⁴ Wu⁴, Superintendent of the Imperial Construction Office. The usual subordinate officials (*see* No. 76) are styled 兼理工程處事務 Chien¹ Li³ Kung¹ Ch'êng² Ch'u⁴ Shih⁴ Wu⁴.

96. 織染局 Chih¹ Jan³ Chu², Imperial Weaving and Dyeing Office (where tissues for the Court use are woven and dyed); supervised by a Prince or Minister of the Household, called 管織染局大臣 Kuan¹ Chih¹ Jan³ Chü² Ta⁴ Ch'ên², Director of the Weaving and Dyeing Office. Subordinate to him, in addition to the usual officials (*see* No. 76), styled 兼攝織染局務司官 Chien¹ Shê⁴ Chih¹ Jan³ Chü² Wu⁴ Ssu¹ Kuan¹, are:

1 司庫 Ssu¹ K'u⁴, Inspector, 6 庫使 K'u⁴ Shih⁵, Overseers, 2 司匠 Ssu¹ Chiang⁴, Clerks of Works, and 6 領催 Ling³ Ts'ui¹ (idem.).

97. 內旗 Nei⁴ Ch'i², Household Division of the Banners.

The Eight Banners 八旗 Pa¹ Ch'i² (*see* No. 718) are divided into the 內旗 Nei⁴ Ch'i², Inner or Household Division, and 外旗 Wai⁴ Ch'i², Outer Division.

The Household Division of the Banners is under the control of the Imperial Household (*see* No. 75) and its duties consist chiefly in guarding the different parts of the Forbidden City (*see* No. 104). It is composed of the so-called 包衣 Pao¹ I¹, Bond-servants, a class formed at the beginning of the rise of the Manchu dynasty, when, for the Emperor and Princes, there were appointed from the Banners a certain number of families who continued to serve, from one generation to another, the Imperial Household and the Princes of the Blood. They receive a fixed salary from the government treasury and retain their status even if they are employed on other service.

Like the Banner Forces, the Household Division of the Banners is made up from the Eight Banners and is divided into:

[24]

1 上三旗 Shang⁴ San¹ Ch'i², The Three Superior
Banners, or 內三旗 Nei⁴ San¹ Ch'i², The Three Imperial
Banners (composed of Bordered Yellow, Plain Yellow and Plain
White Banners), and

2 下五旗 Hsia⁴ Wu³ Ch'i², The Five Lower Banners
(composed of the five remaining Banners; compare No. 718).

The Three Superior Banners appertain to the Imperial
Household, and the Bond-servants composing them are called
皇包衣 Huang² Pao¹ I¹, the Imperial Household Bond-servants.

The Five Lower Banners are attached to the various
Princely Houses, and the Bond-servants composing them are
called 王包衣 Wang² Pao¹ I¹, Bond-servants of Princes of the
Blood.

The Three Imperial Banners are divided into the following
brigades:

97A. 內護軍營 Nei⁴ Hu⁴ Chün¹ Ying², The Imperial
Guards. Its organisation is similar to that of the 護軍營
Hu⁴ Chün¹ Ying², the Guards (see No. 734).

97B. 內驍騎營 Nei⁴ Hsiao¹ Ch'i² Ying², The Household
Brigade of the Line; this must be distinguished from 驍騎營
Hsiao¹ Ch'i² Ying², Brigade of the Line (see Nos. 718 to 732A).

97C. 內前鋒營 Nei⁴ Ch'ien² Fêng¹ Ying², The Household
Vanguard; its organisation is similar to the 前鋒營 Ch'ien²
Fêng¹ Ying², Banner Vanguard (see No. 735).

97D. 圓明園內旗護軍營 Yüan² Ming² Yüan² Nei⁴
Ch'i² Hu⁴ Chün¹ Ying², The Imperial Guards at the Summer
Palace, Yüan Ming Yüan. Its organisation is the same as the
圓明園八旗護軍營 Yüan² Ming² Yüan² Pa¹ Ch'i² Hu⁴
Chün¹ Ying², The Guards Brigade at the Summer Palace, Yüan
Ming Yüan (see No. 741).

97E. 南苑護衛營 Nan² Yüan⁴ Hu⁴ Wei⁴ Ying², The
Guards Brigade at the Nan² Yüan⁴ (The Southern Park; also
海子 Hai³ Tzu³). The staff includes 1 總管 Tsung³ Kuan³,

[25]

**98
to
99**

Commandant; 4A, 8 防禦 Fang² Yü⁴, Captains; 5A, 10 領催 Ling³ Ts'ui¹, Corporals, and 90 驍騎 Hsiao¹ Ch'i², Privates.

98. 領侍衞府 (also 侍衞處 Shih⁴ Wei⁴ Ch'u⁴) Ling³ Shih⁴ Wei⁴ Fu³, Office of the Imperial Body-guard. This office controls the affairs of the 親軍營 Ch'in¹ Chün¹ Ying², the Imperial Body guard, composed of 侍衞親軍 Shih⁴ Wei⁴ Ch'in¹ Chün¹.

The duty of the Body-guard is to escort the Emperor, perform various offices in the interior of the Palace, and guard the Emperor's person. It is chiefly composed of young men from the Three Imperial Banners (*see* No. 97.)

The administration of the Imperial Body-guard is vested in:

1. Six 領侍衞內大臣 Ling³ Shih⁴ Wei⁴ Nei⁴ Ta⁴ Ch'ên², Chamberlains of the Imperial Body-guard; 1A. Whether the Emperor is abroad or in the Capital, two of these are selected as 後扈大臣 Hou⁴ Hu⁴ Ta⁴ Ch'ên², Chamberlains of the Rear-guard.

2. Six 內大臣 Nei⁴ Ta⁴ Ch'ên², Senior Assistant Chamberlains of the Imperial Body-guard; 1B.

3. An indefinite number of 散秩大臣 San⁴ Chih⁴ Ta⁴ Ch'ên², Junior Assistant Chamberlains of the Imperial Body-guard; 2B. This title of 散秩大臣 is often conferred as a hereditary title.

From the Senior and Junior Assistant Chamberlains of the Imperial Body-guard there are appointed (similarly to the Chamberlains) ten 前引大臣 Ch'ien² Yin³ Ta⁴ Ch'ên², Chamberlains of the Van-guard.

99. The Imperial Body-guard is composed of:

1. 侍衞 Shih⁴ Wei⁴, also 花翎侍衞 Hua¹ Ling² Shih⁴ Wei⁴, the Senior Body-guards (wearing the Peacock Feather); Sixty are 一等 I¹ Têng³, First Rank; 3A, One Hundred and

Fifty 二 等 Erh Têng[3], Second Rank ; 4A, and Two Hundred and Seventy 三 等 San[1] Têng[3], Third Rank ; 5A, and 四 等 Ssu[4] Têng[3], Fourth Rank ; 5B.

2. 藍 翎 侍 衛 Lan[2] Ling[2] Shih[4] Wei[4], the Junior Body-guards (wearing the Blue Feather) ; 6A. There are Ninety of the 一.

3. 宗室侍衛 Tsung[1] Shih[4] Shih[4] Wei[4], also 三 旗 宗室 侍 衛 San[1] Ch'i[2] Tsung[1] Shih[4] Shih[4] Wei[4], the Clansmen Corps of the Imperial Body-guards. Nine of these are 一 等 I[1] Têng[3], First Rank, Eighteen are 二 等 Erh Têng[3], Second Rank, and Sixty-three are 三 等 San[1] Têng[3], Third Rank.

From the above-mentioned Body-guards, commonly known as 三 旗 侍 衛 San[1] Ch'i[2] Shih[4] Wei[4], there are selected an indefinite number of 御 前 侍 衛 Yü[4] Ch'ien[2] Shih[4] Wei[4], Guards of the Ante-chamber, and 乾 清 門 侍 衛 Ch'ien[2] Ch'ing[1] Mên[2] Shih[4] Wei[4], Guards at the Ch'ien Ch'ing Gate.

In addition, there are Sixty 豹 尾 班 侍 衛 Pao[4] Wei[3] Pan Shih[4] Wei[4], the Imperial Body-guards wearing the Leopard's Tail.

4. 漢 侍 衛 Han[4] Shih[4] Wei[4], Chinese Corps of the Imperial Body-guards ; these are of three ranks.

When engaged on guard duty, the Body-guards are divided into 6 班 Pan[1], Reliefs, which, in turn, are divided into 2 翼 I[4], Wings.

In command of each relief is a 侍 衛 班 領 Shih[4] Wei[4] Pan[1] Ling[3], Commander of a Relief of the Body-guards, and below him is a 署 班 領 Shu[4] Pan[1] Ling[3], Second in Command of a Relief of the Body-guards.

For every ten Privates there is a 侍 衛 什 長 Shih[4] Wei[4] Shih[2] Chang[3], Sergeant.

100. The Emperor's personal detachment of the Body-guards consists of 77 親 軍 校 Ch'in[1] Chün[1] Hsiao[4], Lieutenants ; 6A, 70 署 親 軍 校 Shu[4] Ch'in[1] Chün[1] Hsiao[4], Sub-Lieutenants ;

101 to 103

8B, 7 委署親軍校 Wei³ Shu⁴ Ch'in¹ Chün¹ Hsiao⁴, Sergeants, and 1,756 親軍 Ch'in¹ Chün¹, Privates.

101. 御前大臣 Yü⁴ Ch'ien² Ta⁴ Ch'ên², Adjutant General; there are four of these, appointed from the Princes or Ministers of the Household.

101A. 御前行走 Yü⁴ Ch'ien² Hsing² Tsou³, Attaché to the Emperor's Suite. This title is usually conferred on Mongolian Princes.

102. 總司稽查守衛事宜處 Tsung³ Ssu¹ Chi² Ch'a² Shou³ Wei⁴ Shih⁴ I² Ch'u⁴, Vigilance Office (office of the General Inspectors charged with the safety and tranquillity of the Palace precincts).

This office was established in accordance with an Edict of the 13th December, 1908, and is under the control of 3 總司稽查守衛事宜大臣 Tsung³ Ssu¹ Chi² Ch'a² Shou³ Wei⁴ Shih⁴ I² Ta⁴ Ch'ên², General Inspectors (charged with the safety and tranquillity of the Palace precincts). These officials are appointed from the Princes or High Officials.

Two reports of the Vigilance Office, approved on the 19th December, 1908, and the 9th January, 1909, show its administration and staff to be as follows:

The actual management is vested in a 總辦 Tsung³ Pan⁴, Manager, and 1 幇辦 Pang¹ Pan⁴, Assistant. Below these are 4 稽查章京 Chi² Ch'a² Chang¹ Ching¹, Secretaries, and 10 稽查委員 Ch'² Ch'a² Wei³ Yüan², Supervisors (these are chiefly charged with keeping a sharp watch over the Palace Guard).

103. 禁衛軍 Chin⁴ Wei⁴ Chün¹, New Palace Guard.

The organisation of this body was decreed by Imperial Edict of the 25th December, 1908, the tenor of which was as follows:

"Prince Tsai Tao, Prince of the 3rd Order, Prince Yü "Lang, Prince of the 3rd Order, and T'ieh Liang, President

103A
to
103B

" of the Ministry of War, are appointed Superintendents for the
" organisation and drilling of an Imperial Guards Corps. They
" are authorised to select from any of the Banner Corps men of
" good physique and health for these Guards and they are to be
" conscientious and diligent in this work. The Corps will be
" under the special command of the Prince Regent. A further
" Edict will be issued when the Corps is functioning smoothly.
" Such is the Emperor's pleasure."

103A.   The New Palace Guards are, so it seems, to replace
the original Imperial Guards. They are to be organised as
divisions of, and will be in type similar to, the New Army.

It is proposed to first complete the formation of one division
of the New Palace Guards, recruits to be drawn from the First
and Sixth Divisions of the New Army. With this object in view
there has been established the 禁衛軍訓練處 Chin^4 Wei^4
Chün^1 Hsün^4 Lien^4 Ch'ü^4, Office for Drilling of the New Palace
Guards, under the supervision of three 專司訓練禁衛軍大臣
Chuan^1 Ssu^1 Hsün^4 Lien^4 Chin^4 Wei^4 Chün^1 Ta^4 Ch'ên^2, Supervisors of the Drilling of the New Palace Guards.   To these are
attached :

103B.   A. 軍諮官 Chun^{1,}Tzu^1 Kuan^1, Military Instructors ;
six in all (one is of the 一 等 I^1 Têng^3, First Rank, two are of
the 二 等 Erh^4 Têng^2, Second Rank, and three are of the
三 等 San^1 Têng^3, Third Rank). These Officers manage
correspondence, supervise sections of the staff, are responsible for
instruction, and are in charge of the four sub-offices attached to
the Chief Drilling Office (see below, No. 103C).

Directly subordinated to the above-mentioned are :
1.   10 執事員 Chih^2 Shih^4 Yüan^2, Adjutants,
2.   5 書記員 Shu^1 Chi^4 Yüan^2, Writers (of three ranks),
3.   2 繪圖員 Hui^4 T'u^2 Yüan^2, Draftsmen,
4.   1 印刷員 Yin^4 Shua^1 Yüan^2, Manager of Printing
Office,

103c
to
103D

5. 1 收支員 Shou[1] Chih[1] Yüan[2], Treasurer,

6. 1 庶務員 Shu[4] Wu[4] Yüan[2], General Supervisor,

7. 2 遞事員 Ti[4] Shih[4] Yüan[2], Registrars.

103c. B. To the Office for Drilling of the New Palace Guards there are attached the following four sub-offices :

1. 軍械科 Chün[1] Hsieh[4] K'o[1], Armoury,

2. 軍法科 Chün[1] Fa[3] K'o[1], Office of Military Jurisprudence,

3. 軍需科 Chün[1] Hsü[1] K'o[1], Commissariat Department, and

4. 軍醫科 Chün[1] I[1] K'o[1], Medical Department.

In each of the sub-offices, or sections, there is a 監督 Chien[1] Tu[1], Section Chief, and from three to five 科員 K'o[1] Yüan[2], Secretaries. In addition, there are :

1. 17 司書生 Ssu[1] Shu[1] Shêng[1], Writers,

2. 11 司事生 Ssu[1] Shih[4] Shêng[1], Clerks,

3. 10 刷印手 Shua[1] Yin[4] Shou[3], Compositors, and

4. 26 夫役 Fu[1] I[4], Servants.

103D. As has been stated above (*see* No. 103A), the formation of the New Palace Guards, with very few exceptions, is identical with that of the 陸軍各鎮 Lu[4] Chün[1] Ko[4] Chên[4], Divisions of the New Army. The artillery detachment, for instance, consists of three companies of field artillery. Also, there are :

1. 交通營 Chiao[1] T'ung[2] Ying[2], Military Communications composed of two companies, *i.e.* 鐵路隊 T'ieh[3] Lu[4] Tui[4], Railway Company, and 電信隊 Tien[4] Hsin[4] Tui[4], Telegraph Company.

2. 1 營 Ying[2], Corps, of 機關礮隊 Chi[1] Kuan[1] P'ao[4] Tui[4], Machine-gun Corps (this is a temporary organisation and will be abolished when the complete formation of the New Palace Guards has been effected), and 1 營 Ying[2], 重礮隊 Chung[4] P'ao[4] Tui[4], Corps of Heavy Artillery.

[30]

3. Later it is planned to organise a 軍鴿隊 Chün[1] Kê[1] Tui[4], Carrier Pigeon Corps, and a 氣球隊 Ch'i[4] Ch'iu[2] Tui[4], Aeronautic Corps.

104
to
104A

To the Commander of each brigade, regiment or battalion there will be attached a 副官 Fu[4] Kuan[1], Adjutant.

104. The Imperial Palaces in Peking are situated in the 紫禁城 Tzu[3] Chin[4] Ch'êng[2], Red Forbidden City, which lies within the 皇城 Huang[2] Ch'êng[2], Imperial City, where most of the buildings and offices pertaining to the Imperial Household are to be found.

Four gates afford access to the Forbidden City :

1. On the North, 神武門 Shên[2] Wu[3] Mên[2].
2. On the East, 東華門 Tung[1] Hua[2] Mên[2].
3. On the South, 午門 Wu[3] Mên[2].
4. On the West, 西華門 Hsi[1] Hua[2] Mên[2].

104A. Within the Forbidden City there is a series of 宮 Kung[1], Palaces, 殿 Tien[4], Halls, and 閣 Ko[2], Pavilions.

The best known of the Palaces are :.

1. 乾清宮 Ch'ien[2] Ch'ing[1] Kung[1], where the most brilliant receptions take place, audiences are granted to Foreign Representatives (since a few years ago), Chinese officials are received, and state business transacted.

2. 坤寧宮 K'un[1] Ning[2] Kung[1], Palace of an Empress, or Shamanic Chapel (see Nos. 79c and 573c).

3. 毓慶宮 Yü[4] Ch'ing[4] Kung[1], Palace of the Heir Apparent.

4. 寧壽宮 Ning[2] Shou[4] Kung[1]. To this Palace there are six gates ; the main gate, on the South, is called 皇極門 Huang[2] Chi[2] Mên[2]. Beyond the gates there is the Throne Hall, 皇極殿 Huang[2] Chi[2] Tien[4], and behind this is the Palace Ning[2] Shou[4] Kung[1], where the Empress Dowager 孝欽顯皇后 Hsiao[4] Ch'in[1] Hsien[3] Huang[2] Hou[4] resided.

104B

5. 齋宮 Chai[1] Kung[1], Palace of Expiation or Abstinence. The Emperor visits this Palace to fast previous to important sacrifices.

6. 雍和宮 Yung[1] Ho[2] Kung[1], Buddhist Temple (Iakhinf calls it the Tibetan Monastery). At the head of this temple, is one of the four Hutukhtus living in Peking (*see* No. 917).

104B. The best known of the Halls are:

1. 太和殿 T'ai[4] Ho[2] Tien[4], Hall of Perfect Harmony (or Hall of Harmony in Nature). Here the Emperor holds levees on New Year's Day, his birthday, and on the Winter solstice.

2. 中和殿 Chung[1] Ho[2] Tien[4], Throne Hall. In this Hall the Emperor scrutinises prayers written for state worship and examines the corn and implements provided for the ploughing ceremony.

3. 保和殿 Pao[3] Ho[2] Tien[4], Throne Hall. In this Hall the Emperor attends examinations for highest literary degrees.

4. 文華殿 Wên[2] Hua[2] Tien[4], Throne Hall. Here the Emperor, in the second moon, attends for explanation of the Classics.

5. 武英殿 Wu[3] Ying[1] Tien[4], Throne Hall where stereotype plates are stored (properly Printing Office, *see* No. 94).

6. 奉先殿 Fêng[4] Hsien[1] Tien[4], Hall where the Emperor worships his ancestors.

7. 養心殿 Yang[3] Hsin[1] Tien[4], Hall to which the Emperor retires for relaxation. At the present time t'' Hall is given up to the Prince Regent for studying government affairs and for small audiences which he may hold (*see* No. 86).

8. 中正殿 Chung[1] Chêng[4] Tien[4], Buddhist Cha el. Of the Pavilions the best known are:

1. 文淵閣 Wên² Yüan¹ Ko², The Library. Here found a full collection of books, labelled in Chinese 四庫全書 Ssu⁴ K'u⁴ Ch'iian² Shu¹.

In charge of the Library is a Grand Secretary (compare No. 131), assisted by :

1 提舉閣事 T'i² Chü³ Ko² Shih⁴, Director of the Library,

2 領閣事 Ling³ Ko² Shih⁴, Assistant Directors of the Library,

6 值閣事 Chih¹ Ko² Shih⁴, Officials on duty at the Library, and

6 檢閱 Chien³ Yüeh², Inspectors,

2 紫光閣 Tzu³ Kuang¹ Ko² (situated on the Western side of the Imperial City), Pavilion of Purple Lustre, where vassals are received and entertained.

104c. The most commonly known gates of the Forbidden City are the 太和門 T'ai⁴ Ho² Mên² and the 乾清門 Ch'ien² Ch'ing¹ Mên² ; the first leads to the Hall of the same name (*see* No. 104B) and the second to the Ch'ien² Ch'ing¹ Palace (*see* No. 104A).

To the Imperial City there are the following gates at the South :—

1. 大清門 Tai⁴ Ch'ing¹ Mên², serving as the main entrance to the Imperial City. Before this gate there is a square court surrounded by a granite palisade, called the 棋盤街 Ch'i P'an Chieh.

2. 天安門 T'ien¹ An¹ Mên²

3. 端門 Tuan¹ Mên². Beyond this gate, entrance to the Forbidden City is obtained through the 午門 Wu³ Mên² (*see* No. 104).

104D. In charge of the Palaces there are (in number from 2 to 3) Ministers of the Household, Princes of the Blood or Grand Secretaries, styled 管理某宮事務 Kuan³ Li³

104c
to
104D

104ᴇ to 105

(Mou³) Kung¹ Shin⁴ Wu⁴, Superintendents of Affairs of such and such a Palace. Subordinated to them, deputed from the Imperial Household, are 郎中 Lang² Chung¹, Department Directors, 員外郎 Yüan² Wai⁴ Lang², Assistant Department Directors, and 內管領 Nei⁴ Kuan³ Ling³, Overseers, bearing the title 兼理某宮事務 Chien¹ Li³ (Mou³) Kung¹ Shih⁴ Wu⁴, Managers of Affairs of such and such a Palace.

In addition to the officials above-mentioned there are a number of 主事 Chu³ Shih⁴ and 委署主事 Wei⁴ Shu⁴ Chu³ Shih⁴, Secretaries, and 筆帖式 Pi³ T'ieh³ Shih⁴, Clerks.

The management of Palace Halls and Pavilions is arranged on the same basis as the Palace management.

104ᴇ. 頤和園 I² Ho² Yüan², Summer Palace of the Emperor. This Palace was the fixed Summer residence of the late Emperor and Empress Dowager. At the present time it is under seal until the Emperor reaches his majority. The grounds, however, are opened on the 5th, 15th and 25th of each moon to the inspection of Diplomatic Representatives and eminent foreigners.

The Summer Palace is under the supervision of the Bureau of Imperial Gardens and Hunting Parks (*see* Nos. 90 and 741).

避暑山莊 Pi⁴ Shu³ Shan¹ Chuang¹, Summer Palace at 熱河 Jehol (in the prefecture of 承德府 Ch'êng² Tê² Fu³, to the North-east of Peking). Until 1860 this Palace was the Summer residence of the Emperors.

105. 奏事處 Tsou⁴ Shih⁴ Ch'u⁴, Chancery of Memorials to the Emperor. At the Chancery are stationed 6 奏事官 Tsou⁴ Shih⁴ Kuan¹, Chancellors of Memorials to the Emperor, who receive memorials from the provinces which, if found to be written in accordance with fixed etiquette, are handed over to the Grand Council for presentation to the Emperor (Metropolitan establishments present their memorials to the Grand Council direct).

[34]

The Chancery of Memorials to the Emperor is divided into 105A to 111 two sections; one for Chinese and Manchu and one for Mongolian memorials.

The general supervision of the Chancery is the duty of 御前大臣 Yü⁴ Ch'ien² Ta⁴ Ch'ên², Adjutant Generals (*see* No. 101).

105A. 欽奉上諭事件處 Ch'in¹ Fêng⁴ Shang⁴ Yü⁴ Shih⁴ Chien⁴ Ch'u⁴, Chancery for the publication of Imperial Edicts. At the head of this Chancery is a 稽察 Chi² Ch'a², Inspector (usually appointed from the ranks of the Grand Secretaries).

106. 稽查壇廟大臣 Chi² Ch'a² T'an² Miao⁴ Ta⁴ Ch'ên², Superintendent of Altars and Temples, and 備查壇廟大臣 Pei⁴ Ch'a² T'an² Miao⁴ Ta⁴ Ch'ên², Assistant Superintendent of Altars and Temples. By these titles are designated the officials charged with the preparations for sacrifices at altars and temples.

107. 喜起舞大臣 Hsi³ Ch'i³ Wu³ Ta⁴ Ch'ên², Director of the Court Ballet.

108. 司鑰長 Ssu¹ Yao¹ Chang³, Keeper of Palace Keys.

THE IMPERIAL EQUIPAGE DEPARTMENT.

109. 鑾輿衞 Luan² Yü² Wei⁴ (previously 鑾儀衞 Luan² I² Wei⁴), the Imperial Equipage Department. This has charge of the preparation of carriages, chairs, regalia, etc., necessary when the Emperor goes abroad.

110. 掌衞事大臣 Chang³ Wei⁴ Shih⁴ Ta⁴ Ch'ên², Superintendent of the Imperial Equipage Department, usually appointed from the Princes of the Blood (literary designation 煖卿 Nuan³ Ch'ing¹).

111. 鑾輿使 Luan² Yü² Shih³ (formerly 鑾儀使 Luan² I² Shih³), Commissioner of the Imperial Equipage Department; 2A. Literary designation 衞尉卿 Wei⁴ Yü⁴ Ch'ing¹ and 大威衞 Ta⁴ Wei¹-wei⁴. There are two of these officials.

[35]

112
to
121

112. 漢鑾輿使 Han⁴ Luan² Yü² Shih³, Chinese Commissioner of the Imperial Equipage Department; 2A. There is one of these officials.

113. 總理事務冠軍使 Tsung³ Li³ Shih⁴ Wu⁴ Kuan⁴ Chün¹ Shih³, Chief Marshals of the Imperial Equipage Department. There are two of these and they have the general supervision of the five sub-departments into which the Equipage Department is divided (*see* Nos. 118 to 123).

114. 協理事務雲麾使 Hsieh² Li³ Shih⁴ Wu⁴ Yün² Hui¹ Shih³, Assistant Chief Marshals of the Imperial Equipage Department (*see* No. 113); two officials of this rank.

115. 陪祀冠軍使 P'ei² Ssu⁴ Kuan⁴ Chün¹ · Shih³, Sacrificial Marshals of the Imperial Equipage Department; two officials of this rank.

116. 堂主事 T'ang² Chu³ Shih⁴, Chief Secretary (compare No. 288); one official of this rank.

117. 經歷廳 Ching¹ Li⁴ T'ing¹, Registry: supervised by two 經歷 Ching¹ Li⁴, Registrars; 6A.

118. 左所 Tso³ So³, First Sub-department, divided into two sections:

1. 鑾輿司 Luan² Yü² Ssu¹, Carriage Section, and
2. 馴馬司 Hsün⁴ Ma³ Ssu¹, Equestrian Section.

119. 右所 Yu⁴ So³, Second Department, consisting of two sections:

1. 擎蓋司 Ch'ing² Kai⁴ Ssu¹, Umbrella Section, and
2. 弓矢司 Kung¹ Shih¹ Ssu¹, Bow and Arrow Section.

120. 中所 Chung¹ So³, Third Sub-department, consisting of two sections:

1. 旌節司 Ching¹ Chieh⁴ Ssu¹, Pennons Section, and
2. 旛幢司 Fan¹ T'ung² Ssu¹, Flags and Signals Section.

121. 前所 Ch'ien² So³, Fourth Sub-department, consisting of two sections:

1. 扇手司 Shan⁴ Shou³ Ssu¹, Fan Section, and

2. 斧鉞司 Fu³ Yüeh⁴ Ssu¹, Halberd Section.

122 後所 Hou⁴ So³, Fifth Sub-department, divided into eight sections:

1. 班劍司 Pan¹ Chien⁴ Ssu¹, Sword Section,
2. 戈戟司 Ko² Chi³ Ssu¹, Spear Section,
3: 馴象所 Hsün⁴ Hsiang⁴ So³, Elephant-training Section.
4. 東司 Tung¹ Ssu¹, Eastern Section,
5. 西司 Hsi¹ Ssu¹, Western Section,
6. 旗手衞 Ch'i² Shou³ Wei¹, Standard-bearers Section,
7. 左司 Tso³ Ssu¹, Left Section, and
8. 右司 Yu⁴ Ssu¹, Right Section.

123. At the head of each of the above-mentioned sub-departments there is a 掌印冠軍使 Chang³ Yin⁴ Kuan⁴ Chün¹ Shih³, Sub-department Chief; 3ᴀ, to whom is attached one 掌所事雲麾使 Chang³ So⁵ Shih⁴ Yün² Hui¹ Shih³, Assistant Sub-department Chief; 4ᴀ.

Each section is directed by a 掌印雲麾使 Chang³ Yin⁴ Yün² Hui¹ Shih³, Section Chief; 4ᴀ, (for the Elephant-training and Standard-bearers Section called 掌印冠軍使 Chang³ Yin⁴ Kuan⁴ Chün Shih³), to whom is attached one 掌司事治宜正 Chang³ Ssu¹ Shih⁴ Chih⁴ I² Chêng⁴ (formerly 治儀正 Chih⁴ I² Chêng⁴), Assistant Section Chiefs; 5ᴀ; but for the Elephant-training and Standard-bearers Sections the title is, for the former, 掌所事雲麾使 Chang³ So³ Shih⁴ Yün² Hui¹ Shih³, and, for the latter, 掌所事冠軍使 Chang³ So³ Shih⁴ Kuan⁴ Chün¹ Shih³.

In the Sub-departments and Sections of the Equipage Department are also employed 筆帖式 Pi³ T'ieh³ Shih⁴, Clerks (number not fixed).

124. 管理 Kuan³ Li³, Overseers. There are twelve attached to the Equipage Department:

1. 靜鞭管理 Ching⁴ Pien¹ Kuan³ Li³, Overseer of Heralds and Whips.

[37]

125

2. 駕庫管理 Chia⁴ K'u⁴ Kuan³ Li³, Overseer of Carriage Houses,

3. 步輦管理 Pu⁴ Nien³ Kuan³ Li³, Overseer of Imperial Carriages,

4. 玉輅管理 Yü⁴ Lo⁴ Kuan³ Li³, Overseer of the Jade Carriage,

5. 象輅管理 Hsiang⁴ Lo¹ Kuan³ Li³, Overseer of the Elephant Carriage,

6. 金輅管理 Chin¹ Lo⁴ Kuan³ Li³, Overseer of the Golden Carriage,

7. 革輅管理 Ko² Lo⁴ Kuan³ Li³, Overseer of the Leather Carriage,

8. 木輅管理 Mu⁴ Lo⁴ Kuan³ Li³, Overseer of the Wooden Carriage,

9. 棕毯管理 Tsung¹ T'an⁵ Kuan³ Li³, Overseer of Coir Mats,

10. 拜褥管理 Pai⁴ Ju⁴ Kuan³ Li³, Overseer of Kneeling Rugs,

11. 梳頭管理 Shu¹ T'ou² Kuan³ Li³, Overseer of Combs, and

12. 駕衣管理 Chia⁴ I¹ Kuan³ Li³, Overseer of Livery for Servants and Chair-bearers.

125. To the Overseer of Heralds and Whips (*see* No. 124) there are attacheu :

3 鳴贊鞭官 Ming² Tsan⁴ Pien¹ Kuan¹, Heralds ; 7ᴀ, and

1 鳴贊鞭使 Ming² Tsan⁴ Pien¹ Shih³, Assistant Herald.

To the Overseer of Carriage Houses (*see* No. 124) there are attached :

1 雲麾使 Yün² Hui¹ Shih³, Assistant Marshal ; 4ᴀ,

1 治宜正 Chih⁴ I² Chêng⁴ (formerly 治儀正 Chih⁴ I² Chêng⁴), Controller of the Fifth Class ; 5ᴀ, and

1 整宜尉 Chêng³ I² Yü⁴ (formerly 整儀尉 Chêng³ I² Yü¹) Controller of the Sixth Class ; 6ᴀ.

To the Overseer of the Imperial Carriages (*see* No. 124) **126** there are attached :

1 雲麾使 Yün² Hui¹ Shih³, Assistant Marshal ; 4A, and

2 治宜正 Chih¹ I² Chêng⁴, Controllers of the Fifth Class ; 5A.

To the remaining Overseers there are subordinated, to each :

1 治宜正 Chih⁴ I² Chêng⁴, Controller of the Fifth Class ; 5A, and

1 整宜尉 Chêng³ I² Yü , Controller of the Sixth Class.

REGENCY.

126. 監國攝政王 Chien¹ Kuo² Shê⁴ Chêng⁴ Wang², Prince Regent. During the minority of the present Emperor, known from his reign as 宣統 Hsüan¹ T'ung³, that is, until he has completed his education and has married, his father, 醇親王 載灃 Ch'un² Ch'in¹ Wang² Tsai³ Fêng¹, Prince of the First Degree, Ch'un, personal name Tsai³ Fêng¹, will govern the Chinese Empire as Regent, having been empowered to assume his title by the late Empress Dowager 孝欽顯皇后 Hsiao⁴ Ch'in¹ Hsien³ Huang² Hou⁴, on the 13th November, 1908.

Rules defining the rights and the authority of the Prince Regent, elaborated by the Grand Secretariat, in conjunction with the Ministries and Chief Government Establishments, were approved by the Emperor in an Edict dated 13th November, 1908.

All government affairs are transacted by the Prince Regent and decisions are published as Edicts of the Emperor under his seal. In very important cases the Prince Regent requests the Empress Dowager 隆裕皇太后 Lung² Yü⁴ Huang² T'ai⁴ Hou⁴ to issue an Edict.

**126A
to
127**
The Prince Regent is Commander-in-Chief of all Naval and Military Forces and, as the Emperor's representative, will attend sessions of the National Assembly. He will also open Parliament.

All reports addressed to the Emperor are presented to the Prince Regent and, in connection with foreign affairs, he concludes treaties, appoints representatives abroad, and receives the credentials of the representatives of Foreign Powers appointed to China.

For the expenses of the Prince Regent there are allotted, yearly, One Hundred and Fifty Thousand Taels by the Ministry of Finance (for details *see* Rules, in 16 Articles).

126A. 議政王 I⁴ Chêng⁴ Wang², Prince Regent. This title was borne by 恭親王奕訢 Kung¹ Ch'in² Wang² I² Hsin¹, Prince of the First Degree, Kung, personal name I² Hsin¹, during the minority of the Emperor T'ung Chih, when, with the Empresses, 慈安 T'zu² An¹ and 慈禧 T'zu² Hsi³, he was in charge of the government of the Empire.

126B. 居攝 Chü¹ Shê⁴, another designation of Prince Regent. This title was held by the usurper 王莽 Wang² Mang³ during the minority of the Emperor 孺子嬰 Ju² Tzu³ Ying¹, of the 漢 Han⁴ Dynasty (in B.C. 6).

126C. 皇太后臨朝 Huang² T'ai⁴ Hou⁴ Lin² Ch'ao², Empress Dowager Regent; also called 垂簾聽政 Ch'ui² Lien² T'ing¹ Chêng⁴ (or 垂簾訓政 Ch'ui² Lien² Hsün⁴ Chêng⁴), literally "to drop the curtain and administer the government." This title was applied to the late Empress Dowager 孝欽顯皇后 Hsiao² Ch'in¹ Hsien³ Huang² Hou⁴ during the minority of the Emperor 光緒 Kuang¹ Hsü⁴ (1875-1908.)

PARLIAMENT.

127. 議院 I⁴ Yuan⁴, Parliament; projected Deliberative Assembly of China; to be opened in 1913. It will consist of

two Houses, *i.e.* 上 議 院 Shang⁴ I⁴ Yüan⁴, Upper House, and   **128**
下 議 院 Hsia⁴ I⁴ Yüan⁴, Lower House.

Rules and Regulations for Parliament and for the Electoral Laws are to be drawn up by the Department for Drawing up Regulations for Constitutional Government and will be promulgated in 1912.

The establishment of a Parliament was foreshadowed by the Emperor's approval of a general outline of the principles of constitutional government, together with laws concerning parliament and the election of its members, (*see* Edict dated 27th August, 1908, in reply to a report from the Bureau for the Investigation of the Principles of Constitutional Government, with two enclosures).

As the Parliament will have deliberative authority alone, having no executive authority whatsoever, it will only be allowed to discuss questions touching the whole Empire and assist in working out the Budget. Its resolutions will be carried out only after the Emperor's approval of the same (*see* details in article " China on the eve of a Constitution " in the " Messenger of Asia," No. 1, July, 1909, pages 57 to 74, translation from the Chinese, by the authors of the Imperial Edict dated 27th August, 1908, and the " Scheme of State Laws and Programme of Constitutional Reforms during the period 1908-1916.")

From the year 1910 until the opening of Parliament there will be a National Assembly as a preliminary deliberative body (*see* Nos. 164 to 167c).

COUNCIL OF STATE.

128. 軍 機 處 Chün¹ Chi¹ Ch'u⁴, Council of State (or Grand Council). This is the Highest Central Establishment, being in charge of the government of the Empire, and was established about 1730 A.D. It was originally a Military Council at which the first Emperors of the present Dynasty

**129
to
129B**

discussed State Affairs. Now, having become the Privy Council of the Emperor, most Decrees are issued from this establishment, as well as orders concerning State Administration.

The Council of State is composed of :

129. 軍機大臣 Chün[1] Chi[1] Ta[4] Ch'ên[2], Grand Councillors, having daily audiences with the Emperor. The number of these officials is not fixed but for many years past there have not been more than five, *i.e.* two Manchus, two Chinese, and one of the Princes of the Blood as President.

Members of the Council of State are usually appointed from the ranks of officials of the grade of Minister of State or Assistant Minister of State and they usually hold substantive posts other than in the Council.

At present the members of the Council of State countersign (署名 Shu[3] Ming[2]) all Decrees issued in the name of the Emperor over the seal of the Prince Regent.

129A. 軍機行走 Chün[1] Chi[1] Hsing[2] Tsou[3], also 在軍機大臣上學習行走 Tsai[4] Chün[1] Chi[1] Ta[4] Ch'ên[2] Shang[4] Hsueh[2] Hsi[2] Hsing[2] Tsou[3], Probationary Grand Councillor. Newly-appointed Grand Councillors are often thus designated.

129B. 軍機章京 Chün[1] Chi[1] Chang[1] Ching[1], also 小軍機 Hsiao[3] Chün[1] Chi[1], Secretaries of the Council of State ; sixty in all. They attend to the clerical work of the Council and are divided into four sections :

1. 滿頭班 Man[3] T'ou[2] Pan[1], and 滿二班 Man[3] Êrh[4] Pan[1], First and Second Manchu, and

2. 漢頭班 Han[4] T'ou[2] Pan[1], and 漢二班 Han[4] Êrh[4] Pan[1], First and Second Chinese.

At the head of each section there is a 領班 Ling[3] Pan[1], Chief of Section ; 3A, assisted by a 幫領班 Pang[1] Ling[3] Pan[1], Assistant Chief of Section ; 4A.

The titles 領班章京上行走 Ling³ Pan¹ Chang¹ Ching¹ Shang⁴ Hsiang² Tsou³, Chief of Section, and 幫領班章京上行走 Pang¹ Ling³ Pan¹ Chang¹ Ching¹ Shang⁴ Hsiang² Tsou³, Assistant Chief of Section, are often borne as honorary titles by some of the Secretaries.

129c
to
131

129c. 記名 Chi⁴ Ming², thus is designated a day-book, kept at the Council of State, for recording praiseworthy actions of officials.

GRAND SECRETARIAT OR IMPERIAL CHANCERY.

130. 內閣 Nei⁴ Ko², Grand Secretariat; technically the highest government establishment; organized in the Ming Dynasty.

Before the establishment of the Grand Council, early in the 18th century (*see* No. 128), the duties of the Grand Secretariat included the preliminary examination of reports from the Provincial Authorities, the making of recommendations as to these before presentation to the Emperor, and the composition and promulgation of Imperial Decrees. It has now, however, lost much of its importanc d its duties at present consist, for the most part, in promulgating Edicts and in keeping State Papers.

The Grand Secretariat is composed as follows :

131. Four 大學士 Ta⁴ Hsüeh² Shih⁴, Grand Secretaries; 1A (colloquial designation 中堂 Chung¹ T'ang², epistolary designation 宰相 Tsai³ Hsiang⁴ and 相國 Hsiang⁴ Kuo²). Two of these are Manchus and two are Chinese, chosen from the most distinguished officials of the Empire who are *sine qua non*, Metropolitan Graduates.

Each of the Grand Secretaries is entitled Ta Hsüeh Shih of one or other of the Throne Halls or Pavilions of the Imperial

Palace, *i.e.* 保和殿 Pao³ Ho² Tien⁴, 文華殿 Wên² Hua² Tien⁴, 武英殿 Wu³ Ying¹ Tien⁴, 體仁閣 T'i³ Jên² Ko², 文淵閣 Wên² Yüan¹ Ko² and 東閣 Tung¹ Ko² (the selection of a particular Hall or Pavilion depends on the Emperor's will).

Under the Ming Dynasty the Grand Secretaries were familiarly designated 閣老 Ko² Lao³, Elders of the Imperial Chancery (rendered by the Jesuit Missionaries as Colao).

132. Two 協辦大學士 Hsieh² Pan⁴ Ta⁴ Hsüeh² Shih⁴, Assistant Grand Secretaries ; 1B (colloquial designation 中堂 Chung¹ T'ang², epistolary designation 協揆 Hsieh² K'uei²). One is Manchu and one Chinese.

Grand Secretaries and Assistant Grand Secretaries are usually also members of the Council of State, Ministers of State or Assistant Ministers of State.

133. Ten 內閣學士 Nei⁴ Ko² Hsüeh² Shih⁴, Sub-Chancellors of the Grand Secretariat ; 2B (literary designation 閣學 Ko² Hsüeh²). Six are Manchus and four are Chinese ; they act as registrars of certain departments of the State Archives.

134. Eight 內閣侍讀學士 Nei⁴ Ko² Shih⁴ Tu² Hsüeh² Shih⁴, Readers of the Grand Secretariat ; 4B. Six are Manchus and two Chinese. They compare the texts, in Manchu and Chinese, of State Papers.

135. Sixteen 內閣侍讀 Nei⁴ Ko² Shih⁴ Tu², Assistant Readers of the Grand Secretariat ; 6A. Fourteen of these are Manchus and two are Chinese.

136. Six 內閣典籍 Nei⁴ Ko² Tien³ Chi², Archivists of the Grand Secretariat ; 7A ; four Manchus and two Chinese.

137. 130 內閣中書 Nei⁴ Ko² Chung¹ Shu¹, Secretaries of the Grand Secretariat ; 7B (literary designation 中翰 Chung¹ Han⁴). Six of these do duty at :

[44]

137A. 中書科 Chung[1] Shu[1] K'o[1], Imperial Patent Office, as 中書科中書 Chung[1] Shu[1] K'o[1] Chung[4] Shu[1], Secretaries of the Imperial Patent Office; 7B. Their duty is to prepare patents and charters.

At the head of the Imperial Patent Office there are:

137B. Two 稽查中書科事務大臣 Chi[2] Ch'a[2] Chung[1] Shu[1] K'o[1] Shih[4] Wu[4] Ta[4] Ch'ên[2], Controllers of the Imperial Patent Office; appointed from the ranks of the Sub-Chancellors of the Grand Secretariat.

138. To the Grand Secretariat, in addition to the Office above-mentioned, there are attached:

3 Copying Offices, *i.e.* 滿本房 Man[3] Pên[3] Fang[2], Manchu, 漢本房 Han[4] Pên[3] Fang[2], Chinese, and 蒙古房 Mêng[3] Ku[3] Fang[2], Mongolian.

2 Registries, *i.e* 滿票簽處 Man[3] P'iao[4] Ch'ien[1] Ch'u[4], Manchu, and 漢票簽處 Han[4] P'iao[4] Ch'ien[1] Ch'u[4], Chinese, specially charged with making extracts from State Documents.

1 批本處 P'i[1] Pên[3] Ch'u[4], Office for copying the Emperor's endorsements of documents,

1 收發紅本處 Shou[1] Fa[1] Hung[2] Pên[3] Ch'u[4], Receiving and Forwarding Office, and

1 副本庫 Fu[4] Pên[3] K'u[4], Archives Office.

139. 方畧館 Fang[1] Lio[4] Kuan[3], Military Archives Office. This office is specially charged with the drawing up of records of military undertakings and achievements of the present Dynasty. It is under the supervision and control of the Grand Secretariat; one of the members of the latter usually holds the position of President. 總裁 Tsung[3] Ts'ai[2]. To him there are subordinated four 提調 T'i[2] Tiao[4], Revisers, four 收掌 Shou[1] Chang[3], Archivists, and nine 纂脩 Tsuan[3] Hsiu[1], Proof Readers.

140. 內繙書房 Nei[4] Fan[1] Shu[1] Fang[2], Manchu-Chinese Translation Office; translates State Papers from Chinese into Manchu and is subject to the control of the Grand Secretar at.

COMMITTEE OF MINISTERS.

141. 政務處.Chêng⁴ Wu⁴ Ch'u⁴, Bureau of Government Affairs; established in 1901 for the examination of reports and memorials, dealing with reforms, coming from officials and the people.

When first formed, this Bureau was composed of four members, with Prince Ch'ing as its head. Officials of the various Ministries have been appointed as members of this Bureau, at the same time continuing to hold their original posts.

In the year 1905 the Bureau was reorganized as:

141A. 內閣會議政務處 Nei⁴ Ko² Hui⁴ I⁴ Chêng⁴ Wu⁴ Ch'u⁴, Committee of Ministers; its functions were unchanged but the number of its members was increased.

At the present time the Committee of Ministers is composed as follows:

142. 政務大臣 Chêng⁴ Wu⁴ Ta⁴ Ch'ên², Ex-officio Members of the Committee of Ministers. These are the Grand Secretaries, the Assistant Grand Secretaries and the President of the Council of State. The last-named acts as President.

143. 參預政務大臣 Ts'an¹ Yü⁴ Chêng⁴ Wu⁴ Ta⁴ Ch'ên², Consulting Members of the Committee of Ministers. The Presidents of the various Ministries (Boards) comprise these (eleven, there now being eleven Boards).

144. Two 提調 T'i² Tiao⁴, Proctors; chosen from the Sub-chancellors of the Grand Secretariat.

145. Three 幫提調 Pang¹ T'i² Tiao⁴, Assistant Proctors.

146. Two 總辦 Tsung³ Pan¹, Chief Secretaries.

147. Two 幫總辦 Pang¹ Tsung³ Pan¹, Assistant Chief Secretaries.

148. 文案 Wên² An⁴, Secretaries. These are chosen from the ranks of the Secretaries of the Grand Secretariat; number not fixed.

149. 遞事官 Ti⁴ Shih⁴ Kuan¹, Registrars; chosen from
the Secretaries of the Grand Sec) tariat; number not fixed.

149
to
153

COMMITTEE FOR DRAWING UP REGULATIONS FOR CONSTITUTIONAL GOVERNMENT.

150 考查政治館 K'ao³ Ch'a² Chêng⁴ Chih⁴ Kuan³,
Committee for the Investigation of the Principles of Modern
Politics and Government; established in 1905 for the supervision
of everything connected with the introduction of constitutional
government, for the compilation of a code of constitutional laws,
and for the discussion of the most important questions of State
administration.

In 1907 an Imperial Edict, dated 13th August, directed
that the name of the Committee be changed to:

150A. 憲政編查館 Hsien⁴ Chêng⁴ Pien¹ Ch'a² Kuan³,
Committee for Drawing up Regulations for Constitutional
Government. This Committee was charged with the supervision
of the introduction of Constitutional Government in China.

By the Rules, elaborated by the Committee itself, approved
by the Emperor on the 24th August, 1907, at the head of the
Committee for Drawing up Regulations for Constitutional Government there are two members of the Council of State, styled:

151. 管理憲政編查事務 Kuan³ Li³ Hsien⁴ Chêng⁴
Pien¹ Ch'a² Shih⁴ Wu⁴, Permanent Members of the Committee
for Drawing up Regulations for Constitutional Government.
These officials, for the actual management of affairs, appoint two

152. 提調 T'i² Tiao⁴, Proctors (from the ranks of Vice-
Presidents of Ministries, or Officials of similar rank).

153. 總核員 Tsung³ Ho² Yüan², Examiners; two. These
officials supervise the preparation of reports, manage correspondence, and control the publication of a newspaper.

154. At the Committee for Drawing up Regulations for Constitutional Government there are two Bureaux, *i.e.* Revising Bureau and Statistical Bureau.

154A. 編 制 局 Pien[1] Chih[4] Chü[2], Revising Bureau; composed of three 科 K'o[1], Sections.

154B. 統 計 局 T'ung[3] Chi[4] Chü[2], Statistical Bureau; composed of three 科 K'o[1], Sections.

154C. At the head of each of the afore-mentioned Bureaux there is a 局 長 Chü[2] Chang[3], President, assisted by a 副 局 長 Fu[4] Chü[2] Chang[3], Vice-President.

Each Section is under a 正 科 員 Chêng[4] K'o[1] Yüan[2], Section Chief, to whom are attached a number of 副 科 員 Fu[4] K'o[1] Yüan[2], Assistant Section Chiefs (the number of these depends on the needs of the various Sections).

155. 總 務 處 Tsung[3] Wu[4] Ch'u[4], Chancery. This is directed by a 總 辦 Tsung[3] Pan[1], Chief of the Chancery; he is assisted by 科 員 K'o[1] Yüan[2], Assistant Chiefs.

The Chancery was established to deal with the registering of in-coming and out-going documents and for controlling the income and expenditure. It was formerly called 庶 務 處 Shu[4] Wu[4] Ch'u[4].

156. 譯 書 處 I[4] Shu[1] Ch'u[4], Translating Office (Interpreting Office)

... to the Committee for Drawing up Regulations for Constitutional Government. The staff of this office is not fixed.

157. 圖 書 處 T'u[2] Shu[1] Ch'u[4], Library; directed by 收 掌 Shou[1] Chang[3], Librarian. Here are kept works in Chinese and foreign languages, as well as maps.

158. 官 報 局 Kuan[1] Pao[4] Chü[2], Government Newspapers Office. This is directed by a 總 辦 Tsung[3] Pan[1], Superintendent, who is responsible for the editorial, proof reading and printing sections into which the Office is divided, *i.e.*

1. 編輯科 Pien¹ Chi⁴ K'o¹, Editorial Section,
2. 校對科 Chiao⁴ Tui⁴ K'o¹, Proof Reading Section, and
3 印刷科 Yin⁴ Shua¹ K'o¹, Printing Section.

159
to
160ᴀ

159. At the Committee for Drawing up Regulations for Constitutional Government there are many somewhat unofficial posts, namely :

159ᴀ. 憲政編查館行走 Hsien⁴ Chêng⁴ Pien¹ Ch'a² Kuan³ Hsing² Tsou³, Attaché of the Committee for the Drawing up of Regulations for Constitutional Government. These officials are appointed from the ranks of expectant Metropolitan officials of the 3rd to the 5th classes.

159ʙ. 一等諮議員 I¹ Têng³ Tzu¹ I⁴ Yüan², Advisers of the First Class, and 二等諮議員 Erh Têng³ Tzu¹ I⁴ Yüan², Advisers of the Second Class. These are, at the Capital, chosen from officials of the ranks of Vice-President of a Ministry to Secretary of a Ministry and, in the provinces, from officials of the ranks of Taot'ai to Governor.

160. 考核專科 K'ao³ Ho² Chuan¹ K'o¹, Investigation Bureau. This Bureau was established at the Committee for Drawing up Regulations for Constitutional Government in consequence of a report by the Committee approved by Imperial Edict of the 2nd January, 1909, for keeping a watch that constitutional reform schemes are properly carried out.

In Peking, the Ministries, and, in the provinces, the Governor-Generals or Governors, must report every six months as to what has been accomplished, whence the Investigation Bureau is kept informed as to the progress of the preliminary efforts with regard to the introduction of constitutional government in China.

160ᴀ. 總辦 Tsung³ Pan¹, Bureau Chief; at the head of the Investigation Bureau. This official is under the control of the Proctors of the Committee for Drawing up Regulations for Constitutional Government (*see* No. 152). He has subordinated to him :

5

161
to
162ʙ

2 帮辦 Pang¹ Pan⁴, Assistants,

2 正科員 Chêng⁴ K'o¹ Yüan², Senior Secretaries, and

8 副科員 Fu⁴ K'o¹ Yüan², Junior Secretaries.

161. By an Imperial Edict, dated 22nd October, 1907, it was directed, in reply to a report of the Committee for Drawing up Regulations for Constitutional Government, that there be established, in the Capital at the Ministries and important Government Offices, 統計處 T'ung³ Chi⁴ Ch'u⁴, Statistical Bureaux, and, in the provinces, in the yamen of the Governor-Generals or Governors, 調查局 Tiao⁴ Ch'a² Chü², Information Bureaux, with the object of furnishing the Committee with necessary information.

162. 統計處 T'ung³ Chi⁴ Ch'u⁴, Statistical Bureaux; first established at six of the Ministries, i.e. Board of Home Affairs, Board of Rites, Board of Finance, Board of Posts and Communications, Board of Agriculture, Works and Commerce, and Board of Justice. Later these bureaux are to be established at the remaining Ministries.

The organization of the Statistical Bureaux is not the same for all the Boards.

162ᴀ. The Statistical Bureau at the Board of Rites has at its head a 總核 Tsung³ Ho², Superintendent, and is divided into two sections :

1. 調查處 Tiao⁴ Ch'a² Ch'u⁴, Information Section, and

2. 編制處 Pien¹ Chih⁴ Ch'u⁴, Revising Section. Each Section has a staff consisting of 1 提調 T'i² Tiao⁴, Proctor, and 10 科員 K'o¹ Yüan², Secretaries.

162ʙ. At the Board of Finance the Statistical Bureau is supervised by a 領辦 Ling³ Pan¹, Chief Director, to whom there are subordinated 4 總辦 Tsung³ Pan¹, Directors, 10 帮辦 Pang¹ Pan¹, Vice-Directors, and 2 坐辦 Tso⁴ Pan⁴, Junior Vice-Directors.

163. 調查局 Tiao⁴ Ch‘a² Chü², Information Bureaux ; established in each province. These are under the control of the respective Governor-General or Governor and their organization is based on a Memorial from the Committee for Drawing up Regulations for Constitutional Government, approved by the Emperor on the 22nd October, 1907.

163A. 總辦 Tsung³ Pan⁴, Director. This official, appointed by the Committee for Drawing up Regulations for Constitutional Government, on the recommendation of the local Governor-General or Governor, for managing the Information Bureaux, may, at the same time, do duty as Adviser to the Committee (compare No. 159B).

163B. The Information Bureaux are each divided into two sections :

1. 法制科 Fa⁴ Chih⁴ K‘o¹, Section of Laws and Regulations, and

2. 統計科. T‘ung³ Chi⁴ K‘o¹, Statistical Section.

Each of these Sections is divided into three 股 Ku³, Sub-sections.

At the head of each section there is a 科長 K‘o¹ Chang³, Section Chief, who, under the supervision of the Director, manages the affairs of his section.

Sub-sections are managed by 管股委員 Kuan³ Ku³ Wei³ Yüan², Secretaries (from one to three in each Sub-section), under the supervision of the Section Chief.

163C. For correspondence there are, at the Sections and Sub-sections, (1) 2 總書記 Tsung³ Shu¹ Chi⁴, Senior Secretaries, (2) 2 幫總書記 Pang¹ Tsung³ Shu¹ Chi⁴, Assistant Senior Secretaries, (3) 2 科書記 K‘o¹ Shu¹ Chi⁴, Section Secretaries, (4) 2 股書記 Ku³ Shu¹ Chi⁴, Sub-section Secretaries, (5) 2 管卷書記 Kuan³ Chüan⁴ Shu¹ Chi⁴, Archivists, and (6) 2 收發書記 Shou¹ Fa¹ Shu¹ Chi⁴, Registrars.

163D
to
165

163D. 庶務處 Shu⁴ Wu⁴ Ch'u⁴, Chancery; for managing the affairs of this establishment the Bureau Chief appoints 2 庶務委員 Shu⁴ Wu⁴ Wei³ Yüan², Chancery Deputies.

THE NATIONAL ASSEMBLY AND PROVINCIAL ASSEMBLIES.

164. 資政院 Tzu¹ Chêng⁴ Yüan⁴, The National Assembly; its establishment was foreshadowed by an Edict of the 20th September, 1907. The tenor of this Edict was:

"A Constitution is necessary to the country. As the two "Houses of Parliament cannot at once be inaugurated, it will be "necessary at first to establish an Assembly of Ministers to "confer on State matters and to prepare the foundations of "Constitutional Government. Prince P'u Lun, Prince of the "4th Order, and the Grand Secretary, Sun Chia Nai, are "appointed to preside over the said Assembly and they are "commanded to confer with the Council of State on details and "modes of procedure. Having settled upon these, details are "to be presented to the Throne for Imperial sanction. Respect "This."

165. The first National Assembly, organized on the authority of the Edict mentioned (*see* No. 164), is merely a temporary establishment entrusted with the special task of drawing up regulations for, and organizing elections to, future National Assemblies, which will serve as a foundation for the Parliament that will be opened in 1917. According to an Imperial Decree of the 4th of November, 1910, Parliament is to be opened in 1913 (*see* No. 127).

Similarly, officials previously employed in connection with the preparations for the Assembly have also had temporary posts.

165A.　As at first constituted, there were at the head of the National Assembly two 總裁 Tsung³ Ts'ai², Presidents, and, attached to them, five 協理資政院事務 Hsieh² Li³ Tzu¹ Chêng⁴ Yüan⁴ Shih⁴ Wu⁴, Senior Supervisors, three 資政院幫辦事務 Tzu¹ Chêng⁴ Yüan⁴ Pang¹ Pan⁴ Shih⁴ Wu⁴, Junior Supervisors, and an indefinite number of 資政院參議 Tzu¹ Chêng⁴ Yüan² Ts'an¹ I⁴, Advisers (at the last session there were six).

165A to 166

166.　By Rules drawn up by the National Assembly (consisting of 10 headings—the first two of which were sanctioned on the 9th July, 1908, and later amended and, with the others, approved on the 23rd August, 1909) the subjects that may be discussed by the Assembly are :

National Income and Expenditure, Methods of Taxation and the National Debt, New Codes of Laws and the Amendment of existing Codes (the right of amendment of constitutional laws is removed from the sphere of influence of the Assembly).

All measures handed over to the National Assembly for its decision must first be considered by the Council of State or the High Officials.　The Assembly, however, in connection with questions relating to methods of taxation, the public debt and the preparation or amendment of codes of laws, may initiate discussion and propose draft measures (articles 14 and 15 of the Rules).

When the Assembly has arrived at a decision on any subject, a Memorial must be prepared by the Presidents and Supervisors of that body, in consultation with the Council of State, or with the President of the Board concerned ; this Memorial, in the usual manner, must await the final decision of an Imperial Edict (article 16).

Matters of disagreement between the National Assembly and the Council of State or the High Officials are to be decided by the Emperor (article 18):

167   As regards the Provincial Assemblies, the National Assembly acts as high controller, deciding differences between the individual Provincial Assemblies and between the Provincial Assemblies and the High Provincial Authorities (articles 22 to 24).

Sessions of the National Assembly are of two kinds, *i.e.* ordinary and extraordinary. Ordinary sessions are to be held each year, during the 9th, 10th and 11th moons (article 31); an extraordinary session may be summoned by Imperial Edict whenever occasion demands (article 32).

In the Rules it is clearly pointed out for what reasons the Emperor may adjourn (article 52), or even dissolve, the National Assembly and call for a new election (article 53).

The scheme of constitutional reforms provides for a general election, in 1910, of delegates to the National Assembly and its opening the same year. Also, it calls for the erection of a hall in the Eastern part of the Tartar City at the 朝 陽 門 Ch'ao² Yang² Mên² (also 齊 化 門 Ch'i² Hua⁴ Mên²), to the North-west of the 觀 象 台 Kuan¹ Hsiang⁴ T'ai², the Observatory, where were formerly the 貢 院 Kung⁴ Yüan⁴, Examination Halls, for the use of the Assembly.

167.   At the head of the National Assembly there is now a 總 裁 Tsung³ Ts'ai², President, appointed by Imperial Edict from the ranks of Princes of the Blood or from officials of the highest rank (article 2). To him there is attached one 副 總 裁 Fu⁴ Tsung³ Ts'ai², Vice-President, appointed by the Emperor from officials of rank not lower than the 3rd (article 3).

While the Assembly is in session, the President and Vice-President do duty as 議 長 I⁴ Chang³, Chairman, and 副 議 長 Fu⁴ I⁴ Chang³, Vice-Chairman of Sessions of the National Assembly (article 30). 資 政 院 議 員 Tzu¹ Chêng⁴ Yüan⁴ I⁴ Yüan², Members of the National Assembly (the number is fixed at two hundred). One hundred of these are appointed by the

Emperor and one hundred elected from the Provincial Assemblies **167A**
(article 4).   **to**

All members of the.National Assembly are to rank equally   **167B**
irrespective of the positions they may hold (article 5).

Eligible for membership in the National Assembly are
persons over 30 years of age who belong to the following classes:

    (a)   Hereditary Princes of the Blood,

    (b)   Manchus and Chinese holding hereditary titles,

    (c)   Hereditary Princes of Mongolia, Tibet and Turkestan,

    (d)   Imperial Clansmen (irrespective of degree of kin),

    (e)   Officials of Metropolitan Establishment between the
4th and 7th ranks (with the exception of officials of justice,
prosecutors and police officials),

    (f)   Eminent scholars,

    (g)   Large tax-payers, and

    (h)   Members of the Provincial Assemblies (*see* details in
articles 9 to 13 of the Rules).

Detailed Regulations, drawn up by the National Assembly
itself and sanctioned by the Emperor on the 26th October, 1909,
define clearly those who come within the eight categories
mentioned above.   The appointment of members and the electoral
procedure are also elaborated in these Regulations.

167A.   Immediately on opening a session, the members of
the National Assembly are, by lot, divided into various 股 Ku³,
committees, for dealing with special questions.   The members of
the committees, 股 員 Ku³ Yüan², elect their respective chairman,
股 長 Ku³ Chang³.

167B.   For the clerical work of the National Assembly
there is a: 秘書廳 Pi⁴ Shu¹ T'ing¹, Secretariat.   At the head of
this is a 秘 書 長 Pi⁴ Shu¹ Chang³, Senior Secretary ; 4A,
appointed by the Emperor.   To him are subordinated 一 等 秘
書 官 I¹ Têng³ Pi⁴ Shu¹ Kuan¹, Secretaries of the First Class;

37c to 68

5A, 二等秘書官 Êrh⁴ Têng³ Pi⁴ Shu¹ Kuan¹, Secretaries of the Second Class; 6A, and 三等秘書官 San¹ Têng³ Pi⁴ Shu¹ Kuan¹, Secretaries of the Third Class; 7A (there are four Secretaries of each class; in all twelve).

The Secretariat is composed of four Sections, *i.e.* (1) 機要科 Chi¹ Yao⁴ K'o¹, Secret Affairs, (2) 議事科 I⁴ Shih⁴ K'o¹, Projects, (3) 速記科 Su² Chi⁴ K'o¹, Stenography, and (4) 庶務科 Shu⁴ Wu⁴ K'o¹, Miscellaneous Affairs. The First Class Secretary at each of the Sections ranks as Chief, 科長 K'o¹ Chang³, the others as his assistants.

In addition to the foregoing there are 書記 Shu¹ Chi⁴, Writers, and 速記生 Su² Chi⁴ Shêng¹, Stenographers on the staff of the Secretariat, and there is also a 圖書室 T'u² Shu Shih¹, Library, in charge of one of the Secretaries, who is styled 管理員 Kuan³ Li³ Yüan², Librarian.

167c. At the Assembly there are special 守衛警官 Shou³ Wei³ Ching¹ Kuan¹, Guards, completely under the authority of the President and Vice-President.

168. 諮議局 Tzu¹ I⁴ Chü², Provincial Assemblies. These are the National Assembly's representatives in the provinces and their establishment was directed by Imperial Edict dated 19th October, 1907.

On the 22nd July, 1908, Regulations for the Provincial Assemblies drawn up by the Committee for Drawing up Regulations for Constitutional Government were sanctioned by the Emperor and, in 1909, in all the provinces, with the exception of the New Dominion—where, owing to the ignorance of the people the assembly will be, at least at first, drawn up on different lines —elections for members of the Assemblies were held.

In the New Dominion members of the Assembly will be appointed, not elected (*see* the report of the Governor, Lien K'uei, dated early in 1909).

[56]

On the 14th October, 1909, the Provincial Assemblies had **169** their first session (*see* Edict dated 13th October, 1909).

As directed by the first article of the Regulations, Provincial Assemblies are established in the cities at which the Governor-Generals or Governors reside, their chief duty being to bring the opinions of the people to the notice of the chief provincial executive that he may- be fully informed of the needs of his district and maintain order therein.

For the election of members of the Provincial Assemblies there is a double election, that is, there is an election of delegates by the people and these, in turn, elect certain of their number as members of the Assemblies.

The number of members of the Provincial Assembly is not the same for all the provinces but ranges from 30 (for the provinces of Kirin, Heilungchiang and Hsinchiang) to 140 (for Chihli province).

The electoral franchise is given to all males of twenty five years of age or more, provided they are natives of the province and possess any of the qualifications stated in detail in the Regulations (articles 3 and 4).

Membership in the Provincial Assembly is open to all males of thirty years of age or more, natives, and non-natives, provided they have been resident in the province concerned for ten years, who are free of the disqualifications enumerated in detail in articles 5 to 8 of the Regulations.

169. In the internal organization of the Provincial Assemblies there are :

1. 議 長 I⁴ Chang³, President,

2. 副 議 長 Fu⁴ I⁴ Chang³, Vice-President, and 常 駐 議 員 Ch'ang² Chu⁴ I⁴ Yüan², Resident Members of the Assembly. The number of these is one fifth the total number of members of the Assembly (articles 10 to 14 of the Regulations).

[57]

170 to 172

The members of the Provincial Assemblies are elected for a term of three years; the President and Vice-Presidents retain their offices during the entire term, the Resident Members serve one year only (articles 15 to 17 of the Regulations).

170. The Provincial Assemblies may discuss affairs dealing with finance, yearly income and expenditure, methods of taxation, the raising of loans for provincial needs, the election of members to the National Assembly, and questions submitted to them by the National Assembly, etc. (*see* articles 21   30 of the Regulations, in which, also, is defined in detail the relation of the Provincial Assemblies to the Governor-Generals, Governors and the National Assembly).

171. To the Provincial Assembly there is attached a 辦事處 Pan⁴ Shih⁴ Ch'u⁴, Chancery, under the control of the President and Vice-Presidents, for dealing with correspondence, accounts and the current affairs of the Assembly. This office is directed by 1 書記長 Shu¹ Chi⁴ Chang³, Chief Secretary, and 4 書記 Shu¹ Chi⁴, Secretaries, who are selected by the President, subject to the approval of the Governor-General or Governor (*see* articles 51 and 52 of the Regulations).

172. The management of elections for members of the Provincial Assemblies is undertaken by special committees in which the local officials act as 初選監督 Ch'u¹ Hsuan³ Chien¹ Tu¹, Executive Supervisors of the First Election, or 複選監督 Fu⁴ Hsuan³ Chien¹ Tu¹, Executive Supervisors of the Second Election.

To the above-mentioned officials there are subordinated during elections:

1. 投票管理員 T'ou² P'iao⁴ Kuan³ Li³ Yüan², Supervisors of Balloting,

2. 投票監查員 T'ou² P'iao⁴ Chien¹ Ch'a² Yüan², Inspectors of Balloting,

3. 開票管理員 K'ai¹ P'iao⁴ Kuan³ Li³ Yüan², Supervising Tellers, and

[58]

4. 開 票 監 查 員 Kʻai¹ Pʻiao⁴ Chien¹ Chʻa² Yüan², **173**
Tellers (*see* details in articles 18 to 20 of the Regulations dealing **to**
with the Provincial Assemblies and the election of members, being **175**
additional articles to the Regulations).

173. 諮 議 局 籌 辦 處 Tzu¹ I⁴ Chü² Chʻou² Pan⁴ Chʻu⁴,
Offices for arranging for Provincial Assemblies, established in
the various provinces in accordance with the instructions issued
by the Department for Drawing up Regulations for Constitutional
Government, in 1908, with the object of organizing the elections
of members of the Provincial Assemblies. After the opening of
the Councils, on the 14th October, 1909, these offices ceased to
exist.

COMMITTEE FOR REVISING AND COMPILING CIVIL AND CRIMINAL CODES.

174. 脩 訂 法 律 館 Hsiu¹ Ting⁴ Fa⁴ Lü⁴ Kuan³, Committee
for Revising and Compiling Civil and Criminal Codes. This
came into existence because of an Imperial Edict of the 11th
October, 1907, the tenor of which was :

"The Committee for Drawing up Regulations for
" Constitutional Government has presented a Memorial urging
" the appointment of officials to compile new civil and criminal
" codes.

" Shên Chia-pên, Junior Vice-President of the Ministry of
" Justice, Yu Lien-san, ex-Governor of Shansi, and Ying Jui,
" President of the Supreme Court, are appointed as officials for
" the compilation of new civil and criminal codes. They are to
" study the codes of Foreign Powers, make a study of the
" customs and conditions in China, and draw up regulations for
" presentation to us. Respect This."

175. The Committee for Revising and Compiling Civil
and Criminal Codes has at its head two 脩 訂 法 律 大 臣 Hsiu¹
Ting⁴ Fa⁴ Lü⁴ Ta⁴ Chʻen², Presidents, who control :

176 to 183

176. Two 提調 Ti² Tiao⁴, Proctors,

177. 第一科 Ti⁴ I¹ K'o¹, First Section ; its duty is to draw up a code of commercial law. This Section is in charge of a :

177A. 總纂 Tsung³ Tsuan³, Chief Reviser, assisted by 4 纂脩 Tsuan³ Hsiu¹, Revisers, 4 協脩 Hsieh² Hsiu¹, Assistant Revisers and 1 or 2 調查員 Tiao⁴ Ch'a² Yüan², Correctors.

178. 第二科 Ti⁴ Erh⁴ K'o¹, Second Section ; in charge of the compilation of civil and criminal codes.

178A. The staff at the Second Section is identical to that of the First Section (see No. 177A).

179. 譯書處 I⁴ Shu¹ Ch'u⁴, Translating Office (Interpreting Office) ; in charge of the translation from foreign languages of laws and judicial works generally. This office is under a 總纂 Tsung³ Tsuan³, Chief Reviser, assisted by 譯員 I⁴ Yüan², Translators (Interpreters) (number not fixed).

180. 編案處 Pien¹ An⁴ Ch'u⁴, Codifying Office. At the head of this office is a 總纂 Tsung³ Tsuan³, Chief Reviser, and subordinated to him there are 2 纂脩 Tsuan³ Hsiu¹, Revisers and 2 協脩 Hsieh² Hsiu¹, Assistant Revisers.

181. 庶務處 Shu⁴ Wu⁴ Ch'u⁴, Chancery ; in charge of clerical work, accounts and economical administration. At its head is a 庶務總辦 Shu⁴ Wu⁴ Tsung³ Pan⁴, Chancery Chief, assisted by 委員 Wei³ Yüan², Deputies (number indefinite).

182. 諮議官 Tzu¹ I⁴ Kuan¹, Advisers ; appointed to an indefinite number by the Presidents of the Committee. All the Provincial Judges are, ex-officio, Advisers to the Committee (for details see the Memorial from the Committee, with three enclosures, sanctioned by the Emperor on the 22nd June, 1908).

183. 調查員 Tiao⁴ Ch'a² Yüan², Legal Experts ; appointed in an indefinite number, by the Presidents of the Committee, from its staff or from the most experienced lawyers to supply the Committee with necessary information.

GENERAL STAFF OF THE ARMY.

184. 軍諮府 Chün[1] Tzu[1] Fu[3], General Staff Office ; not in existence as yet ; to be organized on the same lines as that of Germany or Japan.

In an Edict, dated the 6th November, 1906, ruling the re-organization of the Board of War, it was directed that, as no General Staff Office was in existence, all matters pertaining to such an office were to be attended to by the :

184A. 軍諮處 Chün[1] Tzu[1] Ch'u[4], General Staff Council, which is attached to the Board of War (compare Nos. 184B, 417 and 418).

By an Imperial Edict, dated the 15th July, 1909, the General Staff Council was made independent of the Board of War and its functions as :

184B. 軍諮處 Chün[1] Tzu[1] Ch'u[4], General Staff Council, which assists the Emperor as Commander-in-Chief of the Army and Navy.

The General Staff Council as at present constituted is not the same as the similar office in Russia but is a preliminary step to the establishment of a General Staff Office (*see* No. 184).

With regard to all questions relating to defences or the command of the forces, the General Staff Council makes recommendations which, after the Emperor's sanction, are transmitted to the Board of War or the Admiralty for execution.

Under the supervision of the General Staff Council there are :

The Military Academy (*see* No. 712 ; the school for Officers at Paotingfu, *see* No. 712A, is to be under the General Staff Council until the Military Academy is established), Schools for Military Draftsmen (*see* No. 715D), Military Attachés at the Legations abroad (*see* No. 329),

Field Officers of the Army and Navy, etc.

184c to 184i

Provisional Regulations for the General Staff Council have been drawn up by itself and were sanctioned by the Emperor on the 22nd September, 1909.

At the head of the General Staff Council there are :

184c. Two 管理軍諮處事務 Kuan³ Li³ Chün¹ Tzu¹ Ch'u⁴ Shih⁴ Wu⁴, Chiefs of the General Staff Council ; these officials have the privilege of making personal reports to the Emperor. To them are directly subordinated :

184d. Two 軍諮使 Chün¹ Tzu¹ Shih³, Chiefs of the Chancery of the General Staff Council (officials of the rank of Lieutenant-General, Major-General or Colonel), who are in charge of the :

184e. 總務廳 Tsung³ Wu⁴ T'ing¹, Chancery ; the duties of this office have not been determined.

184f. To the General Staff Council, in addition to the offices already mentioned, there are attached, with functions yet to be fixed :

1. 第一廳 Ti⁴ I¹ T'ing¹, First Section,
2. 第二廳 Ti⁴ Erh⁴ T'ing¹, Second Section,
3. 第三廳 Ti⁴ San¹ T'ing¹, Third Section,
4. 第四廳 Ti⁴ Ssu⁴ T'ing¹, Fourth Section,
5. 第五廳 Ti⁴ Wu³ T'ing¹, Fifth Section, and
6. 海軍廳 Hai³ Chün¹ T'ing¹, Naval Section.

At the head of each Section there is a :

184g. 廳長 T'ing¹ Chang³, Section Chief (from officials of the rank of Major-General or Colonel). This official directs, under the supervision of the Directors of the General Staff Council, all affairs pertaining to the Sub-sections of his respective Section. Each is assisted by a :

184h. 副官 Fu⁴ Kuan¹, Adjutant (from officials of the rank of Captain or Lieutenant), who manages the general affairs.

184i. Each Section is composed of 科 K'o¹, Sub-sections (their number, functions and staff have still to be particularly determined).

[62]

At the head of each Sub-section is a :

184J. 科長 K‘o¹ Chang³, Sub-section Chief (from officials of the rank of Colonel or Lieutenant Colonel), who is in charge of the affairs of the Sub-section and is assisted by :

1. 一等科員 I¹ Têng³ K‘o¹ Yüan², Secretaries of the First Class (from Lieutenant Colonels and Captains, or civil officials of similar rank),

2. 二等科員 Êrh⁴ Têng³ K‘o¹ Yüan², Secretaries of the Second Class, and

3. 三等科員 San¹ Têng³ K‘o¹ Yüan², Secretaries of the Third Class (these two latter are officials of the rank of Captain or Lieutenant, or civil officials of corresponding rank.)

For the clerical work of the Sub-sections there are attached to the Sub-section Chiefs :

1. 一等錄事 I¹ Têng³ Lu⁴ Shih⁴, Writers of the First Class,

2. 二等錄事 Êrh⁴ Têng³ Lu⁴ Shih⁴, Writers of the Second Class, and

3. 三等錄事 San¹ Têng³ Lu⁴ Shih⁴, Writers of the Third Class.

184K. 顧問官 Ku⁴ Wên⁴ Kuan¹, Advisers. The number of these is not fixed. They are appointed by the Emperor on the recommendation of the General Staff Council.

184L. Having under its control (as stated above in No. 184B) all the Field Officers of the Army and Navy, 參謀官 Ts‘an¹ Mou² Kuan¹, the General Staff Council has drawn up Regulations concerning the ranks of Field Officers, in six articles (sanctioned by the Emperor on the 5th October, 1909), which empower the Council to issue commissions to persons of a rank not lower than 1st Lieutenant, who have passed the examinations at the Military Academy (*see* No. 712; until its establishment, the School for Field Officers at Paotingfu, *see* No. 712A) and to persons who have completed the course of study

**185
to
185B**

at foreign Military Schools and have served in the line for more than one year.

These officers, being directly subordinated to the Directors of the General Staff Council, are obliged to assist the Commanders of the Forces where they may be stationed by drawing up schemes of defence and by drilling the troops.

Field Officers must, yearly, serve two months in the line; they may choose the district in which they wish to serve. For distinction they wear particular stripes similar to those of the New Palace Guards.

COMMISSION FOR THE REORGANIZATION OF THE NAVY

185. 籌辦海軍事務處 Ch'ou² Pan⁴ Hai³ Chün¹ Shih⁴ Wu⁴ Ch'u⁴, Commission for the Reorganization of the Navy. This was established by Imperial Edict of the 19th February, 1909, under the supervision of three 籌畫海軍基礎大臣 Ch'ou² Hua⁴ Hai³ Chün¹ Chi¹ Ch'u³ Ta⁴ Ch'ên², Commissioners in charge of the Reorganization of the Navy (Prince Su, President of the Board of Home Affairs, Prince Tsai Tsê, President of the Board of Finance, and T'ieh Liang, President of the Board of War), and the presidency of Prince Ch'ing, for elaborating plans for the formation of the nucleus of a Navy.

Its preliminary work accomplished, the Commission was reorganized by Edict of the 15th July, 1909, with:

185A. Two 籌辦海軍大臣 Ch'ou² Pan⁴ Hai³ Chün¹ Ta⁴ Ch'ên², Presidents of the Commission for the Reorganization of the Navy (the brother of the Prince Regent, 載洵 Tsai³ Hsün¹, Prince of the 3rd Degree, and Admiral 薩鎮氷 Sa¹ Chên⁴ Ping¹), who were directed to formulate plans for an independent Ministry of the Navy (*see* No. 185B).

185B. 海軍部 Hai³ Chün¹ Pu⁴, Ministry of the Navy; not yet organized.

185c to 185G

In an Imperial Edict, dated 6th November, 1906, it was ruled that until a Ministry of the Navy should be established, matters appertaining to such an office were to be attended to at the Board of War.

185c. 海軍處 Hai³ Chün¹ Ch'u⁴, Naval Council; attached to the Board of War (*see* Nos. 417 and 419). The staff for this office was arranged by the Board of War in 1907 (sanctioned by the Emperor on the 7th June, 1907).

185d. By Imperial Edict of the 15th July, 1909, the Naval Council was made independent of the Board of War and directly subordinated to the Presidents of the Commission for the Reorganization of the Navy (*see* No. 185A).

185e. At the head of the Naval Council there are a 正 使 Chêng⁴ Shih³, Superintendent, and a 副 使 Fu⁴ Shih³, Assistant Superintendent, who, under the supervision of the Presidents of the Commission for the Reorganization of the Navy (*see* No. 185A), attend to the affairs of the Council, *i.e.* the staff of the Navy, the drawing up of Rules and Regulations for the Navy, supervising of shipbuilding, Naval Schools, etc. They are assisted by 2 承 發 官 Ch'êng² Fa¹ Kuan¹, Registrars, and 4 錄 事 Lu⁴ Shih⁴, Writers.

185f. The Naval Council is to consist of 6 司 Ssu¹, Departments; three of these have already been organized and three will later be arranged for.

185g. 機 要 司 Chi¹ Yao⁴ Ssu¹, Department of Urgent Affairs; dealing with the drawing up of naval codes and regulations, armament of ships, navigation and marine engineering. It is divided into four Sections:

1. 制 度 科 Chih⁴ Tu⁴ K'o¹, Section for Naval Codes and Regulations,

2. 籌 械 科 Ch'ou² Hsieh⁴ K'o¹, Section for Naval Armament,

3. 駕 駛 科 Chia⁴ Shih³ K'o¹, Navigation Section, and

5

185ʜ
to
185ᴊ

4. 輪機科 Lun² Chi¹ K'o¹, Section for Marine Engineering.

For each Department there is a 司長 Ssu¹ Chang³, Department Director, assisted by a 承發官 Chêng² Fa¹ Kuan¹, Registrar.

For each Section there is a 科長 K'o¹ Chang³, Section Chief, assisted by 12 科員 K'o¹ Yüan², Secretaries (of the First, Second and Third Classes), and 6 錄事 Lu⁴ Shih⁴, Writers.

185ʜ. 船政司 Ch'uan² Chêng⁴ Ssu¹, Construction Department; supervises construction and repair of men-of-war. This is not divided into Sections. Its staff comprises a 司長 Ssu¹ Chang³, Department Director, a 承發官 Ch'êng² Fa¹ Kuan¹, Registrar, 5 考工官 K'ao³ Kung¹ Kuan¹, Inspectors of Works (of the First, Second and Third Classes), a 藝師 I⁴ Shih¹, Chief Engineer, 2 藝士 I⁴ Shih⁴, Engineers, and 6 錄事 Lu⁴ Shih⁴, Writers.

185ɪ. 運籌司 Yün⁴ Ch'ou² Ssu¹, Department of Naval Tactics; supervises matters of strategy, instruction and hydrographical affairs. It is divided into three Sections:

1. 謀畧科 Mou² Lüeh⁴ K'o¹, Section of Strategy,
2. 教務科 Chiao¹ Wu⁴ K'o¹, Instruction Section, and
3. 測海科 Ts'ê⁴ Hai³ K'o¹, Hydrographical Section.

The staff of the Department of Naval Tactics includes a 司長 Ssu¹ Chang³, Department Director, a 承發官 Ch'êng² Fa¹ Kuan¹, Registrar, and for each Section, a 科長 K'o¹ Chang³, Section Chief, 6 科員 K'o¹ Yüan², Secretaries (of the First, Second and Third Classes), 2 藝師 I⁴ Shih¹, Chief Engineers, 3 藝士 I⁴ Shih⁴, Engineers, and 6 錄事 Lu⁴ Shih⁴, Writers.

185ᴊ. 儲備司 Ch'u³ Pei⁴ Ssu¹, Department of Communications and Accounts; not yet in operation. This is to be composed of three Sections:

1. 會計科 Hui⁴ (K'uai) Chi⁴ K'o¹, Accounts Section,

185ᴋ
to
185ᴘ

2. 服用科 Fu² Yung⁴ K'o¹, Ammunition Section, and

3. 屯積科 T'un² Chi² K'o¹, Supplies Section.

Its staff will include a 司長 Ssu¹ Chang³, Department Director, a 承發官 Ch'êng² Fa¹ Kuan¹, Registrar, and, for each Section, a 科長 K'o¹ Chang², Section Chief, 9 科員 K'o¹ Yüan², Secretaries (of the First, Second and Third Classes), and 6 錄事 Lu⁴ Shih⁴, Writers.

185ᴋ. 醫務司 I¹ Wu⁴ Ssu¹, Medical Department; not yet functioning; to supervise medical affairs of the Navy. This Department will not be divided into Sections. Its staff will include a 司長 Ssu¹ Chang³, Department Director, a 承發官 Chêng² Fa¹ Kuan¹, Registrar, 5 醫官 I¹ Kuan¹, Medical Officers (of the First, Second and Third Classes), and 6 錄事 Lu⁴ Shih⁴, Writers.

185ʟ. 法務司 Fa⁴ Wu⁴ Ssu¹, Department of Naval Law; for drawing up naval laws. This Department will not be sub-divided into Sections. Its staff will consist of a 司長 Ssu¹ Chang³, a 承發官 Ch'êng². Fa¹ Kuan¹, Registrar, 4 司法官 Ssu¹ Fa⁴ Kuan¹, Legal Advisers (of the First, Second and Third Classes), and 6 錄事 Lu⁴ Shih⁴, Writers.

185ᴍ. 編譯局 Pien¹ I⁴ Chü², Translation Office (Interpreting Office). This is directed by a 總辦 Tsung³ Pan⁴, Chief, assisted by a 正監督 Chêng⁴ Chien¹ Tu¹, Director, and two 提調 T'i² Tiao⁴, Proctors.

185ɴ. 兵學館 Ping¹ Hsüeh² Kuan³, Military Instruction Office; at its head is a 提調 T'i² Tiao⁴, Proctor.

185ᴏ. 醫學館 I¹ Hsüeh² Kuan³, Medical Institute; at its head is a 監督 Chien¹ Tu¹, Director.

185ᴘ. For details concerning the Four Squadrons, Staff of the Commander-in-Chief of the Naval Forces at Shanghai, Naval Schools, Shipbuilding Dockyards, Arsenals and Docks *see* Nos. 756, 756ᴀ to 756ᴄ, 757 and 757ᴀ to 757ᴄ.

COMMISSION FOR THE REVISION OF THE
BANNER ORGANIZATION.

186. 變通旗制處 Pien⁴ T'ung¹ Ch'i² Chih⁴ Ch'u⁴, Commission for the Revision of the Banner Organization. This s
established by an Imperial Edict dated the 17th December,
1908, under the direction of six officials, chosen from the ranks
of Princes of the Blood and Presidents and Vice-Presidents of
the Ministries (Manchu), who were directed to consider the
revision of the Banner regulations in consultation with the
Council of State.

This Commission (the establishment of which was foreseen
by the programme of Constitutional Reforms) has, as is stated in
an Edict of the 26th December, 1908, to revise the regulations
of " the Banner organization so as to fit present conditions of the
Empire and to devise means for teaching every Bannerman to
earn a living and become independent." Further, the same
Decree adds that " there is no intention at present of stopping
the pensions and allowances issued to every Bannerman, and all
are to continue, as usual, to draw the same, that there shall be
no misapprehension on the part of Bannermen."

To the Commission has been given the task of reorganizing
the Banner Corps, the main idea in view being to annul the
differences between Manchus and the Chinese population by 1915.

186A. 總司變通旗制處大臣 Tsung³ Ssu¹ Pien⁴ T'ung¹
Ch'i² Chih⁴ Ch'u⁴ Ta⁴ Ch'ên², Presidents of the Commission for
the Revision of the Banner Organization ; at present, as stated
above (see No. 186), there are six. The staff of the Commission
has not as yet been arranged for.

THE ANTI-OPIUM COMMISSION.

187. The Anti-Opium Commission (The Opium Prohibition
Commission) was established by an Imperial Edict, dated the

7th April, 1908, which appointed four 禁煙大臣 Chin[4] Yen[1] Ta[4] Ch'ên[2], Opium Prohibition Commissioners, with 恭親王 溥偉 P'u[3] Wei[3], Prince Kung[1], Prince of the First Degree, at its head. The Commission was given great power with reference to the examination of officials and populace and it was directed that the expenses of the Commission be defrayed from local Opium Taxes. For its administration the Commission was instructed to draw up suitable Regulations.

188 to 188ʙ

Originally composed of four officials only as stated above, there were later appointed 提調 T'i[2] Tiao[4], Proctors (3 to 4 in number) to assist the Commission and, by Regulations drawn up by the Commission (sanctioned by the Emperor on the 7th June, 1908), there have been established at all the Provincial capitals :

188. 禁煙公所 Chin[4] Yen[1] Kung[1] So[3], Anti-Opium Bureaux, at the head of which are officials of high local rank (Provincial Treasurers, Commissioners of Education, Police Taot'ais) as 督辦 Tu[1] Pan[4]; also 總理 Tsung[3] Li[3], Superintendents.

As regards the actual management of these Bureaux, the Governor-General or Governor appoints an official, as 總辦 Tsung[3] Pan[4], Bureau Chief.

At places other than provincial capitals there are established, either by the Government or on private account, offices called :

188ᴀ. 戒煙局 Chieh[4] Yen[1] Chü[2], Anti-Opium Offices. The internal organization and the functions of the Anti-Opium Offices are similar to those of the Anti-Opium Bureaux (see No. 188).

Finally, the Authorities everywhere exhort the Gentry to establish :

188ʙ. 戒煙會社 Chieh[4] Yen[1] Hui[4] Shê[4], Anti-Opium Societies, the aim of which is to struggle by every means (including the issue of newspapers) against opium-smoking (see details in article by V. V. Hagelstrom, " Summary of Measures

189   taken by the Chinese Government for abolishing Opium-smoking in China," in the "Chinese Good News" of the 28th June, 1909, issue 9–10, pages 1–13).

COMMITTEE IN CHARGE OF CONSTRUCTION OF THE IMPERIAL MAUSOLEUM, "CH'UNG LING."

189. 崇陵工程處 Ch'ung² Ling² Kung¹ Ch'êng- Ch'u⁴, Committee in Charge of Construction of the Imperial Mausoleum, "Ch'ung Ling"; appointed by Imperial Edict of the 5th January, 1909.

This Committee of four 承脩崇陵工程大臣 Ch'êng² Hsiu¹ Ch'ung² Ling² Kung¹ Ch'êng² Ta⁴ Ch'ên², Commissioners in Charge of Construction of the Imperial Mausoleum, "Ch'ung Ling" (Princes 載洵 Tsai³ Hsün¹, 溥倫 P'u³ Lun², and 載澤 Tsai³ Tsê², and the late Grand Secretary, 鹿傳霖 Lu⁴ Ch'uan²-lin²), under the presidency of Prince Ch'ing, was detailed to take charge of the construction of a mausoleum, to be styled 崇陵 Ch'ung² Ling², for the reception of the remains of the late Emperor 德宗景皇帝 Tê² Tsung¹ Ching³ Huang² Ti⁴, from his reign known as 光緒 Kuang¹ Hsü⁴ (1875–1908), near the Western Mausolea (*see* No. 569c), in the valley 金龍峪 Chin¹ Lung² Yü⁴ (of the Golden Dragon).

The work of constructing the Mausoleum is going on under the supervision of officials, holding office at the Capital selected by the Commission, styled 監督 Chien¹ Tu¹, Inspectors (eight, *see* Memorial of the Commission, dated 16th January, 1909), and 監脩 Chien¹ Hsiu¹, Overseers (about 35 of these; *see* Memorial of the Commission, dated 12th February, 1909).

The Edict of the 16th January, 1909, directed that the Emperor Kuang Hsu's Mausoleum should be constructed on the same lines as that of the Emperor T'ung Chih (1862–1875), the 惠陵 Hui⁴ Ling², and that it should be completed within five years; the Commission then to be dissolved.

HISTORIOGRAPHICAL COMMISSION.

190. 實錄館 Shih² Lu⁴ Kuan³, Commission of Historiography; appointed by Imperial Edict of the 21st February, 1909, at the Grand Secretariat (*see* No. 130), for the compilation— 春秋 Ch'un¹ Ch'iu¹, *i.e.* in chronological order—of the annals of the reign of the Emperor 德宗景皇帝 Tê² Tsung¹ Ching³ Huang² Ti⁴, from his reign called 光緒 Kuang¹ Hsü⁴ (1875— 1908).

Detailed Rules for the Commission, defining its duties and determining its staff, drawn up by the Commission itself, were submitted to the Throne and received Imperial Sanction on the 23rd September, 1909.

At the head of the Commission of Historiography is a 監脩總裁 Chien¹ Hsiu¹ Tsung³ Ts'ai², Director-General (one of the Grand Secretaries). His staff consists of :

1. 5 總裁 Tsung³ Ts'ai², Directors (chosen from the Grand Secretaries, Ministers of State and President of the Censorate ; of these, 2 are 滿總裁 Man³ Tsung³ Ts'ai², Manchu Directors, 2 are 漢總裁 Han⁴ Tsung³ Ts'ai², Chinese Directors, and 1 is 蒙古總裁 Mêng³ Ku³ Tsung³ Ts'ai², Mongol Director) ;

2. 6 副總裁 Fu⁴ Tsung³ Ts'ai², Vice-Directors (chosen from the Vice-Presidents of Ministries ; 3 are Manchus and 3 are Chinese),

3. 3 提調 T'i² Tiao⁴, Proctors (1 Manchu, 1 Chinese and 1 Mongol),

4. 6 總纂 Tsung³ Tsuan³, Chief Revisers (2 Manchus, 2 Chinese and 2 Mongols),

5. 42 纂脩 Tsuan³ Hsiu¹, Revisers (14 Manchus, 20 Chinese and 8 Mongols),

6. 40 協脩 Hsieh² Hsiu¹, Assistant Revisers (12 Manchus, 20 Chinese and 8 Mongols),

7. 收掌 Shou¹ Chang³, Archivists (no fixed number),

191
to
197

8. 校對 Chiao⁴ Tui⁴, Correctors (number not fixed),

9. 繙譯 Fan¹ I⁴, Translators (number not fixed), and

10. 供事 Kung¹ Shih⁴, Clerks (number not fixed).

THE NATIONAL ACADEMY.

191. 翰林院 Han⁴ Lin² Yüan⁴, The National Academy ; the highest establishment of learning in the Empire. The drawing up of government documents, histories and other works devolves upon this institution. Its chief officers direct the various classes, encouraging them to the acquisition of the highest literary degrees, which afford access to the most eminent government posts (for instance, that of Grand Secretary).

The chief officers of the National Academy are :

192. 掌院學士 Chang³ Yüan⁴ Hsüeh² Shih⁴, Chancellors of the National Academy ; 2B, (one Manchu and one Chinese). These officials are usually Grand Secretaries, Presidents or Vice-Presidents of Ministries.

193. 學士 Hsüeh² Shih⁴, Members of the Academy (Academician) ; 3A, (two; one Manchu and one Chinese). This post was established on the 3rd April, 1908, in consequence of a Memorial from the Committee of Ministers.

194. 侍讀學士 Shih⁴ Tu² Hsüeh² Shih⁴, Readers of the Academy (two ; one Manchu and one Chinese) ; 4A. The rank of this post was, in 1903, raised from 4B to 4A.

195. 侍講學士 Shih⁴ Chiang³ Hsüeh² Shih⁴, Expositors of the Academy (two Manchus and three Chinese) ; 4A. In 1909 the rank of this post was raised from 4B to 4A.

196. 侍讀 Shih⁴ Tu², Sub-reader of the Academy (two are Manchus and three are Chinese) ; 4B. The rank of this post was raised from 5B to 5A in 1903, and to 4B in 1909.

197. 侍講 Shih⁴ Chiang³, Sub-expositor (two Manchus and three Chinese) ; 4B. In 1909 the rank of this post was raised from 5B to 4B.

198
to
201

198. 撰文 Chuan[4] Wên[2], Composers (four in number);
5A. This post was established in 1903 and its rank raised from
6A to 5A in 1909.

199. 秘書郎 Pi[4] Shu[1] Lang[2], Secretaries (four in number);
5A. This post was established on the 3rd April, 1908, in
response to a Memorial from the Council of State. In 1909 its
rank was raised from 6B to 5A.

200. Besides the foregoing there are, relating to the
Academy, the following degrees, formerly open to successful
candidates at the triennial examinations, 進士 Chin[4] Shih[4] (see
No. 629C), in future to be bestowed on graduates of Chinese
Universities, at present, a transitory stage, bestowed on persons
educated abroad (see No. 630).

200A. 脩撰 Hsiu[1] Chuan[4], Compiler of the First Class;
5A. The rank of this title was raised from 6B to 5A in 1909.
For particulars as to attaining it see Nos. 593C and 629C.

200B. 編脩 Pien[1] Hsiu[1], Compiler of the Second Class
(literary designation, 太史 T'ai[4] Shih[3]); 5B (in 1909 rank
raised from 7A to 5B). For particulars as to its attainment see
Nos. 593C and 629C.

200C. 檢討 Chien[3] T'ao[3], Corrector; 5B (rank raised from
7B to 5B in 1909). For particulars as to its attainment see Nos.
593C and 629C.

201. 庶常館 Shu[4] Ch'ang[2] Kuan[3], Department of Study
of the National Academy; made up of 庶吉士 Shu[4] Chi[2] Shih[4],
Bachelors; or graduates of the lowest degree. These graduates
pursue an advanced course of study at the Shu Ch'ang Kuan and,
by subsequent examination, held by a special commission within
the Palace, may attain the degrees of Compiler of the Second
Class and Corrector (see Nos. 200B–C). Those successful are
styled 留館 Liu[2] Kuan[3], i.e. retained at the Academy; those
unsuccessful are described as 散館 San[4] Kuan[3], released from

study, and receive appointments as District Magistrates or as Secretaries of Boards.

At the head of the Department of Study are :

201A.　Two 教習大臣 Chiao⁴ Hsi² Ta⁴ Ch'ên², Senior Professors (one Manchu and one Chinese).　They are assisted by two 提調 T'i² Tiao⁴, Proctors, and 教習 Chiao⁴ Hsi², Professors (number indefinite).

For dealing with correspondence there is a staff of 筆帖式 Pi³ T'ieh³ Shih⁴, Clerks.

202.　典簿廳 Tien³ Pu⁴ T'ing¹, Record Office ; stationed here are two 典簿 Tien³ Pu⁴, Senior Archivists (one Manchu and one Chinese) ; 8B, and two 孔目 K'ung³ Mu⁴, Junior Archivists (one Manchu and one Chinese) ; of unclassed rank.

For correspondence work there is a staff of 筆帖式 Pi³ T'ieh³ Shih⁴, Clerks.

203.　待詔廳 Tai⁴ Chao⁴ T'ing¹, Office for Compilation of Edicts (Manifests).　To this office there are attached two 待詔 Tai⁴ Chao⁴, Compilers ; 9B, and a staff of 筆帖式 Pi³ T'ieh³ Shih⁴, Clerks.

204.　起居注館 Ch'i³ Chü¹ Chu⁴ Kuan³, Office for Keeping a Diary of the Emperor's Movements.　To this office there are attached 20 日講起居注官 Jih⁴ Chiang⁴ Ch'i³ Chü¹ Chu⁴ Kuan¹, Diarists (8 Manchus and 12 Chinese), 3 主事 Chu³ Shih⁴, Assistant Diarists (two Manchus and one Chinese), and a staff of 筆帖式 Pi³ T'ieh³ Shih⁴, Clerks.

The officials attached to this office are on duty at the Palace daily.

205.　國史館 Kuo² Shih³ Kuan³, State Historiographer's Office ; where a chronicle of the reign is written up.　This chronicle, written in triplicate in what are called 實錄 Shih² Lu⁴, is kept secret until the death of the reigning Emperor, when one copy is deposited at the National Academy, one sent to the

Grand Secretariat, and one copy is preserved at the old capital of the Manchu Dynasty, Moukden.

On the State Historiographer's Office devolves the task of compiling official biographies of eminent statesmen, for embodiment in the history of the reign affected, when directed by special Edict to do so.

In charge of the State Historiographer's Office is a :

205ᴀ. 總裁 Tsung³ Ts'ai², Director-General (usually one of the Ministers of State), and a 副總裁 Fu⁴ Tsung³ Ts'ai², Assistant Director-General. These are assisted by 4 提調 T'i² Tiao⁴, Proctors (two Manchus and two Chinese), 10 總纂 Tsung³ Tsuan³, Revisers (four Manchus and six Chinese), 34 纂修 Tsuan³ Hsiu¹, Compilers (12 Manchus and 22 Chinese), and 16 校對 Chiao⁴ Tui⁴, Correctors (eight Manchus and eight Chinese).

THE CENSORATE.

206. 都察院 Tu¹ Ch'a² Yüan⁴, The Censorate (literary designation, 御史臺 Yü⁴ Shih³ T'ai²); by the code of laws entrusted with the duty of censuring officials, when necessary, for their neglect or incompetency in official affairs, their behavior and private life, and charged with the care of the public morals.

In addition to their official title, members of the Censorate are often called 耳目官 Erh³ Mu⁴ Kuan¹, The Eyes and Ears (through which the Emperor is made aware of the state of the Empire), and 言官 Yen² Kuan¹, Speech Officials, *i.e.* Officials having freedom of speech.

The Censorate institution in China is extremely old ; it is spoken of in the 秦 Ch'in² dynasty, *i.e.* two centuries B.C.

Some reforms in the Censorate were made in 1906 in accordance with a Memorial, emanating from that body itself, sanctioned by the Emperor on the 25th December, 1906.

At the head of the Censorate there is a :

[75]

207. 都御史 Tu¹ Yü⁴ Shih³, President of the Censorate (literary designation, 總憲 Tsung³ Hsien⁴); 1B.

207A. Before its reform at the head of the Censorate were two 左都御史 Tso³ Tu¹ Yü⁴ Shih³, Senior Presidents of the Censorate (one Manchu and one Chinese).

207B. 右都御史 Yu⁴ Tu¹ Yü⁴ Shih³, Junior President of the Censorate. This title is borne by Governor-Generals.

208. 左副都御史 Tso³ Fu⁴ Tu¹ Yü⁴ Shih³, Senior Vice-President of the Censorate (literary designation, 副憲 Fu⁴ Hsien⁴); 3A.

208A. Before the reform of the Censorate there were two 左副都御史 Tso³ Fu⁴ Tu¹ Yü⁴ Shih³, Senior Vice-Presidents of the Censorate (one Manchu and one Chinese).

209. 右副都御史 Yu⁴ Fu⁴ Tu¹ Yü⁴ Shih³, Junior Vice-President of the Censorate (literary designation, 副憲 Fu⁴ Hsien⁴); 3A. This title is borne by Governors.

209A. Before its reform there were four 右副都御史 Yu⁴ Fu⁴ Tu¹ Yü⁴ Shih³, Junior Vice-Presidents of the Censorate (two Manchus and two Chinese).

210. 給事中衙門 Chi³ Shih⁴ Chung¹ Ya² Mên², Office for Scrutiny of Metropolitan Officials. Its staff consists of two 掌印給事中 Chang³ Yin⁴ Chi³ Shih⁴ Chung¹, Senior Metropolitan Censors (literally, "Keepers of the Seal"); 4A, 18 給事中 Chi³ Shih⁴ Chung¹, Junior Metropolitan Censors; 5A, and, for correspondence, 30 筆帖式 Pi³ T'ieh² Shih⁴, Clerks.

210A. At the 給事中衙門 Chi³ Shih⁴ Chung¹ Ya² Mên² (*see* No. 210) it is intended to establish a 研究所 Yen² Chiu¹ So³, Reference Library, containing various works, and where Foreign and Chinese newspapers will be kept on file, so that the Censors may be enabled to follow political events at home and abroad and thus carry out their duties more thoroughly.

210ʙ
to
212ʙ

For managing the Reference Library there are to be two 提 調 T'i² Tiao⁴, Proctors, and two 編 譯 Pien¹ I⁴, Translators (Interpreters).

210ʙ. Previous to the reform of the Censorate the Office for Scrutiny of Metropolitan Officials was organized somewhat differently than at present: it consisted of 六 科 Liu⁴ K'o¹, Six Sections (there being six Ministries), for scrutinizing the doings of the various Ministrie⁻. In each Section there were two 掌印給事中 Chang³ Yin⁴ Chi³ Shih⁴ Chung¹, Senior Metropolitan Censors, as Section Chiefs, assisted by two 給 事 中 Chi³ Shih⁴ Chung¹, Junior Metropolitan Censors (literary designation, 大 給 諫 Ta⁴ Chi³ Chien⁴).

211. 都事廳 Tu¹ Shih⁴ T'ing¹, Chancery of the Censorate; here are stationed two 都事 Tu¹ Shih⁴, Officials of the Censorate Chancery; 6ᴀ.

212. 經歷廳 Ching¹ Li⁴ T'ing¹, Registry of the Censorate. At the Registry there are two 經 歷 Ching¹ Li⁴, Registrars; 6ᴀ.

212ᴀ. At the Chancery (see No. 211) and the Registry (see No. 21 ·. ⸗ there is a staff of 筆帖式 Pi³ T'ieh³ Shih⁴ (30 in all). Also, at the Chancery there are an indefinite number of 額外都事 Ê² Wai⁴ Tu¹ Shih⁴, Supernumerary Chancery Officials, and at the Registry there are an indefinite number of 額外經歷 Ê² Wai⁴ Ching¹ Li⁴, Supernumerary Registrars.

212ʙ. 承 發 科 Ch'êng² Fa¹ K'o¹, Transmission Office. This office existed before the reorganization of the Censorate, and it is now the intention to bring it again into being as an office similar to the 司 務 廳 Ssu¹ Wu⁴ T'ing¹, Chanceries (see No. 296) which are found at all the Ministries. It is to be styled the 收 發 文 書 處 Shou¹ Fa¹ Wên² Shu¹ Ch'u⁴, Transmission Office, and have a staff of 都 事 Tu¹ Shih⁴, Chancery Officials, 經 歷 Ching¹ Li⁴, Registrars (see No. 212), and 筆帖式 Pi³ T'ieh³ Shih⁴, Clerks (see No. 212ᴀ). Should the idea be

213
to
214A

acted upon, the Chancery (*see* No. 211) and the Registry (*see* No. 212) will, in all probability, be abolished.

213. 御 史 Yü⁴ Shih³, Provincial Censors (literary designation, 侍 御 Shih⁴ Yü⁴, colloquial designation, 都 老 爺 Tu¹ Lao³ Yeh²); 5B. There are 44 Provincial Censors, distributed over 20 道 Tao⁴, or Circuits, which, excepting two, only bear the names of various provinces (for instance, 江 蘇 道 Chiang¹ Su¹ Tao⁴, Kiangsu Censor Circuit). The two exceptions are the Chihli Censor Circuit, which is styled 京 畿 道 Ching¹ Chi¹ Tao⁴, Metropolitan Circuit, and the Manchurian Censor Circuit, one for the three provinces, which is called 遼 瀋 道 Liao² Shên³ Tao⁴, Liaoyang Moukden Censor Circuit (遼 Liao², abbreviation of 遼 陽 Liao² Yang², and 瀋 Shên³ for 瀋 陽 Shên³ Yang²—the ancient name of Moukden).

The Metropolitan and the Manchurian Censor Circuits have each four Censors, for the others there are two for each.

The full title of a Provincial Censor, taking Anhui Province for an example, is 掌 安 徽 道 監 察 御 史 Chang³ An¹ Hui¹ Tao⁴ Chien¹ Ch'a² Yü⁴ Shih³, Censor overseeing the Anhui Circuit.

For the Metropolitan and Manchurian Circuits the two Junior Censors are styled, for the former, 京 畿 道 監 察 御 史 Ching¹ Chi¹ Tao⁴ Chien¹ Ch'a² Yü⁴ Shih³, and for the latter, 遼 瀋 道 監 察 御 史 Liao² Shên³ Tao⁴ Chien¹ Ch'a² Yü⁴ Shih³.

214. Formerly, in Peking, a number of the Censors were employed as Superintendents of Police (*see* details in No. 796A) for the five divisions of the city and suburbs and were styled 五 城 御 史 Wu³ Ch'êng² Yü⁴ Shih³, Censors of the Five Cities (these are the Centre, North, South, East and West Divisions into which Peking is divided).

214A. 查 倉 御 史 Ch'a² Ts'ang¹ Yü⁴ Shih³, Censors Supervising the Government Granaries (at Peking and T'ung-chow); also in charge of portage of Tribute Rice which is brought from the South by the Grand Canal. At present these

SUPREME COURT OF JUSTICE.

215. 大理寺 Ta⁴ Li³ Ssu⁴, Court of Judicature and Revision ; the duty of this Court was the general supervision of the administration of criminal law, and the examination, by this Court, of criminal cases where judgment had been delivered was necessary before the decree became operative. This Court, with the Board of Punishment (*see* No. 438) and the Censorate (*see* No. 206), was styled by the general title 三法司 San¹ Fa⁴ Ssu¹, Three High Courts of Judicature, and formed something similar to the Supreme Criminal Court.

By Imperial Edict, dated the 7th December, 1906, the Court of Judicature and Revision was reorganized as :

215A. 大理院 Ta⁴ Li³ Yüan⁴, Supreme Court of Justice ; specially entrusted with the administration of justice in the Empire. At the present time this Court is the supreme tribunal of justice in connection with all cases which are brought, in the first instance, before the District Court (*see* No. 760), and, secondly, before the Court of Assizes (*see* No. 759). Also, it functions (as Court of first and last appeal) with reference to crimes committed by Imperial Clansmen (宗室 Tsung¹ Shih⁴) and officials, crimes against State Offices and State Officials, and, finally, in cases of extreme importance that are outside the scope of inferior Courts (of Justices of Peace, of District Courts or of Courts of Assizes). For the last-mentioned, the Supreme Court of Justice must, after having examined the substance of the case and delivered judgment, forward its decision to the Ministry of Justice for approval.

Although, as we have seen above, to the Ministry of Justice (*see* No. 440) belongs the supreme control of the actions of the

216 to 217

Supreme Court of Justice, nevertheless the latter is an independent establishment, having the privilege of direct reports to the Throne.

A new arrangement of the Supreme Court of Justice, devised by the Ministry of Justice, with the assistance of the Council of State, was proposed to the Throne in a Memorial and was sanctioned by the Emperor on the 10th June, 1907.

216. The personnel of the Court of Judicature and Revision was :

1. 1 大理寺卿 Ta⁴ Li³ Ssu⁴ Ch'ing¹, Director of the Court of Judicature and Revision (literary designation, 廷則 T'ing² Tsê²) ; 3A,

2. 1 大理寺少卿 Ta⁴ Li³ Ssu⁴ Shao⁴ Ch'ing¹, Sub-Director of the Court of Judicature and Revision (literary designation, 佐棘 Tso³ Chi·) ; 4A,

3. 1 左寺丞 Tso³ Ssu⁴ Ch'êng², Senior Secretary of the Court of Judicature and Revision (literary designation, 議司 I⁴ Ssu¹) ; 6A,

4. 1 右寺丞 Yu⁴ Ssu⁴ Ch'êng², Junior Secretary of the Court of Judicature and Revision (literary designation, 議司 I⁴ Ssu¹) ; 6A,

5. 1 左評事 Tso³ P'ing² Shih⁴, Senior Assistant Secretary of the Court of Judicature and Revision ; 7A, and

6. 1 右評事 Yu⁴ P'ing² Shih⁴, Junior Assistant Secretary of the Court of Judicature and Revision ; 7A.

216A. At the head of the Supreme Court of Justice there is a 大理院正卿 Ta⁴ Li³ Yüan⁴ Chêng⁴ Ch'ing¹, President of the Supreme Court of Justice ; 2A, assisted in the administration of the affairs of the Court and in the general supervision of matters of justice in the Empire by a :

217. 大理院少卿 Ta⁴ Li³ Yüan⁴ Shao⁴ Ch'ing¹, Vice-President of the Supreme Court of Justice ; 3A.

218
to
220

218. 刑科推丞 Hsing² K'o¹ T'ui¹ Ch'êng², Director of the Department of Criminal Cases ; 4A. This official has subordinated to him 19 刑科推事 Hsing² K'o¹ T'ui¹ Shih⁴, Secretaries of the Department of Criminal Cases ; 5A. He is in charge of the :

218A. 刑科 Hsing² K'o¹, Department of Criminal Cases ; this Department consists of 4 庭 T'ing², Sections, namely :

1. 第一庭 Ti⁴ I¹ T'ing², First Section ; supervising cases inspired by the Emperor and also cases concerning crimes against the State,

2. 第二庭 Ti⁴ Êrh⁴ Ting², Second Section ; supervising cases concerning crimes committed by Imperial Clansmen, 宗室 Tsung¹ Shih⁴, and officials,

3. 第三庭 Ti⁴ San¹ T'ing², Third Section ; supervising appeals against judgments of the Metropolitan Court of Assizes, and

4. 第四庭 Ti⁴ Ssu⁴ T'ing², Fourth Section ; supervising appeals against judgments of Provincial Courts of Assizes.

219. 民科推丞 Min² K'o¹ T'ui¹ Ch'êng², Director of the Department of Civil Cases ; 4A. This official has subordinated to him 9 民科推事 Min² K'o¹ T'ui¹ Shih⁴, Secretaries of the Department of Civil Cases ; 5A. He is in charge of the :

219A. 民科 Min² K'o¹, Department of Civil Cases, consisting of 2 庭 T'ing¹, as shown below :

1. 第一庭 Ti⁴ I¹ T'ing¹, First Section ; dealing with civil cases concerning 宗室 Tsung¹ Shih⁴, Imperial Clansmen, and with appeals, in civil cases, against judgments of the Metropolitan Court of Assizes, and

2. 第二庭 Ti⁴ Êrh⁴ T'ing¹, Second Section ; dealing with appeals, in civil cases, against judgments of Provincial Courts of Assizes.

220. 典簿廳 Tien³ Pu⁴ T'ing¹, Chancery and Record Office. This office is supervised by a 都典簿 Tu¹ Tien³ Pu⁴,

221
to
223

Chief Archivist; 5B, as Chancery Chief, who is assisted by 4 典簿 Tien³ Pu⁴, Archivists; 6B, 6 主簿 Chu³ Pu⁴, Registrars; 7A, and 30 錄事 Lu⁴ Shih⁴, Writers (of the eighth and ninth ranks).

221. 看守所 K'an¹ Shou³ So³, House of Detention. This is in charge of a 看守所長 K'an¹ Shou³ So³ Chang³, Chief Supervisor of the House of Detention; 5B, who is assisted by 4 看守所官 K'an¹ Shou³ So³ Kuan¹, Supervisors of the House of Detention; 8A, and 2 錄事 Lu⁴ Shih⁴, Writers; 9A (*see* No. 767).

Because of the pressure of affairs, there was established in 1908, in accordance with a Memorial from the Supreme Court of Justice, the unclassed post of 看守所協理 K'an¹ Shou³ So³ Hsieh⁴ Li³, Assistant Chief Supervisor of the House of Detention, for performing the duties of which there are deputed officials from the Supreme Court.

222. 總檢察廳 Tsung³ Chien³ Ch'a² T'ing¹, Attorney-General's Office; established at the Supreme Court of Justice on lines similar to those of Prosecutors of judicial organizations of lower rank (*see* Nos. 762 to 765).

Besides functioning as public prosecutor, the Attorney-General's Office holds inquests, where necessary, in cases in which the Supreme Court is the court of first and last appeal (*see* No. 215A) and has control over Prosecutors of lower courts.

At the head of the Attorney-General's Office is a 總檢察廳廳丞 Tsung³ Chien³ Ch'a² T'ing¹ T'ing¹ Ch'êng², Attorney-General; 3B. He has subordinated to him 6 檢察官 Chien³ Ch'a² Kuan¹, Attorneys; 5A, 1 主簿 Chu³ Pu⁴, Registrar; 7A, and 4 錄事 Lu⁴ Shih⁴, Writers; 9A.

IMPERIAL BOARD OF ASTRONOMY.

223. 欽天監 Ch'in¹ T'ien¹ Chien⁴, Imperial Board of Astronomy; compiles the calendar, makes astronomical and

meteorological observations, and selects so-called 吉 日 Chi² Jih⁴, "lucky days," for important State undertakings.

At the head of the Board is a :

224. 管理欽天監事務 Kuan³ Li³ Ch'in¹ T'ien¹ Chien⁴ Shih⁴ Wu⁴, Chancellor of the Imperial Board of Astronomy ; appointed by the Emperor, usually one of the Princes of the Blood.

225. 欽天監監正 Ch'in¹ T'ien¹ Chien⁴ Chien⁴ Chêng⁴, Directors of the Imperial Board of Astronomy ; 5ᴀ (one Manchu and one Chinese).

226. 欽天監左監副 Ch'in¹ T'ien¹ Chien⁴ Tso³ Chien⁴ Fu⁴, Senior Vice Directors of the Imperial Board of Astronomy ; 6ᴀ (one Manchu and one Chinese).

227. 欽天監右監副 Ch'in¹ T'ien¹ Chien⁴ Yu⁴ Chien⁴ Fu⁴, Junior Vice-Director of the Imperial Board of Astronomy ; 6ʙ (one Manchu and one Chinese).

227ᴀ. Formerly there were 2 監 副 Chien⁴ Fu⁴, Vice-Directors ; 6ᴀ, 1 左 監 副 Tso³ Chien Fu⁴, Senior Assistant Vice-Director ; 6ʙ, and 1 右 監 副 Yu⁴ Chien⁴ Fu⁴, Junior Assistant Vice-Director ; 6ʙ, on the Board of Astronomy.

227ʙ. The 大 清 會 典 Tai⁴ Ch'ing¹ Hui⁴ Tien³, or the " Institutes of the Empire of the Ta Ch'ing Dynasty," contains the proviso that the posts of Director, and Senior and Junior Assistant Vice-Director, of the Imperial Board of Astronomy are to be held by Europeans.

228. 主 簿 Chu³ Pu⁴, Registrar ; 8ᴀ (one Manchu and one Chinese).

229. 時 憲 科 Shih Hsien⁴ K'o¹, Calendar Section ; here the calendar is compiled, the seasons are defined and the 24 periods of the year, arranged. The staff of this Section is composed of :

1. 5 五官正 Wu³ Kuan¹ Chêng⁴, Astronomers ; charged with general astronomical calculations,

230
to
232

2. 1 春官正 Ch'un[1] Kuan[1] Chêng[4], Astronomer for the Spring, 1 夏官正 Hsia[4] Kuan[1] Chêng[4], Astronomer for the Summer, 1 中官正 Chung[1] Kuan[1] Chêng[4], Astronomer for the Mid-year, 1 秋官正 Ch'iu[1] Kuan[1] Chêng[4], Astronomer for the Autumn, 1 冬官正 Tung[1] Kuan[1] Chêng[4], Astronomer for the Winter,

3. 1 司書 Ssu[1] Shu[1], Compiler; charged with issuing the calendar,

4. 20 博士 Po[2] Shih[4], Mathematicians; 9B, and

5. 筆帖式 Pi[3] T'ieh[3] Shih[4], Clerks (number not fixed).

230. 天文科 T'ien[1] Wên[2] K'o[1], Astronomical Section; makes astronomical and meteorological observations. The staff of this Section is composed of:

1. 8 靈臺郎 Ling[2] T'ai[2] Lang[2], Supervisors of the Observatory; 7B,

2. 6 博士 Po[2] Shih[4], Mathematicians; 9B,

3. 1 監候 Chien[4] Hou[4], Observer; 9A, and

4. 筆帖式 Pi[3] T'ieh[3] Shih[4], Clerks (number not fixed).

231. 漏刻科 Lou[4] K'o[4] K'o[1], Section of the Clepsydra; observes time by the clepsydra and selects "lucky" days for important affairs. This Section is carried on by:

1. 4 挈壺正 Hsieh[4] Hu[2] Chêng[4], Keepers of Clepsydra; 8A,

2. 1 司晨 Ssu[1] Ch'ên[2], Assistant Keeper of the Clepsydra,

3. 6 博士 Po[2] Shih[4], Mathematicians; 9B, and

4. 筆帖式 Pi[3] T'ieh[3] Shih[4], Clerks (number indefinite).

232. 天文算學 T'ien[1] Wên[2] Suan[4] Hsüeh[2], Astronomical College; where those who are desirous of joining the service at the Observatory are examined and where lectures on the sciences necessary to the proper performance of astronomical duties are held. The College is administered by:

1. 管理欽天監天文算學事務 Kuan[3] Li[3] Ch'in[1] T'ien[1] Chien[4] T'ien[1] Wên[2] Suan[4] Hsüeh[2] Shih[4] Wu[4], Superintendent of the Astronomical College; this post is an

[84]

adjunct of that of Chancellor of the Imperial Board of Astronomy (*see* No. 224), and

2. 協理欽天監天文算學事務 Hsieh² Li³ Ch'in¹ T'ien¹ Chien⁴ T'ien¹ Wên² Suan⁴ Hsüeh² Shih⁴ Wu⁴, Assistant Superintendent of the Astronomical College; this post is an adjunct of that of Director of the Imperial Board of Astronomy (*see* No. 225).

232ᴀ. 助教廳 Chu⁴ Chiao⁴ T'ing¹, Preceptory; under a 助教 Chu⁴ Chiao⁴, Preceptor, and 2 教習 Chiao⁴ Hsi², Teachers.

THE IMPERIAL MEDICAL DEPARTMENT.

233. 太醫院 T'ai⁴ I¹ Yüan⁴, The Imperial Medical Department; for the Emperor and his associates. At the head of this Department is a:

234. 管理太醫院事務 Kuan³ Li³ T'ai⁴ I¹ Yüan⁴ Shih⁴ Wu⁴, Superintendent of the Imperial Medical Department; this post is usually given to a Minister of the Household.

235. 太醫院院使 T'ai⁴ I¹ Yüan⁴ Yüan⁴ Shih³, Commissioner of the Imperial Medical Department; 5ᴀ.

236. 太醫院左院判 T'ai⁴ I¹ Yüan⁴ Tso³ Yüan⁴ P'an⁴, Senior Vice-Commissioner of the Imperial Medical Department; 6ᴀ.

236ᴀ. 太醫院右院判 T'ai⁴ I¹ Yüan⁴ Yu⁴ Yüan⁴ P'an⁴, Junior Vice-Commissioner of the Imperial Medical Department; 6ᴀ.

237. 首領廳 Shou³ Ling³ T'ing¹, Office of Administration; managed by 2 吏目 Li⁴ Mu⁴, Secretaries, 1 御醫 Yü⁴ I¹, Imperial Physician, and 1 醫士 I¹ Shih⁴, Physician, all entitled 兼首領廳事 Chien¹ Shou³ Ling³ T'ing¹ Shih⁴, *i.e.* Administrators.

238. 御醫 Yü⁴ I¹, Imperial Physician; 7ᴀ (15).

239. 八品吏目 Pa⁴ P'in³ Li⁴ Mu⁴, Secretary of the Eighth Rank (12).

9A   239A. 九品吏目 Chiu³ P'in³ Li⁴ Mu⁴, Secretaries of the
Ninth Rank (15).

240. 醫士 I¹ Shih⁴, Physician (the rules call for 24 but
sometimes they number as many as 30).

BOARD OF CUSTOMS CONTROL.

241. 稅務處 Shui⁴ Wu⁴ Ch'u⁴, Board of Customs
Control. This came into existence in accordance with an Edict
dated the 9th May, 1906, and controls all Chinese and Foreign
employés of the Customs (*see* Nos. 253 and 311).

At the Board of Customs Control there are :

242. Two 督辦稅務大臣 Tu¹ Pan⁴ Shui⁴ Wu⁴ Ta⁴ Ch'ên²,
Superintendents of the Board of Customs Control (this post is an
additional office held by a President or a Vice-President of a
Ministry).

243. One 幫辦稅務大臣 Pang¹ Pan⁴ Shui⁴ Wu⁴ Ta⁴
Ch'ên², Assistant Superintendent of the Board of Customs Control
(this post is an additional office held by a President or a Vice-
President of a Ministry).

244. 提調 T'i² Tiao⁴, Proctor.

245. 幫提調 Pang¹ T'i² Tiao⁴, Assistant Proctor.

246. The Board of Customs Control consists of 4 股 Ku³,
Sections. For each Section there is a 總辦 Tsung³ Pan⁴, Section
Chief, assisted by 3 or 4 幫辦 Pang¹ Pan⁴, Assistants, and 1 or
2 委員 Wei³ Yüan², Deputies (these posts are usually held by
junior officials of the Ministries of Foreign Affairs and Finance
or by Expectants of provincial offices, up to and inclusive of
Taotais).

247. 第一股 Ti⁴ I¹ Ku³, First Section ; considers duties
on mechanical and manufactured goods and minerals, gives
decisions on Customs Regulations, audits Customs revenue returns
and studies trade conditions at the ports.

248. 第二股 Ti⁴ Êrh⁴ Ku³, Second Section; deals with
duties collected by "Native" (old Chinese) Customs and
exemption of goods from duty, looks into foreign loans and their
acquittance—including the 1900 Indemnity—and supervises
certain taxes, *i.e.* the salt gabelle and Likin, collected by the
Maritime Customs, settles the tariff of import and export duties
and takes measures to prevent the smuggling of goods into the
country.

249. 第三股 Ti⁴ San¹ Ku³, Third Section; supervises
the tax collected on foreign and native opium and the issue of
Transit Certificates for foreign goods sent to the interior, controls
inland waters shipping, construction of harbours, lighthouses and
pontoons, and tonnage dues and studies the Customs of foreign
countries.

250. 第四股 Ti⁴ Ssu⁴ Ku³, Fourth Section; deals with
Postal affairs of the Empire, the transfer and appointment of
Customs Officials, as well as their reward, the staff of the Board
of Customs Control, and keeps the accounts of the last-mentioned.

251. 收發處 Shou¹ Fa¹ Ch'u⁴, Registry or Chancery;
keeps the seal, looks over incoming and out-going despatches and
telegrams, archives, etc. At this office there are 3 委員 Wei³
Yüan², Deputies, and 1 雜務委員 Tsa² Wu⁴ Wei³ Yüan²,
Unclassed Deputy.

252. 稅務學堂 Shui⁴ Wu⁴ Hsüeh² T'ang², Customs
College; attached to the Board of Customs Control. This
College was established in 1908 for preparing young men for
service in the Customs.

The Customs College is divided into two sections, *i.e.* 補習科
Pu³ Hsi² K'o¹, Preparatory Section, and 本科 Pên³ K'o¹, Special
Section. For the first there are accepted pupils between the ages
of 14 and 20 years who have passed the Middle School
examinations (*see* Nos. 580 to 582), after a competitive
examination; for the Special Section there are chosen scholars

[87]

253 between the ages of 16 and 22 years—who have passed the Middle School examinations and speak English—after a competitive examination.

The enrollment of the Preparatory Section is 50 and that of the Special Section is 36.

The course of study in the Special Section covers four years. Besides Chinese, there is instruction in foreign languages (Russian, French, German and Japanese, all optional, and English, compulsory), history, geography, mathematics, physics, political economy, international law, commercial law, history of the development of trade, differentiation of merchandise, statistics, political and commercial treaties, Customs regulations, book-keeping, etc.

Graduates of the College are entitled to the same privileges as graduates of High Schools (*see* No. 583).

At the head of the Customs College is a 總辦 Tsung³ Pan⁴, Director, and subordinated to him are 1 Inspector (*see* No. 649), 1 總教習 Tsung³ Chiao⁴ Hsi², Senior Teacher, 8 教習 Chiao⁴ Hsi², Teachers, 1 齋務委員 Chai¹ Wu⁴ Wei³ Yüan², Supervisor of Dormitories (*see* No. 645), 1 庶務委員 Shu⁴ Wu⁴ Wei³ Yüan², Steward (compare No. 641), 1 醫官 I¹ Kuan¹, Physician, 1 Writer (*see* No. 642), 1 Book-keeper (*see* No. 643), 2 Secretaries (*see* No. 650) and 2 司書 Ssu¹ Shu¹, Clerks.

Regulations for the Customs College, drawn up by the Superintendents of the Board of Customs Control, were sanctioned by the Emperor on the 21st May, 1909.

THE IMPERIAL MARITIME CUSTOMS.

253. 海關 Hai³ Kuan¹, Chinese Imperial Maritime Customs; functions at all ports open to foreign trade (通商口岸 T'ung¹ Shang¹ K'ou³ An⁴).

The Imperial Maritime Customs was started in 1854, at the initiative of the British, French and American Consuls, at

Shanghai, when, the native city having been captured by the rebels, the authorities were unable to collect the duties on foreign goods. Proving very successful, it was extended to other ports.

At the head of the Service, by order of the Governor-General, was placed an Englishman, Lay, as Inspector General of Customs.

In 1863 Mr. Lay was replaced by Sir (then Mr.) Robert Hart, who has retained his post to the present and to whose ability in organization and indefatigable zeal the Chinese owe that the Maritime Customs is now one of the great sources of revenue to the Treasury.

The staff of the Imperial Maritime Customs, mostly recruited from Foreigners (at least, they hold most of the high positions), was formerly under the supervision of the Yamen of Foreign Affairs,—up to 1901,—and, later, under the Board of Foreign Affairs (*see* No. 311). However, in 1906, the Imperial Maritime Customs was subordinated, by Imperial Edict, to the Board of Customs Control (*see* Nos. 241 and 311), a purely Chinese organization, with a view to closer supervision of the foreign administration of Chinese interests.

The administration of the Chinese Imperial Maritime Customs is arranged as follows :

254. 總 稅 務 司 署 Tsung³ Shui⁴ Wu⁴ Ssu¹ Shu³, Inspectorate General of Customs.

255. 總 稅 務 司 Tsung³ Shui⁴ Wu⁴ Ssu¹, Inspector General of Customs, to whom appertains the supreme direction of the Imperial Maritime Customs throughout the Empire and the general supervision of Postal affairs (*see* No. 273).

256. 副 總 稅 務 司 Fu⁴ Tsung³ Shui⁴ Wu⁴ Ssu¹, Deputy Inspector General of Customs.

257. 總 理 文 案 稅 務 司 Tsung³ Li³ Wên² An⁴ Shui⁴ Wu⁴ Ssu¹, Chief Secretary.

258. 管理漢文文案稅務司 Kuan³ Li³ Han⁴ Wên² Wên² An⁴ Shui⁴ Wu⁴ Ssu¹, Chinese Secretary.

259. 委巡各口欵項事稅務司 Wei³ Hsün² Ko⁴ K'ou³ K'uan³ Hsiang⁴ Shih⁴ Shui⁴ Wu⁴ Ssu¹, Audit Secretary.

260. 駐英稅務司 Chu⁴ Ying¹ Shui⁴ Wu⁴ Ssu¹, Non-resident Secretary.

261. 造冊處稅務司 Tsao⁴ Ts'ê⁴ Ch'u⁴ Shui⁴ Wu⁴ Ssu¹, Statistical Secretary.

262. 襄辦文案副稅務司 Hsiang¹ Pan⁴ Wên² An⁴ Fu⁴ Shui⁴ Wu⁴ Ssu¹, Assistant Secretary.

263. 襄辦漢文文案副稅務司 Hsiang¹ Pan⁴ Han⁴ Wên² Wên² An⁴ Fu⁴ Shui⁴ Wu⁴ Ssu¹, Assistant Chinese Secretary.

264. 襄查各口欵項事副稅務司 Hsiang¹ Ch'a² Ko⁴ K'ou³ Kuan³ Hsiang⁴ Shih⁴ Fu⁴ Shui⁴ Wu⁴ Ssu¹, Assistant Audit Secretary.

265. 造册處副稅務司 Tsao⁴ Ts'ê⁴ Ch'u⁴ Fu⁴ Shui⁴ Wu⁴ Ssu¹, Assistant Statistical Secretary.

266. 總司錄事司 Tsung³ Ssu¹ Lu⁴ Shih⁴ Ssu¹, Private Secretary.

267. 通商各關 T'ung¹ Shang¹ Ko⁴ Kuan¹, The Maritime Customs at the Open Ports.

The administration of the Maritime Customs at the open ports is arranged as follows :

1. 稅務司 Shui⁴ Wu⁴ Ssu¹, Commissioner of Customs.

2. 署稅務司 Shu⁴ Shui⁴ Wu⁴ Ssu¹, Acting Commissioner of Customs.

3. 副稅務司 Fu⁴ Shui⁴ Wu⁴ Ssu¹, Deputy Commissioner of Customs.

4. 署副稅務司 Shu⁴ Fu⁴ Shui⁴ Wu⁴ Ssu¹, Acting Deputy Commissioner of Customs.

5. 代理稅務司 Tai⁴ Li³ Shui⁴ Wu⁴ Ssu¹, Assistant in Charge.

6. 超等幫辦 Ch'ao¹ Têng³ Pang¹ Pan⁴, Chief Assistant.

7. 頭等幫辦 T'ou² Têng³ Pang¹ Pan⁴, First Assistant.

8. 二等幫辦 Êrh⁴ Têng³ Pang¹ Pan⁴, Second Assistant.

9. 駐京學習漢文幫辦 Chu⁴ Ching⁴ Hsüeh² Hsi² Han⁴ Wên² Pang¹ Pan⁴, Assistant Studying Chinese.

10. 供事 Kung⁴ Shih⁴, Clerk.

There are also Third and Fourth Assistants.

268. For the examination of cargo there are the following officers of the Customs :

1. 超等總巡 Ch'ao¹ Têng³ Tsung³ Hsün², Chief Tide-surveyor.

2. 頭等總巡 T'ou² Têng³ Tsung³ Hsün², Tidesurveyor.

3. 署理頭等總巡 Shu⁴ Li³ T'ou² Têng³ Tsung³ Hsün², Acting Tidesurveyor.

4. 二等總巡 Êrh⁴ Têng³ Tsung³ Hsün², Assistant Tide-surveyor.

5. 三等總巡 San¹ Têng³ Tsung³ Hsün², Boat Officer.

6. 署理三等總巡 Shu⁴ Li³ San¹ Têng³ Tsung³ Hsün², Acting Boat Officer,

7. 頭等驗貨 T'ou² Têng³ Yen⁴ Huo⁴, Chief Examiner.

8. 二等驗貨 Êrh⁴ Têng³ Yen⁴ Huo⁴, Examiner.

9. 三等驗貨 San¹ Têng³ Yen⁴ Huo⁴, Assistant Examiner.

10. 頭等鈐字手 T'ou²'Têng³ Ch'ien¹ Tzu⁴ Shou³, First Class Tidewaiter.

11. 試用鈐字手 Shih⁴ Yung⁴ Ch'ien¹ Tzu⁴ Shou³, Probationary Tidewaiter.

12. 巡役 Hsün² I⁴, Watcher.

269. For patrolling the coast there is a Customs cruising flotilla.

In charge of each cruiser is a 巡船管駕官 Hsün² Ch'uan² Kuan³ Chia⁴ Kuan¹, Commander, with the following subordinate officers :

1. 巡船管駕副 Hsün² Ch'uan² Kuan³ Chia⁴ Fu⁴, First Officer.

2. 巡船管駕二副 Hsün² Ch'uan² Kuan³ Chia⁴ Êrh⁴ Fu⁴, Second Officer.

3. 巡船管駕三副 Hsün² Ch'uan² Kuan³ Chia⁴ San¹ Fu⁴, Third Officer.

4. 巡船管輪正 Hsün² Ch'uan² Kuan³ Lun² Chêng⁴, First Engineer.

5. 巡船管輪副 Hsün² Ch'uan² Kuan³ Lun² Fu⁴, Second Engineer.

6. 礮手首領 P'ao⁴ Shou³ Shou³ Ling³, Gunner.

7. 水手首領 Shui³ Shou³ Shou³ Ling³, Quarter-master.

8. 巡艇弁 Hsün² T'ing² Pien⁴, Launch Officer.

270. Within the Customs there is a 營造處 Ying² Tsao⁴ Ch'u⁴, Engineers' Office, supervised by a 總營造司 Tsung³ Ying² Tsao⁴ Ssu¹, Engineer-in-Chief. To him there are subordinated :

1. 副營造司 Fu⁴ Ying² Tsao⁴ Ssu¹, Assistant Engineers.

2. 工師 Kung¹ Shih¹, Clerks of Works, and

3. 匠董 Chiang⁴ Tung³, Mechanics.

271. Supervision of the harbour is the duty of the 理船處 Li³ Ch'uan² Ch'u⁴, Harbour Office. General supervision of all the harbours is entrusted to a 巡工司 Hsün² Kuang¹ Ssu¹, Coast Inspector.

In charge of the Harbour Office is a 理船廳 Li³ Ch'uan² T'ing¹, Harbour Master, who is assisted by 指泊所 Chih³ Po⁴ So³, Berthing Officers.

In addition, there are :

1. 信旗吏 Hsin⁴ Ch'i² Li⁴, Signalmen,

2. 巡江吏 Hsün² Chiang¹ Li⁴, River Police, and

3. 入水匠 Ju⁴ Shui³ Chiang⁴, Pilots.

272. The Customs also administers a 鐙塔處 Têng¹ T'a³ Ch'u⁴, Lights Department, in charge of a 巡鐙司 Hsün² Têng¹ Ssu¹, Inspector of Lights. To him are subordinated :

1. 鐙船主 Têng¹ Ch'uan² Chu³, Lightship Captains,

2. 鐙 船 大 副 Têng¹ Ch'uan² Ta⁴ Fu⁴, Lightship Mate, **273** and

3. 鐙 塔 值 事 人 Têng¹ T'a³ Chih² Shih⁴ Jên², Light-keepers.

273. There is as yet no uniformity in the Postal organization of China. In addition to the old Government Post (*see* No. 754), which is under the supervision of the Board of War and the local provincial authorities, at the most important centres (for detailed list *see* the edition of the Imperial Maritime Customs "Alphabetical Index of Imperial Post Offices,") there have been established (the first in 1874) by Sir Robert Hart, the Inspector General of Customs (*see* No. 255), Post Offices working on the lines of those of European countries. These are controlled by a Postal Department, at the head of which is a 總 郵 政 司 Tsung³ Yu¹ Chêng⁴ Ssu¹, Inspector General of Posts (this post has always been an adjunct of that of Inspector General of Customs).

For Postal work there are subordinated to the Inspector General of Customs a 郵 政 總 辦 Yu¹ Chêng⁴ Tsung³ Pan⁴, Postal Secretary, and a 郵 政 副 總 辦 Yu¹ Chêng⁴ Fu⁴ Tsung³ Pan⁴, Assistant Postal Secretary.

Post Offices are of two descriptions, *i.e.* 郵 政 總 局 Yu¹ Chêng⁴ Tsung³ Chü², Head Offices, and 郵 政 分 局 Yu¹ Chêng¹ Fên¹ Chü², Branch Offices.

PART II.

MINISTRIES

MINISTRIES (BOARDS).

MINISTRIES (BOARDS) IN GENERAL.

274. In addition to establishments already mentioned, having very special or temporary functions, there are in China eleven Ministries (Boards) whose authority extends to all parts of the Empire. Although a development of the old 六 部 Liu⁴ Pu⁴, Six Ministries (Boards) and other offices, the new Ministries are gradually changing the former practice of administration of metropolitan affairs only and the leaving of the greatest initiative in provincial affairs to Governor-Generals and Governors.

Being convinced of the detrimental influence of a system of decentralization, the Government is bending itself to a policy of subordinating to the Ministries everything that is of general importance (education, finance, military affairs, police and justice)

The eleven Ministries (Boards) are :

1. 外 務 部 Wai⁴ Wu⁴ Pu⁴, Ministry (Board) of Foreign Affairs (*see* Nos. 305 to 332A),

2. 吏 部 Li⁴ Pu⁴, Ministry (Board) of Civil Appointments (*see* Nos. 333 to 338),

3. 民 政 部 Min² Chêng⁴ Pu⁴, Ministry (Board) of the Interior (*see* Nos. 339 to 348).

4. 度 支 部 Tu⁴ Chih¹ Pu⁴, Ministry (Board) of Finance (*see* Nos. 349 to 375),

5. 禮 部 Li³ Pu⁴, Ministry (Board) of Rites (*see* Nos. 376 to 394),

6. 學 部 Hsüeh² Pu⁴, Ministry (Board) of Education (Nos. 395 to 414),

7

7. 陸軍部 Lu⁴ Chün¹ Pu⁴, Ministry (Board) of War (*see* Nos. 415 to 437),

8. 法部 Fa⁴ Pu⁴, Ministry (Board) of Justice (*see* Nos. 438 to 459),

9. 農工商部 Nung² Kung¹ Shang¹ Pu⁴, Ministry of Agriculture, Industry and Commerce (Nos. 460 to 471),

10. 郵傳部 Yu¹ Ch'uan² Pu⁴, Ministry of Posts and Communications (*see* Nos. 472 to 490), and

11. 理藩部 Li³ Fan¹ Pu⁴, Ministry (Board) of Dependencies (*see* Nos. 491 to 499).

275. Each 部 Pu⁴, Ministry, is composed of a number (from 4 to 10) of 司 Ssu¹, Departments, which, again, are divided into 科 K'o¹, Sections, and 股 Ku³, Sub-sections. Also, at the majority of the Ministries there is a 承政廳 Ch'êng² Chêng⁴ T'ing¹, Council, and a 參議廳 Ts'an¹ I⁴ T'ing¹, Secretarial Office, as well as 局 Chü², Offices, and 處 Ch'u⁴, Committees (for various affairs).

276. The head of all but one of the Ministries is the 尚書 Shang⁴ Shu¹, President; at the Ministry of Foreign Affairs, the exception, this official is subordinated to a 總理外務部事務 Tsung³ Li³ Wai⁴ Wu⁴ Pu⁴ Shih⁴ Wu⁴, Controller, to whom appertains the supreme control of affairs of the Ministry *see* No. 305ʙ).

At one period—from 1907 to 1909—there were Controllers at other Ministries, for instance, at the Ministry of War (管理陸軍部事務 Kuan³ Li³ Lu⁴ Chün¹ Pu⁴ Shih⁴ Wu⁴) and at the Ministry of Education (管理學部事務 Kuan³ Li³ Hsüeh² Pu⁴ Shih⁴ Wu⁴), holding which position, were, respectively, Prince Ch'ing and 張文襄公 Chang¹ Wên² Hsiang¹ Kung¹ (the late Grand Secretary 張之洞 Chang¹ Chih¹ Tung⁴).

277. In addition to the afore-mentioned, at the Ministry of Foreign Affairs there is the post of 會辦大臣 Hui⁴ Pan⁴ Ta⁴ Ch'ên², Assistant Controller, which title is sometimes

conferred on the President of that Ministry, his title then becoming 外 務 部 尚 書 會 辦 大 臣 Wai⁴ Wu⁴ Pu⁴ Shang⁴ Shu¹ Hui⁴ Pan⁴ Ta⁴ Ch'ên² (*see* Nos. 305C and 305D).

278. As has been stated above (*see* No. 276), at the head of each Ministry (with the exception mentioned) there is a 尚 書 Shang⁴ Shu¹ (official designation, 部 堂 Pu⁴ T'ang²) President ; 1B, to whom are subordinated :

279. 左 侍 耶 Tso³ Shih⁴ Lang² (official designation, 部 院 Pu⁴ Yüan²), Senior Vice-President ; 2A ; one at each Ministry.

280. 右 侍 耶 Yu⁴ Shih⁴ Lang² (official designation, 部 院 Pu⁴ Yüan²), Junior Vice-President ; 2A ; one at each Ministry.

281. 左 丞 Tso³ Ch'êng², Senior Councillor ; 3A ; one at each Ministry, with the exception of the Ministry of Dependencies (*see* No. 492).

282. 右 丞 Yu⁴ Ch'êng², Junior Councillor ; 3A ; one at each Ministry, with the exception of the Ministry of Dependencies (*see* No. 492).

283. 左 參 議 Tso³ Ts'an¹ I⁴, Senior Secretary ; 4A ; one at each Ministry, with the exception of the Ministry of Dependencies (*see* No. 492).

284. 右 參 議 Yu⁴ Ts'an¹ I⁴, Junior Secretary ; 4A ; one at each Ministry, with the exception of the Ministry of Dependencies (*see* No. 492).

284A. Under the old regime, previous to 1901, at the head of each Ministry there were two Presidents (Manchu and Chinese respectively), to whom were subordinated two Senior Vice-Presidents (Manchu and Chinese respectively) and two Junior Vice-Presidents (Manchu and Chinese respectively). The posts of Councillor and Secretary did not exist ; these were first established at the Ministry of Foreign Affairs, in 1901, and, later, in 1905, at the Ministries of Education, of the

**285
to
285c**

Interior and of Agriculture, Industry and Commerce, and, finally, in the Autumn of 1906, at the remaining Ministries, with the exception of the Ministry of Dependencies.

285. 承 政 廳 Ch'êng[2] Chêng[4] T'ing[1], Council of a Ministry (Board) ; with Councillors (*see* Nos. 281 and 282) in charge. This office is found at the Ministries of the Interior (*see* No. 340), of Finance (*see* No. 350), of War (*see* No. 422), of Justice (*see* No. 441) and of Posts and Communications (*see* No. 473).

285A. 參 議 廳 Ts'an[1] I[4] T'ing[1], Secretarial Office ; with Secretaries (*see* Nos. 283 and 284) in charge. This office is found at the Ministries of the Interior (*see* No. 341), of Finance (*see* No. 351), of War (*see* No. 423), of Justice (*see* No. 442) and of Posts and Communications (*see* No. 474).

285B. Besides Councillors (*see* Nos. 281 and 282), attached to the Councils of the Ministries (*see* No. 285) are :

Section Chiefs (*see* No. 290); three at the Ministry of Finance,

Assistant Section Chiefs (*see* No. 291) ; four at the Ministries of the Interior and of Finance,

Second Class Secretaries (*see* No. 292) ; four at the Ministry of the Interior, three at the Ministry of Finance, and

Assistant Secretaries (*see* No. 286) ; two at the Ministries of Justice and of Posts and Communications.

The Council of the Ministry of War has a peculiar organization (for details *see* No. 422B).

285C. In addition to Secretaries (*see* Nos. 283 and 284), the members of the Secretarial Offices of the Ministries (*see* No. 285A) are :

Section Chiefs (*see* No. 290); three at the Ministry of Finance,

Assistant Section Chiefs (*see* No. 291) ; four at the Ministry of Finance.

[100]

286
to
291

Second Class Secretaries (*see* No. 292); three at the Ministry of Finance, and

Assistant Secretaries (*see* No. 286); two at the Ministries of the Interior, of Justice and of Posts and Communications.

The Secretarial Office of the Ministry of War has a peculiar organization (for details *see* No. 423A).

286. 參事 Ts'an¹ Shih⁴ or, at the Ministry of Posts and Communications, 僉事 Chien¹ Shih⁴, Assistant Secretary of a Ministry; 5A. These officials, as seen above, are attached to the Councils (*see* No. 285B) and to the Secretarial Offices (*see* No. 285C). Also, four Assistant Secretaries are stationed at the Ministry of Education (*see* No. 396).

287. 丞參上行走 Ch'êng² Ts'an¹ Shang⁴ Hsing² Tsou³, Expectant Councillors or Expectant Secretaries. These are attached to the various Ministries in an indefinite number.

288. 堂主事 T'ang² Chu³ Shih⁴,˙ Secretaries (of the President of a Ministry); 6A. They are found at the Ministries of Civil Appointments (*see* No. 334; five), of Rites (*see* No. 377; four) and of Dependencies (*see* No. 492A; six).

289. The Departments composing the various Ministries are organized on uniform lines with the exception of those of the Ministry of War. The last mentioned have a peculiar organization (for details *see* No. 434).

290. 郎中 Lang² Chung¹, Department Directors; 5A, (literary designation, 正郎 Chêng⁴ Lang²); 1 to 9 in each Department; stationed at the Councils (*see* No. 285B) and at the Secretarial Offices (*see* No. 285C).

291. 員外郎 Yüan² Wai⁴ Lang², Assistant Department Directors (literary designation, 副郎 Fu⁴ Lang²; also 計郎 Chi⁴ Lang²); 5B; 2 to 8 in each Department; stationed at the Councils (*see* No. 285B) and at the Secretarial Offices (*see* No. 285C).

292
to
298

292. 主事 Chu³ Shih⁴, Second Class Secretaries of Ministries (literary designation, 主政 Chu³ Chêng⁴); 6ᴀ; 1 to 6 in each Department; stationed at the Councils (*see* No. 285ʙ) and at the Secretarial Offices (*see* No. 285ᴄ).

293. 筆帖式 Pi³ T'ieh³ Shih⁴, Clerks, of the seventh to the ninth ranks, (literary designation, 筆政 Pi³ Chêng⁴).

294. 司長 Ssu¹ Chang³, Department Controllers. 承發官 Ch'êng² Fa¹ Kuan¹, Registrars. 科長 K'o¹ Chang³, Section Chiefs. 科員 K'o¹ Yüan², Section Secretaries (of the first, second and third ranks). 錄事 Lu⁴ Shih⁴, Writers (of the eighth and ninth ranks).

The above-mentioned officials are found at all the Ministries, in the various Departments and Councils, including the Ministry of War.

295. 書記官 Shu¹ Chi⁴ Kuan¹, Clerks (of the first, second and third ranks); 7ᴀ, 8ᴀ and 9ᴀ. Thus are styled the Clerks at the Ministry of Education (*see* Nos. 403 and 413ᴀ); they correspond to the 筆帖式 Pi³ T'ieh³ Shih⁴ of other Ministries.

296. 司務廳 Ssu¹ Wu⁴ T'ing¹, Chancery; with two 司務 Ssu¹ Wu⁴, Chancery Chiefs; 8ᴀ, in charge. This office is found at the Ministries of Foreign Affairs (*see* No. 307), of Civil Appointments (*see* No. 334ᴀ), of Rites (*see* No. 378), of Finance (*see* No. 365), of Education (*see* No. 397) and of Dependencies (*see* No. 494, and, for details, No. 495ᴀ).

297. 額外司員 Ê² Wai⁴ Ssu¹ Yüan², Supernumerary Department Officials; having the titles of Department Director (*see* No. 290), Assistant Department Director (*see* No. 291), Second Class Secretary (*see* No. 292) and Clerk (*see* No. 293). They are attached to the various Departments in an indefinite number, sometimes very great.

298. 司庫 Ssu¹ K'u⁴, Treasurer; 7ᴀ, and 庫使 K'u⁴ Shih³, Treasury Overseer. These Officials are stationed at the Treasuries of the Ministries (for example, *see* No. 384ᴀ).

299. 七品小京官 Ch'i¹ P'in³ Hsiao³ Ching¹ Kuan¹, Official of the seventh rank, and 八品小京官 Pa¹ P'in³ Hsiao³ Ching¹ Kuan¹, Official of the eighth rank. These are attached to the Councils and Secretarial Offices in an indefinite number (compare No. 475).

300. 議員 I⁴ Yüan², Advisers; consisting of 礦務議員 Kung³ Wu⁴ I⁴ Yüan², Mining Advisers, and 商務議員 Shang¹ Wu⁴ I⁴ Yüan², Commercial Advisers, at the Ministry of Agriculture, Industry and Commerce (see No. 468), and 路務議員 Lu⁴ Wu⁴ I⁴ Yüan², Railway Advisers, at the Ministry of Posts and Communications (see No. 484).

301. 藝師 I⁴ Shih¹, Chief Engineers of the. first and second rank; 6A and 7A, and 藝士 I⁴ Shih⁴, Engineers of the first and second rank; 8A and 9A. These are found at the Ministries of the Interior (see No. 345B), of War (see Nos. 427B and 428B), of Agriculture, Industry and Commerce (see No. 469) and of Posts and Communications (see No. 487).

301A. 醫官 I¹ Kuan¹, Physicians (of the sixth and seventh rank); stationed at the Ministry of the Interior (see No. 346B).

302. 諮議官 Tzu¹ I⁴ Kuan¹, Consulting Experts (of the first, second, third and fourth rank); found at the Ministries of Education (see No. 405), and of War (see No. 423A; they are here members of the Secretarial Office). The number of these officials is indefinite.

302A. 顧問官 Ku⁴ Wên⁴ Kuan¹, Advisers (of the first, second, third and fourth rank); stationed at the Ministries of Agriculture, Industry and Commerce (see No. 468) and of Posts and Communications (see No. 483) in an indefinite number.

302B. Advisers and Experts of the first rank (see Nos. 302 and 302A) have the rank of Councillor (see Nos. 281 and 282), of the second rank, that of Senior or Junior Secretary (see Nos. 283 and 284), of the third rank, that of Department Director or

303

Assistant Department Director (*see* Nos. 290 and 291), and of the fourth rank, that of Second Class Secretary (*see* No. 292).

The title of Adviser is sometimes bestowed on persons distinguished for some particular service (for instance, with regard to home industries, commerce, etc.) The title of Adviser of the fourth rank was bestowed, in accordance with a Memorial from the Ministry of Agriculture, Industry and Commerce, on 張 煜 南 Chang[1] I[4]-nan[2] and 陳 宜 禧 Ch'ên[2] I[2]-hsi[3], who initiated the building of two private railways in Kwangtung Province, 潮 汕 鐵 路 Ch'ao[2] Shan[3] T'ieh[3] Lu[4], the Ch'ao-chou-Shan-t'ou (Swatow) Railway, and 新 寗 鐵 路 Hsin[1] Ning[2] T'ieh[3] Lu[4], Hsin Ning Railway.

303. 檢 查 官 Chien[3] Ch'a[2] Kuan[1], Inspectors of Military affairs (of the first, second and third rank); attached in an indefinite number to the Secretarial Office of the Ministry of War (*see* No. 423A).

304. 堂 官 T'ang[2] Kuan[1], a designation common to all the High Officials of the Ministries, Secretaries included. 司 官 Ssu[1] Kuan[1], common designation of all officials of the Ministries below the rank of Secretary ("dignitaries" and "officers.")

MINISTRY (BOARD) OF FOREIGN AFFAIRS.

305. 總 理 各 國 事 務 衙 門 Tsung[3] Li[3] Ko[4] Kuo[2] Shih[4] Wu[4] Ya[2] Mên[2], Office of Foreign Affairs (shorter; 總 理 衙 門 Tsung[3] Li[3] Ya[2] Mên[2]; also 總 署 Tsung[3] Shu[3]); established by Imperial Edict of the 31st January, 1861, for dealing with all matters concerning China and the Foreign Powers, the representatives of the latter having been granted by Treaties (Tientsin; 1858, and Peking; 1860) the privilege of residing at the Capital (previously all dealings between China and Russia were carried on through the Ministry of Dependencies and those with other Powers through the Ministry of Rites; *see* Nos. 376

and 491). 恭親王奕訢 Kung[1] Ch'in[1] Wang[2] I[2] Hsin[1], Kung,
Prince of the First Degree, personal name 奕訢 I Hsin (the
sixth brother of the Emperor 咸豐 Hsien[2] Fêng[1], 1851-1861),
was its first President and 桂良 Kuei[4] Liang[2], a Grand
Secretary, and 文祥 Wên[2] Hsiang[2], Vice-President of the
Ministry of War, were detailed to this office.

The number of members of the Tsung Li Ya Mên, known
by the general title of 王大臣 Wang[2] Ta[4] Ch'ên[2], "Prince and
Ministers" was not defined and sometimes reached eleven. High
Officials holding substantive posts, which they retained, were
detailed to this office, but it is worthy of remark that, for thirty
years after the institution of the Tsung Li Ya Mên, its existence
was ignored by the 縉紳錄 Chin[4] Shên[1] Lu[4], "Red Book,"
which was otherwise a complete directory of Metropolitan and
Provincial State Establishments and indicated their personnel.
The omission was rectified in 1890.

The clerical work of the Tsung Li Ya Mên was performed
by 章京 Chang[1] Ching[1], Secretaries (official designation, 司員
Ssu[1] Yüan[2] or 司官 Ssu[1] Kuan[1]), who were originally drafted
from the staff of the Council of State (see No. 129B). The six
senior Secretaries, all of whom held either substantive or
expectant rank, were usually styled 總辦 Tsung[3] Pan[4].

The members of the Tsung Li Ya Mên, being only
temporarily deputed to that office, naturally paid attention
mainly to the duties of their substantive posts, leaving no time
for seriously attending to those of their additional office, which
were, in addition, quite unknown to them. Also, there being a
numerous staff of members of equal standing, sometimes having
entirely different views on international questions, the practice of
referring questions from one memb r to another during negotiations, the absence of initiative and fear of the consequences of any
initiative, and, finally, the little knowledge, or even complete
ignorance, of the members of the Tsung Li Ya Mên of questions

305A under discussion, made negotiations very difficult for the Foreign Representatives, who continually pointed out to China the necessity for the reform of this establishment. These recommendations remained fruitless and, at last, the Powers insisted on an Article being inserted in the " Peace Protocol between China and the Foreign Powers," signed on the 7th December, 1901 ;—Article 12—reading as follows :

" An Imperial Edict of 24th July, 1901, has reformed the " Office of Foreign Affairs in the direction indicated by the " Powers, that is to say, has transformed it into a Ministry of " Foreign Affairs, which takes precedence of the other Six " Ministries.

" The same Edict has named the principal member of this " Ministry."

305A. 外 務 部 Wai⁴ Wu⁴ Pu⁴, Ministry of Foreign Affairs ; established, as stated above, by Imperial Edict of the 24th July, 1901, the tenor of which was as follows :

On the ninth day of the sixth moon the Grand Secretariat received an Edict, as follows :

" The appointment of officials and the determination of their " duties have, until now, been regulated by the needs of the " moment. Henceforth, however, when a Treaty of Peace is " concluded, international relations are to be placed in the first " rank of important affairs and it is more than ever necessary to " call for the assistance of clever men and give them opportunity " to study everything having reference to the establishment of " friendly relations and confidence in intercourse.

" It is true that the Office of Foreign Affairs, previously " established for dealing with international affairs, has existed for " many years, but the ' Prince and Ministers ' composing its " staff, holding office there as a complement to other substantive " posts, have been unable to devote themselves entirely to its

" affairs and it is necessary to create distinctive positions that 305ʙ
" each may recognize his duties. to

" In view of this we direct that the Office of Foreign 305ᴄ
" Affairs be transformed into a Ministry of Foreign Affairs,
" which shall take precedence of the other Six Ministries of
" State.

" We appoint I K'uang, Prince Ch'ing, Prince of the First
" Degree, President of the Ministry of Foreign Affairs ; Wang
" Wên-shao, Grand Secretary of the T'i Jên Ko, to be Vice-
" President, and Ch'ü Hung-chi, President of the Ministry of
" Works, to retain his title but act as Vice-President, Hsü
" Shou-p'êng, Director of the Palace Stud, and Lien Fang,
" Expectant Metropolitan Vice-Director of the third or fourth
" rank, to be First and Second Directors (Assistant Secretaries).

" As regards the appointment of a staff, regulations and
" salaries to be paid, we direct that these be arranged by the
" Council of State and the Ministry of Civil Appointments as
" soon as possible and a Memorial on the subject be presented to
" Us. Respect This."

The internal organization of the Ministry of Foreign Affairs
is based on Memorials of the Bureau of Government Affairs,
in collaboration with the Ministry of Civil Appointments, dated
the 11th August, 1901, and of the Ministry of Foreign Affairs
itself, dated the 29th December of the same year.

The reform of the political organization of the State, undertaken in the autumn of 1906, did not affect the Ministry of
Foreign Affairs (see Edict dated 6th November).

305ʙ.　總理外務部事務　Tsung³ Li³ Wai⁴ Wu⁴ Pu⁴ Shih⁴
Wu⁴, Controller of the Ministry of Foreign Affairs (see No. 276).

305ᴄ.　外務部會辦大臣　Wai⁴ Wu⁴ Pu⁴ Hui⁴ Pan⁴ Ta⁴
Ch'ên², Assistant Controller of the Ministry of Foreign Affairs
(see No. 277).

305D. 外務部尚書會辦大臣 Wai[4] Wu[4] Pu[4] Shang[4] Shu[1] Hui[4] Pan[4] Ta[4] Ch'ên[2], President and Assistant Controller of the Ministry of Foreign Affairs (*see* No. 277).

306. The Ministry of Foreign Affairs is composed of the following four Departments :

1. 和會司 Ho[2] Hui[4] Ssu[1], Department of Intercourse ; arranges receptions for Foreign Representatives, requests audiences for them and recommends decorations to be bestowed on them, supervises the appointment and transfer of Chinese Representatives abroad and Chinese Consuls, the personal staff of the Ministry, and the recommendation of rewards for these officials, etc.

2. 考工司 K'ao[3] Kung[1] Ssu[1], Department of Technical Affairs ; controls the engagement of foreigners for service in the Railways, Mines, Telegraph Service, Arsenals, etc., and the sending of Students abroad.

3. 榷算司 Ch'üeh[4] Suan[4] Ssu[1], Accounts Department ; supervises Customs Duties, Foreign Trade, Steam Navigation, Foreign Loans, Postal Affairs, Expenditure of the Ministry, paying the salaries of Chinese Representatives abroad, etc.

4. 庶務司 Shu[4] Wu[4] Ssu[1], Department of General Affairs ; in charge of Frontier and Missionary Affairs, the issue of Passports for travel in the interior, etc.

307. 司務廳 Ssu[1] Wu[4] T'ing[1], Chancery (*see* No. 296) ; in charge of 2 司務 Ssu[1] Wu[4], Chancery Chiefs ; 8A.

308. In each Department there are two Department Directors (*see* No. 290), two Assistant Department Directors (*see* No. 291) and two Second Class Secretaries (*see* No. 292). These all have distinctive titles, distinguishing them from similar officials of the other Ministries, namely :

1. 掌印 Chang[3] Yin[4], Keeper of the Seal,
2. 主稿 Chu[3] Kao[3], Keeper of Drafts,
3. 幫掌印 Pang[1] Chang[3] Yin[4], Assistant Keeper of the Seal.

4. 帮主稿 Pang¹ Chu³ Kao³, Assistant Keeper of Drafts. **309**

5. 帮掌印上行走 Pang¹ Chang³ Yin⁴ Shang⁴ Hsing² **to**
Tsou³, Expectant Assistant Keeper of the Seal, and **310**

6. 帮主稿上行走 Pang¹ Chu³ Kao³ Shang⁴ Hsing²
Tsou³, Expectant Assistant Keeper of Drafts.

309. Interpreters (Translators) attached to the Ministry of Foreign Affairs are divided, in the first instance, into various ranks :

1. 七品繙譯官 Ch'i¹ P'in³ Fan¹ I⁴ Kuan¹, Interpreters of the seventh rank.

2. 八品繙譯官 Pa¹ P'in³ Fan¹ I⁴ Kuan¹, Interpreters of the eighth rank, and

3. 九品繙譯官 Chiu³ P'in³ Fan¹ I⁴ Kuan¹, Interpreters of the ninth rank.

They are further divided, from their specialities, into sections (now 股 Ku³, formerly 處 Ch'u⁴) *i.e.* 俄 Ê⁴, Russian, 德 Tê², German, 法 Fa⁴, French, 英 Ying¹, English, and 日本 Jih⁴ Pên³, Japanese, each section having one Interpreter of each rank.

310. 儲才館 Ch'u³ Ts'ai² Kuan³, Preceptory of the Ministry of Foreign Affairs ; established in accordance with a Memorial from the Ministry itself, dated the 13th June, 1906.

The internal organization of this establishment was treated in Memorials dated 14th December, 1906, 26th April, 7th May and 3rd June, 1907. The object of its establishment is the training of officials for service at the Ministry of Foreign Affairs, both at Headquarters and at Establishments abroad.

The administration of the Preceptory is in the hands of the following (officials of the Ministry) :

1. 1 提調 T'i² Tiao⁴, Proctor,

2. 1 帮提調 Pang¹ T'i² Tiao⁴, Assistant Proctor,

3. 1 文案員 Wên² An⁴ Yüan², Secretary,

4. 1 支應員 Chih¹ Ying¹ Yüan², Treasurer,

5. 1 庶務員 Shu⁴ Wu⁴ Yüan², Steward,

[109]

6. 書記員 Shu[1] Chi[4] Shêng[1], Clerks (number not fixed).

7. 1 講員 Chiang[3] Yüan[2], Senior Teacher, and

8. 課員 K'o[4] Yüan[2], Teachers (of specialities; up to the number of 26).

311. Formerly, under the direct supervision of the Ministry of Foreign Affairs were:

1. 同文館 T'ung[2] Wên[2] Kuan[3], College of Languages; established in 1862. At first only courses in English, Frénch and Russian were given; later, in 1867, there were added courses in certain sciences; namely, mathematics, astronomy, chemistry and physics and a course in international law. This college is now non-existent; on its abolition (1900) the teaching of foreign languages was transferred, at Peking, to the College of Interpreters (*see* No. 625), and, in the provinces, to the Colleges of Languages (*see* No. 626).

2. The Imperial Maritime Customs (*see* No. 253), which, on the establishment of the Board of Customs Control in 1906 (*see* No. 241), was placed under the control of the latter.

312. 駐洋大臣 Chu[4] Yang[2] Ta[4] Ch'ên[2], Diplomatic Representatives and 駐外使府 Chu[4] Wai[4] Shih[3] Fu[3], Legations.

In accordance with the reply of the Ministry of Foreign Affairs to a Memorial from 劉式訓 Liu[2] Shih[4]-hsün[4], Minister at Paris, at Chinese Government Establishments abroad there are the following (sanctioned by the Emperor on the 25th January, 1907):

313. 頭等出使大臣 T'ou[2] Têng[3] Ch'u[1] Shih[3] Ta[4] Ch'ên[2], Ambassador—first rank (salary 1,400 taels per month).

314. 二等出使大臣 Êrh[4] Têng[3] Ch'u[1] Shih[3] Ta[4] Ch'ên[2], Envoy Extraordinary and Minister Plenipotentiary—second rank (salary 1,000 taels per month).

315. 三等出使大臣 San[1] Têng[3] Ch'u[1] Shih[3] Ta[4] Ch'ên[2] Minister Resident—third rank (salary 800 taels per month).

316. 頭等參贊 T'ou² Têng³ Ts'an¹ Tsan⁴, First Councillor, third rank (salary 500 taels per month).

317. 總領事 Tsung³ Ling³ Shih⁴, Consul-General—fourth rank (salary 500 taels per month).

318. 二等參贊 Êrh⁴ Têng³ Ts'an¹ Tsan⁴, Second Councillor—fourth rank (salary 400 taels per month).

319. 頭等通譯官 T'ou² Têng³ T'ung¹ I⁴ Kuan¹, First Interpreter—fifth rank (salary 400 taels per month).

320. 領事 Ling³ Shih⁴, Consul—fifth rank (salary 400 taels per month).

321. 商務委員 Shang¹ Wu⁴ Wei³ Yüan², Commercial Agent—sixth rank (salary 240 taels per month).

322. 三等參贊 San¹ Têng³ Ts'an¹ Tsan⁴, Third Councillor—fifth rank (salary 300 taels per month).

323. 二等通譯官 Êrh⁴ Têng³ T'ung¹ I⁴ Kuan¹, Second Interpreter—fifth rank (salary 300 taels per month).

324. 副領事 Fu⁴ Ling³ Shih⁴, Vice-Consul—fifth rank (salary 300 taels per month).

325. 一等書記官 I¹ Têng³ Shu¹ Chi⁴ Kuan¹, First Secretary—fifth rank (salary 300 taels per month).

326. 三等通譯官 San¹ Têng³ T'ung¹ I⁴ Kuan¹, Third Interpreter—sixth rank (salary 240 taels per month).

327. 二等書記官 Êrh⁴ Têng³ Shu¹ Chi⁴ Kuan¹, Second Secretary—sixth rank (salary 240 taels per month).

328. 三等書記官 San¹ Têng³ Shu¹ Chi⁴ Kuan¹, Third Secretary—seventh rank (salary 200 taels per month).

329. 武隨員 Wu³ Sui² Yüan², Military Attaché; subordinated directly to the General Staff Council (*see* No. 184B). There is one for Great Britain and France, one for Russia and Germany, one in America and one in Japan (*see* report of the Ministry of War, dated 10th January, 1907).

330. 使館 Shih³ Kuan³, Legation (also 使署 Shih³ Shu³; colloquially, 欽差府 Ch'in¹ Ch'ai¹ Fu³ and 欽差衙門 Ch'in¹

Ch'ai[1] Ya[2] Mên[2]) ; with a 欽命出使某國大臣 Ch'in[1] Ming[4] Ch'u[1] Shih[3] Mou[u] Kuo[2] Ta[4] Cl'ên[2], Minister (also 公使 Kung[1] Shih[3] or 使臣 Shih[3] Ch'ên[2]; literary designation, 星使 Hsing[1] Shih[3]; colloquially, 欽差 Ch'in[1] Ch'ai[1]) in charge ; China has no Embassies.

There are Chinese Legations at Tokyo, London, Washington, Vienna, Rome, Berlin, Paris, St. Petersburg, Brussels and The Hague.

330ᴀ.   Staff of various Legations :

1. Tokyo, London, Washington, Berlin, Paris and St. Petersburg :

Second and Third Councillors (one at each).   Second and Third Interpreters (one at each).   Commercial Agents and First and Second Secretaries (one at each).

2.   Vienna, Rome, Brussels and The Hague :

Second Councillors, Second Interpreters and First and Second Secretaries (one at each).

331. 分館 Fên[1] Kuan[3], Subsidiary Legations ; with 代辦使事 Tai[4] Pan[4] Shih[3] Shih[4], Chargé d'Affaires (also 代辦使臣 Tai[4] Pan[4] Shih[3] Ch'ên[2], 代理公使 Tai[4] Li[3] Kung[1] Shih[3] or 臨時代理公使 Lin[2] Shih[2] Tai[4] Li[3] Kung[1] Shih[3], Chargé d'Affaires *ad interim*), in charge ; usually a Second Councillor (*see* No. 318).

There are subsidiary Legations :

A.   Subordinated to the Minister at Washington :

1. 墨分館 Mo[4] Fên[1] Kuan[3], Subsidiary Legation in Mexico,

2.   秘分館 Pi[4] Fên[1] Kuan[3], Subsidiary Legation in Peru (at Lima), and

3.   古分館 Ku[3] Fên[1] Kuan[3], Subsidiary Legation in Cuba (at Havana).

B.   Subordinated to the Minister at Paris :

1. 日分館 Jih⁴ Fên¹ Kuan³, Subsidiary Legation in Spain (at Madrid), and

2. 葡分館 P'u² Fên¹ Kuan³, Subsidiary Legation in Portugal (at Lisbon).

331A. The staff of the Subsidiary Legations in Mexico, Peru, Cuba, Spain and Portugal is composed of a Second Councillor as Charge d'Affaires (*see* No. 331)—in Mexico and Cuba also acting as Consul-General,—a Second Interpreter and a Second Secretary—acting in Peru as Consul.

332. 總領事館 Tsung³ Ling³ Shih⁴ Kuan³, Consulate-General (also 總領事署 Tsung³ Ling³ Shih⁴ Shu³ and 總領事府 Tsung³ Ling³ Shih⁴ Fu³).

There are Consulates-General at 横濱 Hêng² Ping², Yokohama, Seoul, 新嘉坡 Hsin¹ Chia¹ P'o¹, Singapore, 南菲 Nan² Fei⁴, South Africa, 澳洲 Ao⁴ Chou¹, Australia, 坎拿大 K'an³ Na² Ta⁴, Canada (Montreal), 金山 Chin¹ Shan¹, California (San Francisco), 小呂宋 Hsiao³ Lü³ Sung⁴, Philippines (Manila), and 海参威 Hai³ Shên¹ Wei⁴, Vladivostock.

領事館 Ling³ Shih⁴ Kuan³ or 正領事館 Chêng⁴ Ling³ Shih⁴ Kuan³ (also 領事署 Ling³ Shih⁴ Shu³ and 領事府 Ling³ Shih⁴ Fu³), Consulate.

There are Consulates at 神戶 Shên² Hu⁴, Kobe, 長崎 Ch'ang² Ch'i², Nagasaki, 仁川 Jên² Ch'uan¹, Chemulpo, 釜山 Fu³ Shan¹, Fusan, 紐絲綸 Niu³ Ssu¹ Lun², New Zealand, 仰光 Yang³ Kuang¹, Rangoon (British Burma), 溫哥埠 Wên¹ Ko¹ Fu⁴, Vancouver, 紐約 Niu³ Yüeh¹, New York, and 檀香山 T'an² Hsiang¹ Shan¹, Honolulu.

副領事館 Fu⁴ Ling³ Shih⁴ Kuan³ (also 副領事署 Fu⁴ Ling³ Shih⁴ Shu³ and 副領事府 Fu⁴ Ling³ Shih⁴ Fu³), Vice-Consulate.

There are Vice-Consulates at 鎮南浦 Chên⁴ Nan² P'u³, Chinnanpo, 元山 Yüan² Shan¹, Gensan, and 檳榔嶼 Pin¹ Lang² Yü⁴, Penang.

[113]

332A. The staff of a Consulate-General is composed of a Second Interpreter, a First Secretary (at Seoul alone), a Second Secretary and a Third Secretary.

The staff of a Consulate consists of a Second Interpreter (at Chemulpo a Third Secretary), Interpreter (at Chemulpo there is a Third Interpreter instead ; at Fusan there is no Second Interpreter) and a Second Secretary.

At Vice-Consulates there is stationed a Second Secretary.

MINISTRY (BOARD) OF CIVIL APPOINTMENTS.

333. 吏部 Li⁴ Pu⁴, Ministry (Board) of Civil Appointments (literary designation, 銓曹 Ch'üan² Ts'ao², Board of Elections, also 天曹 T'ien¹ Ts'ao², Celestial Board) ; this is one of the oldest establishments in China, for which reason, in the hierarchy, it is placed immediately after the Ministry of Foreign Affairs. This Ministry controls and directs the personnel of the Civil Service in the Empire ; its duties are defined as including " whatever appertains to selection, rank and gradation, rules defining degradation or promotion, and ordinances as to the granting of investitures or rewards."

The Imperial Edict, dated the 6th November, 1906, reorganizing the Ministries, did not affect the Ministry of Civil Appointments.

333A. The literary designation of the President of the Ministry of Civil Appointments is 太宰 T'ai⁴ Tsai³, and, of Vice-President, 少宰 Shao⁴ Tsai³.

334. 堂主事 T'ang² Chu³ Shih⁴, Secretary (of the President ; five in all) ; 6A (*see* No. 288).

334A. 司務廳 Ssu¹ Wu⁴ T'ing¹, Chancery (*see* No. 296).

335. 文選司 Wen² Hsuan³ Ssu¹, Department of Selection ; controls selection, appointment and transfer of civil officials.

336. 考 功 司 K'ao³ Kung¹ Ssu¹, Department of Scrutiny; supervises rewards to be granted and penalties to be inflicted, also prescribes furloughs.

337. 稽 勳 司 Chi² Hsun¹ Ssu¹, Record Department; keeps a record of official titles, regulates retirement on account of mourning, amount of pensions to civil officials and the bestowal of hereditary titles on Bannermen.

338. 驗 封 司 Yen⁴ Feng¹ Ssu¹, Department of Grants; regulates the bestowal of titles, patents and presents, and hereditary titles on heads of tribes.

MINISTRY (BOARD) OF THE INTERIOR.

339. 巡 警 部 Hsun² Ching³ Pu⁴, Ministry (Board) of Police. This was established by Imperial Decree dated the 8th October, 1905 (till that time there was no special Ministry overseeing the policing of the Empire), which reads as follows:

" Police affairs are of the utmost importance and we " have repeatedly issued instructions for their improvement, " both in the Capital and in the provinces. It is necessary " that a special establishment be in charge of these affairs and " we now direct the organization of a Ministry of Police and " appoint Hsu Shih-ch'ang, Senior Vice-President of the " Ministry of War, as its President, Yü Lang, Sub-Chancellor " of the Grand Secretariat, as Senior Vice-President, and " Chao Ping-chun, Expectant Taotai of Chihli, now raised to " the rank of Metropolitan Official of the 3rd rank, as Acting " Junior Vice-President. This Ministry will be in charge of " everything pertaining to policing and the maintenance of " good order in the Manchu and Chinese sections of the " Capital as well as the policing of the provinces. The above- " mentioned President and other officials are to earnestly " devise measures, exert themselves to the utmost in the " performance of their duties, take no heed of reproaches and "draw up strict regulations. They must exercise a complete "control that everything remain calm and the people undis-"turbed. As regards questions not arranged for by this "Edict, the Ministry is to deliberate and report. Respect this."

By an Imperial Decree of the 6th November, 1906, the Ministry of Police was transformed into :

339ᴀ. 民 政 部 Min² Chêng⁴ Pu⁴, Ministry (Board) of the Interior (or Ministry of the Administration of the People).

The Ministry of the Interior controls police affairs generally, local self-government, census taking, sanitary matters, land boundary questions, buildings, etc.

The proposed internal organization of the Ministry was presented to the Throne in a Memorial from the Ministry itself and received Imperial sanction on the 1st January, 1907.

340. 承 政 廳 Ch'êng² Chêng⁴ T'ing¹, Council (for organization *see* No. 285) ; considers the most important questions ; attends to correspondence, accounting and general administration of the Ministry.

341. 叅 議 廳 Ts'an¹ I⁴ T'ing¹, Secretarial Office (for organization *see* No. 285ᴀ). This office is charged with the drafting of rules and regulations.

341ᴀ. Two 叅 事 Ts'an¹ Shih⁴, Assistant Secretaries (*see* No. 286) ; 5ᴀ, and one 編 譯 員 Pien¹ I⁴ Yüan², Translator (Interpreter), are stationed in the Secretarial Office.

342. 民 治 司 Min² Chih⁴ Ssu¹, Department of Administration of the People ; supervises local self-government, census taking, the improvement of the customs and manners of the people, questions of emigration, colonization, etc.

To this Department was transferred :

342ᴀ. The 戶 籍 科 Hu⁴ Chi² K'o¹, Census Section ; from the former 警 政 司 Ching³ Chêng⁴ Ssu¹, Department of Police Affairs.

[116]

343. 警政司 Ching³ Chêng⁴ Ssu¹, Department of Police Affairs ; controls administrative and judicial police, police instruction, etc.

343ᴀ. To the Department of Police Affairs were transferred the 行政科 Hsing² Chêng⁴ K'o¹, Section of Administration —from the previous 警政司 Ching³ Chêng⁴ Ssu¹, Department of Police Affairs— 司法科 Ssu¹ Fa⁴ K'o¹, Judicial Section, and 國際科 Kuo² Chi⁴ K'o¹, Section of International Affairs—from the former 警法司 Ching³ Fa⁴ Ssu¹, Police Judicial Department— 保安科 Pao³ An¹ K'o¹, Section of Public Safety—from the former 警保司 Ching³ Pao¹ Ssu¹, Department of Police Defence— 營業科 Ying² Yeh⁴ K'o¹, Section of Industry and Handicraft—from the same Department—and 課程科 K'o⁴ Ch'êng² K'o¹, Section of Instruction—from the former 警學司 Ching³ Hsüeh² Ssu¹, Department of Police Instruction.

343ʙ. 習藝所 Hsi² I¹ So³, Workhouse. This was formerly under the supervision of the Police Judicial Department (*see* No. 343ᴀ) ; it is now controlled by the Department of Police Affairs (*see* No. 343). Its staff consists of one Assistant Department Director (*see* No. 291) and two Second Class Secretaries (*see* No. 292) ; compare No. 514.

344. 疆理司 Chiang¹ Li³ Ssu¹, Department of Land Boundaries ; supervises the determination of the boundaries of plots of land, the measurement of all the land in the Empire, topographic surveys, the making of maps and the clearing of public and private land.

345. 營繕司 Ying² Shan⁴ Ssu¹, Building Department. This Department supervises all the buildings of the Ministry, as well as State buildings in the capital, keeps monuments of antiquity in repair, and supervises the maintenance of altars, temples, etc., in good condition.

345ᴀ. To the above-mentioned Department there has been transferred the 工築科 Kung¹ Chu⁴ K'o¹, Building Section ;

345B
to
349

from the former 警保司 Ching³ Pao³ Ssu¹, Department of Police Defence.

345B. Two 藝師 I⁴ Shih¹, Chief Engineers, of the sixth and seventh ranks (*see* No. 301), are attached to the Building Department (*see* No. 345).

346. 衛生司 Wei⁴ Shêng¹ Ssu¹, Sanitary Department ; combats epidemics, considers all questions of sanitation, has the supervision of physicians, medicine compounding and the establishment of hospitals, etc.

346A. To the Sanitary Department there has been transferred the 衛生科 Wei⁴ Shêng¹ K'o¹, Sanitary Section, of the former 警保司 Ching³ Pao³ Ssu¹, Department of Police Defence.

346B. Two 醫官 I¹ Kuan¹, Physicians, of the sixth and seventh ranks (*see* No. 301A), are attached to the Sanitary Department (*see* No. 346).

347. 統計處 T'ung³ Chi⁴ Ch'u⁴, Statistical Bureau (for its organization *see* No. 162).

348. Under the control of the Ministry of the Interior are:

1. The Metropolitan Police (*see* Nos. 500—518),

2. Police Taotais (*see* Nos. 840 and 840A), and through them,

3. The Provincial Police (*see* Nos. 520 and 521),

4. Judicial Police (*see* No. 519),

5. Police Schools (*see* Nos. 522 and 523),

6. Local Self Government Establishment (*see* Nos. 524—527A), and·

7. Establishments supervising the taking of the Census (*see* Nos. 528—532).

MINISTRY (BOARD) OF FINANCE.

349. 戶部 Hu⁴ Pu⁴, Ministry (Board) of Revenue (literary designation, 農部 Nung² Pu⁴ and 民部 Min² Pu⁴ ; of its President—in the 夏 Hsia⁴ and 殷 Yin¹ Dynasties—大司徒

Ta⁴ Ssu¹ T'u², and its Vice-President, 少 司 徒 Shao³ Ssu¹ T'u², and—in the 周 Chou¹ Dynasty—地 官 Ti⁴ Kuan¹, Land Official).

349ᴀ
to
353

In the Hu Pu there were fourteen Departments, corresponding to the number of Governor-General and Governors.

349ᴀ. 財 政 處 Ts'ai² Chêng⁴ Ch'u⁴, Committee of Finance; established in 1903 in connection with a proposed general reform of the financial affairs of the Empire.

By Imperial Edict of the 6th November, 1906, the Ministry of Revenue was reorganized, with it being amalgamated the Committee of Finance, as the :

349ʙ. 度 支 部 Tu⁴ Chih¹ Pu⁴, Ministry (Board) of Finance. This Ministry is in charge of all financial affairs of the Empire, regulates the levying and collection of duties and taxes, supervises transportation and storage of grain, arranges State loans, controls mints, banks, financial establishments, schools, etc.

This Ministry has authority to depute officials to reorganize the finances of any of the provinces.

The internal organization of the Ministry is in accordance with a Memorial from the Ministry itself, sanctioned by the Emperor on the 26th April, 1907.

350. 承 政 廳 Ch'êng² Chêng⁴ T'ing¹, Council (for its organization see No. 285). This supervises the most important financial questions and the translation of financial regulations of Foreign Powers, as well as works on political economy.

351. 叅 議 廳 Ts'an¹ I⁴ T'ing¹, Secretarial Office (for its organization see No. 215ᴀ); compiles reports to the Emperor, drafts despatches and frames rules and regulations.

352. 田 賦 司 T'ien² Fu⁴ Ssu¹, Department of Land Taxes ; in charge of the levy and collection of land taxes, exemption from or postponement of payment of these taxes, the colonization of lands, etc.

353. 漕 倉 司 Ts'ao² Ts'ang¹ Ssu¹, Department of Tithes; charged with the control of tribute grain, its storage in

354 to 360

metropolitan and provincial granaries and distribution to the people in time of calamity, and the payment, in money, of taxes in kind.

354. 稅課司 Shui[4] K'o[4] Ssu[1], Department of Duties; has supervision of the income and expenditure of Native and Maritime Customs, Customs duties, excise on opium and wine, likin, duties leviable on mechanical and manufactured goods, stamp duties, granting of Customs certificates, etc.

355. 筦榷司 Kuan[3] Ch'üeh[4] Ssu[1], Department of Excise; in charge of the excise on salt, tea and native opium and the consideration of measures for the monopoly of the last-mentioned, etc.

356. 通阜司 T'ung[1] Fu[4] Ssu[1], Currency Department; superintends the provision of gold, silver, copper and tin for, and their conversion into, currency, the making of bank notes, the framing of regulations concerning the organization of banks and mints, and the maintenance of a sufficient supply of currency in circulation.

357. 庫藏司 K'u[4] Ts'ang[2] Ssu[1], Department of the State Treasury; supervises the income and expenditure of the State Treasury, scrutinizes financial reports from the provinces, as well as reports from the Imperial silk factories in Kiangsu and Chekiang, reorganizes provincial treasuries, etc.

358. 廉俸司 Lien[2] Fêng[4] Ssu[1], Department of Emoluments. This Department is in charge of the payment of salaries and allowances to officials and Princes and the issue of allowances of Bannermen.

359. 軍餉司 Chün[1] Hsiang[3] Ssu[1], Department of Military Supplies; superintends the distribution of supplies to the Military and Naval Forces of the Empire.

360. 制用司 Chih[4] Yung[4] Ssu[1], Department of Expenditure. This Department regulates the expenditure of funds provided by the provinces for use in the Capital, as well as the

expenditure on buildings, railways, mines, telegraphs and postal administration.

361. 會計司 Hui⁴ (K'uai⁴) Chi⁴ Ssu¹, Audit Department; audits the income and expenditure of the State Treasury, prepares the budget, determines extraordinary expenditure, revises accounts, etc.

362. 收發稽查處 Shou¹ Fa¹ Chi² Ch'a² Ch'u⁴, Registry; in charge of the reception of incoming, and issue of outgoing, despatches, looks after matters of economy and has control of the several Departments' correspondence with other establishments.

363. 金銀庫 Chin¹ Yin² K'u⁴, State Treasury. Here State funds are stored, in currency, bullion and bank notes.

364. 統計處 T'ung³ Chi⁴ Ch'u⁴, Statistical Bureau (for its organization see No. 162B).

365. 司務廳 Ssu¹ Wu⁴ T'ing¹, Chancery (see No. 296).

366. 寶泉局 Pao³ Ch'üan² Chü², Coinage Office; charged with the reception of copper and tin and the coinage of copper money.

366A. 兼理錢法堂事務 Chien¹ Li³ Ch'ien² Fa⁴ T'ang² Shih⁴ Wu⁴. Thus was formerly designated one of the Junior Vice-Presidents of the Ministry, under whose supervision the Coinage Office was placed (see No. 366).

366B. The administration of the Coinage Office is now carried out by three 大使 Ta⁴ Shih³, Overseers, each being in charge of one of the 廠 Ch'ang³, Mints, 北廠 Pei³ Ch'ang³, Northern, 中廠 Chung¹ Ch'ang³, Middle, and 西廠 Hsi¹ Ch'ang³, Western.

367. 核捐處 Ho² Chüan¹ Ch'u⁴, Subscription Bureau. This is a temporary establishment, organized for recommending rewards for subscribers to national needs.

368. 印刷局 Yin⁴ Shua¹ Chü², Printing Office.

368A. 造紙廠 Tsao⁴ Chih³ Ch'ang³, Official Paper Mill.

369
to
374A

369. 督辦鹽政大臣 Tu¹ Pan⁴ Yen² Chêng⁴ Ta⁴ Ch'ên², Controller-General of the Salt Gabelle; this post (associated with that of President of the Ministry of Finance) was established by Imperial Edict of the 31st December, 1909, in order that the control of the salt affairs of the Empire might be under one head.

369A. The Controller-General of the Salt Gabelle is in charge of the 督辦鹽政處 Tu¹ Pan⁴ Yen² Chêng⁴ Ch'u⁴, Office of the Controller-General of the Salt Gabelle, which was established in accordance with a Memorial from the Controller-General (*see* No. 369), of the 19th January, 1910. Arrangements for the staff of this office have not yet been completely defined, but it is known that the direct management of affairs is to be vested in 總辦 Tsung³ Pan⁴, Office Chiefs.

For particulars as to the salt administration in the provinces *see* Nos. 835, 835A, 835B, and 841.

370. 財政研究所 Ts'ai² Chêng⁴ Yen² Chiu¹ So³, Section for the Study of Financial Affairs.

371. 財政調查處 Ts'ai² Chêng⁴ Tiao⁴ Ch'a² Ch'u⁴, Office for the Study of Financial Affairs.

372. 編譯所 Pien¹ I⁴ So³, Translating (Interpreting) Office.

373. 幣制調查局 Pi⁴ Chih⁴ Tiao⁴ Ch'a² Chü², Commission for the Study of the Currency System; established for the purpose of defining the weight and type of currency to be coined according to the new regulations concerning currency (*see* Memorial of the Ministry of Finance, dated 24th May, 1909).

374. 清理財政處 Ch'ing¹ Li³ Ts'ai² Chêng⁴ Ch'u⁴, Committee for the Reorganization of the Financial Affairs of the Empire (for details *see* Nos. 533—535).

374A. 度支部簿記講習所 Tu⁴ Chih¹ Pu⁴ Pu⁴ Chi⁴ Chiang³ Hsi² So³, Courses in Book-keeping at the Ministry of Finance; instituted in the Summer of 1911 (provisionally at the

School of the Ta Ch'ing Government Bank; *see* No. 548) for training book-keepers for government offices generally. Eligible for admission to these courses are officials of the Ministry of Finance, and other metropolitan offices, who have sufficient education along general lines, in mathematics and jurisprudence, and are between 20 and 35 years of age.

The courses supply instruction in general accounting (普通, 簿記, P'u³ T'ung¹ Pu⁴ Chi⁴), official accounting (官廳簿記 Kuan¹ T'ing¹ Pu⁴ Chi⁴), general principles of financial law (財政大綱 Ts'ai² Chêng⁴ Ta⁴ Kang¹), the preparation of estimates (會計法 Hui⁴ Chi⁴ Fa⁴) and mathematics (算術 Suan⁴ Shu⁴) and extend over half a year.

Those successfully completing the studies prescribed receive diplomas (文憑 Wên² P'ing²) from the Ministry of Finance which entitle them to employment in the accounts offices of various government establishments. In future persons holding such diplomas are to be employed as auditors, 檢查官 Chien³ Ch'a² Kuan¹, in the Audit Department (審計院 Shên³ Chi⁴ Yüan⁴).

At the head of the Book-keeping Courses at the Ministry of Finance there is a 所長 So³ Chang³, who has subordinated to him two 教務員 Chiao⁴ Wu⁴ Yüan², Preceptors, and two 庶務員 Shu⁴ Wu⁴ Yüan², Stewards. The teaching staff includes one 簿記主課教習 Pu⁴ Chi⁴ Chu³ K'o⁴ Chiao⁴ Hsi², Teacher of the Science of Book-keeping, and two 助教 Chu⁴ Chiao⁴, Assistant Teachers, and, for subjects of secondary importance, 附課 Fu⁴ K'o⁴, there are five 教習 Chiao⁴ Hsi², Teachers.

375. Under the control of the Ministry of Finance are the following:

1. Provincial Branch Offices for the Reorganization of the Financial Affairs of the Empire (*see* Nos. 536—541).

2. Ta Ch'ing Government Bank, with its branches as well as other banks (*see* Nos. 542—550c).

3. The Central Mint at Tientsin, with branches in the provinces (*see* Nos. 551—551B).

4. Office for the collection of excise on native opium, at Wuch'ang, with its branches in the provinces (*see* Nos. 552—555).

5. Customs Office at the Ch'ung Wên Mên Gate of Peking (*see* Nos. 556—560).

6. Native Customs (*see* Nos. 561—561B).

7. Office of the Government Granaries at Peking (*see* Nos. 562—567A), and

8. Financial (Political Economy) Colleges (*see* No. 568).

MINISTRY (BOARD) OF RITES.

376. 禮部 Li³ Pu⁴, Ministry (Board) of Rites (literary designation, 詞部 Tz'u² Pu⁴, of its President, 大宗伯 Ta⁴ Tsung¹ Po², and, of its Vice-Presidents, 少宗伯 Shao³ Tsung¹ Po²). This Ministry is one of the oldest, as well as one of the most important, of the Empire. It supervises the code of ceremonies, rites and forms binding every man, irrespective of rank and position in society, from the Emperor to the most humble subject, both as regards himself alone and his intercourse with others, after death as well as during life, and those appertaining to the various unknown powers influencing the life of everyone.

Before the establishment of the Ministry of Education in 1905 (*see* No. 395) the Ministry of Rites supervised national education and customs and controlled the literary examinations which serve as a stepping-stone to the government service.

Also, before the establishment of the Office of Foreign Affairs in 1861 (*see* No. 305), the Ministry of Rites was in charge of all dealings with the West, and the reception of Ambassadors thence, and supervised relations with the former tributary states of Annam, Siam, Burma, Nepal, Corea and the Loochoo Islands (now belonging to Japan).

376ᴀ. Before its reform (*see* No. 376ʙ) the Ministry of Rites was composed of the following four Departments :

1. 儀 制 司 I² Chih⁴ Ssu¹, Department of Ceremonies,
2. 祠 祭 司 T'zu² Chi⁴ Ssu¹, Department of Sacrifices,
3. 主 客 司 Chu³ K'o⁴ Ssu¹, Reception Department, and
4. 精 膳 司 Ching¹ Shan⁴ Ssu¹, Banqueting Department.

376ʙ. By Imperial Edict of the 6th November, 1906, the Ministry of Rites was reformed and with it were amalgamated the Courts 太 常 寺 T'ai⁴ Ch'ang² Ssu⁴, of Sacrificial Worship (*see* No. 933), 光 祿 寺 Kuang¹ Lu⁴ Ssu⁴, of Banqueting (*see* No. 934), and 鴻 臚 寺 Hung² Lu⁴ Ssu⁴, of State Ceremonial (*see* No. 935), which had been previously quite independent institutions.

The internal organization of the Ministry of Rites is as recommended by the Ministry itself in a Memorial to the Throne, sanctioned by the Emperor on the 5th January, 1907.

The Ministry of Rites superintends ceremonies of the Court, sacrifices, sacrificial altars, Imperial mausolea, ancestral temples, the Office of Music and the Buddhist, Taoist and Confucian religions.

377. 堂 主 事 T'ang² Chu³ Shih⁴, Secretaries (of the President); 6ᴀ. There are four of these officials (*see* No. 288).

378. 司 務 廳 Ssu¹ Wu⁴ T'ing¹, Chancery (*see* No. 296).

379. 滿 檔 房 Man³ Tang¹ Fang², Record and Registry Office ; besides various other duties this Office was in charge of making translations into Manchu. This Office no longer exists.

380. 典 制 司 Tien³ Chih⁴ Ssu¹, Department of Ceremonies ; regulates the etiquette to be observed at the Court on all occasions, organizes ceremonials, determines posthumous honours of the Imperial Family, etc.

380ᴀ. The Department of Ceremonies (*see* No. 380) is a development of the former Department of Ceremonies (*see* No· 376ᴀ), with which was amalgamated the Reception Department

**381
to
382B**

(see No. 376A) and the Court of State Ceremonial (see Nos. 376B and 935), in accordance with a Memorial from the Ministry, sanctioned by the Emperor on the 6th February, 1909.

381. 祠祭司 Tz'u² Chi⁴ Ssu¹, Department of Sacrifices (or Department of Sacrificial Affairs); this arranges the rites to be observed at sacrifices on solemn occasions—in "saving the sun and moon" when eclipsed—etc.

This Department is identical with the former Department of Sacrifices (see No. 376A); likewise its staff.

382. 太常司 T'ai⁴ Ch'ang² Ssu¹, Department of Sacrificial Worship; directs sacrifices, determines the musical instruments to be used and decides the magnitude of sacrifices to be performed.

382A. The Department of Sacrifical Worship (see No. 382) was organized from the former Court of Sacrificial Worship, which was a separate institution (see Nos. 376B and 933).

382B. In addition to Department Directors (see No. 290), Assistant Department Directors (see No. 291) and Second Class Secretaries (see No. 292), common to all Departments, the Department of Sacrificial Worship employs the following:

1. 六品贊禮官 Liu⁴ P'in³ Tsan⁴ Li³ Kuan¹, Ceremonial Usher of the sixth rank (one),

2. 六品讀祝官 Liu⁴ P'in³ Tu² Ch'u⁴ Kuan¹, Reciter of Prayers of the sixth rank (one),

3. 贊禮郎 Tsan⁴ Li³ Lang², Ceremonial Ushers; 7A (28 in all),

4. 讀祝官 Tu² Chu⁴ Kuan¹, Reciters of Prayers; 7A (10 in all),

5. 鳴贊 Ming² Tsan⁴, Heralds; 7A (63 in all) and

6. 序班 Hsü⁴ Pan¹, Ushers; 9B (four).

Officials of the Department of Sacrificial Worship are often deputed to the Offices of the Imperial Mausolea, Eastern and Western (see No. 570).

[126]

383. 光祿司 Kuang¹ Lu⁴ Ssu¹, Banqueting Department; supervises food supplies for banquets and sacrifices.

383A. The Banqueting Department (*see* No. 383) was evolved from the former Banqueting Court, which was an independent institution (*see* Nos. 376B and 934), and the old Banqueting Department (*see* No. 376A).

384. 禮器庫 Li³ Ch'i⁴ K'u⁴, Store of Sacrificial and Ceremonial Instruments. Here are stored all sacrificial and ceremonial instruments formerly kept at the Courts of Sacrificial Worship (*see* Nos. 376B and 933) and of Banqueting (*see* Nos. 376B and 934). At the head of this Store is a :

384A. Department Director (*see* No. 290), as Superintendent of the Store, assisted by one Assistant Department Director (*see* No. 291) and :

1. 4 簿正 Pu⁴ Chêng⁴, Overseers ; 6B,

2. 4 典簿 Tien³ Pu⁴, Assistant Overseers,

3. 2 司庫 Ssu¹ K'u⁴, Inspectors ; 7A, and

4. 8 庫使 K'u⁴ Shih³, Assistant Inspectors ; 7B.

384B. The post of 簿正 Pu⁴ Chêng⁴ (*see* No. 384A) replaces that of 署正 Shu³ Chêng⁴ (*see* Nos. 389 and 391) of the former Banqueting Court ; 典簿 Tien³ Pu⁴ (*see* No. 384A) replaces those of 博士典簿 Po² Shih⁴ Tien³ Pu⁴ of the former Court of Sacrificial Worship and 典簿 Tien³ Pu⁴ of the former Banqueting Court. Concerning the posts 司庫 Ssu¹ K'u⁴ and 庫使 K'u⁴ Shih³ (*see* No. 298).

385. 統計處 T'ung³ Chi⁴ Ch'u⁴, Statistical Bureau (for its organization *see* No. 162A).

386. 鑄印局 Chu⁴ Yin⁴ Chü², Office of Seal-casting ; supervising the casting of seals for all government establishments of the Empire. This Office is administered by one Assistant Department Director (*see* No. 291), one Second Class Secretary (*see* No. 292 , and one 大使 Ta⁴ Shih³, Inspector.

383
to
386

[127]

387 to 391

387. 樂部 Yüeh⁴ Pu⁴, Board of State Music ; determines the music, singing and posturing for sacrifices and solemn occasions generally. It is directed by :

387A. Two 管理樂部事務 Kuan³ Li³ Yüeh⁴ Pu⁴ Shih⁴ Wu⁴, Director-Generals of the Board of Music ; usually Princes of the Blood or Ministers of the Household.

388. 和聲署 Ho² Shêng¹ Shu³, Music Office (at the Board of Music ; *see* No. 387) ; superintends the training of musicians, provision of musical instruments, etc. It is in charge of :

389. One 和聲署署正 Ho² Shêng¹ Shu³ Shu³ Chêng⁴, Director of the Office of Music, who is assisted by two 和聲署署丞 Ho² Shêng¹ Shu³ Shu³ Ch'êng², Assistant Directors of the Office of Music (左 Tso³, Senior, and 右 Yu⁴, Junior) ; 7B.

At the Office of Music there are also :

1. 5 協律郎 Hsieh² Lü⁴ Lang², Chief Musicians ; 8A,
2. 25 司樂郎 Ssu¹ Yüeh⁴ Lang², Bandmasters ; 9B,
3. 180 樂生 Yüeh⁴ Shêng¹, Musicians, and
4. 300 舞生 Wu³ Shêng¹, Posturers.

390. 神樂署 Shên² Yüeh⁴ Shu³, Office of Sacred Music ; supervises an orchestra which attends sacrifices and other solemn ceremonies where music is required.

The office of Sacred Music is attached to the Board of State Music (*see* No. 387) and is directed by :

391. One 神樂署署正 Shên² Yüeh⁴ Shu³ Shu³ Chêng⁴, Director of the Office of Sacred Music ; 6A. To this official there are subordinated two 神樂署署丞 Shên² Yüeh⁴ Shu³ Shu³ Ch'êng², Assistant Directors of the Office of Sacred Music (左 Tso³, Senior, and 右 Yu⁴, Junior) ; 8B, and :

1. 1 贊禮郎 Tsan⁴ Li³ Lang², Ceremonial Usher ; 7A,
2. 協律郎 Hsieh² Lü⁴ Lang², Chief Musicians (in an indefinite number) ; 8A, and

392
to
393

3. 司 樂 耶 Ssu¹ Yüeh⁴ Lang², Bandmasters (in an indefinite number) ; 9B.

392. 會同四譯館 Hui⁴ T'ung² Ssu⁴ I⁴ Kuan³, Residence for Envoys of the Four Tributary States ; here were domiciled Envoys from Korea, Siam, Tonkin and Burma ; no longer existing.

In charge of the Residence there was a 提督館務 T'i² Tu¹ Kuan³ Wu⁴, Superintendent, who had under his control one 大使 Ta⁴ Shih³, Residence Keeper ; 9A, two 序班 Hsu⁴ Pan¹, Ceremonial Ushers ; 9B, and a staff (8) 通官 T'ung¹ Kuan¹, Interpreters (of the sixth, seventh and eighth ranks).

393. 禮學館 Li³ Hsüeh² Kuan³, School of Ceremonials. This school was established by Imperial Edict of the 11th July, 1907, which read as follows :

" The most potent forces in the maintenance of peace and
" in the government of the people are the natural laws governing
" the phenomena of nature. Being aware of this, former
" Emperors of Our Dynasty gave their greatest attention to the
" improvement of rites and education.

" In the reigns of Ch'ien Lung (1736-1796) and Tao
" Kuang (1821-1850) the code of rites was repeatedly revised
" and, in its improved form, promulgated for general observance
" throughout the Empire.

" With the new order of things that have come into the
" lives of the people, such as changes that have taken place in
" education, in the Army and in social intercourse, it has become
" evident that steps must be taken to adapt, or reorganize, the
" customs hitherto observed by the populace with regard to the
" details of funerals, sacrifices, head dresses, marriage ceremonies
" and articles of use and for adornment.

" On a previous occasion the Ministry of Rites memorialised
" Us with regard to the establishment of a School of Ceremonials.
" The said Ministry has now presented a detailed report as to

[129]

9

394   " the execution of this project and we hereby give it Our " sanction that it may be immediately put into force.

" We hereby further command that the Ministers of the " said Ministry of Rites, with their subordinates, take the lead in " the said School of Ceremonials, carefully consider the ancient " and modern customs and the everyday habits of the people, " select the best and bring them to Our notice that We may " promulgate them to the people of the Empire.

" This is in proof of Our earnest desire for the preparation " of the way towards the granting of a constitution and " parliamentary representation to the country. Respect This."

In charge of the School of Ceremonials are the officials of the two highest ranks of the Ministry of Rites (President and Vice-Presidents) as 總裁 Tsung³ Ts'ai². The direct management of affairs is, however, vested in the 總理禮學館事務 Tsung³ Li³ Li³ Hsüeh² Kuan³ Shih⁴ Wu⁴, Director of the School of Ceremonials, and the following :

1.   2 to 3 提調 T'i² Tiao⁴, Proctors,

2.   1 幫提調 Pang¹ T'i² Tiao⁴, Assistant Proctor,

3.   1 總纂 Tsung³ Tsuan³, Chief Reviser,

4.   11 纂脩 Tsuan³ Hsiu¹, Revisers,

5.   協脩 Hsieh² Hsiu¹, Assistant Revisers (in an indefinite number),

6.   校對 Chiao⁴ Tui⁴, Correctors (in an indefinite number),

7.   文案 Wên² An¹, Secretaries, and

8.   各省顧問官 Ko² Shêng³ Ku⁴ Wên⁴ Kuan¹, Provincial Advisers (the schedule calls for 46 of these).

394.   The Ministry of Rites supervises :

1.   Imperial Mausolea (*see* Nos. 569—571A),

2.   Metropolitan Temples and Sacrifices performed therein (*see* No. 572) and

3.   Religions (Buddhist, Taoist and Shamanist Priests; *see* Nos. 573, 573A to 573C).

MINISTRY (BOARD) OF EDUCATION.

395. 學部 Hsüeh² Pu⁴, Ministry (Board) of Education ; established in 1905 for the supervision of the educational affairs of the Empire (before that time this duty devolved upon the Ministry of Rites ; *see* No. 376.)

The internal organization of the Ministry of Education, as proposed by the Ministry itself, was sanctioned by the Emperor on the 11th June, 1906.

395A. 管理學部事務 Kuan³ Li³ Hsüeh² Pu⁴ Shih⁴ Wu⁴, Controller of the Ministry of Education (*see* No. 276).

396. 叅事 Ts'an¹ Shih⁴, Assistant Secretaries ; 5A, (*see* No. 286 ; there are four of these officials).

397. 司務廳 Ssu¹ Wu⁴ T'ing¹, Chancery (*see* No. 296).

398. 總務司 Tsung³ Wu⁴ Ssu¹, Department of General Affairs ; superintends the most important matters, correspondence, archives, compilation of Memorials, framing of rules and regulations and is in charge of education throughout the Empire.

This Department is composed of three 科 K'o¹, Sections, *i.e.*

1. 機要科 Chi¹ Yao⁴ K'o¹, Section of Confidential Affairs,

2. 案牘科 An⁴ Tu³ K'o¹, Correspondence Section, and

3. 審定科 Shên³ Ting⁴ K'o¹, Inspection Section.

399. 專門司 Chuan¹ Mên² Ssu¹, Department of Higher and Special Schools ; charged with the supervision of Universities, Higher and Special Schools.

This Department consists of two Sections :

1. 專門教務科 Chuan¹ Mên² Chiao⁴ Wu⁴ K'o¹, Higher and Special School Instruction Section, and

2. 專門庶務科 Chuan¹ Mên² Shu⁴ Wu⁴ K'o¹, Higher and Special School Maintenance Section.

400. 普通司 P'u³ T'ung¹ Ssu¹, Department of Common Schools ; supervises Normal, Middle and Elementary Schools.

[131]

This Department has three Sections :

1. 師範教育科 Shih[1] Fan[4] Chiao[4] Yü[4] K'o[1], Normal School Section,

2. 中等教育科 Chung[1] Têng[3] Chiao[4] Yü[4] K'o[1], Middle School Section, and

3. 小學教育科 Hsiao[3] Hsüeh[2] Chiao[4] Yü[4] K'o[1], Elementary School Section.

401. 實業司 Shih[2] Yeh[4] Ssu[1], Department of Industrial Schools ; controls Manual Training, Commercial and Agricultural Schools, etc.

There are two Sections to this Department, *i.e.*

1. 實業教務科 Shih[2] Yeh[4] Chiao[4] Wu[4] K'o[1], Industrial School Instruction Section, and

2. 實業庶務科 Shih[2] Yeh[4] Shu[4] Wu[4] K'o[1], Industrial School Maintenance Section.

402. 會計司 Hui[4] (K'uai[4]) Chi[4] Ssu[1], Audit Department ; examines income and expenditure, prepares estimates, furnishes, builds and repairs schools, etc.

This Department is divided into two Sections :

1. 度支科 Tu[4] Chih[1] K'o[1], Finance Section, and

2. 建築科 Chien[4] Chu[4] K'o[1], Construction Section.

403. Besides a Department Director (*see* No. 290), an Assistant Department Director (*see* No. 291) and one or two Second Class Secretaries (*see* No. 292) there are attached to each Department and the Chancery (*see* Nos. 396 and 397) a number of 書記官 Shu[1] Chi[4] Kuan[1], Clerks, of the first, second and third ranks (*see* No. 295).

404. 視學官 Shih[4] Hsüeh[2] Kuan[1], Inspectors of Education ; there are two of these officials for each educational circuit, of which there are 12 (*vide* regulations drawn up by the Ministry of Education and sanctioned by the Emperor on the 11th December, 1909), as tabulated below :

1. The provinces of Fengtien, Kirin and Heilungchiang,

2. The provinces of Chihli and Shansi,
3. The provinces of Shantung and Honan,
4. The provinces of Shensi and Szechwan,
5. The provinces of Hupeh and Hunan,
6. The provinces of Kiangsu, Anhui and Kiangsi,
7. The provinces of Fukien and Chekiang,
8. The provinces of Kuangtung and Kuangsi,
9. The provinces of Kweichow and Yünnan,
10. The provinces of Kansu and Hsinkiang.
11. Inner and Outer Mongolia, and
12. K'uk'unor and Tibet.

Certain of the Inspectors of Education are deputed, yearly, for the inspection of from three to four educational circuits, so that all the circuits may be inspected within a three years' period.

The Inspectors of Education are selected from officials of the Ministry of Education and to each there is attached one 書記生 Shu[1] Chi[4] Shêng[1], Clerk.

Originally the post of Inspector of Education was a substantive position (namely, 5A) and the number of Inspectors was 12 ; from the 1st November, 1909, in accordance with a report from the Ministry of Education, the position was made supernumerary in character and a corresponding number of substantive posts were established at the Ministry—of Department Director (*see* No. 290 ; five), of Assistant Department Director (*see* No. 291 ; four) and of Second Class Secretary (*see* No. 292 ; three).

404A. 編訂名詞館 Pien[1] Ting[4] Ming[2] Tz'u[2] Kuan[3], Committee for the Compilation of Technical Terms established in accordance with a report of the Ministry of Education, sanctioned by the Emperor on the 29th October, 1909, with a staff consisting of one 總纂 Tsung[3] Tsuan[3], Chief Reviser, and an indefinite number of 分纂 Fên[1] Tsuan[3], Revisers, for compiling a dictionary of physical, mathematical, political, judicial, historical, pedagogical, etc., expressions.

405
to
407

When completed, the use of the expressions appearing in the dictionary spoken of above will be obligatory for both public and private purposes.

405. 諮議官 Tzu[1] I[4] Kuan[1], Consulting Experts; number indefinite; of four 等 Têng[3], Ranks.

Consulting Experts of the first rank have the rank of Councillor; of the second rank, that of Secretary; of the third rank, that of Department Director or Assistant Department Director, and of the fourth rank, that of Second Class Secretary (*see* No. 302.)

406. 編譯圖書局 Pien[1] I[4] T'u[2] Shu[1] Chü[2], Book Compilation and Translation Office (developed from the 編書局 Pien[1] Shu[1] Chü[2], Book Compilation Office, of the 學務處 Hsüeh[2] Wu[4] Ch'u[4], Committee of Educational Affairs).

At the head of this Office is a 局長 Chü[2] Chang[3], Chief of Office, and subordinated to him are a number of 局員 Chü[2] Yüan[2], Office Attachés.

In the Book Compilation and Translation Office there is a:

406A. 研究所 Yen[2] Chiu[1] So[3], School Books Compilation Bureau.

407. 京師督學局 Ching[1] Shih[1] Tu[1] Hsüeh[2] Chü[2], Committee for Superintendence of Metropolitan Schools; divided into three 科 K'o[1], Sections:

1. 師範教育科 Shih[1] Fan[4] Chiao[4] Yü[4] K'o[1], Normal School Section,

2. 中等教育科 Chung[1] Têng[3] Chiao[4] Yü[4] K'o[1], Middle School Section, and

3. 小學教育科 Hsiao[3] Hsüeh[2] Chiao[4] Yü[4] K'o[1], Elementary School Section.

As chief of the Committee there is a Chü[2] Chang[3], President, and at the head of the Sections there are 科長 K'o[1] Chang[3], Section Chiefs (from the ranks of officials of the Ministry of Education).

408. 學制調查局 Hsüeh² Chih⁴ Tiao⁴ Ch'a² Chü², Commission for the Study of Educational Regulations; in charge of the making of a comparative study of the educational situation in foreign countries.

At the head of the Commission there is a 局長 Chü² Chang³, President, who is assisted by a number of 局員 Chü² Yüan², Attachés, and a staff of 譯官 I⁴ Kuan¹, Translators (Interpreters).

408A. The Chief of the Book Compilation and Translation Office (*see* No. 406), the President of the Committee for Superintendance of Metropolitan Schools (*see* No. 407) and the President of the Commission for the Study of Educational Regulations (*see* No. 408) rank as Councillors (*see* Nos. 281—282) or Secretaries (*see* Nos. 283—284) of the Ministry of Education.

409. 高等教育會議所 Kao¹ Têng³ Chiao⁴ Yü⁴ Hui⁴ I⁴ So³, Deliberative Convention of Higher Education; called once a year (or more often if occasion demands); under the general control of the President and Vice-Presidents of the Ministry of Education.

Delegates to this Convention comprise officials of the Ministry of Education, Directors of Metropolitan and Provincial Schools (Middle and Higher) and persons with great experience in educational matters.

The Delegates, who must be approved by the Emperor, elect the 議長 I⁴ Chang³, President of the Convention.

From the officials of the Ministry of Education there are selected two 庶務員 Shu⁴ Wu⁴ Yüan², Stewards, for the management of the general affairs of the Convention.

410. 教育研究所 Chiao⁴ Yü⁴ Yen² Chiu¹ So³, Section of Instruction; here are given lectures on educational questions for the benefit of officials of the Ministry of Education.

To this Section there are attached:

411 to 412

1 庶 務 員 Shu⁴ Wu⁴ Yuan², Steward (for its general management) and

1 編 輯 員 Pien¹ Chi⁴ Yüan², Compiler.

Both are chosen from amongst the officials of the Ministry.

411. 八 旗 學 務 處 Pa¹ Ch'i² Hsüeh² Wu⁴ Ch'u⁴, Committee of Banner Schools ; established in accordance with a Memorial from the Ministry of Education, sanctioned by the Emperor on the 22nd September, 1909, for the control of Primary and Middle Schools for Bannermen (*see* Nos. 717 and 717ᴀ)

At the head of the Committee there is a 總 理 Tsung³ Li³, Director-General, and two 協 理 Hsieh² Li³, Assistant Directors. The Committee consists of two Sections, *i.e.*

1. 敎 務 科 Chiao⁴ Wu⁴ K'o¹, Instruction Section, and

2. 庶 務 科 Shu⁴ Wu⁴ K'o¹, Maintenance Section.

Each Section is directed by a 科 長 K'o¹ Chang³, Section Chief, to whom there are subordinated an indefinite number of 科 員 K'o¹ Yüan², Secretaries.

For the inspection of schools the Committee periodically deputes 査 學 員 Ch'a² Hsüeh² Yüan², Inspectors of Education.

Attached to the Committee of Banner Schools, in addition to the officials mentioned above, are 評 議 員 P'ing² I⁴ Yüan², Advisers, the chief of whom is styled 評 議 長 P'ing² I⁴ Chang³, Senior Adviser.

Later (in 1915), when the Manchus and Chinese are placed on an equal footing, this Committee will be abolished.

412. 國 子 監 Kuo² Tzu³ Chien⁴, National College or Imperial Academy of Learning (literary designation, 太 學 T'ai⁴ Hsüeh², 成 均 Ch'êng² Chün¹, 司 成 館 Ssu¹ Ch'êng² Kuan³).

This institution was divided into 六 堂 Liu⁴ T'ang², six classes or sections, and its students (known as 監 生 Chien⁴ Shêng¹) received a stipend from the Government.

Worthy of remark is the hall 辟雍 Pi⁴ Yung¹, where the   **412ᴀ**
Emperor discusses the classics in the presence of learned men.   **to**

At the Imperial Academy there were :   **413ᴀ**

412ᴀ. 管理國子監大臣 Kuan³ Li³ Kuo² Tzu³ Chien⁴
Ta⁴ Ch'ên², Chancellor of the Imperial Academy (usually one of
the senior Grand Secretaries), and the following :

1. 2 祭酒 Chi⁴ Chiu³, Libationers (literary designation,
大司成 Ta⁴ Ssu¹ Ch'êng²) ; 4ʙ, one Manchu and one Chinese,

2. 3 司業 Ssu¹ Yeh⁴, Tutors (literary designation, 少司
成 Shao³ Ssu¹ Ch'êng²) ; 6ᴀ, one Manchu, one Mongol and one
Chinese, .

3. 監丞 Chien⁴ Ch'êng², Proctor ; 7ᴀ,

4. 博士 Po² Shih⁴, Doctor ; 7ʙ.

5. 典簿 Tien³ Pu⁴, Archivist ; 8ʙ,

6. 典籍 Tien³ Chi², Sub-Archivist ; 9ʙ,

7. 助教 Chu⁴ Chiao⁴, Preceptor ; 7ʙ,

8. 四氏學錄 Ssu⁴ Shih⁴ Hsüeh² Lu⁴, Registrar ; 8ᴀ,

9. 學錄 Hsüeh² Lu⁴, Sub-Registrar ; 8ᴀ, and

10. 學正 Hsüeh² Chêng⁴, Director of Studies ; 8ᴀ.

413. 國子丞衙門 Kuo² Tzu³ Ch'êng² Ya² Mên², The
Government Institute ; this establishment is the result of the
reformation of the Imperial Academy of Learning (*see* No. 412)
in accordance with a Memorial from the Ministry of Education
(sanctioned by the Emperor on the 11th June, 1906). It regulates
the rites and ceremonies performed at the 文廟 Wên² Miao⁴,
Temple of Confucius, and at the 辟雍殿 Pi⁴ Yung¹ Tien⁴, Pi
Yung Hall (*see* No. 412).

In charge of the Government Institute is a :

413ᴀ. 國子丞 Kuo² Tzu³ Ch'êng², Director of the
Institute ; 4ᴀ. He has subordinated to him :

1. 4 典簿 Tien³ Pu⁴, Archivists ; 7ᴀ,

2. 4 典籍 Tien³ Chi², Sub-Archivists ; 8ᴀ,

414 to 415A

3. 2 七品奉祀官 Ch'i[1] P'in[3] Fêng[4] Ssu[4] Kuan[1], Overseers of Sacrifices of the 7th Class,

4. 2 八品奉祀官 Pa[1] P'in[3] Fêng[4] Ssu[4] Kuan[1], Overseers of Sacrifices of the 8th Class,

5. 2 九品奉祀官 Chiu[3] P'in[3] Fêng[4] Ssu[4] Kuan[1], Overseers of Sacrifices of the 9th Class,

6. 2 正通贊官 Chêng[4] T'ung[1] Tsan[4] Kuan[1], Senior Heralds ; 7A,

7. 2 副通贊官 Fu[4] T'ung[1] Tsan[4] Kuan[1], Junior Heralds ; 8B,

8. 3 二等書記官 Êrh[4] Têng[3] Shu[1] Chi[4] Kuan[1], Clerks of the 2nd Class ; 8A, and

9. 3 三等書記官 San[1] Têng[3] Shu[1] Chi[4] Kuan[1], Clerks of the 3rd Class ; 9A.

414. The Board of Education has the supreme control of various educational institutions, as shown below :

Common Schools (Primary, Middle and Higher),

Universities, Professional Schools, Institutes, etc. (details *see* Nos. 574—654).

MINISTRY (BOARD) OF WAR.

415. 兵部 Ping[1] Pu[4], Ministry (Board) of War (literary designation of Ministry, 犀部 Hsi Pu, of its President, 大司馬 Ta[4] Ssu[1] Ma[3], and of its Vice-Presidents, 少司馬 Shao[3] Ssu[1] Ma[3]). This Ministry, in addition to the administration of the land, sea and river forces of the Empire, supervised the examinations for military skill, which consisted of drawing the bow, military gymnastics and lifting the stone (these examinations were abolished by Imperial Edict of the 29th August, 1901).

415A. Before its reorganization the Ministry of War was composed of four Departments :

1. 武選司 Wu[3] Hsüan[3] Ssu[1], Department of Selection,

2. 職方司 Chih[2] Fang[1] Ssu[1], Department of Discipline,

3. 車駕司 Ch'ê[1] Chia[4] Ssu[1], Remount Department, and

4. 武庫司 Wu[3] K'u[4] Ssu[1], Commissariat Department.

416 to 419

416. 練兵處 Lien[4] Ping[1] Ch'u[4], Commission for Army Reorganization; established in 1903 at the initiative of 袁世凱 Yuan[2] Shih[4] K'ai[3] (who was made its President) for the reorganization of the Chinese army on western lines.

417. The reorganization of the Ministry of War was commanded by Imperial Edict of the 6th November, 1906, which read as follows:

" 兵部 Ping[1] Pu[4], the Ministry of War, is now to become "the 陸軍部 Lu[4] Chün[1] Pu[4], Board of War, the Commission "for Army Reorganization (see No. 416) and the 太僕寺 T'ai[4] "P'u[2] Ssu[1], Court of the Imperial Stud (see No. 936B), to be "assimilated by the latter. The proposed 海軍部 Hai[3] Chün[1] "Pu[4], Ministry of the Navy (see No. 185B), and the 軍諮府 "Chün[1] Tzu[1] Fu[3], General Staff Office (see No. 184), not being "regularly organized, affairs appertaining to these are to be "attended to in the Ministry of War, by a 海軍處 Hai[3] Chün[1] "Ch'u[4], Naval Council (see No. 185C), and a 軍諮處 Chün[1] "Tzu[1] Ch'u[4], Army Staff Council (see No. 184A), respectively."

The internal organization of the Ministry of War, as proposed by the Ministry itself, received Imperial sanction on the 7th June, 1907.

418. 軍諮處 Chün[1] Tzu[1] Ch'u[4], General Staff Council (see No. 417); for its organization see enclosure to a report of the Ministry of War, dated 7th June, 1907.

For particulars as to the removal of the General Staff Council from the supervision of the Ministry of War, and its establishment as an independent institution, see Nos. 184A to 184L.

419. 海軍處 Hai[3] Chün[1] Ch'u[4], Naval Council (see No. 417). For particulars as to the transfer of this Council from the supervision of the Ministry of War to that of the Commission for the Reorganization of the Navy, see Nos. 185C to 185o.

420 to 422A

420. 陸軍部 Lu⁴ Chün¹ Pu⁴, Ministry (Board) of War or Ministry (Board) of Land Forces. This Ministry is now the administrative head of all the land forces of the Empire, directs Military Schools, has charge of ordnance stores and arsenals, etc. The postal system, for Government use exclusively, in China proper and in the outlying dependencies, is maintained by this Ministry.

421. 管理陸軍部事務 Kuan³ Li³ Lu⁴ Chün¹ Pu⁴ Shih⁴ Wu⁴, Controller of the Ministry of War (see No. 276).

422. 承政廳 Ch'êng² Chêng⁴ T'ing¹, Council (see No. 285); attends to the most important questions; supervises finances correspondence, staff, etc.

The Council is divided into four 科 K'o¹, Sections, i.e. 秘書科 Pi⁴ Shu¹ K'o¹, Secret Affairs Section, and 典章科 Tien³ Chang¹ K'o¹, Section of Army Regulations—under the control of the Senior Councillor (see No. 281)—and 庶務科 Shu⁴ Wu⁴ K'o¹, Section of General Affairs, and 收支科 Shou¹ Chih¹ K'o¹, Finance Section—in charge of the Junior Councillor (see No. 282).

422A. The Council (see No. 422) was organized from:

1. The following offices of the former Ministry of War (see No. 415):

滿檔房 Man³ Tang⁴ Fang², Record and Registry Office (compare No. 379), 司務廳 Ssu¹ Wu⁴ T'ing¹, Chancery (compare No. 296), 派辦處 P'ai⁴ Pan⁴ Ch'u⁴, Office for Deputation of Officials for Special Duty, 收支所 Shou¹ Chih¹ So³, Finance Office, and 俸餉股 Fêng⁴ Hsiang³ Ku³, Office for issue of Salaries and Supplies (see No. 415A), from the Commissariat Department.

2. The following offices of the Commission for Army Reorganization (see No. 416):

文案處 Wên² An¹ Ch'u⁴, Chancery, and 收支處 Shou¹ Chih¹ Ch'u⁴, Treasury.

422B. The staff of the Council (*see* No. 422) is made up of two Councillors (*see* Nos. 281 and 282), two 承發官 Ch'êng² Fa¹ Kuan¹, Registrars (*see* No. 294), four 科長 K'o¹ Chang³, Section Chiefs (corresponding to the number of Sections ; *see* No. 422), 20 科員 K'o¹ Yüan², Secretaries (of the 1st, 2nd and 3rd ranks), five 譯員 I⁴ Yüan², Translators (Interpreters ; of the 1st, 2nd and 3rd ranks), 14 錄事 Lu⁴ Shih⁴, Writers (*see* No. 294), one 正從事官 Chêng⁴ Ts'ung² Shih⁴ Kuan¹, Adjutant, and one 副從事官 Fu⁴ Ts'ung² Shih⁴ Kuan¹, Second Adjutant.

423. 參議廳 Ts'an¹ I⁴ T'ing¹, Secretarial Office (*see* No. 285A) ; draws up rules and regulations for the Ministry of War, Military Scholars, etc.

423A. Attached to the Secretarial Office are :

Two Secretaries (*see* Nos. 283 and 284), one Registrar (*see* No. 294), 諮議官 Tzu¹ I⁴ Kuan¹, Advisers (of the 1st, 2nd and ?rd ranks ; *see* No. 302), and 檢查官 Chien³ Ch'a² Kuan¹, Inspectors of Military Affairs (of the 1st, 2nd and 3rd ranks ; *see* No. 303), in an indefinite number, and 12 Writers (*see* No. 294).

424. 軍衡司 Chün¹ Hêng² Ssu¹, Department of Selection ; supervises appointment and transfer of military officials, granting of hereditary titles, etc.

This Department has four Sections :

1. 遴材科 Lin² Ts'ai² K'o¹, Section of Appointments.
2. 任官科 Jên⁴ Kuan¹ K'o¹, Section of Distribution of Posts,
3. 襲廕科 Hsi² Yin⁴ K'o¹, Section of Hereditary Titles, and
4. 旗務科 Ch'i² Wu⁴ K'o¹, Section of Banner Affairs.

424A. The Department of Selection (*see* No. 424) is a development of the 武選司 Wu³ Hsüan³ Ssu¹, Department of Selection (*see* No. 415A), of the old Ministry of War.

425. 軍乘司 Chün¹ Ch'êng² Ssu¹, Department of Military Posts ; in charge of the Military Posts and the horses for couriers employed therein.

425ᴀ
to
426ᴀ

This Department consists of three Sections :

1. 驛傳科 I⁴ Ch'uan² K'o¹, Military Posts Section,
2. 銷算科 Hsiao¹ Suan⁴ K'o¹, Expenditure Section, and
3. 配戍科 P'ei⁴ Shu⁴ K'o¹, Convoy Section (supervising the convoying of exiles to their places of banishment).

425ᴀ. To the Department of Military Posts (*see* No. 425) were transferred certain of the functions of the 車駕司 Ch'ê¹ Chia⁴ Ssu¹, Remount Department (*see* No. 415ᴀ), and the 武庫司 Wu³ K'u⁴ Ssu¹, Commissariat Department (*see* No. 415ᴀ), of the old Ministry of War (*see* No. 415).

425ʙ. In addition to the customary officials (*see* No. 434), attached to the Department of Military Posts (*see* No. 425) are the following :

1. 提報處 Chieh² Pao⁴ Ch'u⁴, Couriers Office, directed by a 總辦 Tsung³ Pan⁴, Chief, assisted by six 辦事官 Pan⁴ Shih⁴ Kuan¹, Secretaries, and two 錄事 Lu⁴ Shih⁴, Writers, and
2. 馬館 Ma³ Kuan³, Depôt of Military Horses, in charge of a 監督 Chien¹ Tu¹, Superintendent, and two 錄事 Lu⁴ Shih⁴, Writers.

426. 軍計司 Chün¹ Chi⁴ Ssu¹, Discipline Department ; directs the issue of rewards or the levy of penalties.

This Department is divided into four Sections :

1. 考績科 K'ao³ Chi⁴ K'o¹, Section for Investigation of Merit,
2. 策勳科 Ts'ê⁴ Hsün¹ K'o¹, Section for Definition of Grade of Merit,
3. 邮賞科 Hsü⁴ Shang³ K'o¹, Rewards Section, and
4. 議罰科 I⁴ Fa⁴ K'o¹, Section of Punishments.

426ᴀ. To the Discipline Department (*see* No. 426) were transferred the functions of the 職方司 Chih² Fang¹ Ssu¹, Department of Discipline (*see* No. 415ᴀ), of the old Ministry of War (*see* No. 415), and of the 考功科 K'ao³ Kung¹ K'o¹,

Section for Investigation of Merit, of the Commission for Army Reorganization (*see* No. 416).

427. 軍 實 司 Chün[1] Shih[2] Ssu[1], Department of Arms Supply ; consisting of two Sections, *i.e.*

    1. 製 造 科 Chih[4] Tsao[4] K'o[1], Section of Manufacture, and

    2. 保 儲 科 Pao[3] Ch'u[4] K'o[1], Storage Section.

427ᴀ. The affairs of the 武 庫 司 Wu[3] K'u[4] Ssu[1], Commissariat Department (*see* No. 415ᴀ), of the old Ministry of War, and of the 器 械 科 Ch'i[4] Hsieh[4] K'o[1], Arms Section, of the Commission for Army Reorganization (*see* No. 416), were handed over to the Department of Arms Supply (*see* No. 427).

427ʙ. In addition to the usual officials (*see* No. 434), at the Department of Arms Supply (*see* No. 427), are found :

    1 繪 圖 員 Hui[4] T'u[2] Yüan[2], Draughtsman,

    1 藝 師 I[4] Shih[1], Chief Engineer (*see* No. 301), and

    1 藝 士 I[4] Shih[4], Engineer (*see* No. 301).

428. 軍 制 司 Chün[1] Chih[4] Ssu[1], Army Inspection Department ; of seven Sections :

    1. 蒐 簡 科 Sou[1] Chien[3] K'o[1], Training Section,

    2. 步 兵 科 Pu[4] Ping[1] K'o[1], Infantry Section,

    3. 馬 兵 科 Ma[3] Ping[1] K'o[1], Cavalry Section,

    4. 礮 兵 科 P'ao[4] Ping[1] K'o[1], Artillery Section,

    5. 工 兵 科 Kung[1] Ping[1] K'o[1], Engineers Section,

    6. 輜 重 兵 科 Tzu[1] Chung[4] Ping[1] K'o[1], Military Trains Section, and

    7. 臺 壘 科 T'ai[2] Lei[3] K'o[1], Sappers Section.

428ᴀ. The Army Inspection Department was developed from the 蒐 討 科 Sou[1] T'ao[3] K'o[1], Battle Training Section, of the Commission for Army Reorganization (*see* No. 416).

428ʙ. In addition to the customary officials (*see* No. 434), the staff of the Army Inspection Department (*see* No. 428) includes one 繪 圖 員 Hui[4] T'u[2] Yüan[2], Draughtsman (compare

429 to 430B

No. 427B), one 藝 師 I⁴ Shih¹, Chief Engineer (*see* No. 301), and one 藝 士 I⁴ Shih⁴, Engineer (*see* No. 301).

429. 軍需司 Chün¹ Hsü¹ Ssu¹, Commissariat Department; of three Sections :

1. 統計科 T'ung³ Chi⁴ K'o¹, Statistical Section,
2. 糧服科 Liang² Fu² K'o¹, Supplies Section, and
3. 建造科 Chien⁴ Tsao⁴ K'o¹, Construction Section.

429A. The Commissariat Department was formed from the 糧餉科 Liang² Hsiang³ K'o¹, Section of Supplies, of the Commission for Army Reorganization (*see* No. 416).

430. 軍學司 Chün¹ Hsüeh² Ssu¹, Department of Military Education consisting of seven Sections :

1. 教育科 Chiao⁴ Yü⁴ K'o¹, Section of Instruction,
2. 步隊科 Pu⁴ Tui⁴ K'o¹, Infantry Section,
3. 馬隊科 Ma³ Tui⁴ K'o¹, Cavalry Section,
4. 礮隊科 P'ao⁴ Tui⁴ K'o¹, Artillery Section,
5. 工程隊科 Kung¹ Ch'êng² Tui⁴ K'o¹, Engineers Section,
6. 輜重隊科 Tzu¹ Chung⁴ Tui⁴ K'o¹, Military Trains Section, and
7. 要塞礮隊科 Yao⁴ Sai⁴ P'ao⁴ Tui⁴ K'o¹, Fortress Artillery (or Heavy Artillery) Section.

430A. The Department of Military Education (*see* No. 430) was formed from the 訓練科 Hsün⁴ Lien⁴ K'o¹, Training Section, and the 教育科 Chiao⁴ Yü⁴ K'o¹, Instruction Section, of the 軍學司 Chün¹ Hsüeh² Ssu¹, Department of Military Education of the Commission for Army Reorganization (*see* No. 416).

430B. 編譯局 Pien¹ I⁴ Chü², Translation Office; attached to the Department of Military Education (*see* No. 430); directed by a 總辦 Tsung³ Pan⁴, Chief, assisted by a 提調 T'i² Tiao⁴, Proctor, a 收掌 Shou¹ Chang³, Librarian (Keeper)

編纂 Pien¹ Tsuan³, Revisers, 譯述 I⁴ Shu¹, Translators **431** (Interpreters), and other officials (of an indefinite number). **to**

431. 軍醫司 Chün¹ I¹ Ssu¹, Army Medical Department; **434** consisting of two Sections:

1. 醫務科 I¹ Wu⁴ K'o¹, Medical Section, and
2. 馬醫科 Ma³ I¹ K'o¹, Veterinary Section.

431A. The Army Medical Department (*see* No. 431) was formed by the reorganization of the 醫務科 I¹ Wu⁴ K'o¹, Medical Section of the Commission for Army Reorganization (*see* No. 416).

432. 軍法司 Chün¹ Fa⁴ Ssu¹, Department of Military Law; supervises military law proceedings and military prisons It has no Sections.

432A. The Department of Military Law (*see* No. 432) was formed by the reorganization of the 法律科 Fa⁴ Lü⁴ K'o¹, Section of Laws, of the Commission for Army Reorganization (*see* No. 416).

432B. In addition to the usual officials (*see* No. 434), the Department of Military Law (*see* No. 432) furnishes employment for six 司法官 Ssu¹ Fa⁴ Kuan¹, Officers of Justice (of the first, second and third ranks).

433. 軍牧司 Chün¹ Mu⁴ Ssu¹, Department of the Military Stud; composed of two Sections:

1. 均調科 Chün¹ T'iao² K'o¹, Distributing Section, and
2. 蕃殖科 Fan¹ Chih² K'o¹, Breeding Section.

433A. The Department of the Military Stud was formed from the Court of the Imperial Stud (*see* Nos. 417 and 936B), and assimilated, in part, the functions of the 車駕司 Ch'ê¹ Chia⁴ Ssu¹, Remount Department (*see* No. 415A) of the old Ministry of War (*see* No. 415).

434. Each Department of the Ministry of War employs:

司長 one Ssu¹ Chang³, Controller (*see* No. 294), one 承發官 Ch'êng² Fa¹ Kuan¹, Registrar (*see* No. 294), 科長 K'o¹ Chang³,

435 to 437A

Section Chiefs (of the same number as there are Sections), 科員 K'o[1] Yüan[2], Secretaries (of the first, second and third ranks; from six to thirty-four), and 錄事 Lu[4] Shih[4], Writers (from six to twelve).

Special officials are treated under their respective Departments.

435. 提塘 T'i[2] T'ang[2], Superintendents of Military Posts; further distinguished as:

435A. 駐京提塘 Chu[4] Ching[1] T'i[2] T'ang[2], Superintendents of Military Posts residing at Peking, of whom there are sixteen.

435B. 駐省提塘 Chu[4] Shêng[3] T'i[2] T'ang[2], Superintendents of Military Posts residing in the Provinces (compare No. 754).

435C. 報房 Pao[4] Fang[2], Printing Office; formerly the 京報 Ching[1] Pao[4], *Peking Gazette*, was printed at this Office, which was under the direction of the Superintendents of Military Posts residing at Peking (see No. 435A).

436. 陸軍部差官 Lu[4] Chün[1] Pu[4] Ch'ia[1] Kuan[1], Officials for Special Duty; attached to the Ministry of War in an indefinite number (up to thirty-four).

437. Under the supervision of the Ministry of War are:

1. The Military Forces of China:

A. Lu Chün, Regular Troops, and

B. Hsün Fang Tui, Reserves (see Nos. 655 to 707),

2. Military Schools (see Nos. 708 to 717B),

3. Banner Troops (see Nos. 718 to 748),

4. Old Chinese Troops (see Nos. 749 to 753),

5. Military Posts (see No. 745), and

6. Office of the Government Stud (see No. 755).

437A. 紅十字會 Hung[2] Shih[2] Tzu[4] Hui[4], The Red Cross Society. Provisional regulations (中國紅十字會試辦章程 Chung[1] Kuo[2] Hung[2] Shih[2] Tzu[4] Hui[4] Shih[4] Pan[4] Chang[1] Ch'êng[2]) were drawn up by 呂海寰 Lü Hai-huan, and sanctioned by

[146]

an Imperial Decree of the 27th February, 1910. The same **438** Decree appointed 盛宣懷 Shêng Hsüan-huai as 紅十字會長 Hung² Shih² Tzu⁴ Hui⁴ Chang³, President of the Red Cross Society.

A special Memorial from the General Staff Office, suggesting certain changes and amendments in the provisional regulations mentioned above, was sanctioned by the Emperor on the 20th May, 1910. Accordingly, the 中國紅十字總會 Chung¹ Kuo² Hung² Shih² Tzu⁴ Tsung³ Hui⁴, Central Office of the Red Cross Society, is to be established at Peking, 分會 Fên¹ Hui⁴, Branch Offices, will be founded in provincial capitals, ports open to foreign trade and sea ports. Also, there is a proposal to form a corps of 醫員 I¹ Yüan², Physicians, and 看護人 K'an¹ Hu⁴ Jên², "Brothers and Sisters of Mercy." Furthermore, a 製藥廠 Chih⁴ Yao⁴ Ch'ang³, Laboratory, is to be founded for the manufacture of medical instruments and the preparation of medicines.

The insignia of the Chinese Red Cross Society is:

1. 白地紅十字旗 Pai² Ti⁴ Hung² Shih² Tzü⁴ Ch'i², Red Cross on a White Ground, or

2. 雙龍嵌十字記章 Shuang¹ Lung² Ch'ien⁴ Shih² Tzu⁴ Chi⁴ Chang¹, Red Cross and Two Dragons, of Gold, Silver, or Bronze (the ensign of members of the Red Cross Society).

MINISTRY (BOARD) OF JUSTICE.

438. 刑部 Hsing² Pu⁴, Ministry (Board) of Punishments, or Criminal Affairs (literary designation, 比部 Pi³ Pu⁴ and 西曹 Hsi¹ Ts'ao²; of its President, 大司寇 Ta⁴ Ssu¹ K'ou⁴; of its Vice-Presidents, 少司寇 Shao³ Ssu¹ K'ou⁴ or 秋官 Ch'iu¹ Kuan¹, Autumn Official).

The duties of this Ministry, according to "The Institutes of the T'ai Ch'ing Dynasty, consisted in: firstly, the enforcement and direction of punishments inflicted on offenders; secondly, at

439 to 440 the Autumn Assizes, preceding the time of executions (which take place in China on the eve of the Winter solstice), the Ministry, together with the Censorate (*see* No. 206) and the Court of Judicature and Revision (*see* No. 215), carefully examined decisions of provincial judges, in cases of capital punishment, submitted to them before presentation to the Emperor (before decisions of capital punishment of provincial judges became effective it was necessary that the assent of all the members of the Three High Courts of Judicature be obtained); finally, the Ministry of Punishments partook of the nature of both a criminal and civil court of the Metropolitan Circuit, for instance, every important criminal case occurring therein—after being carefully considered by a certain Department of the Ministry, in the first instance, by all the Department Controllers assembled, in the second instance, and by the Presidents of the Ministry, finally—was brought for final decision before the above-mentioned Three High Courts of Judicature.

439. In accordance with the former division of China into 18 provinces, the Ministry of Punishments (*see* No. 438) was composed of 18 Departments—one for each province.

In addition, to the Ministry there was attached a 律例館 Lü[4] Li[4] Kuan[3], Commission of Laws, whose duty consisted in the promulgation, every five years, of the code of criminal laws, with all amendments and supplements that had taken place since its previous issue.

At the head of the Commission, as Superintendent, was one of the Princes of the Blood or one of the highest officials of the Empire, appointed by the Emperor, and, to his service, there were deputed, from the higher Metropolitan Establishments, officials skilled in jurisprudence.

440. 法部 Fa[4] Pu[4], Ministry (Board) of Justice; formed by the reorganization of the Ministry of Punishments (*see* No. 438), as directed by Imperial Edict of the 6th November, 1906.

[148]

This Ministry controls and directs all the Judicial Establishments of the Empire, the Supreme Court of Justice (*see* No. 215A) included, attends to all prison affairs and renders the final decision with regard to the infliction of capital punishment.

441 to 446

The internal organization of the Ministry is as proposed in a Memorial to the Throne by the Ministry itself, sanctioned by the Emperor on the 31st January, 1907.

441. 承政廳 Ch'êng² Chêng⁴ T'ing¹, Council (*see* No. 285); considers the most important questions of the Ministry, controls the granting of pardons and the personnel of judicial establishments, defines the scope of judicial establishments and judicial police, etc.

442. 叅議廳 Ts'an¹ I⁴ T'ing¹, Secretarial Office (*see* No. 285A); frames rules and regulations, compiles reports and attends to correspondence generally.

443. Four 叅事 Ts'an¹ Shih⁴, Assistant Secretaries (*see* No. 286); 5A. There are two at the Council (*see* No. 441) and two at the Secretarial Office (*see* No. 442).

444. 審錄司 Shên³ Lu⁴ Ssu¹, Department of Judicial Affairs. Under the supervision of this Department are:

Criminal cases submitted for the Emperor's decision, the revision of decisions of the Supreme Court of Justice (*see* No. 215A) and of other judicial establishments and the criminal and civil cases of the provinces of Chihli, Kwangtung, Kwangsi, Yünnan and Kweichow and the Left Wing of the Ch'ahars.

445. 制勘司 Chih⁴ K'an¹ Ssu¹, Department of Revision. This Department supervises:

Revision of sentences of death passed by Higher Courts, the promulgation of death sentences and the criminal and civil cases of the provinces of Szechwan, Honan, Shensi and Hsinkiang and, also, of Uliasut'ai and Kobdo.

446. 編置司 Pien¹ Chih⁴ Ssu¹, Department of Banishment Affairs; supervising cases where the extreme penalty

defined by law is not inflicted, the determination of places of banishment and the civil and criminal cases of the provinces of Fengtien, Kírin, Heilungchiang, Shantung and Shansi and, also, of the Left Wing of Ch'ahars, Suiyuanch'êng and Kueihua-ch'êng.

447. 宥恤司 Yu⁴ Hsü¹ Ssu¹, Department of Pardons. This Department is charged with the publication of Benevolent Edicts and Manifests, questions concerning pardons, and the civil and criminal cases of the provinces of Kiangsu, Kiangsi, Anhui, Fukien, Chekiang, Hunan and Hupeh.

448. 舉叙司 Chü³ Hsü⁴ Ssu¹, Department of Personnel; controls the personnel of the Ministry and of judicial establishments in general and recommends rewards to be granted to, or punishments to be inflicted on, judicial officials.

449. 典獄司 Tien³ Yü⁴ Ssu¹, Department of Prisons; supervising prisons and workhouses attached to them (*see* No. 767A). Under the direct control of this Department is the prison at the Ministry of Justice (*see* No. 766).

450. 會計司 Hui⁴ (K'uai⁴) Chi⁴ Ssu¹, Audit Department registers receipts and expenditure of the Ministry, prepares estimates, collects fines and takes control of property confiscated.

451. 都事司 Tu¹ Shih⁴ Ssu¹, Department of General Affairs; prepares translations from Manchu into Chinese and *vice versâ*, copies reports, has the custody of the seal, etc.

452. The staff of each Department of the Ministry of Justice consists of three Department Directors (*see* No. 290), four Assistant Department Directors (*see* No. 291), and four Second Class Secretaries (*see* No. 292).

453. 收發所 Shou¹ Fa¹ So³, Registry; deals with correspondence concerning prisoners, prepares and stores instruments of torture, e.c. Its staff consists of two Assistant Department Directors (*see* No. 291) and two Second Class Secretaries (*see* No. 292).

454. 統計處 T'ung³ Chi⁴ Ch'u⁴, Statistical Bureau (*see* No. 162).

455. 當月司 Tang¹ Yüeh⁴ Ssu¹, Record and Registry Office; managed by one Department Director (*see* No. 290), one Assistant Department Director (*see* No. 291) and three Second Class Secretaries (*see* No. 292). Now abolished.

456. 藏罰庫 Tsang¹ Fa² K'u⁴, Treasury; where fines were deposited. Its staff consisted of one 司庫 Ssu¹ K'u⁴, Treasurer; 7A, and from one to two 庫使 K'u⁴ Shih³, Overseers (*see* No. 298). This is now non-existent (compare No. 450).

457. 提牢廳 T'i² Lao² T'ing¹, Prison Office; formerly in charge of two prisons of the Ministry, *i.e.* 南監 Nan² Chien¹, the Southern, and 北監 Pei³ Chien¹, the Northern, and with a staff consisting of two 提牢 T'i² Lao², Inspectors of Prisons (one Manchu and one Chinese). With the establishment of the Department of Prisons (*see* No. 419) this Office was abolished (for details *see* No. 766).

457A. 司獄司 Ssu¹ Yü⁴ Ssu¹, Section of Warders (of the Prison Office; *see* No. 457). This Section furnished employment for eight 司獄 Ssu¹ Yü⁴, Warders; 9B. It is now non-existent (for details *see* No. 766).

458. 編查處 Pien¹ Ch'a² Ch'u⁴, Compiling Office; collects information, frames rules and regulations, compiles drafts of laws, etc.

459. The Ministry of Justice supervises supreme control over:

1. Shên P'an T'ing, Local Courts (*see* Nos. 758 to 761A),

2. Chien Ch'a T'ing, Prosecuting Attorneys, and

3. Prisons (*see* Nos. 766 to 767A).

460

MINISTRY (BOARD) OF AGRICULTURE, INDUSTRY AND COMMERCE.

460. 工部 Kung¹ Pu⁴, Ministry (Board) of Works (literary designation, 水部 Shui³ Pu⁴; of its President 大司空 Ta⁴ Ssu¹ K'ung¹, literally, "Superintendent of Caves"; of its Vice-Presidents, 少司空 Shao³ Ssu¹ K'ung¹). This Ministry controlled and directed all government buildings and works, *i.e.* government ship-building, construction and repair of bridges, sluices, canals, embankments, mausolea, temples and city walls. Also, the Ministry defined weights and measures and furnished the army with contrivances and utensils necessary to its use

460A. The Ministry of Works was composed of the following Departments, Sections, Offices, etc.

1. 營膳司 Ying² Shan⁴ Ssu¹, Building Department (compare No. 345),

2. 虞衡司 Yü² Hêng² Ssu¹, Department of Weights and Measures,

3. 都水司 Tu¹ Shui³ Ssu¹, Department of Waterways and Dikes,

4. 料估所 Liao⁴ Ku¹ So³, Department of Estimates,

5. 寶源局 Pao³ Yüan² Chü², Coinage Office, directed by two 監督 Chien¹ Tu¹, Superintendents, and two 大使 Ta⁴ Shih², Overseers (compare No. 366); also 錢法堂 Ch'ien² Fa⁴ T'ang², Coinage Office which was under the control of the Junior Vice-President of the Ministry of Revenue to whose title was added 兼理錢法堂事務 Chien¹ Li³ Ch'ien² Fa⁴ T'ang² Shih⁴ Wu⁴, (*see* No. 366A).

6. 窖廠 Chiao⁴ Ch'ang³, Icehouse (for supplying the Court), supervised by two 監督 Chien¹ Tu¹, Overseers,

7. 木倉 Mu⁴ Ts'ang¹, Fire-wood Store, supervised by two 監督 Chien¹ Tu¹, Overseers, and

8. 司匠 Ssu¹ Chiang⁴, Overseers of Works ; 9в, etc.

461. 商部 Shang¹ Pu⁴, Ministry (Board) of Trade ; established by Imperial Edict of the 7th December, 1903.

461A. In accordance with a Memorial from the Ministry of Trade (sanctioned by the Emperor on the 26th September, 1903) its organization was as follows :

1. 保惠司 Pao³ Hui⁴ Ssu¹, Department of Trade,

2. 平均司 P'ing² Chün¹ Ssu¹, Department of Agriculture and Forestry,

3. 通藝司 T'ung¹ I⁴ Ssu¹, Department of Industry,

4. 會計司 Hui⁴ (K'uai⁴) Chi⁴ Ssu¹, Audit Department,

5. 司務廳 Ssu¹ Wu⁴ T'ing¹, Chancery,

6. 律學館 Lü⁴ Hsüeh² Kuan³, Commission for the Study of Commercial Legislation, directed by two 總纂官 Tsung³ Tsuan³ Kuan¹, Chief Revisers, and two 纂脩官 Tsuan³ Hsiu¹ Kuan¹, Revisers, and

7. 商報館 Shang¹ Pao⁴ Kuan³, Commercial Newspaper Office, directed by one 提調官 T'i² Tiao⁴ Kuan¹, Proctor.

In addition to two Councillors and two Secretaries for the Ministry (*see* Nos. 281 to 284), there were also established the posts of Department Director, Assistant Department Director and Second Class Secretary (*see* Nos. 290 to 292) ; two officials of each of the latter three ranks were attached to every Department.

For information as to the staff of the Chancery (*see* No. 296).

462. 農工商部 Nung² Kung¹ Shang¹ Pu⁴, Ministry (Board) of Agriculture, Industry and Commerce ; established by Imperial Edict of the 6th November, 1906 ; an amalgamation of the Ministry of Works (*see* No. 460) and the Ministry of Trade (*see* No. 461).

The internal organization of the Ministry of Agriculture, Industry and Commerce is as proposed in a Memorial from the

463 to 464

Ministry itself, sanctioned by the Emperor on the 22nd January, 1907.

The Ministry of Agriculture, Industry and Commerce supervises agriculture, industry, trade, forestry, mining, fisheries, the issue of trade marks, and schools having connection with the afore-mentioned.

463. 農務司 Nung² Wu⁴ Ssu¹, Department of Agriculture; directs agriculture, colonization, forestry, sericulture, tea planting, horticulture, fisheries, the building of wharves, bunds and dikes, the conservancy of rivers and harbours, etc.

This Department is in direct control of :

1. Agricultural Schools at the Capital and in the provinces (*see* Nos. 600 to 603 and 770),

2. Agricultural Guilds, their branches and sections (*see* No. 770), and

3. The Botanical Garden at Peking, and the Agricultural Office and School attached to it as well as Botanical Gardens in the provinces (*see* Nos. 770, 770A and 603A).

464. 工務司 Kung¹ Wu⁴ Ssu¹, Department of Industry ; supervises industry in all its branches, *i.e.* mechanical and with the hands, mining, the issuing of patents for prospecting and working of mines, the engagement of mining experts, etc.

Under the direct control of this Department are :

1. Schools of Craft and Mining at the Capital and in the provinces (*see* Nos. 604 to 608),

2. Metropolitan Professional Schools (*see* No. 598A),

3. School of Crafts (*see* No. 605A ; now reorganized),

4. Industrial Institute at Peking (and other places ; *see* No. 771),

5. Exhibitions for the Encouragement of Industry, at Peking (*see* No. 771A) and, in the provinces (*see* No. 771), and

6. Embroidery Workship (*see* No. 771).

464A. 化 分 礦 質 所 Hua⁴ Fên¹ Kung³ Chih⁴ So³, Chemical Laboratory for analysis of Mining Products (opened in 1910).

464B. 權 衡 度 量 局 Ch'üan² Hêng² Tu⁴ Liang⁴ Chü², Office of Weights and Measures.

465. 商 務 司 Shang¹ Wu⁴ Ssu¹, Department of Commerce; controls Chambers of Commerce in China (as well as Chinese Chambers of Commerce abroad), trade marts, exhibitions, the insurance business, fosters commerce, etc.

Directly supervised by this Department are :

1. Commercial Schools at Peking and in the provinces (see Nos. 609 to 612), and

2. Chambers of Commerce (see No. 774).

465A. 商 律 館 Shang¹ Lü⁴ Kuan³, Commercial Laws Committee.

465B. 商 報 館 Shang¹ Pao⁴ Kuan³, Commercial Newspaper Office (compare No. 461A).

465C. 公 司 註 册 局 Kung¹ Ssu¹ Chu⁴ Ts'ê⁴ Chü², Company Registration Bureau (see No. 776A).

465D. 商 標 局 Shang¹ Piao¹ Chü², Trade Marks Registration Bureau (see No. 776A).

466. 庶 務 司 Shu⁴ Wu⁴ Ssu¹, Department of General Affairs; checks the income and expenditure of the Ministry, keeps its accounts and supervises the staff—appointments, transfers, promotions,—etc.

Under the direct supervision of this Department is the :

466A. 承 值 所 Ch'êng² Chih⁴ So³, Registry and Record Office ; the duties of the Chancery, now abolished (see No. 461A), in connection with the supervision of incoming and outgoing correspondence, ciphering of telegrams, custody of the seal, etc., were transferred to this office.

167
to
171

467. The staff of the four Departments of the Ministry of Agriculture, Industry and Commerce (*see* Nos. 463 to 466) includes 12 Department Directors, 16 Assistant Department Directors and 18 Second Class Secretaries (*see* Nos. 290 to 292).

468. The following appointments at the Ministry of Trade were left unchanged on the formation of the Ministry of Agriculture, Industry and Commerce :

1. 顧問官 Ku[4] Wên[4] Kuan[1], Advisers (*see* No. 302A),

2. 礦務議員 Kung[3] Wu[4] I[4] Yüan[2], Mining Advisers (*see* No. 775),

3. 商務議員 Shang[1] Wu[4] I[4] Yüan[2], Commercial Advisers, and

4. 商務隨員 Shang[1] Wu[4] Sui[2] Yüan[2], Commercial Agents (Attachés).

469. To the Ministry of Agriculture, Industry and Commerce there are attached an indefinite number of :

1. 一等藝師 I[1] Têng[3] I[4] Shih[1], Chief Engineers of the first rank ; 6A,

2. 二等藝師 Êrh[4] Têng[3] I[4] Shih[1], Chief Engineers of the second rank ; 7A,

3. 一等藝士 I[1] Têng[3] I[4] Shih[4], Engineers of the first rank ; 8A, and

4. 二等藝士 Êrh[4] Têng[3] I[4] Shih[4], Engineers of the second rank ; 9A.

470. 統計處 T'ung[3] Chi[4] Ch'u[4], Statistical Bureau (*see* No. 162).

471. Under the control of the Ministry of Agriculture, Industry and Commerce are :

1. The Industrial Taotais (*see* Nos. 839 to 839B), and

2. Various establishments and officials discussed in Nos. 768 to 782.

MINISTRY (BOARD) OF POSTS AND COMMUNICATIONS.

472. 郵 傳 部 Yu¹ Ch'uan² Pu⁴, Ministry (Board) of Posts and Communications established by Imperial Edict of 6th November, 1906, which directed as follows :

" Shipping communication, Railways, Telegraphs and " Postal communications are to be jointly supervised by a " Ministry of Posts and Communications."

The Ministry of Posts and Communications is in supreme control of navigation, railways, telegraphs, and schools of these specialities. The Posts are still under the control of the Inspector General of Customs.

The organization of the Ministry is as proposed by the Ministry itself and sanctioned by the Emperor on the 1st August, 1907.

473. 承 政 廳 Ch'êng² Chêng⁴ T'ing¹, Council (*see* No. 285) ; the most important and most confidential affairs of the Ministry are managed by this office, which controls the staff and regulates expenditure, etc..

474. 叅 議 廳 Ts'an¹ I⁴ T'ing¹, Secretarial Office (*see* No. 285A) ; frames rules, initiates projects, examines plans, supervises correspondence, etc.

475. Four 僉 事 Ch'ien¹ Shih⁴, Assistant Secretaries (*see* No. 286) ; 5A, and four 七 品 小 京 官 Ch'i¹ P'in⁸ Hsiao³ Ching¹ Kuan¹, Officials of the seventh rank (*see* No. 299), are employed at the Ministry of Posts and Communications,—two at the Council (*see* No. 473) and two at the Secretarial Office (*see* No. 474).

476. 船 政 司 Ch'uan² Chêng⁴ Ssu¹, Department of Navigation ; supervises marine and riverine shipping, the construction of docks, the improvement of harbours, erection of lighthouses, etc.

477 to 481

The actual administration of the majority of the functions just mentioned is carried out by the 北 洋 大 臣 Pei³ Yang² Ta⁴ Ch'ên², Superintendent of Trade for the Northern Ports, and the 南 洋 大 臣 Nan² Yang² Ta⁴ Ch'ên², Superintendent of Trade for the Southern Ports (*see* No. 820B).

477. 路 政 司 Lu⁴ Chêng⁴ Ssu¹, Department of Land Communications; controls land communications within the Empire and legislation having reference thereto, collects funds and arranges loans for railway construction, etc. (compare No. 482).

478. 電 政 司 Tien⁴ Chêng⁴ Ssu¹, Department of Telegraphs; controls the telegraph affairs of the Empire, the erection of land lines and the laying of cables, construction of telephone and electric lighting systems, etc.

479. 郵 政 司 Yu¹ Chêng⁴ Ssu¹, Department of Posts; superintending, in theory, the entire postal affairs of the Empire, the improvement of postal communications, the sale of money orders and stamps and the transmission of postal parcels. Actually, the postal administration is under the supervision of the Imperial Maritime Customs (*see* No. 273).

480. 庶 務 司 Shu⁴ Wu⁴ Ssu¹, Department of General Affairs; recommends the transfer or promotion of officials, has the custody of the seal, supervises reception and despatch of correspondence and telegrams, keeps the accounts, oversees buildings, etc.

In the Autumn of 1909 the Department of General Affairs was abolished and its duties were transferred to the Council of the Ministry (*see* No. 473).

481. At each Department of the Ministry of Posts and Communications there are stationed two Department Directors (*see* No. 290), two to three Assistant Department Directors (*see* No. 291) four to six Second Class Secretaries (*see* No. 292), two Officials of the seventh rank (*see* No. 299), and an indefinite

number of 八品錄事 Pa[1] P'in[3] Lu[4] Shih[4], Writers of the eighth rank, and 九品錄事 Chiu[3] P'in[3] Lu[4] Shih[4], Writers of the ninth rank.

482. 鐵路總局 T'ieh[3] Lu[4] Tsung[3] Chü[2], Chief Railway Bureau, administrated by a 局長 Chü[2] Chang[3], Inspector, and 局員 Chü[2] Yüan[2], Attachés. This Bureau was formed in accordance with a Memorial from the Ministry of Posts and Communications, dated the 22nd December, 1907, for the supervision of Government and private railways.

The Bureau is the executive organ of the Department of Land Communications (*see* No. 477) and was developed from the 提調處 T'i[2] Tiao[4] Ch'u[4], Railway Section (now abolished) which was under the supervision of a 各路提調 Ko[4] Lu[4] T'i[2] Tiao[4], Inspector of Railways.

483. 顧問官 Ku[4] Wên[4] Kuan[1], Advisers (of the first, second and third ranks; *see* No. 302A). The number is indefinite.

484. 議員 I[4] Yüan[2], Advisers (*see* Nos. 300 and 468); similar to the 路務議員 Lu[4] Wu[4] I[4] Yüan[2], Railway Advisers of the Board of Trade (now abolished; *see* Nos. 461 and 461A); distinguished by their specialities (船路電郵 Ch'uan[2] Lu[4], Tien[4] and Yu[1], Navigation, Railways, Telegraphs and Posts).

485. 圖書館 T'u[2] Shu[1] Kuan[3], Library; containing many special works in Chinese and foreign languages.

486. 講習所 Chiang[3] Hsi[2] So[3], Lecture Hall; here are given lectures for the benefit of officials of the Ministry. Attached to this Hall is the :

486A. 閱報所 Yüeh[4] Pao[4] So[3], Reading Room.

487. 考工局 K'ao[3] Kung[1] Chü[2], Engineering Office.

At this Office are stationed: 測繪員 Ts'ê[2] Hui[4] Yüan[2], Draughtsmen, 藝師 I[4] Shih[1], Chief Engineers (of the first and second ranks; *see* No. 301), and 藝士 I[4] Shih[4], Engineers (of the first and second ranks; *see* No. 301).

488 to 491

488. 通譯局 T'ung¹ I⁴ Chü², Translation Office (Interpreting Office); with 繙譯 Fan¹ I⁴, Interpreters (Translators), and 編輯 Pien¹ Chi⁴, Compilers.

This Office is to be established later; its duties are now being performed by the Secretarial Office (see No. 474).

489. 統計處 T'ung³ Chi⁴ Ch'u⁴, Statistical Bureau (see No. 162).

490. The Ministry of Posts and Communications has supreme control of the following :

1. Railways (see Nos. 783 and 784).

2. Railway Schools and other Schools (see Nos. 785 to 788A),

3. The China Merchants' Steam Navigation Company (see No. 789),

4. Telegraphs and Telephones (see Nos. 790 and 791), and

5. The Bank of Communications (see No. 792).

MINISTRY (BOARD) OF DEPENDENCIES.

491. 藩理院 Li³ Fan¹ Yüan⁴, Court of Colonial Affairs ; established in the 17th century for the management of relations with Mongolia, K'uk'unor and the Mohammedan Princedoms in Western China.

Until 1861, all relations with Russia were supervised by this Court. In Russia these matters were attended to by the Ruling Senate.

In carrying out its duties the Court of Colonial Affairs was guided by the 理藩院則律 Li³ Fan⁴ Yüan² Tsê² Li⁴, Institutes of the Colonial Court (this book was translated into Russian, "Institutes of the Chinese Colonial Office," by S. Lipovzev, in two volumes ; St. Petersburg, 1828).

The reorganization of the Court of Colonial Affairs, in the sense of increasing its scope, was simultaneous with the general reform of the political organization of the Empire, in the Autumn of 1906, when, by Imperial Edict of the 6th November, the Court of Colonial Affairs became the :

491ᴀ. 理 藩 部 Li³ Fan¹ Pu⁴, Ministry (Board) of Dependencies ; charged with the control of the Mongolian, Tibetan and Mohammedan tribes inhabiting Mongolia, Tibet and districts bordering on Tibet and Hsining.

The organization of the Ministry is based on three Memorials (of the 3rd January and 30th July, 1907, and the 2nd January, 1908) presented by the Ministry itself, which left almost unchanged, as will be seen below, the old arrangements of the Court of Colonial Affairs (*see* No. 491).

492. As regards the various Ministries, the following are peculiarities of the Ministry of Dependencies :

1. 額 外 侍 郎 Ê¹ Wai⁴ Shih⁴ Lang², Supernumerary Vice-President ; an appointment usually conferred on some Mongol Prince.

2. There are no Councillors (*see* Nos. 281 and 282), Secretaries (*see* Nos. 283 to 284), Council (*see* No. 285) nor Secretarial Office (*see* No. 285ᴀ).

These, however, will come into existence when the Departments of Colonization and Frontier Defence are organized (*see* No. 496).

492ᴀ. 堂 主 事 T'ang² Chu³ Shih⁴, Secretaries (of the President of the Ministry) ; 6ᴀ. There are six in all (*see* No. 288).

493. 領 辦 處 Ling³ Pan⁴ Ch'u⁴, Orderly Office. This was formed from the following establishments of the Court of Colonial Affairs (*see* No. 491) :

1. 滿 檔 房 Man³ Tang⁴ Fang², Record and Registry Office.

2. 漢 檔 房 Han⁴ Tang⁴ Fang², Translation Office (for Manchu and Chinese),

[161]

11

**494
to
495**

3. 俸檔房 Fêng⁴ Tang⁴ Fang², Treasury, and

4. 督催所 Tu¹ Ts'ui¹ So³, Office of Incitement (to ensure the prompt despatch of business) ; the officials of this Office were charged with " the unfailing duty of keeping a strict watch for the prompt despatch of documents in general and the certification of all returns of questions settled and unsettled " (*see* Lipovzev, Preface, page xv).

The staff of the Orderly Office is composed of two 領辦 Ling³ Pan⁴, Chiefs, two 帮辦 Pang¹ Pan⁴, Assistants, four 稽核文移 Chi² Ho² Wên² I², Secretaries, four 總看奏摺 Tsung³ K'an⁴ Tsou⁴ Chê², Inspectors of Memorials, four 委署 主事 Wei³ Shu⁴ Chu³ Shih⁴, Assistant Secretaries, four 正繕寫 Chêng⁴ Shan⁴ Hsieh³, Senior Writers, and eight 副繕寫 Fu⁴ Shan⁴ Hsieh³, Junior Writers.

494. 司務廳 Ssu¹ Wu⁴ T'ing¹, Chancery (*see* No. 296) ; with two 司務 Ssu¹ Wu⁴, Chancery Directors ; 8A. For details as to other officials *see* No. 495A.

495. The six Departments (Lipovzev styles "Registries") of the Court of Colonial Affairs (*see* No. 491), were left unchanged in the Ministry of Dependencies :

1. 旗籍司 Ch'i² Chi² Ssu¹, Department of the Inner Mongols (managing the affairs of the Inner Mongols),

2. 典屬司 Tien³ Shu³ Ssu¹, Department of the Outer Mongols (managing the affairs of the Outer Mongols, Dzungaria (Sungaria), K'uk'unor and Tibet),

3. 王會司 Wang² Hui⁴ Ssu¹, Department for Receiving Princes of Inner Mongolia (in charge of the collection of tributes paid yearly by the Princes of the tribes and the issue of presents and allowances to Princes of Inner Mongolia, etc.),

4. 柔遠司 Jou² Yuan³ Ssu¹, Department for Receiving Princes of Outer Mongolia (in charge of the collection of tributes paid yearly by Princes of Outer Mongolia and the Lamas and the issue of presents from the Court to these persons),

5. 徠遠司 Lai² Yuan³ Ssu¹, Department of Eastern Turkestan (manages the affairs of the Mohammedan tribes in Hami, Turfan and other districts of Eastern Turkestan), and

6. 理刑司 Li³ Hsing² Ssu¹, Judicial Department (in charge of civil and criminal cases occurring in Inner and Outer Mongolia).

495A. At each Department, as well as at the Chancery (*see* No. 494), there are stationed:

1. 1 掌印 Chang³ Yin⁴, Keeper of the Seal (as Department Controller); from the ranks of Department Directors (*see* No. 290) or Assistant Department Directors (*see* No. 291).

2. 1 to 2 副印 Fu⁴ Yin⁴, Assistant Keepers of the Seal; from the ranks of Department Directors (*see* No. 290), Assistant Department Directors (*see* No. 291) or Second Class Secretaries (*see* No. 292),

3. 1 to 2 主稿 Chu³ Kao³, Keepers of Drafts (in all Departments; not in the Chancery; *see* No. 494); officials similar to the Assistant Keepers of the Seal,

4. 2 to 4 委署主事 Wei³ Shu⁴ Chu³ Shih⁴, Assistant Secretaries.

5. 3 to 4 正繕寫 Chêng⁴ Shan⁴ Hsieh³, Senior Writers, and

6. 3 to 4 副繕寫 Fu⁴ Shan⁴ Hsieh³; Junior Writers; from the ranks of Clerks (*see* No. 293).

496. In accordance with a Memorial from the Ministry, sanctioned by the Emperor on the 3rd January, 1907, there are later to be established two additional Departments, *i.e.*

1. 殖產司 Chih⁴ Ch'an³ Ssu¹, Department of Colonization, which will be in charge of the colonization of Mongolia, the conservation of forests, the improvement of cattle breeding, wild animal preservation, fur curing, railway construction, the development of mines and fisheries and the reorganization of the salt administration, and

495A to 496 (margin)

496A
to
497

2. 邊衛司 Pien[1] Wei[4] Ssu[1], Department of Frontier Defence, which will control the drilling of troops of Mongols and Tibetans, the spread of education, expansion of trade, etc.

496A. As proposed in a report of the Ministry of Dependencies, dated the 30th July, 1907, to perform the duties of the two above-mentioned Departments (*see* No. 496) for the time being there have been established two temporary offices, from which will be developed the Departments of Colonization and Frontier Defence, namely :

1. 調查局 Tiao[4] Ch'a[2] Chü[2], Investigation Office, and

2. 編纂局 Pien[1] Tsuan[3] Chü[2], Revising Office.

Each of these Offices is composed of a number of 股 Ku[3], Sections, at which are stationed Department Directors, Assistant Department Directors, Second Class Secretaries and Writers (*see* Nos. 290 to 293), from other Departments of the Ministry, to perform duties as 正管股 Chêng[4] Kuan[3] Ku[3], Section Chiefs, 副管股 Fu[4] Kuan[3] Ku[3], Assistant Section Chiefs, and 繙譯官 Fan[1] I[4] Kuan[1], Interpreters (Translators),

497. The following Offices, Sections, etc., of the Court of Colonial Affairs (*see* No. 491) have been left unchanged in the Ministry of Dependencies :

1. 當月處 Tang[1] Yüeh[4] Ch'u[4], Record Office ; here the Seal is kept,

2. 銀庫 Yin[2] K'u[4], Treasury ; issues maintenance allowances to Mongols arriving in Peking on business, discounts. by payments in money, allotments of hay and oats for their horses and firewood for their lodgings.

3. 飯銀處 Fan[4] Yin[2] Ch'u[4], Mess Allowance Office ; audits accounts of sums issued, in accordance with regulations, as table money,

4. 喇嘛印務處 La³ Ma³ Yin⁴ Wu⁴ Ch'u⁴, Lama Office, and

498 to 499

5. 蒙古房 Mêng³ Ku³ Fang², Mongolian Translation Office; translates despatches of all kinds written in Mongolian, especially those which must be presented in Manchu to the Emperor.

498. 內館 Nei⁴ Kuan³, Inner Inn, and 外館 Wai⁴ Kuan³, Outer Inn. These were maintained for Mongolian Princes visiting the Court with tribute or for duty.

In charge of the Inn there was a 監督 Chien¹ Tu¹, Inspector.

As proposed in a Memorial from the Ministry, dated the 2nd January, 1908, the Inns were abolished.

499. 殖邊學堂 Chih² Pien¹ Hsüch² T'ang², School of Mongolian and Tibetan (at the Ministry of Dependencies).

This was established in accordance with a Memorial from the Ministry, sanctioned by the Emperor on the 30th January, 1909, with the object of preparing men for service at the Ministry of Dependencies and along the frontiers. It consists of two Sections, namely, 蒙部科 Meng³ Pu⁴ K'o¹, Mongolian Section, and 藏衛科 Tsang⁴ Wei⁴ K'o¹, Tibetan Section, and the course of study in each is of 3 years' duration.

Admission to the School of Mongolian and Tibetan is open to all males between the ages of 18 and 32 years, who are physically fit and have a certificate showing that they have completed a Middle School course (*see* Nos. 580 to 582), provided they can pass a test examination.

The enrollment of each section of the school is 100.

On completion of their courses of study, students of the School are examined by the Ministry; those satisfactory are retained for service at the Ministry or given appointments on the frontier.

In addition to the study of Mongolian and Tibetan languages, literature, history and geography, students of the School attend lectures on political economy and finance.

POLICE.

500. 巡警 Hsün[2] Ching[3], Police (another designation is 警察 Ching[3] Ch'a[2]).

The metropolitan and provincial police are to a great extent organized on similar lines, the great difference being in the terminology used.

A. Metropolitan Police:

501. 巡警總廳 Hsün[2] Ching[3] Tsung[3] T'ing[1], Central Police Bureau. There are two of these, one in the 內城 Nei[4] Ch'êng[4], Tartar City, and one in the 外城 Wai[4] Ch'êng[2], Chinese City.

At the head of each is a :

502. 巡警總廳廳丞 Hsün[2] Ching[3] Tsung[3] T'ing[1] T'ing[1] Ch'êng[2], Police Superintendent.

Directly subordinated to the Police Superintendent are :

503. 巡警總廳僉事 Hsün[2] Ching[3] Tsung[3] T'ing[1] Ch'ien[1] Shih[4], Director of the Chancery of the Central Police Bureau ; 4B, and three Office Chiefs ; 5A.

504. The Central Police Bureau is composed of a Chancery of General Affairs and three Offices.

504A. 總務處 Tsung[3] Wu[4] Ch'u[4], Chancery of General Affairs ; composed of five Sections :

1. 警事股 Ching[3] Shih[4] Ku[3], Section of Police Matters,

2. 機要股 Chi[1] Yao[4] Ku[3], Section of Secret Affairs,

3. 文牘股 Wên[2] Tu[3] Ku[3], Section of Current Correspondence,

4. 支應股 Chih[1] Ying[1] Ku[3], Section of Finances, and

5. 統計股 T'ung[3] Chi[4] Ku[3], Section of Statistics and Accounts.

[167]

**504B
to
506**

504B. 衛 生 處 Wei⁴ Shêng¹ Ch'u⁴, Sanitary Office ; divided into four Sections :

1. 清道股 Ch'ing¹ Tao⁴ Ku³, Street Cleaning Section,
2. 防疫股 Fang² I⁴ Ku³, Disinfecting Section,
3. 醫學股 I¹ Hsüeh² Ku³, Medical Section, and
4. 醫務股 I¹ Wu⁴ Ku³, Medical Examinations Section.

504C. 司法處 Ssu¹ Fa⁴ Ch'u⁴, Judicial Office ; has one 刑事股 Hsing² Shih⁴ Ku³, Section of Judicial Affairs.

504D. 行 政 處 Hsing¹ Chêng⁴ Ch'u⁴, Administrative Office ; consisting of eight Sections :

1. 護衛股 Hu⁴ Wei⁴ Ku³, Section of Public Protection,
2. 治安股 Chih⁴ An¹ Ku³, Section of Public Peace,
3. 交涉股 Chiao¹ Shê⁴ Ku³, Section of Affairs concerning Foreigners,
4. 戶籍股 Hu⁴ Chi² Ku³, Census Section,
5. 正俗股 Chêng⁴ Su² Ku³, Section for the improvement of the Habits of the People,
6. 交通股 Chiao¹ T'ung¹ Ku³, Section of Communications,
7. 營業股 Ying² Yeh⁴ Ku³, Section of Industry and Handicrafts, and
8. 建築股 Chien⁴ Chu² Ku³, Construction Section.

505. Each Section is directed by a 正管股 Chêng⁴ Kuan³ Ku³, Section Chief, and 副 管 股 Fu⁴ Kuan³ Ku³, Assistant Section Chief.

In addition to the above-mentioned there are 警官 Ching³ Kuan¹, Police Officers of the fifth, sixth and seventh ranks (one of each in every Section) and Police Officers of the eighth and ninth ranks (two of each in every Section).

506. 巡 警 分 廳 Hsün² Ching³ Fên¹ T'ing¹, Police Bureau ; directed by a 知事 Chih¹ Shih⁴, Deputy Police Superintendent ; 5A.

There were originally five of these Bureaux in Peking but, towards the end of 1908 and with a view to economy, they were all abolished and their functions transferred to the corresponding Police Stations.

507. 巡警區 Hsün² Ching³ Ch'ü¹, Police Station ; directly under the control of the Central Police Bureaux.

At the head of each Police Station there is a 區長 Ch'ü¹ Chang³, Police Captain of the sixth or seventh rank. He is assisted by 區員 Ch'ü¹ Yüan², Police Officers of the eighth and ninth ranks (one of each at every Police Station).

At the Capital there are 23 Police Stations.

In addition to those already mentioned, there are the following Police Establishments in Peking :

508. 探訪局 T'an⁴ Fang³ Chü², Detective Office.

509. 工巡捐局 Kung¹ Hsün² Chüan¹ Chü², Municipal Tax Collection Office.

510. 路工局 Lu⁴ Kung¹ Chü³, Office for Supervision of Streets.

510A. 衛生局 Wei⁴ Shêng¹ Chü², Sanitary Office (see No. 859).

511. 濟良所 Chi⁴ Liang² So³, House of Correction (for prostitutes and female offenders who have just completed a term of imprisonment).

512. 緝捕局 Chi⁴ Pu³ Chü², Office for the Apprehension of Law-breakers.

512A. 待質所 Tai⁴ Chih⁴ So³, House of Detention ; consisting of three Sections :

1. 紳商 Shên¹ Shang¹, for the educated classes,
2. 婦女 Fu⁴ Nü³, for females, and
3. 平民 P'ing² Min², for the masses.

513. 消防隊 Hsiao¹ Fang² Tui⁴, Fire Brigade.

514. 京師習藝所 Ching¹ Shih¹ Hsi² I⁴ So³, Metropolitan Workhouse (or House of Correction). This was established in

August, 1905, and provisional rules for its administration, drawn up by the Ministry of Police, were sanctioned by the Emperor on the 30th July, 1906.

In this institution there are confined, and kept at work, those who have been condemned for petty misdemeanours to imprisonment for a period of three months or more; the Workhouse is also open to the poorest of the masses (compare No. 343B).

The management of the Workhouse is carried on by five 處 Ch'u⁴, Sections, and two 科 K'o¹, Sub-sections, *i.e.*

1. 文案處 Wên² An⁴ Ch'u⁴, Correspondence Section,
2. 會計處 Hui⁴ Chi⁴ Ch'u⁴, Accounts Section,
3. 考工處 K'ao³ Kung¹ Ch'u⁴, Handicraft Section,
4. 庶務處 Shu⁴ Wu⁴ Ch'u⁴, Section of General Affairs,
5. 稽巡處 Chi² Hsün² Ch'u⁴, Inspection Section,
6. 診治科 Chên³ Chih⁴ K'o¹, Sick Ward, and
7. 教授科 Chiao⁴ Shou⁴ K'o¹, School.

At the head of the Metropolitan Workhouse is a 監督 Chien¹ Tu¹, Director (of the rank of Ts'an¹ I⁴; *see* Nos. 283 and 284), who has attached to his staff:

1. 1 提調兼典獄官 T'i² Tiao⁴ Chien¹ Tien³ Yü⁴ Kuan¹, Proctor and Inspector,
2. 2 分判所官 Fên¹ P'an⁴ So³ Kuan¹, Senior Overseers (acting as assistants to the Inspector; having general supervision of the five Sections and two Sub-sections),
3. 7 所官 So³ Kuan¹, Overseers (carry on the actual management of their respective Sections and Sub-sections).
4. 1 醫官 I¹ Kuan¹, Physician,
5. 1 總教習官 Tsung³ Chiao⁴ Hsi² Kuan¹, Senior Teacher,
6. 6 看守長 K'an¹ Shou³ Chang³, Senior Warders,
7. 7 看守 K'an¹ Shou³, Warders,
8. 1 分授習官 Fên¹ Chiao⁴ Hsi² Kuan¹, Teacher,

    9.   1 教誨師 Chiao[4] Hui[4] Shih[1], Teacher of Morality,   **514A**

  10. 2 書記 Shu[1] Chi[4], Clerks, and   **to**

  11. 8 技師 Chi[4] Shih[1], Craftsmen.   **519**

514A. In the provinces 習藝所 Hsi[2] I[4] So[3], or 罪犯習 藝所 Tsui[4] Fan[4] Hsi[2] I[4] So[3], Workhouses (Houses of Correction), are established in the provincial capitals and their organization is on the same lines as that at the Capital (*see* No. 514 ; compare, also, No. 767A).

515. 博濟工場 Po[2] Chi[4] Kung[1] Ch'ang[3], Home for Unemployed Males.

516. 教養局 Chiao[4] Yang[3] Chü[2], Free Meal Station.

517. 官醫院 Kuan[1] I[1] Yüan[4], Public Dispensary (compare No. 859).

518. 自治研究所 Tzu[4] Chih[4] Yen[2] Chiu[1] So[3], Self-government Instruction Office (compare No. 527A).

519. 司法警察 Ssu[1] Fa[4] Ching[3] Ch'a[2], Judicial Police ; established (in accordance with a Memorial from the Ministry of Justice, dated the 27th January, 1908), to serve the needs of the Prosecuting Attorneys' Offices (*see* No. 762), at various Police Stations. They are under the supervision of the local police officials as well as the Prosecuting Attorneys.

The duties of the Judicial Police consist in apprehending law-breakers and bringing them to the Courts of Justice, the making of searches (under order of a Court of Justice), the gathering of evidence, the giving of information, the escorting of accused persons, the collection of bail and the examination, in company with officials from the Prosecuting Attorney's Office, of corpses or wounded people, etc.

Judicial Police have come into existence wherever the new Judicial Establishments have been instituted.

The ranks of the Judicial Police are :

519A
to
521

519A. 巡官 Hsün² Kuan¹, Chief of Judicial Police, 巡長 Hsün² Chang³, Captain of Judicial Police, and 巡警 Hsün² Ching³, Judicial Police Officer.

B. *Provincial Police*:

520. Throughout the provinces there has not as yet been introduced a uniform police organization; in some districts the police are similar in type to the Metropolitan police (*see* Nos. 501 to 518), in others there is difference.

Below is described the police organization of the Capital of Honan province:

At the head of the 巡警總局 Hsün² Ching³ Tsung³ Chü², Central Police Bureau, there is a 總辦 Tsung³ Pan⁴, Police Superintendent. He has directly subordinated to him:

1 副辦 Fu⁴ Pan⁴, Deputy Police Superintendent,

1 提調 T'i² Tiao⁴, Proctor,

1 正文案 Chêng⁴ Wên² An⁴, Senior Secretary,

1 副文案 Fu⁴ Wên² An⁴, Junior Secretary,

1 考功 K'ao³ Kung¹, Registrar, and

1 發審 Fa¹ Shên³, Judicial Officer.

In addition to the above-mentioned there are eight (corresponding to the 八隅分局 Pa¹ Yü² Fên¹ Chü², eight Police Stations of the city) 總巡官 Tsung³ Hsün² Kuan¹, Chief Police Inspectors, eight 巡官 Hsün² Kuan¹, Police Inspectors, eight 巡記 Hsün² Chi⁴, Police Secretaries, five (corresponding to the 五城門 Wu³ Ch'êng² Mên², five City Gates) 稽查官 Chi² Ch'a² Kuan¹, Inspectors of Gates, six 總局書識 Tsung³ Chü² Shu¹ Shih⁴, Clerks of the Central Police Bureau, six 總局差役 Tsung³ Chü² Ch'ai¹ I⁴, Runners of the Central Police Bureau, 16 分局局役 Fên¹ Chü² Chü² I¹, Runners of the Police Stations (two at each), and 14 總局護勇 Tsung³ Chü² Hu⁴ Yung³, Guards at the Central Police Bureau.

521. In charge of the police employed in patrolling the streets is a 帶管 Tai⁴ Kuan³, Chief of the Street Patrolling

Police, who is at the head of a force composed of one 督操 Tu[1] Ts'ao[1], Senior Police Instructor, four 巡弁 Hsün[2] Pien[4], Police Captains, four 副巡弁 Fu[4] Hsün[2] Pien[4], Police Lieutenants, 16 巡長 Hsün[2] Chang[3], Police Sergeants, four 號兵 Hao[4] Ping[1], Special Policemen, 40 巡目 Hsün[2] Mu[4], Police Corporals, 400 巡兵 Hsün Ping[1], Policemen, 40 火夫 Huo[3] Fu[1], Cooks, 80 工兵 Kung[1] Ping[1], Labourers, one 清書 Ch'ing[1] Shu[1], Clerk and four 書識 Shu[1] Shih[4], Writers.

POLICE SCHOOLS.

522. 高等巡警學堂 Kao[1] Têng[3] Hsün[2] Ching[3] Hsüeh[2] T'ang[2], formerly called 警務學堂 Ching[3] Wu[4] Hsüeh[2] T'ang[2] or 警察學堂 Ching[3] Ch'a[2] Hsüeh[2] T'ang[2], Higher Police Schools. These have been established, as proposed in a Memorial of the Ministry of the Interior (sanctioned by the Emperor on the 3rd October, 1908) at the provincial capitals, with the object of preparing men for the police service. The course of study extends over 3 years and the number of students is never less than fifty.

In charge of a Higher Police School there is a 監督 Chien[1] Tu[1], Director. He is in charge of a staff composed of 1 教務提調 Chiao[4] Wu[4] T'i[2] Tiao[4], Inspector of Education, 1 庶務提調 Shu[4] Wu[4] T'i[2] Tiao[3], Steward, and an indefinite number of 教習 Chiao[4] Hsi[2], Teachers.

The Higher Police Schools have, also, a :

522A. 簡易科 Chien[3] I[4] K'o[1], Abridged Course of Study (for the education of policemen) of one year's duration.

523. 巡警教練所 Hsün[2] Ching[3] Chiao[4] Lien[4] So[3], Police Instruction Bureaux ; established in the principal towns of prefectures, sub-prefectures, departments and districts. The course of study covers one year and the number of students is not less than 100.

**523ᴀ
to
525**

In charge of every Instruction Bureau is a 所 長 So³ Chang³, Director. He is assisted by a 教務委員 Chiao⁴ Wu⁴ Wei³ Yüan², Inspector of Education, a 庶務委員 Shu⁴ Wu⁴ Wei³ Yüan², Steward, and an indefinite number of 教習 Chiao⁴ Hsi², Teachers.

523ᴀ. It has been arranged to establish a 監獄學堂 Chien¹ Yü⁴ Hsüeh² T'ang², School of Prison Management, to be attached to the Higher Police School of the province of Kuangsi. The date fixed for its opening is the year 1910 (*see* details in No. 766ʙ).

LOCAL SELF-GOVERNMENT.

524. Among the projects to be accomplished during the preparatory period preceding the institution of constitutional government (1908—1916) is the establishment of self-government or public administration institutions, whose duties will consist in the provision and maintenance of good local organization, the control of local agriculture, industry, commerce, schools, sanitary affairs, charity, public buildings, etc.

By the programme of reform schemes drawn up by the Commission for Drawing up Regulations for Constitutional Government, with the National Assembly, sanctioned by the Emperor on the 27th August, 1908, the introduction of local self-government was to be begun in 1909, so that the establishment of local self-government institutions for cities, towns and villages (*see* Nos. 525, 525ᴀ and 525ʙ) might be completed in 1913, and, for prefectures, sub-prefectures, departments and districts (similar to the Russian provincial establishments—Zemstvo; *see* No. 526), in 1914.

525. 地 方 自 治 Ti⁴ Fang¹ Tzu⁴ Chih⁴, Local Self-Government; projected for universal introduction within the periods 1909—1913 4 (compare No. 524).

As regards local self-government for cities, towns and **525A** villages there is a division into :

. 1. 京師地方自治 Ching¹ Shih¹ Ti⁴ Fang¹ Tzu⁴ Chih⁴, Peking Municipal Administration (*see* No. 525A), and

2. 城鎭郷地方自治 Ch'êng² Chên⁴ Hsiai g Ti⁴ Fang¹ Tzu⁴ Chih⁴, Municipal Administration of Cities, Towns and Villages (*see* No. 525B).

525A. 京師地方自治 Ching¹ Shih¹ Ti⁴ Fang¹ Tzu⁴ Chih⁴, Peking Municipal Administration (*see* No. 525); introduced in accordance with regulations drawn up by the Commission for Drawing up Regulations for Constitutional Government (following a proposal of the Ministry of the Interior, dated the 10th September, 1909), and promulgated, with regulations as to the necessary elections, in an Imperial Edict of the 3rd February, 1910 (the regulations concerning the Peking Municipal Administration consist of 8 headings and 136 articles; the regulations as to elections consist of 7 headings and 87 articles).

Within the scope of the Peking Municipal Administration are all affairs of local utility or necessity, *i.e.* educational matters (Elementary and Middle Schools, Associations for the Fostering of Public Education, Public Education Societies, Libraries, etc.), the maintenance of good order in the city (the keeping in order of the streets, markets, pavements, etc.), building affairs, public charity and public utilities (tramways, electric lighting, waterworks, etc.)

All people living in Peking are considered 居民 Chü¹ Min², Residents ; those who are Chinese subjects, are not less than 25 years of age, have resided at the Capital for three consecutive years, and pay a direct tax or contribute not less than two dollars for local public needs, are considered as 選民 Hsüan³ Min², Electors, have the right of voting for (選舉自治職員之權

Hsüan³ Chü³ Tzu⁴ Chih⁴ Chih² Yüan² Chih¹ Ch'üan²), and may be elected as (被選舉爲自治職員之檔 Pei⁴ Hsüan³ Chü³ Wei² Tzu¹ Chih⁴ Chih² Yüan² Chih¹ Ch'üan²), Members of the Municipal Administration.

The Peking Municipal Administration (自治職員 Tzu⁴ Chih⁴ Chih² Yüan²) is arranged as follows :

A. 1. 區議事會 Ch'ü¹ I⁴ Shih⁴ Hui⁴, Ward Councils, and

2. 區董事會 Ch'ü¹ Tung³ Shih⁴ Hui⁴, Ward Executive Boards.

B. 1. 總議事會 Tsung³ I⁴ Shih⁴ Hui⁴, Municipal Council, and

2. 總董事會 Tsung³ Tung³ Shih⁴ Hui⁴, Municipal Executive Board.

A. 1. Ward Councils are established, one at each, at Police Stations (區 Ch'ü ; see No. 507).

The regulations contain a provision for the establishment of one Ward Council only, for two Wards, should the paucity of the population make this desirable.

Ward Councils are made up of from 15 to 30 議員 I⁴ Yüan², Ward Councilmen, who are elected for a term of two years (by delegates chosen by the electors directly; see above).

The Ward Councilmen themselves elect one of their number as their 議長 I⁴ Chang³, President, and another as their 副議長 Fu⁴ I⁴ Chang³, Vice-President, both for a term of two years.

Under the control of the Ward Councils are the affairs of their respective Wards.

A. 2. Ward Executive Boards are established at the Ward Councils and their duty consists in the execution of decisions of the Councils. They are made up of a 總董 Tsung³ Tung³, President, one to three 董事 Tung³ Shih⁴, Members (the number being one-tenth of the number of Councilmen of the

[176]

Ward Council concerned), and from three to six 名譽董事 Ming[2] Yü[4] Tung[3] Shih[4], Honorary Members (in number equal to one-fifth of the number of Councilmen of the Ward Council in question), who are elected, for a term of two years, by the Ward Councilmen, from the electors (*see* above) of the Ward concerned.

The names of the Presidents-elect of the Ward Executive Boards are presented to the Chief Inspector of Municipal Administration for approval; those of Members of the Ward Executive Boards are presented to the respective Inspector of Municipal Administration for approval (*see* below).

B. 1. The Municipal Council attends to affairs relating to the city as a whole and its suburbs. The various Ward Councils at a general meeting elect, from their own members, one 議長 I[4] Chang[3], President (of the Municipal Council), one 副議長 Fu[4] I[4] Chang[3], Vice-President, and 議員 I[4] Yüan[2], Members of the Municipal Council (in number equal to one-tenth the total number of members of the Ward Council concerned) for a term of two years.

B. 2. The Municipal Executive Board (*see* above), the executive organ of the Municipal Council, is composed of one 總董 Tsung[3] Tung[3], President, five 董事 Tung[3] Shih[4], Members, and 12 名譽董事 Ming[2] Yü[4] Tung[3] Shih[4], Honorary Members of the Municipal Executive Board, who are elected for a term of two years by the members of the Municipal Council— from the electors of the city. Their names are presented for approval to the Ministry of the Interior, through the Chief Inspector of Municipal Administration.

As regards 文牘員 Wên[2] Tu[3] Yüan[2], Secretaries 庶務員 Shu[4] Wu[4] Yuan[2], Stewards, and other officials who may be attached to the Councils and Executive Boards, their number and engagement is left entirely in the hands of the Presidents and Vice-Presidents.

[177]

525ʙ   Supervision over the actions of the Peking Municipal Administration, as regards justice and legality, is exercised, within the
precincts of the city, by the Central Police Bureaux (*see* No. 501)
and, in the suburbs, by the Office of the General Commandant
of the Gendarmerie (*see* No. 798). In this connection the Police
Superintendents of the Central Police Bureaux are styled
自治總監督 Tzu⁴ Chih⁴ Tsung³ Chien¹ Tu¹, Chief Inspectors
of Municipal Administration, and Police Captains (*see* No. 507)
are called 自治監督 Tzu⁴ Chih⁴ Chien¹ Tu¹, Inspectors of
Municipal Administration (in the suburbs of the city the latter
title is applied to officials deputed from the Office of the General
Commandant of the Gendarmerie). These officials are subordinated, as regards the duties mentioned, to the control of the
Ministry of the Interior (compare Nos. 339ᴀ and 342).

   525ʙ. 城鎮鄉地方自治 Ch'êng² Chên⁴ Hsiang¹ Ti⁴
Fang¹ Tzu⁴ Chih⁴, Municipal Administration of Cities, Towns and
Villages (*see* No. 525) ; to be introduced throughout the Empire
within the period 1909-1913, as defined in regulations drawn up
by the Commission for Drawing up Regulations for Constitutional
Government (as called for by a proposal of the Ministry of the
Interior, dated the 24th August, 1908), which were promulgated,
together with regulations regarding the necessary elections, in an
Imperial Decree of the 18th January, 1909 (the regulations
regarding Municipal Administration consist of eight headings and
112 articles ; those regarding the elections are divided into six
headings and 81 articles).

   As 城 Ch'êng², Cities, are considered administrative centres
of prefectures, sub-prefectures, departments and districts, with
their suburbs ; as 鎮 Chên⁴, Towns, are considered places, not
administrative centres, having a population of more than 50,000 ;
as 鄉 Hsiang¹, Villages, are considered places having a population
of less than 50,000.

The scope of the Municipal Administrations of the places mentioned above is similar to that of the Peking Municipal Administration (*see* No. 525A).

The organs of municipal administration (自治職員 Tzu⁴ Chih⁴ Chih² Yüan²) in cities and towns are 城鎮議事會 Ch'êng² Chên⁴ I⁴ Shih⁴ Hui⁴, City and Town Councils, as deliberative bodies, and 城鎮董事會 Ch'êng² Chên⁴ Tung³ Shih⁴ Hui⁴, City and Town Executive Boards, as executive bodies ; in villages there are the 鄉議事會 Hsiang¹ I⁴ Shih⁴ Hui⁴, Village Councils, and 鄉董 Hsiang¹ Tung³, Village Reeves.

The Municipal Councils are made up of 議員 I⁴ Yüan², Members (in cities and towns they number from 20 to 50 and in villages from 6 to 18, depending on the population) ; elected, by delegates chosen by the electors directly (compare No. 525A), for a term of two years.

The members of the Municipal Councils elect one of their number as 議長 I⁴ Chang³, President, and another as 副議長 Fu⁴ I⁴ Chang³, Vice-President, both for a term of two years.

Municipal Executive Boards (for cities and towns) are made up of a 總董 Tsung³ Tung³, President, one to three 董事 Tung³ Shih⁴, Members (in number equal to one-twentieth of the total number of members of the corresponding Municipal Council), and from four to 12 名譽董事 Ming² Yü⁴ Tung³ Shih⁴, Honorary Members (in number equal to one-fifth of the total number of members of the corresponding Municipal Council), who are elected, from the ranks of the electors, by the Municipal Councils. The name of the President-elect is presented for approval to the Governor-General or Governor ; the names of the others are presented for the approval of the local authorities (*see* below).

In villages the members of the Municipal Council elect (from the ranks of the electors) a 鄉董 Hsiang¹ Tung³, Village

526 Reeve, and a 鄉佐 Hsiang¹ Tso³, Assistant Village Re-- there is no Executive Board.

To the above-mentioned municipal establishments (Councils and Boards) there may be attached 文牘員 Wên² Tu³ Yüan², Secretaries, 庶務員 Shu⁴ Wu⁴ Yüan², Stewards, and 辦事員 Pan⁴ Shih⁴ Yüan², Attendants.

Supervision over the actions of the Municipal Administrations in Cities, Towns and Villages (自治監督 Tzu⁴ Chih⁴ Chien¹ Tu¹; compare Nos. 525A and 526) as regards their regularity and legality, is exercised by the 地方官 Ti⁴ Fang¹ Kuan¹, Local Authorities, who, in this connection, forward detailed reports of the proceedings of the local self-government institutions to the Governor-General or Governor of the province. The supreme control (in the direction indicated) appertains to the Ministry of the Interior (*see* Nos. 339A and 342; compare No. 525A).

526. 府廳州縣地方自治 Fu³ T'ing¹ Chou¹ Hsien⁴ Ti⁴ Fang¹ Tzu⁴ Chih⁴, Public Administration (Zemstvo; compare No. 524) in Prefectures, Sub-prefectures, Departments and Districts; to be introduced throughout the Empire within the period 1910-1914, as defined in regulations drawn up by the Commission for Drawing up Regulations for Constitutional Government (complementary to a recommendation of the Ministry of the Interior, dated the 19th December, 1909), which were promulgated, with regulations for the necessary elections, in an Imperial Decree of the 6th February, 1910 (the regulations as to the Public Administration consist of eight headings and 105 articles; those referring to the elections are in 47 articles).

The regulations mentioned above cover:

1. Prefectures. 2. Independent Sub-prefectures. 3. Dependent Prefectures. 4. Independent Departments. 5. Departments and 6. Districts (*see* No. 846).

Within the scope of the Public Administration of Prefectures, Sub-prefectures, Departments and Districts (Public Administration of Counties) are placed all affairs concerning public utility or necessity, either of the country as a whole or of its component parts—should the local self-government institutions of the city, town or village concerned be unable to cope with them.

The Public Administration of Prefectures, Sub-prefectures, Departments and Districts (自治職員 Tzu⁴ Chih⁴ Chih² Yüan²) is carried on by :

1. 府廳州縣議事會 Fu³ T'ing¹ Chou¹ Hsien⁴ I⁴ Shih⁴ Hui⁴, County Councils (Councils of Prefectures, Sub-prefectures, Departments and Districts), and

2. 府廳州縣叅事會 Fu³ T'ing¹ Chou¹ Hsien⁴ Ts'an¹ Shih⁴ Hui⁴, Board of County Councillors (a deliberative and, to some extent, executive body), and

3. 府廳州縣長官 Fu³ T'ing¹ Chou¹ Hsien⁴ Chang³ Kuan¹, Government Representatives in Prefectures, Sub-prefectures, Departments and Districts (the executive officials).

County Councils are made up of 議員 I⁴ Yüan², Members (from 20 to 60 according to the population), elected for a term of three years.

The members of the County Councils elect their respective 議長 I⁴ Chang³, President, and 副議長 Fu⁴ I⁴ Chang³, Vice-President, for a term of three years.

As to the franchise and eligibility for election to the Public County Administration Establishments, the rules are similar to those referring to cities, towns and villages (*see* No. 525A). Persons attached to local officials, as well as officials at local police establishments, lose the franchise and are ineligible for election ; teachers in elementary schools are eligible for election but may not vote.

Affairs after being discussed by the County Council are brought before the Board of County Councillors.

Sessions of the County Councils (會議 Hui⁴ I⁴) are held once a year—in the ninth moon—and are of 30 to 40 days' duration; should occasion arise, extraordinary sessions (臨時會議 Lin² Shih² Hui⁴ I⁴), of 10 days' duration, may be convened.

Boards of County Councillors are made up of 叅事員 Ts'an¹ Shih⁴ Yüan², Councillors, numbering one-fifth the number of members of the respective County Council; also, there are elected a similar number of 候補叅事員 Hou⁴ Pu³ Ts'an¹ Shih⁴ Yüan², Expectant Councillors. The Government Representative acts as 會長 Hui⁴ Chang³, President.

The Board of County Councillors revises decisions of the County Council, considers questions submitted by the local officials and determines ways and means for putting resolutions of the County Council into practice.

For the audit of the income and expenditure of the County Council there may be appointed a number of officials of the Board of County Councillors (so-called 委員 Wei³ Yüan²).

Sessions of the Boards of County Councillors are held once a month. Also, should occasion arise, extraordinary sessions may be called by the local officials or by the initiative of a majority of the County Councillors of the Board affected.

To the County Establishments mentioned above (Councils and Boards) there may be attached 文牘員 Wên² Tu³ Yüan², Secretaries, and 庶務員 Shu⁴ Wu⁴ Yüan², Stewards.

The establishment of one County Council and one Board of County Councillors for two administrative centres is permissible (compare No. 525A) should the number of members be between 30 and 100. In the event of this the senior Government Representative becomes President of the Board of County Councillors; the next in rank becomes 副會長 Fu⁴ Hui⁴ Chang³, Vice-President. Also, the Council is divided into two 股 Ku³, Sections, in which questions referring to the two administrative units are separately discussed (*see* detailed rules, consisting of 11 **527** articles, annexed to the regulations).

The executive officials of the Public County Administration Establishments (自 治 行 政 Tzu⁴ Chih⁴ Hsing² Chêng⁴) are, as stated before, the local Government representatives, *i.e.* Prefects (*see* No. 848), Sub-prefects (*see* Nos. 852 and 854), Department Magistrates (*see* Nos. 851 and 855) and District Magistrates (*see* No. 856), and attached to them, as assistants, are a number of 自 治 委 員 Tzu⁴ Chih⁴ Wei³ Yüan², Deputies of Self-government Affairs. Their duties consist in : 1. The execution of measures of the County Councils and Boards of Councillors, 2. The transmission of proposals to the County Councils and Boards of Councillors for discussion, 3. The management of correspondence, etc. Also, under certain conditions, they may suspend sessions for 10 days.

Differences between the local officials and the County Councils and Boards of County Councillors are to be settled by the 行 政 審 判 衙 門 Hsing² Chêng⁴ Shên³ P'an⁴ Ya² Mên², Administrative-Judicial Offices, or, until the establishment of this office, by the Councils attached to the Governors-General and Governors (*see* No. 823).

Supervision over the regularity and legality of actions of the County Councils and Boards of County Councillors (自 治 監 督 Tzu⁴ Chih⁴ Chien¹ Tu¹ ; compare Nos. 525A and 525B) is exercised by the provincial Governors-General and Governors, to whom the local officials are constrained to make detailed reports as to the proceedings of the Public County Administration Establishments. The supreme control, in the direction just spoken of, appertains to the Ministry of the Interior (*see* Nos. 339A and 342 ; compare Nos. 525A and 525B).

527. 自治籌辦處 Tzu⁴ Chih⁴ Ch'ou² Pan⁴ Ch'u⁴, Offices for the Organization of Local Self-government ; established at provincial capitals (for the time being at the Offices for Arrang-

527A ing for Provincial Assemblies; compare No. 173), under the direction of the higher provincial officials, with the object of organizing local self-government institutions throughout the country.

527A. 自治究研所 Tzu⁴ Chih⁴ Yen² Chiu¹ So³, Self-government Instruction Offices; established, in 1909, as arranged for by the general outline of constitutional reforms (*see* No. 127), at provincial capitals. Later these Offices are to be established in the administrative centres of prefectures, sub-prefectures, departments and districts.

The object of the establishment of Self-government Instruction Offices is the spreading of the principles of local self-government among the people.

According to regulations, consisting of 14 articles, drawn up by the Commission for Drawing up Regulations for Constitutional Government (as arranged for in a proposal from the Ministry of the Interior, dated the 3rd April, 1909), and sanctioned by the Emperor on the 5th of May, 1909, eligible for enrollment (學員 Hsueh² Yüan²) at the Self-government Instruction Offices are persons having the franchise (*see* No. 525A).

Concerning the staff of Self-government Instruction Offices the Regulations for Local Self-government define as follows:

The Lecturers (講員 Chiang³ Yüan²) are appointed on the recommendation of the Local Office for the Organization of Local Self-government (*see* No. 527) and one of them acts as 所長 So³ Chang³, Director of Courses.

In administrative centres of prefectures, sub-prefectures, departments and districts, as Directors and Teachers, there may be appointed persons who have completed the course at the Self-government Instruction Offices of the provincial capitals. Concerning the Peking Self-government Instruction Office, compare No. 518.

GENERAL CENSUS.

528. The programme of constitutional reforms, sanctioned by the Emperor, calls for the taking of a census of the Empire within the period 1909–1912. During the first two years (1909–1910) a census of the families in China will be taken; during 1911–1912 the number of persons of both sexes will be ascertained.

By the Census Regulations, 調查戶口章程 Tiao⁴ Ch'a² Hu⁴ K'ou³ Chang¹ Ch'êng², drawn up by the Ministry of the Interior (sanctioned by the Emperor on the 14th January, 1909), the taking of the census is to be supervised by the following officials:

529. 總監督 Tsung³ Chien¹ Tu¹, Chief Census Supervisor; in the provinces this position is an adjunct to that of Police Taotai or Provincial Treasurer (for provinces as yet having no Police Taotai). In Chihli province this post is held also, in addition to the Provincial Treasurer, by the following:

In the prefecture of Shun T'ien Fu; by the Prefect (*see* No. 793).

In Peking; by the Police Superintendents of the Central Police Bureaux (*see* No. 502).

530. 監督 Chien¹ Tu¹, Census Supervisor; this post is an adjunct to those of Prefect, Department Magistrate, District Magistrate, or their Assistants.

531. 調查長 T'iao⁴ Ch'a² Chang³, Chief Census Inspector; this post is an adjunct to those of 總董 Tsung³ Tung³, President of the Municipal Executive Board, and 鄉長 Hsiang¹ Chang³, Village Elder.

532. 調查員 Tiao⁴ Ch'a² Yüan², Census Inspector; this post is an adjunct to those of 董事 Tung³ Shih⁴, Member of the Municipal Executive Board, and 鄉董 Hsiang¹ Tung³, Village Reeve.

COMMITTEE FOR THE REORGANIZATION OF THE
FINANCIAL AFFAIRS OF THE EMPIRE.

533. In the measures preparatory to the introduction of constitutional government in China the government has aimed at reforms with regard to finances, firstly : looking towards the subordination of all financial affairs to the control of the Ministry of Finance, further : the determination of the State Budget and the estimation from this of the income and expenditure of the State, with a view to the strict control of the latter.

With the object of accomplishing the reforms above-mentioned there was established, by Imperial Edict of the 10th January, 1909, the Committee for the Reorganization of the Financial Affairs of the Empire, (*see* Nos. 534 and 535), in the Ministry of Finance at Peking, and in the provinces, there were established Branch Offices of the Committee for the Reorganization of the Financial Affairs of the Empire (*see* Nos. 536 to to 541), at the Governor-General's and Governor's Yamen. Regulations defining the duties of these establishments—at the Capital and in the provinces—were drawn up by the Ministry of Finance and submitted in a Memorial which was sanctioned by the Emperor on the 21st March, 1909.

534. 清 理 財 政 處 Ch'ing¹ Li³ Ts'ai² Chêng⁴ Ch'u⁴, Committee for the Reorganization of the Financial Affairs of the Empire (*see* Nos. 374 and 533) ; established at the Ministry of Finance and made up of officials of the Ministry, specially deputed for the general guidance of Provincial Branch Offices of the Committee for the Reorganization of the Financial Affairs of the Empire (*see* Nos. 375, 533 and 536 to 541), for verifying information supplied by these and for drawing up an estimate of the State income and expenditure from materials supplied from the provinces.

535. At the head of the Committee there are: one 提調 **535**
T‘i² Tiao⁴, President, one 幫提調 Pang¹ T‘i² Tiao⁴, Vice-
President, one 總辦 Tsung³ Pan⁴, Director, and one 幫辦 Pang¹
Pan⁴, Assistant. All these positions are held by higher officials
of the Ministry of Finance.

The Committee is divided into the following 12 Sections:

1. 總務科 Tsung³ Wu⁴ K‘o¹, Section of General Affairs;
in charge of the compilation of information supplied by the
provincial branch offices and the drawing up of reports based on
such information.

2. 京畿科 Ching¹ Chi¹ K‘o¹, Metropolitan Section (for
Peking, the Metropolitan Prefecture, the province of Chihli and
Ch‘ahar),

3. 遼瀋科 Liao² Shên³ K‘o¹, Manchurian Section
(provinces of Fengtien, Kirin and Heilungchiang),

4. 江贛科 Chiang¹ Kan⁴ K‘o¹, Section for Kiangsu,
Anhui and Kiangsi,

5. 青豫科 Ch‘ing¹ Yü⁴ K‘o¹, Section for Shantung and
Honan,

6. 湘鄂科 Hsiang¹ Ao⁴ K‘o¹, Section for Hunan and
Hupeh,

7. 閩浙科 Min³ Chê⁴ K‘o¹, Section for Fukien and
Chekiang,

8. 粵桂科 Yüeh⁴ Kuei⁴ K‘o¹, Section for Kuangtung and
Kuangsi,

9. 秦晉科 Ch‘in² Chin⁴ K‘o¹, Section for Shensi and
Shansi (also for places like Urga, Suiyüanchêng, Kueihuachêng,
Uliasut‘ai, Kobdo, Alt‘ai, etc.),

10. 甘新科 Kan¹ Hsin¹ K‘o¹, Section for Kansu and
Hsinchiang (also for Ili, Tarbagatai, Hsining, etc.),

11. 梁益科 Liang² I⁴ K‘o¹, Section for Szechwan, Yünnan
and Kweichow, and Tibet,

12. 收掌科 Shou¹ Chang³ K‘o¹, Section of Archives.

536 to 538   In charge of each Section is a 總核 Tsung³ Ho², Section Chief, assisted by 坐辦 Tso⁴ Pan⁴, Assistants. Also there are an indefinite number of 書記員 Shu¹ Chi⁴ Yüan², Clerks, and 諮議官 Tzu⁴ I⁴ Kuan¹, Advisers ; the necessary qualification of the first is the possession of a good handwriting ; the latter are selected from persons experienced in finance and well acquainted with the financial position of the provinces.

BRANCH OFFICES OF THE COMMITTEE FOR THE REORGANIZATION OF THE FINANCIAL AFFAIRS OF THE EMPIRE.

536. 清理財政局 Ch'ing¹ Li³ Ts'ai² Chêng⁴ Chü², Branch Offices of the Committee for the Reorganization of the Financial Affairs of the Empire (*see* Nos. 375 and 533). These are established in all the provinces with the object of furnishing the Committee itself (*see* Nos. 533 to 535) with information necessary to the drawing up of a State Budget, namely, by submitting reports as to provincial income and expenditure, by furnishing information as to the working out of the budget of the previous year and by supplying materials for the preparation of the yearly budget.

537. 總辦 Tsung³ Pan⁴, Chief of a Branch Office of the Committee for the Reorganization of the Financial Affairs of the Empire ; in charge of a branch office of the Committee. This post is an adjunct to that of Provincial Treasurer (*see* No. 825) or Commissioner of Finance (*see* No. 808).

538. 會辦 Hui⁴ Pan⁴, Associate Chief of a Branch Office of the Committee for the Reorganization of the Financial Affairs of the Empire ; this post is an adjunct to those of Salt Commissioner (*see* No. 835), Superintendent of Customs (*see* No. 842), Salt Intendant (*see* No. 841), Grain Intendant (*see* No. 836) and, also, of Expectant Taotais in charge of provincial financial establishments.

539. 正監理官 Chêng[4] Chien[1] Li[3] Kuan[1], Financial Supervisor; these are appointed for a term of two years, one to each branch office of the Committee, on the recommendation of the Ministry of Finance—approved by the Emperor—to observe what success attends the efforts of the Branch Offices of the Committee for the Reorganization of the Financial Affairs of the Empire.

540. 副監理官 Fu[4] Chien[1] Li[3] Kuan[1], Assistant Financial Supervisor; deputed in a similar manner to Financial Supervisors (*see* No. 539) and with the same object.

541. Branch Offices of the Committee for the Reorganization of the Financial Affairs of the Empire are made up of three Sections:

1. 編輯科 Pien[1] Chi[4] K'o[1], Compiling Section; in charge of drawing up rules, reports, Memorials and returns of income and expenditure,

2. 審覈科 Shên[3] Ho[2] K'o[1], Revising Section; for the examination of returns of income and expenditure forwarded from the various government establishments, and

3. 庶務科 Shu[4] Wu[4] K'o[1], Section of General Affairs; among other duties, manages the correspondence.

Each Section is administered by a 科長 K'o[1] Chang[3], Section Chief, to whom there are subordinated 科員 K'o[1] Yüan[2], Secretaries (the number depending on the business of the Section), 書記 Shu[1] Chi[4], Clerks and 議紳 I[4] Shên[1], Advisers (chosen from the local gentry).

BANKS (GOVERNMENT AND OTHERS).

542. 戶部銀行 Hu[4] Pu[4] Yin[2] Hang[2], Bank of the Ministry of Revenue; established in accordance with a Memorial from the Committee of Finance (*see* Nos. 349A and 932A) and

542ᴀ to 544

the Ministry of Revenue (*see* No. 349), dated the 14th March, 1904, and opened to business, at Peking, on the 27th September, 1905.

The original regulations of the bank were drawn up by the Ministry of Revenue and submitted to the Throne in Memorials dated April, 1904, and 22nd August, 1905 (supplementary). The capital was fixed at four million taels, divided into forty thousand shares of one hundred taels; half the shares were taken up by the Government and half were issued to the public.

As recommended in a report from the Ministry of Finance, sanctioned by the Emperor on the 17th February, 1908, the Bank of the Ministry of Revenue became the :

542ᴀ. 大清銀行 Ta⁴ Ch'ing¹ Yin² Hang², Ta Ch'ing Government Bank. The original capital was, at the same time, raised (to ten million taels) by the issue of sixty thousand additional shares.

By the new regulations (consisting of 24 articles), submitted in the report above-mentioned (of the 17th February, 1908), the Ta Ch'ing Government Bank is a 股分有限公司 Ku³ Fên¹ Yu³ Hsien⁴ Kung¹ Ssu¹, Limited Joint-stock Company (*see* No. 776.)

The Board of Directors of the Ta Ch'ing Government Bank is made up of one Governor (*see* No. 543), one Deputy Governor (*see* No. 544) and four Directors (*see* No. 545) a control over the operations of the bank is exercised by two Official Supervisors (*see* No. 546) and three Inspectors (*see* No. 546ᴀ).

543. 正監督 Chêng⁴ Chien¹ Tu¹, Governor (formerly styled 總辦 Tsung³ Pan⁴); 3ᴀ. Appointed by the Emperor, on the recommendation of the Ministry of Finance, for a term of service of five years.

544. 副監督 Fu⁴ Chien¹ Tu¹, Deputy Governor (formerly styled 副辦 Fu⁴ Pan⁴); 4ᴀ. Appointed by the Emperor, on

the recommendation of the Ministry of Finance, for a term of five years.

545. 理 事 Li[3] Shih[4], Directors (four in all). They are elected at a general meeting of the shareholders, from the ranks of holders of 100 or more shares, and their names are presented for the approval of the Ministry of Finance. Their term of service is four years.

546. 監 理 官 Chien[1] Li[3] Kuan[1], Official Supervisors (two); appointed by the Emperor, on the recommendation of the Ministry of Finance, for general control of the bank's operations.

546A. 監 事 Chien[1] Shih[4], Inspectors (three); elected at a general meeting of the shareholders from those who hold 40 or more shares. Their term of service is three years.

547. In addition to its Head Office at Peking, the Ta Ch'ing Government Bank has the following branches in the provinces : Tientsin (Chihli province ; the first branch opened ; established in October, 1905), Moukden (Fengtien province), Yingk'ou (Fengtien province), Ch'ang Ch'un (also Kwanchêng-tzu ; Kirin province), Kalgan (Chihli province), Urga (Mongolia), Nanking (Kiangsu province), Shanghai (Kiangsu province), Anking (Anhui province), Taiyüanfu (Shansi province), Chinanfu (Shantung province), Hsianfu (Shensi province), Hangchow (Chekiang province), Foochow (Fukien province), Kiukiang (Kiangsi province), Hankow (Hupeh province), Chungking (Szechwan province), Changsha (Hunan province) and Canton (Kuangtung province).

At each branch there is a 總 辦 Tsung[3] Pan[4], Superintendent, chosen by the Board of Directors, and approved by the Emperor, on the recommendation of the Ministry of Finance, for a period of service of five years. Subordinated to him there are a 經 理 Ching[1] Li[3], Manager, and a 協 理 Hsieh[4] Li[3], Sub-manager (not as yet appointed for all the branches), appointed by the Board of Directors.

[191]

**548
to
550A**

548. At Peking, under the supervision of the Ta Ch'ing Government Bank, there are:

1. 北京儲蓄銀行 Pei³ Ching¹ Ch'u³ Hsü⁴ Yin² Hang², Peking Savings-bank, which is directed by a 總辦 Tsung³ Pan⁴, Superintendent; opened to business in the Summer of 1908 (compare No. 550c), and

2. 大清銀行學堂 Ta⁴ Ch'ing¹ Yin² Hang² Hsüeh² T'ang², School of the Ta Ch'ing Government Bank; established in 1908 with the object of training, gratis, young men for the bank's service; there are now 80 pupils at this school.

549. 官銀號 Kuan¹ Yin² Hao⁴, also 官錢局 Kuan¹ Ch'ien² Chü², Government Banks; these are in existence at places where branches of the Ta Ch'ing Government Bank have not been established and their functions consist in the regulating of the local money market and the issue of bank-notes. From them it usually happens that branches of the Ta Ch'ing Government Bank are evolved.

550. The report of the Ministry of Finance spoken of above (dated 17th February, 1908), dealing with the reorganization of the Bank of the Ministry of Revenue as the Ta Ch'ing Government Bank (*see* Nos. 542 and 542A), foreshadowed the formation of three additional types of banks throughout China, namely :

550A 銀行 Yin² Hang², Banks (also 普通銀行 P'u³ T'ung¹ Yin² Hang², General or Universal Banks) ; these are to replace the private credit establishments, such as 銀號 Yin² Hao⁴, 票莊 P'iao⁴ Chuang¹, and 錢莊 Ch'ien² Chuang¹. Banks of this type (they may be called Banking Houses) will discount bills and drafts, accept deposits, make advances, buy and sell bullion, exchange money, issue time-drafts (期票 Ch'i¹ P'iao⁴), bills of exchange (匯票 Hui⁴ P'iao⁴), etc.

The regulations for this type of bank consist of 15 articles.

[192]

550B. 殖業銀行 Chih² Yeh⁴ Yin² Hang², Banks of Agriculture and Industry ; these banks will assist agricultural and commercial enterprises. Of this type are : one 交通銀行 Chiao¹ T'ung¹ Yin² Hang², the Bank of Communications (see details in No. 792), two 興業銀行 Hsing¹ Yeh⁴ Yin² Hang², Industrial Bank (founded to satisfy the needs of railway construction in Chekiang province), and three 農業銀行 Nung² Yeh⁴ Yin² Hang², Agricultural Banks (yet to be established), etc.

For the supervision (examination) of the operations of Banks of Agriculture and Industry the Ministry of Finance has authority to depute some of the local officials as 監理 Chien¹ Li³, Official Supervisors. The regulations concerning this type of bank consist of 34 articles.

550C. 儲蓄銀行 Ch'u³ Hsü⁴ Yin² Hang², Savings-banks; with a minimum paid-up capital of fifty thousand taels. These banks accept small sums for deposit (other types of banks may carry on this kind of banking business with the permission of the Ministry of Finance). The regulations for their control consist of 13 articles.

For the Peking Savings-bank *see* No. 548.

MINTS.

551. 天津銀錢總廠 T'ien¹ Tsin¹ Yin² Ch'ien² Tsung³ Ch'ang³, Central Mint at Tientsin (official designation, 戶部造幣總廠 Hu⁴ Pu⁴ Tsao⁴ Pi⁴ Tsung³ Ch'ang³, Central Mint of the Ministry of Revenue); established in accordance with a Memorial from the Committee of Finance (*see* No. 349A) and the Ministry of Revenue (*see* No. 349), sanctioned on the 22nd August, 1905, for the minting of silver and copper coins.

This mint is now styled :

551A. 造幣總廠 Tsao⁴ Pi⁴ Tsung³ Ch'ang³, Central Mint. It is directed by a 造幣總廠正監督 Tsao⁴ Pi⁴ Tsung³ Ch'ang³

[193]

13

**551ʙ
to
555**

Chêng⁴ Chien¹ Tu¹, Superintendent of the Central Mint ; 3ᴀ, and a 造幣總廠副監督 Tsao⁴ Pi⁴ Tsung³ Ch'ang³ Fu⁴ Chien¹ Tu¹, Assistant Superintendent of the Central Mint ; 4ᴀ.

551ʙ. 造幣分廠 Tsao⁴ Pi⁴ Fên¹ Ch'ang³, Mints (or Branches of the Central Mint). These are situated in the provinces and each is directed by a 造幣分廠正監督 Tsao⁴ Pi⁴ Fên¹ Ch'ang³ Chêng⁴ Chien¹ Tu¹, Mint Superintendent (or Superintendent of a Branch of the Central Mint) ; 3ᴀ, and a 造幣分廠副監督 Tsao⁴ Pi⁴ Fên¹ Ch'ang³ Fu⁴ Chien¹ Tu¹, Assistant Mint Superintendent (or Assistant Superintendent of a Branch of the Central Mint) ; 4ᴀ.

HEAD OFFICE FOR THE COLLECTION OF EXCISE ON NATIVE OPIUM.

552. 土藥統稅總局 T'u³ Yao⁴ T'ung³ Shui⁴ Tsung³ Chü², Head Office for the Collection of Excise on Native Opium ; established (a temporary institution) in 1906 at 武昌府 Wu³ Ch'ang¹ Fu³ (Hupeh province). It is directed by a :

553. 督辦土藥統稅事務大臣 Tu¹ Pan⁴ T'u³ Yao⁴ T'ung³ Shui⁴ Shih⁴ Wu⁴ Ta⁴ Ch'ên², Superintendent of the Native Opium Excise. This official is assisted by two :

554. 幫辦土藥統稅事務大臣 Pang¹ Pan⁴ T'u³ Yao⁴ T'ung³ Shui⁴ Shih⁴ Wu⁴ Ta⁴ Ch'ên², Assistant Superintendents of the Native Opium Excise.

555. 土藥統稅分局 T'u³ Yao⁴ T'ung³ Shui⁴ Fên¹ Chü², Offices for the Collection of Excise on Native Opium. In charge of each of these offices there is an official, ranking as Taotai (*see* No. 838), styled 正辦 Chêng⁴ Pan⁴, Office Chief.

The Offices for the Collection of Excise on Native Opium number nine, *i.e.* one for the provinces of Chihli and Shantung, one for the provinces of Honan and Shansi, one for the provinces of Szechwan, Yünnan and Kweichow, one for the province of

Hupeh, one for the provinces of Kiangsi and Hunan, one for the provinces of Kiangsu and Anhui, one for the provinces of Fukien and Chekiang, one for the provinces of Shensi and Kansu and one for the provinces of Kuangtung and Kuangsi.

OFFICE OF THE CUSTOMS AND OCTROI OF PEKING AT THE CH'UNG WÊN GATE.

556. 崇文門稅務衙門 Ch'ung² Wên² Mên² Shui⁴ Wu⁴ Ya² Mên², Head Office of the Customs and Octroi at the Ch'ung Wên Gate (colloquially, 哈達門 Ha¹ T'a² Mên² or 海岱門 Hai³ T'ai⁴ Mên²); out-stations of this office are established in a cordon about Peking, at distances ranging from 10 to 30 miles.

In charge of the Head Office of the Customs and Octroi at the Ch'ung Wên Gate are:

557. 崇文門正監督 Ch'ung² Wên² Mên² Chêng⁴ Chien¹ Tu¹, Superintendent of the Customs and Octroi at the Ch'ung Wên Gate, and 崇文門副監督 Ch'ung² Wên² Mên² Fu⁴ Chien¹ Tu¹, Assistant Superintendent of the Customs and Octroi at the Ch'ung Wên Gate; both are appointed by the Emperor, for a term of one year, from the high officials of the Empire. They are assisted by:

558. 左翼監督 Tso³ I⁴ Chien¹ Tu¹, Superintendent of the House Tax and Livestock Tax for the East Division of Peking.

559. 右翼監督 Yu⁴ I⁴ Chien¹ Tu¹, Superintendent of the House Tax and Livestock Tax for the West Division of Peking.

560. 崇文門宣課副使 Ch'ung² Wên² Mên² Hsüan¹ K'o⁴ Fu⁴ Shih³, Customs Examiner.

561
to
566

NATIVE (LAND) CUSTOMS.

561. 各關稅口監督 Ko[4] Kuan[1] Shui[4] K'ou[3] Chien[1] Tu[1], Superintendents of the Native (Land) Customs (Barriers). These officials are in charge of the collection of taxes on goods imported into China from Mongolia.

561A. 張家口監督 Chang[1] Chia[1] K'ou[3] Chien[1] Tu[1], Inspector of Customs at Kalgan.

561B. 殺虎口監督 Sha[1] Hu[3] K'ou[3] Chien[1] Tu[1], Inspector of Customs at Shahuk'ou.

GOVERNMENT GRANARIES.

562. 倉塲 Ts'ang[1] Ch'ang[3], Government Granaries at the Capital. These are managed by the :

563. 倉塲總督衙門 Ts'ang[1] Ch'ang[3] Tsung[3] Tu[1] Ya[2] Mên[2], Head Office of the Government Granaries at the Capital. At the head of this Office are two :

564. 欽命總督倉塲度支部右侍郎 Ch'in[1] Ming[4] Tsung[3] Tu[1] Ts'ang[1] Ch'ang[3] Tu[4] Chih[4] Pu[4] Yu[4] Shih[4] Lang[2], Superintendents of the Government Granaries at the Capital with the rank of Junior Vice-President of the Ministry of the Ministry of Finance (shorter, 總督倉塲 Tsung[3] Tu[1] Ts'ang[1] Ch'ang[3] and 倉塲侍郎 Ts'ang[1] Ch'ang[3] Shih[4] Lang[2]).

565. 坐粮廳 Tso[4] Liang[2] T'ing[1], also 坐粮廳監督 Tso[4] Liang[2] T'ing[1] Chien[1] Tu[1], Supervisors of the Government Granaries at the Capital. There are two of these officials (one Manchu and one Chinese) and they are appointed from Department Directors of the Ministry of Finance.

566. 各倉塲監督 Ko[4] Ts'ang[1] Ch'ang[3] Chien[1] Tu[1], Inspectors of the Government Granaries at the Capital. These officials number 16 (half are Manchus and half are Chinese), two for each Granary—there being eight Granaries in Peking.

[196]

566A. The names of the Granaries at Peking are: **566A**
1. 大通橋 Ta⁴ T'ur Ch'iao², 2. 祿米倉 Lu⁴ Mi³ Ts'ang¹, **to**
3. 南新倉 Nan² Hsin¹ Ts'ang¹, 4. 舊太倉 Chiu⁴ T'ai⁴ **568**
Ts'ang¹, 5. 北新倉 Pei³ Hsin¹ Ts'ang¹, 6. 富新倉 Fu⁴
Hsin¹ Ts'ang¹, 7. 興平倉 Hsin¹ P'ing² Ts'ang¹, and 8. 豐益
倉 Fêng¹ I⁴ Ts'ang¹.

567. 內倉 Nei⁴ Ts'ang¹, Court Granaries; managed by
two 監督 Chien⁴ Tu¹, Inspectors.

567A. For particulars as to 查倉御史. Ch'a² Ts'ang¹ Yü⁴
Shih³, Censors Supervising the Government Granaries, *see*
No. 214A.

FINANCIAL COLLEGE.

568. 財政學堂 Ts'ai² Chêng⁴ Hsüeh² T'ang², Financial
(Political Economy) College. The establishment of this institution was outlined in a report of the Ministry of Finance, dated
the 26th April, 1907, and detailed regulations, in 50 articles,
were drawn up and submitted to the Throne in a report dated
the 5th March, 1909.

The object of the Financial College is the supplying of a
higher financial education for those who are desirous of devoting
themselves to service in the various establishments under the
control of the Ministry of Finance, *i.e.* Banks, Customs, etc.

The College consists of two Sections:

1. 中等科 Chung¹ Têng³ K'o¹, Middle Section; with a
course of three years and a curriculum similar to that of Middle
Professional Schools (*see* No. 598). The course includes foreign
languages and literature and subjects of general education having
reference to finances.

2. 高等科 Kao¹ Têng³ K'o¹, Higher Section; with a
special course of three years for those who have successfully
completed the course in the Middle Section. This Section

569
to
569A
supplies instruction in special financial subjects, financial policy, financial legislation, etc.

The Financial College also maintains a 別科 Pieh² K'o¹, Special Course—for persons in the Government service—similar to the course of Colleges of Law and Administration (*see* No. 623A), a 稅務專科 Shui⁴ Wu⁴ Chuan¹ K'o¹, Course of Customs Administration, and a 銀行講習科 Yin² Hang² Chiang³ Hsi² K'o¹, Banking Course.

At the head of the Financial College there is a 監督 Chien¹ Tu¹, Director. He is in charge of a staff made up of one Preceptor (*see* No. 636), one Steward (*see* No. 641), one Inspector of Dormitories (*see* No. 645), an indefinite number of Teachers (*see* No. 637), three Proctors (*see* No. 646), one Librarian (*see* No. 639), one Secretary (*see* No. 642), one Accountant (*see* No. 643), one Clerk of Works (*see* No. 644) and one Assistant Inspector of Dormitories (*see* No. 647).

IMPERIAL MAUSOLEA.

569. 陵寢 Ling² Ch'in³, Imperial Mausolea; under the supervision of the Ministry of Rites.

The Emperors of the reigning (Manchu) Dynasty are buried in three separate groups of mausolea; one is situated in Manchuria and the others in Chihli province.

While the Emperor is living his mausoleum is sometimes euphemistically called 萬年吉地 Wan⁴ Nien² Chi² Ti⁴, " The Happy Land of a Myriad Years."

569A. The group of Imperial Mausolea in Manchuria is situated near Moukden and Hsinching and includes 三陵 San¹ Ling², Three Mausolea :

1. 永陵 Yung³ Ling², situated near Hsinching (80 miles from Moukden) on the hill 啓運山 Chi³ Yün⁴ Shan¹. Here are buried the first four Manchu Sovereigns, styled (since 1648)

from their names in the Temple of Ancestors and their posthumous titles by the following :

A. 肇祖原皇帝 Chao⁴ Tsu³ Yüan² Huang² Ti⁴, B. 興祖直皇帝 Hsing¹ Tsu³ Chih² Huang² Ti⁴, C. 景祖翼皇帝 Ching³ Tsu³ I⁴ Huang² Ti⁴, and D. 顯祖宣皇帝 Hsien³ Tsu³ Hsüan¹ Huang² Ti⁴.

2. 福陵 Fu² Ling², situated seven miles from Moukden on the hill 天桂山 T'ien¹ Kuei⁴ Shan¹. Here is buried the Emperor 太祖高皇帝 T'ai⁴ Tsu³ Kao¹ Huang² Ti⁴, known from his reign as 天命 T'ien¹ Ming⁴ (1616–1626).

3. 昭陵 Chao¹ Ling², situated three miles from Moukden on the hill 隆業山 Lung² Yeh⁴ Shan¹. Here are buried the Emperor 太宗文皇帝 T'ai⁴ Tsung¹ Wên² Huang² Ti⁴, known from his reign as 天聰 T'ien¹ Ts'ung¹ (1626–1636), and the Emperor 崇德 Ch'ung² Te² (1636–1643).

569B. 東陵 Tung¹ Ling², The Eastern Imperial Mausolea; situated 80 miles to the North-east of Peking, in the Department of 遵化州 Tsun¹ Hua⁴. They include the following mausolea of Emperors and Empresses :

1. 昭西陵 Chao¹ Hsi¹ Ling²; situated in the pass 馬蘭峪 Ma³ Lan² Yü⁴. Here is buried the Empress 孝莊 Hsiao⁴ Chuang¹ (deceased in 1725), the mother of the Emperor 世祖 Shih⁴ Tsu³.

2. 孝陵 Hsiao⁴ Ling². Here are buried the Emperor 世祖 Shih⁴ Tsu³, known from his reign as 順治 Shun⁴ Chih⁴ (1644–1661), and the Empresses 孝獻 Hsiao⁴ Hsien³ and 孝康 Hsiao⁴ K'ang¹.

3. 孝東陵 Hsiao⁴ Tung¹ Ling². Here was buried (in 1718) the Empress 孝惠 Hsiao⁴ Hui⁴ (deceased in 1717), the Consort of the Emperor 世祖 Shih⁴ Tsu³.

4. 景陵 Ching³ Ling². Here are buried the Emperor 聖祖 Shêng⁴ Tsu³, known from his reign as 康熙 K'ang¹ Hsi¹ (1662–1722), and four Empresses, i.e. 孝誠 Hsiao⁴ Ch'êng²,

[199]

569c 孝昭 Hsiao⁴ Chao¹, 孝懿 Hsiao⁴ I², and 孝恭 Hsiao⁴ Kung¹.

5. 裕 陵 Yü⁴ Ling². Here are buried the Emperor 高宗 Kao¹ Tsung¹, known from his reign as 乾隆 Ch'ien² Lung² (1736-1795), who died and was buried in 1799, and the two Empresses 孝賢 Hsiao⁴ Hsien² and 孝儀 Hsiao⁴ I².

6. 定 陵 Ting⁴ Ling². Here are buried the Emperor 文宗 Wên² Tsung¹, known from his reign as 咸豐 Hsien² Fêng¹ (1851-1861), and the Empress 孝德 Hsiao⁴ Tê².

7. 定東陵 Ting⁴ Tung¹ Ling². Here are buried the Empresses 孝貞 Hsiao⁴ Chên¹ (deceased in 1881) and 孝欽 Hsiao⁴ Ch'in¹ (deceased in 1908), the consorts of the Emperor 文宗 Wên² Tsung¹. The former (by name 慈安 Tz'u² An¹) is buried at a place called 普祥峪 P'u³ Hsiang² Yü⁴ and the latter (by name 慈禧 Tz'u² Hsi³) at 普陀峪 P'u³ T'o² Yü⁴.

8. 惠 陵 Hui⁴ Ling². Here are buried the Emperor 穆宗 Mu⁴ Tsung¹, known from his reign as 同治 T'ung² Chih⁴, (1862-1875), and the Empress 孝哲 Hsiao⁴ Chê².

569c. 西 陵 Hsi¹ Ling², Western Imperial Mausolea; situated 93 miles to the South-west of Peking in the Department of 易州 I⁴ Chou¹, in a valley formerly called 太平峪 T'ai⁴ P'ing² Yü⁴, its name was changed, in 1736, to 永寧山 Yung³ Ning² Shan¹, "Mountains of Eternal Peace."

This group of Imperial Mausolea includes those of Emperors and Empresses as follows :

1. 泰 陵 T'ai⁴ Ling². Here are buried the Emperor 世宗 Shih⁴ Tsung¹, known from his reign as 雍正 Yung¹ Chêng⁴, (1723-1735), and the Empress 孝敬 Hsiao⁴ Ching⁴.

2. 泰東陵 T'ai⁴ Tung¹ Ling². Here is buried the Empress 孝聖 Hsiao⁴ Shêng⁴ (deceased and buried in 1777), the consort of the Emperor 世宗 Shih⁴ Tsung¹.

3. 昌陵 Ch'ang¹ Ling². Here are buried the Emperor **570** 仁宗 Jên² Tsung¹, known from his reign as 嘉慶 Chia¹ Ch'ing⁴, (1796–1820), and the Empress 孝淑 Hsiao⁴ Shu².

4. 昌西陵 Ch'ang¹ Hsi¹ Ling². Here is buried the Empress 孝和 Hsiao⁴ Ho² (deceased in 1849 ; buried in 1853), the Consort of the Emperor 仁宗 Jên² Tsung¹.

5. 慕陵 Mu⁴ Ling². Here are buried the Emperor 宣宗 Hsüan¹ Tsung¹, known from his reign as 道光 Tao⁴ Kuang¹ (1821–1850), and the Empresses 孝穆 Hsiao⁴ Mu⁴ 孝慎 Hsiao⁴ Shên⁴ and 孝全 Hsiao⁴ Ch'üan².

6. 慕東陵 Mu⁴ Tung¹ Ling². Here is buried the Empress 孝靜 Hsiao⁴ Ching⁴ (deceased in 1855 ; buried in 1857), the Consort of the Emperor 宣宗 Hsüan¹ Tsung¹.

7. 崇陵 Ch'ung² Ling². Here is buried the Emperor 德宗 Tê² Tsung¹, known from his reign as 光緒 Kuang¹ Hsü⁴ (1875–1908). For full details *see* No. 189.

570. 承辦事務衙門 Ch'êng² Pan⁴ Shih⁴ Wu⁴ Ya² Mên², Office of the Imperial Mausolea. The 總管 Tsung³ Kuan³, Controller-General of the Banner Garrison, is at the head of this office, being styled (as regards its affairs) 守護陵寢大臣 Shou³ Hu⁴ Ling² Ch'in³ Ta⁴ Ch'ên². For each group of Mausolea in Chihli there is one Office of the Imperial Mausolea (at the Eastern and at the Western Mausolea).

To the Chief of the Office of the Imperial Mausolea there is attached a staff of officials deputed from the Ministry of Rites (郎中 Lang² Chung¹, Department Directors, 員外郎 Yüan² Wai⁴ Lang², Assistant Department Directors and 主事 Chu³ Shih⁴, Secretaries, and officials of the 太常司 T'ai⁴ Ch'ang² Ssu¹, Department of Sacrificial Worship—*see* No. 382B) and from the Imperial Household (尚茶正 Shang⁴ Ch'a² Chêng⁴, Chief Cup-bearers, 尚膳正 Shang⁴ Shan⁴ Chêng⁴, Chief Trencher Knight (*see* No. 91), 內管領 Nei⁴ Kuan³ Ling³,

571 to 572

Overseers, 副 內 管 領 Fu⁴ Nei⁴ Kuan³ Ling³, Assistant Overseers *see* No. 85), etc.

For the General supervision of each group of Imperial Mausolea there are deputed two or three Department Directors (or Assistant Department Directors) from the Ministry of Rites.

571. 陵 寢 駐 防 Ling² Ch'in³ Chu⁴ Fang² (*see* No. 743B), Garrisons at the Imperial Mausolea ; charged with the guarding of Imperial Mausolea.

At the head of each Garrison there is a 陵 寢 總 管 Ling² Ch'in³ Tsung³ Kuan³, Controller-General ; 3A. He is assisted by an 陵 寢 副 總 管 Ling² Ch'in³ Fu⁴ Tsung³ Kuan³, Assistant Controller-General ; 4A, a 陵 寢 翼 長 Ling² Ch'in³ I⁴ Chang³, Brigadier ; 4A, 陵 寢 防 禦 Ling² Ch'in³ Fang² Yü⁴, Captains, and other officials of the same grades as those of provincial Banner garrisons (*see* No. 746).

571A. In addition to the officials mentioned above, for the supervision of repairs to, and the maintenance in order of, Imperial Mausolea there are the following :

1. 陵 寢 司 工 匠 Ling² Ch'in³ Ssu¹ Kung¹ Chiang⁴, Overseers of Works at the Imperial Mausolea ; 4A,

2. 陵 寢 管 理 燒 造 磚 瓦 官 Ling² Ch'in³ Kuan³ Li³ Shao¹ Tsao⁴ Chuan¹ Wa³ Kuan¹, Overseers of Brick and Tile Making for the Imperial Mausolea ; 5A, and

3. 陵 寢 祭 祀 供 應 官 Ling² Ch'in³ Chi⁴ Ssu⁴ Kung¹ Ying¹ Kuan¹, Commissioner of Sacrifices at the Imperial Mausolea ; 6A.

METROPOLITAN TEMPLES,—SACRIFICES,—BUDDHISM, TAOISM AND SHAMANISM.

572. The Ministry of Rites (*see* No. 376) not only has the general supervision of temples but also directs the sacrifices performed therein.

Sacrifices are of three grades :

1. 大祀 Ta⁴ Ssu⁴, Great Sacrifices (at which jade, silk tissues and animals are offered),

2. 中祀 Chung¹ Ssu⁴, also 次祀 Tz'u⁴ Ssu⁴, Superior Sacrifices (at which silk tissues and animals are offered), and

3. 羣祀 Ch'ün² Ssu⁴, also 小祀 Hsiao³ Ssu⁴, Inferior Sacrifices (at which animals are offered).

Great Sacrifices are performed at :

1. 天壇 T'ien¹ T'an¹, The Altar or Temple of Heaven (also called 南郊 Nan² Chiao¹, The Southern Suburbs ; erected in 1420) ; three times yearly :

A. In the first moon, the so-called 祈穀 Ch'i² Ku³, Prayer for a Bountiful Harvest, at the 祈年殿 Ch'i² Nien² Tien¹, Altar of Supplication for a Bountiful Harvest,

B. In the fourth moon, the so-called 雩祀 Yü² Ssu⁴, Prayer for Rain (also 常雩 Ch'ang² Yü²), at the 圜丘 Yüan² Ch'iu¹, Round Hill, and

C. In the eleventh moon, because of the Winter Solstice (冬至 Tung¹ Chih⁴), at the 圜丘 Yüan² Ch'iu¹, Round Hill.

2. At the 地壇 Ti⁴ T'an², Altar or Temple of Earth (also 方澤壇 Fang¹ Tsê² T'an², Altar with the Square Cistern, or 北郊 Pei³ Chiao¹, Northern Suburbs) ; in the fifth moon ; because of the Summer Solstice, 夏至 Hsia⁴ Chih⁴ (this temple was built in 1530).

3. At the 太廟 T'ai⁴ Miao⁴, Great Temple (or Temple of Ancestors of the Reigning Dynasty) ; five times a year :

A. In the first moon, because of the 孟春 Mêng⁴ Ch'un¹, Beginning of Spring,

B. In the fourth moon, because of the 孟夏 Mêng⁴ Hsia⁴, Beginning of Summer,

C. In the seventh moon, because of the 孟秋 Mêng⁴ Ch'iu¹, Beginning of Autumn,

[203]

D. In the tenth moon, because of the 孟 冬 Mêng⁴ Tung¹, Beginning of Winter, and

E. In the twelfth moon, because of the 年 終 Niên² Chung¹, End of the Year, the so-called 祫 祭 Hsia² Chi⁴.

4. At the 社 稷 壇 Shê⁴ Chi³ T'an², Altar of the Spirits Shê and Chi (Spirits—Patrons of the Dynasty); twice yearly :

A. 春 社 Ch'un¹ Shê⁴, in the second or third moon, and

B. 秋 社 Ch'iu¹ Shê⁴, in the eighth moon.

5. At the 文 廟 Wên² Miao⁴, or 孔 聖 廟 K'ung³ Sheng⁴ Miao⁴, Temple of Confucius, also 國 學 Kuo² Hsüeh², State School (先 師 孔 子 Hsien¹ Shih¹ K'ung³ Tzu³); twice yearly :

A. In the second moon (the so-called 春 祭 Ch'un¹ Chi¹, Spring Sacrifice), and B. In the eighth moon (the so-called 秋 祭 Ch'iu¹ Chi¹, Autumn Sacrifice). Superior Sacrifices are offered :

1. At the 朝 日 壇 Chao¹ Jih⁴ T'an², Altar of the Morning Sun ; once a year ; on the 春 分 Ch'un¹ Fên¹, Spring Equinox.

2. At the 夕 月 壇 Hsi¹ Yüeh⁴ T'an², Altar of the Evening Moon ; once a year ; on the 秋 分 Ch'iu¹ Fên¹, Autumn Equinox (in the eighth moon).

3. At the 歷 代 帝 王 廟 Li³ Tai⁴ Ti⁴ Wang² Miao⁴ (or 帝 王 廟 Ti⁴ Wang² Miao⁴), Temple of the Emperors of all Dynasties (built in 1522), twice yearly :

A. In the third moon (the so-called 春 祭 Ch'un¹ Chi¹, Spring Sacrifices), and B. In the ninth moon (the so-called 秋 祭 Ch'iu¹ Chi¹, Autumn Sacrifice).

4. At the 先 農 壇 Hsien¹ Nung² T'an², Altar of the Father of Agriculture ; once a year ; in the third moon.

5. At the 先 蠶 壇 Hsien¹ Ts'an² T'an², Altar of the Mother of Agriculture ; once a year ; in the third moon (this altar was built in 1742).

[204]

6. At the 天 神 壇 T'ien[1] Shên[2] T'an[2], Altar of the Heavenly Spirits ; in case of natural calamities.

7. At the 地 祇 壇 Ti[4] Ch'i[2] T'an[2], Altar of the Spirits of Earth ; in case of natural calamities. (The Altars of the Heavenly Spirits and the Spirits of Earth bear the general name of 神 祇 壇 Shên[2] Ch'i[2] T'an[2]).

8. At the 太 歲 壇 T'ai[4] Sui[4] T'an[2], Altar of Jupiter (King of the Year); twice yearly, *i.e.* in the first and tw lfth moons.

Four of the latter-mentioned altars, *i.e.* those of the Father of Agriculture, of the Spirits of Heaven and Earth, and of Jupiter, are situated in the Temple of Agriculture, which is also known as the 山 川 壇 Shan[1] Ch'uan[1] T'an[2], Temple of Mountains and Rivers.

Inferior Sacrifices are offered :

1. At the 先 醫 廟 Hsien[1] I[1] Miao[4], Temple of Famous Physicians of Antiquity ; twice a year; in the second and eleventh moons.

2. At the 火 神 廟 Huo[3] Shên[2] Miao[4], Temple of the God of Fire ; once a year ; in the sixth moon.

3. At the 文 昌 廟 Wên[2] Ch'ang[1] Miao[4], Temple of the Patron of Education; twice a year ; in the second and eighth moons.

4. At the 關 帝 廟 Kuan[1] Ti[4] Miao[4], Temple of the General 關 羽 Kuan[1] Yü[3], three times yearly ; in the second, fifth and eighth moons.

5. At the 賢 良 祠 Hsien[2] Liang[2] Tz'u[2], Temple of Eminent Statesmen (those who have rendered great service to the present Dynasty ; founded in 1734); twice yearly ; in the second and eighth moons.

6. At the 昭 忠 祠 Chao[1] Chung[1] Tz'u[2], Temple of Zealots of the Dynasty (founded in 1724) ; twice a year; in t second and eighth moons.

[205]

7. At the 雙忠祠 Shuang[1] Chung[1] Tz'u[2]; twice yearly; in the second and eighth moons.

8. At the 獎忠祠 Chiang[3] Chung[1] Tz'u[2]; twice yearly; in the second and eighth moons.

9. At the 褒忠祠 Pao[1] Chung[1] Tz'u[2]; twice yearly; in the second and eighth moons.

10. At the 顯忠祠 Hsien[3] Chung[1] Tz'u[2]; twice a year; in the second and eighth moons.

11. At the 表忠祠 Piao[3] Chung[1] Tz'u[2]; twice yearly; in the second and eighth moons.

12. At the 惠濟祠 Hui[4] Chi[3] Tz'u[2]; twice yearly; in the second and eighth moons.

13. At the 龍神祠 Lung[2] Shên[2] Tz'u[2], Temple of the Dragon Spirit; twice a year; in the second and eighth moons.

14. At the 河神廟 Ho[2] Shên[2] Miao[4], Temple of the River Spirit; twice a year; in the second and eighth moons.

15. At the 旋勇祠 Ching[1] Yung[3] Tz'u[2]; twice yearly; in the second and eighth moons.

16. At the 黑龍潭 Hei[1] Lung[2] T'an[2], Black Dragon Pool (here there is a temple, built in 1771, called 龍王亭 Lung[2] Wang[2] T'ing[2]); twice a year; in the second and eighth moons.

17. At the 白龍潭 Pai[2] Lung[2] T'an[2], White Dragon Pool; twice a year; in the second and eighth moons.

18. At the 玉泉山 Yü[4] Ch'üan[2] Shan[1]; twice a year; in the second and eighth moons.

1⁰. At the 昆明湖 K'un[1] Ming[2] Hu[2] (also 西湖 Hsi[1] Hu[2], lake at the foot of the hill 萬壽山 Wan[4] Shou[4] Shan[1]); twice yearly; in the second and eighth moons.

20 to 26. To the Princes: 睿忠親王 Jui[4] Chung[1] Ch'in[1] Wang[2], 定南武壯王 Ting[4] Nan[2] Wu[3] Chuang[1] Wang[2], 宏毅公 Hung[2] I[4] (Ni) Kung[1], 恪禧公 Ch'üeh[4] Hsi[3] Kung[1], 勤襄公

Ch'in² Hsiang¹ Kung¹, 恪僖公 Ch'üeh¹ Hsi³ Kung¹, and 文襄 公 Wên² Hsiang¹ Kung¹.

27. At the 太廟後殿 T'ai⁴ Miao⁴ Hou¹ Tien⁴, Rear Hall of the Temple of Ancestors (*see* above); on the first day of the first moon and, also, on the birthdays of the Emperor (the thirteenth day of the first moon) and the Empress Dowager (the tenth day of the first moon).

28. At the 顯佑宮 Hsien³ Yu⁴ Kung¹, Temple of the Polar Star (founded in 1415); on the birthdays of the Emperor and the Empress Dowager.

29. At the 東嶽廟 Tung¹ Yüeh⁴ Miao⁴, Temple of the Eastern Sacred Mountain (built in 1317); on the birthdays of the Emperor and the Empress Dowager.

30. At the 都城隍廟 Tu¹ Ch'êng² Huang² Miao⁴, (commonly called 城隍廟 Ch'êng² Huang² Miao⁴; compare No. 573ʙ), Temple of the Patron of the City; on the birthdays of the Emperor and the Empress Dowager.

At the Temples and Altars there are found 奉祀 Fêng⁴ Ssu⁴, Priests, 祀丞 Ssu⁴ Ch'êng², Assistant Priests and a staff of officials of the fourth to sixth ranks.

573. In China, in addition to the predominant religion 儒教 Ju² Chiao⁴, Confucianism (also 名教 Ming² Chiao⁴ or 聖教 Shêng⁴ Chiao⁴), there are the recognized general religions of 佛教 Fo² Chiao⁴ (also 釋教 Shih⁴ Chiao⁴) Buddhism, and 道教 Tao⁴ Chiao⁴, Taoism. With a view to control of the priesthood of these religions there exist certain official ranks.

573ᴀ. 僧錄司 Sêng¹ Lu⁴ Ssu¹, Superior of the Buddhist Priesthood. Two office bearers invested with this title are appointed in each district, department and prefecture throughout the Empire, as principal and deputy, the chief being designated as 正印 Chêng⁴ Yin⁴, or principal, and the second in order as 副印 Fu⁴ Yin⁴, or Deputy, Holder of the Seal. These appointments are made by the local authorities from the leading abbots

573B (方 仗 Fang[1] Chang[4]) of the monasteries and are submitted for approval, when made by subordinate officials, to the provincial government. The Superior acts as a medium of communication between the secular authorities and the priesthood, and depending on the rank of the territorial division with which he is concerned, bears one of the following distinctive titles :

1. 僧 綱 Sêng[1] Kang[1], Superior of the Buddhist Priesthood in a Prefecture ; 9B (the full title is 僧 綱 司 都 綱 Sêng[1] Kang[1] Ssu[1] Tu[1] Kang[1]),

2. 僧 正 Sêng[1] Chêng[4], Superior of the Buddhist Priesthood in a Department, and

3. 僧 會 Sêng[1] Hui[4], Superior of the Buddhist Priesthood in a District.

In addition to the foregoing, in the Buddhist priesthood there are the following ranks (they are very little, if at all, used at present) :

1. 左 善 司 Tso[3] Shan[4] Shih[4], Principal Preceptor, and 右 善 司 Yu[4] Shan[4] Shih[4], Secondary Preceptor ; 6A,

2. 左 闡 教 Tso[3] Ch'an[4] Chiao[4], Principal Preacher, and 右 闡 教 Yu[4] Ch'an[4] Chiao[4], Secondary Preacher ; 6B,

3. 左 講 經 Tso[3] Chiang[3] Ching[1], Principal Expositor, and 右 講 經 Yu[4] Chiang[3] Ching[1], Secondary Expositor ; 8A, and

4. 左 覺 義 Tso[3] Chüeh[2] I[4], Principal Clerk, and 右 覺 義 Yu[4] Chüeh[2] I[4], Secondary Clerk ; 8B.

573B. In the Taoist priesthood the primacy appertains to the hereditary patriarch 張 天 師 Chang[1] T'ien[1] Shih[1], so-called Heavenly Master Chang—in whose body it is believed the spirit of one of the earliest of the Taoist mystics has taken up its abode. This Patriarch (called also 正 一 眞 人 Chêng[1] I[4] Chên[1] Jên[2]) resides on the hill 龍 虎 山 Lung[2] Ju[3] Shan[1], in the district of 貴 溪 縣 Kuei[4] Ch'i[1] Hsien[4], 江 西 Kiangsi province. Excepting the foregoing, the organization of the Taoist priesthood is similar to that of the Buddhist priesthood (compare

No. 573A). Thus, in each district, department and prefecture **573c**
there are two 道 錄 司 Tao⁴ Lu⁴ Ssu¹, Superiors of the Taoist
Priesthood, bearing, from the rank of the territorial division to
which they appertain, one of the following distinctive titles:

1. 道 紀 Tao⁴ Chi⁴, Superior of the Taoist Priesthood in a
Prefecture (the full title is 道 紀 司 道 紀 Tao⁴ Chi⁴ Ssu¹ Tao³
Chi⁴) ; 9ʙ,

2. 道 正 Tao⁴ Chêng⁴, Superior of the Taoist Priesthood
in a Department, and

3. 道 會 Tao⁴ Hui⁴, Superior of the Taoist Priesthood in a
District.

Besides the above-mentioned, in the Taoist priesthood there
are the following ranks :

1. 左 正 Tso³ Chêng⁴, Principal Director, and 右 正 Yu⁴
Cheng⁴, Secondary Director ; 6ᴀ,

2. 左 演 法 Tso³ Yen³ Fa⁴, Principal Hierophant, and
右 演 法 Yu⁴ Yen³ Fa⁴, Secondary Hierophant (performing
certain sacrificial observances in the Imperial temples); 6ʙ,

3. 左 至 靈 Tso³ Chih⁴ Ling², Principal Thaumaturgist,
and 右 至 靈 Yu⁴ Chih⁴ Ling², Secondary Thaumaturgist; 8ᴀ,
(these "miracle workers" conduct services at State temples, of
propitiatory nature, during times of floods or drought ; a similar
duty is performed by Taoist priests, called 陰 陽 正 術 Yin¹
Yang² Chêng⁴ Shu⁴, in temples dedicated to the tutelar spirits of
the various prefectural cities,—the 城 隍 廟 Ch'êng² Huang²
Miao⁴), and

4. 左 至 義 Tso³ Chih⁴ I⁴, Principal Priest of the Lowest
Grade, and 右 至 義 Yu⁴ Chih⁴ I⁴, Secondary Priest of the
Lowest Grade ; 8ʙ.

573c. In addition to the general religions of Buddhism
and Taoism (see Nos. 573A and 573B), there is the religion of
Shamanism, enjoying the official patronage of the Chinese
Government. The substance of this cult consists in the offering

[209]

of sacrifices to Heaven (according to the doctrine of the Shamans, Heaven is understood to be the power ruling the world—God) and to the Saints—as Saints are considered those who benefited mankind during their lives and continue to benefit mankind after death.

In Peking Shamanic services are held at the :

1. 坤寧宮 K'un[1] Ning[2] Kung[1], Palace of the Empress or Shamanic Chapel (daily), and

2. 堂子 T'ang[2] Tzu[3], Shamanic Temple (founded in 1664; monthly).

A peculiarity of Shamanic places of worship is the absence of any sacred vessels or ornaments and the simplicity of their exterior (跳神 T'iao[4] Shên[2], to practice Shamanism ; to dance before an idol and invoke the spirits).

As the Empress, in whose presence no man may appear, sometimes attends Shamanic services, sacrifices at both places of worship mentioned above are, for the most part, offered by women—Shamanic Priestesses and Sub-priestesses (colloquially called, 薩滿太太 Sa[1] Man[3] T'ai[4] T'ai[4]; *see* No. 79c).

The staff of Shamanic priestesses of the Court numbers twelve ; they are usually the wives of members of the Imperial Bodyguards. For their services they receive nothing but the dresses used and they are called, officially, 司祝 Ssu[1] Chu[4], Readers of Prayers. Also, there are : 1. 36 司俎婦人 Ssu[1] Tsu[3] Fu[4] Jên[2], Shamanic Sub-priestesses or Supervisors of Sacrificial Attributes, 2. 37 司碓婦人 Ssu[1] Tui[4] Fu[4] Jên[2], Supervisors of Powdering of Bark, and 3. 19 司香婦人 Ssu[1] Hsiang[1] Fu[4] Jên[2], Supervisors of the Preparation of Incense (for Shamanic services) ; these are wives of the Palace soldiers and receive from one half a tael to two taels and a bag of rice per month from the Court.

In 1747 a mass-book for the Shamanic service was published (in the Manchu language) called " Hosei T'okt'opuha Manchu-sai Vechere Medere Cooli Pitho."

EDUCATION.

574. Until the beginning of the present century education in China was principally based on assiduous study of the classics and their numerous commentaries, the knowledge of which was tested by general examinations of three leading grades (in the prefectural cities, the provincial capital, and, finally, in Peking) and, when recognized as satisfactory, furnished the lucky candidate with a passport to the public service. With such a system there was, of course, no instruction in the applied sciences; even a knowledge of history and geography was required only so far as necessary to commenting on places mentioned in the classics, these studies having a place similar to that of Greek and Latin in our schools furnishing instruction in the ancient languages.

The defects and imperfections of this system were at last recognized by the Chinese Government and, among other reforms undertaken after the Boxer movement, it was resolved, in 1903, to make gradual changes in educational affairs, following the methods serving as the basis of the educational systems of other countries.

The first step in the direction indicated was the establishment of the 學務處 Hsüeh[2] Wu[4] Ch'u[4], Committee of Educational Affairs (compare No. 406; until this time all matters concerning education were in the hands of the Ministry of Rites—compare Nos. 376 and 395).

At the head of the Committee there was placed a 總理 Tsung[3] Li[3], Superintendent, and to him there were attached two 管學大臣 Kuan[3] Hsüeh[2] Ta[4] Ch'ên[2], Members of the Committee of Educational Affairs; in 1905 the Committee was expanded into the Ministry of Education (compare No. 395).

The members of the Committee of Education, 張百熙 Chang[1] Po[2]-hsi[1], 榮慶 Jung[2] Ch'ing[4], and 張之洞 Chang[4]

Chih[1]-tung[4], Governor-General of Hukuang (now dead), were simultaneously directed to compile a new scheme of education, to draw up regulations for schools and colleges, to define the type of educational institutions from the character of the subjects and sciences taught (common, professional and special), and to determine the grade of the education attained on completion of the courses of the educational establishments (elementary, primary, middle, higher, etc.). The results of the labour of the officials mentioned took the form of a voluminous report (with 20 enclosures) which has since served as the basis of all educational advancement in China. This report not only laid down general principles but also expanded regulations for schools and colleges of the most divergent types, beginning with elementary schools and reaching to the "Academy of Sciences" which, in China, is not the highest "institution of science" but, rather, a high institution of learning where those who wish, after completion of their university courses, may extend their knowledge. On the 13th January, 1904, the report was sanctioned by the Emperor and a Decree to this effect was issued the same day.

By the new scheme of education all schools in China may be classed, from the type of education suppled, into the following four groups :

A. General Educational Institutions ; supplying 普通教育 P'u[3] T'ung[1] Chiao[4] Yü[4], General Education ; elementary schools, primary schools of the senior and junior grades, middle schools, higher schools, universities, etc. (see Nos. 575 to 595).

B. Professional Educational Institutions ; supplying 實業 教育 Shih[2] Yeh[4] Chiao[4] Yü[4], Professional Education ; agricultural, industrial and commercial schools of all classes (see Nos. 598 to 617).

C. Normal Schools ; supplying 師範教育 Shih[1] Fan[4] Chiao[4] Yü[4], Pedagogic Education ; normal schools of the senior and junior grades (see Nos. 618 to 620).

[212]

D. Special Educational Institutions; supplying 專門教育 Chuan[1] Mên[2] Chiao[4] Yü[4], Special Education; colleges of all types, *i.e.* Interpreters, Foreign Languages, Law, etc. (*see* Nos. 621 to 627).

ELEMENTARY AND PRIMARY SCHOOLS.

575. 蒙養院 Mêng[2] Yang[3] Yüan[4], Elementary Schools or Preparatory Schools for Infants (from 3 to 7 years of age). These schools aim at furnishing a substitute for 家庭教育 Chia[1] T'ing[2] Chiao[4] Yü[4], Home Instruction, to the extent required by the educational regulations for admittance to Elementary Schools. They are the nearest approach to the 幼稚園 Yu[4] Chih[4] Yüan[2] (also 幼稚舍 Yu[4] Chih[4] Shê[4]), Kindergartens, of foreign countries.

Elementary Schools are established at 育嬰堂 Yü[4] Ying[1] T'ang[2], Orphan Asylums, and at 敬節堂 Ching[4] Chieh[2] T'ang[2], Widows Homes, and sessions, of not more than four hours duration, are held daily under the direction of 乳媼 Ju[3] Ao[4], Wetnurses, and 保姆 Pao[3] Mu[3], Nurses.

At the head of each Elementary School there is a 院董 Yüan[4] Tung[3], Director.

575A. 蒙學堂 Mêng[2] Hsüeh[2] T'ang[2], Elementary Schools; the proposed establishment of these schools was not carried out as it was seen that they would be of practically the same type as the Elementary Schools mentioned above.

576. 小學 Hsiao[3] Hsüeh[2], Primary Schools; including 初等小學堂 Ch'u[1] Teng[3] Hsiao[3], Hsüeh[2] T'ang[2] (also 尋常小學堂 Hsün[2] Ch'ang[2] Hsiao[3] Hsüeh[2] T'ang[2]), Primary Schools of the Junior Grade, 高等小學堂 Kao[1] Têng[3] Hsiao[3] Hsüeh[2] T'ang[2], Primary Schools of the Senior Grade, and, when both grades are combined in one establishment, 兩等小學堂 Liang[3] Teng[3] Hsiao[3] Hsüeh[2] T'ang[2], Primary Schools of the Junior and Senior Grades.

577. At the initiative of the Ministry of Education, and sanctioned by Imperial Edict of the 15th May, 1909, Primary Schools of the Junior Grade were reformed so as to provide three courses of study, *i.e.* 1. 完全科 Wan² Ch'üan² K'o¹, Full Course of five years, and 2 and 3. 簡易科 Chien³ I⁴ K'o¹, Abridged Course of three and four years. Accordingly, there are now three types of Primary Schools of the Junior Grade:

1. 初等小學堂完全科 Ch'u¹ Têng³ Hsiao³ Hsüeh² T'ang² Wan² Ch'üan² K'o¹, Primary School of the Junior Grade giving Full Course of Study.

2. 四年級小學簡易科 Ssu⁴ Nien² Chi² Hsiao³ Hsüeh² Chien³ I⁴ K'o¹, Primary School of the Junior Grade with Abridged Course of four years, and

3. 三年級小學簡易科 San¹ Nien² Chi² Hsiao² Hsiao³ Hsüeh² Chien³ I⁴ K'o¹, Primary School of the Junior Grade with Abridged Course of three years.

The number of subjects taught was reduced from eight to five (history, geography and the natural sciences were discarded; ethics, literature, arithmetic, the classics and callisthenics were retained) and 隨意科 Sui² I⁴ K'o¹, Optional Subjects were introduced (manual training, drawing, music and singing).

On completion of the course of study of the Primary Schools of the Junior Grade, pupils proceed to Professional Schools (*see* below) or to:

577ᴀ. 高等小學堂 Kao¹ Têng³ Hsiao³ Hsüeh² T'ang², Primary Schools of the Senior Grade. These schools furnish instruction in the same subjects as do the Primary Schools of the Junior Grade, but more thoroughly and to a greater number of hours per week (36 instead of 30). Their course of study covers years.

Primary Schools are established in cities, towns, villages and marts (of the Junior Grade, obligatory; of the Senior Grade, optional) according to the following scheme:

[214]

In administrative centres of departments and districts the
establishment of at least one Primary School of the Senior Grade
is obligatory, the establishment of Primary Schools of the Junior
Grade in these centres, as well as the establishment of Primary
Schools of both grades in other administrative centres, is
obligatory, to a number depending on the population of these
places.

Besides 官 立 Kuan[1] Li[4], Government Schools, the founding
of 公 立 Kung[1] Li[4], Municipal, and 私 立 Ssu[1] Li[4], Private,
Schools is urged by the Government.

577B. For a Primary School (of either grade) there is
a 校 長 Hsiao[4] Chang[3], Director (*see* No. 635A), who has a staff
made up of 正 教 員 Chêng[4] Chiao[4] Yüan[2], Teachers (*see* No.
637), 副 教 員 Fu[4] Chiao[4] Yüan[2], Assistant Teachers (*see* No.
638) and 1 to 2 司 事 Ssu[1] Shih[4], Secretaries (*see* No. 650).

577c. Satisfactory completion of the course of a Primary
School of the Senior Grade carries with it the following
privileges :

Those who complete the course with one of the first three
ratings (1st, 2nd or 3rd) may, after a test examination, join the
Middle Schools, Normal Schools of the Junior Grade, or Middle
Professional Schools. Should they join one of these, and
complete the course, they receive the degree 廩 生 Lin[3] Shêng[1],
if they attain the first rating, 增 生 Tsêng[1] Shêng[1], if they
attain the second rating, and 附 生 Fu[4] Shêng[1], if they attain
the third rating (*see* Nos. 629A and 631); should they attain the
fourth rating, they are detained with the degree 佾 生 I[4] Shêng[1],
for continued study and, should they again fail to qualify for
one of the three first ratings and be unwilling to remain another
year, they receive a document certifying that they have
completed the course of study of a Primary School of the Senior
Grade. Those who attain the fifth rating merely receive a list
of their examination marks.

578 578. 女學 Nü³ Hsüeh², Female Schools. A scheme for the establishment of such schools was brought forward by the Ministry of Education in 1907 (sanctioned by the Emperor on the 8th March, 1907), it being clearly recognized that the domestic education mapped out for females in the educational programme of 1903 was incomplete, provision being made for the founding of 女子小學堂 Nü³ Tzu³ Hsiao³ Hsüeh² T'ang², Female Primary Schools, to include, as in the case of male schools :

1. 女子初等小學堂 Nü³ Tzu³ Ch'u¹ Têng³ Hsiao³ Hsüeh² T'ang², Female Primary Schools of the Junior Grade,

2. 女子高等小學堂 Nü³ Tzu³ Kao¹ Têng³ Hsiao³ Hsüeh² T'ang², Female Primary Schools of the Senior Grade, and

3. 女子兩等小學堂 Nü³ Tzu³ Liang³ Têng³ Hsiao³ Hsüeh² T'ang², Female Primary Schools of the Junior and Senior Grades, when both grades are combined in one establishment (*see* No. 576).

Female Primary Schools of the Junior Grade accept as pupils girls of from seven to 14 years of age ; the course of study covers four years and from 24 to 28 hours of instruction are given weekly ; Female Primary Schools of the Senior Grade accept as pupils girls of from 11 to 14 years of age ; the course of study covers four years and from 28 to 30 hours of instruction are given weekly.

Schools of the junior grade furnish instruction in ethics, literature, arithmetic, handiwork and callisthenics. Also, instruction is given in drawing, music and singing to those who desire it.

Schools of the senior grade follow the same programme as do those of the junior grade with the exception that the history and geography of China, natural sciences and drawing are added to the obligatory studies.

In charge of each Female School is a 堂長 T'ang² Chang³, **579**
Head Schoolmistress, whose staff consists of 正教習 Chêng⁴
Chiao⁴ Hsi², Schoolmistresses, 副教習 Fu⁴ Chiao⁴ Hsi²,
Assistant Schoolmistresses. General affairs are attended to by
a 經理 Ching¹ Li³, Manager, a 書記 Shu¹ Chi⁴, Clerk, and a
庶務員 Shu⁴ Wu⁴ Yüan², Steward (the latter two officials are
found only at schools with a large enrollment; most schools
having a Manager only).

579. To the number of Primary Schools there must be
added the following :

1. 蒙養學堂 Mêng² Yang³ Hsüeh² T'ang², Elementary
Schools ; established in the Dependencies of China and having a
course of study similar to that of Primary Schools of the Junior
Grade (*see* No. 577).

2. 半日學堂 Pan⁴ Jih⁴ Hsüeh² T'ang², Half-day Schools.
(holding sessions part of the day only—in the morning, the
afternoon or the evening, as the students have leisure time), with
a course of study similar to that of Primary Schools of the
Junior Grade. These schools are found in the majority of cities
of China proper. The Acting Imperial Agent, 三多 San¹ To¹,
at K'urun (Urga) urged that these schools be established in
Mongolia and Outer China in general with a view to spreading
the study of Chinese amongst the population of these places;
this scheme was, however, not acted upon as, owing to the
existence of schools of the type 蒙養學堂 Mêng² Yang³
Hsüeh² T'ang², it was feared that the enrollment would be
insufficient.

3. 模範學堂 Mu² Fan⁴ Hsüeh² T'ang², also, 模範學
塾 Mu² Fan⁴ Hsüeh² Shu², Model Schools. These schools,
with a course of study of Primary Schools of the Junior Grade,
are established at provincial capitals to serve as a model for
Primary Schools of the Junior Grade.

[217]

580 4. 簡 易 識 字 學 (堂) 塾 Chien[3] I[4] Shih[4] Tzu[3] Hsüeh[2] (T'ang[2]) Shu[2], Schools for Teaching the Commonly Used Chinese Characters. According to the programme of constitutional reforms, schools of this type were to be inaugurated in 1909 and the number of characters taught was to be reduced to a minimum—special manuals to be prepared by the Ministry of Education. By regulations prepared by the Ministry of Education, sanctioned by the Emperor on the 10th January, 1910, these schools were established for illiterate adults and children of the poor, with a course of from one to three years, two to three lessons daily, and gratuitous instruction. The text books used are the 簡 易 識 字 課 本 Chien[3] I[4] Shih[4] Tzu[3] K'o[4] Pên[3], Manuals of Common Characters, and the 國 民 必 讀 課 本 Kuo[2] Min[2] Pi[4] Tu[2] K'o[4] Pên[3], Popular Science Manuals, and there is some instruction in arithmetic. Those who complete the course of three years may join Primary Schools of the Junior Grade (*see* No. 577) in the class which has already completed three years of the course.

5. 土 司 學 堂 T'u[3] Ssu[1] Hsüeh[2] T'ang[2], Schools for Native Tribes; these are established in provinces where native tribes are found (for instance, in Kuangsi; *see* report of the Governor 張 鳴 岐 Chang[1] Ming[2]-ch'i[1], dated the 5th November, 1909), with a view to the training of a staff of officials from the tribesmen themselves.

6. Particulars as to 八 旗 小 學 堂 Pa[1] Ch'i[2] Hsiao[3] Hsüeh[2] T'ang[2], Primary Schools for Bannermen, and 駐 防 滿 營 小 學 堂 Chu[4] Fang[2] Man[3] Ying[2] Hsiao[3] Hsüeh[2] T'ang[2], Primary Schools at the Manchu Garrisons are given in Nos. 717A and 717B.

MIDDLE SCHOOLS.

580. 中 學 堂 Chung[1] Hsüeh[2] T'ang[2], Middle Schools; for those who have completed the course of Primary Schools of

581
to
582

the Senior Grade (*see* No. 577A); with a course of study of five years and 36 hours instruction weekly. These schools are established in prefectural cities (obligatory) and in departmental and district towns (optional). The enrollment of each is between 300 and 400 students, who follow a course of study similar to that of Normal Schools of the Junior Grade (*see* No. 618), with the exception that much more stress is laid on the study of foreign languages.

581. By a Memorial from the Ministry of Education, sanctioned by the Emperor on the 15th May, 1909, the organization of Middle Schools was revised so as to supply two distinct courses of study: 1. 文 科 Wên² K'o¹, Classical Course, and 2. 實 科 Shih² K'o¹, Scientific Course. The Classical Course comprises the following subjects:

A. Major Subjects: The Classics and commentaries, Chinese language and literature, foreign languages (English or German—by choice—and, also, others when local surroundings seem to demand them), history and geography.

B. Minor Subjects: Ethics, mathematics, physics, natural history, jurisprudence, political economy, drawing and callisthenics.

The Scientific Course comprises the following subjects:

A. Major Subjects: Foreign languages, mathematics, physics, chemistry, and natural history.

B. Minor Subjects: Ethics, the Classics, and their commentaries, Chinese language and literature, history, geography, drawing, manual training, jurisprudence, political economy and callisthenics.

In addition to the above-mentioned subjects, both courses supply instruction in music and singing to those who desire it.

582. At the head of each Middle School there is a Director (*see* No. 635); instruction is supplied by Teachers (*see* No. 637). Also, there are one Librarian (one of the Teachers *see* No. 639), one Secretary (*see* No. 642), one

582A
to
583

Accountant (*see* No. 643), one Steward (*see* No. 641) and two Proctors (at schools where there are dormitories, *see* No. 646).

582A. Satisfactory completion of the course of the Middle Schools carries with it the following privileges :

Those who complete the course with one of the first three ratings (first, second or third) may, after a test examination, join the Higher Schools, Normal Schools of the Senior Grade and Higher Professional Schools. Should they join one of these, and complete the course they receive the degree 拔 貢 Pa² Kung⁴, if they attain the first rating, 優 貢 Yu¹ Kung⁴, if they attain the second, and 歲 貢 Sui² Kung⁴, if they attain the third (*see* Nos. 629 and 631); should they attain the fourth rating, they are detained for continued study, with the degree 優 廩 生 Yu¹ Lin³ Shêng¹, and, should they again fail to qualify for one of the three first ratings and be unwilling to remain another year, they receive a document certifying they that have completed the course of study of a Middle School. Those who attain the fifth rating merely receive a list of their examination marks.

HIGHER SCHOOLS.

583. 高等學堂 Kao¹ Têng³ Hsüeh² T'ang², Higher Schools ; for those who have completed the course of study of Middle Schools (*see* Nos. 580 to 582); having 36 hours of instruction weekly and a course of study of three years. These schools are established at the provincial capitals, each with an enrollment of from 300 to 500 scholars, and their raison d'être is the preparation of students for the University.

The Higher Schools have three courses of study ; subjects obligatory in all courses are : ethics, the essentials of the Classics, Chinese language and literature and callisthenics.

In addition to the foregoing, the course preparatory to study in the Classical Department (*see* No. 585), the Department of Law and Administration (*see* No. 586), the Department of History and Philology (*see* No. 587) and the Commercial Department (*see* No. 592) of the University calls for the study of history, geography, logic, common and financial law and foreign languages—English is obligatory, French or German, as the student elects, and Latin is optional.

The course preparatory to study in the Department of Mathematics and Physics (*see* No. 589), the Engineering Department (*see* No. 591) and the Department of Agriculture (*see* No. 590) of the University demands, in addition to the subjects common to all courses, study of the following : mathematics, physics, chemistry, geology, mineralogy and foreign languages— English (and in some cases German) is obligatory, French or German, as the student elects, and Latin is optional. Also, for those who wish, and as an aid in the speciality they intend to follow, instruction is given in botany, zoology, topography, etc.

The course preparatory to study in the Medical Department of the University comprises mathematics, physics, chemistry, zoology, botany, Latin and foreign languages—German is obligatory and English or French is studied as the student elects.

Completion of the course of a Higher School carries with it the following rewards and distinctions :

1. Those who graduate with the first rating receive the degree 舉 人 Chü³ Jên² (*see* Nos. 629B and 631) and are appointed, after a 覆 試 Fu⁴ Shih¹, Test Examination, 內 閣 中 書 Nei⁴ Ko² Chung¹ Shu¹ (*see* No. 137), at the Capital—or 知 州 Chih¹ Chou¹ (*see* No. 855)—in the provinces.

2. Those who graduate with the second rating receive the degree 舉 人 Chü³ Jên² (*see* Nos. 629B and 631) and are appointed, after a test examination (*see* above), as 中 書 科 中 書

583A
to
583C

Chung¹ Shu¹ K'o¹ Chung¹ Shu¹ (*see* No. 137A)—at the Capital—or as 知 縣 Chi¹ Hsien⁴ (*see* No. 856)—in the provinces.

3. Those who graduate with the third rating receive the degree 舉人 Chü³ Jên² (*see* Nos. 629B and 631) and are appointed, after a test examination, as 司 務 Ssu¹ Wu⁴ (*see* No. 296)—at the Capital—or as 通 判 T'ung¹ P'an⁴ (*see* No. 849A)—in the provinces.

4. Those who graduate with the fourth rating are detained for continued study and, should they again fail to attain one of the three first ratings and be unwilling to remain another year, they receive a document certifying that they have completed the course of a Middle School.

5. Those who graduate with the fifth rating merely receive a list of their examination marks.

583A. At each Higher School there is a Director (*see* No. 635), who is directly in control of a Preceptor (*see* No. 636), a Steward (*see* No. 641) and an Inspector of Dormitories (*see* No. 645).

The Preceptor is in charge of Teachers (*see* No. 637), Assistant Teachers (*see* No. 638) and the Librarian (*see* No. 639).

The Steward's staff consists of a Secretary (*see* No. 642), an Accountant (*see* No. 643) and a Clerk of Works (*see* No. 644).

To the Inspector of Dormitories there are subordinated Proctors (*see* No. 646) and Assistant Inspectors of Dormitories (*see* No. 647).

583B. For particulars concerning 宗 室 覺 羅 八 旗 高 等 學 堂 Tsung¹ Shih⁴ Chüeh² Lo² Pa¹ Ch'i² Kao¹ Têng³ Hsüeh² T'ang², Higher Schools for Imperial Clansmen and Bannermen, *see* No. 717A.

583C. The majority of the so-called 專 門 學 堂 Chuan¹ Mên² Hsüeh² T'ang², Special Schools, such as the College of

Interpreters (*see* No. 626), may be considered as Higher Schools.

UNIVERSITIES.

584. 大學堂 Ta⁴ Hsüeh² T'ang², Universities; for students who have completed the course of Higher Schools (*see* No. 583); with a three years (in the Law and Medical Departments, four years) course. These are to be established in all the provinces; at present there is only one University—at Peking, composed of eight 分科大學 Fên¹ K'o¹ Ta⁴ Hsüeh², Departments.

585. 經學科大學 Ching¹ Hsüeh² K'o¹ Ta⁴ Hsüeh², Classical Department; with eleven courses of instruction:

1. 周易學門 Chou¹ I⁴ Hsüeh² Mên², Course in the "Book of Changes," as revised in the Chou Dynasty.

2. 尚書學門 Shang⁴ Shu¹ Hsüeh² Mên², Course in the "Book of History."

3. 毛詩學門 Mao² Shih¹ Hsüeh² Mên², Course in the "Book of Odes," as revised by Mao Ch'ang.

4. 春秋左傳學門 Ch'un¹ Ch'iu¹ Tso³ Chuan⁴ Hsüeh² Mên², Course in the "Annals," with the commentary of Tso-chuan.

5. 春秋三傳學門 Ch'un¹ Ch'iu¹ San¹ Chuan⁴ Hsüeh² Mên², Course in the "Annals," with three commentaries.

6. 周禮學門 Chou¹ Li³ Hsüeh² Mên², Course in the Book of Rites" of the Chou Dynasty compiled by Chou-kung.

7. 儀禮學門 I² Li³ Hsüeh² Mên², Course in the "Ritual of Deportment."

8. 禮記學門 Li³ Chi⁴ Hsüeh² Mên², Course in the "Book of Rites."

9. 論語學門 Lun² Yü³ Hsüeh² Mên², Course in the "Analects of Confucius."

10. 孟子學門 Mêng⁴ Tzu³ Hsüeh² Mên², Course in the Writings of Mencius, and

11. 理學門 Li³ Hsüeh² Mên², Course in Natural Philosophy (of China).

585ᴀ. In accordance with a recommendation from the Ministry of Education, dated the 10th January, 1910, and sanctioned by the Emperor, foreigners are permitted to attend lectures and exercises at the classical Department of the University and brief regulations for their observance have been drawn up by the Ministry mentioned.

586. 法政科大學 Fa⁴ Chêng⁴ K'o¹ Ta⁴ Hsüeh², Department of Law and Administration; this gives two courses of instruction :

1. 政治學門 Cheng⁴ Chih⁴ Hsüeh² Mên², Course in Administration, and

2. 法律學門 Fa⁴ Lü⁴ Hsüeh² Mên², Course in Law.

587. 文學科大學 Wên² Hsüeh² K'o⁴ Ta⁴ Hsüeh², Department of History and Philology; consisting of nine courses :

1. 中國史學門 Chung¹ Kuo² Shih³ Hsüeh² Mên², Course in Chinese History,

2. 萬國史學門 Wan⁴ Kuo² Shih³ Hsüeh² Mên², Course in History of the World,

3. 中外地理學門 Chung¹ Wai⁴ Ti⁴ Li³ Hsüeh² Mên², Course in Geography of China and other Countries.

4. 中國文學門 Chung¹ Kuo² Wên² Hsüeh² Mên², Course in Chinese Literature,

5. 英國文學門 Ying¹ Kuo² Wên² Hsüeh² Mên², Course in English Literature,

6. 法國文學門 Fa⁴ Kuo² Wên² Hsüeh² Mên², Course in French Literature,

7. 德國文學門 Tê² Kuo² Wên² Hsüeh² Mên², Course in German Literature,

8. 俄國文學門 Ê⁴ Kuo² Wên² Hsüeh² Mên², Course in Russian Literature, and

9. 日本國文學門 Jih⁴ Pên³ Kuo² Wên² Hsüeh² Mên², Course in Japanese Literature.

588. 醫科大學 I¹ K'o¹ Ta⁴ Hsüeh², Department of Medicine; with two courses:

1. 醫學門 I¹ Hsüeh² Mên², Course in Medicine, and
2. 藥學門 Yao⁴ Hsüeh² Mên², Course in Pharmaceutics.

589. 格致科大學 Ko² Chih⁴ K'o¹ Ta⁴ Hsüeh², Department of Mathematics and Physics; having six courses of study:

1. 算學門 Suan⁴ Hsüeh² Mên², Course in Mathematics,
2. 星學門 Hsing¹ Hsüeh² Mên², Course in Astronomy,
3. 物理學門 Wu⁴ Li³ Hsüeh² Mên², Course in Physics,
4. 化學門 Hu⁴ Hsüeh² Mên², Course in Chemistry,
5. 動植物學門 Tung⁴ Chih² Wu⁴ Hsüeh² Mên², Course in Botany and Zoology, and
6. 地質學門 Ti⁴ Chih⁴ Hsüeh² Mên², Course in Geology.

590. 農科大學 Nung² K'o¹ Ta⁴ Hsüeh², Department of Agriculture; with four courses:

1. 農學門 Nung² Hsüeh² Mên², Course in Agriculture,
2. 農藝化學門 Nung² I⁴ Hua⁴ Hsüeh² Mên², Course in the Chemistry of Agriculture,
3. 林學門 Lin² Hsüeh² Mên², Course in Forestry, and
4. 獸醫學門 Shou⁴ I¹ Hsüeh² Mên², Course in Veterinary Surgery.

591. 工科大學 Kung¹ K'o¹ Ta⁴ Hsüeh², Polytechnic Department; with courses:

1. 土木工學門 T'u³ Mu⁴ Kung¹ Hsüeh² Mên², Course in Engineering,
2. 機器工學門 Chi¹ Ch'i⁴ Kung¹ Hsüeh² Mên², Course in Machine Designing,
3. 造船學門 Tsao⁴ Ch'uan² Hsüeh² Mên², Course in Shipbuilding,

592
to
592ᴀ

4. 造兵器學門 Tsao⁴ Ping¹ Ch'i⁴ Hsüeh² Mên², Course in Arms Manufacture,

5. 電氣學門 Tien⁴ Ch'i⁴ Hsüeh² Mên², Course in Electricity,

6. 應用化學門 Ying¹ Yung⁴ Hua⁴ Hsüeh² Mên², Course in Industrial Chemistry,

7. 建築學門 Chien⁴ Chu² Hsüeh² Mên², Course in Building.

8. 火藥學門 Huo³ Yao⁴ Hsüeh² Mên², Course in Explosives, and

9. 採礦及冶金學門 Ts'ai³ Kung³ Chi² Yeh³ Chin¹ Hsüeh² Mên², Course in Mining and Metallurgy.

592. 商科大學 Shang¹ K'o¹ Ta⁴ Hsüeh², Commercial Department; having three courses of study:

1. 銀行及保險學門 Yin² Hang² Chi² Pao³ Hsien³ Hsüeh² Mên², Course in Banking and Insurance,

2. 貿易及販運學門 Mao⁴ I⁴ Chi² Fan⁴ Yün⁴ Hsüeh² Mên², Course in Business and Transportation, and

3. 關稅學門 Kuan¹ Shui⁴ Hsüeh² Mên², Course in Customs Administration.

592ᴀ. 豫備科 Yü⁴ Pei⁴ K'o¹, Preparatory Department; this Department came into existence at the University in December, 1904, to prepare students for enrollment in the regular classes, thus playing the role of a Higher School (*see* No. 583). Early in 1909 its first class was graduated and, in the Autumn of that year, these students were enrolled in the various Departments of the University.

For the reason mentioned above, the Ministry of Education submitted a report (sanctioned by the Emperor on the 25th April, 1909), recommending that the 京師大學堂豫備科 Ching¹ Shih¹ Ta⁴ Hsüeh² T'ang² Yü⁴ Pei⁴ K'o¹, Preparatory Department of the Peking (Metropolitan) University be

[226]

reorganized as the 京師高等學堂 Ching[1] Shih[1] Kao[1] Têng[3] Hsueh[2] T'ang[2], Peking (Metropolitan) Higher School.

592B. 師範館 Shih[1] Fan[4] Kuan[3], also 優級師範科 Yu[1] Chi[2] Shih[1] Fan[4] K'o[1], Normal Department; organized at the University in December, 1904, with a programme similar to that of Normal Schools of the Senior Grade (*see* Nos. 618 to 620). Its first class was graduated early in 1909. This Department is later to be removed from University control and reorganized as a Normal School of the Senior Grade (*see* Nos. 618 to 620).

593. The senior official of the University is the Rector (*see* No. 633), and he is directly in charge of the Deans of the various Departments (*see* No. 634; eight in all, there being eight Department).

To each Dean there are subordinated : one Preceptor (*see* No. 636), one Steward (*see* No. 641) and one Inspector of Dormitories.

The Preceptor is directly in charge of Professors (*see* No. 637) and Assistant Professors (*see* No. 638); the Steward controls Secretaries (*see* No. 642), the Accountants (*see* No. 643) and the Clerks of Works (*see* No. 644); while the Inspector of Dormitories supervises Proctors (*see* No. 646), Assistant Inspectors of Dormitories (*see* No. 647) and the Health Officers (*see* No. 648).

In addition to the officials mentioned above, the Rector is directly in charge of the various Professors who are deputed to carry on the duties of the positions given below ;

1. 植物園經理官 Chih[2] Wu[4] Yüan[2] Ching[1] Li[3] Kuan[1], Curator of the Botanical Gardens,

2. 天文臺經理官 T'ien[1] Wên[2] T'ai[2] Ching[1] Li[3] Kuan[1], Director of the Observatory,

3. 動物園經理官 Tung[4] Wu[4] Yüan[2] Ching[1] Li[3] Kuan[1], Curator of the Zoological Gardens,

592B to 593

[227]

4. 演習林經理官 Yen³ Hsi² Lin² Ching¹ Li³ Kuan¹, Director of the Forestry Station,

5. 圖書館經理官 T'u² Shu¹ Kuan³ Ching¹ Li³ Kuan¹, Librarian, and

6. 醫院經理官 I¹ Yuan⁴ Ching¹ Li³ Kuan¹, Supervisor of the Hospital.

593A. 會議所 Hui⁴ I⁴ So³, University Council; under the presidency of the Rector (*see* No. 633). This meets for the discussion of questions affecting the University as a whole and the Deans (*see* No. 634), the Preceptor (*see* No. 636), the Professors (*see* No. 637), the Assistant Professors (*see* No. 638) and the Proctors make up its membership.

593B. 教員監學會議所 Chiao⁴ Yüan² Chien¹ Hsüeh² Hui⁴ I⁴ So¹, Department Councils; under the presidency of the Dean of the Department concerned. These Councils, made up of the Preceptor and the Professors, the Assistant Professors and the Proctors of the respective Departments (compare No. 593A) meet to discuss questions affecting the Department alone.

593c. Completion of the course of the University carries with it the following rewards in the public service:

1. Those who graduate with the first rating receive the degree of 進士出身 Chin⁴ Shih⁴ Ch'u¹ Shên¹ (*see* Nos. 629c and 631), are enrolled at the National Academy as 編脩 Pien¹ Hsiu¹ (*see* No. 200B) and 檢討 Chien³ T'ao³ (*see* No. 200c), and are expected to join the Academy of Sciences (*see* No. 594), should they be unwilling to join, they receive appointments in the provinces.

The reward to be bestowed on the student graduating with the highest rank (optimus), who receives an appointment to the Academy of Sciences as 脩撰 Hsiu¹ Chuan⁴ (*see* No. 200A), will be decided when the first class is graduating.

2. Those who graduate with the second rating are given the degree of 進士出身 Chin⁴ Shih⁴ Ch'u¹ Shên¹ (*see* Nos.

629c and 631), are enrolled in the National Academy as **594**
庶 吉 士 Shu⁴ Chi² Shih⁴ (*see* No. 201), and are expected to join
the Academy of Sciences (*see* No. 594), should they not desire
to join, they receive appointments in the provinces.

3. Those who graduate with the third rating receive the
Degree of 進 士 出 身 Chin⁴ Shih⁴ Ch'u¹ Shên¹ (*see* Nos. 629c
and 631), are enrolled in the Ministries as 主 事 Chu³ Shih⁴
(*see* No. 292), and are called upon to join the Academy of
Sciences (*see* No. 594), in cases of unwillingness to join, appointments are granted in the provinces.

4. Those who graduate with the fourth rating receive the
degree of 同 進 士 出 身 T'ung² Chin⁴ Shih⁴ Ch'u¹ Shên¹ (*see* Nos.
629c and 631) and remain at the University for another year's
study. Should they then fail to attain one of the three senior
ratings, and be unwilling to remain for further study, they
receive appointments in the provinces as 知 縣 Chih¹ Hsien⁴ (*see*
No. 856).

5. Those who attain the fifth rating on graduation merely
receive a list of their examination marks and are not permitted
to remain for further study.

594. 通 儒 院 T'ung¹ Ju² Yüan⁴ (also 大 學 院 Ta⁴
Hsiieh² Yüan⁴), Academy of Sciences (compare No. 574); this
institution is intended for those who complete the University
course (*see* No. 584) and wish to perfect themselves in their
chosen lines of study. The course covers five years.

At the Academy of Sciences there is no fixed course;
the students themselves arrange the subjects they wish to study—
by order of the Dean (of the University); under the guidance
of one of the Professors (of the University) of the Department
conforming to the speciality followed. On completion of their
studies each student is called upon to prepare a thesis which,
when approved by the Department Council concerned (*see* No.
593ʙ), is submitted through the Rector of the University and

595 the President of the Ministry of Education to the Emperor and a reward is requested for the author.

Students at the Academy of Sciences pay no fees and may, with the permission of the University Council (*see* No. 593A), be sent to various places by the Government for studying questions pertaining to their specialities.

At the end of each year all those who are studying at the Academy of Sciences submit the results of their researches to the various Deans, who transmit them to the University Council for examination.

The Rector of the University (*see* Nos. 593 and 633) is at the head of the Academy of Sciences ; the direct supervision of its affairs appertains to the Deans of the various Departments of the University (*see* Nos. 593 and 634).

595. 仕學館 Shih⁴ Hsüeh² Kuan³, College for Officials ; established at the Peking (Metropolitan) University. At the present time this College is not functioning as its work—the supplementing of the education of officials—is now carried on by the College of Law and Administration (*see* No. 623).

Completion of the course of study of the College for Officials carried with it the following rewards :

1. Those who graduated with the first and second ratings received the degree of 副榜 Fu⁴ Pang³ (*see* Nos. 629B and 631), unless, of course, they already possessed the degree of 舉人 Chü³ Jên², and according to their official position were recommended for promotion.

2. Those who graduated with the third rating were recommended for promotion, but got no degree.

3. Those who graduated with the fourth rating were detained for further study and, should they again fail to attain one of the three senior ratings and be unwilling to study further, they received a document certifying that they had attended

the full course of the College and were granted a one degree promotion in rank (加 一 級 Chia[1] I[1] Chi[2]).

4. Those who graduated with the fifth rating merely received a list of their examination marks (考試分數單 K'ao[3] Shih[4] Fên[1] Shu[4] Tan[1]).

595ᴀ. 仕 學 館 Shih[4] Hsüeh[2] Kuan[3], Colleges for Officials (in the provinces); compare No. 595. These have been established with the same object as were the 課吏館 K'o[4] Li[4] Kuan[3] (see No. 597); when Colleges of Law and Administration (see Nos. 623 and 623ᴀ) have been established these will be abolished.

595ʙ. For particulars concerning 仕學速成科 Shih[4] Hsüeh[2] Su[2] Ch'êng[2] K'o[1], Accelerated Course of Study for Officials, at the 課 吏 館 K'o[4] Li[4] Kuan[3], see No. 597ᴀ.

596. 進 士 館 Chin[4] Shih[4] Kuan[3], College for Metropolitan Graduates ; established in accordance with regulations drawn up in 1903—supplementary regulations were compiled on the 26th September, 1904, at Peking. The aim of this institution is to give modern education to those who have obtained the literary degree 進 士 Chin[4] Shih[4], Metropolitan Graduate, at the competitions held according to the former scheme of education (see Nos. 628 and 629ᴄ). The course of study covers three years and there are 24 lectures weekly. Attendance is obligatory for Metropolitan Graduates of less than 35 years of age ; those over 35 years of age may request appointments as District Magistrates in the provinces but they are compelled to attend the local 仕 學 館 Shih[4] Hsüeh[2] Kuan[3] (see No. 595ᴀ) or 課 吏 館 K'o[4] Li[4] Kuan see No. 597), Colleges for Officials, or, when these are abolished, the Colleges of Law and Administration (see Nos. 623 and 623ᴀ).

The course of study at the College for Metropolitan Graduates includes the following :

History, geography, pedagogy, jurisprudence, political economy, international law, strategy, engineering, commerce

597
to
597ᴀ

and natural science. Optional subjects include European and Japanese languages and literature, mathematics and callisthenics.

Those who successfully complete the three years course are presented to the Emperor and receive rewards according to their attainments.

At the head of the College for Metropolitan Graduates there is a Director (*see* No. 635) and, subordinated to him, there are one Preceptor (*see* No. 636), one Steward (*see* No. 641) and one Inspector of Dormitories (*see* No. 645).

The Preceptor is in charge of the Chinese and foreign Professors (*see* No. 637) and the 助教 Chu⁴ Chiao⁴, Assistant Professors (*see* No. 638).

The Steward is in charge of the Secretary (*see* No. 642), the Accountant (*see* No. 638) and the Clerk of Works (*see* No. 644).

Under the supervision of the Inspector of Dormitories are the Proctors (*see* No. 646) and the Assistant Inspectors of Dormitories (*see* No. 647).

597. 課吏館 K'o⁴ Li⁴ Kuan³, Colleges for Officials (for providing officials with modern education; compare No. 595ᴀ). These institutions are found throughout the provinces; they are to be abolished on the institution of Colleges of Law and Administration (*see* Nos. 623 to 623ᴀ).

597ᴀ. 仕學速成科 Shih⁴ Hsüeh² Su² Ch'êng² K'o¹, Accelerated Course of Study for Officials; this was instituted, as proposed in a Memorial from the President of the Ministry of Education (sanctioned by the Emperor on the 3rd August, 1905), at the 課吏館 K'o⁴ Li⁴ Kuan³ (*see* No. 597) and the complete course covers one and one-half years. The studies are those of the Judicial Course of the Department of Law and Administration of the University.

PROFESSIONAL SCHOOLS. 598

598. 實業學堂 Shih² Yeh⁴ Hsüeh² T'ang², Professional Schools; these are intended to contribute towards the development of the country along the lines of agriculture, industry and trade. From the character of the instruction, Professional Schools may be arranged in the following groups :

1. 實業教員講習所 Shih² Yeh⁴ Chiao⁴ Yüan² Chiang³ Hsi² So³, Schools for Training Teachers for Professional Schools (*see* No. 620).

2. 農業學堂 Nung² Yeh⁴ Hsüeh² T'ang², Agricultural Schools (*see* Nos. 600 to 603),

3. 工業學堂 Kung¹ Yeh⁴ Hsüeh² T'ang², Schools of Trades and Handicrafts (*see* Nos. 604 to 608),

4. 商業學堂 Shang¹ Yeh⁴ Hsüeh² T'ang², Commercial Schools (*see* Nos. 609 to 612), and

5. 商船學堂 Shang¹ Ch'uan² Hsüeh² T'ang², Mercantile Marine Schools (*see* Nos. 613 to 616),

Depending on the extent of their courses of study, Professional Schools are divided into three classes :

1. 高等實業學堂 Kao¹ Têng³ Shih² Yeh⁴ Hsüeh² T'ang², Higher Professional Schools (of the grade of Higher Schools, *see* Nos. 583 to 583B),

2. 中等實業學堂 Chung¹ Têng³ Shih² Yeh⁴ Hsüeh² T'ang², Middle Professional Schools (of the grade of Middle Schools, *see* Nos. 580 to 582), and

3. 初等實業學堂 Ch'u¹ Têng³ Shih² Yeh⁴ Hsüeh² T'ang², Lower Professional Schools (of the grade of Primary Schools of the Senior Grade, *see* No. 577A).

Also, 實業補習普通學堂 Shih² Yeh⁴ Pu³ Hsi² P'u³ T'ung¹ Hsüeh² T'ang², Schools of Professional and General Education (*see* No. 599), and 藝徒學堂 I⁴ T'u² Hsüeh² T'ang², Schools of Crafts (*see* No. 605), may be established at Primary and

Middle Schools, being considered, however, below these as regards educational rating.

實業教員講習所 Shih² Yeh⁴ Chiao⁴ Yüan² Chiang³ Hsi² So³, Schools for Training Teachers for Professional Schools, may be considered as equal in grade to Normal Schools (*see* Nos. 618 to 620).

Completion of the course of study of Middle Professional Schools carries with it the following privileges :

Those who graduate with the first rating may join Higher Professional Schools and, should they do so, receive, according to their rating, the literary degrees bestowed on graduates of Middle Schools (*see* No. 582A). Should they not care to attend Higher Professional Schools, they receive a document certifying completion of the course of a Middle Professional School and are appointed to the provinces as 州判 Chou¹ P'an⁴ (*see* No. 851A), 府經 Fu³ Ching¹ (*see* No. 850), or 主簿 Chu³ Pu⁴ (*see* No. 857). Those who graduate with the fourth rating remain for continued study ; should they again fail to attain one of the principal ratings, and be unwilling to study longer, they receive a document certifying attendance at a Middle Professional School. Those who attain the fifth rating merely receive a list of their examination marks.

On those who complete the course of study of Higher Professional Schools the following privileges are conferred :

Students who attain one of the three senior ratings are eligible for teaching and administrative posts at Middle Professional Schools, receive the degree of 舉人 Chü³ Jên² (*see* Nos. 629B and 631) and are enrolled as preferential candidates, ¹n the provinces, for the posts of 知州 Chih¹ Chou¹ (*see* No. 855), 知縣 Chih¹ Hsien⁴ (*see* No. 856) or 州同 Chou¹ T'ung² (*see* No. 855A).

Those who attain the fourth rating are detained for continued study ; should they again fail to attain one of the three senior ratings, and be unwilling to study further, they receive a document certifying attendance at a Higher Professional School and become eligible for administrative posts at Higher Professional Schools.

Those who attain the fifth rating merely receive a list of their examination marks.

The administration of Professional Schools is entirely similar to that of Schools of General Education of corresponding grades (*see* Nos. 577B, 582 and 583A).

598A. 京師實業學堂 Ching¹ Shih¹ Shih² Yeh⁴ Hsüeh² T'ang², Peking (Metropolitan) Professional Schools; these are under the joint control of the Ministries of Education and of Agriculture, Industry and Commerce (Department of Industry; *see* No. 464).

598B. In the provinces the Professional Schools are under the joint control of the Commissioner of Education (*see* No. 827) and the Industrial Taotai (*see* Nos. 839 to 839B).

598C. 上海高等實業學堂 Shang⁴ Hai³ Kao¹ Têng³ Shih² Yeh⁴ Hsüeh² T'ang², Shanghai Higher Professional School; this is under the control of the Ministry of Posts and Communications (*see* No. 787).

599. 實業補習普通學堂 Shih² Yeh⁴ Pu³ Hsi² P'u³ T'ung¹ Hsüeh² T'ang², Schools of Professional and General Education. These are found at Primary or Middle Schools, or at Professional Schools, and are open to those who have, at least, completed the course of a Primary School of the Junior Grade (*see* No. 577). The instruction includes 普通科 P'u³ T'ung¹ K'o¹, Course of General Education (ethics, Chinese literature, mathematics and callisthenics), and 實業科 Shih² Yeh⁴ K'o¹, Course of Professional Education. The latter is sub divided into:

1. 農業科 Nung² Yeh⁴ K'o¹, Course in Agriculture,
2. 工業科 Kung¹ Yeh⁴ K'o¹, Course in Handicrafts, 3. 商業科

600 to 602

Shang¹ Yeh⁴ K'o¹, Commercial Course, and 水產科 Shui³ Ch'an³ K'o¹, Course in Marine Industries.

The duration of the course of study, as well as the determination of the subjects to be taught in these schools, depends on local conditions.

A. Agricultural Schools:

600. 農業學堂 Nung² Yeh⁴ Hsüeh² T'ang² (also 農務學堂 Nung² Wu⁴ Hsüeh² T'ang²), Agricultural Schools. In Peking these schools are under the joint control of the Ministries of Education and of Agriculture, Industry and Commerce (Department of Agriculture; *see* No. 463); in the provinces they are under the control of the Commissioner of Education (*see* No. 827) and the Industrial Taotai (*see* Nos. 839 to 839B).

601. 初等農業學堂 Ch'u¹ Têng³ Nung² Yeh⁴ Hsüeh² T'ang², Lower Agricultural Schools; open to those who have completed the course of Primary Schools of the Junior Grade (*see* No. 577). The course of study covers three years and 30 hours of instruction are given weekly. The instruction given includes 普通科 P'u³ T'ung¹ K'o¹, Course of General Education (ethics, Chinese literature, mathematics, natural science and callisthenics), and 實習科 Shih² Hsi² K'o¹, Practical Course. The latter is sub-divided into: 1. 農業科 Nung² Yeh⁴ K'o¹, Course in Agriculture, 2. 蠶業科 Ts'an² Yeh⁴ K'o¹, Course in Sericulture, 3. 林業科 Lin² Yeh⁴ K'o¹, Course Forestry, and 4. 獸醫科 Shou⁴ I¹ K'o¹, Course in Veterinary Surgery.

602. 中等農業學堂 Chung¹ Têng³ Nung² Yeh⁴ Hsüeh² T'ang², Middle Agricultural Schools; open to those who have completed the course of Primary Schools of the Senior Grade (*see* No. 577A). The course consists of two years in the 豫科 Yü⁴ K'o¹, Preparatory Section, and three years in the 本科 Pên³ K'o¹, Specializing Section. The Preparatory Section supplies

instruction in ethics, Chinese literature, mathematics, geography, history, natural science, drawing, callisthenics and foreign languages (optional). The Special Section has the following five courses : 1. 農業科 Nung² Yeh⁴ K'o¹, Course in Agriculture, 2. 蠶業科 Ts'an² Yeh⁴ K'o¹, Course in Sericulture, 3. 林業科 Lin² Yeh⁴ K'o¹, Course in Forestry, 4. 獸醫業科 Shou⁴ I¹ Yeh⁴ K'o¹, Course in Veterinary Surgery, and 5. 水產業科 Shui³ Ch'an³ Yeh⁴ K'o¹, Course in Marine Industries.

602A to 603

Should local conditions demand it, the course of study at the Specializing Section may be shortened to two years or lengthened to five years.

602A. 水產學校 Shui³ Ch'an³ Hsüeh² Hsiao⁴, Schools of Marine Industries ; the establishment of these, in all the maritime and riverine provinces, was recommended in 1909 (see Memorials from the Ministry of Agriculture, Industry and Commerce, dated the 8th April, 1909, and the 23rd January, 1910). At present this type of school is found only at 吳淞 Wu² Sung¹, Shanghai, and 烟台 Yen¹ T'ai², Chefoo.

603. 高等農業學堂 Kao¹ Têng³ Nung² Yeh⁴ Hsüeh² T'ang², Higher Agricultural Schools ; open to students who have graduated from Middle Schools (see Nos. 580 to 582). The course of study includes one year at the 豫科 Yü⁴ K'o¹, Preparatory Section, and three or four years (depending on the course of study) at the 本科 Pên³ K'o¹, Specializing Section ; with 36 hours of instruction weekly. At the Preparatory Section there are taught ethics, Chinese literature and foreign languages (English and German for students of the Agricultural Course), mathematics, zoology, botany, physics, chemistry, drawing and callisthenics. The Specializing Section is made up of three Courses : 1. 農學科 Nung² Hsüeh² K'o¹, Course in Agriculture, 2. 林學科 Lin² Hsüeh² K'o¹ Course in Forestry, and 3. 獸醫學科 Shou⁴ I¹ Hsüeh² K'o¹, Course in Veterinary Surgery (at schools on the frontier there is also a

603A
to
605

土木工科 T'u³ Mu⁴ Kung¹ K'o¹, Course in Wood and Earth Defences).

603A. 高等農學堂 Kao¹ Têng⁵ Nung² Hsüeh² T'ang², Higher Agricultural School, at the 農事試驗場 Nung² Shih⁴ Shih⁴ Yen⁴ Ch'ang³, Botanical Garden at Peking ; under the control of the Ministry of Agriculture, Works and Commerce (*see* No. 463).

B. Schools of Trades and Handicrafts :

604. 工業學堂 Kung¹ Yeh⁴ Hsüeh² T'ang², Schools of Trades and Handicrafts ; these are under the joint control, at Peking, of the Ministries of Education and of Agriculture, Industry and Commerce (namely, the Department of Industry ; *see* No. 464), and, in the provinces, of the Commissioner of Education (*see* No. 827) and the Industrial Taotai (*see* Nos. 839 to 839B).

605. 藝徒學堂 I⁴ T'u² Hsüeh² T'ang², Schools of Crafts; for boys over 12 years of age who have completed the course of Primary Schools of the Junior Grade (*see* No. 577). These schools are found at Primary Schools of the Junior grade and of the Senior grade and the course covers, at most, four years, at least, six months. Instruction is supplied in two courses : 1. 普通科 P'u³ T'ung¹ K'o¹, Course of General Education (ethics, Chinese literature, mathematics, physics, chemistry, drawing and callisthenics), and 2. 工業科 Kung¹ Yeh⁴ K'o¹, Course in Crafts.

Detailed regulations for Schools of Crafts were submitted in 1906 to the Throne by the Ministry of Commerce. By these the enrollment of Schools of Crafts (to be equal in educational rating to Lower Schools of Trades and Handicrafts ; *see* No. 606) was fixed at 300, divided into six 班 Pan¹, Classes. Four classes follow (for from one half to two years) the 速成科 Su² Ch'êng² K'o¹, Accelerated Course of Study ; the other two classes follow (for from three to four years) the 完全科 Wan² Ch'üan²

K'o¹, Complete Course. The first four classes include boys of from twelve to fifteen years of age and the last two are made up of boys from fourteen to twenty years of age. The subjects of instruction are arranged as 通 脩 T'ung¹ Hsiu¹, General, or 專 脩 Chuan¹ Hsiu¹, Special. Under the former are ethics, arithmetic, natural science, chemistry, history, drawing, callisthenics, Chinese literature, singing and character writing; under the latter are metal working, wood working, lacquering, dyeing, pottery and manufacture of articles used in writing.

605A to 606

By a Memorial from the Ministry of Agriculture, Industry and Commerce (dated the 6th August, 1909), and a Memorial from the Ministry of Finance, reporting on the former (dated 22nd August, 1909), Schools of Crafts were reorganized as 中初兩等工業學堂 Chung¹ Ch'u¹ Liang³ Têng³ Kung¹ Yeh⁴ Hsüeh² T'ang², Lower and Middle Schools of Trades and Handicrafts (*see* Nos. 606 and 607).

605A. 京師藝徒學堂 Ching¹ Shih¹ I⁴ T'u² Hsueh² T'ang², Peking (Metropolitan) School of Crafts. This institution, under the control of the Department of Industry of the Ministry of Agriculture, Industry and Commerce (*see* No. 464), has been reorganized, following the general rule, as a Lower and Middle School of Trades and Handicrafts (*see* Nos. 606 and 607).

606. 初等工業學堂 Ch'u¹ Têng³ Kung¹ Yeh⁴ Hsüeh² T'ang², Lower Schools of Trades and Handicrafts. These have been established in accordance with a Memorial from the Ministry of Education—sanctioned by the Emperor on the 3rd January, 1909,—for those who have completed the course of Primary Schools of the Junior grade (*see* No. 577); with a course of study covering three years. The instruction is arranged as 普通科 P'u³ T'ung¹ K'o¹, Course of General Education (ethics, Chinese literature, mathematics, physics chemistry, drawing and callisthenics—geography, history, natural science, music and singing; optional), and 實習科 Shih² Hsi²

[239]

607 to 608　K'o¹, Practical Course (wood working, metal working, ship-building, electricity, mining, dyeing, pottery, lacquering, surveying and drawing).

607. 中等工業學堂 Chung¹ Têng³ Kung¹ Yeh⁴ Hsüeh² T'ang², Middle Schools of Trades and Handicrafts; open to those who have completed the course of Primary Schools of the Senior grade (*see* No. 577A); with a course of study of two years at the 豫科 Yü⁴ K'o¹, Preparatory Section, and three years at the 本科 Pên³ K'o¹, Specializing Section. At the Preparatory Section instruction is given in ethics, Chinese literature, mathematics, geography, history, natural science, drawing and callisthenics (also foreign languages—optional), 30 hours per week. The Specializing Section includes ten Courses of Study: 1. 土木科 T'u³ Mu⁴ K'o¹, Course in Wood and Earth Defences, 2. 金工科 Chin¹ Kung¹ K'o¹, Course in Metal Working, 3. 造船科 Tsao⁴ Ch'uan² K'o¹, Course in Ship-building, 4. 電氣科 Tien⁴ Ch'i⁴ K'o¹, Course in Electricity, 5. 木工科 Mu⁴ Kung¹ K'o¹, Course in Wood Working, 6. 礦業科 Kung³ Yeh⁴ K'o¹, Course in Mining, 7. 染織科 Jan³ Chih¹ K'o¹, Course in Dyeing, 8. 窰業科 Yao² Yeh⁴ K'o¹, Course in Pottery, 9. 漆工科 Ch'i¹ Kung¹ K'o¹, Course in Lacquering, and 10. 圖稿繪畫科 T'u² Kao³ Hui⁴ Hua⁴ K'o¹, Course in Surveying and Drawing. There are 30 hours of nstruction weekly at the Specializing Section, excluding practical exercises.

608. 高等工業學堂 Kao¹ Têng³ Kung¹ Yeh⁴ Hsüeh² T'ang², High f Schools of Trades and Handicrafts. Those who have completed the course of Middle Schools (*see* Nos. 580 to 582) are eligible for enrollment in this type of school. The course of study covers three years and there are 36 hours of instruction weekly, under two courses: 普通科 P'u³ T'ung¹ K'o¹, Course of General Education (ethics, mathematics, physics, chemistry, applied mechanics, drawing, tracing, experimental chemistry, legislation

[　240　]

affecting workmen, factory hygiene, English, callisthenics, etc.), and 專門科 Chuan[1] Mên[2] K'o[1], Specializing Course, which is divided into 13 courses : 1. 應用化學科 Ying[1] Yung[4] Hua[4] Hsüeh[2] K'o[1], Course in Industrial Chemistry, 2. 染色科 Jan[3] Se[4] K'o[1], Course in Dyeing, 3. 機織科 Chi[1] Chih[1] K'o[1], Course in Weaving Machinery, 4. 建築科 Chien[4] Chu[2] K'o[1], Course in Construction, 5. 窰業科 Yao[2] Yeh[4] K'o[1], Course in Pottery, 6. 機器科 Chi[1] Ch'i[4] K'o[1], Course in Machinery, 7. 電氣科 Tien[4] Ch'i[4] K'o[1], Course in Electricity, 8. 電氣化學科 Tien[4] Ch'i[4] Hua[4] Hsüeh[2] K'o[1], Course in Electro-Chemistry, 9. 土木科 T'u[3] Mu[4] K'o[1], Course in Wood and Earth Defences, 10. 礦業科 Kung[3] Yeh[4] K'o[1], Course in Mining, 11. 造船科 Tsao[4] Ch'uan[2] K'o[1], Course in Shipbuilding, 12. 漆工科 Ch'i[1] Kung[1] K'o[1], Course in Lacquering, and 13. 圖稿繪畫科 T'u[2] Kao[3] Hui[4] Hua[4] K'o[1], Course in Surveying and Drawing.

C. Commercial Schools :

609. 商業學堂 Shang[1] Yeh[4] Hsüeh[2] T'ang[2], Commercial Schools. These are under the joint supervision of the Ministries of Education and of Agriculture, Industry and Commerce (Department of Commerce ; *see* No. 465)—at the Capital—and of the Commissioner of Education (*see* No. 827) and the Industrial Taotai (*see* Nos. 839 to 839B)—in the provinces.

610. 初等商業學堂 Ch'u[1] Têng[3] Shang[1] Yeh[4] Hsüeh[2] T'ang[2], Lower Commercial Schools ; open to scholars who have completed the course of Primary Schools of the Junior Grade see No. 577); having a course of three years and 30 hours of instruction weekly. Instruction is given in ethics, Chinese literature, mathematics, geography, book-keeping, differentiation of merchandise, callisthenics and various sciences pertaining to commerce.

611. 中等商業學堂 Chung[1] Têng[3] Shang[1] Yeh[4] Hsüeh[2] T'ang[2], Middle Commercial Schools ; eligible for enrollment are

612 those who have completed the course of Primary Schools of the Senior Grade (*see* No. 577A). The course of study consists of two years at the 豫 科 Yü⁴ K'o¹, Preparatory Section, and three years at the 本 科 Pên³ K'o¹, Specializing Section. At the former 30 hours of instruction are given weekly, at the latter there are 34 hours of instruction weekly.

At the Preparatory Section instruction is given in ethics, Chinese literature, mathematics, geography, history, foreign languages, natural science, drawing and callisthenics.

The Specializing Section is made up of two Courses of Study: 普 通 科 P'u³ T'ung¹ K'o¹, Course of General Education (ethics, Chinese literature, mathematics and callisthenics), and 實 習 科 Shih² Hsi² K'o¹, Practical Course (commercial geography, history of trade, foreign languages, general principles of the laws of trade and finance, the commercial code, book-keeping, differentiation of merchandise, etc.).

612. 高 等 商 業 學 堂 Kao¹ Têng³ Shang¹ Yeh⁴ Hsüeh² T'ang², Higher Commercial Schools; open to those who have completed the course of Middle Schools (*see* Nos. 580 to 582). The course includes one year at the 豫 科 Yü⁴ K'o¹, Preparatory Section, and three years at the 本 科 Pên³ K'o¹, Specializing Section. In both Sections there are 36 hours of instruction weekly.

At the Preparatory Section there is instruction in ethics of commerce, commercial correspondence, mathematics, book-keeping, industrial chemistry, foreign languages, callisthenics, etc.

At the Specializing Section there is instruction in ethics of commerce, commercial correspondence, commercial arithmetic, commercial geography, history of trade, book-keeping, differentiation of merchandise, financial law, statistics, civil code, commercial code, international law, foreign languages, laws of commerce, callisthenics, etc.

D. Mercantile Marine Schools:

613. 商 船 學 堂 Shang¹ Ch'uan² Hsüeh² T'ang², Mercantile Marine Schools; under the supervision—at the Capital—of the Ministries of Education, of Agriculture, Industry and Commerce and of Posts and Communications, and, in the provinces, of the Commissioner of Education (*see* No. 827) and the Industrial Taotai (*see* Nos. 839 to 839B).

614. 初 等 商 船 學 堂 Ch'u¹ Têng³ Shang¹ Ch'uan² Hsüeh² T'ang², Lower Mercantile Marine Schools; open to those who have completed the course of Primary Schools of the Junior Grade (*see* No. 577). The course covers two years, and 30 hours of instruction are given weekly. The instruction is arranged as: 1. 航 海 科 Hang² Hai³ K'o¹, Course in Navigation, and 2. 機 輪 科 Chi¹ Lun² K'o¹, Course in Marine Engineering. The former includes instruction in ethics, Chinese literature, mathematics, geography, general principles of navigation and the transport of cargo by water, callisthenics, etc.; the latter comprises ethics, Chinese literature, mathematics, physics, chemistry, general principles of marine engineering, practical machine drawing, callisthenics, etc.

615. 中 等 商 船 學 堂 Chung¹ Têng³ Shang¹ Ch'uan² Hsüeh² T'ang², Middle Mercantile Marine Schools; open to those who have completed the course of Primary Schools of the Senior Grade (*see* No. 577A). The course includes two years at the 豫 科 Yü⁴ K'o¹, Preparatory Section, and three years at the 本 科 Pên³ K'o¹, Specializing Section; there are 30 hours of instruction weekly at each Section.

The Preparatory Section furnishes instruction in ethics, Chinese literature, mathematics, geography, history, natural science, foreign languages, drawing and callisthenics.

The Specializing Section is sub-divided into: 1. 航 海 科 Hang² Hai³ K'o¹, Course in Navigation, and 2. 機 輪 科 Chi¹ Lun² K'o¹, Course in Marine Engineering. As 普 通 科 目

616 to 617

P'u³ T'ung¹ K'o¹ Mu⁴, Subjects of General Education, there are taught in both these Courses : ethics, Chinese literature, mathematics, physics, chemistry, geography, drawing, foreign languages and callisthentics. Also, as 實習科目 Shih² Hsi² K'o¹ Mu⁴, Practical Subjects, instruction is given in :

1. In the Course in Navigation : legislation affecting the mercantile marine, navigation, general principles of marine engineering, shipbuilding (as a science), etc.

2. In the Course in Marine Engineering : mechanics, dynamics, applied dynamics, general principles of electricity, etc.

616. 高 等 商 船 學 堂 Kao¹ Têng³ Shang¹ Ch'uan² Hsüeh² T'ang², Higher Mercantile Marine Schools ; open to those who have completed the course of Middle Schools (*see* Nos. 580 to 582). The course of study is of five and one half years duration for the 航 海 科 Hang² Hai³ K'o¹, Course in Navigation, and of five years duration for the 機 輪 科 Chi¹ Lun² K'o¹, Course in Marine Engineering ; 34 hours of instruction weekly.

The subjects making up the Course in Navigation are ethics, Chinese literature, foreign languages (English is compulsory; Russian, French, German, Japanese and Korean are optional), mathematics, physics, chemistry, commercial law, commercial geography, general principles of law, commercial legislation, navigation, shipbuilding (as a science), the mechanics of shipping, ship hygiene, financial law, marine law, etc.

The Course in Marine Engineering provides for instruction in ethics, Chinese literature, foreign languages (as above), mathematics, physics, dynamics, chemistry, electricity, etc.

617. At Middle Professional Schools there may be established :

1. 別 科 Pieh² K'o¹, Special Courses with shortened programme.

2. 選 科 Hsüan³ K'o¹, Selected Courses ; for providing instruction in one or other branch of professional education.

617ᴀ
to
617ʙ

3. 專功科 Chuan¹ Kung¹ K'o¹, Specializing Courses; for those who have completed the course of Professional Schools and wish to further perfect themselves in their chosen speciality (the course covers one year for the Course in Agriculture, or two years for the Course in Trades and Handicrafts), and

4. 專脩科 Chuan¹ Hsiu¹ K'o¹, Special Courses at Mercantile Marine Schools.

617ᴀ. At Higher Professional Schools there may be established :

1. 專功科 Chuan¹ Kung¹ K'o¹, Specializing Courses; for those who have completed the course of Professional Schools and wish to further perfect themselves in some speciality,

2. 選科 Hsüan³ K'o¹, Selected Courses; for selected branches of professional education (course covering one year),

3. 實業教員講習所 Shih² Yeh⁴ Chiao⁴ Yuan² Chiang³ Hsi² So³, Courses for Training Teachers for Professional Schools (*see* No. 620),

4. 中等實業學堂 Chung¹ Têng³ Shih² Yeh⁴ Hsüeh² T'ang², Middle Professional Schools, and

5. 實業補習普通學堂 Shih² Yeh⁴ Pu³ Hsi² P'u³ T'ung Hsüeh² T'ang², Schools of Professional and General Education (*see* No. 599).

617ʙ. The following schools may be considered as Professional Schools :

1. 礦務學堂 Kung³ Wu⁴ Hsüeh² T'ang², Mining Schools,

2. 農務講習所 Nung² Wu⁴ Chiang³ Hsi² So³, Agricultural Schools (*see* No. 770c),

3. 農林學堂 Nung² Lin² Hsüeh² T'ang², Schools of Agriculture and Forestry,

4. 森林學堂 Sen¹ Lin² Hsüeh² T'ang², Schools of Forestry, and

5. 蠶業講習所 Ts'an² Yeh⁴ Chiang³ Hsi² So³, Schools of Sericulture (in Chekiang ; reorganized, in accordance with a

618 Memorial from the Ministry of Education of the 6th May, 1909, as a Higher Agricultural School ; *see* No. 603).

In addition to the above-mentioned, by the programme of measures to be accomplished by the Ministry of Agriculture, Industry and Commerce during the period 1908 to 1914 (sanctioned by the Emperor on the 8th April, 1909), the following schools, which come into the category of Professional Schools, are to be established in the provinces :

In 1909 :

蠶業講習所 Ts'an² Yeh⁴ Chiang³ Hsi² So³, Schools of Sericulture, and

茶務講習所 Ch'a² Wu⁴ Chiang³ Hsi² So³, Schools of Tea Growing.

In 1910 :

農林學堂 Nung² Lin² Hsueh² T'ang², Schools of Agriculture and Forestry (*see* above).

In 1911 :

礦務學堂 Kung³ Wu⁴ Hsüeh² T'ang², Mining Schools (*see* above).

In 1912 :

農事半日學堂 Nung² Shih⁴ Pan⁴ Jih⁴ Hsüeh² T'ang², Agricultural Schools with half-day sessions (compare No. 579).

In 1913 :

獸醫學堂 Shou⁴ I¹ Hsüeh² T'ang², Schools of Veterinary Surgery.

In 1914 :

美術學堂 Mei³ Shu⁴ Hsüeh² T'ang², Schools of Fine Arts.

Normal Schools :

618. 師範學堂 Shih¹ Fan⁴ Hsüeh² T'ang², Normal Schools (Pedagogic Institutes). These schools train pupils for following the profession of teaching. Normal Schools are arranged as :

1. 初級師範學堂 Ch'u¹ Chi² Shih¹ Fan⁴ Hsüeh² T'ang², Lower Normal Schools,

2. 優級師範學堂 Yu¹ Chi² Shih¹ Fan⁴ Hsüeh² T'ang², **618ᴀ**
Higher Normal Schools (*see* No. 618ʙ).

3. 女子師範學堂 Nü³ Tzu³ Shih¹ Fan⁴ Hsüeh² T'ang²,
Female Normal Schools (*see* No. 619), and

4. 實業教員講習所 Shih² Yeh⁴ Chiao⁴ Yüan² Chiang³
Hsi² So³, Schools for Training Teachers for Professional Schools
(*see* No. 620).

618ᴀ. 初級師範學堂 Ch'u¹ Chi² Shih¹ Fan⁴ Hsüeh²
T'ang², Lower Normal Schools; for the training of teachers for
Primary Schools of the Junior Grade and Senior Grade (*see*
Nos. 577 and 577ᴀ). The full course of study covers five years
hours of instruction are given weekly.

The establishment of Lower Normal Schools at all the
principal towns of Departments and Districts is to be compulsory.
At present they are found only at provincial capitals. The
instruction has been arranged in two courses, *i.e.* 完全學科
Wan² Ch'üan² Hsüeh² K'o¹, Complete Course, and 簡易科
Chien³ I⁴ K'o¹, Abridged Course. Also, in the principal towns
of Departments and Districts there have been instituted 師範傳
習所 Shih¹ Fan⁴ Ch'üan² Hsi² So³, Normal Institutes, at which
scholars who have completed the Abridged Course of the
Lower Normal School (at the provincial capital) act as teachers.

In addition to the above-mentioned, there have been
instituted at Lower Normal Schools: a 預備科 Yü⁴ Pêi⁴ K'o¹,
Preparatory Section, for providing preliminary instruction for
those who desire to join Normal Schools, and 小學師範講習所
Hsiao" Hsüeh² Shih¹ Fan⁴ Chiang³ Hsi² So³, Courses for
Teachers of Primary Schools, for supplementing the education
of Primary School Teachers who have attended the Normal
Institutes mentioned above.

The Complete Course of Lower Normal Schools includes
instruction in ethics, reading and commenting on the Classics,
Chinese literature, pedagogy, history, geography, mathematics,

natural science, physics, chemistry, character writing, drawing and callisthenics—foreign languages, agricultural and commercial subjects and crafts are optional.

The Abridged Course provides for instruction in ethics, pedagogy, Chinese literature, history, geography, mathematics, natural science, drawing and callisthenics.

Eligible for enrollment at Lower Normal Schools are those who have completed the course of Primary Schools of the Senior Grade (*see* No. 577A). At these schools there are Primary Schools where the students give probationary lessons.

At the head of a Lower Normal School there is a Director (*see* No. 635). Subordinated to him are Teachers (*see* No. 637), Assistant Teachers (*see* No. 638) and Proctors (*see* No. 646).

In charge of the Primary School of a Normal School there is a 小 學 辦 事 官 Hsiao[3] Hsüeh[2] Pan[4] Shih[4] Kuan[1], Primary School Inspector, who controls the 小 學 教 員 Hsiao[3] Hsüeh[2] Chiao[4] Yüan[2], Primary School Teachers, and the 庶 務 員 Shu[4] Wu[4] Yüan[2], Steward (*see* No. 641).

Completion of the course of Lower Normal Schools carries with it the following privileges :

Those who graduate with one of the three senior ratings are eligible for appointment as teachers in Primary Schools of various types and receive the degree of 師 範 科 貢 生 Shih[1] Fan[4] K'o[1] Kung[4] Shêng[1]. The first rating carries with it sixth class rank (加 六 品 銜 Chia[1] Liu[4] P'in[3] Hsien[2]); the second rating places the graduate on the list of preferential candidates for the post of 教 諭 Chiao[4] Yü[4] (*see* No. 857); the third rating places the graduate on the list of preferential candidates for the post of 訓 導 Hsün[4] Tao[4] (*see* No. 857).

Those who attain the fourth rating on graduation are given a diploma and are eligible for employment as Assistant Teachers at Primary Schools and, after a period of obligatory service, may be given the degree of 師 範 科 貢 生 Shih¹ Fan⁴ K'o¹ Kung⁴ **618B** Shêng¹, with the title 訓 導 Hsün⁴ Tao⁴ (*see* above).

Those who attain the fifth rating merely obtain a document certifying attendance at a Lower Normal School.

618B.   優 級 師 範 學 堂 Yu¹ Chi² Shih¹ Fan⁴ Hsüeh² T'ang², Higher Normal School; furnishes training for teachers for Lower Normal Schools (*see* No. 618A) and Middle Schools (*see* Nos. 580 to 582). The course of study covers three years and there are 36 hours of instruction weekly. These schools are established at the Capital and at all provincial capitals and the students are drawn from the ranks of graduates of Lower Normal Schools (*see* No. 618A) and Middle Schools (*see* Nos. 580 to 582).

During the first year students of Higher Normal Schools follow the 公共科 Kung¹ Kung⁴ K'o¹, General Course, comprising ethics,   origin of the Classics, Chinese literature, Japanese literature English literature, logic, mathematics and callisthenics. From the second year begins the 分類科 Fên¹ Lei⁴ K'o¹, Specializing Courses, made up of :

1.   Chinese literature and foreign languages,
2.   Geography and history,
3.   Mathematics, chemistry and physics, and
4.   Botany, zoology, mineralogy and physiology.

General subjects taught in all these courses are : ethics, the essence of the Classics, pedagogy, psychology and callisthenics.

The Specializing Courses cover three years and those who complete them may, should they wish, take the 加習科 Chia¹ Hsi² K'o¹, Supplementary Course, which extends one year and calls for the presentation of a thesis on its completion.

There are later to be instituted 專脩科 Chuan¹ Hsiu¹ K'o¹, Special Courses, and 選科 Hsüan³ K'o¹, Selected Courses.

On completion of the course of Higher Normal Schools the following privileges are granted :

Those who graduate with the first rating receive the degree of 師範科舉人 Shih¹ Fan⁴ K'o¹ Chü³ Jên², are eligible for teaching positions at Middle Schools or at Lower Normal Schools and become preferential candidates (儘先補用 Chin⁴ Hsien¹ Pu³ Yung⁴) for the post of 內閣中書 Nei⁴ Ko² Chung¹ Shu¹ (*see* No. 137). They are granted, at the same time, fifth class rank (加五品銜 Chia¹ Wu³ P'in³ Hsien²).

Those who attain the second rating on graduation are granted the degree of 師範科舉人 Shih¹ Fan⁴ K'o¹ Chü³ Jên² (*see* above), are eligible for teaching posts as mentioned above and become preferential candidates for the post of 中書科中書 Chung¹ Shu¹ K'o¹ Chung¹ Shu¹ (*see* No. 137ᴀ).

Those who graduate with the third rating receive the degree of 師範科舉人 Shih¹ Fan⁴ K'o¹ Chü³ Jên² (*see* above), are eligible for employment as teachers in various schools (as above) and become preferential candidates for the post of 司務 Ssu¹ Wu⁴ (*see* No. 296). Those who attain the fourth rating receive a diploma, are eligible for employment as Assistant Teachers at Middle Schools or Primary Schools of the Senior Grade and, after one years obligatory service, receive the degree of 師範科舉人 Shih¹ Fan⁴ K'o¹ Chü³ Jên² and the title 中書科中書 Chung¹ Shu¹ K'o¹ Chung¹ Shu¹.

Those who complete the course with the fifth rating receive a document certifying attendance at a Higher Normal School and are eligible for temporary employment as Assistant Teachers at Primary Schools of the Senior Grade.

At Higher Normal Schools there are found: 1. Middle Schools (*see* Nos. 580 to 582), and 2. Primary Schools of the Junior and Senior Grades (*see* Nos. 577 and 577ᴀ). Also, should necessity arise, there may be established; 1. 半日小學科 Pan⁴ Jih⁴ Hsiao³ Hsüeh² K'o¹, Half-day Courses of Primary School Instruction (*see* No. 579), and 2. 小學補

習 科 Hsiao³ Hsüeh² Pu³ Hsi² K'o¹, Supplementary Courses of Primary School Instruction.

The establishment of a 敎 育 博 物 館 Chiao⁴ Yü⁴ Po² Wu⁴ Kuan², Pedagogic Museum, is obligatory at Higher Normal Schools

The Administration of Higher Normal Schools is similar to that of Higher Schools (*see* No. 583A). For the schools functioning within Higher Normal Schools there are: a 中 學 辦 事 官 Chung¹ Hsüeh² Pan⁴ Shih⁴ Kuan¹, Director of the Middle School, 中 學 敎 員 Chung¹ Hsüeh² Chiao⁴ Yüan², Teachers of the Middle School, a 小 學 辦 事 官 Hsiao³ Hsüeh² Pan⁴ Shih⁴ Kuan¹, Director of the Primary School, and 小 學 敎 員 Hsiao³ Hsüeh² Chiao⁴ Yüan², Teachers of the Primary School.

618c. 優 級 師 範 選 科 Yu¹ Chi² Shih¹ Fan⁴ Asüan³ K'o¹: Selected Higher Courses for Teachers instituted in accordance with regulations promulgated by the Ministry of Education on the 21st July, 1906, in all the provinces. These Courses are for those who have completed the Abridged Course at Lower Normal Schools (*see* No. 618A), or who have spent not less than two years at Middle Schools (*see* Nos. 580 to 582), and are intended to prepare teachers for Lower Normal Schools (*see* No. 618A) and Middle Schools (*see* Nos. 580 to 582). The course includes one year at the 豫 科 Yü⁴ K'o¹. Preparatory Section, and two years at the 本 科 Pên³ K'o¹, Specializing Section.

619. 女 子 師 範 學 堂 Nü³ Tzu³ Shih¹ Fan⁴ Hsüeh² T'ang², Female Normal Schools; these are to be established (in accordance with regulations drawn up by the Ministry of Education—sanctioned by the Emperor on the 23rd February, 1907), at the principal towns of Departments and Districts. As a first effort they are established only at provincial capitals and prefectural cities.

[251]

619ᴀ   Eligible for admission to Female Normal Schools are girls
over 15 years of age who have completed the course of
Primary Schools of the Senior Grade (*see* No. 578.) The object
of Female Normal Schools is to train teachers for Female
Primary Schools. The course covers four years and 34 hours
instruction are given weekly. The instruction includes ethics,
pedagogy, Chinese literature, history, geography, mathematics,
natural science, drawing, sewing, handiwork,ʼ music, singing
and callisthenics.

For girls wishing to join the 師 範 科 Shih¹ Fan⁴ K‘o¹,
Pedagogic Section, and needing improvement in their education,
there may be instituted a 豫 備 科 Yü⁴ Pêi⁴ K‘o¹, Preparatory
Section, with instruction similar to that supplied during the
third and fourth years of study at Female Primary Schools of
the Senior Grade.

Obligatory at Female Normal Schools is the establishment
of : Female Primary Schools (*see* No. 578) and Elementary
Schools (for children of tender age) (*see* No. 575), at which the
students of the Normal Schools act as teachers.

At the head of a Female Normal School there is a 監 督
Chien¹ Tu¹, Mistress. Subordinated to her there are 教 習
Chiao⁴ Hsi², Teachers, 副 教 習 Fu⁴ Chiao⁴ Hsi², Assistant
Teachers, and 監 學 Chien¹ Hsüeh², Proctors. Further, there are
the 小 學 堂 堂 長 Hsiao³ Hsüeh² T‘ang² T‘ang² Chang³,
Inspectress of the Primary School, and the 蒙 養 院 院 長
Mêng² Yang³ Yüan⁴ Yüan⁴ Chang³, Inspectress of the
Elementary School.

To the staff of Female Normal Schools there may be added
a Manager, a Secretary and a Steward (*see* No. 578).

619ᴀ. 京 師 女 子 師 範 學 堂 Ching¹ Shih¹ Nü³ Tzu³
Shih¹ Fan⁴ Hsüeh² T‘ang², Peking (Metropolitan) Female
Normal School ; established in accordance with a Memorial from
the Ministry of Education (sanctioned by the Emperor on the

4th July, 1908). At first only a 簡易科 Chien³ I⁴ K'o¹, **620 to 621** Abridged Course of Study, was supplied, the course covering two years. Later the 完全科 Wan² Ch'üan² K'o¹, Complete Course of Study, was instituted, covering four years.

620. 實業教員講習所 Shih² Yeh⁴ Chiao⁴ Yüan² Chiang³ Hsi² So³, Schools for Training Teachers for Professional Schools; open to those who have completed the course of Middle Schools (*see* Nos. 580 to 582) or Lower Normal Schools (*see* No. 618A) and desire to devote themselves to teaching at the various Professional Schools (*see* No. 598), Schools of Professional and General Education (*see* No. 599) and Schools of Crafts (*see* No. 605). They are established in the Agricultural (*see* No. 590), Polytechnical (*see* No. 591) and Commercial (*see* No. 592) Department of the University or at Higher Agricultural Schools (*see* No. 603), Schools of Trades and Handicrafts. (*see* No. 608) and Commercial Schools (*see* No. 612).

These schools are arranged as: 1. 農業教員講習所 Nung² Yeh⁴ Chiao⁴ Yüan² Chiang³ Hsi² So³, Schools for Training Teachers for Agricultural Schools, 2. 商業教員講習所 Shang¹ Yeh⁴ Chiao⁴ Yüan² Chiang³ Hsi² So³, Schools for Training Teachers for Commercial Schools, and 3. 工業教員講習所 Kung¹ Yeh⁴ Chiao⁴ Yüan² Chiang³ Hsi² So³, Schools for Training Teachers for Schools of Trades and Handicrafts. The course of the first two covers two years; the course of the latter covers three years for the 完全科 Wan² Ch'üan² K'o¹, Complete Course, or one year for the 簡易科 Chien³ I⁴ K'o¹, Abridged Course.

Special Schools :

621. 專門學堂 Chuan¹ Mên² Hsüeh² T'ang², Special Schools; their courses of study place these in the category of Higher Schools (compare No. 583B).

Special Schools include:

[253]

621ᴀ 1. 貴冑法政學堂 Kuei⁴ Chou⁴ Fa⁴ Chêng⁴ Hsüeh² T'ang², College of Law and Administration for Princes and Nobles, at Peking (No. 622).

2. 法政學堂 Fa⁴ Chêng⁴ Hsüeh² T'ang², Colleges of Law and Administration, at Peking and in the provinces (*see* No. 623),

3. 法律學堂 Fa⁴ Lü⁴ Hsüeh² T'ang², College of Law, at Peking (*see* No. 624),

4. 譯學館 I⁴ Hsüeh² Kuan³, College of Interpreters, at Peking (*see* No. 625),

5. 方言學堂 Fang¹ Yen² Hsüeh² T'ang², Colleges of Languages, in the provinces (*see* No. 626),

6. 滿蒙文高等學堂 Man³ Mêng² Wên² Kao¹ Têng³ Hsüeh² T'ang², Higher School of Manchu and Mongolian Languages (*see* No. 627), and

7. 曲阜學堂 Ch'ü¹ Fu⁴ Hsüeh² T'ang², College of History and Philology at Ch'üfu (*see* No. 627ᴀ).

621ᴀ. In addition to the above-mentioned, the following schools, under the joint supervision of the Ministry of Education and various other Government offices, may be considered as Special Schools:

1. 高等巡警學堂 Kao¹ Têng³ Hsün² Ching³ Hsüeh² T'ang², Higher Police Schools, at Peking and in the provinces— directly supervised by the Ministry of the Interior (*see* No. 522).

2. 財政學堂 Ts'ai² Chêng⁴ Hsüeh² T'ang², Financial (Political Economy) College, at Peking—directly supervised by the Ministry of Finance (*see* No. 568),

3. 稅務學堂 Shui⁴ Wu⁴ Hsüeh² T'ang², Customs College, at Peking—directly supervised by the Board of Customs Control (*see* No. 252),

4. 陸軍貴冑學堂 Lu⁴ Chün¹ Kuei⁴ Chou⁴ Hsüeh² T'ang², Military School for Princes and Nobles—directly supervised by the Ministry of War (*see* No. 713),

5. 唐山路礦學堂 T'ang² Shan¹ Lu⁴ Kung³ Hsüeh² T'ang², Railway and Mining College at T'angshan—directly supervised by the Ministry of Posts and Communications (*see* No. 786),

6. 殖邊學堂 Chih² Pien¹ Hsüeh² T'ang², College of Mongolian and Tibetan Languages, at Peking—directly supervised by the Ministry of Dependencies (*see* No. 499), and

7. 速記學堂 Su² Chi⁴ Hsüeh² T'ang², School of Stenography—directly supervised by the National Assembly (*see* Supplement, No. 167B).

621B. In accordance with the programme of measures to be accomplished by the Ministry of Education within the period 1908–1916 (sanctioned by the Emperor on the 18th April, 1909), the following schools, coming into the category of Special Schools, are to be instituted:

1. In 1910:

存古學堂 Ts'un² Ku³ Hsüeh² T'ang², Colleges of History and Philology—in all provinces (compare No. 627A),

2. In 1911:

專門醫學堂 Chuan¹ Mên² I¹ Hsüeh² T'ang², Special College of Medicine, at Peking,

3. In 1911:

專門農業學堂 Chuan¹ Mên² Nung² Yeh⁴ Hsüeh² T'ang² Special College of Agricultural Science, at Peking,

4. 1912:

專門工業學堂 Chuan¹ Mên² Kung¹ Yeh⁴ Hsüeh² T'ang², Special College of Technology, at Peking,

5. 1912:

專門商業學堂 Chuan¹ Mên² Shang¹ Yeh⁴ Hsüeh² T'ang², Special Commercial College, at Peking, and

6. In 1915:

音樂學堂 Yin¹ Yüeh⁴ Hsüeh² T'ang², Conservatory of Music, at Peking.

622

622. 貴胄法政學堂 Kuei⁴ Chou⁴ Fa⁴ Chêng⁴ Hsüeh²
T'ang², College of Law and Administration for Princes and
Nobles ; established, at Peking, in accordance with a Memorial
from the Committee for Drawing up Regulations for Constitutional
Government, by Imperial Edict of the 9th April, 1909. This
Edict also approved of the regulations for the College, drawn up
by the said committee. The object of the College is to train
those of princely and noble birth—as well as their sons—for
judicial and administrative service.

The instruction supplied by the College of Law and
Administration for Princes and Nobles is arranged as :

1. 正科 Chêng⁴ K'o¹, Complete Course ; covering four
years. During the first year the teaching is in 普通學 P'u³
T'ung¹ Hsüeh², General Education ; during the last three years
the instruction is in 法政專科 Fa⁴ Chêng⁴ Chuan¹ K'o¹, Legal
and Administrative Subjects.

2. 簡易科 Chien³ I⁴ K'o¹, Abridged Course ; covering
two years. The first half year is devoted to general education
and the remainder of the course to legal and administrative
subjects.

At the College there is also a course of lectures—lasting one
year and a half—for 聽講員 T'ing¹ Chiang³ Yüan², Lecture
Students, who are persons of princely birth, more than 30 years
of age, in the Government service ; officials of Manchu and
Chinese birth, holding posts not lower than the fourth rank, are
also enrolled for this Lecture Course.

At the request of 貝勒毓朗 Pei¹ Lê¹ Yü⁴ Lang³, Prince
of the third degree, Yü Lang, Curator of the College of Law
and Administration for Princes and Nobles, there have been
introduced some changes in the regulations of the College
(sanctioned by the Emperor on the 11th November, 1909), i.e.
the term of the Complete Course has been extended to five
years—two years of general education and three years of legal

[256]

and administrative education ; the Lecture Course has been extended to three years—one year of general education and two years of special (legal and administrative) education ; and a 預 備 科 Yü⁴ Pêi⁴ K‘o¹, Preparatory Section, with a course of study of two years duration, and providing 32 hours instruction weekly, has been introduced. At the Preparatory Section there are taught : ethics, Chinese literature, history, geography, mathematics, natural science, drawing and callisthenics.

All males between the ages of 18 and 30 years who are Clansmen, Princes or bearers of hereditary titles—as well as their sons—if they are not in the Government service or enrolled in Government schools, are obliged to join the College. Children of Clansmen, as well as Manchu and Chinese officials of the first two ranks, are accepted at the College, on completion of the course of Middle Schools (see Nos. 580 to 582), after a test examination.

Supplementary Regulations for the College of Law and Administration for Princes and Nobles (providing for the changes mentioned above) were drawn up by the Curator and sanctioned by the Emperor on the 21st December, 1909.

622A. At the head of the College of Law and Administration for Princes and Nobles there is a 總理 Tsung³ Li³, Curator. Subordinated to him there are : 1. two Directors (see No. 635), 2. one 提調 T‘i² Tiao⁴, Preceptor, 3. Teachers (number not fixed ; see No. 637), 4. two Proctors (see No. 646), 5. 書 記 官 Shu¹ Chi⁴ Kuan¹, Secretaries, 6. Accountant (see No. 643), 7. Steward, and 8. Tutor (see No. 640).

623. 京 師 法 政 學 堂 Ching¹ Shih¹ Fa⁴ Chêng⁴ Hsüeh² T‘ang², College of Law and Administration, at Peking ; established in accordance with a Memorial from the Ministry of Education, sanctioned by the Emperor on the 2nd February, 1907, for the purpose of preparing students for a judicial or administrative career. The course of study covers five years ;

622A to 623

the first two years are spent at the 豫 科 Yü⁴ K'o¹, Preparatory Section, and the remaining three at the 正 科 Chêng¹ K'o¹, Specializing Section. The latter has two courses of study: 1. 政治門 Chêng⁴ Chih⁴ Mên², Course in Administration, and 2. 法律門 Fa⁴ Lü⁴ Mên², Course in Law.

At this College there are also found: 1. 別科 Pieh⁴ K'o¹, Special Course, of three years duration, and 2. 講習科 Chiang³ Hsi² K'o¹, Lecture Course, covering one year and a half, providing lectures, on administrative and financial law, for officials.

For the Preparatory Section there are yearly accepted, after a test examination, 200 students. They must be between the ages of twenty and twenty-five years, of good behaviour, physically strong and educated to the standard reached by Middle Schools (*see* Nos. 580 to 582). For the Special Course there are yearly accepted, after a test examination, 100 students. These must be less than 35 years of age, be employed at the various Ministries or other Government offices, or possess literary degrees—not higher than 舉 人 Chü³ Jên², Graduate (Bachelor of Arts). For the Specializing Section of the College there are chosen 200 students from the ranks of those who have completed the course of the Preparatory Section, or externs of corresponding education, after a test examination.

The subjects of study at the Preparatory Section include: ethics, Chinese literature, Japanese, history, geography, mathematics, natural science logic, general outline of law, principles of financial law and call sthenics. The Course in Administration of the Specializing Section provides instruction in: ethics, "Institutes of the Reigning Dynasty," laws of the Ta Ch'ing Empire, State law, constitutional law, administrative law, civil law, criminal law, commercial law, general international law, special international law, political economy, financial law, sociology, history of international relations, statistics, Japanese, English and callisthenics. The subjects taught in the Course in

Law of the Specializing Section are : ethics, "Institutes of the 623A
Reigning Dynasty," laws of the Ta Ch'ing Empire, history of
Chinese legislation, history of foreign legislation, constitutional
law, administrative law, civil law, criminal law, commerical law,
civil law proceedings, criminal law proceedings, general international law, special international law, prison administration,
Japanese and callisthenics.

At the head of the College of Law and Administration, at
Peking, there is a Director (*see* No. 635). He has subordinated
to him : 1. One Preceptor (*see* No. 636), 2. Teachers (number
not fixed ; *see* No. 637), 3. Two Tutors (*see* No. 640), 4.
Librarian (*see* No. 639), 5. Steward (*see* No. 641), 6. Secretary (*see* No. 642), 7. Accountant (*see* No. 643), 8. Two
Clerks of Works (*see* No. 644), and a 講習科辦事官 Chiang³
Hsi² K'o¹ Pan⁴ Shih⁴ Kuan¹, Inspector of Lecture Course for
officials (*see* above).

623A. 法政學堂 Fa⁴ Chêng⁴ Hsüeh² T'ang², Colleges of
Law and Administration, in the provinces. The course of study
of these Colleges is similar to that of the Special Course of the
College of Law and Administration at Peking (*see* No. 623) ; the
duration of the course is not uniform in all provinces. In Chihli
the course covers two years- a year at the 豫科 Yü⁴ K'o¹,
Preparatory Section, and one year and a half at the 本科 Pên³ K'o¹,
Specializing Section ; in Anhui the course includes two years for
the 簡易科 Chien³ I⁴ K'o¹, Abridged Course, and one year for
the 補習科 Pu³ Hsi² K'o¹, Supplementary Course ; in Chekiang
the course covers one year and a half, etc.

The enrollment of the Colleges of Law and Administration
varies in different provinces (in Chekiang it is 200, in Chihli 120,
and in Shantung and Anhui 60).

Instructions from the Ministry of Education, dated the
9th March, 1907, directed that the provincial Colleges of Law and
Administration introduce—following the example of the Peking

623B
to
624

College of Law and Administration (*see* No. 623), a course of 監獄學專科 Chien¹ Yü⁴ Hsüeh² Chuan¹ K'o¹, Prison Administration, as a speciality to which students of the first section of Higher Schools (preparing to attend the Department of Law of the University ; *see* No. 583) may devote themselves for a year and a half

623B. For particulars as to 司法講習科 Ssu¹ Fa⁴ Chiang³ Hsi² K'o¹, also 審判講習所 Shen³ P'an⁴ Chiang³ Hsi² So³, Courses of Lectures on Law, instituted at Colleges of Law, *see* No. 758B.

624. 法律學堂 Fa⁴ Lü⁴ Hsüeh² T'ang², College of Law, at Peking ; founded in accordance with a Memorial from the President of the Ministry of Education—sanctioned by the Emperor on the 3rd August, 1905—with the object of providing judicial education for officials. The course of study covers three years (also, there is a 速成科 Su² Ch'êng² K'o¹, Abridged Course, of one year and a half).

At the College are taught: laws of the Ta Ch'ing, Ming and T'ang Dynasties, legislation now in force, history of legislation in China (from olden times), general outline of law, principles of political economy, State law, Roman law, civil law, criminal law, constitutional law, commercial law, civil and criminal law proceedings, international law (general and special), administrative law, prison administration, judicial practice, laws of commercial companies, laws of bankruptcy, general principles of finance, foreign languages and callisthenics.

At the Head of the College of Law at Peking there is a Director (*see* No. 635); subordinated to him are: 1. The Preceptor (*see* No. 636), 2. Eight Teachers (*see* No. 637), 3. Librarian (*see* No. 639), 4. Steward (*see* No. 641), 5. Secretary (*see* No. 642), 6. Accountant (*see* No. 643), 7. Clerk of Works (*see* No. 644), 8. Inspector of Dormitories (*see* No.

645), 9. Proctors (*see* No. 646) and 10. Assistant Inspector **625** of Dormitories (*see* No. 647).

625. 譯學館 I⁴ Hsüeh² Kuan³, College of Interpreters, at Peking; established with the object of preparing young men who have completed the course of Middle Schools (*see* Nos. 580 to 582) for transacting affairs dealing with foreigners. The enrollment is 200; the course of study covers five years and 36 hours of instruction are given weekly. There are five courses for instruction in foreign languages, *i.e.* 1. 英文科 Ying¹ Wên² K'o¹, Course in English, 2. 法文科 Fa⁴ Wên² K'o¹, Course in French, 3. 俄文科 Ê⁴ Wên⁴ K'o¹, Course in Russian, 4. 德文科 Tê² Wên² K'o¹, Course in German, and 5. 日本文科 Jih⁴ Pên³ Wên² K'o¹, Course in Japanese.

In addition to language study, in each of the courses mentioned above there is instruction during the first two years in 普通學 P'u³ T'ung¹ Hsüeh², General Education (ethics, Chinese literature, history, geography, mathematics, natural science, physics, chemistry, drawing and callisthenics), and, during the remaining three years, in 專門學 Chuan¹ Mên² Hsüeh², Special Education (international law, political economy and pedagogy).

Young men between the ages of 12 and 20 years, having a good knowledge of Chinese, free from impediments in speech and physically strong, are accepted as 附學 Fu⁴ Hsüeh², Special Students. They are not distinguished from the ordinary students as regards study and privileges granted.

At the head of the College of Interpreters there is a Director (*see* No. 635). He is in charge of a staff made up of: 1. Preceptor (*see* No. 636; also 副監督 Fu⁴ Chien¹ Tu¹, Assistant Director), 2. 專門學教員 Chuan¹ Mên² Hsüeh² Chiao⁴ Yüan², Teachers of Special Subjects, 3. 外國文教員 Wai⁴ Kuo² Wên² Chiao⁴ Yüan², Teachers of Foreign Languages, 4. 普通學教員 P'u³ T'ung¹ Hsüeh² Chiao⁴ Yüan², Teachers of General Subjects, 5. 助教 Chu⁴ Chiao⁴,

Assistant Teachers, 6. Steward (*see* No. 641; also 副監督 Fu[4] Chien[1] Tu[1], Assistant Director), 7. Secretary (*see* No. 642), 8. 收支官 Shou[1] Chih[1] Kuan[1], Treasurer, 9. Clerk of Works (*see* No. 644), 10. Inspector of Dormitories (*see* No. 645), 11. Proctor (*see* No. 646), and 12. Assistant Inspector of Dormitories (*see* No. 647).

Completion of the course of the College of Interpreters carries with it the following privileges :

Those who graduate with the first rating receive the degree of 舉人出身 Chü[3] Jên[2] Ch'u[1] Shên[1], are enrolled as preferential candidates for the post of 主事 Chu[3] Shih[4] (*see* No. 292)—at the Capital—or 直隸州 Chih[2] Li[4] Chou[1] (*see* No. 851)— in the provinces, and join the Faculty of the University (in whatever department they choose) or are sent abroad for further study.

Those who complete the course with the second rating receive the degree Chü[3] Jên[2] Ch'u[1] Shên[1] (as above), perform duty as interpreters at the Wai Wu Pu in Peking, with the title 內閣中書 Nei[4] Ko[2] Chung[1] Shu[1] (*see* No. 137), or are appointed to the provinces for interpreting, or for dealing with affairs concerning foreigners, as 知縣 Chih[1] Hsien[4] (*see* No. 856). A staff of interpreters and Consuls for service abroad is chosen from the ranks of those who attain the second rating. Those who attain the third rating receive the degree of 舉人 Chü[3] Jên[2] (*see* Nos. 629B and 631) and are appointed, at the Capital, to the various Ministries as Officials of the seventh rank (*see* No. 299) or, in the provinces, as 通判 T'ung[1] P'an[4] (*see* No. 849A). They may also take positions as teachers of foreign languages in Middle Schools. Those who attain the fourth rating remain for repeated study ; should they again fail to attain one of the three senior ratings, and be unwilling to study longer, they receive a document certifying attendance for the full period at the College of Interpreters and are eligible for employment as teachers of foreign languages. The students who graduate with the fifth rating merely receive a list of their examination marks.

625A
to
626

625A. 文典處 Wên² Tien³ Ch'u⁴, Committee for Dictionary Compilation; at the College of Interpreters. This Committee is to compile a dictionary for English and Chinese, French and Chinese, Russian and Chinese, German and Chinese, and Japanese and Chinese. Each dictionary is to be arranged in three divisions, *i.e.* Chinese Language—Foreign Language, Foreign Language—Chinese Language, and Special Expressions.

The Committee is under the supervision of the Director of the College of Interpreters (*see* No. 625) and consists of: 1. a 總纂 Tsung³ Tsuan³, Chief Compiler, 2. Two 分纂 Fên¹ Tsuan³, Compilers, 3. a 繙譯 Fan¹ I⁴, Translator (Interpreter), and 4. a 書籍 Shu¹ Chi², Secretary.

626. 方言學堂 Fang¹ Yen² Hsüeh² T'ang², Colleges of Languages, in the provinces. The object of these institutions is identical with that of the College of Interpreters at Peking (*see* No. 625; compare also No. 311), *i.e.* to prepare men qualified for diplomatic service and for teaching in Middle Schools (*see* Nos. 580 to 582). The course of study is arranged in two sections: 1. Preparatory, providing a course in English, a course in Russian and a course in Japanese, extending over two years, and 2. Special, with a course covering three years.

The Special Course supplies instruction in: arithmetic, Chinese, geography, history, chemistry, philosophy, psychology, international law, natural science and callisthenics. The Preparatory Course includes the study of: arithmetic, the first principles of algebra, Chinese literature, geography, history, principles of chemistry, principle of natural philosophy, the Classics, natural science, drawing and callisthenics.

As students at the Colleges of Languages there are accepted those who have completed the course of a Middle School.

[263]

626A
to
627

The description of the organization of Colleges of Languages given above is that of the College in Fengt'ien province ; those of other provinces are of practically similar organization.

Completion of the course of study of Colleges of Languages carries with it the privileges attained by those who complete the course of the College of Interpreters at Peking (*see* No. 625).

626A. 方言肄習所 Fang¹ Yen² I⁴ Hsi² So³, Practical Courses in Foreign Languages ; held at Moukden. These were instituted for the benefit of substantive and expectant officials of 奉天 Fengt'ien province. They owe their inception to a Memorial of the ex-Governor-General of Manchuria, 徐世昌 Hsü² Shih⁴-ch'ang², sanctioned by the Emperor on the 25th April, 1909.

The students attending these courses are divided into two groups : one group is taught at day sessions (the full course covers two years) and one group attends night sessions (the full course covers three years).

627. 滿蒙文高等學堂 Man³ Mêng² Wên² Kao¹ Têng³ Hsüeh² T'ang², Higher School of Manchu and Mongolian languages ; established in 1908, at Peking, to provide men versed in the Manchu and Mongolian languages. The school has two Courses : 1. 滿蒙文科 Man³ Mêng² Wên² K'o¹, Course in Manchu and Mongolian Languages, and 2. 藏文科 Tsang⁴ Wên² K'o¹, Course in Tibetan. Each Course, in turn, is made up of two sub-divisions : 1. 豫科 Yü⁴ K'o¹, Preparatory Course (covering two years) and 2. 本科 Pên³ K'o¹, Specializing Course (extending over three years). Also, there is a 別科 Pieh⁴ K'o¹, Special Course, with a term of three years, for those not over 35 years of age who possess a literary degree not higher than 舉人 Chü³ Jên², Graduate (Bachelor of Arts), or are in the Government service.

The enrollment of the Preparatory and Specializing Courses is 120 for each ; that of the Special Course is 80.

As students at the Higher School of Manchu and   **627ᴀ**
Mongolian Languages there are accepted persons who have
completed the course of Middle Schools (580 to 582). At
first, as an exception, there were accepted as students persons
not over 25 years of age who were well versed in Chinese and
had some knowledge of Manchu and Mongolian.

The subjects of study include philosophy (Chinese), Chinese
literature, general outline of law, history, geography, arithmetic,
natural science, physics, algebra, trigonometry, general principles
of financial law and political economy, statistics, criminal law,
administrative law, international law, topography, drawing and
tracing, constitutional legislation, laws of the Ta Ch'ing Dynasty,
theory of colonization, geography and history of Manchuria,
Mongolia and Tibet, callisthenics, etc. Russian, Japanese and
veterinary surgery are optional subjects.

At the head of the School there is a Director (*see* No. 635).
He has a staff consisting of: 1. Preceptor (*see* No. 636),
2. 滿蒙語文教員 Man³ Mêng² Yü³ Wên² Chiao⁴ Yüan²,
Teachers of Manchu and Mongolian, 3. 藏語藏文教員
Tsang⁴ Yü³ Tsang⁴ Wên² Chiao⁴ Yüan², Teachers of Tibetan,
4. 各種科學教員 Ko⁴ Chung³ K'o¹ Hsüeh² Chiao⁴ Yüan²,
Teachers of Sciences, 5. 俄文英文東文教員 Ê⁴ Wên²
Ying¹ Wên² Tung¹ Yang² Wên² Chiao⁴ Yüan², Teachers of
Russian, English and Japanese, 6. Steward (*see* No. 641),
7. Secretary (*see* No. 642), 8. Treasurer (*see* No. 643), 9.
Clerk of Works (*see* No. 644), 10. Inspector of Dormitories
(*see* No. 645), 11. Proctor (*see* No. 646), and 12. Assistant
Inspector of Dormitories (*see* No. 647).

627ᴀ. 曲阜學堂 Ch'ü¹ Fu⁴ Hsüeh² T'ang², College
of History and Philology at Ch'üfu (*see* No. 621 ; compare,
also, No. 621ʙ). This College was established on the recommendation of 梁鼎芬 Liang² Ting³-fên¹, late Provincial Judge
of Hupeh (*see* No. 830), *see* Decrees dated the 6th and 14th

628 January, 1907, with sums granted by the Throne, at the district town of Ch'üfu (in the 兗州府 Yen³ Chou¹ Fu³ prefecture of Shantung), the birth-place and burial-place of Confucius.

The College has two courses of study: 豫科 Yu⁴ K'o¹, Preparatory Course, similar to the programme of Middle Schools (*see* No. 580), and 正科 Chêng⁴ K'o¹, Specializing Course, supplying instruction in the Classics, history and literature.

For the Preparatory Course there are accepted scholars who have completed the course of Primary Schools of the Senior Grade (*see* No. 577A); for the Specializing Course there are accepted scholars who have completed the Classical Course of Middle Schools (*see* Nos. 580 and 581) or the course of Lower Normal Schools (*see* No. 618A).

At the head of the College there is a 監督 Chien¹ Tu¹, Director (*see* No. 635); to this position the above-mentioned Liang Ting-fen was appointed (*see* report of the Ministry of Education, dated 7th February, 1910).

A college similar to the College of History and Philology at Ch'üfu has existed for many years in Hupeh province under the title of 存古學堂 Ts'un² Ku³ Hsüeh² T'ang² (compare also No. 621B).

EXAMINATIONS AND LITERARY DEGREES.

628. It has already been mentioned (*see* No. 574) that the occupancy of public posts in China was dependent—until a short time ago—upon the possession of literary degrees (of Metropolitan Graduate, Provincial Graduate or Licentiate— with their various gradations). These degrees were obtained at 考試 K'ao³ Shih⁴, Examinations, of three kinds: 1. 鄉試 Hsiang¹ Shih⁴, Provincial Examinations (held, as a rule, triennially, in the autumn, at the provincial capital), followed by 2. 會試 Hui⁴ Shih⁴, Metropolitan Examination (held at

Peking the following spring), and 3. 殿 試 Tien⁴ Shih⁴, Palace Examination (following immediately after the Metropolitan Examination), after which the award of final degrees was made. Also, there were special examinations—in celebration of auspicious public events—styled 恩 試 Ên¹ Shih⁴, Examinations held by Imperial Favour. The Provincial and Metropolitan Graduates were respectively styled 科 K'o¹ and 甲 Chia³ (the combination of the two terms 科 甲 K'o¹ Chia³, commonly meant "Graduate").

On the 2nd September, 1905, following a Memorial from 袁 世 凱 Yüan² Shih⁴-k'ai³, ex-Governor-General of Chihli, an Imperial Decree was promulgated recognizing that the system of competition for literary degrees was effete—as events had shown—and directing its abolition from the year 1906. At the same time the various Governors-General and Governors were instructed to take steps towards increasing the number of schools—the completion of the courses of these to replace the competitive examinations as a means of obtaining the various literary degrees. However, as a special case (*see* report of the Committee of Ministers, dated the 19th March, 1906) permission has been granted for holding the examinations in 1909 and 1912 for the degrees of 拔 貢 生 Pa² Kung⁴ Shêng¹ and 優 貢 生 Yu¹ Kung⁴ Shêng¹ (*see* No. 629A).

At present, a transitory period, the Higher Schools (previous to 1909) and, furthermore, the University—completion of the courses of which serves as a means of attaining the highest literary degrees—having graduated no classes, the acquisition of degrees is possible only to those who have been educated abroad—after passing examinations at the Ministry of Education and at the Palace (*see* Nos. 630 and 652c to 652E).

All who attained literary degrees previous to the promulgation of the Edict (of 1905) mentioned above have been directed, with a view to the advancement of their education, to join the

629 to 629A 仕學館 Shih⁴ Hsüeh² Kuan³ (*see* Nos. 595 and 595A), the 進士館 Chin⁴ Shih⁴ Kuan³ (*see* No. 596) or the 課吏館 K'o⁴ Li⁴ Kuan³ (*see* Nos. 597 and 597A).

629. By the old system of examinations, abolished by the Decree of the 2nd September, 1905 (*see* No. 628), a person wishing to obtain the first literary degree 秀才 Hsiu⁴ Ts'ai² (*see* No. 629A)—such a person was designated as 俊秀 Chün⁴ Hsiu⁴, had first to pass an examination before the Magistrate of his district. A certificate of merit from the Magistrate enabled the candidate for literary honours to style himself 童生 T'ung² Shêng¹, which may be taken as equivalent to "Student."

The candidate ranking first on the Magistrate's list received the distinguishing title of 案首 An¹ Shou³.

629A. 秀才 Hsiu⁴ Ts'ai², Licentiate; the first literary degree (literary designation, 生員 Shêng¹ Yüan²). This degree was awarded by the Literary Chancellor (*see* No. 827A) at examinations held in prefectural cities (the highest candidate on the list also received the title 案首 An¹ Shou³; compare No. 629). The successful candidates were divided into two groups: 附生 Fu⁴ Shêng¹, Licentiates of the First Class, and 增生 Tsêng¹ Shêng¹, Licentiates of the Second Class. Also, the highest candidates were granted 膏火 Kao¹ Huo³, Government Stipends, and for this reason they were known as 廩生 Lin³ Shêng¹ or 廩膳生 Lin³ Shan⁴ Shêng¹, Stipendiaries.

The Licentiates as a whole were known generally as 貢生 Kung⁴ Shêng¹, Senior Licentiates, *i.e.*, 1. 恩貢生 Ên¹ Kung⁴ Shêng¹, Senior Licentiates by Imperial Favour—having passed at one of the so-called 恩試 Ên¹ Shih⁴ (*see* No. 628), 2. 拔貢生 Pa² Kung⁴ Shêng¹, Senior Licentiates of the First Class—having passed at the examination held every 12 years, 3. 副貢生 Fu⁴ Kung⁴ Shêng¹, or 歲貢生 Sui⁴ Kung⁴ Shêng¹, Senior Licentiate of the Second Class—senior by virtue of the date of their success at the examination or because of

their age; Unsalaried Licentiates, and 4. 優貢生 Yu⁴ Kung⁴ **629ʙ**
Shêng¹, Senior Licentiates of the Third Class—those having
shown noteworthy achievements at the regular examination.
Also, Licentiates of the First Class (Fu⁴ Shêng¹; *see* above)
might obtain the degree of 附貢生 Fu⁴ Kung⁴ Shêng¹ by
purchase.

629ʙ. 舉人 Chü³ Jên² (literary designation, 孝廉
Hsiao⁴ Lien²), Provincial Graduate (Bachelor of Arts); the
second literary degree; conferred at the so-called 鄉試 Hsiang¹
Shih⁴ (*see* No. 628) by the 正考官 Chêng⁴ K'ao³ Kuan¹
(literary designation, 大總裁 Ta⁴ Tsung³ Ts'ai²; ordinary
designation, 大主考 Ta⁴ Chu³ K'ao³), Examiner appointed from
Peking.

Of 'some ten to twelve thousand competitors, commonly
described as 士子 Shih⁴ Tzu³, Scholars, barely three hundred at
the utmost received degrees. The successful candidates, whose
names appeared in an official list styled 龍虎榜 Lung² Hu²
Pang³, were said to have 中舉 Chung¹ Chü³, Attained a Degree,
and were thenceforth known as 舉人 Chü³ Jên², Promoted Men.

In addition to the list of successful scholars, about forty
candidates, whose showing was adjudged as scarcely inferior to
their successful companions, were enrolled in a secondary list,
styled 副榜 Fu⁴ Pang³, a description of proxime accessit, their
names in this manner securing the honour of publicity although
they failed to secure the degree.

The first on the list of graduates received the honorary title
of 解元 Chieh⁴ Yüan², the following four were styled 經魁
Ching¹ K'uei², while the next thirteen received the designation
魁 K'uei² or 鄉魁 Hsiang¹ K'uei². Finally, the degree of 舉人
Chü³ Jên², was sometimes bestowed as an honorary reward upon
candidates over 80 or 90 years of age who had presented
themselves at successive examinations without success—on their
complying with certain specified requirements.

629c   629c. 進士 (hin⁴ Shih⁴, Metropolitan Graduate (Doctor);
the third and highest literary degree; conferred at the 會試
Hui⁴ Shih⁴ (see No. 628) following a 覆試 Fu⁴ Shih⁴, Test
Examination. Those proving successful at this examination
(usually some three hundred and twenty-five to three hundred
and fifty out of six thousand competitors) were known by the
general designation of 貢士 Kung⁴ Shih⁴. Some were
distinguished further, i.e. the first as 會元 Hui⁴ Yüan², the
second to the fifth as 經魁 Ching¹ K'uei², and the sixth to the
thirteenth as 會魁 Hui⁴ K'uei². The degree of Chin⁴ Shih⁴
was bestowed only after the so-called 殿試 Tien⁴ Shih⁴ (see No.
628), Palace Examination. The essays composed at this
examination were scrutinized and classified by a special
committee of Imperial Revisers, called 閱卷大臣 Yüeh⁴ Chüan⁴
Ta⁴ Ch'ên², and the confirmation of the degree was made after
the 朝考 Ch'ao² K'ao³, Court Examination, at which the theme
of the essay to be composed was selected by the Emperor himself.

The examinations completed, the successful scholars were
received in audience by the Emperor and those highest on the
list received various posts at the National Academy (see supra);
the others were given appointments either to provincial posts—
District Magistrate—or to minor positions in the Six Boards at
Peking or the Grand Secretariat.

The scholar ranking first among the Metropolitan Graduates
received the title of 狀元 Chuang⁴ Yüan². The recipient of
this, the highest literary award, attained the rank of 修撰
Hsiu¹ Chuan⁴ (see No. 200A). The graduate ranking second in
order of merit at the Court Examination received the title of
榜眼 Pang³ Yen³ and the third that of 探花 T'an⁴ Hua¹; both
these candidates were invested with the rank of 編修 Pien¹
Hsiu¹ (see No. 200B). The three graduates mentioned made up
the 一甲 I¹ Chia³, First Class, of the year and were styled
進士及第 Chin⁴ Shih⁴ Chi² Ti⁴.

Those graduating highest in the Second Class, 二 甲 Êrh⁴ **629ᴅ**
Chia³, at the Court Examination received the title of 傳臚 **to**
Ch'uan² Lu² and were invested with the rank of 檢討 Chien³ **631**
T'ao³ (see No. 200c) ; the remainder of this class received the
title of 進 士 出 身 Chin⁴ Shih⁴ Ch'u¹ Shên¹ and the rank of
庶 吉 士 Shu⁴ Chi² Shih⁴ (see No. 201).

Of the graduates of the third and last class, designated by
the general name of 同 進 士 出 身 T'ung² Chin⁴ Shih⁴ Ch'u¹
Shên¹; the highest received the rank of 庶 吉 士 Shu⁴ Chi² Shih⁴
(see No. 201) and were attached to the National Academy, the
others were known simply as Chin Shih and received appointments
in the various offices at Peking and in the provinces.

629ᴅ. Examinations for military degrees followed a
precisely similar course and gave access to the same degrees as
did those for the civil career, with the exception that the
character 武 Wu³ (Military) was prefixed (for instance, 武 舉 人
Wu³ Chü³ Jên², or 武 進 士 Wu³ Chin⁴ Shih⁴). These were
abolished by Imperial Edict of 29th August, 1901.

629ᴇ. On Manchus competing in the examinations, employing their own language rather than Chinese, there were conferred
the degrees mentioned above with the distinguishing term 繙 譯
Fan¹ I⁴ prefixed (for instance, 繙 譯 進 士 Fan¹ I⁴ Chin⁴ Shih⁴).

630. Since the abolition of the old system of examinations
(see No. 628) there is operating what may be considered a
transitory system according to which students who have completed
their education abroad are required to undergo, on their return
to Peking, examinations of three grades (for details see Nos.
652c to 652ᴇ), following which, dependent on the literary degree
attained, they receive various appointments.

631. The Imperial Degree of the 2nd September, 1905
(see No. 628), touching the school regulations of 1903,
introduced a new system of competition for literary degrees,

directing their bestowal on students completing the courses of the various types of schools in a satisfactory manner.

There are five distinct examinations held at the schools:

1. 臨 時 考 試 Lin[2] Shih[2] K'ao[3] Shih[4], Periodic Examination (once a month),

2. 學 期 考 試 Hsüeh[2] Ch'i[1] K'ao[3] Shih[4], Semestral Examination (held twice a year), and

3. 學 年 考 試 Hsüeh[2] Nien[2] K'ao[3] Shih[4], Annual Examination.

The above-mentioned examinations are carried on by the administration of the school concerned.

4. 畢 業 考 試 Pi[4] Yeh[4] K'ao[3] Shih[4], Final Examination, and

5. 升 學 考 試 Shêng[1] Hsüeh[2] K'ao[3] Shih[4], Examination for Advancement to a School of Higher Grading.

The two last-mentioned examinations are carried on—at Peking—by officials deputed by the Ministry of Education and—in the provinces—by deputies of the Governor-General or Governor.

At all examinations the "one hundred mark total" is used. Conforming to the percentages received in the examinations students are arranged according to five ratings: 1. 最 優 等 Tsui[4] Yu[1] Têng[3], Excellent (80 to 100, 2. 優 等 Yu[1] Têng[3], Good (60 to 80), 3. 中 等 Chung[1] Têng[3], Satisfactory (40 to 60), 4. 下 等 Hsia[4] Têng[3], Unsatisfactory (20 to 40), and 5. 最 下 等 Tsui[4] Hsia[4] Têng[3], Very Poor (1 to 20).

Dependent on the type of school and on the attainments of the candidates at the final examinations, the following degrees are conferred (in ascending scale): 1. 佾 生 I[4] Shêng[1], 2. 附 生 Fu[4] Shêng[1], 3. 增 生 Tsêng[1] Shêng[1], 4. 廩 生 Lin[3] Shêng[1], 5. 優 廩 生 Yu[1] Lin[3] Shêng[1], 6. 歲 貢 Sui[4] Kung[4], 7. 優 貢 Yu[1] Kung[4], 8. 拔 貢 Pa[2] Kung[4], 9. 貢 生 Kung[4] Shêng[1], 10. 副 榜 Fu[4] Pang[3], 11. 舉 人 Chü[3] Jên[2],

and 12. 進士 Chin⁴ Shih⁴ (of two grades, *i.e.* 同進士出身 **632**
T'ung² Chin⁴ Shih⁴ Ch'u¹ Shên¹ and 進士出身 Chin⁴ Shih⁴ **to**
Ch'u¹ Shên¹).   **635ᴀ**

For particulars as to which schools appertain the various
degrees see the descriptions of the several types of schools.

ADMINISTRATION OF SCHOOLS.

632. 總理 Tsung³ Li³, Curator; at the head of the College
of Law and Administration for Princes and Nobles (*see* No. 622ᴀ).
This post is held by a Prince or High Official of the Empire.

632ᴀ. 總辦 Tsung³ Pan⁴, Curator; formerly at the head
of the Military School for Princes and Nobles. This post is now
abolished (*see* No. 713ᴀ).

633. 大學總監督 Ta⁴ Hsüeh² Tsung³ Chien¹ Tu¹, Rector of
the University; 3ᴀ, at the head of the University (*see* No. 593).

634. 大學分科監督 Ta⁴ Hsüeh² Fên¹ K'o¹ Chien¹
Tu¹, Department Dean; at the head of the Faculty of a
Department of the University (*see* No. 593); directly subordinate
to the Rector of the University (*see* No. 633).

635. 監督 Chien¹ Tu¹, Director. This official is found at
Middle and Higher Schools (*see* Nos. 582 and 583ᴀ), Middle
and Higher Professional Schools (*see* No. 598), Normal Schools
of Lower (*see* No. 618ᴀ) and Higher (*see* No. 618ʙ) Grades,
College of Law and Administration for Princes and Nobles (*see*
No. 622ᴀ), Colleges of Law and Administration, at Peking (*see*
No. 623) and in the province (*see* No. 623ᴀ), College of Law
(*see* No. 624), College of Interpreters (*see* No. 625), Colleges of
Languages (*see* No. 626), College of Manchu and Mongolian
Languages (*see* No. 627), College of History and Philology at
Ch'üfu (*see* No. 627ᴀ), etc. He is the direct and administrative
chief of these institutions.

635ᴀ. 校長 Hsiao⁴ Chang³, Director; at Primary Schools
of both grades (*see* No. 577ʙ) and at Lower Professional Schools
(*see* No. 598).

**635ᴮ
to
639**

635ᴮ. 堂長 T'ang² Chang³, Head Mistress; at Female Primary Schools of both grades (*see* No. 578).

635ᴄ. 小學辦事官 Hsiao³ Hsüeh² Pan⁴ Shih⁴ Kuan¹ and 中學辦事官 Chung¹ Hsüéh² Pan⁴ Shih⁴ Kuan¹, Inspector of Primary School and Director of Middle School at Normal Schools, of the lower (*see* No. 618ᴀ) and higher (*see* No. 618ʙ) grades.

636. 教務提調 Chiao⁴ Wu⁴ T'i² Tiao⁴ or 教務長 Chiao⁴ Wu⁴ Chang³, Preceptor. With the first title, this official is found at the University (*see* No. 593) and at the College of Interpreters (*see* No. 625) and, with the second title, at Higher Schools (*see* No. 583ᴀ), Higher Professional Schools (*see* No. 598) and Higher Special Schools. At the University he is subordinated to the Dean; at other schools to the Director (*see* No. 635).

637. 正教員 Chêng⁴ Chiao⁴ Yüan², Professor (at the University; *see* No. 593). At other schools: 正教員 Chêng⁴ Chiao⁴ Yüan², 教員 Chiao⁴ Yüan², or 教習 Chiao⁴ Hsi², Teacher.

Professors are subordinated to the Preceptor (*see* Nos. 593 and 636). Teachers are subordinated—at Higher Schools, Higher Professional Schools, Higher Normal Schools and Higher Special Schools—to the Preceptor (*see* No. 636) and—at other schools—directly to the Director (*see* No. 635); at the College of Law and Administration for Princes and Nobles (*see* No. 622ᴀ) and at the Military School for Princes and Nobles (*see* No. 713ᴀ) they are subordinated to the Preceptor (*see* No. 649).

638. 副教員 Fu⁴ Chiao⁴ Yüan², Assistant Professor (at the University; *see* No. 598). At other schools: 副教員 Fu⁴ Chiao⁴ Yüan² or 助教 Chu⁴ Chiao⁴, Assistant Teacher. Subordinated tc the Preceptor (*see* No. 636) or, there being no Preceptor, to the Director (*see* No. 635; compare also No. 637).

639. 掌書 Chang³ Shu¹ or 掌書官 Chang³ Shu¹ Kuan¹, Librarian; subordinated to the Preceptor (*see* No. 636) or, there being no Preceptor, to the Director (*see* No. 635; compare also No. 637).

639A. 司書員 Ssu¹ Shu¹ Yüan², Librarian; at the
Military School for Princes and Nobles (see No. 713A); subordinated to the Preceptor (see No. 649).

640. 管課官 Kuan³ K'o⁴ Kuan¹, Tutor; subordinated, at
the College of Law and Administration for Princes and Nobles
(see No. 622A), to the Preceptor (see No. 649), and, at the
College of Law and Administration at Peking (see No. 623) to
the Preceptor (see No. 636).

641. 庶務提調 Shu⁴ Wu⁴ T'i² Tiao⁴, Steward; at the
University (see No. 593) and at the College of Interpreters (see
No. 625). 庶務長 Shu⁴ Wu⁴ Chang³, Steward; at Primary
Schools of the Senior Grade, Higher Schools, etc. 庶務員
Shu⁴ Wu⁴ Yüan² or 庶務委員 Shu⁴ Wu⁴ Wei³ Yüan²,
Steward; at other schools.

The Steward is subordinated, at the University (see No.
593), to the Dean (see No. 634) and, at other schools, to the
Director (see No. 635).

642. 文案 Wên² An⁴, also 文案官 Wên² An⁴ Kuan¹ or
文案員 Wên² An⁴ Yüan², Secretary; at the University, Higher
and Middle Schools and schools of corresponding grades;
subordinated to the Steward (see No. 641).

642A. 書記官 Shu¹ Chi⁴ Kuan¹, Secretary; at the College
of Law and Administration for Princes and Nobles (see No. 622A).

643. 會計 Hui⁴ Chi⁴, also 會計官 Hui⁴ Chi⁴ Kuan¹, or
會計員 Hui⁴ Chi⁴ Yüan², Accountant; at the University,
Higher and Middle Schools and schools of corresponding grades;
subordinated to the Steward (see No. 641).

643A. 收支官 Shou¹ Chih¹ Kuan¹, Treasurer, with duties
of Accountant (see No. 643); at the College of Interpreters (see
No. 625) and at the Military School for Princes and Nobles (see
No. 713A).

643B. 支應官 Chih¹ Ying¹ Kuan¹, Assistant Treasurer
(see No. 643A); at the Military School for Princes and Nobles
(see No. 713A).

639A
to
643B

[275]

644 to 650

644. 雜務官 Tsa² Wu⁴ Kuan¹ or 雜務員 Tsa² Wu⁴ Yüan², Clerk of Works; at the University and Higher Schools and schools of corresponding grade : subordinated to the Steward (*see* No. 641).

645. 齋舍提調 Chai⁴ Shê⁴ T'i² Tiao⁴ (at the University), 齋舍長 Chai⁴ Shê⁴ Chang³, 齋務長 Chai⁴ Wu⁴ Chang³, or 齋務委員 Chai⁴ Wu⁴ Wei³ Yüan² (at other schools—where there are dormitories)—Inspector of Dormitories; subordinated, at the University (*see* No. 593), to the Dean (*see* No. 643), and, at other schools, to the Director (*see* No. 635); appointed from the ranks of Professors or Teachers (*see* No. 637).

646. 監學官 Chien¹ Hsüeh² Kuan¹ or 監學員 Chien¹ Hsüeh² Yüan², Proctor; at the University and Higher Schools and schools of corresponding grade; subordinated to the Inspector of Dormitories; appointed from the ranks of Professors or Teachers (*see* No. 637).

647. 檢察官 Chien³ Ch'a² Kuan¹ or 檢察員 Chien³ Ch'a² Yüan², Assistant Inspector of Dormitories; at the University and Higher Schools and schools of the corresponding grade; subordinated to the Inspector of Dormitories (*see* No. 645).

648. 衛生官 Wei⁴ Shêng¹ Kuan¹, Health Officer; at the University (*see* No. 593); subordinated to the Inspector of Dormitories (*see* No. 645); appointed from the ranks of Professors of the Departments of Medicine, Agriculture or Polytechnic.

649. 提調 T'i² Tiao⁴, Preceptor; at the College of Law and Administration for Princes and Nobles (*see* No. 622A) and at the Military School for Princes and Nobles (*see* No. 713A). This official performs the duties of Preceptor (*see* No. 636) and Steward (*see* No. 641) and assists the Director.

650. 司事 Ssu¹ Shih⁴ or 司事官 Ssu¹ Shih⁴ Kuan¹, Secretary; at Primary Schools of both grades (*see* No. 577B) and at the Customs College (*see* No. 252); subordinated to the Director (*see* No. 635).

[276]

651. Scheme of gradation of schools of various types :

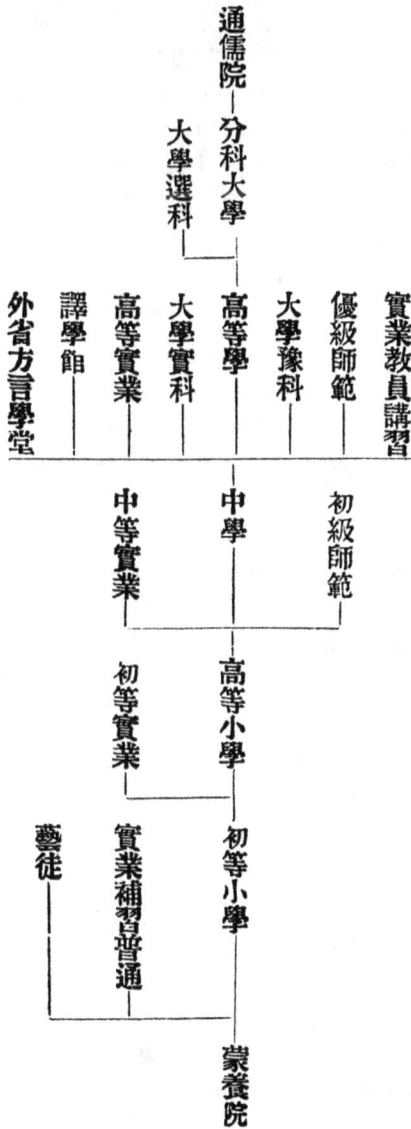

各學堂階級程度統系圖

CHINESE STUDENTS ABROAD.

652. 管理日本游學生監督處 Kuan³ Li³ Jih⁴ Pên³ Yu² Hsüeh² Shêng¹ Chien¹ Tu¹ Ch'u⁴, Inspectorate of Chinese Students in Japan; at the Chinese Legation at Tokyo. At the head of the Inspectorate is a 監督 Chien¹ Tu¹, Controller, appointed from the Legation Secretaries, on the recommendation of the Chinese Minister at Tokyo, by the Ministry of Education.

The Inspectorate is arranged in four sections or departments :

1. 庶務科 Shu⁴ Wu⁴ K'o¹, Section of General Affairs,
2. 會計科 Hui⁴ (K'uai⁴) Chi⁴ K'o¹, Section of Accounts,
3. 文牘科 Wên² Tu³ K'o¹, Section of Correspondence, and
4. 通譯科 T'ung¹ I⁴ K'o¹, Translating (Interpreting) Section.

Each Section is under the control of 科長 K'o¹ Chang³, Section Chiefs, who are assisted by two or three 科員 K'o¹ Yüan², Secretaries.

At the Inspectorate there is also a 編報所 Pien¹ Pao⁴ So³, Office for Compilation of Reports, under a 管理員 Kuan³ Li³ Yüan², Superintendent, where official reports, giving necessary information as to the Chinese students in Japan, arrangements for their education, etc., are compiled, and ten 諮議員 Tzu¹ I⁴ Yüan², Consulting Experts, appointed, on the recommendation of the Controller, by the Minister.

652A. 游美學務處 Yu² Mei³ Hsüeh² Wu⁴ Ch'u⁴, Office for Selection of Students for America ; established in 1909 at Peking. This Office is under the control of the Ministries of Foreign Affairs and of Education. Under the control of the Office there is the 游美肄業館 Yu² Mei³ I⁴ Yeh⁴ Kuan³, Preparatory College, from which students are selected for despatch to America.

By an agreement between the Chinese and American **652B** Governments, dated 1908, the former bound itself to despatch, **to** yearly, for four years (beginning from 1909), 100 students to **652D** America ; thereafter 50 men are to be sent yearly.

The control of Chinese students in America as regards allotment to various schools, etc., rests with a specially appointed 監 督 Chien[1] Tu[1], Controller.

652B.   歐 州 遊 學 生 監 督 Ou[1] Chou[1] Yu[2] Hsüeh[2] Shêng[1] Chien[1] Tu[1], Controller of Chinese Students in Europe ; this post was established in 1907 with a view to control of all Chinese students in Europe.   Practice having shown the unsuitability of the system of control, a Memorial from the Ministry of Education (sanctioned by the Emperor on the 7th November, 1909), arranged for the appointment of five Controllers, to reside in England, France, Germany, Russia and Belgium, and be subordinated to the Chinese Ministers at London, Paris, Berlin, St. Petersburg and Brussels respectively.

Regulations relating to the ccntrol of students in Europe, similar to those for students in Japan, are to be later drawn up (*see* No. 652).

652C.   Having studied abroad for a period of not less than three years, possessing a diploma from a Middle School, or for a period of not less than four year, possessing no diploma, and having successfully completed the course of study of Government Universities or of Special Higher Schools, Chinese students on their return to Peking are called upon to undergo examinations of three types : 1.   甄 錄 Chên[1] Lu[4], Test Examination, 2. 正 場 考 試 Cheng[4] Ch'ang[3] K'ao[3] Shih[4], Ministerial Examination, and 3.   廷 試 T'ing[2] Shih[4], Examination at the Palace.

652D.   The Test Examination is held at the Ministry of Education and consists of foreign languages and subjects of general education.   On satisfactory completion of this examination students are admitted to the Ministerial Examination.

652E
to
652F

652E. At the Ministerial Examination (*see* No. 652C) there are set three examination papers, *i.e.* one of foreign languages and two of selected special educational subjects. Those proving successful at this examination are arranged, in order of merit, in three classes : 1. 最優等 Tsui⁴ Yu¹ Têng³, Excellent, 2. 優等 Yu¹ Têng³, Good, and 3. 中等 Chung¹ Têng³, Satisfactory.

Those attaining the grade of "excellent" receive the degree of 進士 Chin⁴ Shih⁴, Doctor, and those graded as "good" or "satisfactory" receive the degree of 舉人 Chü³ Jên², Bachelor.

The candidates at the examination themselves select the special education in which they wish to be examined. The list of special subjects numbers seven : 1. 法政科 Fa⁴ Chêng⁴ K'o¹, Legal and Administrative Subjects, 2. 醫科 I¹ K'o¹, Medicine, 3. 農科 Nung² K'o¹, Agriculture, 4. 工科 Kung¹ K'o¹, Polytechnics, 5. 格致科 Ko² Chih⁴ K'o¹, Natural Sciences, 6. 商科 Shang¹ K'o¹, Commercial Subjects and 7. 文科 Wên² K'o¹, Literature. The literary degree attained is qualified by the speciality examined in *i.e.* 法政科舉人 Fa⁴ Chêng⁴ K'o¹ Chü³ Jên², Bachelor of Law and Administration, or 醫科進士 I¹ K'o¹ Chin⁴ Shih⁴, Doctor of Medicine.

The final confirmation of literary degrees is made only after the examination at the Palace (*see* No. 652C), which takes place in the 保和殿 Pao³ Ho² Tien⁴, with Princes and High Officials of the Empire as the examiners.

652F. The Ministerial Examination is held yearly, in the 8th moon, and is carried on by the officials following :

1. 主試官 Chu³ Shih⁴ Kuan¹, Chief Examiners (number indefinite); supervise the preparation of examination papers and their subsequent marking.

2. 襄校官 Hsiang¹ Chiao⁴ Kuan¹, Assistant Examiners (the number of these depends on the number of candidates to be examined).

3. 監臨官 Chien[1] Lin[2] Kuan[1], Supervisors; charged with the supervision and control of candidates while the examination is in progress and assist in compiling the examination marks.

4. 提調官 T'i[2] Tiao[4] Kuan[1], Proctors; distribute examination papers and maintain order in the examination hall, etc.

5. 庶務官 Shu[4] Wu[4] Kuan[1], Stewards.

6. 收掌官 Shou[1] Chang[3] Kuan[1], Collectors; receive completed examination papers (marked with secret designations) from the candidates and hand same to the Examiners.

7. 彌封官 Mi[2] Fêng[1] Kuan[1], Sealers of Examinations; seal the examination papers of candidates with a secret designation—on the first page.

8. 監塲官 Chien[1] Ch'ang[3] Kuan[1], Inspectors; watch that no abuses take place in the examination hall.

9. 內塲監試御史 Nei[4] Ch'ang[3] Chien[1] Shih[4] Yü[4] Shih[2], Examination Censers; appointed from the ranks of officials of the Ministry of Education to keep a watch for malpractices on the part of the above-enumerated officials. Should any irregularities be detected they present Memorials accusing the guilty parties.

653. 青島特別高等專門學堂 Ch'ing[1] Tao[3] T'ieh[4] Pieh[4] Kao[1] Têng[3] Chuan[1] Mên[2] Hsüeh[2] T'ang[2], Privileged Special Higher School at Tsingtau; established in 1909 at the initiative of the German Government, which allotted three hundred thousand marks for preliminary expenses and bound itself to contribute seventy thousand marks yearly towards its upkeep—the Chinese Government contributed forty thousand marks as preliminary expenses and has bound itself to pay forty thousand marks yearly, for the first ten years, towards its maintenance. The object of the school is to enable Chinese to receive a modern education in their native land.

The school is organized into two sections :

1. 預備班 Yü⁴ Pei⁴ Pan¹, Preparatory, or 初級習普通學班 Ch'u¹ Chi² Hsi² P'ü³ T'ung¹ Hsüeh² Pan¹, General Education Section ; with a course of six years. For this section there are accepted scholars between the ages of 13 and 15 years, who have completed the course of a Primary School of the Senior Grade, after a test examination.

2. 高等班 Kao¹ Têng³ Pan¹, Higher Section, consisting of four courses: 1. 法政科 Fa⁴ Chêng⁴ K'o¹, Course in Law and Administration, 2. 醫科 I¹ K'o¹, Course in Medicine, 3. 工科 Kung¹ K'o¹, Course in Technology, and 4. 農林科 Nung² Lin² K'o¹, Course in Agriculture and Forestry. Each of these courses covers three years,—with the exception of the Course in Medicine, which is made up of a four years course at the school and a year of training, immediately after, at one of the city hospitals. For the Higher Section there are accepted scholars who have successfully completed the Primary Section course of study and after a test examination, scholars possessing a diplomas from a Middle School.

At the head of the Tsingtau School there is a 監督 Chien¹ Tu¹, Director, appointed by the German Government. This official is charged with the supreme control of the affairs of the school.

For the supervision of the instruction, as regards its conformity to the programme of education of Chinese Government schools, there is a 總稽查 Tsung³ Chi² Ch'a², Chief Inspector, appointed by the Ministry of Education and independent of the Director.

The teachers of Chinese are appointed on the recommendation of the Shantung Commissioner of Education, and the local 視學官 Shih⁴ Hsüeh² Kuan¹, Inspectors of Education have the right of supervision of the school.

For attendance at examinations the Ministry of Education deputes a special official who, with the Director and the Chief Inspector, signs diplomas bestowed on graduates.

On completion of the course of study of the Tsingtau School students join the University at Peking for further study or are appointed to various Government offices—according to their courses of study.

At the school there has been established a 譯 書 局 I⁴ Shu⁴ Chü², Translating Office, for the translation of text books from German into Chinese.

Regulations for the school at Tsingtau, in 18 articles, were drawn up by the Ministry of Education and received Imperial Sanction on the 14th August, 1909.

PUBLIC LIBRARIES.

654. 京 師 圖 書 館 Ching¹ Shih¹ T'u² Shu¹ Kuan³, Metropolitan Public Library; established in accordance with a Memorial from the Ministry of Education, sanctioned by Imperial Decree of the 8th September, 1909, not only for old and modern Chinese books but for foreign works as well. By the Decree mentioned it was directed that there be delivered to the Metropolitan Library : 1. Old plates of the 宋 Sung⁴, and the 元 Yüan², Dynasties, kept at the Grand Secretariat, 2. "Great Record" of the Emperor Yung³ Lo⁴ 永 樂 大 典 Yung³ Lo⁴ Ta² Tien³, from the National Academy, 3. A full collection of books labelled in Chinese 四 庫 全 書 Ssu⁴ K'u⁴ Ch'üan² Shu¹, from the hall 文 津 閣 Wên² Chin¹ Ko², at 熱 河 Je² Ho², and 4. All the works previously kept at the 避 署 山 莊 Pi⁴ Shu³ Shan¹ Chuang¹, Summer Palace at Jehol.

For the library there were granted, close to the 德 勝 門 Tê² Shêng⁴ Mên² gate (see No. 801B), two plots of land known as 淨 業 湖 Ching⁴ Yeh⁴ Hu² and 滙 通 祠 Hui⁴

654. T'ung¹ Tz'u², belonging to the Imperial Household and under the control of the 奉宸苑 Fêng⁴ Ch'ên² Yüan² (*see* No. 90).

The general supervision of the library appertains to the Ministry of Education; the real control is vested in a 監督 Chien¹ Tu¹, Director, who has a staff made up of 副監督 Fu⁴ Chien¹ Tu¹, Assistant Director, and 提調 T'i² Tiao⁴, Proctor.

At the Metropolitan Library there is to be established a 古物保存會 Ku³ Wu⁴ Pao³ Ts'un² Hui⁴, Museum of Antiques.

654A. 圖書館 T'u² Shu¹ Kuan³, Public Libraries, in the provinces; these are to be opened throughout the provinces, according to the scheme of constitutional reforms of the Ministry of Education (*see* report of the Ministry dated the 18th April, 1909), in 1910; at present they are found only in Shantung, Shansi, Heilungchiang and some others. Libraries are under the general supervision of the Commissioners of Education (*see* No. 827) who are styled, as supervisors of the Librarians, 總理 Tsung³ Li³.

General Regulations, in 20 articles, for the Metropolitan and Provincial Public Libraries have been drawn up by the Ministry of Education (*see* report of the Ministry dated the 27th January, 1910).

Public Libraries at provincial capitals are designated 某省圖書館 Mou³ Shêng³ T'u² Shu¹ Kuan³, those at administrative centres of prefectures, sub-prefectures, departments and districts are called 某府廳州縣圖書館 Mou³ Fu³ T'ing¹ Chou¹ Hsien⁴ T'u² Shu¹ Kuan³ (article 3).

Public Libraries are to consist of a 藏書室 Ts'ang² Shu¹ Shih⁴, Library, 閱書室 Yüeh Shu¹ Shih⁴, Reading Room, and 辦事室 Pan⁴ Shih⁴ Shih⁴, Office (Chancery) (article 5).

The general supervision of libraries at provincial capitals appertains to the Governors-General or Governors; at administrative centres of prefectures, sub-prefectures, departments and districts the Commissioners of Education exercise the supreme control. The actual management of affairs appertains to the 監督 Chien¹ Tu¹, Directors and 提調 T‘i² Tiao⁴, Proctors (compare No. 654).

At places where there are few duties at the library there may be appointed a 管理 Kuan³ Li³, Supervisor, alone, this position being associated with that of Director of the Association for the Fostering of Public Education (see No. 829a) or of Director of a School (article 6).

It is arranged that 刊印所 K‘an³ Yin⁴ So³, Printing Offices, with 排印所 P‘ai² Yin⁴ So³, Typesetting Offices, may be established at Libraries (article 12).

MILITARY FORCES OF CHINA.

655. As a basis for the formation of a modern military force in the Chinese Empire a scheme was drawn up by the Committee for Army Reorganization (see No. 416), under the presidency of Prince Ch‘ing, and submitted to the Emperor for sanction on the 12th September, 1904.

The modern troops of China (so-called "New Troops" to distinguish them from the "Troops of the Green Standard and of the Eight Banners") may be divided into two categories: 1. 陸軍 Lu⁴ Chün¹, Land (general for the Empire) Forces, and 2. 巡防隊 Hsün² Fang² T‘ui⁴, Reserve Forces (or "Provincial Troops").

A. Lu Chün or Land Forces:

656. 陸軍 Lu⁴ Chün¹, Land Forces; made up of: 1. 常備軍 Ch‘ang² Pei⁴ Chün¹, Regular Army—in this the term of service is 3 years; at present it is in the process of formation and its full complement of 三十六鎮 San¹ Shih² Liu⁴ Chên⁴, 36 Divisions, will not be reached until 1913,

續備軍 Hsü⁴ Pei⁴ Chün¹, Reserves of the First Call—the

656A   term of service here is 3 years; for each division of the Regula
Army there is to be a division of Reserves of the First Call
corresponding to it in all respects except that there will be two,
instead of three, batallions in each regiment (the complement of
a division of the Reserves comprises 8,640 men in the ranks and
1,200 camp followers and there are eight "yings"), and
3. 後備軍 Hou⁴ Pei⁴ Chün¹, Reserves of the Second Call
(army of reserve, militia)—the term of service of these troops is
4 years; in war time this branch of the Army will furnish a
brigade of four batallions which is given a number as a division
of the Regular Army.

In China there is as yet no conscription and 新兵 Hsin¹
Ping¹, Recruits, are enrolled through the 徵兵總署 Chêng¹
Ping¹ Tsung³ Shu³, Head Recruiting Offices, established at the
provincial 督練處 Tu¹ Lien⁴ Ch'u⁴ (see Nos. 695 and 700B).
The determination of physical fitness for military service is made
according to the 募兵制畧 Mu⁴ Ping¹ Chih⁴ Lüeh⁴, Short
Regulations Concerning Recruiting (forming one of the enclosures
to the Memorial of Prince Ch'ing, already mentioned in
No. 655).

656A. From the types of arms used the Chinese Army is
arranged as: 1. 步隊 Pu⁴ Tui⁴, Infantry, 2. 馬隊 Ma³ Tui⁴,
Cavalry, 3. 礮隊 P'ao⁴ Tui⁴, Artillery (in its turn sub-divided
into 1. 陸路礮隊 Lu⁴ Lu⁴ P'ao⁴ Tui⁴, Field Artillery, and
2. 過山礮隊 Kuo⁴ Shan¹ P'ao⁴ Tui⁴, Mountain Artillery),
4. 工程隊 Kung¹ Ch'êng² Tui⁴, Engineers, 5. 輜重隊 Tzu¹
Chung⁴ Tui⁴, Troops for Transport of Supplies. Also there are
the following auxiliary corps: 1. 軍需 Chün¹ Hsü¹, Commissariat Corps, 2. 軍醫 Chün¹ I¹, Medical Corps, 3. 馬醫
Ma³ I¹, Veterinary Corps, 4. 製械 Chih⁴ Hsieh⁴, Ordnance
Corps, 5. 測繪 Ts'ê⁴ Hui⁴, Topographic Corps, 6. 軍樂
Chün¹ Yüeh⁴, Music Corps, and 7. 憲兵 Hsien⁴ Ping¹,
Gendarmerie.

656B. As regards administration, the Chinese Army is
thus divided: 1. 鎮 Chên⁴, Division, 2. 協 Hsieh², Brigade,
3. 標 Piao¹, Regiment, 4. 營 Ying², Batallion (in infantry);
Division (in cavalry and artillery), 5. 隊 Tui⁴, Company (in
infantry); Squadron (in cavalry); Battery (in artillery), 6. 排
P'ai², Platoon (in infantry, in time of peace; in time of war, 哨
Shao⁴); Half a Squadron (in cavalry), and 7. 棚 P'êng², Squad.

656C. 鎮 Chên⁴, Division; the largest organized unit in
time of peace. The regulations provide for the combination of
three divisions into a 軍 Chün¹, Corps, and the combination of
Chün into a 大 軍 Ta⁴ Chün¹, in time of war.

In time of peace a division is made up of two brigades of
infantry, each of which consists of two regiments of three
batallions each, one regiment of artillery, having nine batteries
(54 guns) and eighteen machine guns, one regiment of cavalry,
made up of twelve squadrons, one batallion of engineers, consisting
of four companies, one batallion of troops for transport of
supplies, having four companies, musicians (51, including a
bandmaster and three servants), and gendarmerie. In time
of peace a division numbers 12,512 men; in war time,
21,000 men.

656D. 協 Hsieh², Brigade (numbered 1 to 72, in
consecutive order, following the numerical order of the divisions).
The brigade is found only in the infantry and consists of two
regiments (it is, however, permissible for a division to have two
regiments of cavalry instead of one, which form a 馬 隊 一 協
Ma³ Tui⁴ I¹ Hsieh², Cavalry Brigade).

656E. 標 Piao¹, Regiment; this organization unit is found
in infantry, cavalry and artillery. In the infantry, regiments
are numbered 1 to 144, in consecutive order, following the order
of their respective divisions, and brigades (see No. 656D);
cavalry and artillery regiments bear the same number as do their
respective divisions. A regiment of infantry consists of three

656F batallions ; cavalry and artillery regiments are made up of three divisions.

656F. 營 Ying[2], Fundamental unit of all branches of the Army (in infantry, Batallion ; in cavalry and artillery, Division); the complement of this unit differs for the various branches and auxiliary parts of the Army.

In the infantry a batallion consists of four 隊 Tui[4], Companies, and numbers, in time of peace, 659 men, in time of war, 1,240 men. Companies are designated as : 前 Ch'ien[2], Company of the Vanguard, 2. 左 Tso[3], Left Company, 3. 右 Yu[4], Right Company, and 4. 後 Hou[4], Company of the Rearguard, the complement of a company is five officers and 149 soldiers, in time of peace, or, in time of war, 294 soldiers. Each company is divided into three 排 P'ai[2], Platoons, composed of three 棚 P'êng[2], Squads, each, in time of peace, or three 哨 Shao[4], Platoons, of six 棚 P'êng[2], Squads, each, in time of war Platoons are designated as 左 Tso[3], Left, 中 Chung[1], Centre, and 右 Yu[4], Right, while squads are designated by the numbers of their respective companies—from one to nine, in time of peace, and from one to eighteen, in time of war—and the first squad is styled 頭 棚 T'ou[2] P'eng[2], Head Squad. Each squad is made up of two sergeants and twelve privates.

A cavalry division consists of four 隊 Tui[4], Squadrons, and numbers, generally speaking, 363 men and 260 horses. It is divided into two 排 P'ai[2], Half Squadrons—left and right— which, in turn, are subdivided into two 棚 P'êng[2], Squads, bearing the numbers (in the squadron) one to four. The complement of a cavalry squadron is three officers, 78 cavalrymen and 64 軍 馬 Chün[1] Ma[3], Cavalry Horses.

A division of field artillery (there are two in a regiment as a rule—should conditions where operations are being carried on demand it, there may be only one division of field artillery, or even none, the divisions of mountain artillery being correspondingly increased) consists of three 礮 隊 P'ao[4] Tui[4], Batteries, having 礮 六 聟 P'ao[4] Liu[4] Tsun[1], six guns, each. Its complement is 568 men and 270 horses.

A battery is made up of three 排 P'ai[2], Platoons (left, centre and right) of three 棚 P'êng[2], Squads, each, which bear the numerical designation of the battery—from one to nine.

A division of mountain artillery, having 18 mountain guns, is organized exactly similarly to a division of field artillery.

The complement of a battery is five officers, 181 men, 48 horses for guns and five chargers.

A batallion of engineers, similarly to the infantry, is composed of four 隊 Tui[4], Companies, and numbers 667 men, in time of peace, or 1,250 men, in time of war. The companies are designated as van, left, right or rear and are distinguished by their specialities : 1. Bridging Company, 2. Sappers Company, 3. Telegraph, Telephone and Search-light Company, and 4. Mining Company.

A transport batallion is divided similarly to a batallion of engineers but, in consequence of the great number of men it operates for, it has in the ranks 748 men in time of peace, and 1,640 men in time of war.

MILITARY RANKS.

657. By temporary regulations, drawn up by the General Staff of the Army and sanctioned by the Emperor on the 11th November, 1909, there were introduced some changes in the military ranks—their number was increased (1A, 8B, 9A and 9B were added), and they were made equal to the corresponding civil ranks.

658. The new regulations (see No. 657) provide for fourteen ranks for officers and sub-officers of the Land Forces :

1. 大 將 軍 Ta⁴ Chiang¹ Chün¹, or 將 軍 Chiang¹ Chün¹, Field Marshal ; 1ᴀ (of the rank of a Grand Secretary—*see* No. 131—of the civil service). This rank is bestowed on very eminent generals (*see* below).

2. 正 都 統 Chêng⁴ Tu¹ T'ung³, General ; 1ʙ (of the rank of a 總 督 Tsung³ Tu¹—*see* No. 820—of the civil service) ; holds the position of Commander of a Corps (*see* No. 661).

3. 副 都 統 Fu⁴ Tu¹ T'ung³, Lieutenant-General ; 2ᴀ (of the rank of 巡 撫 Hsün² Fu³—*see* No. 821—of the civil service) ; holds the position of Commander of a Division (*see* No. 661).

4. 協 都 統 Hsieh² Tu¹ T'ung³, Major-General ; 2ʙ (of the rank of 布 政 使 Pu⁴ Chêng⁴ Shih³—*see* No. 826—of the civil service) ; holds the position of Commander of a Brigade (*see* No. 661), Chief of Staff of a Corps (*see* No. 662) or Commander of an Artillery Corps (*see* No. 670).

Ranks Nos. 2 to 4 form what is known as the 上 等 Shang⁴ Têng³, Highest Class, made up of 三 級 San¹ Chi², Three Grades.

5. 正 參 領 Chêng⁴ Ts'an¹ Ling³, Colonel ; 3ᴀ (of the rank of 按 察 使 An⁴ Ch'a² Shih³—*see* No. 830—of the civil service) ; holds the position of Commander of a Regiment (*see* No. 661), Commander of Engineers of a Corps (*see* No. 671), Senior Adjutant of a Corps (*see* No. 663), Arms Inspector of a Corps (*see* No. 668), Chief of Staff of a Division (*see* No. 662), Judge Advocate of a Corps (*see* No. 672), or Corps Surgeon (*see* No. 675).

6. 副 參 領 Fu⁴ Ts'an¹ Ling³, Lieutenant-Colonel ; 3ʙ (of the rank of 鹽 運 使 Yen² Yün⁴ Shih³—*see* No. 835—of the civil service) ; holds the position of Second in Command of a Regiment (*see* No. 661), Senior Assistant Chief of Staff of a Corps (*see* No. 662), Senior Adjutant of a Division (*see* No. 663), Arms Inspector of a Division (*see* No. 668), Commissary

Officer of a Division (*see* No. 673), Judge Advocate of a Division (*see* No. 672), Surgeon of a Division (*see* No. 675), Corps Veterinary Surgeon (*see* No. 676) or Secretary of the First Class (*see* No. 664).

Ranks Nos. 1 to 6 are bestowed by Imperial Decrees (簡放 Chien³ Fang⁴).

7. 協參領 Hsieh² Ts'an¹ Ling³, Captain; 4A (of the rank of 道員 Tao⁴ Yüan²—*see* No. 838—of the civil service); holds the position of Commander of a Battalion (*see* No. 661), Junior Assistant Chief of Staff of a Corps (*see* No. 662), Senior Assistant Chief of Staff of a Division (*see* No. 662), Arms Inspector of a Regiment (*see* No 668), Senior Adjutant of a Brigade (*see* No. 663), Commissary Officer of a Regiment (*see* No. 673), Surgeon of a Regiment (*see* No. 675), Veterinary Surgeon of a Division (*see* No. 676) or Secretary of the Second Class (*see* No. 664).

The ranks Nos. 5 to 7 form the 中 等 Chung¹ Têng³, Middle Class, divided into three grades (*see* above).

8. 正軍校 Chêng⁴ Chün¹ Hsiao⁴, First Lieutenant; 5A (ranking with the 直隸州 Chih² Li⁴ Chou¹—*see* No. 851—of the civil service); holds the position of Second in Command of a Battalion (*see* No. 661), Commander of a Company (*see* No. 661), Junior Assistant Chief of Staff of a Division (*see* No.662), Adjutant of a Corps (or Brigade, Division and Regiment; *see* No. 663), Arms Inspector of an Artillery Division (*see* No. 668), Commissary Officer of a Battalion (*see* No. 673), Surgeon of a Battalion (*see* No. 675), Veterinary Surgeon of a Regiment (*see* No. 676), Inspector of Couriers and Convoys (*see* No. 665), Inspector of Arms Depôts (*see* No. 669), Remount Officer (in cavalry and artillery) of a Division, or (in transport troops or commissariat troops) of a Battalion (*see* No. 667) or Chief of Musicians (*see* No. 679).

9. 副軍校 Fu⁴ Chün¹ Hsiao⁴, Second Lieutenant; 6A (ranking with the 通判 T'ung¹ P'an⁴—*see* No. 849A—of the

659 civil service); holds the position of Commander of a Platoon (*see* No. 661), Assistant Surgeon (*see* No. 675), Divisional Chief of Signalmen (*see* No. 678), Veterinary Surgeon of a Division or Battalion (*see* No. 676), Senior Clerk (*see* No. 664), Bandmaster (*see* No. 679) or Regimental Standard-Bearer (*see* No. 666).

10. 協軍校 Hsieh² Chün¹ Hsiao⁴, Sub-Lieutenant; 7A (ranking with the 知縣 Chih¹ Hsien⁴—*see* No. 856—of the civil service); holds the position of Adjutant of a Company (*see* No. 663), Brigade and Regimental Chief of Signalmen (*see* No. 678), Assistant Surgeon (*see* No. 675) or Clerk (*see* No. 664).

The ranks Nos. 8 to 10 form the 次等 Tz'u⁴ Têng³, Lower Class, divided in three grades (compare above). The ranks Nos. 7 to 10 are bestowed according to the recommendations of reports (奏補 Tsou⁴ Pu³).

11. 司務長 Ssu¹ Wu⁴ Chang³, Ensign; 8A (ranking with the 縣丞 Hsien⁴ Ch'êng²—*see* No. 857—of the civil service); one of the 額外軍官 Ê² Wai⁴ Chün¹ Kuan¹, "Supernumerary Officers' Ranks."

12. 上士 Shang⁴ Shih⁴, Sergeant of the First Class; 8B (ranking with a 訓導 Hsün⁴ Tao⁴—*see* No. 857—of the civil service).

13. 中士 Chung¹ Shih⁴, Sergeant of the Second Class; 9A (ranking with a 縣主簿 Hsien⁴ Chu³ Pu⁴—*see* No. 857—of the civil service).

14. 下士 Hsia⁴ Shih⁴, Sergeant of the Third Class; 9B (ranking with a 巡檢 Hsün² Chien³—*see* No. 857—of the civil service).

Ranks Nos. 12 to 14 belong to the category of 軍士 Chün¹ Shih⁴, Petty Officers' Ranks.

Ranks Nos. 11 to 14 are bestowed by the officer in command on persons serving under him (咨補 Tzu¹ Pu³).

659. In accordance with the new regulations (*see* No. 657) those of the rank of Colonel, or lower, have their ranks further

defined by the indication of this or that type of arms or this or **659ᴀ**
that auxiliary corps (compare No. 656ᴀ). Thus, a Colonel may
be designated : 1. 警察隊正參領 Ching[3] Ch'a[2] Tui[4] Chêng[4]
Ts'an[1] Ling[3], Colonel of the Military Police (or Gendarmerie)
2. 步隊正參領 Pu[4] Tui[4] Chêng[4] Ts'an[1] Ling[3], Colonel of
Infantry, 3. 馬隊正參領 Ma[3] Tui[1] Chêng[4] Ts'an[1] Ling[3],
Colonel of Cavalry, 4. 礮隊正參領 P'ao[4] Tui[4] Chêng[4] Ts'an[1]
Ling[3], Colonel of Artillery, 5. 工程隊正參領 Kung[1] Ch'êng[2]
Tui[4] Chêng[4] Ts'an[1] Ling[3], Colonel of Engineers, 6. 輜重隊正
參領 Tzu[1] Chung[4] Tui[4] Chêng[4] Ts'an[1] Ling[3], Colonel of Troops
of Transport, 7. 軍需正參領 Chün[1] Hsü[1] Chêng[4] Ts'an[1]
Ling[3], Commissariat Colonel, 8. 軍醫正參領 Chün[1] I[1]
Chêng[4] Ts'an[1] Ling[2], Colonel of the Medical Staff (and 司藥正
參領 Ssu[1] Yao[4] Chêng[4] Ts'an[1] Ling[3], Colonel of the Pharma-
ceutical Staff), 9. 馬醫正參領 Ma[3] I[1] Chêng[4] Ts'an[1] Ling[3],
Colonel of the Veterinary Staff, 10. 製械正參領 Chih[4]
Hsieh[4] Chêng[4] Ts'an[1] Ling[3], Colonel of Ordnance, 11. 測繪正
參領 Ts'ê[4] Hui[4] Chêng[4] Ts'an[1] Ling[3], Colonel of Topographical
Staff, or 12. 軍樂協軍校 Chün[1] Yüeh[4] Hsieh[2] Chün[1]
Hsiao[4], Sub-Lieutenant of the Musical Staff.

The rank of General is modified, to show service in this or
that branch of the Army, in three cases only, namely : 1. 軍需副
都統 Chün[1] Hsü[1] Fu[4] Tu[1] T'ung[3], Commissariat Lieutenant-
General, 2. 軍醫副都統 Chün[1] I[1] Fu[4] Tu[1] T'ung[3], Lieutenant-
General of the Medical Staff, and 3. 製械副都統 Chih[4]
Hsieh[4] Fu[4] Tu[1] T'ung[3], Lieutenant-General of Ordnance.

659ᴀ. Of late, for the designation of military ranks in
Chinese literature (especially in newspapers), the Japanese terms
are becoming more and more current. By these the military
ranks are divided into three classes, which, in turn, are sub-
divided into three grades :

First Class: 大將 Ta[4] Chiang[4], General, 中將 Chung[1] Chiang[4],
Lieutenant-General, and 少將 Shao[4] Chiang[4], Major-General.

**659B
to
660**

Second Class : 大佐 Ta⁴ Tso³, Colonel, 中佐 Chung¹ Tso³, Lieutenant-Colonel, and 少佐 Shao⁴ Tso³, Captain.

Third Class : 大尉 Ta⁴ Yü⁴, First Lieutenant, 中尉 Chung¹ Yü⁴, Second Lieutenant, and 少尉 Shao⁴ Yü⁴, Sub-Lieutenant.

659B. Naval ranks correspond to those of the Army, with the exception that they are prefixed by 海軍 Hai³ Chün¹, Naval, thus : 1. 海軍正都統 Hai³ Chün¹ Chêng⁴ Tu¹ T'ung³, Admiral, 2. 海軍副都統 Hai³ Chün¹ Fu⁴ Tu¹ T'ung³, Vice-Admiral, 3. 海軍協都統 Hai³ Chün¹ Hsieh² Tu¹ T'ung³, Rear-Admiral, 4. 海軍正參領 Hai³ Chün¹ Chêng⁴ Ts'an¹ Ling³, Post-Captain, 5. 海軍副參領 Hai³ Chün¹ Fu⁴ Ts'an¹ Ling³, Commander, 6. 海軍協參領 Hai³ Chün¹ Hsieh² Ts'an¹ Ling³, Lieutenant-Commander, 7. 海軍正軍校 Hai³ Chun¹ Chêng⁴ Chün¹ Hsiao⁴, Senior Lieutenant, 8. 海軍副軍校 Hai³ Chün¹ Fu⁴ Chün¹ Hsiao⁴, Lieutenant, and 9. 海軍協軍校 Hai³ Chün¹ Hsieh² Chün¹ Hsiao⁴, Midshipman.

659C. The Japanese terms for the various naval ranks (compare No. 659A) are :

First Class : 海軍大將 Hai³ Chün¹ Ta⁴ Chiang⁴. Admiral, 海軍中將 Hai³ Chün¹ Chung¹ Chiang⁴, Vice-Admiral, and 海軍少將 Hai³ Chün¹ Shao⁴ Chiang⁴, Rear-Admiral.

Second Class : 海軍大佐 Hai³ Chün¹ Ta⁴ Tso³, Post-Captain, 海軍中佐 Hai³ Chün¹ Chung¹ Tso³, Commander, and 海軍少佐 Hai³ Chun¹ Shao⁴ Tso³, Lieutenant Commander.

Third Class : 海軍大尉 Hai³ Chün¹ Ta⁴ Yü⁴, Senior Lieutenant, 海軍中尉 Hai³ Chün¹ Chung¹ Yü⁴, Lieutenant, and 海軍少尉 Hai³ Chun¹ Shao⁴ Yü⁴, Midshipman.

660. Posts existing in the Army may be arranged under the following categories : 1. Line, 2. Staff, 3. Adjutancy, 4. Secretarial, 5. Orderly and Convoy, 6. Colours, 7. Remount, 8. Arms, 9. Arsenal, 10. Artillery, 11. Engineer, 12. Judicial, 13. Commissariat, 14. Administration of Com-

missariat Office, 15. Medical, 16. Veterinary, 17. Medical Department Administration, 18. Signal, 19. Music, and 20. Camp-follower.

661. Posts of the Line : 1. 總統官 Tsung³ T'ung³ Kuan¹, Corps Commander, 2. 領制官 T'ung³ Chih⁴ Kuan¹, Division Commander, 3. 統領官 T'ung³ Ling³ Kuan¹, Brigade Commander, 4. 統帶官 T'ung³ Tai⁴ Kuan¹, Regiment Commander, 5. 教練官 Chiao⁴ Lien⁴ Kuan¹, Second in Command of a Regiment (in time of peace, " Regimental Instructor," and acts partly as Chief of Staff and Adviser to the Commander ; later, when all Commanders will be drawn from the ranks of officers who have received a proper military education, this post will be abolished), 6. 管帶官 Kuan³ Tai⁴ Kuan¹, Battalion Commander, 7. 督隊官 Tu¹ Tui⁴ Kuan¹, Second in Command of a Battalion, 8. 隊官 Tui⁴ Kuan¹, Company Commander, 9. 排長 P'ai² Chang³, Platoon Chief, 10. 正目 Chêng⁴ Mu⁴, Senior Sergeant (one to a squad), 11. 副目 Fu⁴ Mu⁴, Second Sergeant (one to a squad), 12. 正兵 Chêng⁴ Ping¹, Private of the First Class (four to a squad), and 13. 副兵 Fu⁴ Ping⁴, Private of the Second Class (eight to a squad).

662. Staff Posts : A. Corps staff : 1. 總參謀官 Tsung³ Ts'an¹ Mou² Kuan¹, Chief of Staff. 2. 一等參謀官 I¹ Têng³ Ts'an¹ Mou² Kuan¹, Senior Assistant Chief of Staff (two in all), and 3. 二等參謀官 Êrh⁴ Têng³ Ts'an¹ Mou² Kuan¹, Junior Assistant Chief of Staff (two in all). B. Division Staff : 1. 正參謀官 Chêng⁴ Ts'an¹ Mou² Kuan¹, Chief of Staff, 2. 二等參謀官 Êrh⁴ Têng³ Ts'an¹ Mou² Kuan¹, Senior Assistant Chief of Staff (one), and 3. 三等參謀官 San¹ Têng³ Ts'an¹ Mou² Kuan¹, Junior Assistant Chief of Staff (one).

663. Adjutancy Posts : 1. 護軍官 Hu⁴ Chün¹ Kuan¹, Senior Corps Adjutant (one), 2. 中軍官 Chung¹ Chün¹ Kuan¹, Senior Division Adjutant (one), 3. 參軍官 Ts'an¹ Chün¹

[295]

663ᴀ to 665 Kuan¹, Senior Brigade Adjutant (one), 4. 執事官 Chih² Shih⁴ Kuan¹, Adjutant (one in each Corps, Division, Brigade and Regiment), and 5. 司務長 Ssu¹ Wu⁴ Chang³, Adjutant (in the infantry, four for a battalion or one for each company; in the cavalry, one for a division; in the artillery, three for a division or one for each battery; in the engineers and troops of transport, four for a battalion or one for a company).

663ᴀ. Concerning 副官 Fu⁴ Kuan¹, Adjutant of the New Palace Guards, *see* No. 103ᴅ.

664. Secretarial Posts: 1. 一等書記官 I¹ Têng³ Shu¹ Chi⁴ Kuan¹, Secretary of the 1st Class (four for a corps and three for a division), 2. 二等書記官 Êrh⁴ Têng³ Shu¹ Chi⁴ Kuan¹, Secretary of the 2nd Class (two for a brigade and two for a regiment), 3. 書記長 Shu¹ Chi⁴ Chang³, Senior Clerk (five for a corps, seven for a division, one for a battalion of infantry, engineers or troops of transport, and one for a division of cavalry or artillery), 4. 司事生 Ssu¹· Shih⁴ Shêng⁴, Clerk (three for a corps and five for a division), and 5. 司書生 Ssu¹ Shu¹ Shêng¹, Writer (fifteen for a corps, fifteen for a division, two for a brigade, two for a regiment, six for a battalion of infantry, engineers or troops of transport, six for a division of cavalry, and five for a division of artillery).

665. Orderly and Convoy Posts: 稽查官 Chi² Ch'a³ Kuan¹, Inspector of Mounted Orderlies and Convoys (one for a corps). To this officer there are subordinated A. Orderlies: 1. 弁目 Pien⁴ Mu⁴, Sergeant (three for a corps and one for a division, brigade and regiment), and 2. 馬弁 Ma³ Pien⁴, Privates (thirty for a corps, sixteen for a division, six for a brigade and four for a regiment); B. Convoys: 1. 護目 Hu⁴ Mu⁴, Sergeant (six for a corps, three for a division, one for a brigade and regiment of infantry, one for a battalion of infantry, engineers or troops of transport, and one for a division of cavalry or artillery), and 2. 護兵 Hu⁴ Ping¹, Privates (sixty for a

corps, thirty for a division, ten for a brigade, eight for a regiment, eighteen for a battalion of infantry, engineers or troops of transport, and for a division of artillery, and twelve for a division of cavalry.

666. Colours Posts : 掌旗官 Chang³ Ch'i² Kuan¹, Colour-Bearer (one for a regiment—of infantry).

667. Remount Posts : 查馬長 Ch'a² Ma³ Chang³, Remount Officer (one for artillery and cavalry divisions ; two for a battalion of troops of transport).

668. Arms Posts : 1. 總軍械官 Tsung³ Chün¹ Hsieh⁴ Kuan¹, Corps Inspector of Arms (one), 2. 正軍械官 Chêng⁴ Chün¹ Hsieh⁴ Kuan¹, Division Inspector of Arms (one) 3. 副軍械官 Fu⁴ Chün¹ Hsieh⁴ Kuan¹, Regiment Inspector of Arms (one), and 4. 軍械長 Chün¹ Hsieh⁴ Chang³, Inspector of Arms in a Division of Artillery (one).

669. 軍械局 Chün¹ Hsieh⁴ Chü², Arsenal (for a corps ; the staff is arranged for a corps of two divisions). Supervision of the making, distributing and storing of arms is carried on at the Arsenal. At its head there is a 總辦官 Tsung³ Pan⁴ Kuan¹, Chief, who has the following subordinated to him : 1. Two 查械官 Ch'a² Hsieh⁴ Kuan¹, Inspectors of Arms, 2. Three 司庫官 Ssu¹ K'u⁴ Kuan¹, Arsenal Overseers, 3. One 三等書記官 San¹ Têng³ Shu¹ Chi⁴ Kuan¹, Clerk of the 3rd Class, 4. Two 司事生 Ssu¹ Shih⁴ Shêng¹, Clerks, 5. Two 司書生 Ssu¹ Shu¹ Shêng¹, Writers, 6. One 護目 Hu⁴ Mu⁴, Convoy Sergeant, 7. Eight 護兵 Hu⁴ Ping¹, Convoy Privates, 8. Two 匠目 Chiang⁴ Mu⁴, Senior Mechanics, 9. Eighteen 修械匠 Hsiu¹ Hsieh⁴ Chiang⁴, Arms Repairers, 10. Two 守庫兵目 Shou³ K'u⁴ Ping¹ Mu⁴, Senior Watchmen at the Arsenal. 11. Eighteen 守庫兵 Shou³ K'u⁴ Ping¹, Arsenal Watchmen, and 12. Five 伙夫 Huo³ Fu¹, Cooks.

670. Artillery Posts : 礮隊協領官 P'ao⁴ Tui⁴ Hsieh² Ling³ Kuan¹, Chief of Artillery of a Corps.

**671
to
674**

671. Engineer Posts: 工程隊叅領官 Kung¹ Ch'êng² Tui⁴ Ts'an¹ Ling³ Kuan¹, Chief of Engineers of a Corps.

672. Judicial Posts: 1. 總執法官 Chung³ Chih² Fa⁴ Kuan¹, Corps Judge-Advocate (one), and 2. 正執法官 Chêng⁴ Chih² Fa⁴ Kuan¹, Division Judge-Advocate (one).

In accordance with a Memorial from the Ministry of War, sanctioned by the Emperor on the 27th March, 1909, at all composite brigades (混成協 Hun³ Ch'êng² Hsieh²), as well as at brigades which are independent (so-called 獨立協 Tu² Li⁴ Hsieh²), there will be for the time being—until these brigades are assimilated by the various divisions—the post of 副執法官 Fu⁴ Chih² Fa⁴ Kuan¹, Brigade Judge-Advocate, who will have subordinated to him: one 司事生 Ssu¹ Shih⁴ Shêng¹ (see No. 664), two 司書生 Ssu¹ Shu¹ Shêng¹ (see No. 664) and two 護兵 Hu⁴ Ping¹ (see No. 665.)

673. Commissariat Posts: 1. 總軍需官 Tsung³ Chün¹ Hsü¹ Kuan¹, Corps Commissary Officer (one), 2. 正軍需官 Chêng⁴ Chün¹ Hsü¹ Kuan¹, Division Commissary Officer (one), 3. 副軍需官 Fu⁴ Chün¹ Hsü¹ Kuan¹, Regiment Commissary Officer (one), and 4. 軍需長 Chün¹ Hsü¹ Chang³, Battalion Commissary Officer (for infantry, engineers, troops of transport—one for each—and for divisions of cavalry and artillery—one for each).

674. 糧餉局 Liang² Hsiang³ Chü², Commissary Office (for a corps; its staff is arranged for a corps of two divisions). This office supervises the preparation and issue of supplies and at its head there is a 總辦官 Tsung³ Pan⁴ Kuan¹, Chief. He has the following subordinated to him: 1. Four 製造官 Chih⁴ Tsao⁴ Kuan¹, Providers of Supplies, 2. Four 司糧官 Ssu¹ Liang² Kuan¹, Inspectors of Supplies, 3. Four 司餉官 Ssu¹ Hsiang³ Kuan¹, Paymasters, 4. Two 三等書記官 San¹ Têng³ Shu¹ Chi⁴ Kuan¹, Secretaries of the 3rd Class, 5. Four 司事生 Ssu¹ Shih⁴ Shêng¹, Clerks, 6. Four 司書生 Ssu¹ Shu¹ Shêng²,

Writers, 7. One 護目 Hu⁴ Mu⁴, Convoy Sergeant, 8. Twelve 護兵 Hu⁴ Ping¹, Convoy Privates, and 9. One 伙夫 Huo³ Fu¹, Cook.

675. Medical Posts: 1. 總軍醫官 Tsung³ Chün¹ I¹ Kuan¹, Corps Surgeon (one), 2. 正軍醫官 Chêng⁴ Chün¹ I¹ Kuan¹, Division Surgeon (one), 3. 副軍醫官 Fu⁴ Chün¹ I¹ Kuan¹, Regiment Surgeon (one), 4. 軍醫長 Chün¹ I¹ Chang³, Battalion Surgeon (in the infantry, engineers and troops of transport—one for each) and Division Surgeon (Cavalry and artillery—one for each), 5. 醫生 I¹ Shêng¹, Assistant Surgeon (one for a battalion of infantry, engineers or troops of transport and one for an artillery division), and 6. 醫兵 I¹ Ping¹, Hospital Attendant (four for a battalion of infantry, engineers or troops of transport and for a cavalry division; three for an artillery division).

676. Veterinary Posts: 1. 總馬醫官 Tsung³ Ma³ I¹ Kuan¹, Corps Veterinary Surgeon (one), 2. 正馬醫官 Chêng⁴ Ma³ I¹ Kuan¹, Division Veterinary Surgeon (one), 3. 副馬醫官 Fu⁴ Ma³ I¹ Kuan¹, Regiment Veterinary Surgeon (one), 4. 馬醫長 Ma³ I¹ Chang³, Battalion Veterinary Surgeon (for troops of transport, one; for a division of cavalry or artillery, one), and 5. 馬醫生 Ma³ I¹ Shêng¹, Assistant Veterinary Surgeon (one for a battalion of troops of transport and one for an artillery division).

677. 軍醫局 Chün¹ I¹ Chü², Medical Office (for a corps; the staff is arranged for a corps of two divisions). At the head of this office there is a 總辦官 Tsung³ Pan⁴ Kuan¹. He has under his control: 1. Two 正軍醫官 Chêng⁴ Chün¹ I¹ Kuan¹, Senior Surgeons, 2. Two 軍醫長 Chün¹ I¹ Chang³, Surgeons, 3. Ten 醫生 I¹ Shêng¹, Assistant Surgeons, 4. One 正馬醫官 Chêng⁴ Ma³ I¹ Kuan¹, Senior Veterinary Surgeon, 5. Four 醫兵目 I¹ Ping¹ Mu⁴, Senior Hospital Attendants, 6. Two 司藥官 Ssu¹ Yao⁴ Kuan¹, Pharmacist, 7. One 三等書記官

[299]

678 to 680

San¹ Têng³ Shu¹ Chi⁴ Kuan¹, Secretary of the 3rd Class, 8. Three 司書生 Ssu¹ Shu¹ Shêng¹, Writers, 9. One 護目 Hu⁴ Mu⁴, Convoy Sergeant, 10. Six 護兵 Hu⁴ Ping¹, Convoy Privates, 11. Forty 醫兵 I¹ Ping¹, Hospital Attendants, and 12. Five 伙夫 Huo³ Fu¹, Cooks.

678. Signal Posts: 1. 司號官 Ssu¹ Hao⁴ Kuan¹, Chief of Signalmen of a Division (one), 2. 司號長 Ssu¹ Hao⁴ Chang³, Chief of Signalmen of a Brigade (one), 3. 司號長 Ssu¹ Hao⁴ Chang³, Chief of Signalmen of a Regiment (one), 4. 號目 Hao⁴ Mu⁴, Senior Signalman of a Battalion (one; in infantry, engineers and troops of transport) or of a Division (of cavalry and artillery—one), and 5. 號兵 Hao⁴ Ping¹, Signalmen (two in each company of infantry, engineers and troops of transport, two to a squadron of cavalry, and two to a battery of artillery).

679. Music Posts: At the head of a 軍樂隊 Chün¹ Yüeh⁴ Tui⁴, Company of Musicians, there is a 隊官 Tui⁴ Kuan¹, Chief, who has subordinated to him: 1. 排長 P'ai² Chang³, Bandmaster (one), 2. Two 一等樂兵 I¹ Têng³ Yüeh⁴ Ping¹, Musicians of the 1st Class, 3. Six 二等樂兵 Êrh⁴ Têng³ Yüeh⁴ Ping¹, Musicians of the 2nd Class, 4. 12 三等樂兵 San¹ Têng³ Yüeh⁴ Ping¹, Musicians of the 3rd Class, 5. 24 學習樂兵 Hsüeh² Hsi² Yüeh⁴ Ping¹, Music Pupils, and 6. Five 伙夫 Huo³ Fu¹, Cooks.

680. Camp-follower Posts: 1. 匠目 Chiang⁴ Mu⁴, Senior Mechanic (one to each battalion of infantry, engineers or troops of transport, and to each division of cavalry and artillery), 2. 槍兵 Ch'iang¹ Ping¹, Armourer (four in a battalion of infantry, engineers and troops of transport; two in a division of cavalry), 3. 鐵匠 T'ieh³ Chiang⁴, Metal Worker (four in a battalion of infantry, engineers and troops of transport; three in an artillery division), 4. 礮匠 P'ao⁴ Chiang⁴, Ordnance Mechanic (three in an artillery division), 5. 掌匠 Chang³

Chiang⁴, Blacksmith (eight in a battalion of troops of transport;
four in a cavalry division; six in an artillery division), 6. 木匠
Mu⁴ Chiang⁴, Carpenter (four in a battalion of engineers and
troops of transport; three in an artillery division), 7. 皮匠
P'i² Chiang⁴, Shoemaker (four in a battalion of infantry and
troops of transport; two in a battalion of engineers; two in a
cavalry division; three in an artillery division), 8. 備補兵
Pei⁴ Pu³ Ping¹, Private of Reserve (one in each squad),
9. 伙夫 Huo³ Fu¹, Cook (nine in a corps, five in a division,
two in a brigade, two in a regiment, thirty-eight in an infantry
battalion, eighteen in a cavalry division, thirty-one in an artillery
division, forty in an engineers battalion and forty-one in a
battalion of troops of transport), 10. 駕車兵 Chia⁴ Ch'ê¹
Ping¹, Private of Transport Troops (four in infantry and
engineers battalions and in cavalry division; six in a division of
field artillery), 11. 喂養夫 Wei⁴ Yang³ Fu¹, Foragers (four
in infantry and engineers battalions and in a cavalry division;
six in a division of field artillery; eighteen in a division of
mountain artillery), 12. 馬夫目 Ma³ Fu¹ Mu⁴, Senior
Stableman (eight in a battalion of troops of transport, four in a
division of cavalry and three in a division of artillery), 13. 馬夫
Ma³ Fu¹, Stableman (seventy in a battalion of troops of
transport, thirty-two in a cavalry division, and thirty-nine in an
artillery division), and 14. 管馱兵 Kuan³ To⁴ Ping¹, Packer
(eighteen in a division of mountain artillery).

REVIEWS OF TROOPS.

681. Regulations drawn up by the Ministry of War—
sanctioned by the Emperor on the 12th April, 1908,—call for
reviews of the troops every three years. With this object in
view, the Emperor appoints, on the recommendation of the
Ministry of War, an official skilled in military matters as:

682. 校閲大臣 Hsiao⁴ Yüeh⁴ Ta⁴ Ch'ên², Inspector-General of Troops, who makes a complete inspection of a certain concourse of troops. To assist him the following staff is organized:

683. 參議 Ts'an¹ I⁴, Adviser (one); assists the Inspector-General in making plans, supervises the most important and the confidential correspondence, and has a general control of all questions of expenditure.

684. 步兵科校閲員 Pu⁴ Ping¹ K'o¹ Hsiao⁴ Yüeh⁴ Yüan², Inspector of Infantry; inspects the infantry as regards its efficiency.

685. 馬兵科校閲員 Ma³ Ping¹ K'o¹ Hsiao⁴ Yüeh⁴ Yüan², Inspector of Cavalry; inspects the cavalry as regards its efficiency.

686. 礮兵科校閲員 P'ao⁴ Ping¹ K'o¹ Hsiao⁴ Yüeh⁴ Yüan², Inspector of Artillery; inspects the artillery as regards its efficiency.

687. 工兵科校閲員 Kung¹ Ping¹ K'o¹ Hsiao⁴ Yüeh⁴ Yüan², Inspector of Engineers; inspects the engineers as regards efficiency and organization.

688. 輜兵科校閲員 Tzu¹ Ping¹ K'o¹ Hsiao⁴ Yüeh⁴ Yüan², Inspector of Troops of Transport; inspects the troops of transport as regards efficiency and organization.

689. 軍需校閲員 Chün¹ Hsü¹ Hsiao⁴ Yüeh⁴ Yüan², Inspector of the Commissariat; inspects the commissariat—audits accounts, scrutinizes its books and bills.

690. 軍械校閲員 Chün¹ Hsieh⁴ Hsiao⁴ Yüeh⁴ Yuan², Inspector of Arms; inspects arms and arms stores (arsenals).

691. 軍醫校閲員 Chün¹ I¹ Hsiao⁴ Yüeh⁴ Yüan², Inspector of Medical Department; inspects the medical staff and hospitals and examines sanitary conditions.

692. 軍法校閱員 Chün[1] Fa[4] Hsiao[4] Yüeh[4] Yüan[2], Inspector of Military Judicial Department; examines sentences imposed on members of some certain concourse of troops.

693. 承發員 Ch'êng[2] Fa[1] Yüan[2], Registrar; charged with miscellaneous duties; delivers orders of Inspector-General and Inspectors.

694. There is a Chancery established at the Inspectorate General, the staff of which is made up of: 1. 書記員 Shu[1] Chi[4] Yüan[2], Secretaries (in charge of the drafting of despatches and reports), 2. 收發員 Shou[1] Fa[1] Yüan[2], Registrar (one; forwards and receives correspondence and telegrams), 3. 日記員 Jih[4] Chi[4] Yüan[2], Diarists (charged with the writing up of daily reports of reviews), 4. 繪圖員 Hui[4] T'u[2] Yüan[2], Draftsmen, 5. 司書員 Ssu[1] Shu[1] Yüan[2], Writers, and 6. 收支員 Shou[1] Chih[1] Yüan[2], Treasurer (one).

COMMITTEES FOR DRILLING TROOPS.

695. 督練處 Tu[1] Lien[4] Ch'u[4], or 督練公所 Tu[1] Lien[4] Kung[1] So[3], Committees for Drilling Troops (former designation), or Provincial Staff of New Troops; established in all provinces to arrange the organization and drilling of divisions of the new troops. These Committees are under the supervision of the Governor-General or Governor of the province concerned (as 督辦 Tu[1] Pan[4]).

695ᴀ. 督練大臣 Tu[1] Lien[4] Ta[4] Ch'ên[2] (or, clearer, 督練近畿一帶各鎮大臣 Tu[1] Lien[4] Chin[4] Chi[1] I[1] Tai[4] Ko[4] Chên[4] Ta[4] Ch'ên[2], or 督辦訓練近畿陸軍各鎮事宜 Tu[1] Pan[4] Hsün[4] Lien[4] Chin[4] Chi[1] Lu[4] Chün[1] Ko[4] Chên[4] Shih[4] I[2]), Chief of Staff of Metropolitan Circuit (Post abolished by Imperial Edict of 26th September, 1910, and functions transferred to the Ministry of War).

696. On the Staff there are : 參議官 Ts'an[1] I[4] Kuan[1], Adviser, 文案 Wên[2] An[4], Secretary, 隨員 Sui[2] Yüan[2] Adjutants, 先鋒官 Hsien[1] Fêng[1] Kuan[1], Orderlies, 清書 Ch'ing[1] Shu[1], Writers, 馬弁 Ma[3] Pien[4], Mounted Orderlies, 護兵長 Hu[4] Ping[4] Chang[3], Convoy Chief, and 伙夫 Huo[3] Fu[1], Cooks.

The Staff is arranged according to the needs of the circuit, as detailed in reports from the Governor-General (or Governor).

696A. 總參議 Tsung[3] Ts'an[1] I[4], Senior Adviser ; this post exists in Manchuria alone (*see* report of 徐世昌 Hsü[2] Shih[4]-ch'ang[1], dated the 13th January, 1908).

697. The Staff is arranged in three 處 Ch'u[4], Offices, which, in turn, are subdivided into 科 K'o[1], or 股 Ku[3], Sections. The Offices are under 總辦 Tsung[3] Pan[4], and 幫辦 Pang[1] Pan[4] (*see* Nos. 698, 699 and 700) ; at the Sections, likewise, there are 提調 T'i[2] Tiao[4], Proctors, 幫提調 Pang[1] T'i[2] Tiao[4], Assistant Proctors, or 科長 K'o[1] Chang[3], Section Chiefs. To these officials there are attached : 委員 Wei[3] Yüan[2], Orderlies, 文案 Wên[2] An[4], Secretaries, and 清書 Ch'ing[1] Shu[1], Writers (the number depends on the volume of affairs—compare No. 696).

The offices are designated as : 1. 兵備處 Ping[1] Pei[4] Ch'u[4], Office of the Inspector-General (for details *see* No. 698), 2. 參謀處 Ts'an[1] Mou[2] Ch'u[4], Office of the Quartermaster-General (*see* No. 699), and 3. 教練處 Chiao[4] Lien[4] Ch'u[4], Office of Military Schools (*see* No. 700).

698. 兵備處 Ping[1] Pei[4] Ch'u[4], Office of the Inspector-General, with the 兵備處總辦 Ping[1] Pei[4] Ch'u[4] Tsung[3] Pan[4], Inspector-General, at its head. This Office is responsible that the troops confirm to military regulations and that they obey orders ; is in charge of the issue of rewards, judicial proceedings, current supplies, and the preparation of supplies for the commissariat artillery and medical branches. It is subdivided (in Manchuria) into five Sections : 1. 考功科 K'ao[3] Kung[1]

K'o[1], Section for Examination of Merit (of Staff), 2. 籌 備 科 Ch'ou[2] Pei[4] K'o[1], Section of Readiness (Preparation), 3. 餉 需 科 Hsiang[3] Hsü[1] K'o[1], Commissariat Section, 4. 醫 務 科 I[1] Wu[4] K'o[1], Medical Section, and 5. 執 法 科 Chih[2] Fa[4] K'o[1], Judicial Section.

698A
to
699B

698A. In some other places (for instance, in the provinces of North China) the Sections (not 科 K'o[1], but 股 Ku[3]) are designated differently : 軍 需 股 Chün[1] Hsü[1] Ku[3], Commissariat Section, and 軍 醫 股 Chün[1] I[1] Ku[3], Medical Section.

698B. In the provinces of South China the Office of the Inspector-General (*see* No. 698) has the following Sections : 1. 蒐 討 科 Sou[1] T'ao[3] K'o[1], Section of Organization of Troops and Battle Preparation, 2. 執 法 科 Chih[2] Fa[4] K'o[1], Judicial Section, and 3. 經 理 科 Ching[1] Li[3] K'o[1], Commissariat Section.

699. 參 謀 處 Ts'an[1] Mou[2] Ch'u[4], Office of the Quartermaster-General, with the 參 謀 處 總 辦 Ts'an[1] Mou[2] Ch'u[4] Tsung[3] Pan[4], at its head ; examines the quartermaster organization and arranges for its proper administration ; collects and compiles statistical military information concerning China and neighbouring states. This Office is subdivided (in Manchuria) into four Sections : 1. 謀 畧 科 Mou[2] Lüeh[4] K'o[1], Strategical Section, 2. 調 查 科 Tiao[4] Ch'a[2] K'o[1], Intelligence Section, 3. 運 輸 科 Yün[4] Shu[1] K'o[1], Section of Transport of Troops. ad 4. 測 量 科 Ts'ê[4] Liang[2] K'o[1], Topographical Section.

699A. In some other places (for instance, in the provinces of North China) the Sections—called 股 Ku[3]—are as above with the exception of the 測 繪 股 Ts'ê[4] Hui[4] Ku[3], Topographical Section.

699B. In the provinces of South China the Office of the Quartermaster-General (*see* No. 699) has the following Sections : 1. 運 籌 科 Yün[4] Ch'ou[2] K'o[1], Strategical and Transport

**700
to
702**

Section, 2. 檢閱科 Chien³ Yüeh⁴ K'o¹, Intelligence Section, and 3. 測繪科 Ts'ê⁴ Hui⁴ K'o¹, Topographical Section.

700. 教練處 Chiao⁴ Lien⁴ Ch'u⁴, Office of Military Schools, with the 教練處總辦 Chiao⁴ Lien⁴ Ch'u⁴ Tsung³ Pan⁴, Chief (and 幫辦 Pang¹ Pan⁴, Assistant), in charge. This Office supervises military schools—draws up schemes and regulations and arranges instruction and textbooks for them. It is subdivided (in Manchuria) into four Sections: 1. 學務科 Hsueh² Wu⁴ K'o¹, Section of Instruction, 2. 校兵科 Hsiao⁴ Ping¹ K'o¹, Section of Revision, 3. 編譯科 Pien¹ I⁴ K'o¹, Translating Section, and 4. 海防科 Hai³ Fang² K'o¹, Section of Coast Defence.

700A. In some places (for instance, the provinces of North China) the Section of Instruction (*see* No. 700) is styled 教育股 Chiao⁴ Yü⁴ Ku³.

700B. In the provinces of South China the Office of Military Schools (*see* No. 700) has the following Sections: 1. 訓練科 Hsün¹ Lien⁴ K'o¹, Section of Drilling, and 2. 教育科 Chiao⁴ Yü⁴ K'o¹, Section of Education.

MILITARY PRISONS.

701. 陸軍監獄 Lu⁴ Chün¹ Chien¹ Yü⁴, Military Prisons; regulations for these were drawn up by the Ministry of War and sanctioned by the Emperor on the 26th September, 1908. They are of two types: 1. 部監 Pu⁴ Chien¹, Prison at the Ministry of War—under the supervision of the Department of Military Law; *see* No. 432—and 2. 鎮監 Chên⁴ Chien¹, Prisons for the Divisions, under the supervision of the 司令處 Ssu¹ Ling⁴ Ch'u⁴, Staff of the Division. The latter are for culprits whose sentences are from one month to ten years; those serving longer sentences are imprisoned at the Prison at the Ministry of War.

702. Following is the personnel of the administration of a Military Prison:

A. 專設員 Chuan[1] Shê[4] Yüan[2], Substantive Officials: **703**
1. 監長 Chien[4] Chang[3], Prison Supervisor (4A or 5A), **to**
2. 監副 Chien[4] Fu[4], Assistant Prison Supervisor (5A or 6A; **703A**
one), 3. 司書生 Ssu[1] Shu[1] Shêng[1], Clerk (7A; two),
4. 一等監卒 I[1] Têng[3] Chien[1] Tsu[2], Warder of the 1st Class
(ranks as 護目 Hu[4] Mu[4]; *see* No. 665), 5. 二等監卒 Êrh[4]
Têng[3] Chien[1] Tsu[2], Warder of the 2nd Class (ranks as 護兵
Hu[4] Ping[1]; *see* No. 665), and 6. 伙夫 Huo[3] Fu[1], Cook.

B. 酌派員 Cho[1] P'ai[4] Yüan[2], Deputed Officials:
1. 衛兵長 Wei[4] Ping[1] Chang[3], Chief of Sentries, 2. 衛兵目
Wei[4] Ping[1] Mu[4], Chief Sentries (from the ranks of sergeants),
and 3. 衛兵 Wei[4] Ping[1], Sentries (from the ranks of privates).

MILITARY POLICE (GENDARMERIE).

703. 陸軍警察隊 Lu[4] Chün[1] Ching[3] Ch'a[2] Tui[4],
Military Police (Gendarmerie of the Line); the organization of
this body was first brought forward in 1908, when temporary
regulations for its administration were drawn up by the Ministry
of War and sanctioned by the Emperor on the 6th May. The
object of its inception is "to keep a watch as to the manner in
which officers and men of the Army and Navy perform their
duties."

The Military Police were first organized at Peking, consist-
ing of one 營 Ying[2], Battalion, of men who had completed the
course of the Gendarmerie School established at the Ministry of
War (*see* No. 715E); later these police were organized in 江北
Chiang[1] Pei[3] (*see* a Memorial from 徐紹楨 Hsü[2] Shao[4]-chêng[1],
dated the 29th September, 1909), to the number of one 隊 Tui[4],
Company. Also, there have been established 練習所 Lien[4] Hsi[2]
So[3], Courses for Preparation for Service in the Military Police.

703A. 陸軍警察處 Lu[4] Chün[1] Ching[3] Ch'a[2] Ch'u[4],
Office of the Military Police (Gendarmerie Office); this is to be

704 to 705 established in Peking for the supervision of the provincial Military Police and will be under the control of the Ministry of War.

704. 陸軍警察隊營制 Lu⁴ Chün¹ Ching³ Ch'a² Tui⁴ Ying² Chih⁴, Staff of a Battalion of Military Police: 1. One 管帶官 Kuan³ Tai⁴ Kuan¹, Battalion Commander (see No. 661), 2. One 執事官 Chih² Shih⁴ Kuan¹, Battalion Adjutant (see No. 663), 3. 隊官 Tui⁴ Kuan¹, Company Commander (three, conforming to the number of companies; see No. 661), 4. 排長 P'ai² Chang³, Platoon Commander (six, conforming to the number of platoons; see No. 661), 5. 司務長 Ssu¹ Wu⁴ Chang³, Company Adjutant (three, conforming to the number of companies; see No. 663), 6. 12 正目 Chêng⁴ Mu⁴, Senior Sergeants (see No. 661), 7. 12 副目 Fu⁴ Mu⁴, Junior Sergeants (see No. 661), 8. 96 正兵 Chêng⁴ Ping¹, Privates of the 1st Class (see No. 661), 9. One 軍需長 Chün¹ Hsü¹ Chang³, Battalion Commissary Officer (see No. 673), 10. One 書記長 Shu¹ Chi⁴ Chang³, Senior Clerk (see No. 664), 11. One 軍醫長 Chün¹ I¹ Chang³, Battalion Surgeon (see No. 675), 12. One 馬醫長 Ma³ I¹ Chang³, Battalion Veterinary Surgeon (see No. 676), 13. Five 司書生 Ssu¹ Shu¹ Shêng¹, Writers (see No. 664), 14. Eight 醫兵 I¹ Ping¹, Hospital Attendants (four of these are 馬醫兵 Ma³ I¹ Ping¹, Veterinary Hospital Attendants; see No. 675), 15. Five 護兵 Hu⁴ Ping¹, Convoy Privates (see No. 665), 16. Three 馬夫目 Ma³ Fu¹ Mu⁴, Senior Stablemen (see No. 680), 17. 24 喂養夫 Wei⁴ Yang³ Fu¹, Foragers (see No. 680), 18. 12 伙夫 Huo³ Fu¹, Cooks (see No. 680) and 82 horses.

705. 陸軍警察隊隊制 Lu⁴ Chün¹ Ching³ Ch'a² Tui⁴ Tui⁴ Chih⁴, Staff of a Company of Military Police: 1. One 隊官 Tui⁴ Kuan¹, Company Commander (see No. 661), 2. 排長 P'ai² Chang³, Platoon Commander (two, conforming to the number of platoons; see No. 661), 3. One 司務長 Ssu¹ Wu⁴

Chang³, Company Adjutant (*see* No. 663), 4. Four 正目 Chêng⁴ Mu⁴, Senior Sergeants (*see* No. 661), 5. Four 副目 Fu⁴ Mu⁴, Junior Sergeants (*see* No. 661), 6. 32 正兵 Chêng⁴ Ping¹, Privates of the 1st Class (*see* No. 661), 7. One 司書生 Ssu¹ Shu¹ Shêng¹, Clerk (*see* No. 664), 8. Two 醫兵 I¹ Ping¹, Hospital Attendants (*see* No. 675), 9. One 護兵 Hu⁴ Ping¹, Convoy Private (*see* No. 665), 10. One 馬夫目 Ma³ Fu¹ Mu⁴, Senior Stableman (*see* No. 680), 11. Eight 喂養夫 Wei⁴ Yang³ Fu¹, Foragers (*see* No. 680), 12. Four 伙夫 Huo³ Fu¹, Cooks (*see* No. 680), and 27 horses.

B. Reserve Forces (Hsün Fang Tui):

706. 巡防隊 Hsün² Fang² Tui⁴, Reserve Forces (Provincial Troops; *see* No. 665). Temporary regulations referring to troops of this type were drawn up by the Ministry of War and sanctioned by the Emperor on the 29th June, 1907. In time of peace they are to be employed in catching thieves and robbers; in time of war they are to act as auxiliary forces to the troops of the line. These troops are to be organized from the various branches of the old troops.

In the various provinces there may be (not more than five) 路 Lu⁴, Roads or Detachments, of Reserve Forces designated: 前 Ch'ien², Vanguard, 後 Hou⁴, Rear-Guard, 中 Chung¹, Centre (Middle), 左 Tso³, Left (Eastern), and 右 Yu⁴, Right (Western). Each Detachment is commanded by a 統領官 T'ung³ Ling² Kuan¹, Detachment Commander (Chief; compare No. 661).

The complement of a Detachment is not fixed except that it must not exceed 10 營 Ying², Battalions (Divisions; compare No. 656F) of 步隊 Pu⁴ Tui⁴, Infantry, and 馬隊 Ma³ Tui⁴, Cavalry.

Each infantry battalion consists of: three 哨 Shao⁴, Companies, of eight 棚 P'êng², Platoons, each. Each Platoon is made up of nine 正兵 Chêng⁴ Ping¹, Privates of the 1st Class, and a 什長 Shih² Chang³, Sergeant (Platoon Chief, Headman). The general number of men to a battalion is 301.

**706A
to
706B**

Each cavalry division consists of three 哨 Shao⁴, Squadrons, of four 棚 P'ng², Squads, each. Each Squad is made up of nine 正 兵 Chêng⁴ Ping¹, Privates of the 1st Class, and a 什長 Shih² Chang³, Sergeant (*see* above). A division usually, numbers 189 men and 135 horses.

706A. The General Staff of a detachment (路 Lu⁴) consists of the following: 1. One 統 領 官 T'ung³ Ling³ Kuan¹, Detachment Commander, 2. One 帮 統 官 Pan¹ T'ung³ Kuan¹, Second in Command of a Detachment, 3. One 書 記 官 Shu¹ Chi⁴ Kuan¹, Secretary (*see* No. 664), 4. One 會 計 官 Hui⁴ Chi⁴ Kuan¹, Accountant, 5. One 執 事 官 Chih² Shih⁴ Kuan¹, Adjutant (*see* No. 663), 6. Two 司 書 生 Ssu¹ Shu¹ Shêng¹, Clerks (*see* No. 664), 7. Two 馬 弁 Ma² Pien⁴, Mounted Orderlies (Privates ; *see* No. 665), 8. Fourteen 護 兵 Hu⁴ Ping¹, Convoy Privates' (*see* No. 665), and 9. Two 伙 夫 Huo³ Fu¹, Cooks (*see* No. 680).

706B. 步隊一營之制 Pu⁴ Tui⁴ I¹ Ying² Chih¹ Chih⁴, General Staff of a battalion of infantry : 1. One 管 帶 官 Kuan³ Tai⁴ Kuan¹, Battalion Commander (*see* No. 661), 2. 哨官 Shao⁴ Kuan¹, Company Commander (three, to conform to the number of companies ; *see* No. 706), 3. 哨 長 Shao⁴ Chang³, Second in Command of a Company (three, to conform to the number of companies ; *see* No. 706), 4. 24 什 長 Shih² Chang³, Sergeants (one for each platoon ; *see* No. 706), 5. 216 正兵 Chêng⁴ Ping¹, Privates of the 1st Class (*see* No. 661), 6. One 書 記 長 Shu¹ Chi⁴ Chang³, Senior Clerk (*see* No. 664), 7. Five 司 書 生 Ssu¹ Shu¹ Shêng¹, Writers (*see* No. 664), 8. One 鼓 號 目 Ku³ Hao⁴ Mu⁴, Signal Sergeant (*see* No. 678), 9. Six 鼓 號 兵 Ku³¹ Hao⁴ Ping¹, Signalmen (compare No. 678), 10. One 護 目 Hu⁴ Mu⁴, Convoy Sergeant (*see* No. 665), 11. 16 護兵 Hu⁴ Ping¹, Convoy Privates (*see* No. 665), and 12. 24 伙 夫 Huo³ Fu¹, Cooks (*see* No. 680).

706c. 馬隊一營之制 Ma³ Tui⁴ I¹ Ying² Chih¹ Chih⁴, General Staff of a cavalry division: 1. One 管帶官 Kuan³ Tai⁴ Kuan¹, Division Commander (see No. 661), 2. 哨官 Shao⁴ Kuan¹, Squadron Commander (three, to conform to the number of squadrons; see No. 706), 3. 哨長 Shao⁴ Chang³, Second in Command of a Squadron (three, conforming to the number of squadrons; see No. 706), 4. 12 什長 Shih² Chang³, Sergeants (conforming to the number of squads; see No. 706), 5. 108 正兵 Chêng⁴ Ping¹, Privates of the 1st Class (see No. 661), 6. One 書記長 Shu¹ Chi⁴ Chang³, Senior Clerk (see No. 664), 7. Five 司書生 Ssu¹ Shu¹ Shêng¹, Writers (see No. 664), 8. One 鼓號目 Ku³ Hao⁴ Mu⁴, Signal Sergeant (see No. 678), 9. Six 鼓號兵 Ku³ Hao⁴ Ping¹, Signalmen (see No. 678), 10. One 護目 Hu⁴ Mu⁴, Convoy Sergeant (see No. 665), 11. 16 護兵 Hu⁴ Ping¹, Convoy Privates (see No. 665), 12. 12 伙夫 Huo³ Fu¹, Cooks (see No. 680), 13. 12 馬夫 Ma³ Fu¹, Stablemen (see No. 680), and 135 horses.

706D. For particulars as to the 巡防營務處 Hsün² Fang² Ying² Wu⁴ Ch'u⁴, Staff of Reserve Forces in Manchuria, see No. 805A.

707. 蘇省飛划水師巡防隊 Su¹ Shêng³ Fei¹ Hua² Shui³ Shih¹ Hsün² Fang² Tui⁴, River Flotilla of Kiangsu Province; organized in accordance with a Memorial from the late Governor 陳啓泰 Ch'ên² Ch'i³-t'ai⁴, sanctioned by the Emperor on the 12th August, 1908. The 軍 Chün¹, Squadron, is divided into five 營 Ying² (the First, Second, Third, Fourth and Fifth), which, in turn, are sub-divided into five 哨 Shao⁴ each (中 Chung¹, 前 Ch'ien², 左 Tso³, 右 Yu⁴, and 後 Hou⁴; see No. 706). A 哨 Shao⁴ consists of eight 划船 Hua² Ch'uan², Boats, having a crew of six 兵夫 Ping¹ Fu¹, Privates (one acts as 伙夫 Huo³ Fu¹, Cook) each.

At the head of each 營 Ying² (consisting of 40 boats, and crews numbering 240 men) there is a 管帶 Kuan³ Tai⁴,

708 Flotilla Commander, who has subordinated to him on his own boat (called 先 鋒 舢 板 Hsien¹ Fêng¹ Shan¹ Pan³) eight 官 長 Kuan¹ Chang³, Officers, and 17 Privates (*see* above).

In charge of the entire squadron is the 統 領 T'ung³ Ling³, Squadron Commander, who has on his own boat (called 關 快 船 Kuan¹ K'uai⁴, Ch'uan²) seven Officers and 38 Privates. The total complement of the squadron (of 206 boats) is 253 Officers and 1,323 Privates—1,576 men in all.

MILITARY SCHOOLS.

708. In the general regulations for 陸 軍 學 堂 Lu⁴ Chün¹ Hsüeh² T'ang², Military Schools, of 20 articles, drawn up by the Committee for the Reorganization of the Army and sanctioned by the Emperor on the 12th September, 1904, there was put forth the following scheme for training officers for the New Army :

On completion of the course of Primary Schools of the Junior Grade, students join the 陸 軍 小 學 堂 Lu⁴ Chün¹ Hsiao³ Hsüeh² T'ang², Primary Military School. The course here—of three years duration—being completed, they advance to the 陸 軍 中 學 堂 Lu⁴ Chün¹ Chung¹ Hsüeh² T'ang², Middle Military School, where the course of study covers two years. After finishing their studies here, and having served four months in the infantry (or cavalry, artillery, engineers or troops of transport) as private of the 1st Class and sergeant, the students—called 陸 軍 入 伍 生 Lu⁴ Chün¹ Ju⁴ Wu³ Shêng¹, Cadets—join the 兵 官 學 堂 Ping¹ Kuan¹ Hsüeh² T'ang², School for Military Officers, where they remain for one year and a half. When graduated from this Institution they again join the army, in the ranks, with the title of 學 習 官 Hsüeh² Hsi² Kuan¹, Sub-Officer, for a further period of six months, after which they return to the school for examination. Those who attain a satisfactory rating in the examination are definitely appointed as officers and receive commissions as Commanders of Companies or Platoons (*see* No. 661). After two years service the most distinguished may join the 陸軍大學堂 Lu⁴ Chün¹ Ta⁴ Hsüeh² T'ang², Military Academy, for a course of study of two years duration, and, on graduation from this institution, they receive the title of Military Staff Officer (*see* No. 184L)

708ᴬ to 709

708ᴀ. Under the old system, for those who wished to follow a military career there were similar examinations as for the civil career, consisting of examinations as to knowledge of military "Ching," Classics, with the addition of various tests, chiefly exercises of physical strength, skill in riding, in drawing the bow, in lifting "the weight" and in fencing. These examinations were abolished—as well as the degrees conferred—in 1901 (*see* No. 629ᴅ).

709. 陸軍小學堂 Lu⁴ Chün¹ Hsiao³ Hsüeh² T'ang², Primary Military Schools (Lower Corps of Cadets); for those who have completed the course of Primary Schools of the Junior Grade ; with a course of study covering three years. These schools are found at the Capital, in the provinces, and at the Manchu Garrisons. Regulations for their administration, drawn up by the Committee for the Reorganization of the Army, were sanctioned by the Emperor on the 27th February, 1905. The enrollment varies from 90 to 300 students (dependent on local conditions) and the attendance of 附學 Fu⁴ Hsüeh², Special Students (between the ages of 15 and 18 years) is permissible. In addition to the subjects of general education (ethics, Chinese literature, history, mathematics, geography, etc.), instruction is given in the elementary principles of military sciences.

At the head of a Primary Military School there is a 總辦 Tsung² Pan⁴, Supervisor. He has subordinated to him : 1. One 監督 Chien¹ Tu¹, Director, 2. One 提調 T'i² Tiao⁴,

709ᴀ
to
711

Inspector, 3. 正教員 Chêng⁴ Chiao⁴ Yüan², Teachers, 4. 副 (助) 教員 Fu⁴ (Chu⁴) Chiao⁴ Yüan², Assistant Teachers (at a school with an enrollment of 300 students there are not more than 26 Teachers and Assistant Teachers), 5. Nine 學長 Hsüeh² Chang³, Instructors, 6. One 醫官 I¹ Kuan¹, Surgeon (acting also as 衛生學教員 Wei⁴ Shêng¹ Hsüeh² Chiao⁴ Yüan², Teacher of Hygiene), 7. One 文案 Wên² An⁴, Secretary, 8. One 收支委員 Shou¹ Chih¹ Wei³ Yüan², Treasurer, 9. One 支應司事 Chih¹ Ying⁴ Ssu¹ Shih⁴, Steward, 10. One 管庫司事 Kuan³ K'u⁴ Ssu¹ Shih⁴, Overseer of Accoutrements, 11. Three 司書 Ssu¹ Shu¹, Clerks, 12. Three 差弁 Ch'ai¹ Pien⁴, Messengers, 13. Two 號兵 Hao⁴ Ping¹, Signalmen, and 14. 40 夫役 Fu¹ I⁴, Servants.

709ᴀ. 武備學堂 Wu³ Pei⁴ Hsüeh² T'ang², Military Preparatory School; with a course covering 2 to 3 years. The establishment of schools of this type took place previous to the promulgation (in 1904) of the general regulations for Military Schools (*see* No. 708). On completion of their studies at these schools the best scholars—aged 20 to 28 years—were advanced to the 速成陸軍學堂 Su² Ch'êng² Lu⁴ Chün¹ Hsüeh² T'ang² (*see* No. 711ᴀ).

The Wu³ Pei⁴ Hsüeh² T'ang² have now been reorganized into Primary Military Schools (*see* No. 709).

710. 陸軍中學堂 Lu⁴ Chün¹ Chung¹ Hsüeh² T'ang², Middle Military Schools (Middle Corps of Cadets); open to those who have completed the course of Primary Military Schools (*see* No. 709); with a two years course of study. These schools are to be established in the provinces of Chihli, Shansi, Hupeh and Kiangsu.

Regulations for Military Middle Schools have not as yet been promulgated.

711. 陸軍兵官學堂 Lu⁴ Chün¹ Ping¹ Kuan¹· Hsüeh² T'ang², School for Military Officers; for those who have

completed the course of Military Middle Schools (*see* No. 710)   **711ᴀ**
and have served in the ranks for four months (*see* No. 708);
with a course of study covering one year and a half. This
school is to be established at Peking but the regulations have
not yet been published.

711ᴀ. 陸軍速成學堂 Lu⁴ Chün¹ Su² Ch'êng² Hsüeh²
T'ang², School for Military Officers with Abridged Course;
established in accordance with a Memorial from the Ministry
of War, in 1905, at 保定府 Pao Ting Fu. The enrollment
is 1,140 and the course of study extends over two years and a
half, or one year and a half, as instruction in the subjects of
general education is, or is not, supplied.

Those following the one year and a half course (第一班
Ti⁴ I¹ Pan⁴) make a special study of military sciences during
the complete course; those following the two year and a half
course (第二班 Ti⁴ Êrh⁴ Pan⁴) study subjects of general
education for one year and military sciences during the remaining
one year and a half.

On satisfactory completion of the course the students serve
in the ranks for three months, with the designation 學習官
Hsüeh² Hsi² Kuan¹ (compare No. 708).

At the head of the School for Military Officers with
Abridged Course there is a 總辦 Tsung³ Pan⁴, Superintendent.
Subordinated to him are: 1. One 正監督 Chêng⁴ Chien¹ Tu¹,
Director, 2. One 副監督 Fu⁴ Chien¹ Tu¹, Vice-Director,
3. One 正提調 Chêng⁴ T'i² Tiao⁴, Inspector, 4. One 副提調
Fu⁴ T'i² Tiao⁴, Assistant Inspector, 5. 正教員 Chêng⁴ Chiao⁴
Yüan², Teachers, 6. 副教員 Fu⁴ Chiao⁴ Yüan² and 助教員
Chu⁴ Chiao⁴ Yüan², Assistant Teachers, 7. Five 科長 K'o¹
Chang³, Section Chiefs, 8. 隊官 Tui⁴ Kuan¹, Company
Commanders (10 in all; 120 students form a 隊 Tui⁴, Company),
9. 排官 P'ai² Kuan¹, Platoon Commanders (40 students form a
排 P'ai², Platoon; there are 30 Platoons in all), 10. 正學長

711ʙ to 711c   Chêng⁴ Hsüeh² Chang³, Instructors (10—there being 10 companies), 11. 副學長 Fu⁴ Hsüeh² Chang³, Assistant Instructors (20 in all; two to each company), 12. Two 醫官 I¹ Kuan¹, Surgeons (acting also as Teachers of Hygiene; compare No. 709), 13. Four 醫生 I¹ Shêng¹, Assistant Surgeons, 14. Two 馬醫官 Ma³ I¹ Kuan¹, Veterinary Surgeons (acting also as 馬學正教員 Ma³ Hsüeh² Chêng⁴ Chiao⁴ Yüan², Teacher of Veterinary Sciences, and 馬學副教員 Ma³ Hsüeh² Fu⁴ Chiao⁴ Yüan², Assistant Teacher of Veterinary Sciences), 15. One 一等書記官 I¹ Têng³ Shu¹ Chi⁴ Kuan¹, Secretary of the 1st Class, 16. Three 二等書記官 Êrh⁴ Têng³ Shu¹ Chi⁴ Kuan¹, Secretaries of the 2nd Class, 17. One 收支正委員 Shou¹ Chih¹ Chêng⁴ Wei³ Yüan², Treasurer, 18. Three 收支副委員 Shou¹ Chih¹ Fu⁴ Wei³ Yüan², Assistant Treasurers, 19. One 管馬正委員 Kuan³ Ma³ Chêng⁴ Wei³ Yüan², Inspector of Horses, 20. Three 管馬副委員 Kuan³ Ma³ Fu⁴ Wei³ Yüan², Assistant Inspectors of Horses, 21. Three 支應司事 Chih¹ Ying⁴ Ssu¹ Shih⁴, Stewards, 22. Three 管庫司事 Kuan³ K'u⁴ Ssu¹ Shih⁴, Overseers of Accoutrements, 23. Two 管藥司事 Kuan³ Yao⁴ Ssu¹ Shih⁴, Pharmacists, 24. 16 司書生 Ssu¹ Shu¹ Shêng¹, Clerks, etc.

711ʙ. 將弁學堂 Chiang⁴ Pien⁴ Hsüeh² T'ang², Courses for Military Officers and Sub-Officers. These have been instituted in the provinces of Chihli (北洋將弁學堂 Pei³ Yang² Chiang⁴ Pien⁴ Hsüeh² T'ang²), Hupeh and Kuangtung, and elsewhere. The term of study (in Chihli) is of eight months duration and the enrollment is 120. On completion of the course Officers receive appointments in the troops of the line.

711c. 講武堂 Chiang³ Wu³ T'ang², Courses of Military Instruction; instituted at provincial capitals for officers holding high rank in the New Army but who have not received the military education outlined by the Committee for the Reorgani-

[316]

zation of the Army (*see* No. 708). The programme of studies is similar to that of the 將弁學堂 Chiang⁴ Pien⁴ Hsüeh² T'ang² of Chihli and Hupeh (*see* No. 711B) and these courses function, for military officers, similarly to the 仕學館 Shih⁴ Hsüeh² Kuan³ (*see* No. 595A) and 課吏館 K'o⁴ Li¹ Kuan³ (*see* No. 597) for civil officials.

711D. 弁目學堂 Pien⁴ Mu⁴ Hsüeh² T'ang², Schools for Sergeants. 學兵營 Hsüeh² Ping¹ Ying², Instruction Battalions. 隨營學堂 Sui² Ying² Hsüeh² T'ang², Instruction Commands. The two latter are for training soldiers for the position of sergeant.

712. 陸軍大學堂 Lu⁴ Chün¹ Ta⁴ Hsüeh² T'ang², Military Academy, also 陸軍參謀大學堂 Lu⁴ Chün¹ Ts'an¹ Mou² Ta⁴ Hsüeh² T'ang², General Staff College. By regulations drawn up by the Committee for the Reorganization of the Army, in 1905, this school is to be established at Peking and is to be under the supervision of the General Staff (*see* No. 184B). Temporarily the enrollment is to be 40 officers, between the ages of 20 and 27 years (*see* No. 708). The course of study will cover three years.

At the head of the Military Academy there will be a 監督 Chien¹ Tu¹, Director. He will be assisted by: 1. 總教習 Tsung³ Chiao⁴ Hsi², Senior Professor, 2. 正教習 Chêng⁴ Chiao⁴ Hsi², Assistant Senior Professor, as Inspector, 3. 教習 Chiao⁴ Hsi², Professors of sciences of general education and special military sciences (also acting as 繙譯官 Fan¹ I⁴ Kuan¹, Translators), 4. 漢文主講 Han⁴ Wên² Chu³ Chiang³, Professor of Chinese Literature (acting at the same time as 編纂官 Pien¹ Tsuan³ Kuan¹, Reviser), 5. 文案 Wên² An⁴, Secretary (simultaneously serving as Proof-reader; compare above), 6. 雜務委員 Tsa² Wu⁴ Wei³ Yüan², Steward, 7. 醫官 I¹ Kuan¹, Surgeon, 8. 司事 Ssu¹ Shih⁴, Assistant Steward (*see* above), 9. 清書 Ch'ing¹ Shu¹, Clerk, 10. 書識 Shu¹

712A
to
713

Shih⁴, Writer, 11. 馬弁 Ma³ Pien⁴, Mounted Petty Officer Orderlies, 12. 馬目 Ma³ Mu⁴, Mounted Orderlies, 13. 差目 Ch'ai¹ Mu⁴, Messengers, 14. 刷印匠 Shua¹ Yin⁴ Chiang⁴, Printers, and 15. 夫役 Fu¹ I⁴, Servants.

712A. 軍官學堂 Chün¹ Kuan¹ Hsüeh² T'ang², Military Staff Officers College (at Paotingfu). Previous to the establishment of the Military Academy (*see* No. 712) this institution serves as the school for training officers for staff posts (*see* No. 184L). It is under the supervision of the General Staff (*see* No. 184B), which issued supplementary regulations for its administration in 1909—these were sanctioned by the Emperor on the 6th September of the same year.

For enrollment in this college there are accepted well-behaved young men aged 25 to 30 years who have completed the course of a Primary Military School (or a school of the corresponding grade), or of a Military College abroad, after a test examination in Chinese and foreign languages, general educational subjects and military sciences. The course of study covers three years (formerly there were two courses of study : 速成科 Su² Ch'êng² K'o¹, and 深造科 Shên¹ Tsao⁴ K'o¹, the former extending over one year and a half only).

713. 陸軍貴胄學堂 Lu⁴ Chün¹ Kuei⁴ Chou⁴ Hsüeh² T'ang², Military School for Princes and Nobles ; founded, in accordance with a Memorial from the Committee for the Reorganization of the Army (sanctioned by the Emperor on the 19th October, 1905), with the object of training the sons of Princes and Nobles for military service. The duration of the course was fixed at five years (lately, on a Memorial from the Ministry of War, dated the 7th March, 1908, it has been reduced to three years).

The enrollment is 120 students, arranged in three 班 Pan¹, Sections, of 40 students each. Eligible for admission to the school are the sons of : 1. Princes, 2. Clansmen holding posts

not lower than the fourth rank, 3. Metropolitan and Provincial
Manchu and Chinese military and civil officials holding posts not
lower than the second rank. The age limit for students is 18 to
25 years.

Those who complete the course of study with the first rating
are enrolled in the army as lieutenants, are attached to the
Ministry of War as 主事 Chu³ Shih⁴ (*see* No. 292), or are sent
to the provinces as 通判 T'ung¹ P'an⁴ (*see* No. 849ᴀ).

Those who graduate with the second rating are enrolled in
the army as sub-lieutenants, are attached to one of the Ministries
as 七品筆帖式 Ch'i¹ P'in³ Pi³ T'ieh³ Shih⁴, (*see* No. 293) or
七品小京官 Ch'i¹ P'in³ Hsiao³ Ching¹ Kuan¹ (*see* No. 299),
or are sent to the provinces as 知縣 Chih¹ Hsien⁴ (*see* No. 856).

At the Military School for Princes and Nobles there is a
蒙旗世爵班 Mêng³ Ch'i² Shih⁴ Chüeh² Pan¹, Special Section
for Hereditary Mongolian Princes (regulations for this were
drawn up by 貝勒載潤 Pei¹ Lê¹ Tsai³ Jun⁴, Tsai Jun, Prince
of the 3rd Degree, the superintendent of the school, and
sanctioned by the Emperor on the 20th February, 1910).

713ᴀ. At the head of the Military School for Princes and
Nobles there is a 管理陸軍貴胄學堂事務 Kuan³ Li³ Lu⁴
Chün¹ Kuei⁴ Chou⁴ Hsüeh² T'ang² Shih⁴ Wu⁴, Superintendent,
appointed from the ranks of Princes of the Blood (the post
of 總辦 Tsung³ Pan⁴, Curator, was abolished on a Memorial
from Prince 載潤 Tsai³ Jun⁴, dated the 20th February, 1910).
Directly subordinated to the Superintendent are: 1. Director
(*see* No. 635), 2. Preceptor (*see* No. 649), 3. 普通學正教
員 P'u³ T'ung¹ Hsüeh² Chêng⁴ Chiao⁴ Yüan², Teachers of
subjects of general education, 4. 普通學副教員 P'u³ T'ung¹
Hsüeh² Fu⁴ Chiao⁴ Yüan², Assistant Teachers of subjects of
general education (there are six Teachers and Assistant Teachers
in all), 5. Three 兵學教員 Ping¹ Hsüeh² Chiao⁴ Yüan⁴,
Teachers of military sciences, 6. One 正醫官 Chêng⁴ I¹ Kuan¹,

[319]

714
to
715ʙ

Surgeon, 7. Two 副醫官 Fu⁴ I¹ Kuan¹, Assistant Surgeons, 8. Three Teachers (*see* No. 637) acting as 繙譯 Fan¹ I⁴, Interpreters, 9. Two 漢文正教員 Han⁴ Wên² Chêng⁴ Chiao⁴ Yüan², Teachers of Chinese literature, 10. Two 漢文副教員 Han⁴ Wên² Fu⁴ Chiao⁴ Yüan², Assistant Teachers of Chinese literature, 11. Six 齋長 Chai¹ Chang³, Inspectors of Dormitories (compare No. 645), 12. One Secretary, 13. One 收支委員 Shou¹ Chih¹ Wei³ Yüan², Treasurer, 14. Two 支應司事 Chih¹ Ying⁴ Ssu¹ Shih⁴, Steward, 15. Five 司書 Ssu¹ Shu¹, Clerks, doing duty as 刷印 Shua¹ Yin⁴, Printers, 16. Four 醫兵 I¹ Ping¹, Hospital Attendants, 17. Two 號兵 Hao⁴ Ping¹, Signalmen, 18. Three 差弁 Ch'ai¹ Pien⁴, Messengers, 19. 門丁 Mên² Ting¹, Watchmen, and 20. 夫役 Fu¹ I⁴, Servants (there are 40 Watchmen and Servants).

714. According to the programme of the Committee for the Reorganization of the Army there are still to be established: 1. 步隊專門學堂 Pu⁴ Tui⁴ Chuan¹ Mên² Hsüeh² T'ang², Special Infantry School, 2. 馬隊專門學堂 Ma³ Tui⁴ Chuan¹ Mên² Hsüeh² T'ang², Special Cavalry School, and 3. 礮隊專門學堂 P'ao⁴ Tui⁴ Chuan¹ Mên² Hsüeh² T'ang², Special Artillery School. To these institutions officers of the corresponding branches of the army will be sent for further prefecting themselves.

715. For the training of officers for the auxiliary branches of the army (compare No. 656A) there are the following schools:

715ᴀ. 軍醫學堂 Chün¹ I¹ Hsüeh² T'ang², Military Medical Schools (for instance, at Tientsin, where it is styled 北洋醫學堂 Pei³ Yang² I¹ Hsüeh² T'ang²).

715ʙ. 馬醫學堂 Ma³ I¹ Hsüeh² T'ang², and 獸醫學堂 Shou¹ I¹ Hsüeh² T'ang², Military Veterinary Schools (for instance, 南洋陸軍獸醫學堂 Nan² Yang² Lu⁴ Chün¹ Shou⁴ I¹ Hsüeh² T'ang²).

[320]

715C. 衛生學堂 Wei⁴ Shêng¹ Hsüeh² T'ang², Military Schools for Assistant Surgeo   (Military Sanitary Schools)—for instance 南洋陸軍衛生學堂 Nan² Yang² Lu⁴ Chün¹ Wei⁴ Shêng¹ Hsüeh² T'ang².

715D. 陸軍測繪學堂 Lu⁴ Chün¹ Ts'ê⁴ Hui⁴ Hsüeh² T'ang², Schools for Military Draftsmen (for instance, at Peking : 京師陸軍測繪學堂 Ching¹ Shih¹ Lu⁴ Chün¹ Ts'ê⁴ Hui⁴ Hsüeh² T'ang²), or 測繪學堂 Ts'ê⁴ Hui⁴ Hsüeh² T'ang², Schools for Draftmen (for instance, in Manchuria, 東三省測繪學堂 Tung¹ San¹ Shêng¹ Ts'ê⁴ Hui⁴ Hsüeh² T'ang²). Both are under the control of the General Staff (see No. 184B).

715E. 憲兵學堂 Hsien⁴ Ping¹ Hsüeh² T'ang², Gendarmerie Schools (for training men for ervice in the Military Police—Gendarmerie ;—(see No. 703). In Manchuria, 東三省憲兵學堂 Tung¹ San¹ Shêng³ Hsien⁴ Ping¹ Hsüeh² T'ang².

715F. 兵工學堂 Ping¹ Kung¹ Hsüeh² T'ang², Military Technical Schools.

716. The despatch of military students abroad is carried on according to regulations drawn up by the Committee for the Reorganization of the Army in 1904 and 1905. There are chosen for study abroad (on their satisfaction of certain requirements, with regard to age and good behavior) a number of students from the following :

1. Those who have completed the course of the 武備學堂 Wu³ Pei⁴ Hsüeh² T'ang² (see No. 709A), the 陸軍速成學堂 Lu⁴ Chun¹ Su² Ch'êng² Hsüeh² T'ang² (see No. 711A), or the 陸軍貴胄學堂 Lu⁴ Chün¹ Kuei⁴ Chou⁴ Hsüeh² T'ang² (see No. 713).

2. Those studying at the 陸軍中學堂 Lu⁴ Chün¹ Chung¹ Hsüeh² T'ang² (see No. 710), or other schools, and

3. Bannermen students.

While abroad, military students are under the control of the Chinese Ministers and Military Attachés. On their return to

717
to
717ᴀ

Peking they undergo an examination at the Ministry of War and, according to their attainments in this examination, are arranged in three classes : 優 等 Yu¹ Têng³, 上 等 Shang⁴ Têng³, and 中 等 Chung¹ Têng³.

Those who attain the first class receive the rank of 副 軍 校 Fu⁴ Chün¹ Hsiao⁴ (*see* No. 658). Those attaining the second and third classes receive the rank of 協 軍 校 Hsieh² Chün¹ Hsiao⁴ (*see* No. 658). On all three classes there is conferred the degree of 舉 人 Chü³ Jên² (*see* No. 652ᴇ), qualified by the speciality of the recipient (five in all; compare No. 656), *i.e.* 1. 陸 軍 步 兵 科 Lu⁴ Chün¹ Pu⁴ Ping¹ K'o¹, 2. 陸 軍 馬 兵 科 Lu⁴ Chün¹ Ma³ Ping¹ K'o¹, 3. 陸 軍 礮 兵 科 Lu⁴ Chün¹ P'ao⁴ Ping¹ K'o¹, 4. 陸 軍 工 兵 科 Lu⁴ Chün¹ Kung¹ Ping¹ K'o¹, and 5. 陸 軍 輜 重 兵 科 Lu⁴ Chün¹ Tzu⁴ Chung⁴ Ping¹ K'o¹ (compare also No. 659.)

717. Until 1902 the children of Clansmen of the Imperial House and of Bannermen were taught in special schools styled : 宗 學 Tsung¹ Hsüeh², Schools for Clansmen of the Imperial House, and 八 旗 官 學 Pa¹ Ch'i² Kuan¹ Hsüeh², Government Schools for Bannermen. In the year mentioned a reform was instituted by virtue of which, instead of schools of the type spoken of, there has been begun the establishment of 學 堂 Hsüeh² T'ang², Schools, not distinguishable in title or programme from the common schools (primary, middle and higher), except that only children of Clansmen of the Imperial House and Bannermen are eligible for admission (for this reason the title of the school is followed by the phrase 宗 室 覺 羅 八 旗 Tsung¹ Shih⁴ Chüeh¹ Lo² Pa¹ Ch'i²). Recently all primary and middle schools of this kind have been placed under the general control of the Committee at the Ministry of Education (*see* No. 411).

717ᴀ. There are at present the following schools for Clansmen of the Imperial House and Bannermen at Peking :

[322]

1. 京師宗室覺羅八旗高等學堂 Ching¹ Shih¹ Tsung¹ Shih⁴ Chüeh¹ Lo² Pa¹ Ch'i² Kao¹ Têng³ Hsüeh² T'ang², Higher School for Clansmen of the Imperial House and Bannermen, at Peking ; this is under the control of the Ministry of Education and at it there is a 中 等 班 Chung¹ Têng³ Pan¹, Section with a Middle School programme (*see* No. 583B).

2. Eight 八 旗 高 等 小 學 堂 Pa¹ Ch'i² Kao¹ Têng³ Hsüeh³ Hsüeh² T'ang², Primary Schools of the Senior Grade for Bannermen (title is shortened by omitting Ching Shih Tsung Shih, etc.; *see* No. 579).

3. 15 八 旗 初 等 小 學 堂 Pa¹ Ch'i² Ch'u¹ Têng³ Hsiao³ Hsüeh² T'ang², Primary Schools of the Junior Grade for Bannermen (*see* No. 579).

4. 內 務 府 三 旗 小 學 堂 Nei⁴ Wu⁴ Fu³ San¹ Ch'i² Hsiao³ Hsüeh² T'ang², Primary School for the Three· Superior Banners (*see* No. 97).

5. 健 銳 營 小 學 堂 Chien⁴ Jui⁴ Ying² Hsiao³ Hsüeh² T'ang², Primary School for the Light Division of the Banners (*see* No. 738).

6. 火 器 營 小 學 堂 Huo³ Ch'i⁴ Ying² Hsiao³ Hsüeh² T'ang², Primary School for the Artillery and Musketry Division of the Banners (*see* No. 737).

717B. Schools established at the Provincial Manchu Garrisons (*see* No. 743C) are styled 駐 防 滿 營 小 學 堂 Chu⁴ Fang² Man³ Ying² Hsiao³ Hsüeh² T'ang², Primary Schools at the Manchu Garrisons (compare No. 579). Similarly to common schools they are divided into two grades : 初 等 Ch'u¹ Têng³, Junior, and 高 等 Kao¹ Têng³, Senior (compare No. 576).

BANNER FORCES.

718. 八 旗 Pa¹ Ch'i², Banner Forces (or Troops of the Eight Banners—Divisions). These are composed of the des-

cendants of : 1. Manchus who aided the first Emperors of the Ta Ch'ing Dynasty in conquering China, at the beginning of the 17th century, 2. Chinese subjects of the Ming Dynasty who transferred their allegiance to the Manchus, and 3. Kharach'in Mongols who transferred their allegiance to the Manchus at the time of the conquest. Accordingly, the Banner Forces are divided, by nationalities, into : 1. 滿洲八旗 Man³ Chou¹ Pa¹ Ch'i², Manchu Banner Troops, 2. 蒙古八旗 Mêng² Ku³ Pa¹ Ch'i², Mongol Banner Troops, and 3. 漢軍八旗 Han⁴ Chün¹ Pa¹ Ch'i², Chinese Banner Troops.

The troops of each nationality are, further, divided under eight banners or divisions, namely : 1. 鑲黃旗 Hsiang¹ Huang² Ch'i², Bordered Yellow, 2. 正黃旗 Chêng⁴ Huang² Ch'i², Plain Yellow, 3. 正白旗 Chêng⁴ Pai² Ch'i², Plain White, 4. 鑲白旗 Hsiang¹ Pai² Ch'i², Bordered White, 5. 正紅旗 Chêng⁴ Hung² Ch'i², Plain Red, 6. 鑲紅旗 Hsiang¹ Hung² Ch'i², Bordered Red, 7. 正藍旗 Chêng⁴ Lan² Ch'i², Plain Blue, and 8. 鑲藍旗 Hsiang¹ Lan² Ch'i², Bordered Blue. The three first mentioned are called the 上三旗 Shang⁴ San¹ Ch'i², Three Superior Banners ; the remaining five are styled the 下五旗 Hsia⁴ Wu³ Ch'i², Five Inferior Banners.

From their stations the Banner Forces are styled : 1. 京旗 Ching¹ Ch'i², Metropolitan Banner Forces, and 2. 駐防 Chu⁴ Fang², Banner Garrisons (*see* below ; No. 743).

The Metropolitan Banner Forces are sub-divided into : 1. 內旗 Nei⁴ Ch'i², Household, or Inner, Banners (for particulars, *see* No. 97), and 2. 外旗 Wai⁴ Ch'i², Outer Banners.

The Outer Banner Troops are stationed in Peking and the adjacent suburbs and are under the supervision of the 值年旗 Chih² Nien² Ch'i², General Headquarters of the Banners, to which one of the Lieutenant-Generals of each of the Banner Divisions (*see* No. 719) is appointed annually.

719
to
721

The chief contingent of the Banner Forces is the so-called 驍騎營 Hsiao¹ Ch'i² Ying², Banner Corps of the Line (compare No. 97ʙ), and is drawn from the 24 Banner Divisions (eight Banners of each nationality; compare above).

Although the Banner Forces played the chief part in the conquest of China and in the consolidation of the power of the reigning Dynasty, nevertheless, at the present time, they have lost any military importance, the more so as a large percentage of the men enrolled in the forces see no service, or perform duties having not the slightest connection with military affairs. The representatives of the three nationalities composing the Banner Forces form a peculiar caste—or military clique—holding a predominant position in the Empire and serve as a support to the power and influence of the Manchu Dynasty. Recently, however, the Government has taken steps for the gradual equalization of the rights of the Banner Forces and the mass of the population (*see* No. 186).

719. 都統 Tu¹ T'ung³, Lieutenant-General; 1ʙ. There are 24 of these; one to each national division of the Banners (*see* No. 718).

719ᴀ. For particulars as to the 都統 Tu¹ T'ung³, acting as Military Lieutenant-Governors (of Chakhar and of Jehol) *see* Nos. 897 and 898.

720. 副都統 Fu⁴ Tu¹ T'ung³, Deputy Lieutenant-General; 2ᴀ. There are 48 in all; two to each national division of the Banners (*see* No. 718).

720ᴀ. For particulars as to the 副都統 Fu⁴ Tu¹ T'ung³, acting as Assistant Military Lieutenant-Governors and as Deputy Lieutenant-Generals of provincial Manchu Garrisons *see* Nos. 802 and 745.

721. 印務參領 Yin⁴ Wu⁴ Ts'an¹ Ling³, Adjutant-General; 3ᴀ. There are two to each of the 24 Banners (except

the Mongol, which have but one each). They are appointed from the ranks of Colonels (*see* No. 722).

722. 驍騎參領 Hsiao¹ Ch'i² Ts'an¹ Ling³, Colonel; 3A; in command of a sub-division or 甲喇 Chia³ La¹ (Manchurian Chalan), of which there are five to each Manchu and Chinese Banner. In the Mongol Banners there are but two of these sub-divisions to each.

723. 副驍騎參領 Fu⁴ Hsiao¹ Ch'i² Ts'an¹ Ling³, Lieutenant-Colonel; 4A; one to each Chalan or sub-division (*see* No. 722).

724. 印務章京 Yin⁴ Wu⁴ Chang¹ Ching¹, Adjutant; 5B; conducts the correspondence of a Banner.

725. 委印務章京 Wei³ Yin⁴ Wu⁴ Chang¹ Ching¹, Assistant-Adjutant.

726. 佐領 Tso³ Ling³, Captain; 4A. Of officers of this rank there are from 70 to 80, in each of the Manchu Banners, and from 30 to 40, in each of the Chinese Banners. Each is in charge of some 70 to 100 of the Household Bannermen. In some cases they hold their rank by hereditary right, either as 勳舊 Hsün¹ Chiu⁴ or as 世管佐領 Shih⁴ Kuan³ Tso³ Ling³. Those who are appointed by various processes of selection are designated 公中 Kung¹ Chung¹, 分管 Fên¹ Kuan³, and 輪管佐領 Lun² Kuan³ Tso³ Ling³.

726A. 半箇佐領 Pan⁴ Ko⁴ Tso³ Ling³, Half Tso Ling. This title was formerly in use but at the present it is almost—if not completely—obsolete. It designated Captains of companies (*see* No. 726) of less than one hundred.

727. 驍騎校 Hsiao¹ Ch'i² Hsiao⁴, Lieutenant; 6A. Officers of this rank are drawn upon to fill the post of 步軍校 Pu⁴ Chün¹ Hsiao⁴ (*see* No. 799).

728. 委署驍騎校 Wei³ Shu⁴ Hsiao¹ Ch'i² Hsiao⁴, Sub-Lieutenant; 8B.

729. 領催 Ling³ Ts'ui¹, Corporal.

730. 馬甲 Ma³ Chia³ (**Manchurian** Ukesen), Private of
the 1st Class. Also called 驍騎 Hsiao¹ Ch'i².

731. 敖爾布 Ao⁴ Êrh³ Pu⁴ (**Manchurian** Orbo), Private
of the 2nd Class. Also called 鹿角兵 Lu⁴ Chiao² Ping¹. This
rank is found in the 漢軍 Han⁴ Chün¹, Chinese Banners only
(*see* No. 718).

732. 養育兵 Yang³ Yü⁴ Ping¹, Supernumeraries, or
Juniors; awaiting appointment as 馬甲 Ma³ Chia³, or 敖爾布
Ao⁴ Êrh³ Pu⁴, as vacancies occur (*see* Nos. 730 and 731).

732A. 閑散 Hsien² San³ (Manchurian Sula), Bannermen
at Large; without position or pay.

733. From the Banner Forces not coming within the
Banner Corps of the line (*see* **No.** 718) there are organized
various divisions, as follows: 1. 護軍營 Hu⁴ Chün¹ Ying²,
The Guards Division (*see* No. 734), 2. 前鋒營 Ch'ien² Fêng¹
Ying², Vanguard Division (*see* No. 735), **3.** 步軍營 Pu⁴
Chün¹ Ying², Gendarmerie Division (*see* No. 736; for details *see*
No. 797), 4. 火器營 Huo³ Ch'i⁴ Ying², The Artillery and
Musketry Division (*see* No. 737), 5. 健銳營 Chien⁴ Jui⁴
Ying², The Light Division (*see* No. 738), 6. 虎槍營 Hu³
Ch'iang¹ Ying², The Marksmen for Tiger Hunts (*see* No. 739),
7. 神機營 Shên² Chi¹ Ying², The Peking Field Force (*see*
No. 740), 8. 圓明園八旗護軍營 Yüan² Ming² Yüan²
Pa¹ Ch'i² Hu⁴ Chün¹ Ying², The Yüan Ming Yüan Division of
the Banner Force (*see* No. 741), 9. 嚮導處 Hsiang³ Tao⁴
Ch'u⁴, The Guides (*see* No. 742), and 10. 上虞備用處
Shang⁴ Yü² Pei⁴ Yung⁴ Ch'u⁴, The Imperial Hunting Depart-
ment (*see* No. 742A).

734. 護軍營 Hu⁴ Chün² Ying², The Guards Division
(common designation, 大營 Ta⁴ Ying², Main Division. The
former designation was Pa-ya-la, which was exchanged in
A. D. 1660 for the Chinese equivalent now in use). Admission
to this division is the special ambition of the great mass of

730
to
734

734ᴀ
to
735
Bannermen of Peking, to whom it secures the advantages of substantial increase in pay and prospects of a promotion of one degree. The principal duty assigned it is to furnish detachments of guards for the Imperial Palace (*see* No. 104). This division consists of eight sections, corresponding to the eight Banners, and each is under the command of a 護軍統領 Hu⁴ Chün¹ T'ung³ Ling³, Captain-General (2ᴀ). The other ranks are: 1. 護軍參領 Hu⁴ Chün¹ Ts'an¹ Ling³, Colonel (3ᴀ; 32 Mongols and 80 Manchus), 2. 副護軍參領 Fu⁴ Hu⁴ Chün¹ Ts'an¹ Ling³, Lieutenant-Colonel (4ᴀ; 32 Mongols and 80 Manchus), 3. 護軍校 Hu⁴ Chün¹ Hsiao⁴, Lieutenant (6ᴀ; 681 Mongols and 204 Manchus), 4. 委署護軍校 Wei³ Shu⁴ Hu⁴ Chün¹ Hsiao⁴, Sub-Lieutenant; 8ʙ, 5. 護軍 Hu⁴ Chün¹, Privates (14,075 in all).

734ᴀ. For particulars concerning 內護軍營 Nei⁴ Hu⁴ Chün¹ Ying², The Imperial Guards, *see* No. 97ᴀ.

735. 前鋒營 Ch'ien² Fêng¹ Ying², Vanguard Division. This is composed entirely of Manchus or Mongols of all Banners. In time of peace this division performs service without the Palace; when the Emperor goes abroad it precedes the Imperial chairs at a distance of 1 ι. 2 li. In time of war it is sent forward to open battles and prepare a way for the success of the main forces.

The Vanguard Division is divided into two "Wings" (or Sections): 1. Left (including the bordered yellow, plain white, bordered white and plain blue Banners) and 2. Right (including the plain yellow, plain red, bordered red and bordered blue Banners). These are commanded by the 左翼前鋒統領 Tso³ I⁴ Ch'ien² Fêng¹ T'ung³ Ling³, and 右翼前鋒統領 Yu⁴ I⁴ Ch'ien² Fêng¹ T'ung³ Ling³, Commandants of the Left and Right Wings of the Vanguard Division; 2ᴀ. The other ranks are: 1. 前鋒參領 Ch'ien² Fêng¹ Ts'an¹ Ling³, Colonel of the Vanguard Division (3ᴀ; four in each Wing), 2. 前鋒

侍衛 Ch'ien² Fêng¹ Shih⁴ Wei⁴, Imperial Guardsmen of the Vanguard Division (4A; four in each Wing), 3. 委署前鋒 侍衛 Wei³ Shu⁴ Ch'ien² Fêng¹ Shih⁴ Wei⁴, Deputy Imperial Guardsman of the Vanguard Division (5B; two in each Wing), 4. 前鋒校 Ch'ien² Fêng¹ Hsiao⁴, Sergeant of the Vanguard Division (6A; 48 in each Wing), 5. 委署前鋒校 Wei³ Shu⁴ Ch'ien² Fêng¹ Hsiao⁴, Sergeant of the Vanguard Division; 8B, and 6. 前鋒 Ch'ien² Fêng¹, Privates of the Vanguard Division (899 in the left and 865 in the right Wing).

735A. For details regarding 內前鋒營 Nei⁴ Ch'ien² Fêng¹ Ying², The Household Vanguard, see No. 97c.

736. 步軍營 Pu⁴ Chün¹ Ying², Gendarmerie Division. For details see No. 797.

737. 火器營 Huo³ Ch'i⁴ Ying², The Artillery and Musketry Division; consisting of 內 Nei⁴, and 外 Wai⁴, or, Inner and Outer, Detachments. The first is stationed at Peking while the second is at 藍靛廠 Lan² Tien⁴ Ch'ang³ (a short distance from the Summer Palace 圓明園 Yüan² Ming² Yüan²).

The 內火器營 Nei⁴ Huo³ Ch'i⁴ Ying² is formed from the 包衣 Pao¹ I¹ of the several Banners (see No. 97).

The Artillery and Musketry Division is composed of Manchu and Mongol Bannermen and is under the command of 總統 Tsung³ T'ung³, General Commandants (number not fixed; Princes of the Blood). At the head of each Detachment there is a 翼長 I⁴ Chang³, Brigadier; 3A. The other ranks are: 1. 營總 Ying² Tsung³, Commandant of a Garrison (Deputy Brigadier; four in each Detachment), 2. 鳥槍護軍參領 Niao³ Ch'iang¹ Hu⁴ Chün¹ Ts'an¹ Ling³, Colonel of the Imperial Regiment of the Artillery and Musketry Division (3A; four in each Detachment), 3. 鳥槍驍騎參領 Niao³ Ch'iang¹ Hsiao¹ Ch'i² Ts'an¹ Ling³, Colonel of the Artillery and Musketry Division; 3A, 4. 副鳥槍護軍參領 Fu⁴ Niao³ Ch'iang¹

[329]

738 Hu⁴ Chün¹ Ts'an¹ Ling³, Lieutenant-Colonel of the Imperial Regiment of the Artillery and Musketry Division; 4A, 5. 管鳥槍散秩官 Kuan³ Niao³ Ch'iang¹ San⁴ Chih⁴ Kuan¹, Musketry Adjutant, 6. 管礮槍散秩官 Kuan³ P'ao⁴ Ch'iang¹ San⁴ Chih⁴ Kuan¹, Artillery Adjutant, 7. 鳥槍護軍校 Niao³ Ch'iang¹ Hu⁴ Chün¹ Hsiao⁴, Lieutenant of the Imperial Regiment of the Artillery and Musketry Division; 6A, 8. 鳥槍驍騎校 Niao³ Ch'iang¹ Hsiao¹ Ch'i² Hsiao⁴, Lieutenant of Artillery and Musketry; 6A, 9. 管礮驍騎校 Kuan³ P'ao⁴ Hsiao¹ Ch'i² Hsiao⁴, Lieutenant of Artillery; 6A, 10. 鳥槍護軍 Niao³ Ch'iang¹ Hu⁴ Chün¹, Musketeer of the Imperial Guard, 11. 鳥槍驍騎 Niao³ Ch'iang¹ Hsiao¹ Ch'i², Musketeer, and 12. 礮驍騎 P'ao⁴ Hsiao¹ Ch'i², Artillery-man.

738. 健銳營 Chien⁴ Jui⁴ Ying², The Scouts, or the Light Division; quartered near the 香山苑 Hsiang¹ Shan¹ Yüan⁴, or 靜宜園 Ching⁴ I² Yüan², the Imperial Hunting Park, North-west of Peking. This division was formed in the fourteenth year of the reign of 乾隆 Ch'ien Lung (1749), because of the frequent revolts North of the Great Wall, the best men being recruited to it from the 前鋒營 Ch'ien² Fêng¹ Ying² (*see* No. 735). At the present time these troops have merely a nominal existence.

At the head of the Light Division there are 總統 Tsung³ T'ung³, General Commandants (number is not fixed; this post may be held by Princes of the Blood). The Division is divided into two Wings and in command of each there is an 翼長 I⁴ Chang³, Brigadier; 3A. The other ranks are: 1. 前鋒參領 Ch'ien² Fêng¹ Ts'an¹ Ling³, Colonel of the Light Division; 3A, 2. 副前鋒參領 Fu⁴ Ch'ien² Fêng¹ Ts'an¹ Ling³, Senior Lieutenant-Colonel of the Light Division; 4A, 3. 署前鋒參領 Shu⁴ Ch'ien² Fêng¹ Ts'an¹ Ling³, Junior Lieutenant-Colonel of the Light Division; 5B, 4. 前鋒校 Ch'ien² Fêng¹ Hsiao⁴, Lieutenant; 6A, 5. 副前鋒校 Fu⁴ Ch'ien² Fêng¹ Hsiao⁴,

Sub-Lieutenant; 8B, 6. 前 鋒 Ch'ien² Fêng¹, Private of the 1st Class of the Light Division, and 7. 委 前 鋒 Wei³ Ch'ien² Fêng¹, Private of the 2nd Class of the Light Division.

739. 虎槍營 Hu³ Ch'iang¹ Ying², The Marksmen for Tiger Hunts; recruited from the best marksmen of the Three Superior Banners (see No. 718). In command of these marksmen there is a 總統 Tsung³ T'ung³, General Commandant of the Marksmen for Tiger Hunts. The other ranks are: 1. 總領 Tsung³ Ling³, Brigadier of a Wing (six in all) 2. 虎 槍 長 Hu³ Ch'iang¹ Chang³, Senior Marksmen (21 in all), 3. 虎槍副長 Hu³ Ch'iang¹ Fu⁴ Chang³, Junior Marksmen (260 in all) and 4. 虎 槍 Hu³ Ch'iang¹, Marksmen (600 in all).

740. 神 機 營 Shên² Chi¹ Ying². The Peking Field Force (Divine Mechanism Regiments). This force, drawn from the élite of the Banner Troops of all three nationalities forming the 京 旗 Ching¹ Ch'i² (see No. 718), was organized in 1862—because of the disastrous campaign of 1860—and numbered 18 to 20 thousand men, supplied with the three types of arms, using modern breech-loaders and drilled in European style. This force no longer exists.

741. 圓明園八旗護軍營 Yüan² Ming² Yüan² Pa¹ Ch'i² Hu⁴ Chün¹ Ying². The Yüan Ming Yüan Guards Division of the Banner Forces. This is a division organized and appointed to guard the Summer residence of the Emperor. This residence is now at the 頤 和 園 I² Ho² Yüan² (at the foot of the hill 萬 壽 山 Wan¹ Shou⁴ Shan¹), as the Yüan Ming Yüan Palace was destroyed by the European troops in 1860, after the taking of Peking.

At the head of this division is the 總 統 Tsung³ T'ung², General Commandant of the Yüan Ming Yüan Guards Division of the Banner Forces. The other ranks are: 1. 營 總 Ying² Tsung³, Commandant (Assistant General Commandant; eight in all ; 3ᴀ), 2. 護軍參領 Hu⁴ Chün¹ Ts'an¹ Ling³, Colonel of the Yüan Ming Yüan Guards, Division of the Banner Forces (3ᴀ ; eight in all), 3. 副護軍參領 Fu⁴ Hu⁴ Chün¹ Ts'an¹ Ling³, Senior Lieutenant-Colonel of the Yüan Ming Yüan Guards Division of the Banner Forces (4ᴀ ; 16 in all), 4. 署護軍參領 Shu⁴ Hu⁴ Chün¹ Ts'an¹ Ling³, Junior Lieutenant-Colonel of the Yüan Ming Yüan Guards Division of the Banner Forces (32 in all), 5. 護軍校 Hu⁴ Chün¹ Hsiao⁴, Lieutenant of the Yüan Ming Yüan Guards Division of the Banner Forces (6ᴀ ; 128 in all), 6. 副護軍校 Fu⁴ Hu⁴ Chün¹ Hsiao⁴, Sub-Lieutenant of the Yüan Ming Yüan Guards Division of the Banner Forces (8ʙ ; 128 in all), and 7. 護軍 Hu⁴ Chün¹, Privates of the Yüan Ming Yüan Guards Division of the Banner Forces (compare No. 734).

741ᴀ. For particulars as to the 圓明園內旗護軍營 Yüan² Ming² Yüan² Nei⁴ Ch'i² Hu⁴ Chün¹ Ying², the Guards at the Summer Palace, Yüan Ming Yüan, etc., *see* No. 97ᴅ.

742. 嚮導處 Hsiang³ Tao⁴ Ch'u⁴, The Guides. This is a department furnishing outriders, etc., for Imperial progresses. At its head is the 總統 Tsung³ T'ung³, General Commandant of the Guides, appointed from the 八旗副都統 Pa¹ Ch'i² Fu⁴ Tu¹ T'ung³ (*see* No. 720), the 護軍統領 Hu⁴ Chün¹ T'ung³ Ling³ (*see* No. 734), and the 前鋒統領 Ch'ien² Fêng¹ T'ung³ Ling³ (*see* No. 735). For manning this department there are deputed officers and privates from the 護軍營 Hu⁴ Chün¹ Ying² (*see* No. 734 ; an indefinite number of 護軍校 Hu⁴ Chün¹ Hsiao⁴, and 護軍 Hu⁴ Chün¹), and from the 前鋒營 Ch'ien² Fêng¹ Ying² (*see* No. 735) ; four 前鋒侍衛 Ch'ien² Fêng¹ Shih⁴ Wei⁴, and an indefinite number of 前鋒校 Ch'ien² Fêng¹ Hsiao⁴ and 前鋒 Ch'ien² Fêng¹).

742ᴀ. 上虞備用處 Shang¹ Yü² Pei⁴ Yung⁴ Ch'u⁴, The Imperial Hunting Department.

[332]

743. 駐防 Chu⁴ Fang², Manchu Garrisons Without Peking (*see* No. 718). These are divided into three classes as follows :

743A. 畿輔駐防 Chi¹ Fu³ Chu⁴ Fang², Garrisons of the "Military Cordon." These are at 25 cities of Chihli, surrounding Peking. The nine garrisons nearest Peking are styled the 小九處 Hsiao³ Chiu³ Ch‘u⁴, Nine Small Posts.

743B. 陵寢駐防 Ling² Ch‘in³ Chu⁴ Fang², Garrisons at the Imperial Mausolea (for details *see* No. 571).

743C. 各省駐防 Ko⁴ Shêng³ Chú⁴ Fang², Garrisons stationed in the Provinces ; at 1. 歸化城 Kuei¹ Hua⁴ Ch‘êng², 綏遠城 Sui¹ Yüan³ Ch‘êng², and 太原府 T‘ai⁴ Yüan² Fu³, in Shansi, 2. 青州府 Ch‘ing¹ Chou¹ Fu³, and 德州 Tê² Chou¹, in Shantung, 3. 開封府 K‘ai¹ Fêng¹ Fu³, in Honan, 4. 江寧府 Chiang¹ Ning² Fu³, and 鎮江府 Chên⁴ Chiang¹ Fu³, in Kiangsu, 5. 杭州府 Hang² Chou¹ Fu³, and 乍浦 Ch‘a⁴ P‘u³, in Chekiang, 6. 福州府 Fu² Chou¹ Fu³, in Fukien, 7. 廣州府 Kuang³ Chou¹ Fu³, in Kuangtung, 8. 成都府 Ch‘êng² Tu¹ Fu³, in Szechwan, 9. 莉州府 Ching¹ Chou¹ Fu³, in Hupeh, 10. 西安府 Hsi¹ An¹ Fu³, in Shensi, and 11. 寧夏府 Ning² Hsia⁴ Fu³, 涼州府 Liang² Chou¹ Fu³, and 莊浪廳 Chuang¹ Liang³ Ting¹, in Kansu, with the garrisons of 烏魯木齊 Wu¹ Lu³ Mu¹ Ch‘i³, Urumtsi (also, 迪化府 Ti⁴ Hua⁴ Fu³), 巴里坤 Pa¹ La³ K‘un¹, Barkul (also, 鎮西廳 Chên⁴ Hsi¹ T‘ing¹), 古城 Ku³ Ch‘êng², or 孚遠城 Fu² Yüan³ Ch‘êng², and 土魯番廳 T‘u³ Lu³ Fan¹ T‘ing¹, Turfan (also, 廣安城 Kuang³ An¹ Ch‘êng²), which are under the Kansu jurisdiction.

744. 將軍 Chiang¹ Chün¹, Manchu General-in-Chief (or Tartar General) ; 1B ; literary designation, 大元戎 Ta⁴ Yüan² Jung². They reside in eight provinces at 1. 綏遠城 Sui¹ Yüan³ Ch‘êng², in Shansi (*see* Nos. 744A and 899), 2. 江寧城 Chiang¹ Ning² Fu³, Nanking, in Kiangsu, 3. 福州府 Fu² Chou¹ Fu³, in Fukien, 4. 杭州府 Hang² Chou¹ Fu³, in

**744A
to
745A**

Chekiang. 5. 荊州府 Ching¹ Chou¹ Fu³, in Hupeh, 6. 寧夏府 Ning² Hsiao⁴ Fu³, in Kansu (*see* Nos. 744B and 900), 7. 成都府 Ch'êng² Tu¹ Fu³, in Szechwan, and 8. 廣州府 Kuang³ Chou¹ Fu³, Canton, in Kuangtung.

744A. For details as to the 綏遠城將軍 Sui¹ Yüan³ Ch'êng² Chiang¹ Chün¹, *see* No. 899.

744B. For details as to the 寧夏將軍 Ning² Hsia⁴ Chiang¹ Chün¹, *see* No. 900.

744C. For details as to the 伊犁將軍 I¹ Li² Chiang¹ Chün¹, *see* No. 866.

744D. For details as to the 烏里雅蘇台將軍 Wu¹ Li³ Ya³ Su¹ T'ai² Chiang¹ Chün¹, *see* No. 879.

744E. For details as to the Chiang Chün in Manchuria, *see* Nos. 802 and 803.

745. 副都統 Fu⁴ Tu¹ T'ung³, Manchu Brigade-General; 2A; literary designation, 大統制 Ta⁴ T'ung³ Chih⁴. They reside in ten provinces, at: 1. 歸化城 Kuei¹ Hua⁴ Ch'êng², in Shansi, 2. 青州府 Ch'ing¹ Chou¹ Fu³, in Shantung, 3. 江寧府 Chiang¹ Ning² Fu³, and 鎮江府 Chên⁴ Chiang¹ Fu³, in Kiangsu —so-called 京口副都統 Ching¹ K'ou³ Fu⁴ Tu¹ T'ung³, 4. 福州府 Fu² Chou¹ Fu³, in Fukien, 5. 杭州府 Hang² Chou¹ Fu³, and 乍浦 Ch'a⁴ P'u³, in Chekiang, 6. 荊州府 Ching¹ Chou¹ Fu³, in Hupeh (two; one 左翼 Tso³ I⁴ and the other 右翼 Yu⁴ I⁴), 7. 西安府 Hsi¹ An¹ Fu³, in Shensi (two; one 左翼 Tso³ I⁴ and the other 右翼 Yu⁴ I¹), 8. 寧夏府 Ning² Hsia⁴ Fu³, and 涼州府 Liang² Chou¹ Fu³, in Kansu, 9. 成都府 Ch'êng² Tu¹ Fu³, in Szechwan, and 10. 廣州府 Kuang³ Chou¹ Fu³, in Kuangtung (two; one 滿州副都統 Man³ Chou¹ Fu⁴ Tu¹ T'ung³, and the other 漢軍副都統 Han⁴ Chün¹ Fu⁴ Tu¹ T'ung³).

745A. The 副都統 Fu⁴ Tu¹ T'ung³ of Chihli province (one at 密雲縣 Mi⁴ Yün² Hsien⁴ and the other at 山海關

Shan¹ Hai³ Kuan¹) are connected with the garrisons of the "military cordon" (*see* No. 743A).

745B. For details as to the 伊犁副都統 I¹ Li² Fu⁴ Tu¹ T'ung³, and the 塔爾巴哈台副都統 Ta³ Êrh³ Pa¹ Ha¹ T'ai² Fu⁴ Tu¹ T'ung³, *see* No. 867.

745C. For details as to the 歸化城副都統 Kuei¹ Hua⁴ Ch'êng² Fu⁴ Tu¹ T'ung³ (*see* No. 745), *see* No. 899.

745D. For details as to the 寧夏副都統 Ning² Hsia⁴ Fu⁴ Tu¹ T'ung³ (*see* No. 745), *see* No. 900.

745E. For details as to the 察哈爾副都統 Ch'a² Ha³ Êrh³ Fu⁴ Tu¹ T'ung³, *see* No. 898.

745F. For details as to the Fu Tu T'ung in Manchuria, *see* Nos. 802 and 804.

746. The various other ranks in the provincial garrisons are: 1. 城守尉 Ch'êng² Shou³ Yü⁴, Military Commandant of a Minor Manchu Garrison in the Provinces (3A; they are found in such cities as 太原府 T'ai⁴ Yüan² Fu³, 德州 Tê² Chou¹, and 開封府 K'ai¹ Fêng¹ Fu³, where there are neither 將軍 Chiang¹ Chün¹ nor 副都統 Fu⁴ Tu¹ T'ung³), 2. 協領 Hsieh² Ling³, Colonel of a Regiment of the Provincial Manchu Garrisons; 3B, 3. 佐領 Tso³ Ling³, Major Commander of a Company of the Provincial Manchu Garrisons (4A; a position appreciably higher than that of 佐領 Tso³ Ling³ of the Peking Banners; *see* No. 726), 4. 防守尉 Fang² Shou³ Yü⁴, Military Commandant of the 2nd Class of a Minor Provincial Manchu Garrison (they reside in towns of the garrisons of the "military cordon," such as 東安縣 Tung¹ An¹ Hsien⁴, 良鄉縣 Liang² Hsiang¹ Hsien⁴, 霸州 Pa⁴ Chou¹, etc.; *see* No. 743A); 4A, 5. 防禦 Fang² Yü⁴, Captain of a Platoon of the Provincial Manchu Garrisons; 5A, 6. 驍騎校 Hsiao¹ Ch'i² Hsiao⁴, Lieutenant; 5B, 7. 委署驍騎校 Wei³ Shu⁴ Hsiao¹ Ch'i² Hsiao⁴, Sub-Lieutenant; 8B, 8. 前鋒 Ch'ien² Fêng¹, Sergeant (also, 鳥槍前鋒 Niao³ Ch'iang¹ Ch'ien² Fêng¹, Sergeant of

**747
to
748**

Musketry ; compare No. 735), 9. 領催 Ling³ Ts'ui¹, Corporal (also, 鳥槍領催 Niao³ Ch'iang¹ Ling³ Ts'ui¹, Corporal of Musketry, or 礮領催 P'ao⁴ Ling³ Ts'ui¹, Corporal of Artillery), 10. 驍騎 Hsiao¹ Ch'i², Private (also, 鳥槍驍騎 Niao³ Ch'iang¹ Hsiao¹ Ch'i², Musketeer, or 礮驍騎 P'ao⁴ Hsiao¹ Ch'i², Artillery-man ; compare No. 737).

747. 水師營 Shui³ Shih⁴ Ying², Marine Battalion of the Banner Forces. This does river service in provinces where Manchu Garrisons are stationed (*see* No. 743c), for instance, Fukien, Kuangtung, etc.

748. 圍塲 Wei² Ch'ang³, The Imperial Hunting Preserves ; in, and about, 熱河 Je⁴ Ho² (承德府 Ch'êng² Tê² Fu³). For guarding these there was formed, in the reign of 康熙 K'ang¹ Hsi¹ (1661-1722), a detachment called the 守圍塲兵 Shou³ Wei² Ch'ang³ Ping¹, Guards of the Hunting Preserves. At the head of these Guards there are the 圍塲正總管 Wei² Ch'ang³ Chêng⁴ Tsung³ Kuan³, and the 圍塲副總管 Wei² Ch'ang³ Fu⁴ Tsung³ Kuan³, Chief Controller (3A) and Deputy Chief Controller of the Hunting Preserves (residing at Ch'êng² Te² Fu³ ; *see* above). The remaining ranks are : 1. 圍塲翼長 Wei² Ch'ang³ I⁴ Chang³, Brigadier of the Hunting Preserves ; 4A (two in all), 2. 防禦 Fang² Yü⁴, Captain ; 5A (eight in all), 3. 驍騎校 Hsiao¹ Ch'i² Hsiao⁴, Lieutenant ; 6A (eight in all), 4. 領催 Ling³ Ts'ui¹, Corporal, and 5. 驍騎 Hsiao¹ Ch'i², Private (of the last two ranks there are about eight hundred and fifty men).

The Imperial Hunting Preserves are under the general supervision of the Military Lieutenant-Governor of Jehol (*see* No. 897), in which district it is situated and where it forms a separate sub-prefecture, 圍塲廳 Wei² Ch'ang³ T'ing¹ (*see* No. 897).

THE OLD CHINESE ARMY.

749. 綠營 Lu⁴ Ying², The **Army** of the Green Standard, or old Chinese Army. These troops **are divided** into 陸路 Lu⁴ Lu⁴, Land Forces, and 水師 Shui³ Shih¹, Marine Forces, and the bulk of the forces of this category in **any** province are under the command of a 提督 T'i² Tu¹ (*see* **No. 750**), General-in-Chief, and are styled 提標 T'i² Piao¹, or T'i **Tu's** Command. The lesser portion of these forces—allotted to the 總督 Tsung³ Tu¹ (*see* No. 820), or to the 巡撫 Hsün² Fu³ (*see* No. 821)— are called, respectively, 督標 Tu¹ Piao¹, and 撫標 Fu³ Piao¹.

Under the orders of the 河道總督 Ho² Tao⁴ Tsung³ Tu¹ (*see* No. 820ᴅ) and of the 漕運總督 Ts'ao² Yün⁴ Tsung³ Tu¹ (*see* No. 834) there were formerly separate military organizations styled the 河標 Ho² Piao¹, and the 漕標 Ts'ao² Piao¹.

The forces under the command of the General-in-Chief— the 提標 T'i² Piao¹—are divided into 鎮標 Chên⁴ Piao¹, Brigades, these, in turn, being sub-divided into 協標 Hsieh² Piao⁴, Territorial Regiments. The Hsieh are made up of 營 Ying², Battalions (of about 500 infantry and 250 cavalry each), which are composed of two 哨 Shao⁴, Patrols, each—a Right and a Left. The Patrols are distributed throughout two or four 司 Ssu¹, corresponding to the 汛 Hsün⁴, or military posts of different districts.

The Army of the Green Standard is distributed throughout the Empire, in towns, stations and villages, and, in addition to doing military duty, performs various other services—in connection with policing, the posts and the customs.

750. 提督 T'i² Tu¹, Provincial Commander-in-Chief, or General-in-Chief; in (common designation, 提台 T'i² T'ai²; epistolary style, 軍門 Chün¹ Mên²). This officer is in command

750A
to
750B

of the bulk of the troops of the Green Standard (*see* No. 749) stationed in a particular province.

Provincial Commanders-in-Chief are stationed ir fourteen provinces, *i.e.* at 1. 通 州 T'ung¹ Chou¹, in Chihli, 2. 松 江 府 Sung¹ Chiang¹ Fu³ (one ; the 江 南 提 督 Chiang¹ Nan² T'i² Tu¹) and 清 和 縣 Ch'ing¹ Ho² Hsien⁴, in the prefecture of 淮 安 府 Huai² An¹ Fu³ (one ; the 江 北 提 督 Chiang¹ Pei³ T'i² Tu¹), in Kiangsu, 3. 廈 門 廳 Hsia⁴ Mên² T'ing¹, in the prefecture of 泉 州 府 Ch'üan² Chou¹ Fu³, in Fukien, 4. 寗 波 府 Ning² P'o¹ Fu³, in Chekiang; 5. 穀 城 縣 Ku³ Ch'êng² Hsien⁴, in the prefecture of 襄 陽 府 Hsiang¹ Yang² Fu³, in Hupeh, 6. 常 德 府 Ch'ang² Tê² Fu³, in Hunan, 7. 西 安 府 Hsi¹ An¹ Fu³, in Shensi, 8. 甘 州 府 Kan¹ Chou¹ Fu³, in Kansu, 9. 成 都 府 Ch'êng² Tu¹ Fu³, in Szechwan, 10. 惠 州 府 Hui⁴ Chou¹ Fu³, in Kuangtung—the so-called 廣 東 陸 路 提 督 Kuang³ Tung¹ Lu⁴ Lu⁴ T'i² Tu¹, 11. 南 寧 府 Nan² Ning² Fu³, in Kuangsi, 12. 大 理 府 Ta⁴ Li³ Fu³, in Yünnan, 13. 安 順 府 An¹ Shun⁴ Fu³, in Kweichow, and 14. 疏 勒 府 Su¹ Lê¹ Fu³, or 喀 什 噶 爾 Ka¹ Shih² Ka¹ Êrh³, Kashgar, in Hsinkiang.

750A. In the provinces of Shansi, Shantung, Honan, Anhui and Kiangsi—there being no 提 督 T'i² Tu¹—the Governors are invested with the duties of Provincial Commander-in-Chief. Accordingly, they are styled 兼 提 督 Chien¹ T'i² Tu¹, Governors and Generals-in-Chief (for instance, 山 東 巡 撫 兼 提 督 Shan¹ Tung¹ Hsün² Fu³ Chien¹ T'i² Tu¹, Shantung Governor and General-in-Chief of the Forces in Shantung Province).

750B. In addition to 提 督 T'i² Tu¹ (also 陸 路 提 督 Lu⁴ Lu⁴ T'i² Tu¹), Commanders-in-Chief of the Land Forces, there are also 水 師 提 督 Shui³ Shih¹ T'i² Tu¹, Naval Commanders-in-Chief. There are ʿtwo for the provinces lying along the Yangtze—長 江 水 師 提 督 Ch'ang² Chiang¹ Shui³ Shih¹ T'i² Tu¹ (at 太 平 府 T'ai⁴ P'ing² Fu³, in Anhui) and 會 辦 長 江 防 守 事 宜

Hui⁴ Pan⁴ Ch'ang² Chiang¹ Fang² Shou³ Shih⁴ I² (at 浦口 P'u³ K'ou³, or 江浦縣 Chiang¹ P'u³ Hsien⁴, in the prefecture of 江寧府 Chiang¹ Ning² Fu³), and one for the province of Kuangtung—廣東水師提督 Kuang³ Tung¹ Shui³ Shih¹ T'i² Tu¹ (at 虎門 Hu³ Mên², in the prefecture of 廣州府 Kuang³ Chou¹ Fu³).

In the provinces of Chekiang and Fukien the Commanders-in-Chief perform, simultaneously the duties of Naval Commanders-in-Chief and are, accordingly, designated 浙江水陸師提督 Chê⁴ Chiang¹ Shui³ Lu⁴ Shih¹ T'i² Tu¹, and 福建水陸師提督 Fu² Chien⁴ Shui³ Lu⁴ Shih¹ T'i² Tu¹, respectively.

751. 總兵 Tsung³ Ping¹, Brigade General; 2A (common designation, 鎮台 Chên⁴ T'ai² : literary designation, 總戎 Tsung³ Jung²; epistolary designation, 大總制 Ta⁴ Tsung³ Chih⁴); commanding a 鎮標 Chên⁴ Piao¹, Brigade (see No. 749), of which there are from two to seven in a province.

There are seven Brigade Generals in Chihli province, two in Shansi, three in Shantung, five in Kiangsu, two in Anhui, three in Kiangsi, four in Fukien, five in Chekiang, three in Hupeh, three in Hunan, three in Shensi, five in Kansu, four in Szechwan, seven in Kuangtung, two in Kuangsi, four in Kweichow, six in Yünnan, four in Hsinkiang, and three in Honan—75 in all.

751A. In the province of Chihli the Brigade Generals, 泰寧鎮總兵 T'ai² Ning² Chên⁴ Tsung³ Ping¹, at 易州 I⁴ Chou¹, and 馬蘭鎮總兵 Ma³ Lan³ Chên⁴ Tsung³ Ping¹, at 馬蘭峪 Ma³ Lan³ Yü⁴, in the prefecture of 遵化州 Tsun¹ Hua⁴ Chou¹—Commanding the brigades stationed at the Imperial Mausolea (Western and Eastern; see Nos. 569 and 569B) bear the title of minister of the Household and, therefore, are officially designated as 兼總管內務府大臣 Chien¹ Tsung³ Kuan³ Nei⁴ Wu⁴ Fu³ Ta⁴ Ch'ên² (see No. 76).

751B
to
752H

751B. Certain of the 總兵 Tsung³ Ping¹, Brigade Generals (*see* No. 751), are in command of naval forces and, in this capacity, are directly subordinated to the Naval Commanders-in-Chief—four in Kiangsu, one in Kiangsi, one in Hupeh, one in Hunan, three in Chekiang, two in Fukien and five in Kuangtung.

752. 副將 Fu⁴ Ching⁴, Colonel; 2B (common designation, 協台 Hsieh² T'ai²; literary designation, 副戎 Fu⁴ Jung²); in command of a 協標 Hsieh² Piao¹, Regiment (*see* No. 749).

752A. 參將 Ts'an¹ Chiang⁴, Lieutenant-Colonel; 3A (common designation, 參府 Ts'an¹ Fu³; literary designation, 參戎 Ts'an¹ Jung²).

The Lieutenant-Colonel acting as Commandant of a Governor's Brigade (撫標 Fu³ Piao¹; *see* No. 749) is colloquially called 大廳 Ta⁴ T'ing¹.

752B. 游擊 Yu² Chi¹, Major; 3B (common designation, 游府 Yu² Fu³; literary designation, 游戎 Yu² Jung²); in command of a 營 Ying², Battalion (*see* No. 749).

752C. 都司 Tu¹ Ssu¹, First Captain; 4A (literary designation, 都閫 Tu¹ K'un³); may be in command of a Battalion (*see* No. 749).

752D. 守備 Shou³ Pei⁴, Second Captain; 5B (common designation, 守府 Shou³ Fu³); may be in command of a Battalion (*see* No. 749).

752E. 千總 Ch'ien¹ Tsung³, Lieutenant; 6A (common designation, 總爺 Tsung³ Yeh²; literary designation, 千戎 Ch'ien¹ Jung²); in command of a 哨 Shao⁴, Patrol (*see* No. 749).

752F. 把總 Pa² Tsung³, Sub-Lieutenant; 7A (common esignation, 副爺 Fu⁴ Yeh²); in command of a 司 Ssu¹, Squad, and commanding a 汛 Hsün⁴, Military Post (*see* No. 749).

752G. 外委千總 Wai⁴ Wei³ Ch'ien¹ Tsung³, Ensign; 8A.

752H. 外委把總 Wai⁴ Wei³ Pa² Tsung³, Colour-Sergeant; 9A.

7521. 額外外委 Ê² Wai⁴ Wai⁴ Wei³, Sergeant ; 9ʙ.

752ᴊ. 中軍 Chung¹ Chün¹, Adjutant. This post is filled by officers of the rank of 副將 Fu⁴ Chiang⁴ (see No. 752) to 守備 Shou³ Pei⁴ (see No. 752ᴅ) and one adjutant is attached to the commandant of any detachment of the forces. The Officers acting as Adjutants to the Governors-General and Governors are, respectively, the Commandants of the Governors-General's (督標 Tu¹ Piao¹) and Governors' (撫標 Fu³ Piao¹) Brigades (see Nos· 749 and 824).

753. 營總 Ying² Tsung³, Commandant. This title is given to officers in command of special bodies of Troops. This post was formerly found in the 壯勇 Chuang⁴ Yung³, or Militia, and in the 練軍 Lien⁴ Chün¹, Disciplined Forces (which were the foundation for the organization of the present 陸軍 Lu⁴ Chün¹, Land Forces ; see No. 656).

MILITARY POST STATIONS.

754. 驛站 I⁴ Chan⁴, Military Post Stations. These are under the superintendence of the Ministry of War and serve for the conveyance of government despatches between metropolitan and provincial establishments, and vice versa. At the head of the 驛 I⁴ or 站 Chan⁴, Post Stations, are 驛丞 I⁴ Ch'êng² (see No. 850), or 站官 Chan⁴ Kuan¹, Inspectors of Post Stations, with a staff of 筆帖式 Pi³ T'ieh³ Shih⁴, Clerks, 馬撥 Ma³ Po¹, Mounted Couriers, and 步撥 Pu⁴ Po¹, Couriers on Foot, attached to them. The direct management of the Military Post Stations is invested in the local authorities (compare No. 850); the general management throughout a province is invested in the 按察使 An⁴ Ch'a² Shih³ (see No. 830 ; compare No. 839).

In Mongolia the Post Stages are called 軍台 Chün¹ T'ai², and are found along the three main roads—to K'urun, K'obdo and Uliasutai—and, in addition to being postal establishments, serve as a place of banishment of condemned officials (compare the expression 發往軍台効力贖罪 Fa[1] Wang[3] Chün[1] T'ai[2] Hsiao[4] Li[4] Shu[2] Tsui[4].

The general control over the Military Post Stations in Mongolia (situated on the so-called 阿勒泰軍台 A[4] Lê[4] T'ai[4] Chün[1] T'ai[2], Military Post Road of Altai) appertains to the Military Lieutenant-General of Ch'ahar (*see* No. 898). Officials proceeding on duty by this road are given special posting-orders, called 勘合 K'an[4] Ho[2], by the Ministry of War.

In Manchuria the Military Post Stations (they are now abolished and have been replaced by the 文報局 Wên[2] Pao[4] Chü[2], *see* below) were under the control of 驛站監督 I[4] Chan[4] Chien[1] Tu[1], Inspectors of Military Post Stations (in the province of Kirin) or 驛巡道 I[4] Hsün[2] Tao[4], Military Intendant of Couriers (in the province of Fengtien)

In addition to the Military Post Stations there were (and, to some extent still are, for instance, in the province of Hsin-kiang) 塘 T'ang[2], Military Couriers Bureaux, under the control of 提塘 T'i[2] T'ang[2] (compare Nos. 435A and 435B).

Of late there has been manifested a tendency of gradual abolition of the Military Post Stations, as well as Military Couriers Bureaux, and the establishment, instead, of 文報局 Wên[2] Pao[4] Chü[2], Offices for the Transmission of Government Correspondence (divided into 文報總局 Wên[2] Pao[4] Tsung[3] Chü[2] and 文報分局 Wên[2] Pao[4] Fên[1] Chü[2], Head and Branch Offices), with 督辦 Tu[1] Pan[4], or 總理 Tsung[3] Li[3], Superintendents, in charge (this post, for instance in Manchuria, is associated with that of local 民政使 Min[2] Chêng[4] Shih[3]; (*see* No. 807). These offices, being administered on more economical lines than was the case with the Military Post Stations, sometimes serve several provinces simultaneously (for instance, the 南北洋文報局 Nan[2] Pei[3] Yang[2] Wên[2] Pao[4] Chü[2]; *see* report from 張人駿 Chang¹ Jên²-chün⁴, and 端方 Tuan¹ Fang¹, dated 29th November, 1909).

OFFICE OF GOVERNMENT DROVES.

755. 張家口兩翼牧羣統轄總管 Chang¹ Chia¹ K'ou³ Liang³ I⁴ Mu⁴ Ch'ün² T'ung³ Hsia² Tsung³ Kuan³, Superintendent of Government Droves of Horses and Cattle in the two Wings of the Ch'ahar Herdsmen in the Territory surrounding Kalgan; under the control of the Ministry of War. This post was established by virtue of an Imperial Edict of the 15th December, 1909, which was promulgated in reply to a Memorial, from the Ministry of War, pointing out the malpractices in breeding of horses and cattle in the territory of the left and right wings of the Ch'ahar Herdsmen (the duties appertaining to this post were previously performed by the Ch'ahar 都統 Tu¹ T'ung³, see No. 898).

The herds of horses and cattle (57 in all) under the control of the Superintendent are distributed, according to the general division of the Ch'ahar territory (see No. 893), into 兩翼 Liang³ I⁴, Two Wings, in charge of which are the 左翼總管 Tso³ I⁴ Tsung³ Kuan³, Supervisor of the Left Wing, and 右翼總管 Yu⁴ I⁴ Tsung³ Kuan³, Supervisor of the Right Wing. The direct management of each drove is invested in a 牧長 Mu⁴ Chang³, Supervisor of a Drove, and a 牧副 Mu⁴ Fu⁴, Assistant Supervisor of a Drove.

To the Superintendent there are attached: 秘書官 Pi³ Shu¹ Kuan¹, Chief Secretary, 總核官 Tsung³ Ho² Kuan¹, Chief Reviser, and 科員 K'o¹ Yüan², Secretaries (in an indefinite number), arranged in four sections: 1. 文牘科 Wên² Tu¹ K'o¹, Section of Correspondence, 2. 牧養科 Mu⁴ Yang³ K'o¹, Breeding Section, 3. 會計科 Hui⁴ Chi⁴ K'o¹,

[343]

756 Accounts Section, and 4. 庶務科 Shu⁴ Wu⁴ K'o¹, Section of General Affairs.

For the advancement of the knowledge of breeding—a very important part of military administration—there are to be established 兩翼牧羣學堂 Liang³ I⁴ Mu⁴ Ch'ün² Hsüeh² T'ang², Stud Schools, and 模範羣 Mu² Fan⁴ Ch'ün², Model Droves, etc.

NAVAL FORCES OF CHINA.

756. Most of the war vessels of the Chinese fleet are divided into the following four squadrons : 1. 北洋水師 Pei³ Yang² Shui³ Shih¹, Peiyang Squadron, 2. 南洋水師 Nan² Yang² Shui³ Shih¹, Nanyang Squadron, 3. 福建水師 Fu² Chien⁴ Shui³ Shih¹, Fukien Squadron, and 4. 廣東水師 Kuang³ Tung¹ Shui³ Shih¹, Kuangtung (Canton) Squadron. In addition to these there are the so-called 海兵營 Hai³ Ping¹ Ying², Marine Battalions (Flotilla): 1. 廣東魚雷營 Kuang³ Tung¹ Yü² Lei² Ying², Kuangtung (Canton) Torpedo Boat Flotilla, at 黃浦 Huang² P'u³ (Whampoa), 2. 南京魚雷營 Nan² Ching¹ Yü² Lei² Ying², Nanking Torpedo Boat Flotilla, at 南京 Nan² Ching¹ (Nanking), and 3. 煙台海軍練習營 Yen¹ T'ai² Hai³ Chün¹ Lien⁴ Hsi² Ying², Training Battalion of Yent'ai (Chefoo), at 芝罘 Chih¹ Fu⁴ (Chefoo).

The general superintendency of all the naval forces of China is invested, as has been already stated, in the 海軍處 Hai³ Chün¹ Ch'u⁴, Naval Council, at Peking (see Nos. 185c and 185d), which, in its turn, is subordinated to the 籌辦海軍大臣 Ch'ou² Pan⁴ Hai³ Chün¹ Ta⁴ Ch'ên², Presidents of the Commission for the Reorganization of the Navy (see No. 185A). The direct command of the fleet appertains to the 海軍提督 Hai³ Chün¹ T'i² Tu¹, Commander-in-Chief of the Naval Forces, to whom there is attached, at Shanghai, the 海軍事務處 Hai³ Chün¹ Shih⁴ Wu⁴ Ch'u⁴, Staff of the Commander-in-Chief of the Naval Forces, directed by the 參謀官 Ts'an¹ Mou² Kuan¹, Chief of Staff. Other Staff-Officers are: 1. 副官 Fu⁴ Kuan¹, Adjutant (one), 2. 機關監 Chi¹ Kuan¹ Chien⁴, Engineer-Officer (one), 3. 主計長 Chu³ Chi⁴ Chang³, Senior Councillor (one), 4. 主計官 Chu³ Chi⁴ Kuan¹, Councillor (one), 5. 秘書官 Pi⁴ Shu¹ Kuan¹, Secretary (one), 6. 秘書官補 Pi⁴ Shu¹ Kuan¹ Pu³, Assistant Secretaries (three), and 7. 軍醫 Chün¹ I¹, Surgeon (one).

756A. For the ranks of line officers of the fleet *see* No. 659B; for the corresponding Japanese terms *see* No. 659C.

756B. For particulars as to the 水師提督 Shui³ Shih¹ T'i² Tu¹, Naval Commanders-in-Chief, *see* No. 750B.

756C. For particulars as to the 水師營 Shui³ Shih¹ Ying², Marine Battalion of the Banner Forces, *see* No. 747.

757. For the training of Naval Officers, as well as for the building and repairing of vessels, there are now in China the following establishments; 1. 水師學堂 Shui³ Shih¹ Hsüeh² T'ang², or 海軍學堂 Hai³ Chün¹ Hsüeh² T'ang², Naval Schools (*see* No. 757A), 2. 造船所 Tsao⁴ Ch'uan² So³, Shipbuilding Yards (*see* No. 757B), and 船渠 Ch'uan² Ch'ü¹, Docks (*see* No. 757C).

757A. At present there are three Naval Schools in China: 1. 江南水師學堂 Chiang¹ Nan² Shui³ Shih¹ Hsüeh² T'ang², Kiangnan Naval School, at 南京 Nan² Ching¹, (Nanking), 2. 煙台海軍學堂 Yen¹ T'ai² Hai³ Chün¹ Hsüeh² T'ang², Yen'tai Naval School, at 芝罘 Chefoo, and 3. 廣東海軍學堂 Kuang³ Tung¹ Hai³ Chün¹ Hsüeh² T'ang², Kuangtung (Canton) Naval School, at 黃浦 Hua g² P'u³ (*see* No. 756).

757B. For the construction of vessels there is a special shipbuilding yard at 福州 Foochow, the so-called 馬尾船廠 Ma³ Wei³ Ch'uan² Ch'ang³ (Mamoi Arsenal). Also, ships are built at the 江南機器局 Chiang¹ Nan² Chi¹ Ch'i⁴ Chü², Kiangnan Arsenal (at 上海 Shang⁴ Hai³, Shanghai).

**757c
to
758**

For the equipment of vessels with the necessary armaments—guns, shells, etc.—there are the following arsenals : 1. 廣東 兵 廠 Kuang³ Tung¹ Tsao⁴ Ping¹ Ch'ang³, Kuangtung (Canton) Arsenal, 2. 廣東火藥製造所 Kuang³ Tung² Huo³ Yao⁴ Chih⁴ Tsao⁴ So³, Kuangtung (Canton) Powder Mills, and 3. 漢陽槍礮局 Han⁴ Yang² Ch'iang¹ P'ao⁴ Chü², Hanyang Arsenal, at 漢陽 Hanyang, in Hupeh.

757c. For repairing vessels there are the following dockyards : 1. 廣 東 船 塢 Kuang³ Tung¹ Ch'uan² Wu³, Kuangtung (Canton) Dockyard, at 黃 浦 Huang² P'u³ ; see No. 756, 2. 江 南 船 塢 Chiang¹ Nan² Ch'uan² Wu³, Kiangnan Dockyard, at 上 海 Shang⁴ Hai³, Shanghai, and 3. 馬尾船塢 Ma³ Wei³ Ch'uan² Wu³, Mawei Dockyard, at Foochow.

JUDICIAL ESTABLISHMENTS AND PRISONS.

A. Shên P'an T'ing or Judicial Establishments :

758. Until lately the local administrative officials in China, to whom were attached judges and prison officials, performed judicial functions. The Imperial Decree of the 6th November, 1906, which directed a general revision of the government organization, also affected judicial establishments—the Board of Punishments (*see* No. 438) was reorganized as the Ministry of Justice (*see* No. 440), and the Court of Judicature and Revision (*see* No. 215) was reformed as the Supreme Court of Justice (*see* No. 215A), specially charged with the supervision of all judicial matters of the Empire. At the same time the Chinese Government determined to sharply define the scope of administrative and judicial officials and, with this object in view, began the organization of quite independent judicial establishments, so-called 審判衙 門 Shen³ P'an⁴ Ya² Mên², free from any control the part of the administrative authorities (compare the expression 司法獨立 Ssu¹ Fa⁴ Tu² Li⁴). These began to function

[346]

first at Peking ; later they were founded in Manchuria and at **758**
Tientsin. Their establishment throughout the Empire will take
place according to the following schedule : in 1909–1910, at
provincial capitals and ports open to foreign trade ; in 1911–
1913, at the chief cities of prefectures, sub-prefectures, departments and districts ; in 1913–1915, at marts and villages.

The organization of judicial establishments is based on :
1. Memorials from the Supreme Court of Justice, dated the
12th December, 1906, and from the Ministry of Justice, dated
the 4th December, 1907, and the 25th August, 1909, and 2.
Regulations for Judicial establishments, 法院編制法 Fa⁴
Yüan⁴ Pien¹ Chih⁴ Fa⁴, compiled by the Committee for Drawing
up Regulations for Constitutional Government and sanctioned by
the Emperor on the 7th February, 1910, with the enclosures:
1. 法官考試任用暫行章程 Fa⁴ Kuan¹ K'ao³ Shih⁴ Jên⁴
Yung⁴ Chan⁴ Hsing² Chang¹ Ch'êng², Provisional Regulations
for Competitive Examination and Appointment of Judicial
Officials, 2. 司法區域分割暫行章程 Ssu¹ Fa⁴ Ch'ü⁴
Yü⁴ Fên¹ Hua⁴ Chan⁴ Hsing² Chang¹ Ch'êng², Provisional
Regulations Defining Judicial Districts, and 3. 初級暨地方
審判廳管轄案件暫行章程 Ch'u¹ Chi⁵ Chi² Ti⁴ Fang¹ Shên³
P'an⁴ T'ing¹ Kuan³ Hsia² An⁴ Chien⁴ Chan⁴ Hsing² Chang¹ Ch'êng²,
Provisional Regulations Defining the Scope of Local and
District Courts according to the Gravity and Type of Cases.

Judicial establishments are divided into : 高等審判廳
Kao¹ Têng³ Shên³ P'an⁴ T'ing¹, Courts of Assizes, 2. 地方
審判廳 Ti⁴ Fang¹ Shên³ P'an⁴ T'ing¹, District Courts, and
3. 初級審判廳 Ch'u¹ Chi² Shên³ P'an⁴ T'ing¹, Local Courts
(for details *see* Nos. 759 to 761).

For particulars as to the functions of the Supreme Court of
Justice *see* No. 215A, and the Supplement, No. 215A.

758A. 審判廳籌辦處 Shên³ P'an⁴ T'ing¹ Ch'ou² Pan⁴
Ch'u⁴, Offices for the Organization of Judicial Establishments ;

758B
to
758D

founded in all provinces, under the direction of the 提 法 使 Ti⁴ Fa⁴ Shih³ (*see* No. 831) or 按 察 使 An⁴ Ch'a³ Shih³; to function until the introduction of judicial establishments in the provinces has been completed.

758B.   For training officials for service in judicial establishments there have been instituted at local Colleges of Law and Administration (*see* No. 623A), or at the 審 判 廳 籌 辦 處 Shên³ P'an⁴ T'ing¹ Ch'ou² Pan⁴ Ch'u⁴ (*see* No. 758A), 審 判 研 究 所 Shên³ P'an⁴ Yen² Chiu¹ So³ (also, 審 判 講 習 所 Shên³ P'an⁴ Chiang³ Hsi² So³, 司 法 研 究 所 Ssu¹ Fa⁴ Yeu² Chiu¹ So³, or 司 法 講 習 科 Ssu¹ Fa⁴ Chiang³ Hsi² K'o¹), Courses in Jurisprudence, covering one year, and providing for an enrollment of from 60 to 120 students (dependent on local conditions).

758C.   檢 驗 學 習 所 Chien³ Yen⁴ Hsüch² Hsi² So³, Courses in Medical Jurisprudence; for training officials skilled in questions of 法 醫 Fa⁴ I¹, Medical Jurisprudence, styled 檢 驗 吏 Chien³ Yen⁴ Li⁴, Medical Inspectors, who are to replace the 仵 作 Wu³ Tso⁴, Coroners, men quite ignorant and entirely unacquainted with the principles of medical jurisprudence, who have long functioned in China.   These courses are to be founded at Judicial Establishments of higher grades and are to extend over a year and a half.

Courses of Medical Jurisprudence were established at Peking, 檢 驗 傳 習 所 Chien³ Yen⁴ Ch'uan² Hsi² So³, in June, 1909, at the 京 師 高 等 檢 察 廳 Ching¹ Shih¹ Kao¹ Têng³ Chien³ Ch'a² T'ing¹.

758D.   For training judicial officials of lower rank (ushers and clerks), in some provinces (for instance Kuangtung) there are 錄 事 書 記 承 發 吏 學 習 所 Lu⁴ Shih⁴ Shu¹ Chi⁴ Ch'êng² Fa¹ Li⁴ Hsüeh² Hsi² So³, Courses for Clerks and Ushers (extending over half a year).

[348   ]

758E. The new scheme for judicial establishments (*see* No. 758) foreshadows the appearance of 律師 Lü⁴ Shih¹, Attorneys (Advocates; also 辯護士 Pien⁴ Hu⁴ Shih⁴) in civil and criminal cases. Special regulations defining their rights and duties (律師單行法 Lü⁴ Shih¹ Tan¹ Hsing² Fa⁴) are to be drawn up by the Committee for Revising and Compiling Civil and Criminal Codes.

758F. Those desiring to serve in judicial establishments are called upon to pass two examinations. On the successful completion of the first examination they are attached to Local and District Courts for practice (學習 Hsüeh² Hsi², Practising) for two years, after which they undergo the second examination. On successfully passing this they are enrolled as Expectants for posts in Judicial Establishments (so-called 候補推事 Hou⁴ Pu³ T'ui¹ Shih⁴ and 候補檢察官 Hou⁴ Pu³ Chien³ Ch'a² Kuan¹).

759. 高等審判廳 Kao¹ Teng³ Shên³ P'an⁴ T'ing¹, Courts of Assizes (*see* No. 758). Within the scope of these Courts come: 1. Appeals (控訴 K'ung⁴ Su⁴) against judgments (not final, 判決 P'an⁴ Chüeh²) of District Courts, of the first hearing (第一審 Ti⁴ I¹ Shên³), 2. Appeals (上告 Shang⁴ Kao⁴) against judgments (not final) of District Courts, of the second hearing (第二審 Ti⁴ Êrh⁴ Shên³), 3. Cassations (抗告 K'ang⁴ Kao⁴) of judgments (final, 決定 Chüeh² Ting⁴) of District Courts, and 4. Cases concerning 宗室 Tsung¹ Shih⁴ (*see* No. 39) and 覺羅 Chüeh¹ Lo² (*see* No. 40), not within the scope of the Supreme Court of Justice.

Courts of Assizes consist (depending on the volume of affairs) of one (or more) 民事庭 Min² Shih⁴ T'ing², Section of Civil Cases, and one (or more) 刑事庭 Hsing² Shih⁴ T'ing², Section of Criminal Cases.

At the head of a Court of Assizes is a 廳丞 T'ing¹ Ch'êng², President of the Court, and at the head of a Section there are

759A to 760

庭 長 T'ing² Chang³, Section Chiefs, appointed from the ranks of 推 事 T'ui¹ Shih⁴, Court Members, of the respective Section.

Originally Courts of Assizes consisted of two 科 K'o¹, Sections: 民 科 Min² K'o¹, Civil, and 刑 科 Hsing² K'o¹, Criminal, with three (six at Peking) 合 議 推 事 Ho² I⁴ T'ui¹ Shih⁴, Collaborating Members of the Court.

At Courts of Assizes there are found: 典 簿 Tien³ Pu⁴, Archivists, 主 簿 Chu³ Pu⁴, Registrars, 錄 事 Lu⁴ Shih⁴, Writers and (at Peking and ports open to foreign trade) 繙 譯 官 Fan¹ I⁴ Kuan¹, Interpreters (Translators).

Courts of Assizes are found at: 1. Peking, 京 師 高 等 審 判 廳 Ching¹ Shih¹ Kao¹ Têng³ Shên³ P'an⁴ T'ing¹, and 2. Provincial capitals. For details *see* the Scheme for Judicial Establishments (*see* No. 758), section 4, articles 25 to 32.

759A. For particulars as to the 高 等 審 判 分 廳 Kao¹ Têng³ Shên³ P'an⁴ Fên¹ T'ing¹, Branch Courts of Assizes, *see* No. 760B.

759B. 大 理 分 院 Ta⁴ Li³ Fên¹ Yüan⁴, Branches of the Supreme Court of Justice (*see* Supplement to No. 215A). These may be established in provinces distant from Peking, at the local Courts of Assizes (*see* No. 759); composed of a 民 事 庭 Min² Shih⁴ T'ing², Section of Civil Cases, and a 刑 事 庭 Hsing² Shih⁴ T'ing², Section of Criminal Cases.

760. 地 方 審 判 廳 Ti⁴ Fang¹ Shên³ P'an⁴ T'ing¹, District Courts (*see* No. 758). Within the scope of these are: 1. Cases without the scope of Local Courts or the Supreme Court of Justice (for the first hearing; 第 一 審 Ti⁴ I¹ Shên³) and 2. For a second hearing, A. Appeals against judgments (not final) of the Local Courts and B. Cassations of judgments (final) of Local Courts.

District Courts are composed (dependent on the volume of affairs) of one (or more) 民 事 庭 Min² Shih⁴ T'ing², Section of Civil Cases, and one (or more) 刑 事 庭 Hsing² Shih⁴ T'ing²,

Section of Criminal Cases. Also, there are two (or more) 獨任推事 Tu² Jên⁴ T'ui¹ Shih⁴, Independent members of the Court (deciding cases singly).

760A
to
760B

At the head of a District Court is a 廳長 T'ing¹ Chang³ (at the Capital 廳丞 T'ing¹ Ch'êng²), President of the Court (holding, at the same time, the position of Chief of one of the Sections); each Section is under a 庭長 T'ing² Chang³, Section Chief, appointed from the ranks of 推事 T'ui¹ Shih⁴, Members of the Court. of the respective Section.

Formerly the District Courts were divided into two 科 K'o¹, Sections: 民科 Min² K'o¹, Civil, and 刑科 Hsing² K'o¹, Criminal, with three (in Peking twelve) 合議推事 Ho² I⁴ T'ui¹ Shih⁴, Collaborating Members of the Court, in each. At the head of the Court was a 推事長 T'ui¹ Shih⁴ Chang³, Senior Member of the Court.

At District Courts there are found: 典簿 Tien³ Pu⁴, Archivists, 主簿 Chu³ Pu⁴, Registrars, 錄事 Lu⁴ Shih⁴, Writers, 承發吏 Ch'êng² Fa¹ Li⁴, Ushers, and (at Peking and ports open to foreign trade) 繙譯官 Fan¹ I⁴ Kuan¹, Interpreters.

District Courts are established at: 1. Peking, 京師內外城地方審判廳 Chiang¹ Shih¹ Nei⁴ Wai⁴ Ch'êng² Ti⁴ Fang¹ Shên³ P'an⁴ T'ing¹, Metropolitan District Court of the Inner and Outer City, and 2. Each prefecture and independent department (one).

For details as to District Courts *see* the Scheme for Judicial Establishments (*see* No. 758) section 3, articles Nos. 17 to 24.

760A. For particulars as to the 地方審判分廳 Ti⁴ Fang¹ Shên³ P'an⁴ Fen¹ T'ing¹, Branches of District Courts, *see* No. 761A.

760B. 高等審判分廳 Kao¹ Têng³ Shên³ P'an⁴ Fên¹ T'ing¹, Branches of Courts of Assizes (*see* No. 759A); may be established at places distant from provincial capitals, at the Local District Courts (*see* No. 760). These are composed of a

761 to 761A

民事庭 Min² Shih⁴ T'ing², Section of Civil Cases, and a 刑事庭 Hsing² Shih⁴ T'ing², Section of Criminal Cases.

761. 初級審判廳 Ch'u¹ Chi² Shên³ P'an⁴ T'ing¹, Local Courts (*see* No. 758). To the authority of these appertain: 1. Civil cases involving a sum of not more than 200 Taels, and 2. By the present Criminal Code, criminal cases punishable by a fine or by a fine (of not more than $200.00) and imprisonment (for a year or less), or, by other rules, by arrest.

Local Courts are made up of one or two (or more) 推事 T'ui¹ Shih⁴, Members of the Court, who judge cases quite independently (獨任制 Tu² Jên⁴ Chih⁴).

Local Courts (also called 城讞局 Ch'êng² Yen² Chü², City Justice of Peace, and 鄉讞局 Hsiang¹ Yen² Chü², Village Justice of Peace) were formerly composed of from one to two (10 at Peking) 單獨推事 Tan¹ Tu² T'ui² Shih⁴, Independent Members of the Court.

At Local Courts there are: 承發吏 Ch'êng² Fa⁴ Li⁴, Ushers, and 錄事 Lu⁴ Shih⁴, Writers.

Local Courts are established at: 1. Peking, 京師初級審判廳 Ching¹ Shih¹ Ch'u¹ Chi² Shên³ P'an⁴ T'ing¹, Metropolitan Local Courts (the former designation was 京師分區城讞局 Ching¹ Shih¹ Fên¹ Ch'ü¹ Ch'êng² Yen² Chü²), 2. Administrative centres of departments and districts of the Metropolitan Prefecture, 3. Administrative centres of sub-prefectures, departments and districts of the provinces, and 4. Thickly populated towns and villages important by their location. For details *see* the Scheme for Judicial Establishments (*see* No. 758), section 2, articles 14 to 16.

761A. 地方審判分廳 Ti⁴ Fang¹ Shên³ P'an⁴ Fên¹ T'ing¹, Branches of District Courts (*see* No. 760A); may be established at Local Courts (*see* No. 761). These are composed of a 民事庭 Min² Shih⁴ T'ing², Section of Civil Cases, a 刑事庭 Hsing² Shih⁴ T'ing², Section of Criminal Cases, and

[352]

two (or more) 獨任推事 Tu² Jên⁴ T'ui¹ Shih⁴, Independent Members of the Court.

762
to
764

B. Chien Ch'a T'ing or Prosecuting Attorneys' Offices:

762. At judicial establishments of the various grades there are found 檢察廳 Chien³ Ch'a² T'ing¹, or Prosecuting Attorneys' Offices, namely : 1. At the Court of Assizes, 高等檢察廳 Kao¹ Têng³ Chien³ Ch'a² T'ing¹, 2. At the District Court, 地方檢察廳 Ti⁴ Fang¹ Chien³ Ch'a² T'ing¹, and 3. At the Local Court, 初級檢察廳 Ch'u¹ Chi² Chien³ Ch'a² T'ing¹ (for details *see* Nos. 763 to 767).

For details as to the 總檢察廳 Tsung³ Chien³ Ch'a² T'ing¹, attached to the Supreme Court of Justice, *see* No. 222.

Duties appertaining to the Prosecuting Attorneys' Offices include : the initiation of cases of criminal prosecution, the making of searches, the enforcement of sentences, etc.

763. 高等檢察廳 Kao¹ Têng³ Chien³ Ch'a² T'ing¹, Prosecuting Attorney's Office at the Court of Assizes (*see* Nos. 759 and 762); composed of a 檢察長 Chien³ Ch'a² Chang³, Senior Prosecuting Attorney, and two (or more) 檢察官 Chien³ Ch'a² Kuan¹, Prosecuting Attorneys. Also, at this office, there are found 典簿 Tien³ Pu⁴, Archivists, 主簿 Chu³ Pu⁴, Registrars, and 錄事 Lu⁴ Shih⁴, Writers.

763ᴀ. 總檢察分廳 Tsung³ Chien³ Ch'a² Fên¹ T'ing¹, Branches of Attorney-General's Office (*see* Supplement to No. 222); established at Branches of the Supreme Court of Justice (*see* No. 759ʙ).

764. 地方檢察廳 Ti⁴ Fang¹ Chien³ Ch'a² T'ing¹, Prosecuting Attorney's Office at the District Court (*see* Nos. 760 and 762); composed of a 檢察長 Chien³ Ch'a² Chang³, Senior Prosecuting Attorney, and two (or more) 檢察官 Chien³ Ch'a² Kuan¹, Prosecuting Attorneys. Also, at this office there are 典簿 Tien³ Pu⁴, Archivists, 主簿 Chu³ Pu⁴, Registrars, and 錄事 Lu⁴ Shih⁴, Writers.

23

764ᴀ. 高等檢察分廳 Kao¹ Têng³ Chien³ Ch'a² Fên¹ T'ing¹, Prosecuting Attorney's Office at a Branch of the Court of Assizes (*see* No. 760ʙ).

765. 初級檢察廳 Ch'u¹ Chi² Chien³ Ch'a² T'ing¹, Prosecuting Attorney's Office at the Local Court (*see* Nos. 761 and 762); composed of from one to two (or more) 檢察官 Chien³ Ch'a² Kuan¹, Prosecuting Attorneys and 錄事 Lu⁴ Shih⁴, Writers.

765ᴀ. 地方檢察分廳 Ti⁴ Fang¹ Chien³ Ch'a² Fên¹ T'ing¹, Prosecuting Attorney's Office at a Branch of the District Court (*see* No. 761ᴀ).

C. Prisons:

766. At the Capital, for the imprisonment of offenders, there are, at the Ministry of Justice, two prisons: 南監 Nan² Chien¹, Southern, and 北監 Pei³ Chien¹, Northern (*see* No. 457), formerly under the supervision of the 提牢廳 T'i² Lao² T'ing¹, Prison Office, but, since the abolition of this office in 1907, administered by the 典獄司 Tien³ Yü⁴ Ssu¹, Department of Prisons (*see* No. 449). On the change of control the organization of these prisons was revised (*see* a Memorial from the Ministry of Justice, dated the 17th September, 1908), in that, instead of the former two 提牢 T'i² Lao², Prison Inspectors, posts were established for two 總管收掌 Tsung³ Kuan³ Shou¹ Chang³, and, instead of 司獄 Ssu¹ Yü⁴, Warders, there were appointed 正管收掌 Chêng⁴ Kuan³ Shou¹ Chang³ (two; from the ranks of 七品小京官 Ch'i¹ P'in³ Hsiao³ Ching¹ Kuan¹; *see* No. 299). Also, there were appointed 副管收掌 Fu⁴ Kuan³ Shou¹ Chang³, Assistant Warders (six: from the ranks of 八品錄事 Pa¹ P'in³ Lu⁴ Shih⁴, and 九品錄事 Chiu³ P'in³ Lu⁴ Shih⁴; *see* No. 481).

766ᴀ. In the provinces the prisons are at the offices of the local authorities and are under the control of Prison Warders, styled: in prefectures, 司獄 Ssu¹ Yü⁴ (*see* No. 850), in departments, 吏目 Li⁴ Mu⁴ (*see* No. 851A); in districts, 典史 **766ᴿ** Tien³ Shih³ (*see* No. 857).

766ʙ. In the scheme for reform of judicial establishments there appears a measure with regard to prison affairs providing for the institution, at the Capital (in 1909, *see* Memorials from the Ministry of Justice, dated June, 1907, and 31st March, 1909), as well as in the provinces, of so-called 模範監獄 Mu² Fan⁴ Chien¹ Yü⁴, Model Prisons. At present these prisons are to be found in the provinces of Kuangsi (*see* Memorial from 張鳴岐 Chang¹ Ming²-ch'i², dated the 8th December, 1909), and Yünnan (*see* report from 沈秉堃 Shên³ Ping³-k'un¹, dated the 21st September, 1909).

In connection with the prison reform it is proposed to abolish, in the provinces, the posts of 司獄 Ssu¹ Yü⁴, 吏目 Li⁴ Mu⁴, and 典史 Tien³ Shih³ (*see* No. 766A).

Regulations referring to prisons (監獄規則 Chien¹ Yü⁴ Kuei¹ Tsê²), and defining penalties to be inflicted on prison administrations (監獄官吏懲罰規則 Chien¹ Yü⁴ Kuan¹ Li⁴ Chêng³ Fa² Kuei¹ Tsê²), were drawn up in 1909, to be promulgated in 1910, and, accordingly, the organization of the new (model) prisons, treated below, has been arrived at, chiefly, from the above-mentioned Memorial from Chang Ming-ch'i (and, to some extent, on the report of Shên Ping-k'un).

At the head of the Model Prison (in Kuangsi) is a 正典獄官 Chêng⁴ Tien³ Yü⁴ Kuan¹, Prison Inspector; 5ʙ (in Yünnan, 典獄官 Tien³ Yü⁴ Kuan¹), To him there are sub-ordinated: 1. Eight 看守長 K'an¹ Shou³ Chang³, Senior Warders; 8ᴀ (in Yünnan, three 守衞長 Shou³ Wei⁴ Chang³), 2. 60 看守 K'an¹ Shou³, Warders; 9ᴀ (in Yünnan, 守衞 Shou³ Wei⁴), 3. Two 教誨師 Chiao⁴ Hui³ Shih¹, Teachers of Morality; 8ᴀ, 4. Two 醫官 I¹ Kuan¹, Physicians; 9ᴀ (in Yünnan, one 醫師 I¹ Shih¹), 5. Ten 工手 Kung¹ Shou³, Workmen, and 6. 20 押丁 Ya¹ Ting¹, Escorts (the two last-

767 mentioned ranks do not exist in Yünnan, but there are five 書記生 Shu¹ Chi⁴ Shêng¹, Clerks).

The general supervision over the affairs of the prison is invested in four Sections: 1. 文牘科 Wên² Tu³ K'o¹, Section of Correspondence (文書科 Wên² Shu¹ K'o¹ in Yünnan), 2. 會計科 Hui⁴ Chi⁴ K'o¹, Section of Accounts, 3. 工業科 Kung¹ Yeh⁴ K'o¹, Section of Handicrafts, and 4. 庶務科 Shu⁴ Wu⁴ K'o¹, Section of General Affairs (總務科 Tsung³ Wu⁴ K'o¹ in Yünnan). At the head of each Section are Senior Warders, as 科長 K'o¹ Chang³, Section Chiefs (one 科長 K'o¹ Chang³ to each Section in Yünnan), assisted by four 科員 K'o¹ Yüan², Secretaries; 9ᴀ (one 科員 K'o¹ Yüan², in Yünnan).

In Yünnan province there is also the 守衛科 Shou³ Wei⁴ K'o¹, Secret Service Section, directed by a 科長 K'o¹ Chang³.

At the Model Prison in Kuangsi, in the Summer of 1909, there was opened a 監獄學堂 Chien¹ Yü⁴ Hsüeh² T'ang², Prison School, for training officials for service in prison administrations, of two Sections: 1. 高等科 Kao¹ Têng³ K'o¹, Higher Section (with a course of study extending over one year, an enrollment of 50 students and 16 subjects of instruction), and 2. 看守科 K'an¹ Shou³ K'o¹, Section of Guarding (prisoners) (with a course of study of half a year's duration, an enrollment of 120 students and eight subjects of instruction). It has been arranged that this school be reorganized, in September, 1910, on the lines of the Japanese 警監學堂 Ching³ Chien¹ Hsüeh² T'ang², Police and Prison Schools, and it is to be annexed to the local Higher Police School (*see* No. 522).

In the province of Hunan, in connection with prison administration, there are 監獄傳習所 Chien¹ Yü⁴ Ch'uan² Hsi² So³, Courses in Prison Administration.

767. 看守所 K'an¹ Shou³ So³, (also 管收所 Kuan³ Shou¹ So³), Houses of Detention; established at District Courts (*see* No. 760) and, in some instances, at Local Courts (*see*

No. 761). These are administered by from two to four 看 守 所 官 K'an¹ Shou³ So³ Kuan¹ (also 所 官 So³ Kuan¹), Warders of Houses of Detention; 8B.

767A to 769

At the 京 師 地 方 看 守 所 Ching¹ Shih¹ Ti⁴ Fang¹ K'an¹ Shou³ So³, House of Detention of the Metropolitan District Court (*see* No. 760), there is found the post of 看 守 所 長 K'an¹ Shou³ So³ Chang³, (also 所 長 So³ Chang³), Senior Warder of the House of Detention; 6B.

For particulars as to the House of Detention of the Supreme Court of Justice, *see* No. 221.

767A. 習 藝 所 Hsi² I² So³, Workhouses; under the supervision of the Ministry of the Interior (*see* No. 514). Here are incarcerated, and employed in handicrafts, offenders condemned, for petty crimes, to some months imprisonment.

AGRICULTURE, INDUSTRY AND COMMERCE.

768. The direct superintendence over all measures directed towards the development of agriculture, industry and commerce, as well as a general control over all establishments having reference to these, appertains to the Industrial Taotai (*see* Nos. 839 and 839A) who, in this instance, is subordinated to the Ministry of Agriculture, Industry and Commerce, from which he receives all necessary instructions.

769. 農 工 商 總 局 Nung² Kung¹ Shang¹ Tsung³ Chü², Head Bureaux of Agriculture, Industry and Commerce. Previous to the establishment of the post of Industrial Taotai (*see* Nos. 768 and 839–839A) these bureaux performed duties which now appertain to this official. They are still to be found in provinces to which the said Taotai has as yet not been appointed (compare the Memorial from the Ministry of Agriculture, Industry and Commerce, referring to the province of Kweichow, dated the 21st January, 1908), and are composed

[357]

770 of four Sections : 1. 農務所 Nung² Wu⁴ So³, Section of Agriculture, 2. 工務所 Kung⁵ Wu⁴ So³, Section of Industry, 3. 商務所 Shang¹ Wu⁴ So³, Section of Commerce, and 4. 庶務所 Shu⁴ Wu⁴ So³, Section of General Affairs.

770. 農會 Nung² Hui⁴, Agricultural Guilds. In accordance with a report from the Ministry of Agriculture, Industry and Commerce, dated the 20th October, 1907, these are established : at provincial capitals, 農務總會 Nung² Wu⁴ Tsung³ Hui⁴, Central Agricultural Guilds ; at the chief cities of prefectures, sub-prefectures, departments and districts, 農務分會 Nung² Wu⁴ Fên¹ Hui⁴, Branch Agricultural Guilds ; at towns and villages, 農務分所 Nung² Wu⁴ Fên¹ So³, Agricultural Associations (or Sections of Agricultural Guilds). The establishment of these Guilds, Branches and Sections commenced in 1908 and it was provided that their complete inauguration be finished in 1910.

Central Agricultural Guilds have a 總理 Tsung³ Li³, Chairman, and a 協理 Hsieh² Li³, Vice-Chairman, elected from the ranks of 董事 Tung³ Shih⁴, Members (of which there are from 20 to 50), who must be approved by the Ministry of Agriculture, Industry and Commerce.

Branch Agricultural Guilds consist of a 總理 Tsung³ Li³ and from 10 to 30 董事 Tung² Shih⁴, Members, while Sections of Agricultural Guilds are composed of 董事 Tung³ Shih⁴ (the maximum is 5).

At Central Agricultural Guilds there are, or will be, established : a 農業學堂 Nung² Yeh⁴ Hsüeh² T'ang², Agricultural School (*see* No. 600), and a 農事試驗塲 Nung² Shih⁴ Shih⁴ Yen⁴ Ch'ang³, Botanical Garden (by 1910 this is to be established at all Central Agricultural Guilds).

At Branch Agricultural Guilds, as well as at Sections of Agricultural Guilds, there are, or will be, established : a 農事半日學堂 Nung² Shih⁴ Pan⁴ Jih⁴ Hsüeh² T'ang², Agricultural

School with Half-day Sessions (*see* No. 617B; compare No. 579; to be established in 1912), and a 農事演說會塲 Nung² Shih⁴ Yen³ Shuo¹ Hui⁴ Ch'ang³, Society for the Diffusion of Agricultural Knowledge (to be instituted in 1912).

770A to 770c

770A. 京師農務總會 Ching¹ Shih¹ Nung² Wu⁴ Tsung³ Hui⁴, Metropolitan Central Agricultural Guild (*see* No. 770). This, as proposed in a Memorial from the Ministry of Agriculture, Industry and Commerce, sanctioned by the Emperor on the 6th July, 1911, is a development of the former 畿輔農工學會 Chi¹ Fu³ Nung² Kung¹ Hsüeh² Hui⁴, Society for the Encouragement of Agricultural and Industrial Education about Peking. In the new Society the designations 會長 Hui⁴ Chang³, Chairman, and 副會長 Fu⁴ Hui⁴ Chang³, Vice-Chairman, have become 總理 Tsung³ Li³ and 協理 Hsieh² Li³ (compare No. 770), and there have been instituted 工業研究所 Kung¹ Yeh⁴ Yen² Chin¹ So³, Courses in Handicrafts.

770B. 京師農事試驗塲 Ching¹ Shih¹ Nung² Shih⁴ Shih⁴ Yen⁴ Ch'ang³, Metropolitan Botanical Garden; opened in 1908. Here is found a 高等農務學堂 Kao¹ Têng³ Nung² Wu⁴ Hsüeh² T'ang², Higher Agricultural School (*see* No. 603A), and the 農務局 Nung² Wu⁴ Chü², Agricultural Office (*see* No. 463).

770c. In Manchuria, as proposed by 徐世昌 Hsü² Shih⁴-ch'ang¹ (*see* his Memorial of the 5th December, 1908, and the reply of the Ministry of Agriculture, Industry and Commerce, dated the 27th December, 1908), at the main cities of prefectures, sub-prefectures, departments and districts there are established 農政廳 Nung² Chêng⁴ T'ing¹, Agricultural Offices, administered by 農官 Nung² Kuan¹, Experienced Agriculturalists (Agricultural Officials) of the sixth, seventh, eighth and ninth ranks, 藝士 I⁴ Shih⁴, Mechanical Engineers, 技手 Chi⁴ Shou³, Workmen, 書記 Shu¹ Chi⁴, Clerks, and 幹事 Kan⁴ Shih⁴, Attendants.

770D
to
771

770D. In addition to the institutions mentioned above there are to be established the following, having as their object the facilitation of the study, and the assisting of the development, of agriculture, forestry, sericulture and tea planting :

1. 農務講習所 Nung² Wu⁴ Chiang³ Hsi² So³, Agricultural Courses (see No. 617B),

2. 農林學堂 Nung² Lin² Hsüeh² T'ang², Schools of Agriculture and Forestry (by 1910 these are to be established in all the provinces; see No. 617B),

3. 蠶業講習所 Ts'an² Yeh⁴ Chiang³ Hsi² So³, Courses in Sericulture (to be instituted in 1909-1910; see No. 617B), and

4. 茶業講習所 Ch'a² Yeh⁴ Chiang³ Hsi² So³, (also 茶務講習所 Ch'a² Wu⁴ Chiang³ Hsi² So³), Courses in Tea Planting (in accordance with a Memorial from the Ministry of Agriculture, Industry and Commerce, sanctioned by the Emperor on the 23rd January, 1910, these must be established in all provinces producing tea—產茶省分 Ch'an³ Ch'a² Sheng³ Fên¹; see No. 617B).

771. For the encouragement and development of industry there are (or will be established) at Peking, and in the provinces, the following :

1. 工藝局 Kung¹ I⁴ Chü², Industrial Institutes (one has existed at Peking for many years—see No. 464—and they are to be established at ports open to foreign trade in 1911),

2. 勸業會 Ch'üan² Yeh⁴ Hui⁴, Societies for the Encouragement of Industry (to be gradually established, in all provinces, within the period 1912-1913),

3. 京師工業試驗所 Ching¹ Shih¹ Kung¹ Yeh⁴ Shih⁴ Yen⁴ So³, Metropolitan Experimental Workshop ; established in accordance with a Memorial from the Ministry of Agriculture, Industry and Commerce, sanctioned by the Emperor on the 23rd January, 1910, at the Metropolitan Exhibition for the Encouragement of Industry (see No. 771A), with two 科 K'o¹, Sections,

i.e. 化學科 Hua⁴ Hsüeh² K'o¹, Chemical, and 機器科 Chi¹ Ch'i⁴ K'o¹, Mechanical (there is to be instituted also a 理化研究所 Li³ Hua⁴ Yen² Chiu¹ So³, Bureau of Chemical Research), 4. 勸工陳列所 Ch'üan⁴ Kung¹ Ch'ên² Lieh⁴ So³, Exhibitions for the Encouragement of Industry ; to be established in 1911 at all places open to foreign trade (for details as to the Metropolitan Exhibition *see* No. 771A), and 5. 繡工科 Hsiu⁴ Kung¹ K'o¹, Embroidery Workshops (*see* No. 464).

771A. 京師勸工陳列所 Ching¹ Shih¹ Ch'üan⁴ Kung¹ Ch'ên² Lieh⁴ So³, Metropolitan Exhibition for the Encouragement of Industry (*see* Nos. 464 and 771); founded at Peking in 1906 (*see* Memorial from the Ministry of Commerce, covering Regulations). The Exhibition is administered by two 總理 Tsung³ Li³, Superintendents, who are assisted by two 協理 Hsieh² Li³, Assistants, and two 庶務長 Shu⁴ Wu⁴ Chang³, Stewards. It is arranged in four Sections : 1. 支設處 Chih¹ Shê⁴ Ch'u⁴, Exhibition Section, 2. 考驗處 K'ao³ Yen⁴ Ch'u⁴, Technical Section, 3. 調查處 Tiao⁴ Ch'a² Ch'u⁴, Information Section, and 4. 收支處 Shou¹ Chih¹ Ch'u⁴, Treasury.

To each Section there are attached two 理事員 Li³ Shih⁴ Yüan², Expositors.

In 1908 the Exhibition was gutted by fire. Repairs were, however, effected in 1909.

At the Metropolitan Exhibition there is found a 勸業塲 Ch'üan⁴ Yeh⁴ Ch'ang³, Workshop for the Encouragement of Industry.

For particulars as to the 京師工業試驗所 Ching¹ Shih¹ Kung¹ Yeh⁴ Shih⁴ Yen⁴ So³, Metropolitan Experimental Workshop, established at the Exhibition, *see* No. 771.

772. 商船公會 Shang¹ Ch'uan² Kung¹ Hui⁴, Mercantile Marine Societies (*see* Memorial from the Ministry of Commerce, dated the 26th March, 1906) ; established at commercial towns interested in the mercantile marine. These

**773
to
774**

Societies, are of two grades: 總 會 Tsung³ Hui⁴, Central
Societies, and 分 會 Fên¹ Hui⁴, Branch Societies. The former
are directed by a 總 理 Tsung³ Li', Chairman, and a 協 理
Hsieh² Li³, Vice-Chairman, while the latter have a Chairman
alone. The establishment of Mercantile Marine Societies
throughout the Empire must be completed by 1913.

773. Conforming to regulations drawn up by the Ministry
of Commerce in 1906, whenever China participates in 賽 會 Sai⁴
Hui⁴, Exhibitions, abroad provision is made for the organization
of a separate Chinese section (華 商 賽 會 Hua² Shang¹ Sai⁴
Hui⁴), for the direction of which there is appointed a 總事務所
Tsung³ Shih⁴ Wu⁴ So³, Committee, under the direction of a 監 督
Chien¹ Tu¹, Inspector (the duties of Inspector are, in some
instances, carried on by the accredited Diplomatic Representative).

773A. 國 內 賽 會 Kuo² Nei⁴ Sai⁴ Hui⁴, Imperial Exhibition. In accordance with the scheme of constitutional reforms,
drawn up by the Ministry of Agriculture, Industry and Commerce, this Exhibition is to be opened in 1915 (preparations
are to be begun in 1913).

773B. 萬 國 賽 會 Wan⁴ Kuo² Sai⁴ Hui⁴, International
Exhibition. Conforming to the scheme of constitutional reforms
(compare No. 773A), this Exhibition is to be opened in 1916
(preparations are to be started in 1915).

774. 商 會 Shang¹ Hui⁴, Chambers of Commerce. Regulations drawn up by the Ministry of Commerce (sanctioned by the
Emperor on the 11th January, 1904), provide for the establishment of these, in the place of previously existing commercial
associations of various kinds (商 業 公 所 Shang¹ Yeh⁴ Kung¹
So³, 商 務 公 會 Shang· Wu⁴ Kung¹ Hui⁴, etc.), at provincial
capitals and important commercial centres. At the former, as
well as at the most important commercial cities, such as Tientsin,
Chefoo, Shanghai, Hankow, Chungking, Canton and Amoy, there

are found 商 務 總 會 Shang[1] Wu[4] Tsung[3] Hui[4], General Chambers of Commerce, while at other places there are established 商 務 分 會 Shang[1] Wu[4] Fên[1] Hui[4], Branch Chambers of Commerce, which are, to some extent, subordinated to the General Chambers of Commerce.

At General Chambers of Commerce there is a 總 理 Tsung[3] Li[3], Chairman, and a 協 理 Hsieh[2] Li[3], Vice-Chairman, who are elected from the ranks of 董 事 Tung[3] Shih[4], Members (20 to 50 in all), while Branch Chambers of Commerce are composed of a Chairman and from 10 to 30 members.

The scheme of constitutional reforms drawn up by the Ministry of Agriculture, Industry and Commerce provides for the establishment: of General Chambers of Commerce, in 1910; of Chambers of Commerce abroad (so-called 華 商 商 會 Hua[2] Shang[1] Shang[1] Hui[4]), in 1911; of Branch Chambers of Commerce in China, in 1911; of Branch Chambers of Commerce abroad (so-called 華 商 地 方 商 會 Hua[2] Shang[1] Ti[4] Fang[1] Shang[1] Hui[4]), in 1914.

774A. 商 律 講 明 所 Shang[1] Lü[4] Chiang[3] Ming[2] So[3], Associations for the Study and Explanation of Commercial Laws; to be established in 1915.

774B. 商 品 陳 列 館 Shang[1] P'in[3] Ch'ên[2] Lieh[4] Kuan[3], Commercial Exhibitions (Stores). The preliminary organization of these is to be started in 1911 and they will be gradually opened: in 1912, at provincial capitals and ports open to foreign trade; in 1914, at prefectural capitals and important commercial centres; in 1916, at the chief cities of departments and districts.

775. 礦 政 調 查 局 Kung[3] Chêng[4] Tiao[4] Ch'a[2] Chü[2], Mining Committees; organized, in accordance with regulations framed by the Ministry of Commerce (sanctioned by the Emperor on the 27th November, 1905), for the general supervision of mining affairs, in all provinces. Each is directed by a 總 理 Tsung[3] Li[3], President, a 協 理 Hsieh[2] Li[3], Vice-President,

775ᴀ to 776

and a number of 礦務議員 Kung³ Wu⁴ I⁴ Yüan², Mining Advisers.

New mining regulations (sanctioned by the Emperor on the 21st September, 1907), left, for the time being, the Mining Committees unchanged, with the exception that there were attached to them a number of 礦務委員 Kung³ Wu⁴ Wei³ Yüan², Deputies for Mining Affairs, and 礦務顧問官 Kung³ Wu⁴ Ku⁴ Wên⁴ Kuan¹, Consulting Experts for Mining Affairs (*see* No. 468).

At present the Mining Committees are being gradually abolished (compare a Memorial from 陳夔龍 Ch'ên² K'uei²-lung², late Governor-General of Hukuang, dated the 1st July, 1909), and their functions transferred to the Industrial Taotai (*sec* Nos. 839 and 839ᴀ; 礦務科 Kung³ Wu⁴ K'o¹, Mining Section).

775ᴀ. Previous to the establishment of Mining Committees in 1905 (*see* No. 775), mining affairs were supervised in the provinces by 礦務總局 Kung³ Wu⁴ Tsung³ Chü², Central Mining Offices, and 查礦公所 Ch'a² Kung³ Kung¹ So³, Mining Offices.

775ʙ. 礦務學堂 Kung³ Wu⁴ Hsüeh² T'ang², Mining Schools (*see* No. 617ʙ); to be organized in all provinces in 1911.

776. 公司 Kung¹ Ssu¹, Companies or Associations. Conforming to commercial laws, drawn up by the Ministry of Commerce and sanctioned by the Emperor on the 21st January, 1904, these may be classed in four groups: 1. 合資公司 Ho² Tzu¹ Kung¹ Ssu¹, Co-partnerships, 2. 合資有限公司 Ho² Tzu¹ Yu³ Hsien⁴ Kung¹ Ssu¹, Limited Liability Co-partnerships, 3. 股分公司 Ku³ Fên¹ Kung¹ Ssu¹, Joint-stock Companies, and 4. 股分有限公司 Ku³ Fên¹ Yu³ Hsien⁴ Kung¹ Ssu¹, Limited Liability Joint-stock Companies.

For (the direction of) the business of any company there is formed a 董事局 Tung³ Shih⁴ Chü², Board of Directors,

[364]

consisting of from three to thirteen 董 事 Tung³ Shih⁴, Directors,   **776ᴀ**
elected at a general meeting of shareholders from the ranks of   **to**
holders of ten shares or more in the company concerned.   At the   **777**
first general meeting of the shareholders there are elected at least
two 查 賬 人 Ch'a² Chang⁴ Jên², Auditors.

Companies must be registered at the Company Registration
Bureau, 公 司 註 册 局 Kung¹ Ssu¹ Chu⁴ Ts'ê⁴ Chü² (*see* No.
465ʙ).   Temporary regulations as to registration of companies
have been compiled by the Ministry of Commerce (consisting of
18 articles).

776ᴀ.   Registration of trade marks is done, following rules
and regulations framed by the Ministry of Commerce (originally
in 1904) by the 商 標 局 Shang¹ Piao¹ Chü² (also 註 册 局
Chu⁴ Ts'ê⁴ Chü²), Trade Marks Registration Bureau (*see* No.
465ᴅ), and by the 商 標 挂 號 分 局 Shang¹ Piao¹ Kua⁴ Hao⁴
Fên¹ Chü², Branch Trade Marks Registration Bureaux, at
Tientsin and Shanghai.

COLONIZATION.

777.   Of late years the Chinese Government has paid
special attention to the question of colonization, which is now
being carried on under official auspices along the Northern
border of the provinces of Shansi, Chihli, Shensi and Kansu, in
Manchuria, in Inner Mongolia (especially in the Cherim league),
about Hsining (on the order of K'uk'unor), in Szechwan (on the
Tibetan border) and in Yünnan (on the border of Tongking).

In the province of Shansi (the territory of the T'umet tribe,
which occupies the region adjacent to Kuei Hua Ch'êng)
colonization was started, roughly speaking, in 1902, and the
following Colonization Bureaux have been gradually called into
activity :   1.   歸 化 墾 務 總 局 Kuei¹ Hua⁴ K'en³ Wu⁴ Tsung³
Chü², Central Colonization Bureaux at Kuei Hua Ch'êng (K'u

778 K'u Ho To), 2. 豐鎮墾務分局 Fêng¹ Chên¹ K'en³ Wu⁴ Fên¹ Chü², Branch Colonization Bureau at Fêng Chên T'ing, 3. 寧遠墾務分局 Ning² Yüan³ K'en³ Wu⁴ Fên¹ Chü², Branch Colonization Bureau at Ning Yüan T'ing, etc.

Later, colonization penetrating Chihli, the following was established: 察哈爾左翼墾務張家口總局 Ch'a² Ha³ Erh³ Tso³ I⁴ K'en³ Wu⁴ Chang¹ Chia¹ K'ou³ Tsung³ Chü², Central Colonization Bureau of the Left Wing of the Ch'ahars at Kalgan.

In the province of Kansu a Colonization Bureau was established (on a Memorial from the 將軍 Chiang¹ Chün¹, 台布 T'ai² Pu⁴, dated the 14th December, 1908), in 1908, styled 奏辦寧夏滿營墾務總局 Tsou⁴ Pan⁴ Ning² Hsia⁴ Man³ Ying² K'en³ Wu⁴ Tsung³ Chü², Central Colonization Bureau of the Manchu Garrison at Ninghsia, established with Imperial sanction.

In addition to the above-mentioned, Colonization Bureaux (Central and Branch) have been called into being at other places in the Empire.

778. 督辦墾務大臣 Tu¹ Pan⁴ K'en³ Wu⁴ Ta⁴ Ch'ên², Superintendent of Colonization Affairs. This title is held by the Chiang¹ Chün¹ at Sui¹ Yüan³ Ch'êng² (*see* Nos. 744, 744A and 899).

To him there are attached the following · 1. One 總查 Tsung³ Ch'a², Chief Inspector, 2. Six 稽查 Chi² Ch'a², Inspectors, 3. One 文巡捕 Wên² Hsün² Pu³, Civil Orderly Officer, 4. One 武巡捕 Wu³ Hsün² Pu³, Military Orderly Officer, 5. One 監印委員 Chien¹ Yin⁴ Wei³ Yüan², Keeper of the Seal, 6. Two 漢通事 Han⁴ T'ung¹ Shih⁴, Chinese Interpreters, 7. Two 蒙通事 Mêng³ T'ung¹ Shih⁴, Mongolian Interpreters, 8. Four 頭等差官 T'ou² Têng³ Ch'ai¹ Kuan¹, Deputies of the first rank, 9. Six 二等差官 Êrh⁴ Têng³ Ch'ai¹ Kuan¹, Deputies of the second rank, 10. Ten 三等差

779
to
781

官 San¹ Têng³ Ch'ai¹ Kuan¹, Deputies of the third rank, and
11. Twenty 夫役 Fu¹ I⁴, Servants.

In addition to the officials mentioned above, for the
Superintendent of Colonization Affairs, there is a : 1. 文案處
Wên² An¹ Ch'u¹, Chancery (see No. 779), and 2. 收支處
Shou¹ Chih¹ Ch'u⁴, Treasury (see No. 780).

779. 文案處 Wên² An⁴ Ch'u⁴, Chancery (see No. 778);
directed by a 總辦 Tsung³ Pan⁴, Chief, who is assisted by :
1. One 會辦 Hui⁴ Pan⁴, Associate Chief, 2. Two 幫辦
Pang¹ Pan⁴, Assistants, 3. Six 主稿委員 Chu³ Kao³ Wei³
Yüan², Chief Revisers, 4. Two 掌案委員 Chang³ An⁴ Wei³
Yüan², Archivists, 5. Two 收發文件委員 Shou¹ Fa¹ Wên²
Chien¹ Wei³ Yüan², Registrars, 6. Four 繙譯委員 Fan¹ I⁴
Wei³ Yüan², Interpreters, 7. Four 司事 Ssu¹ Shih⁴, Clerks,
8. Two 通事 T'ung¹ Shih⁴, Assistant Interpreters, 9. 書手
Shu¹ Shou³, Writers, 10. Four 差官 Ch'ai¹ Kuan¹ (see No.
778), 11. Four 聽事 T'ing¹ Shih⁴, Runners, and 12. Ten
護局夫 Hu⁴ Chü² Fu¹, Guards.

780. 收支處 Shou¹ Chih¹ Ch'u⁴, Treasury (see No. 778);
directed by a 總辦 Tsung³ Pan⁴, to whom there are subordinated:
1. One 會辦 Hui⁴ Pan⁴, Associate Chief, 2. One 幫辦
Pang¹ Pan⁴, Assistant, 3. Four 總核委員 Tsung³ Ho² Wei³
Yüan², Auditors, 4. Two 主稿委員 Chu³ Kao³ Wei³ Yüan²,
5. One 掌案委員 Chang³ An⁴ Wei³ Yüan², 6. Two 支應
委員 Chih¹ Ying⁴ Wei³ Yüan², Assistant Treasurers, 7. Four
司事 Ssu¹ Shih⁴, 8. Fourteen 書手 Shu¹ Shou³, 9. Four
差官 Ch'ai¹ Kuan¹, 10. Four 聽事 T'ing¹ Shih⁴ and 11. Ten
護局夫 Hu⁴ Chü² Fu¹ (compare No. 779).

781. The personnel of the Central Colonization Bureau at
Kuei Hua Ch'êng (K'u K'u Ho T'o; see No. 777) is as
follows : 1. Two 總辦 Tsung³ Pan², 2. Two 會辦 Hui⁴ Pan⁴,
3. Two 幫辦 Pang¹ Pan⁴, 4. Two 提調 T'i² Tiao⁴, Proctors,
5. Four 主稿委員 Chu³ Kao³ Wei³ Yüan², 6. Four 承審委

員 Ch'êng² Shên³ Wei³ Yüan², Judicial Commissioners, 7. Four 稽核冊報委員 Chi² Ho² Ts'ê⁴ Pao⁴ Wei³ Yüan², Auditors of Colonization Accounts, 8. Four 抽查履丈委員 Ch'ou¹ Ch'a² Lü³ Chang⁴ Wei³ Yüan², Land Surveyors, 9. Two 測繪委員 Ts'ê⁴ Hui⁴ Wei³ Yüan², Draftsmen, 10. Two 掌案委員 Chang³ An⁴ Wei³ Yüan², 11. Two 繙譯委員 Fan¹ I⁴ Wei³ Yüan², 12. Two 通事 T'ung¹ Shih⁴, 13. Four 司事 Ssu¹ Shih⁴, 14. Fourteen 書手 Shu¹ Shou³, 15. Four 差官 Ch'ai¹ Kuan¹, 16. Four 聽事 T'ing¹ Shih⁴, and 17. Twelve 護局夫 Hu⁴ Chü² Fu¹ (compare Nos. 779 and 780).

The personnel of the other Colonization Bureaux mentioned above (Central, at Kalgan; Branches, at Fêng Chên T'ing and Ning Hsia T'ing) is, with almost no exception, similar to that just expanded.

782. 墾務總局 K'en³ Wu⁴ Tsung³ Chü², Central Colonization Bureau at Tsitsihar (in the province of Heilungchiang). This superintends colonization affairs and the selling of public lands to immigrants. At its head is a 總辦 Tsung³ Pan⁴, who has subordinated to him a 提調 T'i² Tiao⁴, Proctor. It is divided into three 科 K'o¹, Sections: 1. 文牘科 Wên² Tu³ K'o¹, Section of Correspondence, 2. 會計科 Hui⁴ (K'uai⁴) Chi⁴ K'o¹, Accounts Section, and 3. 庶務科 Shu⁴ Wu⁴ K'o¹, Section of General Affairs. At the head of each Section there is a 科長 K'o¹ Chang³, Section Chief. He is assisted by a 副 科長 Fu⁴ K'o¹ Chang³, Assistant Chief.

782ᴀ. 黑龍江省邊墾招待處 Hei¹ Lung² Chiang¹ Shêng³ Pien¹ K'en³ Chao¹ Tai⁴ Ch'u⁴, Immigrant Agencies for the Colonization of the Frontier of Heilungchiang. These were established, in accordance with a Memorial from the Governor-General of Manchuria (of the 28th January, 1909), at Hankow, Shanghai, Tientsin, Chefoo, Yingkow and K'uangch'êngtzu. They furnish information and endeavour to attract people for colonization purposes.

RAILWAYS.

783. Railways, all under the supervision of the Ministry of Posts and Communications, may be classed under four headings : 1. 官欵官辦 Kuan¹ K'uan³ Kuan¹ Pan⁴, Government Built and Operated Railways, 2. 借欵官辦 Chieh⁴ K'uan³ Kuan¹ Pan⁴, Government Operated Railways Built with Loan Funds, 3. 借欵商辦 Chieh⁴ K'uan³ Shang¹ Pan⁴, Private Railways Built with Loan Funds, and 4. 商辦 Shang¹ Pan⁴, Private Railways (built with private funds).

At the head of Government Railways there is a 總辦 Tsung³ Pan⁴, Chief, and a 會辦 Hui⁴ Pan⁴, Assistant.

At the head of Private Railways there is a 總理 Tsung³ Li³, Chief Manager (may be 坐辦總理 Tso⁴ Pan⁴ Tsung³ Li³, Actual Chief Manager, or 名譽總理 Ming² Yü⁴ Tsung³ Li³, Honorary Chief Manager) and a 協理 Hsieh² Li³, Assistant Manager.

During the construction period, on important railway lines there are sometimes appointed a 督辦 Tu¹ Pan⁴, Superintendent, and a 幫辦 Pang¹ Pan⁴, Assistant. Construction work is carried on in 叚 Tuan⁴, Sections, which are directed by 總辦 Tsung³ Pan⁴, Chiefs, and 幫總辦 Pang¹ Tsung³ Pan⁴, Assistant Chiefs.

On all Railways—Government or Private—there are found: 總工程司 Tsung³ Kung¹ Ch'êng² Ssu¹ (also 技師長 Chi⁴ Shih¹ Chang³), Chief Engineer, and 副工程司 Fu⁴ Kung¹ Ch'êng² Ssu¹ (also 工程師 Kung¹ Ch'êng² Shih¹, 副技師 Fu⁴ Chi⁴ Shih¹, or 技師 Chi⁴ Shih¹), Engineers.

For the 鐵路局 T'ieh³ Lu⁴ Chü², Railway Bureaux, the personnel has, as yet, not been defined.

784. 護路巡警 Hu⁴ Lu⁴ Hsün² Ching³, Railway Police; conforming to a Memorial from the Ministry of Posts and

785 to 786A

Communications, dated the 7th July, 1909, these police are to be organized on all Railways—Government or Private. The Ministry is now engaged in arranging the personnel of this force and, in this connection, has consulted with the high officials of provinces in which there are railways.

785. 鐵路學堂 T'ieh³ Lu⁴ Hsüeh² T'ang², Railway Schools; there is one for each railway, founded with the object of training employés for the various branches of railway work.

785A. The scheme of constitutional reforms drawn up by the Ministry of Posts and Communications, sanctioned by the Emperor on the 8th April, 1909, called for the establishment at Peking, in 1909, of: 1. A 實業學堂 Shih² Yeh⁴ Hsüeh² T'ang², Professional School (at the Ministry), and 2. A 電氣專門學堂 Tien⁴ Ch'i⁴ Chuan¹ Mên² Hsüeh² T'ang², School of Electrical Engineering.

786. 唐山路礦學堂 T'ang² Shan¹ Lu⁴ Kung³ Hsüeh² T'ang², Railway and Mining School at T'angshan (in the province of Chihli; see No. 621A).

In 1909, in consequence of internal dissensions, this school was reorganized (see report from the Ministries of Education and of Posts and Communications, sanctioned by the Emperor on the 6th June, 1909), as follows: to consist of two Sections, namely, 1. 中等科 Chung¹ Têng³ K'o¹, Middle Section (with the curriculum of a Middle School and a course of study covering three years), and 2. 高等科 Kao¹ Têng³ K'o¹, Higher Section (with the rating of a Higher Professional School and a course of four years). The head of the school is now a 監督 Chien¹ Tu¹, Director (instead of the former 總辦 Tsung³ Pan⁴; see No. 635). He is assisted by a 教務長 Chiao⁴ Wu⁴ Chang³ (see No. 636) and a 齋務長 Chai¹ Wu⁴ Chang³ (see No. 645).

786A. Previous to 1909 the Railway and Mining School at T'angshan (see No. 786) was composed of two Sections:

1. 路礦公共科 Lu⁴ Kung³ Kung¹ Kung⁴ K'o¹, General, and
2. 路礦專門科 Lu⁴ Kung³ Chuan¹ Mên² K'o¹, Special.
The course of study in each covered two years.

787. 上海高等實業學堂 Shang⁴ Hai³ Kao¹ Têng³ Shih² Yeh⁴ Hsüeh² T'ang², Higher Professional School at Shanghai (see No. 598c). Previous to 1909 this school was under the supervision of the Ministry of Agriculture, Industry and Commerce; in that year it was placed under the control of the Ministry of Posts and Communications. It furnishes instruction in a 鐵路科 T'ieh³ Lu⁴ K'o¹, Railway Course, which is arranged in two Sections: a 豫科 Yü⁴ K'o¹, Preparatory Section, with a three or four years' course of study, and a 本科 Pên³ K'o¹, Specializing Section, with a three years' term. At the last mentioned there is a 中學 Chung¹ Hsüeh², Sub-section with the curriculum of a Middle School.

788. 交通傳習所 Chiao¹ T'ung¹ Ch'uan² Hsi² So³ (formerly 鐵路管理傳習所 T'ieh³ Lu⁴ Kuan³ Li³ Ch'uan² Hsi² So³), Courses of Instruction at the Ministry of Posts and Communications. These are arranged in two Sections. 1. 鐵路科 T'ieh³ Lu⁴ K'o¹, Railway Section, and 2. 郵電科 Yu¹ Tien⁴ K'o¹, Section of Posts and Telegraphs. Each Section is sub-divided into two sub-sections: 1. 高等班 Kao¹ Têng³ Pan⁴, Higher (term of course for the Railway Section is three years; for the Section of Posts and Telegraphs, two and a half years), and 2. 簡易班 Chien³ I⁴ Pan⁴, Abridged (covering one year for the Railway Section and one and a half years for the Section of Posts and Telegraphs).

788A. 工匠夜學所 Kung¹ Chiang⁴ Yeh⁴ Hsüeh² So³, Evening Courses for Workmen. In accordance with directions from the Ministry of Posts and Communications (dated August, 1909), these are to be instituted at all Railway Bureaux.

789. 輪船招商局 Lun² Ch'uan² Chao¹ Shang¹ Chü², China Merchants' Steam Navigation Co.; established in 1872

790 to 791 (and until 1909) under the superintendency of the 北洋大臣 Pei³ Yang² Ta⁴ Ch'ên² (*see* No. 820B). In 1909, as directed by Imperial Edict, dated the 4th May, this company was transferred to the control of the Ministry of Posts and Communications (*see* report of the latter, sanctioned by the Emperor on the 26th August).

TELEGRAPHS AND TELEPHONES.

790. In 1908 the telegraph lines of the Empire were redeemed by the Government and their administration was invested in the Ministry of Posts and Communications, which directly manages telegraphic affairs through the 電政司 Tien⁴ Chêng⁴ Ssu¹, Department of Telegraphs (*see* No. 478), and the 上海電政局 Shang⁴ Hai³ Tien⁴ Chêng⁴ Chü², Bureau of Telegraphs at Shanghai. The latter is directed by a 總辦 Tsung³ Pan⁴, Chief, assisted by a 總管電政 Tsung³ Kuan³ Tien⁴ Chêng⁴, Superintendent of Telegraphs.

At the head of 電報局 Tien⁴ Pao⁴ Chü², Telegraph Offices, are 總辦 Tsung³ Pan⁴, Chiefs. To them are attached 理事員 Li³ Shih⁴ Yüan², Managers, 領班 Ling³ Pan¹, Chiefs of Reliefs, and 副領班 Fu⁴ Ling³ Pan¹, Assistant Chiefs of Reliefs.

790A. The scheme of constitutional reforms drawn up by the Ministry of Posts and Communications provides for China's affiliation with the 萬國電政公會 Wan⁴ Kuo² Tien⁴ Chêng⁴ Kung¹ Hui⁴, International Telegraph Union, in 1913.

791. Telephony is also under the supervision of the Ministry of Posts and Communications and, in the latter's scheme of constitutional reforms, it is arranged that telephone installation throughout the Empire shall be completed in 1916.

Telephone Stations are divided into: 1. 電話總局 Tien⁴ 792
Hua⁴ Tsung³ Chü², Central Stations and 2. 電話分局 Tien⁴
Hua⁴ Fên¹ Chü², Branch Stations.

BANK OF COMMUNICATIONS.

792. 交通銀行 Chiao¹ T'ung¹ Yin² Hang², Bank of
Communications; established, as proposed in a Memorial from
the Ministry of Posts and Communications (sanctioned by the
Emperor on the 7th December, 1907), with the object of assisting
in the development of shipping, railways, telegraphs and posts.
Of the total number of shares issued, 40% were taken up by the
Government and 60°/₀ were issued to the public. The 總行
Tsung³ Hang², Head Office, of the Bank is in Peking; 分行
Fên¹ Hang², Branch Offices, were first established at Tientsin,
Shanghai, Hankow, Amoy, Chinkiang and Canton. Later, at
important commercial centres of China, as well as abroad, there
are to be opened Branch Offices or 代辦行 Tai⁴ Pan⁴ Hang²,
Agencies.

For the Head Office, as well as for each Branch
Office, there is a 總辦 Tsung³ Pan⁴, Superintendent,
and to this official there is attached one 副辦 Fu⁴ Pan⁴,
Assistant.

At the head of the 總管理處 Tsung³ Kuan³ Li³ Ch'u⁴,
Board of Directors (at Peking), there is a 總理 Tsung³ Li³,
President, and a 協理 Hsieh² Li³, Vice-President. To render
them any assistance that may be required there are deputed a
number officials from the personnel of the Railway Administration. The President and Vice-President are appointed by the
Ministry of Posts and Communications.

Shareholders, at a general meeting, elect four 董事 Tung³
Shih⁴, Supervisors, who keep a watch over the actions of the

[373]

Board of Directors. For Branch Offices the shareholders elect two 監 事 Chien[1] Shih[1], Inspectors. Other posts in the Bank (for instance, 司 賬 Ssu[1] Chang[4], Book-keepers, and others) are held by persons chosen by the Superintendent.

At the Branch Office at Tientsin the post of 總 辦 Tsung[3] Pan[4], Superintendent, has been abolished and the management of affairs there placed under the direct control of the Head Office at Peking (*see* Memorial from the Ministry of Posts and Communications, dated the 28th April, 1909).

PART III.

METROPOLITAN PREFECTURE AND MANCHURIA; PROVINCIAL ADMINISTRATION AND DEPENDENCIES OF CHINA.

PEKING AND THE METROPOLITAN PREFECTURE.

793. 順 天 府 Shun⁴ T'ien¹ Fu³, The Metropolitan Prefecture. In charge of this prefecture is the 府 尹 Fu³ Yin⁵, Prefect of the Metropolitan Prefecture (3ᴀ; literary designation, 大 京 兆 Ta⁴ Ching¹ Chao¹, or 京 兆 Ching¹ Chao¹), who is, at the same time, Governor of Peking. This official, in his capacity of Prefect, is not subordinated to the 布 政 使 Pu⁴ Chêng⁴ Shih³ (*see* No. 826) of Chihli province. As Governor of Peking he has subordinated to him: 1. 府 丞 Fu³ Ch'êng², Vice-Governor of Peking (4ᴀ; literary designation, 副 京 兆 Fu⁴ Ching¹ Chao¹), and 2. 治 中 Chih⁴ Chung¹, Sub-Prefect of Shun T'ien Fu; 5ᴀ.

793ᴀ. 兼 尹 Chien¹ Yin³ (or, more explicit, 兼 管 順 天 府 府 尹 事 務 Chien¹ Kuan³ Shun⁴ T'ien¹ Fu³ Fu³ Yin³ Shih⁴ Wu⁴), Governor Adjoint. This title is usually borne by one of the Presidents or Vice-Presidents of the various Ministries.

794. The personnel of the staff of the Prefect of the Metropolitan Prefecture includes the following: 1. One 通 判 T'ung¹ P'an⁴ (also 京 府 通 判 Ching¹ Fu³ T'ung¹ P'an⁴, or 粮 馬 通 判 Liang² Ma³ T'ung¹ P'an⁴) 6ᴀ; (*see* No. 849), 2. Two 教 授 Chiao⁴ Shou⁴ (also 順 天 府 學 教 授 Shun⁴ T'ien¹ Fu³ Hsüeh² Chiao⁴ Shou⁴); 7ᴀ (*see* No. 850), 3. Two 訓 導 Hsün⁴ Tao⁴ (also 順 天 府 學 訓 導 Shun⁴ T'ien¹ Fu³ Hsüeh² Hsun⁴ Tao⁴); 7ᴀ (*see* No. 850), 4. One 經 歷 Ching¹ Li'; 7ʙ (*see* No. 850), 5. One 照 磨 Chao⁴ Mo²; 9ʙ (*see* No. 850), and 6. One 司 獄 Ssu¹ Yü⁴; 9ʙ (*see* No. 850).

794ᴀ. The central administration of the Metropolitan Prefecture is concentrated in two districts: 大 興 縣 Ta⁴ Hsing¹

795
to
795D

Hsien⁴ (the Eastern Section of Peking), and 宛平縣 Wan³ P'ing² Hsien⁴ (the Western Section of Peking). At the head of each of these there is a 知縣 Chih¹ Hsien⁴ (also 京縣知縣 Ching¹ Hsien⁴ Chih¹ Hsien⁴); 6A (see No. 856). To these officials there are attached 縣丞 Hsien⁴ Ch'êng² (also 京縣縣丞 Ching¹ Hsien⁴ Hsien⁴ Ch'êng²); 7A (see No. 857).

795. As regards territorial authority, to the Prefect of the Metropolitan Prefecture there are subordinated: 1. Four 廳 T'ing¹ (see No. 846), 2. Five 州 Chou¹ (see No. 846), and 3. 19 縣 Hsien⁴ (see No. 846).

795A. 東路捕盜廳同知 Tung¹ Lu⁴ Pu³ Tao⁴ T'ing¹ T'ung² Chih¹, Sub-Prefect for Police Affairs of the Eastern Section of the Metropolitan Prefecture (compare No. 849); resides at 通州 T'ung¹ Chou¹. Under the control of this official there are two departments and five districts.

795B. 南路捕盜廳同知 Nan² Lu⁴ Pu³ Tao⁴ T'ing¹ T'ung² Chih¹, Sub-Prefect for Police Affairs of the Southern Section of the Metropolitan Prefecture (compare No. 849); resides at 黃村 Huang² Ts'un¹, in the district of 大興縣 Ta⁴ Hsing¹ Hsien⁴. This official has a department and six districts under his control.

795C. 西路捕盜廳同知 Hsi¹ Lu⁴ Pu³ Tao⁴ T'ing¹ T'ung² Chih¹, Sub-Prefect for Police Affairs of the Western Section of the Metropolitan Prefecture (compare No. 849); resides at 蘆溝橋 Lu⁴ Kou¹ Ch'iao², in the district of 宛平縣 Wan³ P'ing² Hsien⁴. Under the supervision of this official there are a department and four districts.

795D. 北路捕盜廳同知 Pei³ Lu⁴ Pu³ Tao⁴ T'ing¹ T'ung² Chih¹, Sub-Prefect for Police Affairs of the Northern Section of the Metropolitan Prefecture (compare No. 849), resides at 鞏華城 Kung³ Hua² Ch'êng², to the South of 昌平州 Ch'ang¹ P'ing² Chou¹. The authority of this official extends over a department and four districts.

[378]

796. 順天府捕盜營 Shun⁴ T'ien¹ Fu³ Pu³ Tao⁴ Ying², 796
Police Corps of the Metropolitan Prefecture. This Corps is to
divided into: 1. A 中營 Chung¹ Ying², Central Detachment, 796c
under the direction of a 千總 Ch'ien¹ Tsung³, and a 把總 Pa²
Tsung³ (*see* Nos. 752E and 752F), 2. A 東路 Tung¹ Lu⁴,
Eastern Detachment, 3. A 西路 Hsi¹ Lu⁴, Western Detachment, 4. A 南路 Nan² Lu⁴, Southern Detachment, and
5. A 北路 Pei³ Lu⁴, Northern Detachment (the last four
detachments mentioned are each under the direction of a 把總
Pa² Tsung³, *see* No. 752F).

796A. According to its former police-judicial organization
Peking was divided into five districts, termed 五城 Wu³ Ch'êng²,
or "Five Cities," under the supervision of two 五城御史 Wu³
Ch'êng² Yü⁴ Shih³, Censors of the Five Districts (Cities), one
Manchu and one Chinese (*see* No. 214). In addition, there was
for each of the five districts, one official of each of the following
ranks: 1. 兵馬司指揮 Ping¹ Ma³ Ssu¹ Chih³ Hui⁴, Police
Magistrate (6A; common designation, 司官 Ssu¹ Kuan¹),
2. 兵馬司副指揮 Ping¹ Ma³ Ssu¹ Fu⁴ Chih³ Hui⁴, Assistant
Police Magistrate (7B; common designation, 坊官 Fang¹
Kuan¹), and 3. 吏目 Li⁴ Mu⁴, Police-master and Jail-Warden.

Under the superintendency of the Police Censors there was
the 街道廳 Chieh¹ Tao⁴ T'ing¹, Roadway Office, which was in
charge of the repair, and maintenance in good order, of the
streets of the Outer (Chinese) City. The preservation of public
order was also included in the duties of this office.

796B. 統計處 T'ung³ Chi⁴ Ch'u⁴, Statistical Bureau at
the Prefectural Office (*see* Memorial from the Prefect, dated the
11th August, 1909); compare No. 162.

796C. 憲政籌備處 Hsien⁴ Chêng⁴ Ch'ou² Pei⁴ Ch'u⁴,
Constitutional Reforms Office at the Prefectural Office (*see* No.
822A, and the Supplement, No. 160); established in accordance
with a Memorial from the Prefect, sanctioned by the Emperor

797 to 798

on the 20th February, 1910, and composed of four 科 K‘o¹, Sections: 1. 民政科 Min² Chêng⁴ K‘o¹, Section of Civil Affairs, 2. 學務科 Hsüeh² Wu⁴ K‘o¹, Section of Educational Affairs, 3. 度支科 Tu⁴ Chih¹ K‘o¹, Section of Financial Affairs, and 4. 司法科 Ssu¹ Fa⁴ K‘o¹, Section of Judicial Affairs.

At the head of each Section there is a 治中 Chih⁴ Chung¹ (*see* No. 793).

The Constitutional Reforms Office assimilated the 警務處 Ching³ Wu⁴ Ch‘u⁴, Office of Police Affairs, and the 學務總匯處 Hsüeh² Wu⁴ Tsung³ Hui⁴ Ch‘u⁴, Head Office of Educational Affairs, both of which were formerly at the Prefectural Office.

797. 步軍營 Pu⁴ Chün¹ Ying², The Division of Gendarmerie (*see* No. 736). With the new Police of the Ministry of the Interior (*see* Nos. 500 to 518), this body performs police duty in the city and suburbs of Peking, and maintains public order. Members of the Gendarmerie patrol the streets day and night, watch the city gates (for details *see* No. 801), arrest malefactors, etc.

At the head of the Division of Gendarmerie there is a 步軍統領 Pu⁴ Chün¹ T‘ung³ Ling³, General Commandant of the Gendarmerie (1B; also bears the designation 提督九門巡捕五營 T‘i² Tu¹ Chiu³ Mên² Hsün² Pu³ Wu³ Ying², and, accordingly, commonly called 九門提督 Chiu³ Mên² T‘i² Tu¹). For particulars as to his administration *see* No. 798.

798. 步軍統領衙門 Pu⁴ Chün¹ T‘ung³ Ling³ Ya² Mên² (*see* No. 797), also 提督衙門 T‘i² Tu¹ Ya² Mên², Office of the Gendarmerie. The personnel of this office includes: 1. 左翼總兵 Tso³ I⁴ Tsung³ Ping¹, Senior Police Provost, or Lieutenant-General of the Gendarmerie (of the Eastern section of the city); 2A, 2. 右翼總兵 Yu⁴ I⁴ Tsung³ Ping¹, Junior Police Provost, or Lieutenant-General of the Gendarmerie (of the Western section of the city); 2A, 3. 左司 Tso³ Ssu¹, First

Department, administered by a 郎中 Lang² Chung¹, Department Director, a 員外郎 Yüan² Wai⁴ Lang², Assistant Department Director, and two 主事 Chu³ Shih⁴, Secretaries, 4. 右司 Yu⁴ Ssu¹, Second Department, administered by two 員外郎 Yüan² Wai⁴ Lang², and one 主事 Chu³ Shih⁴, and 5. 司務廳 Ssu¹ Wu⁴ T'ing¹, Chancery, directed by a 司務 Ssu¹ Wu⁴, Supervisor. At the Departments and the Chancery there are also found 筆帖式 Pi³ T'ieh³ Shih⁴, Clerks, and 額外司員 Ê² Wai⁴ Ssu¹ Yüan², Supernumerary Officials.

799. For policing purposes Peking is divided into two districts: 1. 左翼 Tso³ I⁴, Eastern and 右翼 Yu⁴ I⁴, Western. At the head of each there is a 翼尉 I⁴ Yü⁴, Deputy Provost; 3A, to whom there are subordinated: 副翼尉 Fu⁴ I⁴ Yü⁴ (also 幫辦翼尉 Pang¹ Pan⁴ I⁴ Yü⁴), Senior Assistant Deputy Provost; 3A, and 委翼尉 Wei³ I⁴ Yü⁴, Junior Assistant Deputy Provost; 4A. At the head of the 官廳 Kuan¹ T'ing¹, Guard Stations (24 in all, three to each of the eight Banners), are 協尉 Hsieh² Yü⁴, Police Majors; 4A, who have subordinated to them: 1. 副尉 Fu⁴ Yü⁴, Police Captain; 5A, 2. 步軍校 Pu⁴ Chün¹ Hsiao⁴, Police Lieutenant; 5B, 3. 委署步軍校 Wei³ Shu⁴ Pu⁴ Chün¹ Hsiao⁴, Deputy Police Lieutenant; 6A, 4. 領催 Ling³ Ts'ui¹, Police Sergeant, and 5. 步軍 Pu⁴ Chün¹, Police Privates (Policemen).

800. 京師步軍統領巡捕五營 Ching¹ Shih¹ Pu⁴ Chün¹ T'ung³ Ling³ Hsün² Pu³ Wu³ Ying², Five Battalions of the Police of the General Commandant of the Gendarmerie. These are: 巡捕中營 Hsün² Pu³ Chung¹ Ying², Central Police Battalion, 巡捕南營 Hsün² Pu³ Nan² Ying², Southern Police Battalion, 巡捕北營 Hsün² Pu³ Pei³ Ying², Northern Police Battalion, 巡捕左營 Hsün² Pu³ Tso³ Ying², Left (Eastern) Police Battalion, and 巡捕右營 Hsün² Pu³ Yu⁴ Ying², Right (Western) Police Battalion.

The general supervision of the five Battalions appertains to the General Commandant of the Gendarmerie and his assistants (*see* No. 798). The direct control is the duty of the 中 軍 Chung¹ Chün¹, Adjutant, as 巡捕五營步軍統領 Hsün² Pu³ Wu³ Ying² Pu⁴ Chün¹ T'ung³ Ling³.

The organization of the Five Battalions of Police recalls that of the Old Chinese Forces of the Green Standard (*see* No. 749). Each battalion is headed by a 參 將 Ts'an¹⁻ Chiang¹ (*see* No. 752ᴀ), as Commander, and to him there is attached a 游擊 Yu² Chi¹ (*see* No. 752ʙ), as his assistant. Commanding a detachment stationed at any place (for instance, at the 圓明園 Yüan² Ming² Yüan², or 暢春園 Ch'ang⁴ Ch'un¹ Yüan² ; *see* No. 90) is a 都 司 Tu¹ Ssu¹ (*see* No. 752ᴄ), or a 守備 Shou³ Pei⁴ (*see* No. 752ᴅ) ; commanding a 哨 Shao⁴ (*see* No. 749) is a 千總 Ch'ien¹ Tsung³ (*see* No. 752ᴇ) ; commanding a 司 Ssu¹ (*see* No. 749) is a 把 總 Pa² Tsung³ (*see* No. 752ꜰ).

801. 京師各門守禦千總 Ching¹ Shih¹ Ko⁴ Mên² Shou³ Yü⁴ Ch'ien¹ Tsung³, Gate Guards. At each of the gates (of which there are sixteen, *i.e.* nine in the Tartar, and seven in the Chinese City ; *see* No. 801ʙ) there are : 1. Two (one in the Chinese City) 城門領 Ch'êng² Mên² Ling³, Captains of the Gate ; 4ʙ, 2. Two 門千總 Mên² Ch'ien¹ Tsung³, Lieutenants of the Gate (more explicit, 守禦千總 Shou³ Yü⁴ Ch'ien¹ Tsung³, prefixed by the designation of the respective gate ; for instance, 正陽門守禦千總 Chêng⁴ Yang² Mên² Shou³ Yü⁴ Ch'ien¹ Tsung³) ; 6ᴀ, 3. Two (one in the Chinese City) 城 門 吏 Ch'êng² Mên² Li⁴, Clerks of the Gate ; 7ᴀ, and 4. 門軍 Mên² Chün¹, Gate Guards.

801ᴀ. Formerly, on the towers over each of the gates of Peking there were alarm guns and signal masts. From the latter flags were flown in the daytime and they bore a lantern at night. Should the public safety be threatened, the nearest alarm-signal gun (信 礮 Hsin⁴ P'ao⁴) was fired, the signal guns at the other

towers repeating the signal given, and the men of the 步軍營 **801B**
Pu⁴ Chün¹ Ying², immediately gathered at the places appointed
for each guard station. At present there are no signals from the
gates, nor are there any signal guns. Nevertheless, posts
appertaining to signalling from the gates—now sinecures—have
been retained, namely; 1. 信礮總管 Hsin⁴ P'ao⁴ Tsung³
Kuan³, Controller of Alarm-signal Guns; 4A, and 2. 監守信
礮官 Chien¹ Shou³ Hsin⁴ P'ao⁴ Kuan¹, Assistant Controller of
Alarm-signal Guns; 5A.

801B. As has been already stated (*see* No. 801), the city
of Peking has 16 gates, nine to the 內城 Nei⁴ Ch'êng², Inner
(Tartar) City (also styled 北城 Pei³ Ch'êng², Northern City) and
seven to the 外城 Wai⁴ Ch'êng², Outer (Chinese) City (also
styled 外羅城 Wai⁴ Lo² Ch'êng², Surrounding City, or 南城
Nan² Ch'êng², Southern City).

To the Tartar City there are three gates on the South—the
central one is the 正陽門 Chêng⁴ Yang² Mên² (colloquially,
前門 Ch'ien² Mên²), the Eastern is the 崇文門 Ch'ung² Wên²
Mên² (colloquially, 哈達門 Ha¹ Ta² Mên², or 海代門 Hai³
Tai⁴ Mên²), and the Western is the 宣武門 Hsüan¹ Wu³ Mên²
(colloquially, 順治門 Shun⁴ Chih⁴ Mên², in place of the
designation 順承門 Shun⁴ Ch'êng² Mên², used during the Yüan
Dynasty). On the North there are two gates—the one to the
East is called the 安定門 An¹ Ting⁴ Mên² (during the Yüan
Dynasty 安貞門 An¹ Chên¹ Mên²) and the one to the West is
the 德勝門 Tê² Shêng⁴ Mên² (during the Yüan Dynasty
健德門 Chien⁴ Tê² Mên²). On the East there are two gates—
the Southern is called the 朝陽門 Ch'ao² Yang² Mên²
(colloquially, 齊化門 Ch'i² Hua⁴ Mên²), and the Northern is
the 東直門 Tung¹ Chih² Mên². On the West there are two
gates—that to the South is the 阜城門 Fu⁴ Ch'êng² Mên²
(colloquially, 平則門 P'ing² Tsê² Mên²), and the one to the
North is the 西直門 Hsi¹ Chih² Mên².

[383]

802

To the Chinese City, on the South there are three gates—the central one is called the 永定門 Yung³ Ting⁴ Mên², that to the East is the 左安門 Tso³ An¹ Mên² (colloquially, 蹼礤門 or 江擦門 Chiang¹ Ts'a¹ Mên²) and that to the West is the 右安門 Yu⁴ An¹ Mên² (colloquially, 南西門 Nan² Hsi¹ Mên²). To the Chinese City, on the East there is the 廣渠門 Kuang³ Ch'ü¹ Mên² (colloquially, 沙窩門 Sha¹ Wo¹ Mên²), and, on the West, the 廣安門 Kuang³ An¹ Mên² (colloquially, 彰儀門 Chang¹ I² Mên²). At the North-eastern corner there is found the 東便門 Tung¹ Pien¹ Mên², and, at the North-western corner there is the 西便門 Hsi¹ Pien¹ Mên².

GOVERNMENT OF MANCHURIA.

802. The government of Manchuria, prior to 1907, was organized on a purely military basis and headed by 將軍 Chiang¹ Chün¹, Military Governors, who were assisted by 副都統 Fu⁴ Tu¹ T'ung³, Military Deputy Lieutenant-Governors. The former were the official heads of provinces and resided at the provincial capitals: Moukden (Chinese designation, 奉天 Fêng⁴ T'ien¹, or 盛京 Shêng⁴ Ching¹), Kirin (Chinese designation, 吉林 Chi¹ Lin²), and Tsitsihar (Chinese designation, 齊齊哈爾 Ch'i² Ch'i² Ha¹ Êrh³). The latter were in charge of Military Departments—called "Fu Tu Tungships"—of the provinces, of which there were: four in Fêng T'ien province (奉天 Fêng⁴ T'ien¹, 金州 Chin¹ Chou¹, 錦州 Chin³ Chou¹, and 興京 Hsing¹ Ching¹), six in Kirin province (吉林烏拉 Chi¹ Lin² Wu¹ La¹, 寧古塔 Ning² Ku³ Ta³, 伯都訥 Po² Tu¹ Na⁴, 三姓 San¹ Hsing⁴, 阿勒楚喀 A⁴ Lieh¹ Ch'u³ K'a¹, and 琿春 Hun¹ Ch'un¹), and five in Heilungchiang province (黑龍江 Hei¹ Lung² Chiang¹, or 愛琿 Ai⁴ Hun¹, 墨爾根 Mo⁴ Êrh³ Ken¹, 齊齊哈爾 Ch'i² Ch'i² Ha¹ Êrh³, 呼蘭 Hu¹ Lan², and 呼倫貝爾 Hu¹ Lun² Pei¹ Êrh³).

For the city of Moukden there was a civil administration, similar to that of Peking, headed by the 府尹 Fu³ Yin³ and 府丞 Fu³ Ch'êng², and including five Boards (Ministries), corresponding to the Boards of Revenue, of Ceremonies, of War, of Punishments and of Works at Peking.

Following a tour of Manchuria (in the winter of 1906) made by 徐世昌 Hsü² Shih⁴-ch'ang¹, President of the Ministry of the Interior, and 載振 Tsai³ Chên⁴, President of the Ministry of Commerce, and in consequence of a joint Memorial submitted by them with regard to the condition of affairs there, a change was effected in the system of government of that section of the Empire. By Imperial Decree of the 20th April, 1907, a general reform of the government of Manchuria was made, by which the 將軍 Chiang¹ Chün¹ were abolished and replaced by a Governor-General and three Governors. The officials appointed to these new posts were commanded to draw up a detailed scheme for the government of the Three Eastern Provinces.

In obedience to the Imperial commands of the Decree mentioned above, Hsü Shih-ch'ang, at the beginning of May, 1907, submitted a Memorial (which received Imperial sanction) containing the scheme called for, and providing for a system of government which, with few exceptions (see a Memorial from Hsi Liang, dated the 7th August, 1909), has been in operation since that time.

The main idea of the administrative reforms proposed by Hsü Shih-ch'ang in his Memorial, as well as that gradually being attained by the Central Government since 1876, has been, on the one hand, the bringing of the system of government into harmony with that of the rest of China, *i.e.* the abolition of the posts of Military Deputy Lieutenant-Governors (Fu Tu T'ung) and their replacement by those of Taotais, Prefects, Department Magistrates and District Magistrates, and, on the other, the introduction, as an experimental trial, of the system of

803 to 805 provincial government which was framed by the Committee of Constitutional Reforms in 1906 and which will eventually be introduced throughout the Empire.

During the three years since the promulgation of the Imperial Edict of the 20th April, 1907, many reforms have been attained in Manchuria. Almost everywhere (Moukden and Hsing Ching excepted) the posts of Fu Tu T'ung have been abolished and in their place are found those of Taotais. Many new administrative divisions, especially in the provinces of Kirin and Heilungchiang, have been made, and many posts and government establishments, proved worthless by experience, have been discarded (for details *see* below).

803. 東三省總督 Tung¹ San¹ Shêng³ Tsung³ Tu¹, Governor-General of the Three Eastern Provinces. This official is the administrative head of the government of Manchuria and has his residence at Moukden (later he will transfer his official residence to the prefectural city of Ch'ang Ch'un). As regards the Banner Forces, he ranks as Chiang Chün, this title being accorded to his position (compare Nos. 744 and 820).

804. 巡撫 Hsün² Fu³, Governor; one for each province. With reference to the Banner Forces this official has the authority of a 副都統 Fu⁴ Tu¹ T'ung³, Manchu Brigadier-General (compare Nos. 745, 745F and 821).

Governors reside at the provincial capitals, *i.e.* Moukden, Kirin, and Tsitsihar (there is a project to abolish the governorship at Moukden and to transfer the residence of the Kirin Governor to Ninguta and that of the Heilungchiang Governor to Aihun).

805 左右參贊 Tso³ Yu⁴ Ts'an¹ Tsan⁴, Senior and Junior Councillors (attached to the Governor-General). These officials superintended : the first, the Chancery, and the second, the Council at the Governor-General's Yamen.

承宣廳 Ch'êng² Hsüan¹ T'ing¹, Chancery. Here were considered : the most important and most confidential affairs of the three provinces, reports to the Governor-General and to the Governors, and the selection, appointment and transfer of officials of lower than the fourth rank. It was arranged in a number of 科 K'o[1], Sections. At the head of the 首科 Shou[3] K'o[1], First Section, there was a 僉事 Ch'ien[1] Shih[4], Chief Secretary ; 4B, while at the head of the other Sections there were 僉事 Ch'ien[1] Shih[4], Secretaries (5A ; one for each). Also, there was a definite number of 一等科員 I[1] Têng[3] K'o[1] Yüan[2], Assistant Secretaries of the first rank ; 5B, 二等科員 Êrh[4] Têng[3] K'o[1] Yüan[2], Assistant Secretaries of the second rank ; 6A, and 三等科員 San[1] Têng[3] K'o[1] Yüan[2], Assistant Secretaries of the third rank ; 7A.

諮議廳 Tzu[1] I[4] T'ing[1], Council (compare No. 823). This was in charge of the examination and discussion of local legislation, regulations and rules. It consisted of two 科 K'o[1], Sections, headed by 僉事 Ch'ien[1] Shih[4], Secretaries ; 4B. Its membership was made up of specially appointed officials and well known citizens styled 議員 I[4] Yüan[2], Members of the Council, 副議員 Fu[4] I[4] Yüan[2], Assistant Members of the Council, 額外議員 Ê[2] Wai[4] I[4] Yüan[2], Supernumerary Members of the Council, and 顧問官 Ku[4] Wên[4] Kuan[1], Advisers.

In the Summer of 1909 the posts of Senior and Junior Councillor were abolished, and the Chancery and Council were reorganized. For managing the correspondence of the Governor-General a Chancery of the general type, headed by a 秘書員 Pi[4] Shu[1] Yüan[2], was instituted at the same time (compare No. 822).

805A. 巡防營務處 Hsün[2] Fang[2] Ying[2] Wu[4] Ch'u[4], Staff of the Reserve Force Divisions (forces of the category of 巡防隊 Hsün[2] Fang[2] Tui[4]; see No. 706); found in each province. This was developed from the former 營務處 Ying[2] Wu[4] Ch'u[4] (Military Secretariat of the Governor-General and Governors; see No. 824) and is in charge of the reorganization

806 to 806A

of the old troops (*see* a Memorial from Hsü Shih-ch'ang, dated the 13th January, 1908 ; compare No. 706).

At the head of the Staff there is a 總辦 Tsung³ Pan⁴, Chief of Staff, who is assisted by two Assistants—幇辦 Pang¹ Pan⁴, and 會辦 Hui⁴ Pan⁴.

For carrying on the affairs of the Staff there are four 股 Ku³, Sections: 1. 文牘股 Wên² Tu³ Ku³, Section of Correspondence, 2. 會計股 Hui¹ (K'uai⁴) Chi⁴ Ku³, Accounts Section, 3. 緝操股 Chi⁴ Ts'ao¹ Ku³, Instruction Section, and 4. 考察股 K'ao³ Ch'a² Ku³, Inspection Section. Each Section is in charge of a 文案總理 Wên² An⁴ Tsung³ Li³, Chief Secretary.

To the Staff there are attached : 1. 執事官 Chih² Shih⁴ Kuan¹, Adjutant (one), 2. 委員 Wei³ Yüan², Orderly Officers, and 3. 稽察委員 Chi² Ch'a² Wei³ Yüan², Revisers.

In the province of Fengtien, in addition to the above-mentioned, to the Staff there is attached a 水師巡船管帶官 Shui³ Shih¹ Hsün² Ch'uan² Kuan³ Tai⁴ Kuan¹, Chief of the River Police (along the Liao river). His permanent residence is at 通江子 T'ung¹ Chiang¹ Tzu³ (also 通江口 T'ung¹ Chiang¹ K'ou³).

806. 交涉司 Chiao¹ Shê⁴ Ssu¹, Bureau of Foreign Affairs; headed by a 交涉司使 Chiao¹ Shê⁴ Ssu¹ Shih³, Commissioner for Foreign Affairs (3A ; compare No. 832). This Bureau has been established in the provinces of Fengtien and Kirin for dealing with affairs concerning foreigners. To these Bureaux there are attached 一等譯官 I¹ Têng³ I⁴ Kuan¹, Interpreters of the first rank, and 二等譯官 Êrh⁴ Têng³ I⁴ Kuan¹, Interpreters of the second rank.

806A. 交涉總局 Chiao¹ Shê⁴ Tsung³ Chü², Head Office cf Foreign Affairs ; established at Tsitsihar and takes the place cf a Bureau of Foreign Affairs (compare No. 806) for the

province of Heilungchiang. At the head of this Office there is
a 總辦 Tsung³ Pan⁴, Chief.

806B. 黑龍江省鐵路交涉總局 Hei¹ Lung² Chiang¹
Shêng³ T'ieh³ Lu⁴ Chiao¹ Shê⁴ Tsung³ Chü², Head Office of
Railway Foreign Affairs of Heilungchiang Province, and 吉林
省鐵路交涉總局 Chi¹ Lin² Shêng³ T'ieh³ Lu⁴ Chiao¹ Shê⁴
Tsung³ Chü², Head Office of Railway Foreign Affairs of Kirin
Province. These were established in 1899 (reorganized in 1901)
at Harbin for the management of all affairs of the railway zone,
in which Chinese are concerned.

To supplement the work of the Head Offices of Railway
Foreign Affairs there are, along the Chinese Eastern Railway,
a number of 鐵路交涉分局 T'ieh³ Lu⁴ Chiao¹ Shê⁴ Fên¹
Chü², Branch Offices of Railway Foreign Affairs—at the
stations, 滿洲里 Man³ Chou¹ Li³ (Manchuria), 海拉爾 Hai³
La¹ Êrh³ (Hailar), 昂昂溪 Ang² Ang² Ch'i¹ (Tsitsihar), 博河
多 Po² Ho² To¹ (Puhotu), 札蘭屯 Cha² Lan² T'un², etc.

806c. 交涉局 Chiao¹ Shê⁴ Chü², Offices of Foreign
Affairs (compare No. 832); established at the Yamen of Taotais
and Prefects, of cities where foreign Consuls are in residence,
for the settlement of questions between foreigners and Chinese.

807. 民政司 Min² Chêng⁴ Ssu¹, Bureau of Civil or
Internal Affairs. This is under the direction of 民政司使
Min² Chêng⁴ Ssu¹ Shih³, Commissioner of Civil Affairs; 2B.
The main object of its establishment is the superintendency
of police affairs of Manchuria (compare Nos. 814 and 840).

At the Bureau of Civil Affairs there are found 一等醫官
I¹ Têng³ I¹ Kuan¹, Physicians of the first rank; 6A, and
二等醫官 Êrh⁴ Têng³ I¹ Kuan¹, Physicians of the second
rank; 7A.

In Heilungchiang province the post of Commissioner of
Finance (*see* No. 808) has been abolished (in the Summer of 1909)
and his duties handed over to the Commissioner of Civil Affairs.

806B
to
807

808
to
811

808. 度支司 Tu⁴ Chih¹ Ssu¹, Bureau of Finance; headed by a 度支司使 Tu⁴ Chih¹ Ssu¹ Shih³, Commissioner of Finance; 3B. This is found in the provinces of Fengtien and Kirin (the post of Commissioner of Finance, formerly existing, for the province of Heilungchiang, was abolished in the Summer of 1909 and the duties appertaining to it were transferred to the Commissioner of Civil Affairs; compare No. 807) for the superintendency of financial affairs, the collection of taxes, etc. At the Bureau there are stationed 一等庫官 I¹ Têng³ K'u⁴, Kuan¹, Treasurers of the first rank; 6A, and 二等庫官 Êrh⁴ Têng³ K'u⁴ Kuan¹, Treasurers of the second rank; 7A.

809. 提學司 T'i² Hsüeh² Ssu¹, Bureau of Education; supervised by a 提學司使 T'i² Hsüeh² Ssu¹ Shih³, Commissioner of Education; 3A (compare Nos. 827 to 828A); established in each of the three provinces of Manchuria for the superintendence of educational affairs. At this Bureau there are found: 1. 一等譯官 I¹ Têng³ I⁴ Kuan¹, Interpreters of the first rank; 6A, and 二等譯官 Êrh⁴ Têng³ I⁴ Kuan¹, Interpreters of the second rank (compare No. 806), and 2. 一等編校官 I¹ Têng³ Pien¹ Hsiao⁴ Kuan¹, Revisers of the first rank, and 二等編校官 Êrh⁴ Têng³ Pien¹ Hsiao⁴ Kuan¹, Revisers of the second rank.

810. 提法司 T'i² Fa⁴ Ssu¹, Bureau of Judicial Affairs; directed by a 提法司使 T'i² Fa⁴ Ssu¹ Shih³, Commissioner of Judicial Affairs (3A; see No. 831B); established in all the provinces for the administration of judicial affairs.

811. 旗務司 Ch'i² Wu⁴ Ssu¹, Bureau of Banner Affairs; directed by a 旗務司使 Ch'i² Wu⁴ Ssu¹ Shih³, Commissioner of Banner Affairs; 3A. This Bureau was founded for Fengtien province alone, for the superintendency of the affairs of Manchu Bannermen. In the Summer of 1909 it was abolished and replaced by the:

811A. 旗務處 Ch'i² Wu⁴ Ch'u⁴, Department of Banner Affairs; headed by a 總理 Tsung³ Li³, Chief Controller, a 協理 Hsieh² Li³, Controller, and a 幫辦 Pang¹. Pan⁴, Assistant Controller.

811A
to
812A

In 1908 similar Departments were established for the provinces of Kirin and Heilungchiang.

The Department of Banner Affairs of Heilungchiang consists of three 科 K'o¹, Sections: 1. 軍事科 Chün¹ Shih⁴ K'o¹, Section of Military Affairs, 2. 民事科 Min² Shih⁴ K'o¹, Section of Civil Affairs, and 3. 庶務科 Shu⁴ Wu⁴ K'o¹, Section of General Affairs. At the head of these Sections there are 科長 K'o¹ Chang³, Section Chiefs, who are assisted by 副科長 Fu⁴ K'o¹ Chang³, Assistants.

812. 蒙務司 Mêng³ Wu⁴ Ssu¹, Bureau of Mongolian Affairs; directed by a 蒙務司使 Mêng³ Wu⁴ Ssu¹ Shih³. Commissioner of Mongolian Affairs; 3B. This was projected for establishment in Fengtien province for the supervision of the affairs of the ten Mongolian Banners of the Cherim league appertaining to that province (*see* Nos. 886 and 892). Its proposed staff included 一等譯官 I¹ Têng³ I⁴ Kuan¹, Interpreters of the first rank; 6A, and 二等譯官 Êrh⁴ Têng³ I⁴ Kuan¹, Interpreters of the second rank; 7A (compare Nos. 806 and 809).

In the Summer of 1909 the post of Commissioner of Mongolian Affairs was definitely abolished and the duties appertaining to it vested in the:

812A. 蒙務總局 Mêng³ Wu⁴ Tsung³ Chü², Head Office of Mongolian Affairs. In charge of this office is a 總辦 Tsung³ Pan⁴, Chief, to whom there are subordinated a 提調 T'i² Tiao⁴, Proctor, and a number of 參謀官 Ts'an¹ Mou² Kuan¹, Councillors (the number is indefinite). Formerly, at the head of the Head Office of Mongolian Affairs there was a 督辦 Tu¹ Pan⁴,

Superintendent, but, with a view to economy, this post was abolished.

The Head Office of Mongolian Affairs is divided into four 科 K‘o¹, Sections: 1. 文牘科 Wên² Tu³ K‘o¹, Section of Correspondence, 2. 會計科 Hui⁴ Chi⁴ K‘o¹, Accounts Section, 3. 儲備科 Ch‘u³ Pei⁴ K‘o¹, Section of Economy, and 4. 工築科 Kung¹ Chu⁴ K‘o¹, Construction Section. Each of these is headed by a 科長 K‘o¹ Chang⁸, Section Chief, to whom there are attached 委員 Wei³ Yüan², Deputies of the first, second and third ranks (等 Têng³), and from two to four 司事 Ssu¹ Shih⁴, Clerks (in the Section of Correspondence styled 司書 Ssu¹ Shu¹). Also, at the Section of Correspondence, there are 繙譯 Fan¹ I⁴, Interpreters (in an indefinite number) and, at the Construction Section are found 測繪生 Ts‘ê⁴ Hui⁴ Shêng¹, Surveyors.

For the judicial examination of questions between Mongols, at the Head Office of Mongolian Affairs there has been organized a 發審局 Fa¹ Shên³ Ch‘u⁴, Judicial Department, administered by a 正審官 Chêng⁴ Shên³ Kuan¹, Judge, two 陪審官 P‘ei² Shên³ Kuan¹, Assessors, two 通譯 T‘ung¹ I⁴, Interpreters, and three 司書 Ssu¹ Shu¹, Clerks.

At the Head Office of Mongolian Affairs there is a 護衞馬隊 Hu⁴ Wei⁴ Ma³ Tui⁴, Cavalry Escort, made up of a 管帶 Kuan³ Tai⁴, Escort Chief, three 哨官 Shao⁴ Kuan¹, Junior Officers, 12 什長 Shih² Chang³, Sergeants, 108 正兵 Chêng⁴ Ping¹, Privates, one 書記長 Shu¹ Chi⁴ Chang³, Clerks, four 司書生 Ssu¹ Shu¹ Shêng¹, Writers, one 鼓號目 Ku³ Hao⁴ Mu⁴, Senior Signalman, six 鼓號兵 Ku³ Hao⁴ Ping¹, Signalmen, ten 護兵 Hu⁴ Ping¹, Guards, and 12 伙夫 Huo³ Fu¹, Cooks—in all, 158 men and 131 horses.

The Head Office of Mongolian Affairs is at Moukden (*see* No. 901), and there are Branch Offices (分局 Fên¹ Chü²), in other places (for instance, at 洮南府 T‘ao² Nan² Fu³).

812B. 吉 林 蒙 務 處 Chi¹ Lin² Mêng³ Wu⁴ Ch'u⁴, Bureau of Mongolian Affairs in Kirin Province; founded in 1908 and headed by a 總 理 Tsung³ Li³, Superintendent.

813. 勸 業 司 Ch'üan⁴ Yeh⁴ Ssu¹, Bureaux of Industry; headed by 勸 業 司 使 Ch'üan⁴ Yeh⁴ Ssu¹ Shih³, Commissioners of Industrial Affairs; 3B, with a staff including 一 等 藝 士 I¹ Têng³ I⁴ Shih⁴, Engineers of the first rank; 6A, and 二 等 藝 士 Êrh⁴ Têng³ I⁴ Shih⁴, Engineers of the second rank; 7A.

The projected establishment of Bureaux of Industrial Affairs was not carried out, their place being taken by:

813A. 勸 業 道 Ch'üan⁴ Yeh⁴ Tao⁴, Industrial Taotais; 4A (compare Nos. 839 to 839B); up to now found only in the provinces of Fengtien and Kirin.

814. 巡 警 道 Hsün² Ching³ Tao⁴, Police Taotai; 4A (compare Nos. 840 to 840B). This post was established for the province of Fengtien alone and, later—in the Summer of 1909— it was abolished and the duties appertaining to the Police Taotai were invested in the Commissioner of Civil Affairs (compare No. 807).

815. At each of the Bureaux under the administration of 司 使 Ssu¹ Shih³, Commissioners, or 道 Tao⁴, Taotais, there is one 僉 事 Ch'ien¹ Shih⁴, Secretary; 4B or 5A. Each Bureau consists of 科 K'o¹, Sections, under the management of 科 長 K'o¹ Chang³, Section Chiefs, who have attached to them a number of 科 員 K'o¹ Yüan², Secretaries.

816. 分 巡 兵 備 道 Fên¹ Hsün² Ping¹ Pei⁴ Tao⁴, Military-Administrative Taotais; 4A (compare No. 844). There are 11 Taotais of this category in Manchuria: four in the province of Fengtien (residing at Yingkow, Antung, Liao Yüan Chou and Lin Chiang Hsien), four in the province of Kirin (at Ch'ang Ch'un, Hun Ch'un, San Hsing and Harbin) and three in Heilungchiang province (at T'o Lo Shan Pei, Aihun and Hurunpir, or Hailar).

812₴
to
816

816A. 兵備道衙門 Ping¹ Pei⁴ Tao⁴ Ya² Mên², Office of the Military-Administrative Taotai (compare No. 844c); divided into 科 K'o¹, Sections, the number of which varies in different localities, for instance, at the Office of the Taotai at Ch'ang Ch'un (see No. 816) there are four Sections: 1. 總務科 Tsung³ Wu⁴ K'o¹, Section of General Affairs, 2. 內政科 Nei⁴ Chêng⁴ K'o¹, Section of Civil (Internal) Affairs, 3. 外交科 Wai⁴ Chiao⁴ K'o¹, Section of Outer (Diplomatic) Relations, and 4. 收發處 Shou¹ Fa¹ Ch'u⁴, Registry. At other places there are the following Sections: 邊務科 Pien¹ Wu⁴ K'o¹, Section of Frontier Affairs, 墾務科 K'en³ Wu⁴ K'o¹, Section of Colonization Affairs, etc.

817. 督辦吉林邊務大臣 Tu¹ Pan⁴ Chi¹ Lin² Pien¹ Wu⁴ Ta⁴ Ch'ên² and 幫辦延吉邊務大臣 Pang¹ Pan⁴ Yen² Chi² Pien¹ Wu⁴ Ta⁴ Ch'ên², Frontier Commissioner of Kirin Province and Assistant Frontier Commissioner residing at Yenchi (in Kirin province). Both these posts were established because of the dispute which cropped up in 1907 between Japan and China as to the sovereignty of the district about Chientao. The Frontier Commissioner, having military and civil authority in his guardianship of the borders of Kirin province, is subordinated to the Governor-General of Manchuria but, at the same time, has the privilege of direct reports to the Emperor (compare No. 845A).

818. 東三省督辦鹽務大臣 Tung¹ San¹ Shêng³ Tu¹ Pan⁴ Yen² Wu⁴ Ta⁴ Ch'ên², Controller-General of the Salt Gabelle of the Three Eastern Provinces; residing at Moukden. This Official is in charge of the 鹽務總局 Yen² Wu⁴ Tsung³ Chü², Head Office of Salt Affairs, to which there are subordinated: 1. 官運總局 Kuan¹ Yün⁴ Tsung³ Chü², Head Offices of Salt Transport (one for each province), and 2. 鹽務分局 Yen² Wu⁴ Fên¹ Chü², Branch Offices of Salt Affairs (found at most of the large commercial centres).

Administering each Head Office of Salt Transport is a 督 辦 Tu¹ Pan⁴, Director, to whom there are subordinated a number of 提 調 T'i² Tiao⁴, Proctors, and other officials.

At Yingkow there is a 官 鹽 採 運 局 Kuan¹ Yen² Ts'ai³ Yün⁴ Chü², Government Agency of Salt Transport.

For the prevention of the illegal transport of salt, at Ch'ang Ch'un and other places, there are established 緝 私 總 局 Chi⁴ Ssu¹ Tsung³ Chü², Head Offices for the Prevention of Salt Smuggling, with a corps of guards—mounted and foot.

儲 鹽 倉 Ch'u³ Yen² Ts'ang¹, Salt Stores. These are found at the principal cities of Manchuria and are divided into 總 倉 Tsung³ Ts'ang¹, Head Stores (for instance, at Ch'ang Ch'un), and 分 倉 Fên¹ Ts'ang¹, Branch Stores (for the organization of salt affairs in other provinces *see* Nos. 835 to 835c and 841).

PROVINCIAL ADMINISTRATION.

A. Higher Administration :

819. 二 十 二 行 省 Êrh⁴ Shih² Êrh⁴ Hsing² Shêng³, The Twenty Two Provinces, namely: 1. 直 隸 Chih² Li⁴ (literary designation, 燕 雲 Yen¹ Yün², and 京 畿 Ching¹ Chi¹), 2. 江 蘇 Chiang¹ Su¹ (literary designation, 吳 Wu²), 3. 安 徽 An¹ Hui¹ (literary designation, 皖 Wan³, or Huan³), 4. 江 西 Chiang¹ Si¹ (literary designation, 豫 章 Yü⁴ Chang¹), 5. 山 東 Shan¹ Tung¹ (literary designation, 山 左 Shan¹ Tso³, 東 Tung¹), 6. 山 西 Shan¹ Si¹ (literary designation, 山 右 Shan¹ Yu⁴, 晉 Chin⁴), 7. 河 南 Ho² Nan² (literary designation, 豫 Yü⁴), 8. 陝 西 Shên³ Si¹ (literary designation, 關 中 Kuan¹ Chung¹, 秦 Ch'in², and 隴 Lung³), 9. 甘 肅 Kan¹ Su⁴, 10. 新 疆 Hsin¹ Chiang¹ (more complete 甘 肅 新 疆 省 Kan¹ Su⁴ Hsin¹ Chiang¹ Sheng³), 11. 福 建 Fu² Chien⁴ (literary designation, 閩 Min³), 12. 浙 江 Chê⁴ Chiang¹ (literary designation, 淛 Chê¹, or 越 Yüeh⁴), 13. 湖 北 Hu² Pei³ (literary designation, 楚 北 Ch'u³

819ᴀ Pei³, or 鄂 Ao⁴), 14. 湖南 Hu² Nan² (literary designation, 楚南 Ch'u³ Nan², or 湘 Hsiang¹), 15. 四川 Ssu⁴ Ch'uan¹ (literary designation, 蜀 Shu³), 16. 廣東 Kuang³ Tung¹ (literary designation, 粵東 Yüeh⁴ Tung¹), 17. 廣西 Kuang³ Si¹ (literary designation, 粵西 Yüeh⁴ Si¹), 18. 雲南 Yün² Nan² (literary designation, 滇 Tien¹), 19. 貴州 Kuei⁴ Chou¹ (literary designation, 黔 Ch'ien¹), 20. 奉天 Fêng⁴ T'ien¹ (shorter, 奉 Fêng⁴; literary designation, 盛京 Shêng⁴ Ching¹, 遼東 Liao² Tung³, or 關東 Kuan¹ Tung¹), 21. 吉林 Chi¹ Lin² (shorter, 吉 Chi¹), and 22. 黑龍江 Hei¹ Lung² Chiang¹ (shorter, 江 Chiang¹).

819ᴀ. The modern division of the Chinese Empire into 省 Shêng³, Provinces, dates from the time of the 元 Yüan², Dynasty (the 14th century) when, in addition to the departments of the Central Government, styled 中書省 Chung¹ Shu¹ Shêng³, thirteen Provincial Governorships were established, under the title of 中書行省 Chung¹ Shu¹ Hsing² Shêng³. The Ming Dynasty (1368 to 1644) inherited this system and, with some slight changes, retained it—the title of the Provincial Governors, in the first instance, was altered to 承宣布政使 Ch'êng² Hsüan¹ Pu⁴ Chêng⁴ Shih³, and, later, this was superseded by 巡撫 Hsün² Fu³, Provincial Governor (the present designation; see No. 821). Also, in the 16th century, the appointment of 總督 Tsung³ Tu¹, Governors-General (see No. 820), was commenced.

The fifteen provinces of the Ming Dynasty were: Shan¹ Tung¹, Shan¹ Si¹, Ho² Nan², Shên³ Si¹, Fu² Chien⁴, Chê¹ Chiang¹, Chiang¹ Si¹, Hu² Kuang³, Ssu⁴ Ch'uan¹, Kuang³ Tung¹, Kuang³ Si¹, Yün² Nan², Kuei⁴ Chou¹, 北直隸 Pei³ Chih² Li⁴ (Chih Li), and 江南 Chiang¹ Nan² (or 南直隸 Nan² Chih² Li⁴).

In the reign of K'ang Hi (1662–1722) the province of An Hui was formed from a portion of Kiang¹ Nan², the latter then becoming Chiang¹ Su¹; similarly, Kan¹ Su⁴ was formed by the partition of Shên³ Hsi¹, and Hu² Kuang³ was divided into two provinces which received the designations of Hu² Peh³ and Hu² Nan². At the same time the provinces were entitled 直省 Chih² Shêng³, a designation by which they are still generally recognized (compare above).

The province of Kan¹ Su⁴ Hsin¹ Chiang¹ was called into being by an Edict of the 17th November, 1884, absorbing Eastern Turkestan and the Departments of Hami, Pali K‘un and Urumtsi (later Ili and Tarbagatai) ; compare Nos. 862 to 867.

For the government of the three Manchurian provinces *see* No. 802.

For sub-divisions of the provinces, as regards administration, *see* No. 846.

819B. A reform of the system of provincial government, in the sense of enlarging, or more exactly defining, the scope of authority of the existing organs of local administration, as well as of new establishments, in connection with the gradual abolition of various posts recognized as not answering the purpose of their inauguration, has been going forward since 1906. Since their promulgation, all changes in the provincial government system have been, and will continue to be, made according to "regulations regarding the reform of the official system of the provinces" drawn up by a special committee (總核官制大臣 Tsung³ Ho² Kuan¹ Chih⁴ Ta⁴ Ch‘ên²), sanctioned by the Emperor on the 7th July, 1907. These regulations are referred to below in various instances.

820. 總督 Tsung³ Tu¹, Governor-General ; 1B, official designation, 制軍 Chih⁴ Chün¹; colloquially called 制臺 Chih⁴ T‘ai²; literary designation, 制憲 Chih⁴ Hsien⁴, 制府 Chih⁴ Fu³, 大總制 Ta⁴ Tsung³ Chih⁴, 大樞臺 Ta⁴ Shu¹-t‘ai² and 帥 Shuai⁴. Being, ex officio, invested with the title of President of the Ministry of War and being, also, ex officio, an Associate President of the Court of Censors (陸軍部尚書兼

都察院右都御使 Lu⁴ Chün¹ Pu⁴ Shang⁴ Shu¹ Chien¹ Tu¹ Ch'a² Yüan⁴ Yu⁴ Tu¹ Yü⁴ Shih³ ; *see* No. 207ʙ), he styles himself 部堂 Pu⁴ T'ang².

For the date of the establishment of the post of Governor-General *see* No. 819ᴀ.

To the Governor-General, within the territory under his jurisdiction, appertains the supreme control over civil affairs and the military forces, and he has the right of direct reports to the Throne.

820ᴀ. At present there are nine Governors-General : 1. 直隸總督 Chih² Li⁴ Tsung³ Tu¹, Governor-General of Chihli province, residing at 天津府 T'ien¹ Ching¹ Fu³, Tientsin, 2. 兩江總督 Liang³ Chiang¹ Tsung³ Tu¹, Governor-General of Kiangsu, Kiangsi and Anhui provinces, residing at 江寧府 Chiang¹ Ning² Fu³, Nanking, 3. 閩浙總督 Min⁵ Chê⁴ Tsung³ Tu¹, Governor-General of Fukien and Chekiang provinces, residing at 福州府 Fu² Chou¹ Fu³, Foochow, 4. 湖廣總督 Hu² Kuang³ Tsung³ Tu¹, Governor-General of Hupeh and Hunan provinces, residing at 武昌府 Wu³ Ch'ang¹ Fu³, Wuch'ang, 5. 陝甘總督 Shên³ Kan¹ Tsung³ Tu¹, Governor-General of Shensi, Kansu and Hsinchiang, residing at 蘭州府 Lan² Chou¹ Fu³, Lanchou, 6. 兩廣總督 Liang³ Kuang³ Tsung³ Tu¹, Governor-General of Kuangtung and Kuangsi provinces, residing at 廣州府 Kuang³ Chou¹ Fu³, Canton, 7. 四川總督 Ssu⁴ Ch'uan¹ Tsung³ Tu¹, Governor-General of Szechwan province, residing at 成都府 Ch'êng² Tu¹ Fu³, 8. 雲貴總督 Yün² Kuei⁴ Tsung³ Tu¹, Governor-General of Yünnan and Kueichow, residing at 雲南府 Yün² Nan² Fu³, and 9. The Governor-General of Manchuria (for particulars *see* No. 803).

820ʙ. 三口通商大臣 San¹ K'ou³ T'ung¹ Shang¹ Ta⁴ Ch'ên², Minister-Superintendent of Trade for the Three Ports (*i.e.* Tientsin, Chefoo and Newchwang). This post was

established in 1861 and existed until 1870, when the functions   **820c**
appertaining to it were handed over to the Governor-General of   **to**
Chihli who, therefore, now bears the title of 北洋大臣 Pei³   **820D**
Yang² Ta⁴ Ch'ên², Superintendent of Trade for the Northern
Ports. Similarly the Governor-General of the Liang Kiang
provinces is referred to as the 南洋大臣 Nan² Yang² Ta⁴
Ch'ên², Superintendent of Trade for the Southern Ports (compare
No. 476).

820c. 兼管巡撫事 Chien¹ Kuan³ Hsün² Fu³ Shih⁴,.
Associate Governor. This title is borne by the Governors-
General of Manchuria, Chihli, Minchê, Huhuang, Shenkan,.
Liang Kuang, Szechwan and Yün Kuei (*see* No. 820A), there
being no post of Governor in the provinces of Fengtien, Chihli,
Fukien, Hupeh, Kansu, Kuangtung, Szechwan and Yünnan
(*see* No. 821A).

820D. 河東河道總督 Ho² Tung¹ Ho² Tao⁴ Tsung³
Tu¹, Director-General of the Conservation of the Yellow River
and the Grand Canal; 2A; ordinary designation, 河道總督
Ho² Tao⁴ Tsung³ Tu¹, and 河督 Ho² Tu¹; literary designation,
都水監 Tu¹ Shui³ Chien¹, and 大督河 Ta⁴ Tu¹ Ho². 河東
Ho² Tung¹ is an abbreviation of the names of the two provinces
of Honan and Shantung.

The duties of the Director-General consist in the
superintendency over the embankment of the 黃河 Huang² Ho²,
Yellow River, and the maintenance of the sluices along the 運河
Yün⁴ Ho², Grand or Imperial Canal.

The Yellow River, and the Grand Canal as well are divided
into three Sections : 1. 南河 Nan² Ho², Southern River (that
part in the province of Kiangsu), 2. 東河 Tung¹ Ho², Eastern
River (that portion in the provinces of Shantung and Honan),
and 3. 北河 Pei³ Ho², Northern River (that portion in the
province of Chihli). Following this division there were formerly
three officials called 河督 Ho² Tu¹ : 1. One in charge of the

821
to
821ᴀ

南 河 Nan² Ho², residing at 清 江 浦 Ch'ing¹ Chiang¹ P'u³ (in the prefecture of 淮安府 Huai² An¹ Fu³, of Kiangsu province), whose duties were transferred to the Liang Kiang Governor-General, 2. One in charge of the 東 河 Tung¹ Ho², residing at 濟 寗 州 Chi⁴ Ning² Chou¹, Shantung province, whose duties were handed over (in February, 1902), to. the Governors of Honan and Shantung, the latter, accordingly, being styled 兼理河道 Kuan³ Li³ Ho² Tao⁴, 兼管河道 Chien¹ Kuan³ Ho² Tao⁴, or 兼河工事務 Chien¹ Ho² Kung¹ Shih⁴ Wu⁴, and 3. One in charge of the 北 河 Pei³ Ho², whose duties are now performed by the Governor-General of Chihli.

For particulars as to the military division under the orders of the Director-General (as 兵 部 侍 郞 Ping¹ Pu⁴ Shih⁴ Lang², Vice-President of the Ministry of War), designated the 河標 Ho² Piao¹, *see* No. 749.

821. 巡 撫 Hsün² Fu³, Governor ; 2ʙ ; official designation, 撫院 Fu³ Yüan⁴, colloquially called, 撫臺 Fu³ T'ai², epistolary style, 中 丞 Chung¹ Ch'êng², and 大 中 丞 Ta⁴ Chung¹ Ch'êng² ; literary designation, 撫軍 Fu³ Chün¹, 撫憲 Fu³ Hsien⁴, and 帥 Shuai⁴. This official, ex officio, bears the titles of 陸 軍 部 侍 郞 Lu⁴ Chün¹ Pu⁴ Shih⁴ Lang², Vice-President of the Ministry of War, and 都 察 院 副 都 御 史 Tu¹ Ch'a² Yüan⁴ Fu⁴ Tu¹ Yü⁴ Shih³, Vice-President of the Censorate (*see* No. 209), and, accordingly, styles himself 部院 Pu⁴ Yüan⁴. For the date of origin of the post of Governor *see* No. 819ᴀ.

The Governor, within the territory under his jurisdiction, enjoys the same power and authority as the Governor-General (*see* No. 820), *i.e.* to him appertains the highest control over all sections of the provincial administration.

821ᴀ. There are now fourteen Governors : 1. 江蘇巡撫 Chiang¹ Su¹ Hsün² Fu³, Governor of Kiangsu province, residing at 蘇州府 Su¹ Chou¹ Fu³, Soochow, 2. 安徽巡撫 An¹ Hui¹ Hsün² Fu³, Governor of Anhui province, residing at 安慶府

An¹ Ch'ing⁴ Fu³, Anking, 3. 江西巡撫 Ching¹ Hsi¹ Hsün² Fu³, Governor of Kiangsi province, residing at 南昌府 Nan² Ch'ang¹ Fu³, Nanch'ang, 4. 浙江巡撫 Chê⁴ Chiang¹ Hsün² Fu³, Governor of Chekiang province, residing at 杭州府 Hang² Chou¹ Fu³, Hangchow, 5. 湖南巡撫 Hu² Nan² Hsün² Fu³, Governor of Hunan province, residing at 長沙府 Ch'ang² Sha¹ Fu³, Changsha, 6. 河南巡撫 Ho² Nan² Hsün² Fu³, Governor of Honan province, residing at 開封府 K'ai¹ Fêng¹ Fu³, 7. 山東巡撫 Shan¹ Tung¹ Chün² Fu³, Governor of Shantung province, residing at 濟南府 Chi⁴ Nan² Fu³, 8. 陝西巡撫 Shên³ Hsi¹ Hsün² Fu², Governor of Shensi province, residing at 西安府 Hsi¹ An¹ Fu³, 9. 山西巡撫 Shan¹ Hsi¹ Hsün² Fu³, Governor of Shansi province, residing at 太原府 T'ai⁴ Yüan² Fu³, 10. 新疆巡撫 Hsin¹ Chiang¹ Hsün² Fu³, Governor of Hsinchiang province, residing at 迪化府 Ti¹ Hua⁴ Fu³, Urumtsi, 11. 廣西巡撫 Kuang³ Hsi¹ Hsün² Fu³, Governor of Kuangsi province, residing at 桂林府 Kuei¹ Lin² Fu³, 12 貴州巡撫 Kuei⁴ Chou¹ Hsün² Fu³, Governor of Kueichow province, residing at 貴陽府 Kuei⁴ Yang² Fu³, 13. 吉林巡撫 Chi¹ Lin² Hsün² Fu³, Governor of Kirin province, residing at 吉林府 Chi¹ Lin² Fu³, Kirin, and 14. 黑龍江巡撫 Hei¹ Lung² Chiang¹ Hsün² Fu³, Governor of Heilungchiang province, residing at 齊齊哈爾 Ch'i² Ch'i² Ha¹ Êrh³, Tsitsihar (see No. 804).

The Governors of the provinces of Kiangsu, Anhui, Kiangsi, Chekiang, Hunan, Shensi, Hsinchiang, Kuangsi, Kueichow, Kirin and Heilungchiang are, to some extent, subordinated to the respective Governors-General (i.e. of Liang Kiang, Minchê Hukuang, Shenkan, Liang Kuang, Yün Kuei and Manchuria; see No. 820A), for instance, the more important reports from these Governors, to the Throne, must pass through the hands of the Governor-General concerned and the latter presents them as joint Memorials, 會奏 Hui⁴ Tsou⁴, from himself and the Governor.

822

The Governors of Shansi, Shantung and Honan govern their respective provinces quite independently.

In the provinces of Fengtien, Chihli, Fukien, Hupeh, Kansu, Kuangtung, Szechwan and Yünnan, provinces in which the post of Governor is not found, the respective Governors-General (namely, of Manchuria, Chihli, Minchê, Hukuang, Shenkan, Liang Kuang, Szechwan and Yün Kuei), perform duties appertaining to a Governor and, in virtue of this, bear the title of 兼管巡撫事 Chien¹ Kuan³ Hsün² Fu³ Shih⁴, Associate Governor (see No. 820c).

The Governor-General and Governor are jointly spoken of as 督撫 Tu¹ Fu³, or 兩院 Liang³ Yüan⁴.

822. 督撫衙門幕職 Tu¹ Fu³ Ya² Mên² Mu⁴ Chih², Chancery of the Governor-General (or Governor); directed by one (or two) 秘書員 Pi⁴ Shu¹ Yüan², Chief Secretaries, who superintend the more confidential affairs and the correspondence. The Chancery (compare also No. 805) is composed of 10 Sections : 1. 交涉科 Chiao¹ Shê⁴ K'o¹, Section of Foreign Affairs, 2. 吏科 Li⁴ K'o¹, Section of Personnel, 3. 民科 Min² K'o¹ (also 民政科 Min¹ Chêng⁴ K'o¹), Section of Civil Affairs, 4. 度支科 Tu⁴ Chih¹ K'o¹, Section of Finance, 5. 禮科 Li³ K'o¹, Section of Ceremonies, 6. 學科 Hsüeh² K'o¹, Section of Education, 7. 軍政科 Chün¹ Chêng¹ K'o¹ (in the province of Szechwan, 陸軍科 Lu⁴ Chün¹ K'o¹), Section of Military Affairs, 8. 法科 Fa⁴ K'o¹, Judicial Section, 9. 農工商科 Nung² Kung¹ Shang¹ K'o¹, Section of Agriculture, Industry and Commerce, and 10. 郵傳科 Yu² Ch'uan² K'o¹, Section of Posts and Communications (in Szechwan there is, in addition, a 邊藏科 Pien¹ Tsang⁴ K'o¹, Section of Tibetan Frontier Affairs ; at Moukden, a 旗務科 Ch'i² Wu⁴ K'o¹, Section of Banner Affairs, and a 邊務科 Pien¹ Wu⁴ K'o¹, Section of Frontier Affairs ; and at Tsitsihar, a 旗蒙科 Ch'i² Mêng³ K'o¹, Section

of Banner and Mongolian Affairs, and a 邊務科 Pien¹ Wu⁴ **822ᴀ**
K'o¹, Section of Frontier Affairs).

At the head of one, or more, Sections (not more than
three) there is a 參事員 Ts'an¹ Shih⁴ Yüan², Secretary,
to whom there are attached an indefinite number of 助理員
Chu⁴ Li³ Yüan² (in Kuangtung province, 副員 Fu⁴
Yüan²), Assistants, and 繕寫員 Shan⁴ Hsieh³ Yüan², Clerks (in
Szechwan province called 書記官 Shu¹ Chi⁴ Kuan¹, of the first,
second and third ranks; replacing the former 繕摺 Shan⁴ Chê²,
Writers of Memorials, 譯電 I⁴ Tien⁴, Clerks in charge of
Ciphering of Telegrams, and 繕校 Shan⁴ Hsiao⁴, Writers). In
Szechwan province, in addition to the officials mentioned, there
are two 收發員 Shou¹ Fa¹ Yüan², Registrars, and 書識 Shu¹
Shih⁴, Writers.

Prior to the reform, foreshadowed by articles Nos. 4 and 5
of the "regulations regarding the reform of the official system
of the provinces" (compare No. 819ʙ), attached to the
Governor-General or Governor were officials of the following
ranks: 1. 洋務文案 Yang² Wu⁴ Wên² An⁴, Secretary of
Foreign Affairs, 2. 刑名 Hsing² Ming², Secretary for Judicial
Affairs, 3. 錢穀 Ch'ien² Ku³, Secretary of Finances and
Supplies, 4. 學務文案 Hsüeh² Wu⁴ Wên² An⁴, Secretary for
Educational Affairs, and 5. 營務刑名 Ying² Wu Hsing²
Ming², Secretary for Military Affairs.

822ᴀ. 憲政籌備處 Hsien⁴ Chêng⁴ Ch'ou² Pei⁴ Ch'u⁴,
Bureaux of Constitutional Reforms; established, in accordance
with a Memorial from the Committee for Drawing up
Regulations for Constitutional Government, sanctioned by the
Emperor on the 30th January, 1910, at the Chanceries of the
various Governors-General and Governors (*see* No. 822). Their
object is the same as that of the 憲政籌備處 Hsien⁴ Chêng⁴
Ch'ou² Pei⁴ Ch'u⁴, Bureaux of Constitutional Reforms, instituted
at the Ministries and principal Government Establishments (*see*

Supplement, No. 160), *i.e.* to arrange for the timely carrying out of the proposed constitutional reforms in the provinces concerned, and to present, twice a year, reports regarding the activity in regard to these reforms to the 考核專科 K'ao³ Ho² Chuan¹ K'o¹, Investigation Bureau of the Committee for Drawing up Regulations for Constitutional Government (*see* No. 160).

On the establishment of the Bureaux of Constitutional Reforms, other institutions, having the same object, but differently designated, were abolished, for instance, the 籌備憲政督催處 Ch'ou² Pei⁴ Hsien⁴ Chêng⁴ Tu¹ Ts'ui¹ Ch'u⁴, of Szechwan province, the 憲政籌備考覈處 Hsien⁴ Chêng⁴ Ch'ou² Pei⁴ K'ao³ Ho² Ch'u⁴, of Manchuria, the 籌備憲政考核處 Ch'ou² Pei⁴ Hsien⁴ Chêng⁴ K'ao³ Ho² Ch'u⁴, of Honan and Shensi, etc.

823. 會議廳 Hui⁴ I⁴ T'ing¹, Council of the Governor-General (or Governor). These are established in all the provinces, in accordance with article six of the "regulations regarding the reform of the official system of the provinces" (*see* No. 819B), for the periodical discussion of the most important questions. At meetings of this Council, in addition to the provincial officials, there may be representatives of the people, chosen by the authorities.

823A. 行政會議處 Hsing² Chêng⁴ Hui⁴ I⁴ Ch'u⁴, Administrative Council. Thus is designated the Council of the Governor of Kirin province (compare No. 823) which was formed in accordance with a Memorial from 陳昭常 Ch'ên² Chao¹-ch'ang², dated the 16th August, 1909. This is made up of members of two types, *i.e.* 正議員 Chêng⁴ I⁴ Yüan², Active Members (drawn from local Commissioners and Taotais), and 副議員 Fu⁴ I⁴ Yüan², Associate Members (drawn from the ranks of citizens experienced in judicial-administrative matters).

824. 營務處 Ying² Wu⁴ Ch'u⁴, Military Secretariat of the Governor-General (or Governor)—The Staff of the Old

Troops. This is headed by a 中軍 Chung¹ Chün¹, Adjutant, who, being the Colonel (副將 Fu⁴ Chiang⁴; *see* No. 752), is in active command of the 督標 Tu¹ Piao¹, or 撫標 Fu³ Piao¹, brigade attached to the Governor-General or Governor (*see* Nos. 749 and 752J). Also, this official is entitled to employ a staff of civil and military orderly officers, designated 文巡捕 Wên² Hsün² Pu³ (usually officials of the rank of Expectant District Magistrate; 知縣 Chih¹ Hsien⁴; *see* No. 856), and 武巡捕 Wu³ Hsün² Pu³ (military officers of the rank of lieutenant, 千總 Ch'ien¹ Tsung³; *see* No. 752E).

824A. 巡防營務處 Hsün² Fang² Ying² Wu⁴ Ch'u⁴, Staff of the Reserve Forces in Manchuria (*i.e.* forces of the category of 巡防隊 Hsün² Fang² Tui⁴; *see* No. 706). For details *see* No. 805A.

825. 布政使 Pu⁴ Chêng⁴ Shih³, Lieutenant-Governor or Financial Commissioner (commonly called Treasurer); 2B; official designation, 藩司 Fan² Ssu¹; colloquially called, 藩臺 Fan² T'ai²; epistolary designation, 方伯 Fang¹ Po², 大藩侯 Ta⁴ Fan² Hou², 大方岳 Ta⁴ Fang¹ Yüeh⁴, and 大旬宣 Ta⁴ Hsün¹ Hsüan¹. For the date of origin of this post *see* No. 819A.

The Lieutenant-Governor is the head of the civil service of the province and is also treasurer of the provincial exchequer and represents (暫行護理 Chan⁴ Hsing² Hu⁴ Li³) the Chief of the provincial administration (Governor-General or Governor) should he be absent from his province. There is one Lieutenant-Governor for each of the provinces, with the exception of the three Manchurian provinces, where this post is non-existent, and the province of Kiangsu, where there are two: 江寧布政使 Chiang¹ Ning² Pu⁴ Chêng⁴ Shih³, residing at 江寧府 Chiang¹ Ning² Fu³, Nanking, and 江蘇布政使 Chiang¹ Su¹ Pu⁴ Chêng⁴ Shih³, residing at 蘇州府 Su¹ Chou¹ Fu³, Soochow.

826. 布政使 Pu⁴ Chêng⁴ Ssu¹, Office of the Lieutenant-Governor (*see* No. 825). This Office is administered by:

826A
to
827

1. 經歷 Ching¹ Li⁴ (colloquially called, 經廳 Ching¹ T'ing¹; epistolary designation, 參軍 Ts'an¹ Chün¹; literary designation, 大贊府 Ta⁴ Tsan⁴ Fu³), Commissaries of Records, or Secretaries (6B; 17 for the Empire), 2. 理問 Li³ Wên⁴, Law Secretaries (6B; seven for the Empire), 3. 都事 Tu¹ Shih⁴ (colloquially, 都事廳 Tu¹ Shih⁴ T'ing¹), Assistant Secretary (7B; found only in the province of Fukien), 4. 照磨 Chao⁴ Mo² (colloquially, 照廳 Chao⁴ T'ing¹), Commissaries of the Seal, or Correspondence Secretaries (8B; seven for the Empire), 5 庫大使 K'u⁴ Ta⁴ Shih³ (colloquial designation, 庫廳 K'u⁴ T'ing¹), Treasury Keepers (8A; 20 for the Empire), and 6. 倉大使 Ts'ang¹ Ta⁴ Shih³. Granary Keepers (9B; two only, in the provinces of Kiangsu and Shensi).

826A. Article No. 9 of the "regulations regarding the reform of the official system of the provinces" (see No. 819B) calls for the future reorganization of the Office of the Lieutenant-Governor (see No. 826) and its administration by a staff similar to that of the 提學司 T'i² Hsüeh² Ssu¹ (see No. 828) and the 提法司 T'i² Fa⁴ Ssu¹ (see No. 831A).

827. 提學使 T'i² Hsüeh² Shih³, Commissioner of Education; 3A. This official superintends the educational affairs of the province to which he is accredited, including schools and literary societies. Though subordinated to the Governor-General (or Governor), at the same time he receives instructions from the Ministry of Education. Kiangsu province excepted, there is one Commissioner of Education for each province. For the province mentioned there are two (compare No. 825): one at 江寧府 Chiang¹ Ning² Fu³, Nanking, and the other at 蘇州 Su¹ Chou¹ Fu³, Soochow.

The post of Commissioner of Education was established to replace the former 學政 Hsüeh² Chêng⁴ (see No. 827A), on a Memorial from the Ministry of Education and the Committee of Ministers, dated the 25th April, 1906. Regulations regarding, 1. 提學使

827ᴀ
to
828

T'i² Hsüeh² Shih³ and their Offices, and 2. The authority of the
提學使 T'i² Hsüeh² Shih³, were framed by the Ministry of
Education and received Imperial sanction, the former on the
13th May, 1906, and the latter on the 28th July, 1906.

Under the reign of the Ming (明 Ming²; 1368–1644), as
well as at the beginning of the reign of the present dynasty the
superintendency over provincial educational affairs was vested in
提學道 T'i² Hsüeh² Tao⁴, Taotais of Education, whose title was
changed (in the reign of 雍正 Yung¹ Chêng⁴; 1723–1735) to
提督學政 T'i² Tu¹ Hsüeh² Chêng⁴ (see No. 827ᴀ).

827ᴀ. 學政 Hsüeh² Chêng⁴, Provincial Director of
Education, or Literary Chancellor (official designation, 學院
Hsüeh² Yüan⁴; colloquially called, 學臺 Hsüeh² T'ai²; literary
designation, 文宗 Wên² Tsung¹, 大文宗 Ta⁴ Wên² Tsung¹,
大文衡 Ta⁴ Wên² Heng², and 宗師 Tsung¹ Shih¹; sometimes
styled 督學使者 Tu¹ Hsüeh² Shih³ Chê³). The full official
title of this official was 提督學院 T'i² Tu¹ Hsüeh² Yüan⁴, or
提督學政 T'i² Tu¹ Hsüeh² Chêng⁴. For the date of origin of
the post of Literary Chancellor see No. 827.

The appointment as Provincial Director of Education, or
Literary Chancellor, was a special one and was usually held by
officials with high literary degrees, who left Peking for three
years to serve in this capacity. In addition to the duties of
general superintendency over the educational affairs of their
respective provinces they presided at prefectural examinations
and bestowed the degree of 秀才 Hsiu¹ Ts'ai² (see No. 629ᴀ).

828. 提學司 T'i² Hsüeh² Ssu¹, Office of the Commissioner
of Education (also 學務公所 Hsüeh² Wu⁴ Kung¹ So³). This
was developed, simultaneously with the institution of the post of
Commissioner of Education (see No. 827), from the former
學務處 Hsüeh² Wu⁴ Ch'u⁴, which was under the direction of a
總辦 Tsung³ Pan⁴, Chief. To this Office there are attached:
1. 議長 I⁴ Chang³, Senior Councillor (appointed by the

828A
to
829

Ministry of Education, on the recommendation of the Governor-General or Governor), and four 議 紳 I⁴ Shên¹, or 學 務 議 紳 Hsüeh² Wu⁴ I⁴ Shên¹, Advisers (for educational affairs), chosen by the Commissioner of Education from the ranks of the local gentry.

The Office of the Commissioner of Education is divided into six 科 K'o¹, Sections (altered from 課 K'o⁴ ; *see* instructions from the Ministry of Education, dated the 14th September, 1908): 1. 總 務 科 Tsung³ Wu⁴ K'o¹, Section of General Affairs, 2. 普 通 科 P'u³ T'ung¹ K'o¹, Section of Common Schools, 3. 專 門 科 Chuan¹ Mên² K'o¹, Section of Special Schools, 4. 實 業 科 Shih² Yeh⁴ K'o¹, Section of Professional Schools, 5. 圖 書 科 T'u² Shu¹ K'o¹, Section of Schoolbooks and Manuals, and 6. 會 計 科 Hui⁴ Chi⁴ K'o¹, Accounts Section.

At the head of each Section there is a 科 長 K'o¹ Chang³, Section Chief ; 5A. He is assisted by a 副 科 長 Fu⁴ K'o¹ Chang³ ; 6A. To the officials just mentioned there are attached an indefinite number of 科 員 K'o¹ Yüan², Chief Secretaries (not more than three to a Section), 司 事 Ssu¹ Shih⁴, Secretaries, and 書 記 Shu¹ Chi⁴, Clerks.

To the Commissioner of Education there are attached six 省 視 學 Shêng³ Shih⁴ Hsüeh², Provincial Inspectors of Education ; 6A. They are charged with the reorganization of educational affairs of prefectures, sub-prefectures, departments and districts.

828A. For the 提 學 司 T'i² Hsüeh² Ssu¹ in Manchuria *see* No. 809.

829. Under the control of the Commissioner of Education (*see* No. 827) there are also: 1. 勸 學 所 Ch'üan⁴ Hsüeh² So³, Associations for the Fostering of Public Education (*see* No. 829A), and 2. 教 育 會 Chiao⁴ Yü⁴ Hui⁴, Public Education Societies (*see* No. 829B), the establishment of which was foreshadowed by the regulations referring to the 提 學 使 T'i² Hsüeh² Shih³, and to his Office (*see* No. 827).

829A. 勸 學 所 Ch'üan⁴ Hsüeh² So³, Associations for the Fostering of Public Education (*see* No. 829); these are established, in conformity with regulations framed by the Ministry of Education and sanctioned by the Emperor on the 13th May, 1906, at the main cities of sub-prefectures, departments and districts, for the superintendency of educational affairs of their respective administrative units, and are under the general control of the local authorities who, ex officio, act as 監 督 Chien¹ Tu¹, Honorary Curators of Public Education. Each district under the supervision of an Association for the Fostering of Public Education is divided into a certain number of 學 區 Hsüeh² Ch'ü¹, Educational Sections.

At the head of an Association for the Fostering of Public Education there is a 總 董 Tsung³ Tung³, Director; the local 縣 視 學 Hsien⁴ Shih⁴ Hsüeh², District Inspector of Education, is appointed to this position.

Supervising any Educational Section are 勸 學 員 Ch'üan⁴ Hsüeh² Yüan², Members of the Association for the Fostering of Public Education, who are appointed by the Director.

Throughout the Empire there are found 宣 講 所 Hsüan¹ Chiang³ So³, Lecture Courses, the object of which is to spread education among the people as much as possible. These Courses are under the direct management of the Director of the Association for the Fostering of Public Education and are controlled by the local authorities and the police.

829B. 教 育 會 Chiao⁴ Yü⁴ Hui¹, Public Education Societies (*see* No. 829). Conforming to regulations framed by the Ministry of Education, which received Imperial sanction on the 28th July, 1906, these are established: at provincial capitals, called 教 育 總 會 Chiao⁴ Yü⁴ Tsung³ Hui⁴ (*i.e.* Central), and at the main cities of prefectures, departments and districts, designated 分 會 Fên¹ Hui⁴, Branches. Their aim is to disseminate education by means of schools, public lectures,

**830
to
830B**

libraries, pedagogic museums, etc. Each Society consists of :
1. One 會長 Hui⁴ Chang³ President, 2. 副會長 Fu⁴ Hui⁴
Chang³, Vice-President, 3. 會員 Hui⁴ Yüan², Members
(number indefinite), 4. 書記 Shu¹ Chi⁴, Clerks (number
indefinite), 5. 會計 Hui⁴ Chi⁴, Accountants (number indefinite),
and 6. 名譽會員 Ming² Yü⁴ Hui⁴ Yüan², Honorary Members
(number indefinite).

830. 按察使 An⁴ Ch'a² Shih³, Provincial Judge, or
Judicial Commissioner (more explicit, 提刑按察使司
T'i² Hsing² An⁴ Ch'a² Shih³ Ssu¹, official designation,
臬司 Nieh⁴ Ssu¹; colloquially, 臬臺 Nieh⁴ T'ai²; epistolary
designation, 廉訪 Lien² Fang³ and 大廉憲 Ta⁴ Lien²
Hsien⁴); 3ᴀ. This official is in charge of the judicial affairs of
the province and the military post stations (see No. 754). Also,
he considers questions of administrative and financial character
with the Lieutenant-Governor (see No. 825).

Each province has one Judicial Commissioner, with the
exception of Manchuria where, already, there is found the post
of 提法使 T'i² Fa⁴ Shih³ (see Nos. 810 and 831ᴮ).

For particulars as to the 按察使 An⁴ Ch'a² Shih³, in
Manchuria, under the old regime, see No. 830ᴮ.

830ᴀ. 按察司衙門 An⁴ Ch'a² Ssu¹ Ya² Mên², Office
of the Provincial Judge (see No. 830). The staff includes:
經歷 Ching¹ Li⁴ (see No. 826); 7ᴀ, 2. 知事 Chih¹ Shih⁴,
Archivists; 8ᴀ, 3. 照磨 Chao⁴ Mo² (see No. 826); 9ᴀ, and
4. 司獄 Ssu¹ Yü⁴, Jail Wardens; 9ᴮ.

830ᴮ. In Manchuria, prior to the establishment of the
post of 提法使 T'i² Fa⁴ Shih³ (see Nos. 810 and 831ᴮ), the
title of Judicial Commissioner, 兼按察使銜 Chien¹ An⁴ Ch'a²
Shih³ Hsien² (see No. 830), was borne: 1. In the province of
Fengtien, by the 奉錦山海道 Fêng⁴ Chin³ Shan¹ Hai³ Tao⁴,
Taotai of the prefectures of Chin Chou Fu and Fêng T'ien Fu,
residing at 營口廳 Ying² K'ou³ T'ing¹, Yingkow, 2. In the

province of Kirin, by the 吉 林 分 巡 道 Chi¹ Lin² Fên¹ Hsün² Tao⁴, Taotai of the Kirin Circuit, residing at 吉 林 府 Chi¹ Lin² Fu³, Kirin, and 3. In the province of Heilungchiang, by the 黑 龍 江 分 巡 道 Hei¹ Lung² Chiang¹ Fên¹ Hsün² Tao⁴, Taotai of the Heilungchiang Circuit, residing at 黑 水 廳 Hei¹ Shui³ T'ing¹, Tsitsihar.

830c to 831A

830c. The Financial Commissioner (*see* No. 825) and the Provincial Judge (*see* No. 830) are frequently spoken of together as the 藩 臬 兩 司 Fan² Nieh⁴ Liang³ Ssu¹, Two Chief Commissioners of the Provincial Government.

831. 提 法 使 T'i² Fa⁴ Shih³, Commissioner for Judicial Affairs ; 3A ; superintends the judicial affairs of the province and has control over Judicial Establishments, Prosecuting Attorneys' Offices and Prisons. He is subordinated to the Governor-General (or Governor).

At the present time the post of Commissioner for Judicial Affairs is found in Manchuria alone (*see* Nos. 810, 830 and 831B). A Memorial from the Ministry of Justice, dated the 17th April, 1909, called for the appointment in 1910 of officials bearing this title to all the provinces, replacing the existing Judicial Commissioners (*see* No. 830).

Regulations referring to the 提 法 使 T'i² Fa⁴ Shih³ and his Office (*see* No. 831A) were compiled by the Committee for Drawing up Regulations for Constitutional Government and received Imperial sanction on the 26th, November, 1909 (the original scheme in this connection was submitted by the Ministry of Justice in a Memorial dated the 27th January, 1908).

831A. 提 法 司 T'i² Fa⁴ Ssu¹, Office of the Commissioner for Judicial Affairs. This is arranged in three Sections : 1. 總 務 科 Tsung³ Wu⁴ K'o¹, Section of General Affairs ; in charge of the personnel of the office itself, and that of Judicial Establishments, Prosecuting Attorneys' Offices and Prisons, correspondence and matters of economy, 2. 刑 民 科 Hsing²

[411]

Min² K'o¹, Section of Criminal and Civil Cases, and 3. 典獄科 Tien³ Yü⁴ K'o¹, Section of Prison Affairs.

At the head of each Section there is a 科長 K'o¹ Chang³, Section Chief ; 5ᴀ. This official, under the general control of the Commissioner (*see* No. 831), superintends the affairs of his Section. He has as his assistants : One 一等科員 I¹ Têng³ K'o¹ Yüan², Secretary of the first rank ; 6ᴀ, and from one to four 二等科員 Êrh⁴ Têng³ K'o¹ Yüan², Secretaries of the second rank ; 7ᴀ. At each Section there are also a number (depending on the volume of affairs ; not more than five) 書記 Shu¹ Chi⁴, Clerks (of the eighth and ninth ranks).

831ʙ. The organization of the Office of the Commissioner for Judicial Affairs in Manchuria (*see* No. 810) is somewhat different from that given above (compare No. 831ᴀ), namely, it has four Sections : 1. 總務科 Tsung³ Wu⁴ K'o¹ (*see* No. 831ᴀ), 2. 刑事科 Hsing² Shih⁴ K'o¹, Section of Criminal Cases, 3. 民事科 Min² Shih⁴ K'o¹, Section of Civil Cases, and 4. 典獄科 Tien³ Yü⁴ K'o¹ (*see* No. 831ᴀ).

At the head of each Section, as Section Chief, there is a 僉事 Ch'ien¹ Shih⁴, Chief Secretary, 5ᴀ (*see* No. 815 ; in the first Section this official is styled 首科僉事 Shou³ K'o¹ Ch'ien¹ Shih⁴, and his rank is 4ʙ). To him there are subordinated one 一等科員 I¹ Têng³ K'o¹ Yüan², Secretary of the first rank, one 二等科員 Êrh⁴ Têng³ K'o¹ Yüan², Secretary of the second rank, and two 三等科員 San¹ Têng³ K'o¹ Yüan², Secretaries of the third rank. For each Section there are also 正司書官 Chêng⁴ Ssu¹ Shu¹ Kuan¹, Senior Clerks, 副司書官 Fu⁴ Ssu¹ Shu¹ Kuan¹, Junior Clerks, and 司書生 Ssu¹ Shu¹ Shêng¹, Writers.

832. 交涉使 Chiao¹ Shê⁴ Shih³, Commissioner for Foreign Affairs ; 3ᴀ ; charged with dealing with affairs in which foreigners are interested. Following the inauguration of this post in Manchuria (*see* No. 806) it was instituted in Yünnan

province (in August, 1909). Later this official will be found in all the provinces.

At present the duties appertaining to the Commissioner of Foreign Affairs are performed by the 洋務局 Yang² Wu⁴ Chü², Office of Foreign Affairs (*see* No. 859), attached to the Governor-General (or Governor). Heilungchiang province has a 交涉總局 Chiao¹ Shê⁴ Tsung³ Chü² (*see* No. 806A) for similar duties.

833. 海關監督 Hai³ Kuan¹ Chien¹ Tu¹, Superintendent of Customs. The duties appertaining to this official are usually associated with those of the Military Circuit Taotai (*see* No. 844).

833A. 粵海關部 Yüeh⁴ Hai³ Kuan¹ Pu⁴, Superintendent of Customs for the Province of Kuangtung; appointed from members of the Imperial Household. Europeans commonly styled this official " Hoppo " and, so long as the entire foreign trade was concentrated at Canton, he enjoyed immense power. This official no longer exists.

833B. 兼管閩海關稅事務 Chien¹ Kuan³ Min³ Hai³ Kuan¹ Shui⁴ Shih⁴ Wu⁴, With Associate Duties as Superintendent of Customs at Foochow. This title is borne by the Fukien Viceroy.

833C. For particulars as to the special 海關道 Hai³ Kuan¹ Tao⁴, Customs Taotai, carrying on the functions of Superintendent of Customs at Tientsin (formerly, likewise, at Harbin) *see* No. 842.

834. 漕運總督 Ts'ao² Yün⁴ Tsung³ Tu¹, Director-General of Grain Transport (2A; literary designation, 漕督 Ts'ao² Tu¹, 都轉運司 Tu¹ Chuan³ Yün⁴ Shih³, and 大司漕 Ta⁴ Ssu¹ Ts'ao²). This official had the honorary rank of 兵部侍郎 Ping¹ Pu⁴ Shih⁴ Lang², and resided at 清江浦 Ch'ing¹ Chiang¹ P'u³ (in the 淮安 Huai² An¹, prefecture of Kiangsu). He superintended the system of transport of grain by

835   the 運河 Yün⁴ Ho², Grand Canal, which was constructed for the conveyance of rice from the Southern provinces to Peking. The post is now non-existent.

Under the control of the Director-General of Grain Transport there was a special military organization styled 漕標 Ts'ao² Piao¹ (*see* No. 749), detachments of which were stationed at the 衛 Wei⁴, and 所 So³, First and Second Class Transport Stations, which were located along the Grand Canal, by which the grain transport was effected. At the head of these stations there were 守備 Shou³ Pei⁴ (*see* No. 752D), and 千總 Ch'ien¹ Tsung³ (*see* No. 752E), designated, according to their duties, as 守禦 Shou³ Yü⁴, First Lieutenant on Garrison Duty, and 領運 Ling³ Yün⁴, Lieutenant Charged with the Conduct of Grain Squadrons.

Of late years the grain transport by sea, 海運 Hai³ Yün⁴, carried on by steamers of the 招商局 Chao¹ Shang¹ Chü² (*see* No. 789), is gradually putting an end to that by the Grand Canal.

835. 鹽運使 Yen² Yün⁴ Shih³, Salt Controller (3B; official designation, 運司 Yün⁴ Ssu¹; epistolary designation, 都轉 Tu¹ Chuan³ and 都運 Tu¹ Yün⁴; literary designation, 大鹺憲 Ta⁴ Ts'o² Hsien⁴, 大鹺侯 Ta⁴ Ts'o² Hou⁴. and 大司賦 Ta⁴ Ssu¹ Fu⁴). This official is the Chief Commissioner of the revenue derived from the provincial salt gabelle, or salt monopoly. There are five for the whole Empire: 1. 長蘆鹽運使兼鹽法道 Ch'ang² Lu² Yen² Yün⁴ Shih³ Chien¹ Yen² Fa⁴ Tao⁴, Ch'anglu Salt Controller with associate duties as Salt Intendant, residing at Tientsin, 2. 山東鹽運使兼鹽法道 Shan¹ Tung¹ Yen² Yün⁴ Shih³ Chien¹ Yen² Fa⁴ Tao⁴, Shantung Salt Controller with associate duties as Salt Intendant, residing at Chinanfu, 3. 兩淮鹽運使兼兵備銜 Liang³ Huai² Yen² Yün⁴ Shih³ Chien¹ Ping¹ Pei⁴ Hsien², Lianghuai Salt Controller, with the rank of Military Circuit Taotai, residing at

揚州府 Yang² Chou¹ Fu³, Yangchow, 4. 兩浙江南鹽運使 835₄
Liang³ Chê¹ Chiang¹ Nan² Yen² Yün⁴ Shih³, Liangchê
(Chekiang) Salt Controller, residing at Hangchow, and 5. 廣
東鹽運使 Kuang³ Tung¹ Yen² Yün⁴ Shih³, Kuangtung Salt
Controller, residing at Canton.

835ᴀ. Under the supervision of the Salt Controller (whose
office is designated 鹽運司使衙門 Yen² Yün⁴ Shih³ Ssu¹ Ya²
Mên²) there are the following officials: 1. 運同 Yün⁴ T'ung²,
Assistant Salt Controller (full designation, 鹽運司運同 Yen²
Yün⁴ Ssu¹ Yün⁴ T'ung²; literary designation, 同轉 T'ung²
Chuan², and 輔轉 Fu³ Chuan³, 鹾貳 Ts'o⁴ Êrh⁴, and 大佐賦
Ta⁴ Tso³ Fu⁴, also 分司 Fên¹ Ssu¹); 4ʙ; one in Shantung,
Chihli and Kuangtung provinces. 2. 鹽掣同知 Chien¹ Ch'ê⁴
T'ung² Chih¹ (also 鹽掣官 Chien¹ Ch'ê⁴ Kuan¹), Inspector of
Salt Distribution; 5ᴀ; two in Kiangsu province and one in
Shansi. 3. 運副 Yün⁴ Fu⁴, Deputy Assistant Salt Controller
(full designation, 鹽運使副使 Yen⁴ Yün⁴ Shih³ Fu⁴ Shih³; also
styled 分司 Fên¹ Ssu¹; compare the above Yün⁴ T'ung²); 5ʙ;
one in Chekiang province. 4. 提舉 T'i² Chü³, Salt Inspector
(also 鹽提舉 Yen² T'i² Chü³; full designation, 鹽課提舉 Yen²
K'o⁴ T'i² Chü³, or 鹽課司提舉 Yen² K'o⁴ Ssu¹ T'i² Chü³); 5ʙ;
three in Yünnan province. 5. 運判 Yün⁴ P'an⁴, Sub-Assistant
Salt Controller (full designation, 鹽運司運判 Yen³ Yün⁴ Ssu¹
Yün⁴ P'an⁴; also 副轉 Fu⁴ Chuan³ and 分司 Fên¹ Ssu¹; compare
the above 運同 Yün⁴ T'ung², and 運副 Yün⁴ Fu⁴); 6ʙ; one in
Chihli, one in Chekiang and three in Kiangsu province. 6. 經
歷 Ching¹ Li⁴ (correctly, 鹽經歷 Yen² Ching¹ Li⁴); 7ʙ (see
No. 826), 7 鹽課大使 Yen² K'o⁴ Ta⁴ Shih³ (more explicit,
鹽課司大使 Yen² K'o⁴ Ssu¹ Ta⁴ Shih³) or 鹽場大使 Yen²
Ch'ang² Ta⁴ Shih³ (literary designation, 鹾尹 Ts'o² Yin³), Salt
Receiver; 8ᴀ. 8. 批驗大使 P'i¹ Yen⁴ Ta⁴ Shih³ (more
explicit, 批驗所大使 P'i¹ Yen⁴ So³ Ta⁴ Shih³, or 鹽引批驗
所大使 Yen² Yin³ P'i¹ Yen⁴ So³ Ta⁴ Shih³), Salt Examiner;

835B 8A ; superintends the registration of bags of salt issued, 9. 庫 大使 K'u⁴ Ta⁴ Shih³ (properly, 運庫大使 Yün⁴ K'u⁴ Ta⁴ Shih³) ; 8A (*see* No. 826), 10. 知事 Chih¹ Shih⁴ (properly 鹽知事 Yen² Chih¹ Shih⁴ ; 8B (*see* No. 830A), and 11. 鹽巡 檢 Yen² Hsün² Chin³, Salt Watchers ; 9B.

835B. 會辦鹽政大臣 Hui⁴ Pan⁴ Yeng² Chêng⁴ Ta⁴ Ch'ên², Associate Controller-General of the Salt Gabelle (compare No. 369). The duties appertaining to this post are associated with those of the Governors-General of Manchuria, Chihli, Liang Kiang, Liang Kuang, Minchê, Szechwan, Yün Kuei and Shenkan (*see* No. 820A) and with those of the Governors of Shantung, Shansi and Chekiang (*see* No. 821A)—*see* a Memorial from the Controller-General of the Salt Gabelle, sanctioned by the Emperor on the 25th February, 1910, covering regulations, concerning the Salt Administration, in 35 articles.

Prior to the promulgation of the Imperial Edict of 31st December, 1909 (compare No. 369), the mentioned Governors-General and Governors were entitled 總理鹽政 Tsung³ Li³ Yen² Chêng⁴.

The title 兼會辦鹽政大臣銜 Chien¹ Hui⁴ Pan⁴ Yen² Chêng⁴ Ta⁴ Ch'ên² Hsien², With Associate Duties as Associate Controller-General of the Salt Gabelle, is borne by the Governor-General of Hukuang and by the Governors of Kirin, Heilungchiang, Kiangsu, Anhui, Kiangsi, Honan, Hunan, Kuangsi, Kueichow, Shensi and Hsinchiang (*see* the above-mentioned Memorial from the Controller-General of the Salt Gabelle).

At the beginning of the reign of the present dynasty, at the head of the six Salt Departments (namely, Ch'anglu, Hotung, Lianghuai, Liangchê, Kuangtung and Fukien ; *see* below) there were special officials, appointed from the ranks of Manchus, styled 巡視鹽政御史 Hsün² Shih⁴ Yen² Chêng⁴ Yü⁴ Shih³ (also 巡鹽御史 Hsün² Yen² Yü⁴ Shih³, or 巡鹽直指 Hsün² Yen² Chih² Chih³), Salt Censors.

[416]

There are now thirteen Departments producing salt. **835c**
Accordingly, from its place of origin, salt bears the following **to**
designations : 1. 盛京鹽 Shêng⁴ Ching¹ Yen² (salt from Fêngtien **836**
province, where there are 20 鹽塲 Yen² Ch'ang³, Salt Works),
2. 長蘆鹽 Ch'ang² Lu² Yen² (salt from Chihli province, where
there are ten Salt Works), 3. 蒙古鹽 Mêng³ Ku³ Yen² (salt
from Mongolia), 4. 山東鹽 Shan¹ Tung¹ Yen² (salt from
Shantung), 5. 兩淮鹽 Liang³ Huai² Yen² (salt from Kiangsu
province), 6. 兩浙鹽 Liang² Chê⁴ Yen² (salt from Chekiang
province, where there are 32 Salt Works), 7. 福建鹽 Fu²
Chien⁴ Yen² (salt from Fukien province, where there are 14 Salt
Works), 8. 廣東鹽 Kuang³ Tung¹ Yen² (salt from Kuangtung province, where there are 12 Salt Works), 9. 河東鹽
Ho² Tung¹ Yen² (salt from Shansi province, where there are
three Salt Works), 10. 陝西鹽 Shên³ Hsi¹ Yen² (salt from
Shensi province), 11. 甘肅鹽 Kan¹ Su⁴ Yen² (salt from
Kansu province), 12. 四川鹽 Ssu⁴ Ch'uan¹ Yen² (salt from
Szechwan province, where there are 8,832 Salt Wells), and
13. 雲南鹽 Yün² Nan² Yen² (salt from Yünnan province,
where there are 10 Salt Wells).

835c. For particulars as to the Salt Intendant, which
title is sometimes applied to the Salt Controller, *see* Nos. 835
and 841.

836. 糧道 Liang² Tao⁴, Grain Intendant (literary
designation, 轉運使 Chuan³ Yün⁴ Shih³; 4ᴀ; Chief Controller
of the provincial revenue from the grain tax, whether collected
in money or in kind. At present there are six Grain Intendants
(later they will be retained only in the provinces of Kiangsu and
Chekiang): 1. 江安糧儲道 Chiang¹ An¹ Liang² Ch'u³ Tao⁴,
Grain Intendant of Kiangnan, residing at 江甯府 Chiang¹
Ning² Fu³, Nanking. 2. 蘇松常鎮太糧儲道 Su¹ Sung¹
Ch'ang² Chên⁴ T'ai¹ Liang² Ch'u³ Tao⁴, Grain Intendant of the
Prefectures of Soochow Fu, Sungkiang Fu, Ch'angchow Fu

837 Chenkiang Fu and Tʻai Tsʻang Chih Li Chow, residing at Soochow, 3. 浙江督糧道 Chê⁴ Chiang¹ Tu¹ Liang² Tao⁴, Grain Intendant of Chekiang, residing at Hangchow, 4. 福建督糧道 Fu² Chien⁴ Tu¹ Liang² Tao⁴, Grain Intendant of Fukien, residing at Foochow, 5. 雲南糧儲道兼分巡 Yün² Nan² Liang² Chʻu³ Tao⁴ Chien¹ Fên¹ Hsün², Grain Intendant of Yünnan, with Associate Duties as Intendant of a Circuit (*see* No. 844), residing at Yünnan Fu, and 6. 鎮迪糧務道 Chên⁴ Ti² Liang² Wu⁴ Tao⁴, Grain Intendant, with Associate Duties as Intendant of the Military Circuit of the Prefecture of Tihua Fu and the Department of Chên Hsi Chih Li Chow, residing at 迪化府 Ti² Hua⁴ Fu³, Urumtsi.

Formerly there were Grain Intendants in the following provinces: 1. 山東糧道 Shan¹ Tung¹ Liang² Tao⁴, Grain Intendant of Shantung, residing at Chinan Fu, 2. 開歸陳許鹽法糧務道 Kʻai¹ Kuei¹ Chʻên² Hsü³ Yen² Fa⁴ Liang² Wu⁴ Tao⁴, Salt and Grain Intendant of the Prefectures of Kaifêng Fu, Kueitê Fu and Chênchow Fu, and of the Department of Hsü Chow Chih Li Chow, residing at 開封府 Kʻai¹ Fêng¹ Fu³, 3. 江西督糧道 Chiang¹ Hsi¹ Tu¹ Liang² Tao⁴, Grain Intendant of Kiangsi, residing at Nanchʻang, and 4. 貴州督糧道 Kuei⁴ Chou¹ Tu⸱ Liang² Tao⁴, Grain Intendant of Kueichow, residing at 貴陽府 Kuei⁴ Yang² Fu³, Kueiyang Fu.

837. 督撫司道 Tu¹ Fu³ Ssu¹ Tao⁴, this is the common designation of the Governor-General (*see* No. 820), the Governor (*see* No. 821), the Lieutenant-Governor (*see* No. 825), the Judicial Commissioner (*see* No. 830), the Salt Controller (*see* No. 835), and the Grain Intendant (*see* No. 836), the officials constituting the "Provincial Government." These officials in many provinces form a peculiar committee styled 善後總局 Shan¹ Hou⁴ Tsung³ Chü², Supreme Board of Reorganization. During the Tʻai Pʻing rebellion, when this committee began to function generally, it was called the 軍需總局 Chün¹ Hsü¹

Tsung³ Chü², Supreme · Mili ry Board. It was the custom to
institute the committee after rebellions, warfare or physical
calamities, when the country needed pacification, or order had to
be restored.

838 to 838A

838. 道臺 Tao⁴ T'ai², Taotai (Intendant); 4A; placed in
administrative control over various sections of the provincial
government; official designation, 道 Tao⁴; epistolary designation,
觀察 Kuan¹ Ch'a², and 監司 Chien¹ Ssu¹.

There are the following categories of Taotais : 1. 勸業道
Ch'üan⁴ Yeh⁴ Tao⁴, Industrial Taotai (*see* Nos. 839 and 839A),
2. 巡警道 Hsün² Ching³ Tao⁴, Police Taotai (*see* Nos. 840
and 840A), 3. 鹽法道 Yen² Fa⁴ Tao⁴, Salt Taotai (*see* No.
841), 4. 海關道 Hai³ Kuan¹ Tao⁴, Customs Taotai (*see* No.
842), 5. 河道 Ho² Tao⁴, River Taotai (*see* No. 843), and
6. 分巡道 Fên¹ Hsün² Tao⁴, Intendant of a Circuit, or 兵備
道 Ping¹ Pei⁴ Tao⁴, Military Taotai (*see* No. 844).

For particulars as to the 糧道 Liang² Tao⁴, Grain
Intendant, *see* No. 836.

838A. 司道 Ssu¹ Tao⁴, Taotai Holding Brevet Rank
of Judicial Commissioner (*see* No. 830). Of this type are the
Taotais : at Tihua and Chenhsi in Hsinchiang (鎮迪道兼按
察使銜 Chên⁴ Ti² Tao⁴ Chien¹ An⁴ Ch'a² Shih³ Hsien², Taotai
of the prefecture of Tihua and the department of Chên Hsi
Chih Li Chow, holding brevet rank as Judicial Commissioner);
at Huai-an, Yangchow and Haichow in Kiangsu (淮揚海道
兼按察使銜 Huai² Yang² Hai³ Tao⁴ Chien¹ An⁴ Ch'a² Shih³
Hsien², Taotai of the prefectures of Huai-an Fu and Yangchow
Fu and of the department of Hai Chow Chih Li Chow, holding
brevet rank as Judicial Commissioner).

For particulars as to the Taotais in Manchuria, to whom
there was formerly applied a brevet rank as Judicial Commissioner, *see* No. 830B.

839. 勸業道 Ch'üan⁴ Yeh⁴ Tao⁴, Industrial Taotai (*see* No. 838); 4A. This official is subordinated directly to the Governor-General or Governor of the province to which he is accredited but, in addition, receives instructions from the Ministry of Agriculture, Industry and Commerce (*see* No. 768). He superintends, within his district, all questions concerning agriculture, industry, commerce and ways and means of communication. Also, on the establishment of the post of 提法司 T'i² Fa⁴ Shih³ (replacing the 按察使 An⁴ Ch'a² Shih³; *see* No. 830), he will be in charge of the military post stations. (*see* No. 754).

The "regulations regarding the reform of the official system of the provinces," articles Nos. 14 and 15 (*see* No. 819B), call for the gradual appointment of Industrial Taotais for all the provinces. At present they are found in all provinces with the exception of Heilungchiang and the New Dominion.

Regulations referring to the Industrial Taotai were drawn up originally, by the Ministry of Agriculture, Industry and Commerce (sanctioned by the Emperor on the 7th June, 1908; 14 articles) and, later, by the Committee for Drawing up Regulations for Constitutional Government (with supplements and amendments; sanctioned by the Emperor on the 1st August, 1908; 18 articles).

For the organization of the Office of the Industrial Taotai *see* No. 839A.

839A. For the Industrial Taotai there is a 公所 Kung¹ So³, Office, composed of six Sections: 1. 總務科 Tsung³ Wu⁴ K'o¹, Section of General Affairs, 2. 農務科 Nung² Wu⁴ K'o¹, Section of Agriculture, 3. 工藝科 Kung¹ I⁴ K'o¹, Section of Handicrafts, 4. 商務科 Shang¹ Wu⁴ K'o¹, Section of Commerce, 5. 礦務科 Kung³ Wu⁴ K'o¹, Section of Mining, and 6. 郵傳科 Yu² Ch'uan² K'o¹, Section of Posts and Communications. Each Section is directed by a 科長 K'o¹ Chang³,

Section Chief; 6ᴀ. He is assisted by a 副科長 Fu⁴ K'o¹ **839ʙ**
Chang³, Assistant Section Chief; 7ᴀ. Also, there are a number **to**
(from two to three in the Section of Posts and Communications **840ᴀ**
and from four to five in the Section of General Affairs) of 科員
K'o¹ Yüan², Secretaries; 8ᴀ.

In all sub-prefectures, departments and districts there are
found 勸業員 Ch'üan⁴ Yeh⁴ Yüan², Industrial Deputies, who
are under the control of the Taotai and local authorities (*see* No.
851ʙ).

839ʙ. For particulars as to the Industrial Taotais in
Manchuria *see* Nos. 813 to 813ᴀ.

840. 巡警道 Hsün² Ching³ Tao⁴, Police Taotai (*see* No.
838); 4ᴀ. Although directly subordinated to the Governor-
General (or Governor) this official receive instructions from the
Ministry of the Interior (*see* No. 348). He superintends the
police affairs of the province to which he is accredited.

By the "regulations regarding the reform of the official
system of the provinces" (articles Nos. 14 and 15; *see* No.
819ʙ) it is arranged that Police Taotais be gradually appointed
to all the provinces. At present they are found in all provinces,
Fêngtien, Kirin, Heilungchiang and the New Dominion
excepted.

Regulations referring to the Police Taotai were drawn up,
first by the Ministry of the Interior (sanctioned on the 3rd April,
1908; in 15 articles), and, later, by the Committee for Drawing
up Regulations for Constitutional Government (with supplements
and amendments; 15 articles; sanctioned by the Emperor on the
25th May, 1908).

For particulars as to the organization of the Office of the
Police Taotai *see* No. 840ᴀ.

840ᴀ. For the Police Taotai there has been instituted a
警務公所 Ching³ Wu⁴ Kung¹ So³, Office of the Police Taotai,
consisting of four Sections: 1. 總務科 Tsung³ Wu⁴ K'o¹,

840B
to
841

Section of General Affairs, 2. 行政科 Hsing² Chêng⁴ K'o¹, Section of Administration, 3. 司法科 Ssu¹ Fa⁴ K'o¹, Section of Judicial Affairs (superintending, amongst other things, the Judicial Police ; *see* Nos. 519 to 519A), and 4. 衛生科 Wei⁴ Shêng¹ K'o¹, Section of Sanitary Affairs. Also, in many places, the Section of General Affairs is sub-divided into : 會計科 Hui⁴ Chi⁴ K'o¹, Section of Accounts, 教練科 Chiao⁴ Lien⁴ K'o¹, Section of Instruction, and 文牘科 Wên² Tu³ K'o¹, Correspondence Section.

At the head of each Section there is a 科長 K'o¹ Chang³, Section Chief ; 5A. He is assisted by a 副科長 Fu⁴ K'o¹ Chang³, Assistant Section Chief ; 6A. Also, there is a fixed number (three to four) of 科員 K'o¹ Yüan², Secretaries ; 7A.

In all sub-prefectures, departments and districts there have been instituted posts as 警務長 Ching³ Wu⁴ Chang³, Chiefs of Police, under whose authority there are placed a number of police divisions, directed by 區官 Ch'ü¹ Kuan¹, Police Captains (*see* Nos. 851B and 857B).

840B. For particulars as to the Police Taotais of Manchuria *see* No. 814.

841. 鹽法道 Yen² Fa⁴ Tao⁴, Salt Taotai ; 4A ; performing duties similar to those of the Salt Controller (*see* No. 835) who, in virtue of this, is sometimes styled Salt Taotai (*see* No. 835B).

There are Salt Taotais in nine provinces : 1. 江南鹽巡道 Chiang¹ Nan² Yen² Hsün² Tao⁴, Kiangnan Salt Taotai, residing at Nanking, 2. 江西鹽法道 Chiang¹ Hsi¹ Yen² Fa⁴ Tao⁴, Kiangsi Salt Taotai, residing at Nanch'ang, 3. 河東鹽法道 Ho² Tung¹ Yen² Fa⁴ Tao⁴, Hotung Salt Taotai, residing at P'uchow Fu, 4. 平慶涇固化鹽法道 P'ing² Ch'ing⁴ Ching⁴ Ku⁴ Hua⁴ Yen² Fa⁴ Tao⁴, Salt Taotai of the Prefectures of P'ing Liang Fu and Ch'ing Yen Fu and of the Departments of Ching Chow Chih Li Chow, Ku Yuan Chih Li Chow and Hua

P'ing Chih Li Chow, residing at 平涼府 P'ing² Liang² Fu³, **842**
5. 福建鹽法道 Fu² Chien⁴ Yen² Fa⁴ Tao⁴, Fukien Salt **to**
Taotai, residing at Foochow, 6. 湖北鹽法道 Hu² Pei³ Yen² **844**
Fa⁴ Tao⁴, Hupeh Salt Taotai, residing at Wuch'ang, 7.
鹽法長寶道 Yen² Fa⁴ Ch'ang² Pao³ Tao⁴, Salt Taotai of the
Prefectures of Ch'ang Sh'a Fu and Pao Ch'ing Fu, residing at
Ch'angsha, 8. 四川鹽茶道 Ssu⁴ Ch'uan¹ Yen² Ch'a² Tao⁴,
Salt and Tea Taotai of Szechwan, residing at Ch'êntê Fu, and
9. 雲南鹽法道 Yün² Nan² Yen² Fa⁴ Tao⁴, Yünnan Salt
Taotai, residing at Yünnan Fu. Also, in the province of Shensi,
the duties of Salt Taotai are performed by the Police Taotai
(*see* No. 840), who is styled 兼管鹽法 Chien¹ Kuan³ Yen² Fa⁴
(formerly the Taotai of the Military Circuit performed these
duties, 鳳邠鹽法道 Fêng⁴ Pin¹ Yen² Fa⁴ Tao⁴).

The majority of the Salt Taotais mentioned above act
simultaneously as Military Circuit Taotais (*see* No. 844).

842. 海關道 Hai³ Kuan¹ Tao⁴, Customs Taotai (literary
designation, 権使 Ch'üeh⁴ Shih³, and 關督 Kuan¹ Tu¹);
performing the duties of Superintendent of Customs (*see* No.
833). This is an independent post at Tientsin alone (津海關道
Chin¹ Hai³ Kuan¹ Tao⁴; *see* No. 833c. Formerly there was an
independent Customs Taotai at Harbin (濱江關道 P'in¹ Chiang¹
Kuan¹ Tao⁴).

843. 河道 Ho² Tao⁴, River Taotai; 4A. As an
independent official this Taotai is found in the province of Chihli
alone and is styled 永定河道 Yung³ Ting⁴ Ho² Tao⁴. He
resides at 固安縣 Ku⁴ An¹ Hsien¹. The similar official for
Shantung (山東運河道 Shan¹ Tung³ Yün⁴ Ho² Tao⁴, residing
at 濟寗州 Chi⁴ Ning² Chou¹) and for Honan (開歸陳許河道
K'ai¹ Kuei¹ Ch'ên² Hsü³ Ho² Tao⁴, residing at 開封府 K'ai¹
Fêng¹ Fu³) no longer exists.

844. 分巡道 Fên¹ Hsün² Tao⁴, and 分守道 Fên¹ Shou³
Tao⁴, Taotai (Intendent) of a Circuit; 4A; literary designation,

844A
to
844B
監司 Chien¹ Ssu¹; official designation, 觀察 Kuan⁴ Ch'a², and 道臺 Tao⁴ T'ai². Also 兵備道 Ping¹ Pei⁴ Tao⁴, Military-Administrative Taotai; 4A (sometimes 分巡兵備道 Fên¹ Hsün² Ping¹ Pei⁴ Tao⁴, Military Circuit Taotai). This official is charged with the administration of two, or more, prefectures, independent sub-prefectures or departments, the names of which are prefixed to his title (for instance, the Shanghai Taotai is designated 蘇松太道 Su¹ Sung¹ Tai⁴ Tao⁴, Taotai of the prefectures of Soochow Fu and Sung Chiang Fu and of the sub-prefecture of T'ai Ts'ang Chih Li Chow, the Taotai of Chefoo is styled 登萊青膠道 Têng¹ Lai⁴ Ch'ing¹ Chiao¹ Tao⁴, Taotai of the prefectures of Têngchow Fu, Laichow Fu, and Ch'ingchow Fu and the sub-prefecture of Chiao Chow Chih Li Chow, etc). At ports open to foreign trade he performs diplomatic functions, being intermediary in all intercourse with foreigners. With very few exceptions (compare Nos. 833A and 833C) he is also the Superintendent of Customs (compare No. 833).

At present there are the following Taotais: six in Chihli province, three in Shantung province, two in Shansi province, four in Honan province, four in Kiangsu province, two in Anhui province, two in Kiangsi province, three in Fukien province, four in Chekiang province, four in Hupeh province, three in Hunan province, three in Shensi province, six in Kansu province, four in Szechwan province, six in Kuangtung province, four in Kuangsi province, one in Kueichow province, four in Yünnan province and three in Hsinchiang province. Thus there are 68 Taotais for China proper and, with Manchuria (there are 11 Taotais here; *see* No. 816), there are 79 for the Empire as a whole.

844A. The posts of 茶馬道 Ch'a² Ma³ Tao⁴, Taotai of the Tea and Horse Revenue, and 屯田道 T'un² T'ien² Tao⁴, Taotai of Agricultural Settlements, are now abolished.

844B. The "regulations regarding the reform of the official system of the provinces" (article No. 17; *see* No. 819B) call for the abolition of the post of Taotai of a Circuit (守巡道 Shou³ Hsün² Tao⁴). For each province there will be retained the 兵備道 Ping¹ Pei⁴ Tao⁴, Military Circuit Taotais (from one to three), who will be specially charged with the capturing of criminals and the moving of military forces. Simultaneously there will be abolished the posts of 庫大司 K'u⁴ Ta⁴ Shih³ (see No. 826) and 倉大使 Ts'ang¹ Ta⁴ Shih³ (see No. 826) which are found at the Taotai's Office.

844c. For particulars as to the Office of a Taotai in Manchuria see No. 816A.

845. 織造 Chih¹ Tsao⁴, Superintendents of the Imperial Manufactories (at Nanking, Soochow and Hangchow); appointed from the Manchu members of the Imperial Household; literary designation, 尚衣 Shang⁴ I¹, 司服 Ssu¹ Fu², and 大繡緞 Ta¹ Fu³ Fu³). They superintend the manufacture and despatch of the silk textiles and other requisites for the use of the Court.

845A. 督辦川滇邊務大臣 Tu¹ Pan⁴ Ch'uan¹ Tien¹ Pien¹ Wu⁴ Ta⁴ Ch'ên², Border Commissioner of the Provinces of Szechwan and Yünnan; subordinated to the Governor-General of Szechwan but with the privilege of direct reports to the Emperor. This official superintends the military and civil affairs of the Western portion of Szechwan and the section of Tibet adjacent to this province (compare No. 817).

B. *Local Administration (of Prefectures, Sub-prefectures, Departments and Districts)*:

846. Each province, as regards administrative authority, is divided into a number (ten to a province on an average) of 府 Fu³, Prefectures, 直隸州 Chih² Li⁴ Chou. Independent Departments, and 直隸廳 Chih² Li⁴ T'ing¹, Independent Sub-prefectures. There is a further division into 州 Chou¹, Departments, 廳 T'ing¹, Sub-prefectures, and 縣 Hsien¹, Districts.

[425]

847   Independent Departments and Independent Sub-prefectures differ from ordinary Departments and Sub-prefectures in that they enjoy a government independent of the Prefect (compare No. 848) and are subjected directly to the Taotai (compare No. 844) and other officials of the higher provincial administration.

Prefectures differ from Independent Departments and Independent Sub-prefectures (the number of the latter, as compared with that of prefectures, is small) in that they are completely organized administrative units and contain within their borders a number of departments, sub-prefectures and districts. Independent Departments, by their form of government, approach prefectures (in the majority of cases they have been organized from ordinary departments which have been removed from the prefectural authority) in that they may include districts, though ordinary departments are never subordinated to them.

Independent Sub-prefectures represent a lower form of local government and are in themselves administrative departments which have been made independent of the prefectural government because of their importance or territorial magnitude.

Independent Departments and Sub-prefectures represent intermediate stages in the transformation of ordinary departments and sub-prefectures into prefectures. For this reason they are observed to be most numerous on the borders of the Empire.

The whole Empire includes 214 Prefectures, 75 Independent Departments, 54 Independent Sub-prefectures, 139 Departments, 57 Sub-prefectures and 1,381 Districts.

847. The appointments of officials heading the administration of Prefectures, Departments and Sub-prefectures (independent or otherwise) and Districts, as well as of Taotais (*see* No. 844) are arranged, in dependence on their importance and volume of affairs, into four categories: 1. 最要 Tsui⁴ Yao⁴, Most Important, 2. 要缺 Yao⁴ Ch'üeh¹, Important,

3. 中缺 Chung[1] Ch'üeh[1], Medium, and 4. 簡缺 Chien[3] Ch'üeh[1], Ordinary. They are popularly called " four-character, three character, two character and one character posts," the first being distinguished by having the four characters 衝繁疲難 Ch'ung[1] Fan[2] Pi[2] Nan[2], " Frequented, Troublesome, Wearisome and Difficult," attached to it, the second has any three of these, the third has any two and the fourth has any one.

848. 知府 Chih[1] Fu[3], Prefect ; 4B ; official designation, 守 Shou[3] ; epistolary designation, 太守 T'ai[4] Shou[3] or 太尊 T'ai[4] Tsun[1]. This post originated in the Han Dynasty. The Prefect styles himself, when enumerating his titles, 正堂 Chêng[4] T'ang[2], or, in the literary style, 黃堂 Huang[2] T'ang[2], 五馬 Wu[3] Ma[3], or 二千石 Erh[4] Ch'ien[1] Tan[4].

In principle the Prefect's authority extends to all branches of the administration of his prefecture but latterly the Government has endeavoured to remove certain sections of governmental activity from his control, for instance, police and judicial affairs, education, etc., and leave to him merely the general guidance of the administration.

In the very early days the Prefect was styled 郡首 Chün[4] Shou[3] (also 郡伯 Chün[4] Po[2], 大郡伯 Ta[4] Chün[4] Po[2], and 大郡侯 Ta[4] Chün[4] Hou[2]), from 郡 Chün[4], Prefecture, the then administrative unit (during the time of 秦始皇帝 Ch'in[2] Shê[3] Huang[2] Ti[4], B.C. 221).

The Prefect of the prefecture in which the provincial capital is situated is designated 首府 Shou[3] Fu[3].

849. 同知 T'ung[2] Chih[1], First Class Sub-prefect (see No. 848) ; 5A ; colloquially called, 貳府 Êrh[4] Fu[3], and 貳守 Êrh[4] Shou[3]; epistolary designation, 司馬 Ssu[1] Ma[3], and 分府 Fên[1] Fu[3]; literary designation, 郡丞 Chün[4] Ch'êng[2], 大貳侯 Ta[4] Êrh[4] Hou[2], and 大贊治 Ta[4] Tsan[4] Chih[4]; during the T'ang Dynasty called 少尹 Shao[4] Yin[3].

[427]

849ᴬ   Being direct assistants of the Prefect in the various branches of the prefectural government, 同知 T'ung² Chih¹ are divided, depending on their functions, into several classes, for instance : 1. Assistant Prefects charged with the control of certain classes of offenders are designated 緝捕 Chi⁴ Pu³, 河捕 Ho² Pu³, 捕盜 Pu³ Tao⁴, 總捕 Tsung³ Pu³, 督捕 Tu¹ Pu³, 鹽捕 Yen² Pu³, 軍捕 Chün¹ Pu³, and 糧捕 Liang² Pu³; 2. Assistant Prefects with military jurisdiction are styled 清軍 Ch'ing¹ Chün¹, 軍糧 Chün¹ Liang², 河軍 Ho² Chün¹, and 理事 Li³ Shih⁴, 3. Assistant Prefects in charge of naval construction are called 船政 Ch'uan² Chêng⁴; 4. Assistant Prefects in charge of water communications are styled 河務 Ho² Wu⁴, 管河 Kuan³ Ho², and 水利 Shui³ Li⁴; 5. Assistant Prefects having control over the coast and river defences are designated 江防 Chiang¹ Fang², 分防 Fên¹ Fang², 海防 Hai³ Fang², and 河防 Ho² Fang²; 6. Assistant Prefects with jurisdiction over the population of turbulent districts and savage tribes are styled 撫民 Fu³ Min², 撫夷 Fu³ I², 理猺 Li³ Yao², 理苗 Li³ Miao², 理番 Li³ Fan¹, and 綏猺 Sui¹ Yao².

The foregoing qualifying characters are prefixed to the title 同知 T'ung² Chih¹, for instance, 緝捕同知 Chi⁴ Pu³ T'ung² Chih¹.

For particulars as to Sub-prefects in charge of a sub-prefecture, whether independent or otherwise, see Nos. 852 and 854.

849ᴀ. 通判 T'ung¹ P'an⁴, Second Class Sub-prefect (see No. 848; compare also No. 849); 6ᴀ; colloquially called, 三府 San¹ Fu³; epistolary designation, 別駕 Pieh² Chia⁴; literary designation, 通守 T'ung¹ Shou³, 倅 Ts'ui⁴, 郡倅 Chün⁴ Ts'ui⁴, 大端佐 Ta⁴ Tuan¹ Tso³, or 大贊治 Ta⁴ Tsan⁴ Chih⁴.

As is the case with 同知 T'ung² Chih¹ (see No. 849), 通判 T'ung¹ P'an⁴ are also distinguished, according to their functions, by various designations, namely : 1. 緝捕 Chi⁴ Pu³, 2. 捕河

Pu³ Ho², 3. 捕盜 Pu³ Tao⁴, 4. 總捕 Tsung³ Pu³, 5. 鹽捕 **850**
Yen² Pu³, 6. 清軍 Ch‘ing¹ Chün¹, 7. 理事 Li³ Shih⁴, 8.
分防 Fên¹ Fang², 9. 水利 Shui³ Li⁴, 10. 督理水利
Tu¹ Li³ Shui³ Li⁴, 11. 管糧 Kuan³ Liang², 12. 督糧 Tu¹
Liang², 13. 鹽漕 Yen² Ts‘ao², 14. 撫民 Fu³ Min², 15.
撫彝 Fu³ I², and 16. 理苗 Li³ Miao².

For particulars as to Second Class Sub-prefects administering the government of sub-prefectures, whether independent or
otherwise, *see* Nos. 852 and 854.

850. For carrying on the prefectural government there are,
in addition to the Prefect (*see* No. 848), the First Class Sub-
prefect and Second Class Sub-prefect (*see* Nos. 849 and
849A), the following officials: 1. 經歷 Ching¹ Li⁴ (*see*
No. 826); 8A; (in the Metropolitan Prefecture, 7B; (*see*
No. 794), 2. 照磨 Chao⁴ Mo² (*see* No. 826); 9B, 3. 庫
大使 K‘u⁴ Ta⁴ Shih³ (*see* No. 826); of unclassed rank,
4. 知事 Chih¹ Shih⁴ (*see* No. 830A); 9A, 5. 倉大使
Ts‘ang¹ Ta⁴ Shih³ (*see* No. 826); of unclassed rank, 6. 司
獄 Ssu¹ Yü⁴ (*see* No. 830A); 9B, 7. 教授 Chiao⁴ Shou⁴,
Prefectural Director of Schools; 7A; (literary designation, 儒學
Ju² Hsüeh², 廣文 Kuang³ Wen², 外翰 Wei⁴ Han⁴, 大外翰
Ta⁴ Wai⁴ Han⁴, 學博 Hsüeh² Po², and 大傳經 Ta⁴ Ch‘uan²
Ching¹), 8. 訓導 Hsün⁴ Tao⁴, Prefectural Sub-Director of
Schools (for details *see* No. 857), 9. 稅課司大使 Shui⁴ K‘o⁴
Ssu¹ Ta⁴ Shih³, Prefectural Receiver of Duties and Taxes; 9B,
10. 宣課司正大使 Hsuan¹ K‘o⁴ Ssu¹ Chêng⁴ Ta⁴ Shih³,
Examiner of Taxes: 9B, 11. 宣課司副大使 Hsuan¹ K o⁴
Ssu¹ Fu⁴ Ta⁴ Shih³. Deputy Examiner of Taxes; 9B, 12.
宣課分司大使 Shui⁴ K‘o⁴ Fen¹ Ssu¹ Ta⁴ Shih³, Deputy
Examiner of Taxes, unclassed, 13. 鹽茶大使 Yen² Ch‘a² Ta⁴
Shih³, Tea and Salt Examiner, unclassed, 14. 關大使 Kuan¹
Ta⁴ Shih³, Customs Examiner, unclassed, 15. 河泊所 Ho² Po⁴
So³, River Police Inspector (colloquially called, 河廳 Ho² T‘ing¹),

850A unclassed, 16. 驛丞 I⁴ Ch'êng², Postmaster (*see* No. 754), unclassed, 17. 閘官 Cha² Kuan¹, Sluicekeeper, unclassed, 18. 檢校 Chien³ Hsiao⁴, Prefectural Police Inspector, unclassed, 19. 正科 Chêng⁴ K'o¹ (also 醫學官 I¹ Hsueh² Kuan¹, 大艮相 Ta⁴ Liang² Hsiang⁴, and 大國醫 Ta⁴ Kuo² I¹), Prefectural Physician ; 9B, and 20. 正術 Chêng⁴ Shu⁴ (also 陰陽學官 Yin¹ Yang² Hsueh² Kuan¹, and 大掌術 Ta⁴ Chang³ Shu⁴), Prefectural Inspector of Petty Professions (or Humble Professions).

Coming into the category of followers of humble professions are the following : 1. 算命 Suan⁴ Ming⁴, Fortune-tellers, 2. 相面 Hsiang⁴ Mien⁴, Physiognomists, 3. 測字 Ts'ê⁴ Tzu⁴, Chirographists, 4. 占課 Chan¹ K'o⁴, Diviners, 5. 相風水 Hsiang⁴ Feng¹ Shui³, Geomancers, 6. 巫覡 Wu¹ Chi¹, Jugglers, 7. 江湖賣醫 Chiang¹ Hu² Mai⁴ I¹, Conjurers, 8. 戲子 Hsi⁴ Tzu³, Actors, 9. 賣戲 Mai⁴ Hsi⁴, Jesters, 10. 賣拳 Mai⁴ Ch'üan², Street Wrestlers, 11. 說書 Shuo¹ Shu¹, Story-tellers, 12. 遊脚僧道 Yu² Chiao³ Sêng¹ Tao⁴, and 遊方僧道 Yu² Fang¹ Sêng¹ Tao⁴, Wandering Buddhist and Taoist Priests, 13. 牙婆 Ya² P'o², Women Dentists, 14. 穩婆 Wen³ P'o², Midwives, 15. 丐頭 K'ai⁴ T'ou², Beggar Chiefs and 16. 六色 Liu⁴ Sê⁴, or 六局 Liu⁴ Chü², *i.e.* those belonging to the following six groups: A. 吹手 Ch'ui¹ Shou³, and 鼓吹 Ku³ Ch'ui¹, Pipers and Drummers (so-called 粗樂 Ts'u¹ Yüeh⁴, Coarse or Noisy Music), B. 清音 Ch'ing¹ Yin¹, Flute players (so-called 細樂 Hsi⁴ Yueh⁴, Soft or Melodious Music), C. 礟手 P'ao⁴ Shou³, Fire-cracker Makers, D. 掌禮 Chang³ Li³, Managers of Ceremonies, E. 茶擔 Ch'a² Tan¹, Tea Bearers, F. 擡盤 T'ai² P'an², and 扛橋 K'ang² Chiao⁴, Chair-bearers.

850A. Although the "regulations regarding the reform of the official system of the provinces," articles Nos. 21 and 27 (*see* No. 819B), provide that the Prefects (*see* No. 848) be subordinated to the Governor-General or Governor (*see* Nos. 820 to 821), nevertheless, in addition, they are to receive instructions from the Lieutenant-Governor (*see* No. 825), the Commissioner of Education (*see* No. 827), the Industrial Taotai (*see* No. 839), and the Police Taotai (*see* No. 840).

As regards First and Second Class Sub-prefects (*see* Nos. 849 to 849A), those who are placed in independent control of any district (*see* Nos. 852 and 854) will be appointed as Department Magistrates (*see* No. 855) and District Magistrates (*see* No. 856). The others, acting as Sub-prefects in various branches of the administration (*see* Nos. 849 to 849A), will remain as before, with the exception that their designation 通判 T'ung[1] P'an[4] (*see* No. 849A), will become 同知 T'ung[2] Chih[1] (*see* No. 849).

851. 直隸州知州 Chih[2] Li[4] Chou[1] Chih[1] Chou[1], Magistrate of an Independent Department (*see* No. 846); 5A; official designation, 牧 Mu[4], 州牧 Chou[1] Mu[4] and 大州牧 Ta[4] Chou[1] Mu[4]; epistolary designation, 刺史 Tz'u[4] Shih[3]. When designating himself the Magistrate uses the expression 正堂 Chêng[4] T'ang[2].

The duties and authority of a Magistrate of an Independent Department are similar to those of a Prefect (compare Nos. 846 and 848).

851A. For the administration of an Independent Department, in addition to the Magistrate (*see* No. 851), there are the following: 1. 州同 Chou[1] T'ung[2], First Class Assistant Department Magistrate; 6B (epistolary designation, 別駕 Pieh[2] Chia[4], 州司馬 Chou[1] Ssu[1] Ma[3], and 州貳守 Chou[1] Erh[4] Shou[3]), 2. 州判 Chou[1] P'an[4], Second Class Assistant Department Magistrate; 7B (epistolary designation, 州別駕 Chou[1] Pieh[2] Chia[4], and 叅軍 Ts'an[1] Chün[1]), 3. 吏目 Li[4] Mu[4], Departmental Police-master and Jail Warden; 9B (literary designation, 大功曹 Ta[4] Kung[1] Ts'ao[2], and 大州幕 Ta[4] Chou[1] Mu[4]), 4. 庫大使 K'u[4] Ta[4] Shih[3] (*see* No. 826); unclassed,

851B
to
852

5. 倉大使 Ts'ang¹ Ta⁴ Shih³ (see No. 826); unclassed, 6. 學正 Hsueh² Chêng⁴, Departmental Director of Schools; 8A, 7. 訓導 Hsün⁴ Tao⁴, Departmental Sub-director of Schools; 8B (for details see No. 857), 8. 檢校 Chien³ Hsiao⁴ (see No. 850), unclassed, 9. 關大使 Kuan¹ Ta⁴ Shih³ (see No. 850), unclassed, 10. 典科 Tien³ K'o¹, Departmental Physician, unclassed, and 11. 典術 Tien³ Shu⁴, Departmental Inspector of Petty Professions (or Humble Professions), unclassed.

851B. The "regulations regarding the reform of the official system in the provinces" (articles Nos. 22 and 28; see No. 819B) rule that Magistrates of Independent Departments (see No. 851), although subordinated to the Governor-General or Governor (see Nos. 820 and 821), are to receive instructions also from the Lieutenant-Governor (see No. 825), the Commissioner of Education (see No. 827), the Industrial Taotai (see No. 839), and the Police Taotai (see No. 840), compare No. 850A.

Conforming to the regulations mentioned above, the officials carrying on the administration of Independent Departments and Sub-prefectures, Departments and Districts (see Nos. 851A, 853, 855A and 857)—the so-called 佐貳 Tso³ Erh⁴, and 佐雜 Tso³ Tsa² (see Nos. 858 and 858A)—are later to be done away with and replaced by the following: 1. 警務長 Ching³ Wu⁴ Chang³, Chief of Police (see No. 840A), 2. 視學員 Shih⁴ Hsüeh² Yuan², Inspector of Education, 3. 勸業員 Ch'üan⁴ Yeh⁴ Yüan², Industrial Deputies (see No. 839A), 4. 典獄員 Tien³ Yü⁴ Yüan², Prison Warden (compare Nos. 766A to 766B), and 5. 主計員 Chu³ Chi⁴ Yüan², Inspector of Revenue.

852. 直隸廳同知 Chih² Li⁴ T'ing¹ T'ung² Chih¹, First Class Sub-prefect in charge of an Independent sub-prefecture (properly Sub-prefect; see No. 849; 5A), and 直隸廳通判 Chih² Li⁴ T'ing¹ T'ung¹ P'an⁴, Second Class Sub-prefect in charge of an Independent Sub-prefecture (properly Assistant Sub-prefect;

see No. 849A; 6A). These officials are found in Independent Sub-prefectures (*see* No. 846) and have similar functions to Prefects (*see* No. 848) and Department Magistrates (*see* No. 851).

853. In addition to the Sub-prefect (*see* No. 852), the administration of an Independent Sub-prefecture is carried on by officials almost similar to those of the prefectural administration, namely: 1. 經歷 Ching[1] Li[4], 2. 照磨 Chao[4] Mo[2], 3. 庫大使 K'u[4] Ta[4] Shih[3], 4. 知事 Chih[1] Shih[4], 5. 倉大使 Ts'ang[1] Ta[4] Shih[3], 6. 司獄 Ssu[1] Yü[4], 7. 教授 Chiao[4] Shou[4], 8. 訓導 Hsün[4] Tao[4], 9. 檢校 Chien[3] Hsiao[4], etc. (for details *see* No. 850).

853A. The "regulations regarding the reform of the official system in the provinces" (articles Nos. 23 and 28; *see* No. 819B) call for the later reorganization of those Independent Sub-prefectures which include Districts as Independent Departments. The remainder will be left unchanged administered by the 同知 T'ung[2] Chih[1] (*see* No. 852), who will be subordinated to the Governors-General or Governors (*see* Nos. 820 and 821; compare Nos. 850A and 851B).

For particulars as to the 佐治員 Tso[3] Chih[4] Yüan[2], Auxiliary Ranks, which will be found in the personnel of the administration of an Independent Sub-prefecture *see* No. 851B.

854. At the head of Sub-prefectures which are subject to Prefectures (the so-called 屬廳 Shu[3] T'ing[1], or 散廳 San[3] T'ing[1]; *see* No. 846) there are Assistant Prefects (compare No. 852), *i.e.* 同知 T'ung[2] Chih[1], First Class Sub-prefect (5A; *see* No. 849), and Second Class Sub-prefect (6A; *see* No. 849A).

855. At the head of Departments subject to Prefectures (*see* No. 846) there are (compare No. 851) 知州 Chih[1] Chou[1], Department Magistrates (also 屬州 Shu[3] Chou[1], and 散州 San[3] Chou[1]; epistolary designation, 刺史 Tz'u[4] Shih[3]); 5B. These

855A
to
856B
are under the authority of the Prefects of the respective Prefectures.

855A. For carrying on the government of a Department there are, in addition to the Department Magistrate (*see* No. 855), almost similar officials as for an Independent Department (*see* No. 851A), namely : 1. 州同 Chou¹ T'ung² ; 6B, 2. 州判 Chou¹ P'an⁴ ; 7B, 3. 吏目 Li⁴ Mu⁴ ; 9B, 4. 學正 Hsüeh² Chêng⁴ ; 8A, 5. 訓導 Hsün⁴ Tao⁴ ; 8B, 6. 檢校 Chien³ Hsiao⁴ ; unclassed, 7. 稅課司大使 Shui⁴ K'o⁴ Ssu¹ Ta⁴ Shih³ ; 9B (*see* No. 850), 8. 驛丞 I⁴ Ch'êng² ; unclassed (*see* No. 850), etc.

855B. For particulars as to the 佐治員 Tso³ Chih⁴ Yüan², Auxiliary Ranks, which will be found in the departmental administration *see* No. 851B.

856. 知縣 Chih¹ Hsien⁴, District Magistrate ; 7B ; official designation, 令 Ling⁴, 縣令 Hsien⁴ Ling⁴, 大令 Ta⁴ Ling⁴, and 令尹 Ling⁴ Yin³, (replacing the former 令長 Ling⁴ Chang³) ; epistolary designation, 明府 Ming² Fu³, 廉 Lien², 邑宰 I¹ Tsai³, 大邑宰 Ta⁴ I¹ Tsai³, 邑尊 I¹ Tsun¹, and 大尹 Ta⁴ Yin³ ; styles himself 正堂 Chêng⁴ T'ang², when enumerating his titles.

This official holds office under a Prefect (*see* No. 848) or an Independent Department (*see* No. 851). The Magistrate of the District in which the provincial capital is situated receives the title of 首縣 Shou³ Hsien⁴.

856A. Conforming to the "regulations regarding the reform of the official system in the provinces" (article No. 26 ; *see* No. 819B), the rank of the District Magistrate is to be raised from 7B to 6A (it will thus be on a par with that of the two District Magistrates of a Metropolitan Prefecture ; compare No. 794A).

856B. 父母官 Fu⁴ Mu³ Kuan¹ (literally, officials who are the "father and mother"), Thus are commonly styled the

府州縣 Fu³ Chou¹ Hsien⁴, Prefects and Magistrates, of **857**
the various classes (colloquially spoken of and addressed as
大老爺 Ta⁴ Lao³ Yeh²), who, in the execution of their varied
and very complicated duties, are the nearest to the people (they
are in direct communication with them). The same officials are
known under the general designation of 地方官 Ti⁴ Fang¹
Kuan¹, Local (Territorial) Officials.

857. For carrying on the administration of a District
there are, in addition to the District Magistrate (see No. 856),
the following: 1. 縣丞 Hsien⁴ Ch'êng², Assistant District
Magistrate; 8A (colloquially called, 左堂 Tso³ T'ang²; epistolary
designation, 貳尹 Erh⁴ Yin³; literary designation, 贊府 Tsan⁴
Fu³, and 大贊侯 Ta⁴ Tsan⁴ Hou²), 2. 主簿 Chu³ Pu⁴,
Registrar; 9A (epistolary designation, 三尹 San¹ Yin³; literary
designation, 仇香 Ch'ou² Hsiang¹), 3. 巡檢 Hsün² Chien³,
Sub-district Magistrate; 9B (epistolary designation, 分司 Fen¹
Ssu¹, a Sub-district is called 司 Ssu¹; see No. 857B, 少尹 Shao⁴
Yin³, 巡政廳 Hsün² Chêng⁴ T'ing¹, 巡司 Hsün² Ssu¹, and
大司巡 Ta⁴ Ssu¹ Hsün²), 4. 典史 Tien³ Shih³, Jail Warden
(colloquially called, 捕廳 Pu³ T'ing¹; literary designation, 右堂
Yu⁴ T'ang²; epistolary designation, 少尉 Shao⁴ Yü⁴, 少尹
Shao⁴ Yin³, 廉捕 Lien² Pu³, 少府 Shao⁴ Fu³, 大少府 Ta⁴
Shao⁴ Fu³, 邑尉 I¹ Yü⁴, and 大贊政 Ta⁴ Tsan⁴ Chêng⁴);
unclassed, 5. 教諭 Chiao⁴ Yü⁴, District Director of Schools;
8A (literary designation, 復諭 Fu⁴ Yü⁴; from the full official
title 復設教諭 Fu⁴ Shê⁴ Chiao⁴ Yü⁴, which indicates "the
restoration cf the office after its temporary abolition in the last
century"; epistolary designation, 司教 Ssu¹ Chiao⁴, and 正齋
Chêng⁴ Chai¹), 6. 訓導 Hsün⁴ Tao⁴, Sub-director of Schools;
8B (literary designation, 復訓 Fu⁴ Hsün⁴, from the full official
title 復設訓導 Fu⁴ Shê⁴ Hsün⁴ Tao⁴, see above; epistolary
designation, 司訓 Ssu¹ Hsün⁴, and 副齋 Fu⁴ Chai¹), 7. 倉大
使 Ts'ang¹ Ta⁴ Shih³ (see No. 826); unclassed, 8. 閘官 Cha²

857ᴀ
to
859

Kuan¹ (*see* No. 850); unclassed, 9. 卡官 Ch'ia⁴ Kuan¹, Keeper of a Customs Barrier; unclassed, 10. 訓科 Hsün⁴ K'o¹, District Physician; unclassed, and 11. 訓術 Hsün⁴ Shu⁴, District Inspector of Petty Professions (or Humble Professions).

857ᴀ. For particulars as to the 佐治員 Tso³ Chih⁴ Yüan², Auxiliary Ranks, which will later be found in the district administration, *see* No. 851ʙ.

857ʙ. The "regulations regarding the reform of the official system in the provinces" (article No. 31; *see* No. 819ʙ) define that all Independent Departments and Sub-prefectures, as well as Departments and Districts, be later divided into a certain number of 區 Ch'ü¹, Divisions, which will be under 區官 Ch'ü¹ Kuan¹, Police Captains (*see* No. 840ᴀ), who will be in full control of all police affairs in their respective divisions. Simultaneously, the post of 巡檢 Hsün² Chien³, Sub-district Magistrate (*see* No. 857) will be abolished.

858. 佐貳 Tso³ Erh⁴, Assistant Magistrate; of Prefectures, Departments and Districts; literary designation, 丞倅 Ch'êng² Ts'ui⁴.

858ᴀ. 佐雜 Tso³ Tsa², Petty Officials. In this category come Assistant Magistrates, Secretaries to the Prefect, etc., of the eighth rank, who are styled 佐 Tso³, and minor officials, of the ninth rank and of unclassed rank, who are styled 雜 Tsa².

Later the 佐貳 Tso³ Erh⁴ (*see* No. 858) and the 佐雜 Tso³ Tsa² are to be abolished, being replaced by 佐治員 Tso³ Chih⁴ Yüan², Auxiliary Ranks (for details *see* No. 851ʙ).

859. To the number of government establishments common to nearly all the provinces, and performing special functions, there may be added the following: 1. 洋務局 Yang² Wu⁴ Chü², Office of Foreign Affairs (交涉局 Chiao¹ Shê⁴ Chü² in Manchuria; *see* No. 806c), charged with the negotiation of all questions concerning foreigners at places where there is no special official for this purpose (compare No. 832), 2. 統捐局

T'ung³ Chüan¹ Chü², Office for the Collection of Consolidated **860** Duties (under 統捐 T'ung³ Chüan¹, Consolidated Duties, is meant the simultaneous collection of 起稅 Ch'i³ Shui⁴, Import Duty, and 落稅 Lo⁴ Shui⁴, Duty at the Place of Sale,— 起落並征 Ch'i³ Lo⁴ Ping⁴ Chêng¹), 3. 釐捐局 Li² Chüan¹ Chü², Likin Station, 4. 官報局 Kuan¹ Pao⁴ Chü², Government Newspaper Office (found in provinces where a Government Newspaper is published, for instance, at Tientsin, where the 北洋官報 Pei³ Yang² Kuan¹ Pao⁴ is published), 5. 官醫院 Kuan¹ I¹ Yüan⁴, Public Dispensary (*see* No. 517); supplying free medical advice and having a 牛痘局 Niu² Tou⁴ Chü², Vaccination Office, 6. 支應局 Chih¹ Ying⁴ Chü², Treasury: for the issue of money for public use, 7. 衛生局 Wei⁴ Shêng¹ Chü², Sanitary Office; superintending sanitary conditions of cities, 8. 工程局 Kung¹ Ch'êng² Chü², Building Office; superintending the construction of pavements and roads, the macadamizing of roads and their maintenance in repair, 9. 編譯局 Pien¹ I⁴ Chü², Book Compilation and Translation Office; charged with the translation of foreign books and the compilation of Chinese books, 10. 銀元局 Yin² Yüan² Chü², and 銅元局 T'ung² Yüan² Chü², Mint; formerly minting silver (銀元 Yin² Yüan²) and copper (銅元 T'ung² Yüan²) coins; now being gradually replaced by the 造幣分廠 Tsao⁴ Pi⁴ Fen¹ Ch'ang³ (*see* No. 551B), 11. 籌賑處 Ch'ou² Chên⁴ Ch'u⁴, Relief Committee; established at those places where the people need relief because of natural calamities, and 12. 官書局 Kuan¹ Shu¹ Chü², Provincial Government Printing-Office; found in the majority of the provinces.

860. 文廟奉祀官 Wen² Miao⁴ Fêng⁴ Ssu⁴ Kuan¹, Priest at the Temple of Confucius (7A to 8B; compare No. 572). This official supervises the sacrificial attributes and maintains the temple in good condition. The "regulations regarding the reform of the official system in the provinces" (article No. 32;

**861
to
861A**

see No. 819B) call for the appointment of this official to all prefectures, sub-prefectures, departments and districts to replace the so-called 教職 Chiao⁴ Chih² (*i.e.* 教授 Chiao⁴ Shou⁴, 學正 Hsüeh² Chêng⁴, 教諭 Chiao⁴ Yü⁴, and 訓導 Hsün⁴ Tao⁴; *see* Nos. 850, 851A, 853, 855A and 857).

ADMINISTRATION OF "NATIVE" DISTRICTS.

861. 土官 T'u³ Kuan¹, Administrators of "Native" Districts.

The sections of the provinces of Kuangsi, Kueichow, Yünnan and Szechwan which are inhabited exclusively by the 苗子 Miao² Tzu³, and other aboriginal tribes, are, in some cases, organized into prefectures, departments or districts ruled by hereditary Prefects, Department Magistrates or District Magistrates, who bear the ordinary Chinese official titles with the character 土 T'u³, prefixed, for instance, 土府 T'u³ Fu³, 土州 T'u³ Chou¹, and 土縣 T'u³ Hsien⁴.

The process of changing the status of a tribe, *i.e.* introducing the ordinary system of government in place of the direct government by an hereditary chieftain, is denoted by the phrase 改土爲流 Kai³ T'u³ Wei² Liu² (or 改土歸流 Kai³ T'u³ Kuei¹ Liu²).

861A. 土司 T'u³ Ssu¹, The Native Tribes; and their Chieftains. This is the designation applied to the 苗子 Miao² Tzu³, of Kuangsi, Kueichow and Szechwan, to the 猓玀|玀猓 Lo³ Lo³, of Szechwan and Yünnan, and to the Shans occupying the Southern and Western parts of Yünnan. The last-named are the descendants of the people of 越裳 Yüeh⁴ Shang⁴, and are styled in Chinese literature 老撾 Lao³ Chua¹. The Shans of the borderland of Yünnan and Burmah style themselves, and are commonly known as, 擺夷 Pai³ I².

The chieftains of the above-mentioned and other tribes are invested with ranks of different grades, as shown in the following schedule: 1. 宣慰使司 Hsüan[1] Wei[4] Shih[3] Ssu[1]; 3B, 2. 宣撫使司 Hsüan[1] Fu[4] Shih[3] Ssu[1]; 4B, 3. 招討使司 Chao[1] T'ao[3] Shih[3] Ssu[1]; 5B, 4. 安撫使司 An[1] Fu[3] Shih[3] Ssu[1]; 5B, 5. 同知 T'ung[2] Chih[1]; with rank varying from 3B to 6A, 6. 副使 Fu[4] Shih[3]; with rank varying from 4B to 6B, and 7. 僉事 Ch'ien[1] Shih[4]; with rank varying from 4A to 7A.

Another type of tribal government shows the following ranks: 1. 千戶 Ch'ien[1] Hu[4] (chieftain of one thousand; 5A), 2. 副千戶 Fu[4] Ch'ien[1] Hu[4] (assistant chieftain of one thousand; 5B), 3. 百戶 Po[2] Hu[4] (centurion; 6A), 4. 長官司 長官 Chang[3] Kuan[1] Ssu[1] Chang[3] Kuan[1]; 6A, 5. 副長官 Fu[4] Chang[3] Kuan[1]; 7A, and 6. 長官司吏目 Chang[3] Kuan[1] Ssu[1] Li[4] Mu[4]; unclassed.

EASTERN TURKESTAN.

862. The province of 新疆 Hsin[1] Chiang[1] (full designation, 甘肅新疆省 Kan[1] Su[4] Hsin[1] Chiang[1] Shêng[3]), New Dominion of Kansu (see Nos. 819 to 819A; also called Eastern or Chinese Turkestan), formerly called 西域 Hsi[1] Yü[4], Western Border, was formed in 1884 from the territory situated on the two slopes of the T'ien Shan (天山南北兩路 T'ien[1] Shan[1] Nan[2] Pei[3] Liang[3] Lu[4]) and is governed on lines similar to those of the remaining 18 provinces of China proper, and those of Manchuria, in that the administrative head is the Governor (see No. 821A). Some peculiarities, however, exist in its governmental system, which are explained by its population by Turkish, Mongolian and Manchurian races (see Nos. 863 to 865).

863. The Mussulman population of Hsinchiang (in Chinese, 回民 Hui[4] Min[2]; also 纏頭回回 Ch'an[2] T'ou[2] Hui[2] Hui[2], Turban-wearing Mussulmen) is ruled by its generic chieftains,

**863A
to
864**
the so-called Begs (in Chinese 伯克 Po² K'o⁴), who are graded according to their importance in six classes : 1. 阿齊木伯克 A⁴ Ch'i² Mu⁴ Po² K'o⁴, Ak'im Beg ; Local Governor, 2. 伊什罕伯克 I¹ Shih² Han³ Po² K'o⁴, Ishhan Beg ; Assistant Governor, 3. 商伯克 Shang¹ Po² K'o⁴, Shang Beg ; Collector of Revenues, 4. 噶雜納齊伯克 Ka¹ Tsa² Na⁴ Ch'i² Po² K'o⁴, Katsonatch'i Beg (as above), 5. 哈孜伯克 Ha¹ Tzu¹ Po² K'o⁴, Hatsze Beg ; Judge, and 6. 密喇布伯克 Mi⁴ La³ Pu⁴ Po² K'o⁴, Mirabu Beg ; Superintendent of Agriculture.

The Mussulman tribes in the departments of Hami (哈密 廳 Ha⁴ Mi⁴ T'ing¹, Hamul) and T'urfan (吐魯番廳 T'u³ Lu³ Fan¹ T'ing¹, or 廣安城 Kuang³ An¹ Ch'êng², Kunia-T'urfan) have a type of administration approaching the Mongolian, *i.e.* they are arranged in Princedoms (Banners) ruled by generic chieftains—Dzassaks—who often receive Princely titles (王 Wang², 貝勒 Pei¹ Lê⁴, etc.).

863A. The Kirghis (哈薩克 Ha¹ Sa¹ K'o⁴), nomadizing in the T'arbagatai region, and under the control of the local Amban (*see* No. 867), are ruled by their generic chieftains, 千戶長 Ch'ien¹ Hu⁴ Chang³, Chiefs of One Thousand, and 百戶長 Po² Hu⁴ Chang³, Centurions (compare No. 877A). There are no bearers of Princely titles (Sultan ; 王 Wang²) amongst them ; the only title found is that of 閑散台吉 Hsien² San³ T'ai² Chi², Daidji with no definite rank (*see* No. 873).

864. The Mongolian, or properly, Oelöt (in Chinese 額魯特 Ê⁴ Lu³ T'ê⁴), tribes of the old Tourgouth (in Chinese 舊土爾扈特 Chiu⁴ T'u³ Êrh³ Hu⁴ T'ê⁴) and Khoshoit (in Chinese 和碩特 Ho² Sho⁴ T'ê⁴) divisions, residing in the Ili district (in the valleys of the Yuldoos, K'obuk and K'ur-K'ara-usu rivers, and about Kuldja), are divided, as are all Mongols, into Khoshuns under generic Prince-chieftains, and form two leagues : 1. Unen-Sutzukt'u (in Chinese 烏納恩素珠克圖盟

Wu¹ Na⁴ Ên¹ Su¹ Chu¹ K'o⁴ T'u² Mêng²), of 10 Khoshuns, and

2. Pat'u-Set'khilt'u (in Chinese 巴 圖 色 特 啟 勒 圖 盟 Pa² T'u² Sê⁴ T'ê⁴ Ch'i³ Lê⁴ T'u² Mêng²), of three Khoshuns. They are under the control of the Military Governor of Ili (*see* No. 866).

865
to
868

865. 領 隊 大 臣 Ling³ Tui⁴ Ta⁴ Ch'ên², Commandant of the Forces. Thus are styled the officials at the head of the military colonists, found in the Ili and T'arbagatai regions, drawn from the 錫 伯 Si² Bê², Mongols, from the neighbourhood of of Jehol, 素 倫 So³ Lun², Manchus, from the region of the Amur, Ch'akhars, and Oelöts. There are four in the Ili region and one for the Tarbagatai region.

866. 伊 犁 將 軍 I¹ Li² Chiang¹ Chün¹, The Tartar General and Military Governor of Ili (*see* No. 744c), residing at 綏 定 Sui¹ Ting⁴, Suitun. He is in command of the military forces of Hsinchiang province in general and, tó some extent, is the head of the Manchu Garrison and the two Mongolian leagues (*see* No. 864). The first official of this category was appointed in 1764.

867. As assistants to the Military Governor of Ili (*see* No. 866), for military affairs, there are two 副 都 統 Fu⁴ Tu¹ T'ung³, Brigade-Generals or Assistant Military Governors, (*see* No. 745B), residing, respectively, at Kuldja and Ch'ukuch'ak (in Chinese 塔 城 Ta³ Ch'êng²). His assistants for civil affairs are two 柴 贊 大 臣 Ts'an¹ Tsan⁴ Ta⁴ Ch'ên², Councillors, or Ambans, residing, respectively, at Kuldja and Ch'ukuch'ak. To the latter there is given a great amount of independence in the government of the T'arbagatai region.

THE DEPENDENCIES OF THE EMPIRE.

868. Included in the Dependencies of China governed on peculiar lines—with a government differing from that of the 19

[441]

**869
to
870ᴀ**

provinces of China proper. and the provinces of Manchuria—are: 1. 蒙古 Mêng³ Ku³, Mongolia, 2. 青海 Ch'ing¹ Hai³, K'uk'unor, and 西藏 Hsi¹ Tsang⁴, Tibet.

The Central Government Establishment invested with the superintendency over the Dependencies is the Ministry of Dependencies at Peking (*see* No. 491ᴀ; formerly the Court of Colonial Affairs, *see* No. 491).

A. Mongolia:

869. 蒙古 Mêng³ Ku³, Mongolia (*see* No. 868) is divided into: 1. 外蒙古 Wai⁴ Mêng³ Ku³, Outer, or Northern, Mongolia, and 2. 內蒙古 Nei⁴ Mêng³ Ku³, Inner, or Southern, Mongolia.

869ᴀ. Outer, or Northern, Mongolia (*see* No. 869) comprises: 1. Khalkha (in Chinese 喀爾喀 K'a¹ Êrh³ K'a¹), 2. The region of K'obdo (in Chinese 科布多 K'o¹ Pu⁴ To¹), 3. The region of Altai (in Chinese 阿爾泰 A⁴ Êrh³ T'ai⁴) and 4. The territory of T'annu-Urianghai (in Chinese 唐努烏梁海 T'ang² Nu² Wu¹ Liang² Hai³).

870. The Khalkhas (*see* No. 869ᴀ) consist of four 部 Pu⁴, Tribes (Mongolian, Aimak) (formerly administrative units): 1. The T'ushet'u-Khanate (in Chinese 土謝圖汗部 T'u³ Hsieh⁴ T'u² Han⁴ Pu⁴), 2. The Tsetsen-Khanate (in Chinese 車臣汗部 Ch'ê¹ Ch'ên² Han⁴ Pu⁴), 3. The Sain-noin (in Chinese 賽音諾顏部 Sai⁴ Yin¹ No⁴ Yen² Pu⁴), and 4. The Dzassakt'u-Khanate (in Chinese 丸薩克圖汗部 Cha¹ Sa¹ K'o⁴ T'u² Han⁴ Pu⁴).

870ᴀ. Aimak is the old Mongolian designation of a Princely appanage—group of Banners forming the inheritance of one Banner line. Thus the Aimak is a consolidation of a number of Banners, bound together by ties of race, past history and the former dominion of a common Prince (ruler), an ancestor of its present ruling Princes.

During the lapse of time the Aimaks have been divided into **871** independent Banners, but the ties of relationship have never been **to** forgotten and the eldest Prince is still considered as the chief of **872** his respective Aimak.

After the submission of Mongolia to the Manchu Dynasty now reigning in China the significance of Aimaks and their rulers declined. The Aimaks of Khalkha, as administrative units, are replaced by the Leagues (*see* No. 872) and the power of the Khans (*see* No. 873) by the authority of the Captains-General of the Leagues (*see* No. 872). Throughout the remainder of Mongolia the appurtenance of various Banners to one Aimak is shown by their common designation.

871. Each Aimak, for military purposes, is a division, composed of 旗 Ch'i², Khoshun, or Banners, which are divided into 佐領 Tso³ Ling³, Sumung, or Squadrons, of 150 horsemen each. Six Squadrons form one 甲喇 Chia³ La³, Tsalang, or Regiment (compare No. 874).

871A. In the Khalkhas there are 86 Khoshun (Banners), *i.e.* 20 in the T'ushet'u-Khanate Aimak, 23 in the Tsetsen-Khanate, 24 in the Sain-noin and 19 in the Dzassakt'u, supplying 169 Squadrons (*see* No. 871).

872. The general administration of Mongolia, and the dispensing of justice, appertains, as will be described below (Nos. 879 to 880), to specially appointed Chinese officials. In Khalkha these officials are invested, also, with a peculiar supreme authority.

As regards local government, this is carried on by the Mongols themselves with almost no interference from the Chinese higher authorities.

The higher judicial-administrative institution of the Aimak (*see* No. 870; 愛瑪克 Ai⁴ Ma³ K'o⁴) is the 盟 Mêng², League (Mongolian, Chogolgan), which meets once in three years, and is attended by all the Prince-rulers of the Banners (*see* No.

872A 873), for the discussion of : 1. Judicial affairs in which members of the various Banners are implicated, 2. Affairs of economy affecting the Aimak as a whole, 3. Administrative questions concerning the Aimak as a whole, and 4. Questions relating to the taking of the census.

The Chinese officials do not interfere with the deliberations of the League.

At the head of a League there is a 盟 長 Mêng² Chang³, League Captain-General (Mongolian, Chogolganu Taruga ; at the same time Commander of a Division). He is assisted by a 副 盟 長 Fu⁴ Mêng² Chang³, League Deputy Captain-General (Mongolian, Têd Chogolganu Taruga).

Formerly the Captain-General of a League was the Khan of the Aimak ; the Manchus, after their conquest, made this post elective. At the present time the League Captain-General is elected from the ranks of Prince-rulers of the Banners of the respective Aimak and must be approved by the Emperor.

As Commander of a Division the League Captain-General has as his assistant, for military affairs, one 副 將 軍 Fu⁴ Chiang¹ Chün¹, Assistant Commander of a Division (Mongolian, T'usalakch'ih Chiang Chün), to whom there is attached a Hopei Amban, Adviser. The two last-mentioned posts are elective (members of the League being eligible) and subject to Imperial approval. The Chinese authorities often exert strong pressure to ensure the election of this, or that, person.

872A. The first Khalkha Division (the T'ushet'u-Khanate Aimak ; *see* No. 870) is styled Han-ula (in Chinese 汗 阿 林 盟 Han⁴ A⁴ Lin² Mêng²), from the name of the mountain, near Urga, where the Prince-rulers of this Division meet.

The second Khalkha Division (the Tsetsen-Khanate Aimak) is styled Kerulen-bars-hoto (in Chinese 客 魯 倫 巴 爾 和 屯 盟 K'o⁴ Lu³ Lun² Pa¹ Erh³ Ho² T'un² Mêng²), from the name of the place where its Prince-rulers meet.

The third Khalkha Division (the Sain-noin Aimak) is called Ts'ets'erlikh (in Chinese 齊齊爾里克盟 Ch'i² Ch'i² Erh³ Li³ K'o⁴ Mêng²), from the meeting place of the Prince-rulers of this division.

The fourth Khalkha Division (the Dzassakt'u Aimak) is designated Tsak-gol (in Chinese 札克必喇色欽 Cha¹ K'o⁴ Pi⁴ La³ Sê⁴ Ch'in¹), or Pinduriya-nor (in Chinese 畢都里雅諾爾盟 Pi⁴ Tu¹ Li³ Ya³ No¹ Erh³ Meng²), from the name of a tributary river of the Paidarik, where the Prince-rulers of this division gather.

873. 札薩克 Cha¹ Sa¹ K'o⁴, Dzassak, or Chieftain (in Chinese 旗長 Ch'i² Chang³). This official is at the head of a Banner (*see* No. 871) and must be approved by the Emperor.

The Dzassak are arranged in the following hereditary ranks: 1. 和碩親王 Ho² Shê⁴ Ch'in¹ Wang², Prince of the First Degree, 2. 多羅郡王 To¹ Lo² Chün⁴ Wang², Prince of the Second Degree, 3. 多羅貝勒 To¹ Lo² Pei¹ Lê⁴, Prince of the Third Degree, 4. 固山貝子 Ku¹ Shan¹ Pei¹ Tzŭ³, Prince of the Fourth Degree, 5. 奉恩鎮國公 Fêng⁴ Ên¹ Chên⁴ Kuo² Kung¹, Prince of the Fifth Degree (Mongolian, Ulusung T'ushê Kung), 6. 奉恩輔國公 Fêng⁴ Ên¹ Fu³ Kuo² Kung¹, Prince of the Sixth Degree (Mongolian, Ulus-t'ur T'ussalakh-ch'ih Kung), and 7. 台吉 T'ai² Chi², Daidji (Hereditary Noble). There are four classes (等 Têng³) of the last rank but the first alone carries with it eligibility for election as Commandant, or Chief, of a Banner.

In addition to the titles mentioned there is that of 汗 Han¹, Khan, held by descendants of the Khans of the four Aimaks (*see* No. 870), which is higher even than that of 親王 Ch'in¹ Wang² (*see* above).

873ᴀ. 宰桑 Tsai³ Sang¹, Tsaisang, (the Mongolian word means "a stock"; "chief of a generation.") This title replaces

**873B
to
874**

that of 台吉 T'ai² Chi² (*see* No. 873) in distinguishing the Hereditary Nobles of the Oelöt tribes.

873B. 諸顏 No⁴ Yen², Noyen, or Noin; Ruling Prince. This is an old Mongolian Princely title and was heretofore in use for speaking of, or addressing, Princes.

873C. 塔布囊 T'a³ Pu⁴ Nang², Tabunang (the Mongolian word means "husband of an Imperial, or Royal, Princess.") This title corresponds to the Chinese 額駙 Ê⁴ Fu⁴ (*see* No. 15).

873D. 達爾汗 Ta² Êrh³ Han⁴, Tarkhan (the Mongolian word means "master.") This is an old Mongolian title which is appended to the name of Princes who have distinguished themselves in some way. It has been left by the Manchu Dynasty uncharged and conferred as a hereditary title on certain Princes (for instance on one of the Khorch'in Princes). It carries with it an increased allowance as compared with the other Princes.

873E. 乾清門行走 Ch'ien² Ch'ing¹ Mên² Hsing² Tsou³, Attaché to the Palace Gate, 乾清門 Ch'ien² Ch'ing¹ Mên² (compare Nos. 99 and 104C); a title bestowed on Mongolian Princes.

For particulars as to the 御前行走 Yü⁴ Ch'ien² Hsing² Tsou³, *see* No. 101A.

874 The Chieftain of a Banner (Dzassak; *see* No. 873) is the absolute master of all its affairs. He may present to the Gegens (Living Buddahs) persons belonging to him or he may give them as part of his daughters' wedding portions. He examines into all lawsuits, allots duties, etc.

The system of inheritance of the post of Dzassak, thanks to which men of no capacity have been, and are, appointed as Banner Chieftains as well as the multitude and complexity of Banner affairs, have called into existence the Banner posts of: 1. 協理台吉 Hsieh² Li³ T'ai² Chi², Administrator (Mongolian, T'ussalakch'ih-Taidji), assistant to the Dzassak in the administration of the affairs of his Banner, and 2. 管旗章京 Kuan³ Ch'i² Chang¹

Ching¹, Adjutant (Mongolian, Tzahurukch'ih-Changguin). As practice shows, practically the whole of the management of the affairs of the Banners falls on the shoulders of these assistants, owing to the incapacity of the Dzassak or because of his absence, either at Peking (on duty) or at meetings of the League.

As a general rule all questions discussed at a League meeting are reported direct to the Administrator (it may be mentioned here that this post and that of Adjutant are not hereditary; appointment to them is dependent on the will of the Banner Chieftain). For this reason his post is practically that of the first importance in the Banner.

The Adjutant plays a secondary role to the Administrator. He reviews the forces of the Banner to which he is attached, superintends education, arranges that the horses and arms are in order, appoints men for various services, etc.

To the Adjutant of a Banner Chieftain there are attached one (two when there are more than 10 squadrons to the Banner; see No. 871) 管 旗 副 章 京 Kuan³ Ch'i² Fu⁴ Chang¹ Ching¹, Deputy Adjutant (Mongolian, Meirenu Changguing).

In command of a regiment (Tsa-lang; see No. 871) there is a 叅 領 Ts'an¹ Ling³, Colonel (Mongolian, Tsalangu Changguing. A squadron (Sumung; see No. 871) is commanded by a 佐 領 Tso³ Ling³, Lieutenant-Colonel (Mongolian, Sumungu Changguing), to whom there are subordinated four 曉 騎 校 Hsiao¹ Ch'i² Hsiao⁴, Subalterns (Mongolian, Huntui or Kuntui), and six 領 催 Ling³ Ts'ui¹, Sergeants (Mongolian, Hukekch'ih, Poshk'o; Manchu, Poshok'u).

Under the command of a 佐 領 Tso³ Ling³ there are six 領 催 Ling³ Ts'ui¹, 50 馬 甲 Ma³ Chia³, Cavalrymen, and 100 閑 散 Hsien² San³, Miscellaneous (compare No. 871).

In time of peace the officials of the military organization perform, as a rule, police-administrative duties, being occupied

875 with the collection of revenues, apprehension of criminals and deserters, etc.

Appointment to the Banner posts above-mentioned is not dependent on heredity. They are filled by persons chosen by the Banner Chieftain.

The bulk of the Mongolian population is styled 鄂爾巴圖 Ao⁴ Êrh³ Pa¹ T'u² (Mongolian, Alba, meaning "tribute;" "requisition in kind.") The various families are arranged in groups of ten, under 什長 Shih² Chang³, Decurions.

875. 商卓特巴衙門 Shang¹ Cho¹ T'ê⁴ Pa¹ Ya² Mên², Office of the Shabis. To this office belong those who have been given as presents at various times, by the Mongol Princes, to the Cheptsum Damba Hut'ukht'u (in Chinese 哲布尊丹巴呼圖克圖 Chê² Pu⁴ Tsun¹ Tan¹ Pa¹ Hu¹ T'u² K'o⁴ T'u²; see No. 916ᴀ), the Gegen of Urga. These people, designated 沙必 Sha¹ Pi⁴, or 沙畢那爾 Sha¹ Pi⁴ Na¹ Êrh³, Shabinar, or Novice of the Prelate (Gegen), make up a very large portion of the population. They number 100,000 and, having no land of their own, wander over the lands of the various Khalkha Banners.

At the head of the Office of the Shabis there is the 商卓特巴 Shang¹ Cho¹ T'ê⁴ Pa¹, Shang Chodba, or Treasurer, whose rank was made equal to that of a League Captain General in 1822 (see No. 872). To him there are attached two 達喇嘛 Ta² La³ Ma⁴, Da Lamas—Assistants, whose rank has been made equal to that of Councillors (see No. 872). From the two latter officials the Shang Chodba is usually chosen, the appointment being subject to Imperial approval. The full title of the Treasurer is Erdeni-setsen-dalai-chindamani-t'oin-shang Chodba.

As a controller over the actions of the Shang Chodba and his Assistants there is selected one of the generic Khalkha Princes, who serves for three years.

The Shabis are exempt from military service and are arranged in clans (Mongolian, Ot'ok) headed by Darugui, or Dargui—Generic Elders—who must be approved by the Emperor (12 in all). To these Elders there are subordinated 9 to 10 Junior Darugui, Assistant Generic Elders, who receive their appointments from the Shang Chodba.

At the office of the Shang Chodba there are found 宰桑 Tsai³ Sang¹, Captains (20 to 30 in number), performing police duties, to whom there are subordinated Hia, Sergeants, (numbering about 100), who perform duty as runners.

876. The region of K'obdo (in Chinese 科布多 K'o¹ Pu⁴ To¹; *see* No. 869A) is occupied by the Mongol, properly Oelöt (in Chinese 額魯特 Ê⁴ Lu³ T'ê⁴, and 金山額魯特 Chin¹ Shan¹ Ê⁴ Lu³ T'ê⁴, Altai Oelöts) clans of Durbets (in Chinese 杜爾伯 特 Tu⁴ Êrh³ Po² T'ê⁴), and Khoits (in Chinese 輝特 Hui¹ T'ê⁴), under the control of the K'obdo Hebei-Amban (*see* No. 880). Divided, as are all Mongols, into various Banners under the direction of the generic Princes, the K'obdo Oelöts make up one League (there were two Leagues formerly; compare No. 876A), the Sain-Tsayagat'u (in Chinese 賽音濟雅哈圖盟 Sai⁴ Yin¹ Chi⁴ Ya³ Ha¹ T'u² Mêng²), comprising sixteen Banners, *i.e.* two Banners of Khoits and 14 Banners of Turbets—11 of the Right Wing and three of the Left Wing.

The K'obdo Hebei-Amban, in addition to the above, has authority over: 1. The Dzakhach'in Aimak (in Chinese 札哈 沁部 Cha¹ Ha¹ Ch'in⁴ Pu⁴), of one Banner, which formerly was affiliated with the Ch'ing Setkhilt'u League (*see* No. 876A), 2. The Mingat Aimak (in Chinese 明阿特部 Ming² A⁴ T'ê⁴ Pu⁴, or 明噶特部 Ming² K'a¹ T'ê⁴ Pu⁴), of one Banner with no generic Prince—Dzassak, and 3. One Banner of the Oelöts (in Chinese 額魯特旗 Ê⁴ Lu³ T'ê⁴ Ch'i²), having no generic Prince—Dzassak.

876A. Prior to 1907 (compare No. 877) the following were under the jurisdiction of the K'obdo Hebei-Amban (*see* No. 880): 1. One Aimak of the New Tourgouths (in Chinese

877
to
877ᴀ

新土爾扈特部 Hsin¹ T'u³ Êrh³ Hu⁴ T'ê⁴ Pu⁴), made up of two Banners, 2. One Aimak of the New Khoshoits (in Chinese 新和碩特部 Hsin¹ Ho² Sho⁴ T'ê⁴ Pu⁴), of one Banner, 3. One Aimak of the Altai Urianghais (in Chinese 阿爾泰烏梁海部 A⁴ Êrh³ T'ai⁴ Wu¹ Liang² Hai³ Pu⁴), of seven Banners, 4. The Military-Agricultural Settlements (in Chinese 屯田兵) at Pulunt'o-Khoi (in Chinese 布倫托海 Pu⁴ Lun² T'o¹ Hai³), and 5. The lands of Kirghis (in Chinese 哈薩克 Ha¹ Sa¹ K'o⁴).

Two Banners of the New Tourgouths form the Ch'ing Setkhilt'u League (in Chinese 青色特啓勒圖盟 Ch'ing¹ Sê⁴ T'ê⁴ Ch'i³ Lê⁴ T'u² Mêng²). This League formerly included one Banner of Khoshoits and one Banner of Djakch'ins also (see No. 876).

877. The district of Altai (in Chinese 阿爾泰 A⁴ Êrh³ T'ai⁴, or 金山 Chin¹ Shan¹; see No. 869ᴀ) was made distinct from that of K'obdo (see No. 876) in 1907 (see an Imperial Decree of the 20th January, 1907, issued in consequence of representations by 連魁 Lien² K'uei², the Hebei-Amban of K'obdo, and his Assistant, 錫恒 Hsi² Hêng²) and was allotted to two Banners of the New Tourgouths, one Banner of the New Khoshoits, seven Banners of the Altai Urianghais, the Military-Agricultural Settlements at Bulunt'okhoi and a section of the Kirghis (see Memorials from the Ministries of Dependencies and of Finance, dated the 7th February, 1907, and from the Ministry of War, dated the 9th March of the same year). For details as to its administration see No. 877ᴀ.

877ᴀ. 哈薩克 Ha¹ Sa¹ K'o⁴, Kirghis. Inhabiting Altai, they consist of 12 鄂托克 Ao⁴ T'o¹ K'o⁴, Ot'oks, Clans (11,516 families in all). In addition to a 公 Kung¹, Prince, and three 台吉 T'ai² Chi², Daidjis, their rulers include 12 比阿哈拉克齊 Pi³ A⁴ Ha¹ La¹ K'o⁴ Ch'i² (比 Pi³ is identified as the equivalent of 伯克 Po² K'o⁴; compare No. 863) Pihahalakhch'ih,

Generic Chieftains, or Rulers (in Mongolian, Ukherid; among the Kirghis, Ukurdai; formerly 總管 Tsung³ Kuan³, or 按班 An⁴ Pan¹, in Chinese), or 千戶長 Ch'ien¹ Hu⁴ Chang³, Chiefs of One Thousand ; 3A. Attached to them there are: 1. 副阿哈拉克齊 Fu⁴ A⁴ Ha¹ La¹ K'o⁴ Ch'i², Fu-Ahalakhch'ih, Assistant Generic Chieftains, or 副千戶長 Fu⁴ Ch'ien¹ Hu⁴ Chang³, Assistant Chiefs of One Thousand (5 in all), 2. 札蘭 Cha¹ Lan², Chiefs of a Column, or 五百戶長 Wu³ Po² Hu⁴ Chang³, Chiefs of 500 (4A; 28 in all), 3. 章蓋 Chang¹ Kai⁴, or 百戶長 Po² Hu⁴ Chang³, Centurions (5A; 78 in all), and 4. 昆都 K'un¹ Tu¹ (Kundui), or 五十戶長 Wu³ Shih² Hu⁴ Chang³, Chiefs of 50 (78 in all). For details as to the last-mentioned ranks *see* a memorial from 錫恒 Hsi² Hêng², dated the 22nd October, 1909

878. 878. The territory of Tannu-Urianghai (in Chinese 唐努烏梁海 T'ang² Nu² Wu¹ Liang² Hai³) is situated on the slopes of the Tannu-ula Mountains (in Chinese 唐努鄂拉嶺 T'ang² Nu² Ao⁴ La¹ Ling³). Five squadrons of the Tannu-Urianghais are under the supervision of the Dzassakt'u-Khanate Aimak (*see* No. 872A), 13 are under the Sain-Noin Aimak (*see* No. 872A) and three are under the control of the Cheptsun-Damba-Hut'ukht'u, a Lama dignitary at Urga (*see* No. 916). The remainder (26 squadrons) are subordinated to the administration of the Military Governor of Uliasut'ai (*see* No. 879) and are divided into five sections (similar to Banners), under special rulers—Ukherids (in Chinese 總管 Tsung³ Kuan³), who enjoy the authority of Dzassaks but whose posts are not hereditary. They are elected subject to the Military Governor's approval. Each section, in its turn, is divided into a number of Sumung, Squadrons: 1. Kossogol (four Sumung), 2. Khemch'ihk (10 Sumung), 3. T'uchih (found along the river T'ersek; four Sumung), 4. Salchihk (four Sumung), and 5. T'annu (four Sumung).

879

879. 烏里雅蘇臺將軍 Wu¹ Li³ Ya³ Su¹ T'ai² Chiang¹ Chün¹, Military Governor of Uliasut'ai (compare No. 744D); invested with the title of 定邊左副將軍 Ting⁴ Pien¹ Tso³ Fu⁴ Chiang¹ Chün¹, Representative of Chinese Authority in Northern Mongolia over the Civil and Military Administration.

This post was instituted in the 18th century, while the wars against the Dzumgars were in progress, and originally bore exclusively a military character. For this reason, up to the present, the Military Governor of Uliasut'ai, as Commander of the Forces in Northern Mongolia, has subordinated to him 副將軍 Fu⁴ Chiang¹ Chün¹, Deputy Military Governors (Mongolian, T'usalakch'ih Chiang Chün; see No. 872), in the persons of a Prince of each of the Khalkha tribes.

On the completion of the wars mentioned the Chinese Government not only considered it necessary to maintain the post but, in addition, directed that the occupant of this position, besides directing military affairs, should also have control over the civil affairs of Mongolia.

In the lapse of time the authority of the Military Governor of Uliasut'ai, which once extended over the four tribes of the Khalkhas greatly declined and, on the appointment of Imperial Agents at Urga (see No. 879A), K'obdo and Altai (see No. 880) and, more especially, when their authority was extended, nothing was left to him but the control over two Khalkha tribes—the Sain-noin and the Dzassakt'u-Khanate (see No. 872A)—and 26 squadrons of the Tannu-Urianghais (see No. 878).

The Military Governor of Uliasut'ai is assisted by two subordinates styled 參贊大臣 Ts'an¹ Tsan⁴ Ta⁴ Ch'ên², Assistant Military Governors, or Councillors (one of them is designated 定邊 Ting⁴ Pien¹, Warden of the Marches; see above).

As proposed in a Memorial from the Chiang Chün, 堃岫 K'un¹ Hsiu⁴, dated the 15th February. 1910, at the Chancery of the Military Governor there has been instituted a 新政領

辦處 Hsin¹ Chêng⁴ Ling³ Pan⁴ Ch'u⁴, Bureau of Constitutional Reforms (compare No. 822ᴀ and the Supplement to No. 160).

879ᴀ. 庫倫辦事大臣 K'u⁴ Lun² Pan⁴ Shih⁴ Ta⁴ Ch'ên², Imperial Agent at K'urun (Urga) ; also Hebei-Amban. 庫倫 幇辦大臣 K'u⁴ Lun² Pang¹ Pan⁴ Ta⁴ Ch'ên², Assistant Imperial Agent at K'urun (Urga). These two officials, in Mongolian, are called Dzarlikh-yierh-dzarukhsang Hurieng-dur-saghuchu-herekh-shitkhekch'ih-sait, *i.e.* "officials deputed by Imperial will and directing affairs at Urga."

The Imperial Agent at Urga and his assistant are charged with the control of two Khalkha tribes, *i.e.* the T'ushet'u-Khanate and the Tsetsen-Khanate (*see* No. 872ᴀ), and the Office of the Shabis (*see* No. 875).

Originally the Imperial Agent at Urga acted as the Assistant Military Governor of Uliasut'ai, whose authority, as has been mentioned above (*see* No. 879), once extended over all four tribes of the Khalkhas. Later he received the privilege of direct reports to the Throne and his dependence on the said Governor became nominal (it consists merely in supplying him with copies of reports to Peking).

Lately there has been attached to the Imperial Agent an official styled 理刑司員 Li³ Hsing² Ssu¹ Yuan², Judicial Commissioner (compare No. 495), whose duties consist in assisting in the settlement of affairs in which foreigners are interested and in the administration of justice (*see* a report from the Imperial Agent at Urga, 延祉 Yen² Chih³, dated the 29th March, 1909 ; compare also No. 897).

880. 科布多叅贊大臣 K'o¹ Pu⁴ To¹ Ts'an¹ Tsan⁴ Ta⁴ Ch'ên², Assistant Military Governor (to the Military Governor of Uliasut'ai) residing at K'obdo. This post was established in 1731, when one of the Assistant Military Governors of Uliasut'ai (*see* No. 879) was deputed to K'obdo. In 1834 this official was ordered to reside permanently at K'obdo. Under

881
to
882

his jurisdiction are the Mongol and Oelöt tribes occupying the so-called K‘obdo region (*see* No. 876).

After the removal (in 1907 ; *see* No. 876A) of the Altai region (*see* No. 877) from the jurisdiction of the Hebei-Amban of K‘obdo, for the administration of the former, there was appointed a special 科 布 多 辦 事 大 臣 K‘o¹ Pu⁴ To¹ Pan⁴ Shih⁴ Ta⁴ Ch‘ên², Imperial Agent at K‘obdo (also 阿 爾 泰 辦 事 大 臣 A⁴ Êrh³ T‘ai⁴ Pan⁴ Shih⁴ Ta⁴ Ch‘ên², Imperial Agent at Altai), who resided at first at K‘obdo, later removing to Shara-sumê (in Chinese 承 化 寺 Ch‘êng² Hua⁴ Ssu⁴), near the Black Irtish river.

The Imperial Agent, like the Assistant Military Governor, was originally subordinated to the Military Governor of Uliasut‘ai (*see* No. 879). Since these officials received the privilege of direct reports to the Throne they have enjoyed a great measure of independence, the Amban at Shara-sumê being considered as the senior.

881. The Hebei-Ambans (the Assistant Military Governors and Imperial Agents ; *see* Nos. 879, 879A and 880) represent the High Government authority over Mongolia, according to which the most complex affairs are decided and to which all subjects of the Bogdokhan residing in Mongolia, *i.e.* Chinese, Manchus and Mongols, must conform.

For the consideration of affairs of various types there are found at the office of each Hebei-Amban two inferior establishments : 1. Office of the Dzarghuch‘ih, presided over by a Dzarghuch‘ih (*see* No. 882), and 2. Chihsa, or Office of Appeal, for the discussion of purely Mongolian affairs (*see* No. 883).

882. 司 員 Ssu¹ Yüan² (also 辦 事 司 員 Pan⁴ Shih⁴ Ssu¹ Yüan² and 司 官 Ssu¹ Kuan¹ ; designated in treaties, 部 員 Pu⁴ Yüan² ; also 通 判 T‘ung¹ P‘an⁴)—Dzarghuch‘ih (in Mongolian), or Judicial Commissioner for Chinese Affairs. All Chinese and Manchus in Mongolia come under the jurisdiction of this official.

There are four Dzarghuch'ihs in the Khalkha region, *i.e.*
two attached to the Hebei-Ambans at Urga (*see* No. 879A ; one
at Urga and one at Kiakhta), one attached to the Hebei-Amban
at Uliasut'ai (*see* No. 879), residing at Uliasut'ai, and one
attached to the Hebei-Amban at K'obdo (*see* No. 880), residing
at K'obdo.

883
to
884

Any Chinese workman or trader coming into the Khalkha
region must present his passport to the Dzarghuch'ih of the town
in which he wishes to settle ; he then receives authority to do so.
Should he wish to journey to any of the various Khalkha
Banners it is necessary that he apply to the Dzarghuch'ih, and
the latter, simultaneously with the granting of permission,
notifies the office of the Banners concerned of his contemplated
journey.

All questions raised by, or against, Chinese in the Khalkha
district are examined into by the Dzarghuch'ih and, conforming
to their importance, are either settled by him or referred to the
Hebei-Amban.

883. Chihsa, or Office of Appeal (the Mongolian word
Chihshiyang, or Chihsang, means "turn"). This office examines
into questions raised by, or against, Mongols exclusively. For
attendance at, and the discussion of affairs of, the Chihsang there
is yearly appointed one Dzassak (*see* No. 873) from each of the
Khalkha tribes. Thus each Chihsang is made up of four
members and any Mongol may there find his Prince, or tribal
representative, at whose hands he is sure of protection and
justice. In small matters the Chihsang delivers judgment ; in
more important affairs it sends the Mongol concerned to his
Banner, at the same time forwarding particulars of the matter,
and the inquiries made, for the judgment of the rulers of the
Banner.

884. To Inner, or Southern, Mongolia (*see* No. 869) there
appertain: 1. Six Leagues of the Inner Mongols (in Chinese

[455]

885
to
887

內蒙古六盟 Nei⁴ Mêng³ Ku³ Liu⁴ Mêng²), 2. The Ch'akhars and T'umets of Kuei Hua Ch'êng (in Chinese 察哈爾及 歸化城土默特 Ch'a² Ha¹ Êrh³ Chi² Kuei¹ Hua⁴ Ch'êng³ T'u³ Mo⁴ T'ê⁴), 3. The Mongols of Alashan (properly Oelöt tribes; in Chinese 賀蘭山額魯特蒙古 Ho⁴ Lan² Shan¹ Ê⁴ Lu³ T'ê⁴ Mêng³ Ku³), and 4. The Old Tourgouths of the river Edsinê, or Edsinei (in Chinese 額濟納舊土爾扈特 Ê⁴ Chi⁴ Na⁴ Chiu⁴ T'u³ Êrh³ Hu⁴ T'ê⁴).

885. The Southern, or Inner, Mongols are, in administrative and military reference, divided into six divisions, with six separate Princely Leagues:

1. Cherim League (in Chinese 哲里木盟 Chê² Li³ Mu⁴ Mêng²),

2. Chosot'u League (in Chinese 卓索圖盟 Cho¹ So³ T'u² Mêng²),

3. Chao Uda League (in Chinese 昭烏達盟 Chao¹ Wu¹ Ta² Mêng²),

4. Silinghol League (in Chinese 錫林郭勒盟 Hsi² Lin² Kuo¹ Lê⁴ Mêng²),

5. Ulan Ch'ap League (in Chinese 烏蘭察布盟 Wu¹ Lan² Ch'a² Pu⁴ Mêng²), and

6. Ikh Chao League (in Chinese 伊克昭盟 I¹ K'o⁴ Chao¹ Mêng²).

886. The Cherim League is composed of the following tribes: 1. Khorch'in tribe (in Chinese 科爾沁部 K'o¹ Erh³ Ch'in⁴ Pu⁴), of six Banners, 2. Djalait tribe (in Chinese 扎賚特部 Cha¹ Lai⁴ T'ê⁴ Pu⁴), of one Banner, 3. Durbet tribe (in Chinese 杜爾伯特部 Tu⁴ Êrh³ Po² T'ê⁴ Pu⁴), of one Banner, and 4. Ghorlos tribe (in Chinese 郭爾羅斯部 Kuo¹ Êrh³ Lo² Ssu¹ Pu⁴), of two Banners. Thus it includes ten Banners, supplying 204 squadrons.

887. The Chosot'u League (see No. 885) consists of the following tribes: 1. Kharach'in tribe (in Chinese 喀喇沁部

888
to
890

K‘a¹ La³ Ch‘in⁴ Pu⁴), of three Banners, 2. T‘umet tribe (in Chinese 土默特部 T‘u³ Mo⁴ T‘ê⁴ Pu⁴), of two Banners. As a whole, it has five Banners, giving 223 squadrons.

888. The Chao Uda League (*see* No. 885) is made up of: 1. The Ao-Khan tribe (in Chinese 敖漢部 Ao⁴ Han⁴ Pu⁴), of one Banner, 2. The Naiman tribe (in Chinese 奈曼部 Nai⁴ Man⁴ Pu⁴), of one Banner, 3. The Barin tribe (in Chinese 巴林部 Pa¹ Lin² Pu⁴), of two Banners, 4. The Djarud tribe (in Chinese 扎嚕特部 Cha¹ Lu³ T‘ê⁴ Pu⁴), of two Banners, 5. The Aru-Khorch‘in (in Chinese 阿嚕科爾沁部 A⁴ Lu³ K‘o¹ Êrh³ Ch‘in⁴ Pu⁴), of one Banner, 6. The Ongniod tribe (in Chinese 翁牛特部 Wêng¹ Niu² T‘ê⁴ Pu⁴), of two Banners, 7. The Keshikhtêng tribe (in Chinese 克什克騰部 K‘ê⁴ Shih² K‘ê⁴ T‘êng² Pu⁴), of one Banner, 8. The Khalkha (one tribe from the Left Wing; in Chinese 喀爾喀左翼 K‘a¹ Êrh³ K‘a¹ Tso³ I⁴), of one Banner. It has 11 Banners in all, supplying 298 squadrons.

889. The Silinghol League (*see* No. 885) has the following tribes: 1. Uchumuch‘in tribe (in Chinese 烏珠穆沁部 Wu¹ Chu¹ Mu⁴ Ch‘in⁴ Pu⁴), of two Banners, 2. Khaochit tribe (in Chinese 浩齊特部 Hao⁴ Ch‘i² T‘ê⁴ Pu⁴), of two Banners, 3. Sunit tribe (in Chinese 蘇尼特部 Su¹ Ni² T‘ê⁴ Pu⁴), of two Banners, 4. Abaga tribe (in Chinese 阿巴噶部 A⁴ Pa¹ Ka¹ Pu⁴), of two Banners, and 5. Abaganar tribe (in Chinese 阿巴哈納爾部 A⁴ Pa¹ Ha¹ Na⁴ Êrh³ Pu⁴), of two Banners. Thus it consists of ten Banners, supplying 111 squadrons.

890. The Ulan Ch‘ap League (*see* No. 885) consists of the following tribes: 1. Durban-Keuket tribe (in Chinese 四子部落 Ssu⁴ Tzu³ Pu⁴ Lo⁴), of one Banner, 2. Mao Mingan tribe (in Chinese 茂明安部 Mao⁴ Ming² An¹ Pu⁴), of one Banner, 3. Urat tribe (in Chinese 烏喇特部 Wu¹ La³ T‘ê⁴ Pu⁴), of three Banners, and 4. Khalkha (one tribe from the Right Wing; in Chinese 喀爾喀右翼 K‘a¹ Êrh³ K‘a¹ Yu⁴ I⁴),

[457]

891
to
892

of one Banner. In all it includes six Banners, supplying 62 squadrons.

891. The Ikh Chao League (*see* No. 885) is made up of seven Banners of the Ordos tribe (in Chinese 鄂爾多斯部 Ao⁴ Êrh³ To¹ Ssu¹ Pu⁴), which supply 274 squadrons.

892. As has been seen above, Nos. 886 to 891, the Leagues of Southern Mongolia are not arranged to include people of one stock alone, as is the case with the Khalkhas (compare No. 870), but are composite organizations of various Mongol tribes (Mongolian, Aimak; Chinese, 部落 Pu⁴ Lo⁴), of which there are 24 in Southern Mongolia. Each tribe consists of one, or more, Banners (Khoshuns). There are 49 Banners in the Six Leagues, and they supply 1,172 squadrons.

The government of Southern Mongolia differs from that of Khalkha in that the Chieftains of the Banners—Dzassaks (*see* No. 873)—are subject to much more control on the part of the Chinese Government. The Captains-General, being deprived of personal initiative, simply supervise the execution of resolutions of the League meetings. These meetings are called at the will of the Peking authorities and for opening them there are appointed Chinese officials, who, in fact, act as their Presidents. The expedition of affairs is in the hands of Chinese Secretaries.

It appears that Southern Mongolia is destined to be gradually converted into an ordinary Chinese province, under a government common to China proper. The three Eastern Leagues have already been almost subordinated to the provincial administration of Chihli (the Chosotʻu League, part of the Chao Uda League, the prefecture of 承德府 Chʻêng⁰ Tê² Fu³, and that of 朝陽府 Chʻao⁴ Yang² Fu³)·and Fêngtien (the Cherim League, part of the Chao Uda League, the prefecture of 洮南府 Tʻao² Nan² Fu³, entirely, and the Western parts of the prefectures of 長春府 Chʻang² Chʻun¹ Fu³, 昌圖府 Chʻang² Tʻu² Fu³ and 新民府 Hsin¹ Min² Fu³).

The colonization of the lands of the Leagues mentioned, by Chinese emigrants, is going forward very rapidly (*see* Nos. 777 and 782) and the Chinese are more and more extending their authority over the Mongol Princes, previously rather independent, and their subjects. At places where the Chinese influence becomes predominant, but which are not annexed to one of the adjacent provinces, there is first established the post of 通判 T'ung¹ P'an⁴ (*see* No. 849A). This official not only takes over control of judicial affairs and collection of revenue from the Banner population but also has authority to supervise the transaction of business at the office of the Banner Chieftain.

893. 察哈爾 Ch'a² Ha² Êrh³, The Ch'ahar Mongols (*see* No. 884). These are distinguished from the other Mongol tribes in that they have lost their generic government. Their camps (in Chinese 遊牧 Yu² Mu⁴) lie in immediate proximity to the Great Wall (長城 Ch'ang² Ch'êng²), beyond the borders of the prefectures of 宣化府 Hsüan¹ Hua⁴ Fu³, of Chihli, and 大同府 Ta⁴ T'ung² Fu³, of Shansi. For administrative and military purposes they are organized under eight Banners (on the same footing as the Manchu military forces) which, in turn, are arranged in two Wings, 左翼 Tso³ I⁴, Left, or Eastern, Wing, and 右翼 Yu⁴ I⁴, Right, or Western, Wing.

Purely Banner affairs of the Ch'ahars are discussed by the Military Lieutenant-Governor of Ch'ahar (*see* Nos. 719A and 898). In civil questions relating to Chinese affairs within the Lieutenant-Governorship the Governor-General of Chihli exercises a superior jurisdiction, through an Intendant bearing the title of 口北道 K'ou³ Pei³ Tao⁴, residing at Hsüan-hua Fu. For assisting the latter with regard to control of Government lands, the examination of questions concerning commercial relations between the Ch'ahars and Chinese, and the administration of civil and criminal affairs, there are three Civil Commissioners, styled 撫民同知 Fu³ Min² T'ung² Chih¹ (compare No. 849),

894 stationed, respectively, at 多倫諾爾廳 To¹ Lun² No⁴ Êrh³ T'ing¹, Dolon-nor (also Lama-miao), 張家口廳 Chang¹ Chia¹ K'ou³ T'ing¹, Kalgan, and 獨石口廳 Tu² Shih² K'ou³ T'ing¹.

Within the Ch'ahar territory there are situated the Imperial pasturages, or 牧塲 Mu⁴ Ch'ang³, the superintendence over which has lately been invested in a special official (*see* No. 755). Formerly they were under the control of the Military Lieutenant-Governor of Ch'ahar (*see* No. 898).

894. 歸化城土默特 Kuei¹ Hua⁴ Ch'êng² T'u³ Mo⁴ T'ê⁴, The T'umet Tribe of Kuei Hua Ch'êng (K'u K'u Ho T'o ; *see* No. 884).

The T'umet are divided into two Banners which, in turn, are arranged in two Wings, 左翼 Tso³ I⁴, Left, or Eastern, Wing, and 右翼 Yu⁴ I⁴, Right, or Western, Wing. Their camps lie to the North of Kuei Hua Ch'êng, or K'u K'u Ho T'o, of Shansi province.

The Banner affairs of the T'umet tribe are attended to by the Manchu General-in-Chief of Sui-yüan-ch'êng (*see* Nos. 744A and 899) and the Manchu Brigade-General of Kuei Hua Ch'êng (*see* Nos. 745B and 899).

For the examination of lawsuits and judicial affairs, as well as questions concerning taxes collected from Chinese and Mongols in the camps of the T'umet tribe, there is an Intendant bearing the title 歸綏兵備道 Kuei¹ Sui¹ Ping¹ Pei⁴ Tao⁴, residing at 綏遠城 Sui¹ Yüan³ Ch'êng². He has as his assistant Civil Commissioners styled 理事同知 Li³ Shih⁴ T'ung² Chih¹, 撫民同知 Fu³ Min² T'ung² Chih¹, or 撫民通判 Fu³ Min² T'ung¹ P'an⁴ (*see* Nos. 849 and 849A), who are stationed at 歸化廳 Kuei¹ Hua⁴ T'ing¹, (Kuei Hua Ch'êng—K'u K'u Ho T'o), 和林格爾廳 Ho² Lin² Ko⁴ Êrh³ T'ing¹, Harin-kor-t'ing, 托克托廳 To¹ K'o⁴ T'o¹ T'ing¹, 清水河廳 Ch'ing¹ Shui³ Ho² T'ing¹, 薩拉齊廳 Sa¹ La¹ Ch'i² Ting¹—Sarach'ih-t'ing, 寧遠廳 Ning² Yüan³ T'ing¹, 綏遠廳 Sui¹ Yüan³ T'ing¹,

五 原 廳 Wu³ Yüan² T'ing¹, 陶 林 廳 T'ao² Lin² T'ing¹, 武川廳 Wu³ Ch'uan¹ T'ing¹, and 興 和 廳 Hsing¹ Ho² T'ing¹.

895. 賀 蘭 山 額 魯 特 蒙 古 Ho² Lan³ Shan¹ Ê⁴ Lu³ T'ê⁴ Mêng³ Ku³, The Mongols of Alashan (belonging properly to the Oirad or Oelöt tribes ; see No. 884) ; deriving their name from the region of 阿 拉 善 A⁴ La³ Shan¹ (also 賀 蘭 山 Ho² Lan³ Shan¹ ; compare above), lying North of Ninghia, in the province of Kansu, where they have settled. They form one Banner which is ruled by generic Princes (tracing their genealogy from Khabut'u Khasar, brother of Kinghis Khan), entitled 親 王 Ch'in¹ Wang² (see No. 873), who reside at the small town of 定 遠 營 Ting⁴ Yüan³ Ying². They are divided into eight squadrons.

The higher supervision over the affairs of the Alashan Banner is invested in the Manchu General-in-Chief at 寧 夏 Ning² Hsia⁴, in the province of Kansu (see Nos. 746B and 900), for which reason the Mongols of Alashan are also designated as the " Mongols of the Ninghia Department."

896. 額 濟 納 舊 土 爾 扈 特 Ê⁴ Chi⁴ Na⁴ Chiu⁴ T'u³ Êrh³ Hu⁴ T'ê⁴, The Old Tourgouths of the Edsinê, or Edsinei, River (see No. 884). They consist of one Banner, occupying land lying to the West of the camps of the Alashan Mongols (see No. 895), and are subject to the superior jurisdiction of the Manchu General-in-Chief at Ninghia (compare No. 895 ; see also Nos. 744B and 900).

896A. 河 西 額 魯 特 Ho² Hsi¹ Ê⁴ Lu³ T'ê⁴, Oirad to the West of the River (i.e. the 黃 河 Huang² Ho², Yellow River). This is the general designation of the Mongols of Alashan and the Old Tourgouths of the Edsinê (see Nos. 895 to 896).

897. 熱 河 都 統 Jê⁴ Ho² Tu¹ T'ung³, Manchu General-in-Chief, or Military Lieutenant-Governor of Jêhol (see No. 719A), residing at 熱 河 Jê⁴ Ho² (Jehol ; also called 承 德 府 Ch'êng² Tê⁴ Fu³ ; see No. 104E) ; in charge of the Chosot'u (see No. 887˙

**898
to
899**

and Chao Uda (*see* No. 888) Leagues and the 圍塲 Wei²
Ch'ang³, Imperial Hunting Preserves (also called 木蘭 Mu⁴
Lan², or Muran ; *see* No. 748).

The civil administration of the Jêhol territory is carried on,
under the supervision of the Military Lieutenant-Governor, by
Commissioners styled 理事司員 Li³ Shih⁴ Ssu¹ Yüan², Civil
Commissioners, and 理刑司員 Li³ Hsing² Ssu¹ Yüan², Judicial
Commissioners (compare No. 879A).

The tract in which the Imperial Hunting Preserves (*see*
above) are situated forms a separate Sub-prefecture, the so-called
圍塲廳 Wei² Ch'ang³ T'ing¹, headed by a 撫民同知 Fu³
Min² T'ung² Chih¹ (compare No. 849).

898   察哈爾都統 Ch'a² Ha¹ Êrh³ Tu¹ T'ung³, Manchu
General-in-Chief of Ch'ahar, or Military Lieutenant-Governor of
Ch'ahar (*see* No. 719A). This official, residing at 張家口
Chang¹ Chia¹ K'ou³, Kalgan, conducts the government of the
Mongols of Ch'ahar (*see* No. 893) and also supervises the actions
of the Silinghol League (*see* No. 889). He is assisted by the
察哈爾副都統 Ch'a² Ha¹ Êrh³ Fu⁴ Tu¹ T'ung³, Deputy
Lieutenant-Governor (*see* No. 745E), residing at Kalgan.

Formerly the 牧塲 Mu⁴ Ch'ang³, Imperial Pasturages (*see*
No. 893), were under the supervision of the Military Lieutenant-
Governor of Ch'ahar ; since 1908 they have been managed by a
special Superintendent (*see* No. 755).

The Military Lieutenant-Governor of Ch'ahar is, ex officio,
Controller of the so-called 阿勒泰軍台 A⁴ Lê³ T'ai⁴ Chün¹
T'ai², Military Post Roads of Altai (for details *see* No. 754).

899.   綏遠城將軍 Sui¹ Yüan³ Ch'êng² Chiang¹ Chün¹,
Manchu General-in-Chief at Sui-yüan-ch'êng, or Military
Lieutenant Governor of Sui-yüan-ch'êng (*see* No. 744A). Under
the supervision of this official are the affairs of the T'umot tribe
of Kuei Hua Ch'êng (*see* No. 894). In addition, he keeps a
watch over the actions of the Ulan Ch'ap League (*see* No. 890).

Also, he bears the title of 督辦墾務大臣 Tu¹ Pan⁴ K'en³ Wu⁴ Ta⁴ Ch'ên², Superintendent of Colonization Affairs (*see* No. 778). As his assistant there is the 歸化城副都統 Kuei¹ Hua⁴ Ch'êng² Fu⁴ Tu¹ T'ung³, Deputy Lieutenant-Governor, residing at 歸化城 Kuei¹ Hua⁴ Ch'êng² (K'u K'u Ho T'o).

900. 寧夏將軍 Ning² Hsia⁴ Chiang¹ Chün¹, Manchu General-in-Chief of Ninghia, or Military Lieutenant-Governor of Ninghia (*see* No. 744B); superintending the affairs of the Mongols of Alashan (*see* No. 895) and the Old Tourgouths of the Edsinê (*see* No. 896). He is assisted by the 寧夏副都統 Ning² Hsia⁴ Fu⁴ Tu¹ T'ung³, Deputy Lieutenant-Governor (*see* No. 745D), residing at Ninghia.

901. 蒙務總局 Mêng³ Wu⁴ Tsung³ Chü², Head Bureau of Mongolian Affairs, headed by a 總辦 Tsung³ Pan⁴, Chief. This Bureau is found at the Governor-General's office at Moukden and superintends the affairs of the Mongols of the Cherim League (*see* No. 886) which, as has been mentioned (*see* No. 892), is subordinated to Fêngtien province.

For the detailed organization of the Head Bureau of Mongolian Affairs *see* No. 812A.

For particulars as to the post of 蒙務司使 Mêng³ Wu⁴ Ssu¹ Shih³, Commissioner of Mongolian Affairs (abolished in 1909), *see* No. 812.

B. K'uk'unor (Kokonor):

902. 青海 Ch'ing¹ Hai³, K'uk'unor (*see* No. 868). Its population consists of various Mongolian tribes (*see* No. 903) and Tangouths (designated by the Chinese as 西番 Hsi¹ Fan¹, Western Tribesmen; *see* No. 904), ruled by generic chieftains who are under the sway of the Chinese Amban at Si-ning (*see* No. 905).

903. 額魯特 Ê⁴ Lu³ T'ê⁴, Oelöts. These are under the control of the Imperial Controller-General (Amban) at Si-ning (*see* No. 905). Their local government is invested in the

**904
to
905**

hands of their generic Princes, as with the Khalkhas (*see* No. 870) and the Inner Mongols (*see* No. 884).

The Mongols of K'uk'unor, as is the case with the Mongols of Khalkha and Inner Mongolia, are divided into 29 Banners, the chieftains of which meet yearly at the Ch'aghang-T'ologhoi (one of the islands in Lake K'uk'unor) for a League meeting (*see* No. 872), at which affairs concerning the internal public administration are discussed.

Since the time of the mutiny of Lubsang Tan-ching (in 1723) the President of the League meeting is not an elected Prince (compare No. 872) but, at the ruling of the Peking Government, is either the Imperial Controller-General at Si-ning or an official chosen by him (compare No. 892).

The following are the tribes of K'uk'unor :

1. Khoshoit (in Chinese 和碩特部 Ho² Sho⁴ T'ê⁴ Pu⁴), 21 Banners,

2. Khalkha (in Chinese 喀爾喀部 K'a¹ Êrh³ K'a¹ Pu⁴), 1 Banner.

3. Ch'oros (in Chinese 綽羅斯部 Ch'o¹ Lo² Ssu¹ Pu⁴), 2 Banners,

4. Khoit (in Chinese 輝特部 Hui¹ T'ê⁴ Pu⁴), 1 Banner, and

5. Tourgouth (in Chinese 土爾扈特部 T'u³ Êrh³ Hu⁴ T'ê⁴ Pu⁴), 4 Banners.

904. 唐古忒 T'ang² Ku³ Tê⁴, Tangouth ; also 西番 F. Fan¹, Western Tribesmen (*see* No. 902).

The Tangouths number 40 族 Tsu², Tribes, ruled by 土司 T'u³ Ssu¹, Generic Chieftains, who are, in turn, placed under the control of the Imperial Controller-General at Si-ning (*see* No. 905). In addition to these there are 39 Tangouth tribes under the Dalai Lama (*see* Nos. 906 and 914).

905. 西寧辦事大臣 Hsi¹ Ning² Pan⁴ Shih⁴ Ta⁴ Ch'ên², The Imperial Controller-General at Si-ning, or Amban (full title 總理青海事務大臣 Tsung³ Li³ Ch'ing¹ Hai³ Shih⁴ Wu⁴

Ta⁴ Ch'ên²) ; representative of the higher Chinese authority and invested with the control of the 29 Mongol (properly Oelöt) and the 40 Tangouth tribes mentioned above (*see* Nos. 903 and 904).

C. *Tibet and the Lamaist Hierarchy* :

906. 西藏 Hsi¹ Tsang⁴, Tibet; known during the Ming Dynasty as 烏斯國 Wu¹ Ssu¹ Kuo², or 烏斯藏 Wu¹ Ssu¹ Tsang⁴. The Mongol designation is Parung-t'ala (*i.e.* Western Country), or T'udbod (圖伯特 T'u² Po⁴ Tê⁴). By the Tibetans themselves (吐番 T'u³ Fan¹, or 西番 Hsi¹ Fan¹; also 唐古忒 T'ang² Ku³ T'ê⁴, or 唐古特 T'ang² Ku³ T'ê⁴) it is called Bot, or Bod, and Bod-jul (the land of Bod). The last-mentioned term corresponds, so it seems, to the old Chinese designation 佛國 Fo² Kuo², the Land of Buddha.

There are two main divisions of Tibet, *i.e.* Large Tibet and Small Tibet, the first of which, called by the Chinese 前藏 Ch'ien² Tsang⁴, Anterior, or Eastern, Tibet, consists of the provinces (部 Pu⁴) 衛 Wei⁴ (Yi or Yü in Tibetan ; also called 中藏 Chung¹ Tsang⁴, Central Tibet), and 康 K'ang¹ (in Tibetan Kham ; also called 察木多 Ch'a² Mu⁴ To¹, Chamdo), while the second, called by the Chinese 後藏 Hou⁴ Tsang⁴, Ulterior, or Western, Tibet, embraces the provinces of 藏 Tsang⁴, and 阿里 A⁴ Li³, Nari (Ngari), or Nari-Khorsung.

As regards political status, Tibet, in olden times, was as a large independent State including the whole of K'uk'unor and a great portion of the present provinces of Szechwan and Yünnan. Its relations with China began in the 7th century A.D. when (in 641) 蘇隆藏干布 Su¹ Lung² Tsang⁴ Kan¹ Pu⁴, Strongtsan Gambo, became allied with the Emperor 太宗 T'ai⁴ Tsung¹, of the T'ang Dynasty, through taking as his wife the Princess 文成 Wên Ch'êng, daughter of the latter. For many centuries his descendants, under the title of Gialbo (in Chinese 贊普 Tsan⁴ Pu³), continued to rule over Tibet although, as time passed, the temporal authority to a great extent was encroached upon by the superiors of a religious association—the Sakya, (Chinese 薩迦 Sa¹ Chia¹) known at that period by the name of Brugba, written in Chinese 布魯克巴 Pu⁴ Lu³ K'ê⁴ Pa¹.

Based on the doctrines of Buddhism, which penetrated Tibet already largely corrupted by Hindoo, and especially Sivaitic, forms of worship, the doctrine of the Sakya (also called 紅教 Hung² Chiao⁴, Red Doctrine, from the colour of the vestments and head-dress of the Sakya priesthood) became in the course of time so perverted from the original dogmas of Buddhism that it brought upon itself a strong revolt, under the leadership of a reformer named Tsongkhab'a (1357–1420), in Chinese 宗喀巴 Tsung¹ K'a¹ Pa¹, who founded a new doctrine (黃教 Huang² Chiao⁴, Yellow Doctrine). His nephew, Gegen-Dub, succeeded in 1439 in attaining the predominant position in the Hierarchy of Tibetan Buddhism (Lamaism) and from him there started a line of clerical rulers of Tibet (Dalai Lamas ; see No. 914).

In the 13th century (during the 元 Yüan Dynasty) Tibet became a vassal of China and in 1260 A.D. the Emperor 世祖 Shih⁴ Tsu³ (Khubilai) bestowed on the famous Paghba Lama (八思巴 Pa¹ Ssu¹ Pa¹) the title 國師大寶法王 Kuo² Shih¹ Ta⁴ Pao³ Fa⁴ Wang², State Teacher and Prince of the Precious Doctrine, giving him, conjointly with the secular authorities, authority over Tibet. The dependence was again confirmed at the beginning of the reign of the Manchu Dynasty when, in 1642 A.D., the Emperor, known from his reign as 崇德 Ch'ung² Tê², received at Moukden envoys carrying presents from the Tibetan rulers. At the same period (1643) the Dalai Lama, oppressed by the temporal authorities, applied to Gushi Khar, in Chinese styled 固始汗 Ku⁴ Shih³ Han⁴, the reigning Prince of the Khoshoit Mongols, for assistance. For his assistance the latter annexed the district of K'uk'unor to his dominions and levied taxes on the Kham province. The Dalai Lama rewarded him for his fidelity with the title of 諾們汗 No⁴ Mên² Han¹, **907** Nomên Han, or Prince (Khan) of the Church, the equivalent of the Sanskrit " Dharma Raja."

In the reign of the Emperor 康熙 K'ang¹ Hsi¹, in 1694 A.D., the temporal administrator who, as Regent for the Dalai Lama, had long conducted the government of Tibet under the title of 第巴 Ti⁴ · Pa¹, or 牒巴 Tieh⁴ Pa¹ (compare No. 912), was invested with the title of 圖伯特國王 T'u² Po² T'ê⁴ Kuo² Wang², King of Tibet. Not long after, however, the continual intrigues of the temporal authorities against the secular powers, and also their inclination to throw off the Chinese yoke, incited the Chinese Government to take steps to strengthen its hold over Tibet. Accordingly, in 1727, a large part of the border territory of the Kham province was annexed to the interior dominions of China. At about the same time two Residents (*see* No. 907) were appointed for the supervision of actions of the temporal administrators.

In 1751 A.D. the temporal sovereignty in Tibet was entirely suppressed, the rule of that region being placed in the hands of the Dalai Lama, aided by a council of four laymen, called Kalon, or Kablon, *i.e.* Ministers of State (*see* No. 910), under the superior direction of the two Chinese Residents. The last-mentioned have, since 1792 A.D., been authorized to take a direct part in the government of Tibet, conjointly with the Dalai Lama.

907. 駐藏大臣 Chu⁴ Tsang⁴ Ta⁴ Ch'ên², Imperial Resident of Tibet ; aided by a colleague, or Assistant Resident, styled 帮辦大臣 Pang¹ Pan⁴ Ta⁴ Ch'ên² (this post was instituted in 1727 ; *see* No. 906).

Both the Resident and Assistant Resident of Tibet are usually chosen from the ranks of higher Chinese officials and are under the direction of the Ministry of Dependencies (*see* No. 491A); charged, however, with memorializing the Throne direct on all

**908
to
909**

important questions. Among other duties, they act as the medium of communication between the Chinese Government and the Court of Nepal, which is known in Chinese as 廓爾喀國 Kuo² Êrh³ K'a¹ Kuo², or 白 布 Pai² Pu⁴, and 巴布 Pa¹ Pu⁴, Parbuttiya. They have a staff of 夷情章京 I² Ch'ing² Chang¹ Ching¹, Secretaries for Native Affairs.

The Imperial Resident and Assistant Resident are invested with the supreme command of both the Chinese garrison troops and the Tibetan soldiery (番兵 Fan¹ Ping¹) and, through the 噶厦 Ka¹ Hsia⁴, Council Chamber (*see* No. 910), control the affairs of the entire Tibetan civil administration.

Since 1909, to the Imperial Residents there has been attached a 駐藏叅贊 Chu⁴ Tsang⁴ Ts'an⁴ Tsan⁴, Councillor (*see* the Imperial Decree of the 18th August, 1909).

908. 糧臺 Liang² T'ai², Commissary. Of this rank are three Chinese officials, stationed at 拉薩 La¹ Sa¹, Lhassa, 札什倫布 Cha¹ Shih² Lun² Pu⁴, Tashilumbo, and Ngari, who act as paymasters to the Chinese forces and as deputies of the Imperial Residents in all matters concerning Chinese interests in Tibet.

909. By the Tibetan-Indian Commercial Convention, concluded between China and England on the 21st October, 1908, in Tibet, in addition to 雅東 Ya³ Tung¹, Yatung, opened to foreign trade in 1895, the following are to be opened : 江孜 Chiang¹ Tzu¹, Gyantze Chung, and 噶大克 Ka¹ Ta⁴ K'ê⁴, Gartok. At Yatung there is a 稅關 Shui⁴ Kuan¹, Custom House, now under the direction of the first Commissioner of Customs of Chinese nationality. At the other places mentioned there have been established 關卡 Kuan¹ Ch'ia⁴, Customs Barriers.

For the three towns mentioned there have been organized : 工部局 Kung¹ Pu⁴ Chü², Municipal Council, 巡警局 Hsün² Ching³ Chü², Department of Police, 工程局 Kung¹ Ch'êng²

Chü², Public Works Department, 裁判局 Ts'ai² Pan⁴ Chü²,
Court of Justice, etc. The British Government has the right of
appointing 商務委員 Shang¹ Wu⁴ Wei² Yüan², Commercial
Agents, at these places.

910. 噶厦 Ka¹ Hsia⁴, The Council. This is composed of
four 噶布倫 Ka¹ Pu⁴ Lun², Members of the Council (Kalons,
or Ministers; see Nos. 906 to 907), appointed by Imperial
Decree, on the nomination of the Residents, and, ex officio,
invested with the third degree of Chinese official rank.

911. 商上 Shang¹ Shang⁴, The Treasury. This department is presided over by the Kalons and has supreme control
over all questions relating to the collection of revenue.

The staff of the Treasury includes three 仔琫 Tsai³ Pêng⁴,
Councillors of the Treasury of the 1st Class (invested with
Chinese official rank of the 4th Class), Two 商卓特巴 Shang¹
Cho¹ T'ê⁴ Pa¹, Councillors of the Treasury of the 2nd Class
(invested with rank of the 4th Class), and two 業爾倉巴 Yeh⁴
Êrh² Ts'ang¹ Pa¹ (Yerts'angba), Controllers of Revenue (with
the 5th Class of Chinese official rank).

912. The remaining officials of the secular administration
of Tibet are: 1. Two 郎仔轄 Lang² Tsai³ Hsia², Controllers
of Streets and Roads; fifth rank, 2. Two 協爾帮 Hsieh² Êrh³
Pang¹ (Hierbang), Commissioners of Justice; fifth rank, 3.
Two 碩第巴 Sho⁴ Ti⁴ Pa¹ (Shediba), Superintendents of
Police; fifth rank, 4. Two 達琫 Ta⁴ Pêng⁴, Controllers of the
Stud; sixth rank, 5. Two 中譯 Chung¹ I⁴, Secretaries of the
Council (of two ranks; distinguished by having the character
大 Ta⁴, Great, or 小 Hsiao³, Lesser, prefixed to the title; of the
sixth and seventh rank), 6. 卓尼爾 Cho¹ Ni² Êrh³ (Chonir),
Second Class Secretaries of the Council; sixth rank, and 7. 13
第巴 Ti⁴ Pa¹, or 牒巴 Tieh² Pa¹, Commissioners (divided into
six classes; compare No. 906).

913. In the military organization of Tibet the following ranks are found :

1. 戴琫 Tai⁴ Pêng⁴ (the sound wa formerly denoted by the characters 代奔 Tai⁴ Pên¹), Commandant ; six in all ; invested with the fourth degree of Chinese official rank.

2. 如琫 Ju² Pêng⁴, Assistant Commandant ; fifth rank ; 12 in all,

3. 甲琫 Chia³ Pêng⁴, Centurion ; sixth rank ; 24 in all. and

4. 定琫 Ting⁴ Pêng⁴, Subaltern; seventh rank ; 120 in all.

913ᴀ. 番目 Fan¹ Mu⁴, A generic designation for Tibetan Officers of all ranks, both civil and military. Officers are appointed by selection from the ranks of scions of the ancient aristocracy (世家 Shih⁴ Chia¹), known as Tongkhor (東科爾 Tung¹ K'o¹ Êrh³).

914. 喇嘛 La³ Ma¹, Lama. This designation, applied to all members of the Buddhist priesthood, is derived from a Tibetan word which, according to the Chinese, has the meaning of 無上 Wu² Shang⁴, " Unsurpassed."

914ᴀ. 達賴喇嘛 Ta² Lai⁴ La³ Ma¹, Dalai Lama.

The word Dalai, or Talé, in Mongolian, signifies " Ocean " and corresponds to the Tibetan word Djamts'o, or Chamts'o, which is found in the full title of Dalai Lama, i.e. Cheptsun Djamts'o Rinboch'e, " Venerable Ocean Treasure."

The Dalai Lama, regarded as a re-embodiment (in Mongolian Kubil'han ; in Chinese 呼畢勒罕 Hu¹ Pi⁴ Lê⁴ Han³, or 化身 Hua⁴ Shên¹) of the famous reformer of Buddhism, Tsongkhaba (see No. 906), and, at the same time, as an incarnation, or Avatar (Sanskrit), of the Bodhisattwa Avalokiteswara (in Chinese 觀音菩薩 Kuan¹ Yin¹ P'u² Sa¹; in Mongalian Ariyabalu), is recognized by the Chinese Government as the supreme Pontiff of the Yellow Church (掌黃教首領

Chang³ Huang² Chiao⁴ Shou³ Ling³) and, as such, is the ecclesiastical ruler of Tibet (*see* No. 906).

Gegen-Dub (*see* No. 906), and his nearest successors, were called only Great, or Superior, Lamas. The title of 達賴 Ta⁴ Lai¹ was bestowed in 1640 A.D. upon the fifth Superior Lama (Navang-Lobtsang) by the Gushi Khan, the reigning Prince of the Khoshoit Mongols, and was sanctioned in 1652 A.D. by the Emperor 順治 Shun⁴ Chih⁴ who, during a visit of the said Dalai Lama to Peking, bestowed upon him a golden seal and a brevet for the title of 西天大善自在佛 Hsi¹ T‘ien¹ Ta⁴ Shan¹ Tzu⁴ Tsai⁴ Fo², "Great, Righteous and Complacent Buddha of the Western Heavens." In 1908, during the visit to Peking of the 13th Dalai Lama, to this title the Emperor 光緒 Kuang¹ Hsü⁴, and the late Empress Dowager 慈禧 Tz‘u² Hsi³, added the characters 誠順贊化 Ch‘êng² Shun⁴ Tsan⁴ Hua⁴, "Sincere and Loyal Spreader of Civilization" (*see* Imperial Decree of the 3rd November, 1908).

On the death (圓寂 Yüan² Chi⁴) of the Dalai Lama steps are at once taken for the selection of his successor. With this object in view inquiries are made by the priesthood as to miraculous manifestations (靈異 Ling² I⁴) having been observed attendant upon the birth of children at about the same time. The names of the children chosen are deposited in a golden urn (金本巴瓶 Chin¹ Pên³ Pa¹ P‘ing²) and that drawn forth determines the successor, in whom the deceased Pontiff has been re-embodied.

The monastery and palace of the Dalai Lama (Tabran-Marbu, meaning "Red Town") is situated on Mount 布達拉 Pu⁴ Ta² La¹, or Potala, one of the three sacred mountains of this name, at the foot of which lies the city of Lhassa (the monastery was built in 1643 A.D. by the fifth Superior Lama ; compare above).

[471]

914B　　As has been stated, there are three mountains sacred to the Buddhists bearing one designation. The original is situated in India, another forms the well-known "island of monasteries" off the coast of Chekiang, called in Chinese 普陀山 P'u³ T'o² Shan¹, while the third has already been spoken of.

914B. 班禪額爾德尼喇嘛 Pan¹ Ch'an² Ê⁴ Êrh³ Tê² Ni² La³ Ma¹, Panchen Erdeni Lama, or Panchen Rinpoche (Pearl of Intellect).

The Panchen Erdeni Lama is believed by the Buddhists to be a regeneration of the second of the eminent disciples of Tsongkhab'a (*see* No. 906) and, at the same time, a re-embodiment of the Buddha-Amitaba (one of the Five Buddhas in Meditation; in Chinese 阿彌陀佛 A¹ Mi² T'o² Fo²). He resides at the Jashilumbo, or Serasiar, Monastery, situated about one mile from the city of 日喀則 Ji⁴ K'a¹ Tze², Shighatze, or Jighatze (also Digharch'ih). This monastery was built by Gegen-Dub (*see* No. 906) in 1445 A.D.

The selection of the Panchen Erdeni Lama is made exactly as is the Dalai Lama (compare No. 914A).

The first Panchen Lama was Lobtsang Choichih Chaltsang, the confessor of the fifth Dalai Lama, declared as such by the latter about 1650 A.D.

One of the Panchen Lamas (namely, the sixth in succession of the Panchen Lamas, Lobtsang Tanishi by name) undertook the journey to Peking to take part in the festivities in connection with the Emperor 乾隆 Ch'ien² Lung's², 70th birthday (in 1780 A.D.) At Peking he succumbed to small-pox and a marble obelisk was erected at his place of sepulture in the 欽靜化城廟 Ch'in¹ Ching⁴ Hua⁴ Ch'êng² Miao⁴, which was built in 1783 and is also styled the 西黃寺 Hsi¹ Huang² Ssu¹.

To the Panchen Erdeni Lama there are attached the following: 1. 濟仲喇嘛 Chi⁴ Chung⁴ La³ Ma¹, Chief Councillor, 2. 歲琫喇嘛 Sui⁴ Pêng⁴ La³ Ma¹, Lama of the

Second Degree, 3. 森本喇嘛 Sên¹ Pên³ La³ Ma¹, Lama of the Third Degree, and 4. 卓尼爾喇嘛 Cho¹ Ni² Erh³ La³ Ma¹, Lama of the Fourth Degree. These positions are all filled by appointment of the Imperial Resident, on the nomination of the Panchen Erdeni Lama.

915 to 915ᴀ

915. 諾們罕 No⁴ Mên² Han³, Nomên Han (the Mongolian is equivalent to the Sanskrit Dharma Raja), "Prince of the Church," or "Prince of the True Faith" (in Chinese 法王 Fa⁴ Wang²). This title has, for a long time past, been bestowed upon eminent supporters of the Lamaist Hierarchy; the first recorded instance of its bestowal was, as we have seen above; in the case of Gushi Khan (compare No. 906). It was often conferred upon ecclesiastical dignitaries under whose direction, as Regent, the Tibetan Council (*see* No. 910) was placed during the repeated minorities of the Dalai Lama. For this reason these dignitaries were sometimes colloquially called 藏王 Tsang⁴ Wang², Princes of Tibet. In addition to the title of Nomên Han they bore also a "Ming Hao" (名號) or "title of honour," such as that of Galdan Shiretu (噶爾丹錫哷圖 Ka¹ Êrh³ Tan¹ Hsi² Lê⁴ T'u²) together with the office of Bakhshi, 巴克什 Pa¹ K'ê⁴ Shih², in Mongolian "Teacher," or "Preceptor," the Chinese 師 Shih¹.

The last of the Nomên Han was degraded in 1844 and died in exile in 1854 (compare No. 915ᴀ).

915ᴀ. 察漢諾們罕 Ch'a² Han⁴ No⁴ Mên² Han³, White Prince of the Church; rendered in Chinese as 白佛 Pai² Fo², in Mongolian as Ts'aghang Nomên Han. This title is borne by the hereditary chieftain of one of the Banners of the T'umets (*see* No. 894). The first bearer was Manchusri Hut'ukht'u, a spiritual counsellor sent by the Dalai Lama, about 1580 A.D., to Altan Khan of the T'umets and who was stablished at Hoku Hotu.

**915ʙ
to
916**

On the accession of the Throne by the Manchu Dynasty the successors of Manchusri Hut'ukht'u were compelled to remove to the region South of the Yellow River, where they have remained up to the present wielding great influence over all the Mongol and Tibetan Buddhists (compare No. 915).

915ʙ. 堪 布 K'an¹ Pu⁴, Abbot (Hambo Lama). By a Decree of 1792 A.D. it was ordained that all K'an Pu enthroned (坐 床 Tso⁴ Ch'uang²) in the larger monasteries should be appointed by the Dalai Lama and the Imperial Resident jointly. In the case of smaller monasteries the power of appointment rests with the Dalai Lama alone.

The envoy despatched yearly to Peking with presents—tribute—from the Dalai Lama and Panchen Lama is selected from the ranks of Hambo Lamas of Tibetan monasteries. He is designated in Chinese by the title Elch'in, 額 爾 沁 Ê⁴ Êrh³ Ch'in⁴, a transliteration of the Manchu word meaning "Envoy."

916. 呼 圖 克 圖 Hu¹ T'u² K'ê⁴ T'u², Hut'ukht'u, Pontiff (the Mongolian word is interpreted by the Chinese as meaning 再 來 人 Tsai⁴ Lai² Jên², "one who returns again"). The colloquial designation is 活 佛 Huo² Fo², Living Buddha.

A large class in the Buddhist Hierarchy are considered as re-embodiments (出 呼 畢 勒 罕 Ch'u⁴ Hu¹ Pi⁴ Lê⁴ Han³) of Bodhisattwas and eminent promoters of Buddhism.

The Hut'ukht'us recognized by the Chinese Government and registered at the Ministry of Dependencies number 160, *i.e.* 30 in Tibet, including 12 bearing the distinctive appellation of Shaburung (沙 布 隆 Sha¹ Pu⁴ Lung²), 19 in Northern Mongolia, 57 in Southern Mongolia, 35 in K'uk'unor, five in Chamdo and 14 in, or near, Peking. For particulars as to the last-mentioned see No. 917.

When a Hut'ukht'u dies his successor is chosen in the same manner as is the successor of the Dalai Lama (*see* No. 914ᴀ). The names of the candidates are deposited in the golden urn

(金 瓶 Chin[1] P'ing[2]) and the lot drawn determines the successor, who, however, must be approved by the Emperor. Imperial Edicts are issued whenever a Hut'ukht'u dies (compare the Decree of the 26th October, 1909, issued on the death of Tungkhor Hut'ukht'u ; *see* No. 917).

Many Hut'ukht'us receive from the Chinese Government, for merit shown, the honorary title of Gegen, a Mongolian word meaning "Light."

916A. 哲 布 尊 丹 巴 呼 圖 克 圖 Chê[2] Pu[4] Tsun[4] Tan[1] Pa[1] Hu[1] T'u[2] Kê[4] T'u[2], Cheptsun-damba Hut'ukht'u, the Mongolian Hut'ukht'u, or Pontiff, residing at Urga and ranking third among the dignitaries of the Lamaist church, *i.e.* after the Dalai Lama and the Panchen Erdeni Lama.

The Mongols frequently refer to the Cheptsun-damba Hut'ukht'u as the Maidari Hut'ukht'u (from Maitrêya, the Messiah of Buddhism; in Chinese 彌 勒 佛 Mi[2] Lê[4] Fo[2]). He is also described as Gegen, the title bestowed by Tsetsen Gegen Khan in 1637 A.D. on Ghombo-Dardji, the son of T'ushet'u Khan. This title was afterwards recognized by the Dalai Lama as appertaining to the Kubil Han of Cheptsun-damba.

The official designation of the Cheptsun-damba Hut'ukht'u is T'aranatha Lama, he being considered the re-embodiment of T'aranatha, the famous historian of Buddhism.

For particulars as to the Shabinors, Serfs of Underlings of the Urga Pontiff, *see* No. 875.

917. 駐 京 喇 嘛 Chu[4] Ching[1] La[3] Ma[1], Lamaist Organization in and about Peking.

Thanks to the large patronage extended to the "Yellow Church" by the Emperors of the Manchu Dynasty (beginning from K'ang Hsi, 1662–1722), the Lamas have succeeded in gradually establishing vast and rich monasteries at Jehol (12 寺 Ssu[1], Monasteries), Dolon-nor (also 喇 嘛 廟 La[3] Ma[1] Miao[4]; there are two monasteries here—Shara-sumê, the Yellow, and

Höhö-sumê, the Blue), and, especially, at 五臺山 Wu³ T‘ai² Shan¹, in Shansi province, where there is a famous temple 菩薩頂 P‘u² Sa¹ Ting³ (official designation, 大文殊寺 Ta⁴ Wên² Shu¹ Ssu¹, Large Temple of Wên Shu, or 眞容院 Chên¹ Jung² Yüan⁴, Court of the True Image), built by the monk 法永 Fa⁴ Yung³, during the time of the T‘ang Dynasty and dedicated to the Bêdhisattwa Manchusri (文殊菩薩 Wen² Shu¹ P‘u² Sa¹), which is annually visited by crowds of pilgrims from all parts of Mongolia.

In and about Peking, as well as at the Imperial Mausolea, there are found lamaseries in which services are daily performed in honour of deceased sovereigns.

Among the Metropolitan Hut‘ukht‘us the first place appertains to the 章嘉呼圖克圖 Chang¹ Chia¹ Hu¹ T‘u² Kê⁴ T‘u², Changcha Hut‘ukht‘u (also designated 掌教 Chang³ Chiao⁴) He is acknowledged as the re-embodiment of a Hut‘ukht‘u despatched by the Dalai Lama, under the same title, to represent him at the Chinese Court (towards the close of the 17th century). The latter was received with great respect by the Emperor K‘ang Hsi and was assigned a residence at the Shara-sumê monastery (compare above), built in the Jehol district about 1691. The successor of the original Changcha Hut‘ukht‘u, during the reign of the Emperor 乾隆 Ch‘ien² Lung² (1736–1796), removed his residence to Peking, where he was allotted the monastery 雍和宮 Yung¹ Ho² Kung¹ (where the Emperor 雍正 Yung¹ Chêng⁴, 1723–1735, lived while Heir Apparent; compare No. 104ᴀ).

The principal Metropolitan Hut‘ukht‘u are enumerated below, in order of rank assigned them by a Decree of 1786: 1. Minchur Hut‘ukht‘u (敏珠爾呼圖克圖 Min³ Chu¹ Êrh³ Hu¹ T‘u² Kê⁴ T‘u²), residing at the monastery 東黃寺 Tung¹ Huang² Ssu¹, built in 1691, lying three 里 Li³ North of the 安定門 An¹ Ting⁴ Mên², 2. Galdan Siret‘u Hut‘ukht‘u

(噶勒丹錫哷圖呼圖克圖 Ka¹ Lê⁴ Tan¹ Hsi² Lê⁴ T'u² Hu¹ T'u² Kê⁴ T'u²), 3. Chilung Hut'ukht'u (濟隆呼圖克圖 Chi⁴ Lung² Hu¹ T'u² Kê⁴ T'u²). These all have precedence of the 總堪布 Tsung³ K'an¹ Pu⁴, Abbots-in-Chief of the Imperial Lamaseries.

There are eight other dignitaries of class mentioned, headed by the Tungkhor Hut'ukht'u (洞科爾呼圖克圖 Tung⁴ K'o¹ Êrh³ Hu¹ T'u² Kê⁴ T'u²), dwelling at, or near, Peking, and two at Dolon-nor.

918. The remaining ranks of the Lamaist Hierarchy are as follows: 1. 掌印扎薩克大喇嘛 Chang³ Yin⁴ Cha¹ Sa¹ Kê⁴ Ta⁴ La³ Ma¹, Dzassak Da-Lama, Grand Chancellor of the Lamaseries, having a seal of office, 2. 副掌印扎薩克大喇嘛 Fu⁴ Chang³ Yin⁴ Cha¹ Sa¹ Kê⁴ Ta⁴ La³ Ma¹, Vice-Chancellor, 3. 扎薩克喇嘛 Cha¹ Sa¹ Kê⁴ La³ Ma¹, Dzassak Lama, Ruler of Lamaseries, 4. 達喇嘛 Ta⁴ La³ Ma¹, Prior of a Lamasery; charged with the management and control of services of the monastery to which he is attached, as well as with supervision of the Lamas, to ensure that they perform their duties properly, 5. 副達喇嘛 Fu⁴ Ta⁴ La³ Ma¹, Vice-Prior, 6. 閒散喇嘛 Hsien² San³ La³ Ma¹, Lamas with no fixed post (compare No. 914), 7. 德木齊 Te² Mu⁴ Ch'i² (also 得木奇 Te² Mu⁴ Ch'i²; in Mongolian Demch'i), Demch'i Lama, or Steward of a Lamasery, 8. 格思規 Kê⁴ Ssu¹ Kuei¹ (in Tibetan Gisk-hui; in Mongolian Gebhui, or Gebghei), Gebhui, or Provost; in charge of the maintenance of good order during services, for which reason he is authorized to carry a sceptre while services are in progress (in large monasteries, where there are many Gebhuis, the senior is designated as Ta Gebhui).

There are three degrees of consecration in the Lamaist Hierarchy: 1. 格隆 Kê⁴ Lung², Geleng (Gylong), Higher, 2. 格粗爾 Kê⁴ Ts'u¹ Êrh³, Gets'ul, Middle, and 3. 班第 Pan¹ Ti⁴, Bandi (in Tibetan Gheneng; in Kalmuk Manchih), Lower. In addition there are 沙必 Sha¹ Pi⁴, Novices.

PART IV.

APPENDIX

SPECIALLY DEPUTED OFFICIALS.

919. 特派差使 T'ê⁴ P'ai⁴ Ch'ai¹ Shih³, Specially Deputed Officials.

In China the custom of charging officials with special missions is very widespread, for instance, for conducting negotiations with Foreign Powers in connection with the conclusion of commercial treaties or for investigating the situation of various questions abroad, such as Education, Finance, etc.

920. 考察政治大臣 K'ao³ Ch'a² Chêng⁴ Chih⁴ Ta⁴ Ch'ên², Commissioner for Studying the Political Organization (of Foreign States). Under this designation officials (載澤 Tsai³ Tsê², 端方 Tuan¹ Fang¹, 戴鴻慈 Tai⁴ Hung²-tz'u², and others) were deputed to Europe and America in 1905.

920A. 考察憲政大臣 K'ao³ Ch'a² Hsien⁴ Chêng⁴ Ta⁴ Ch'ên², Commissioner for Studying Constitutional Government (in Foreign Countries). This titles was given to officials deputed, in August, 1907, to England (汪大變 Wang¹ Ta⁴-hsieh⁴), Germany (于式枚 Yü² Shih⁴-mei²) and Japan (first 達壽 Ta⁴ Shou⁴, later 李家駒 Li⁵ Chia¹-chü¹).

920B. 纂擬憲法大臣 Tsuan³ Ni³ (I³) Hsien⁴ Fa⁴ Ta⁴ Ch'ên², Commissioner for Compiling Constitutional Laws. An Imperial Edict of the 5th November, 1910, appointed Princes P'u Lun and Tsai Tse, with this title, to draw up a schedule of essential constitutional laws.

921. 澳門劃界大臣 Ao⁴ Mên² Hua⁴ Chieh⁴ Ta⁴ Ch'ên², Commissioner for Defining the Macao Boundaries. An official bearing this title, 高而謙 Kao¹ Êrh²-ch'ien¹, took part in the deliberations of a mixed Sino-Portuguese Commission convened

for the purpose of defining the boundaries of Macao (in 1909).

922. 考察財政大臣 K'ao³ Ch'a² Ts'ai² Chêng⁴ Ta⁴ Ch'ên², Commissioner for Studying the Financial Organization (in Foreign Countries). Invested with this title, 唐紹怡 T'ang² Shao⁴-i², studied the financial situation of America and the continental Powers during 1908-1909.

922A. A similar charge to the above, namely, the studying of the financial organization (考察財政 K'ao³ Ch'a² Ts'ai² Chêng⁴) of Japan, America and Europe, was laid upon 連甲 Lien² Chia³, the late Lieutenant-Governor of Anhui province, in 1909. He was, at the same time, directed to study the measures taken towards spreading education (兼察各國推廣教育辦法 Chien¹ Ch'a² Ko⁴ Kuo² T'ui¹ Kuang³ Chiao⁴ Yü⁴ Pan⁴ Fa³), extending the postal and telegraph services and the institution of Postal Savings Banks.

923. 考察海軍大臣 K'ao³ Ch'a² Hai³ Chün¹ Ta⁴ Ch'ên², Commissioner for Studying Naval Affairs. Bearing this title, Prince 載洵 Tsai³ Hsün¹, and Admiral 薩鎮氷 Sa¹ Chên⁴-ping¹, left, in the Autumn of 1909, to study the situation of naval affairs in England, France, Italy, Germany and Russia. They visited the United States of America and Japan for a similar purpose in the Autumn of 1910.

923A. 考察陸軍大臣 K'ao³ Ch'a² Lu⁴ Chün¹ Ta⁴ Ch'ên², Commissioner for Studying Military Affairs. Invested with this title, Prince 載濤 Tsai³ T'ao¹ was despatched, in 1910, to Japan, America, England, France, Germany, Italy, Austria and Russia, with the object of studying the military situation in these countries.

924. 欽差辦理商約事務大臣 Ch'in¹ Ch'ai¹ Pan⁴ Li³ Shang¹ Yüeh¹ Shih⁴ Wu⁴ Ta⁴ Ch'ên², Imperial Commissioner for Negotiating Commercial Treaties. This title was borne by 盛宣懷 Shêng⁴ Hsüan¹-huai², 呂海寰 Lü³ Hai³-huan², and

伍廷芳 Wu³ T'ing²-fang¹, who concluded commercial treaties with England (in 1902) and with America and Japan (in 1903).

924A. 會辦商約大臣 Hui⁴ Pan⁴ Shang¹ Yüeh¹ Ta⁴ Ch'ên², Associate Imperial Commissioner for Negotiating Commercial Treaties. This title is borne by Shêng Hsüan-huai, although at present no commercial treaties with Foreign Powers are being negotiated.

925. 專使 Chuan¹ Shih³, Ambassador Extraordinary; the title of officials deputed for extraordinary missions to Foreign Sovereigns. It was borne by 醇親王載灃 Ch'un² Ch'in¹ Wang² Tsai³ Fêng¹, Ch'un, Prince of the First Rank, personal name 載灃 Tsai Fêng, who was deputed to Germany in 1901 to express regret for the killing of Baron von Kettler, and by 那桐 Na¹ T'ung², who was deputed to Japan at the same time to express similar regrets for the killing of Mr. Sugiyama. For tendering China's thanks to America for waiving part of the indemnity of 1900, 唐紹怡 T'ang² Shao⁴-i², as Ambassador Extraordinary, visited that country in 1908 and, similarly, Prince 載振 Tsai³ Chên⁴, and 戴鴻慈 Tai⁴ Hung²-tz'u², were deputed to Japan and Russia respectively to express China's gratitude for the despatch of Special Ambassadors from these countries to the funeral of the Emperor Kuang Hsü.

926. 恭辦喪禮大臣 Kung¹ Pan⁴ San¹ Li³ Ta⁴ Ch'ên², Superintendent of Funeral Rites. This title was borne by various Princes of the Blood and High Officials of the Empire who were deputed in November, 1908, for the supervision of the funeral ceremonies of the Emperor Kuang Hsü and the Empress Dowager T'zu Hsi (20 officials in all).

927. 驗放大臣 Yen⁴ Fang⁴ Ta⁴ Ch'ên², Controller of Examination of Officials. Thus are designated Metropolitan officials who are deputed, in accordance with the law, to receive officials who have obtained appointments to posts not higher than the fourth rank, the Imperial Audience being waived, with the

928 to 929 object of ascertaining whether there is any obstacle to their taking up appointments (for instance, physical defects, bad official record, etc.). The examination of these officials is made in groups, periodically) several times a month), Imperial sanction being obtained for each examination.

ESTABLISHMENTS ABOLISHED OR REORGANIZED.

928. 通政司 T'ung[1] Chêng[4] Ssu[1], Transmission Office; literary designation, 銀臺 Yin[2] T'ai[2]. This office was charged with the reception, recording and transmission to the Council of all Memorials received from the provinces. Also, it was the depôt for the receipt of all petitions addressed to the Emperor direct. The staff included: 1. 通政使司通政使 T'ung[1] Chêng[4] Shih[3] Ssu[1] T'ung[1] Chêng[4] Shih[3], Commissioners of the Transmission Office (literary designation, 銀臺 Yin[2] T'ai[2], 大銀臺 Ta[4] Yin[2] T'ai[2], 納言 Na[4] Yen[2], 大納言 Ta[4] Na[4] Yen[2], 獻納使 Hsien[4] Na[4] Shih[3], 大獻納 Ta[4] Hsien[4] Na[4], and 匭使 Kuei[3] Shih[3]); one Manchu and one Chinese; 3A, 2. 通政使司副使 T'ung[1] Chêng[4] Shih[3] Ssu[1] Fu[4] Shih[3], Deputy Commissioners of the Transmission Office; one Manchu and one Chinese, 4A, 3. 通政司叅議 T'ung[1] Chêng[4] Ssu[1] Ts'an[1] I[4], Secretaries of the Transmission Office; one Manchu and one Chinese; 5A, and 4. 通政司經歷 T'ung[1] Chêng[4] Ssu[1] Ching[1] Li[4], Commissary of Records of the Transmission Office.

In 1902 the Transmission Office was abolished.

929. 詹事府 Chan[1] Shih[4] Fu[3], Supervisorate of Imperial Instruction; literary designation, 端司 Tuan[1] Ssu[1], and 宮詹 Kung[1] Chan[1]; under the Yüan Dynasty called 儲院 Ch'u[3] Yüan[4]. This department was specially charged with the direction of the studies of the Heir Apparent but, as the Emperors of the reigning dynasty, for reasons already mentioned (*see* No. 12), forbore from making the selection of an Heir

Apparent during their lifetime, it was, up to the date of its **930** abolition in 1902, an absolute sinecure for a personnel made up, in view of the important object of its institution, of Members of the National Academy, holding office also in the latter. The staff was made up of: 1. Two 詹事府正詹事 Chan[1] Shih[4] Fu[3] Chêng[4] Chan[1] Shih[4], Chief Supervisors of Instruction; literary designation, 宮正 Kung[1] Chêng[4], 宮尹 Kung[1] Yin[3], 儲端 Ch'u[3] Tuan[1], 端尹 Tuan[1] Yin[3], 大宮端 Ta[4] Kung[1] Tuan[1], 大儲端 Ta[4] Ch'u[3] Tuan[1], and 宮詹 Kung[1] Chan[1]; 3A, 2. Two 詹事府少詹事 Chan[1] Shih[4] Fu[3] Shao[4] Chan[1] Shih[4], Supervisors of Instruction; literary designation, 少尹 Shao[4] Yin[3], 詹事丞 Chan[1] Shih[4] Ch'êng[2], 少端 Shao[4] Tuan[1], and 端丞 Tuan[1] Ch'êng[2]; 4A, 3. Four 春坊庶子 Ch'un[1] Fang[2] Shu[4] Tzu[3], Deputy Supervisors of Instruction, two 左 Tso[3], Senior, and two 右 Yu[4], Junior; literary designation, 宮庶 Kung[1] Shu[4], 中護 Chung[1] Hu[4], and 大中護 Ta[4] Chung[1] Hu[4]; 5A, 4. Four 春坊中允 Ch'un[1] Fang[2] Chung[1] Yün[3], Secretaries of the Supervisorate of Imperial Instruction, two 左 Tso[3], Senior, and two 右 Yu[4], Junior; literary designation, 宮允 Kung[1] Yün[3], and 大宮允 Ta[4] Kung[1] Yün[3]; 6A, 5. Four 春坊贊善 Ch'un[1] Fang[2] Tsan[4] Shan[4], Assistant Secretaries of the Supervisorate of Imperial Instruction; literary designation, 宮贊 Kung[1] Tsan[4], and 大宮贊 Ta[4] Kung[1] Tsan[4]; 6B, 6. Two 司經局 洗馬 Ssu[1] Ching[1] Chü[2] Hsien[1] Ma[3], Librarians; literary designation, 桂坊大夫 Kuei[4] Fang[2] Ta[4] Fu[1], 司經 大夫 Ssu[1] Ching[1] Ta[4] Fu[1], and 大掌經 Ta[4] Chang[3] Ching[1], 5B, and 7. 主簿 Chu[3] Pu[4], Archivist; 7B.

930. 總理各國事務衙門 Tsung[3] Li[3] Ko[4] Kuo[2] Shih[4] Wu[4] Ya[2] Mên[2], or, more explicit, 總理各國通商事務衙門 Tsung[3] Li[3] Ko[4] Kuo[2] T'ung[1] Shang[1] Shih[4] Wu[4] Ya[2] Mên[2], Office of Foreign Affairs; established in 1861 and administered by 總理各國事務大臣 Tsung[3] Li[3] Ko[4] Kuo[2] Shih[4] Wu[4] Ta[4] Ch'ên[2], Members (for details *see* No. 305).

930A
to
933

In 1901 this institution was reorganized as the 外務部 Wai⁴ Wu⁴ Pu⁴, Ministry of Foreign Affairs (*see* No. 305A).

930A. 同文館 T'ung² Wên² Kuan³, College of Foreign Languages; established in 1862 (*see* No. 311) at the Office of Foreign Affairs (*see* Nos. 305 and 930); abolished in 1900.

931. 巡警部 Hsün² Ching³ Pu⁴, Ministry (Board) of Police; established in 1905 (*see* details in No. 339); reorganized in 1906 as the 民政部 Min² Cḥêng⁴ Pu⁴, Ministry of the Interior (*see* No. 339A).

932. 戸部 Hu⁴ Pu⁴, Ministry (Board) of Revenue (*see* No. 349). This Ministry was also designated 地曹 Ti⁴ Ts'ao², 人部 Jên² Pu⁴, 司徒 Ssu¹ T'u², and 司農 Ssu¹ Nung², while its President was called 地卿 Ti⁴ Ch'ing¹, 大司農 Ta⁴ Ssu¹ Nung², or 大司元 Ta⁴ Ssu¹ Yüan², and its Vice-President 少司農 Shao⁴ Ssu¹ Nung². It was reorganized in 1906 as the 度支部 Tu⁴ Chih¹ Pu⁴ (*see* No. 349B).

932A. 財政處 Ts'ai² Chêng⁴ Ch'u⁴, Committee of Finance; formed in 1903 (*see* No. 349A); amalgamated in 1906 with the 度支部 Tu⁴ Chih¹ Pu⁴, Ministry of Finance (*see* No. 349B).

933. 太常寺 T'ai⁴ Ch'ang² Ssu⁴, Court of Sacrificial Worship; literary designation, 奉常寺 Fêng⁴ Ch'ang² Ssu⁴, 司禮寺 Ssu¹ Li³ Ssu⁴, and 曲臺 Ch'ü³ T'ai² (*see* No. 376B); was in charge of all sacrifices performed by the Emperor in person, or by his deputies, and supervised temples and Imperial Mausolea. Its personnel was made up of: 1. Two 太常寺正卿 T'ai⁴ Ch'ang² Ssu⁴ Chêng⁴ Ch'ing¹, Directors of the Court of Sacrificial Worship; literary designation, 司禮寺卿 Ssu¹ Li³ Ssu⁴ Ch'ing¹, 大儀 Ta⁴ I², 奉常寺卿 Fêng⁴ Ch'ang² Ssu⁴ Ch'ing¹, 大典禮 Ta⁴ Tien³ Li³, and 宗伯 Tsung¹ Po²; 3A, and 2. Two 大常寺少卿 T'ai⁴ Ch'ang² Ssu⁴ Shao⁴ Ch'ing¹, Sub-Directors of the Court of Sacrificial Worship; literary designation, 司禮少卿 Ssu¹ Li³ Shao⁴ Ch'ing¹, and

奉 常 大 夫 Fêng⁴ Ch'ang² Ta⁴ Fu¹. These Officials were generically described as 京 堂 Ching¹ T'ang².

For officials additional to the above-mentioned *see* Nos. 382B and 391.

The Court of Sacrificial Worship was amalgamated in 1906 with the 禮 部 Li³ Pu⁴, Ministry (Board) of Rites (*see* No. 376B), *i.e.* with the Department of Sacrificial Worship (*see* No. 382A).

934. 光 祿 寺 Kuang¹ Lu⁴ Ssu⁴, Banqueting Court; literary designation, 司 宰 司 Ssu¹ Tsai³ Ssu¹, and 宣 徽 院 Hsüan¹ Hui¹ Yüan⁴ (*see* No. 376B). This department supervised the food supplies for banquets given in honour of Envoys from vassal states, as well as in honour of new Metropolitan Graduates and Provincial Graduates or, in the case of very worthy officials, on the 60th anniversary of the attainment of their literary degrees, by Imperial direction, at the Court or at the Board of Ceremonies. Its personnel was: 1. Two 光 祿 寺 正 卿 Kuang¹ Lu⁴ Ssu⁴ Chêng⁴ Ch'ing¹, Directors of the Banqueting Court; literary designation, 太 官 令 T'ai⁴ Kuan¹ Ling⁴, 司 宰 卿 Ssu¹ Tsai³ Ch'ing¹, 冷 卿 Lêng³ Ch'ing¹, 大 司 膳 Ta⁴ Ssu¹ Shan⁴, and 大 鼎 相 Ta⁴ Ting³ Hsiang⁴; 3B, and 2. Two 光 祿 司 少 卿 Kuang¹ Lu⁴ Ssu¹ Shao⁴ Ch'ing¹, Sub-Directors of the Banqueting Court; literary designation, 少 司 膳 Shao⁴ Ssu¹ Shan⁴, and 大 和 羹 Ta⁴ Ho² Kêng¹; 5A.

The Banqueting Court was amalgamated with the 禮 部 Li³ Pu⁴, Ministry of Rites (*see* No. 376B), *i.e.* the Banqueting Department (*see* No. 383A) in 1906.

935. 鴻 臚 寺 Hung² Lu² Ssu⁴, Court of State Ceremonial; literary designation, 儀 臺 I² T'ai² (*see* No. 376B). The duty of informing guests at banquets as to the ceremonies required by etiquette devolved upon this Court. Its personnel included: 1. Two 鴻 臚 寺 正 卿 Hung² Lu² Ssu⁴ Chêng⁴ Ch'ing¹, Directors of the Court of State Ceremonial; literary designation,

[487]

936 to 936B

大司儀 Ta⁴ Ssu¹ I², and 大行人 Ta⁴ Hsing² Jên²; 4A, and 2. Two 鴻臚寺少卿 Hung² Lu² Ssu⁴ Shao⁴ Ch'ing¹, Sub-Directors of the Court of State Ceremonial; literary designation, 少行人 Shao⁴ Hsing² Jên²; 5B.

The Court of State Ceremonial was amalgamated, in 1906, with the 禮部 Li³ Pu⁴, Ministry of Rites (*see* No. 376B), *i.e.* with the Department of Ceremonies (*see* No. 380A).

936. 兵部 Ping¹ Pu⁴, Ministry (Board) of War (*see* No. 415). This was also called 駕部 Chia⁴ Pu⁴, 武部 Wu³ Pu⁴, 西曹 Hsi¹ Ts'ao², 兵曹 Ping¹ Ts'ao², and 司馬 Ssu¹ Ma³, while its President was styled 夏官 Hsia⁴ Kuan¹, 夏卿 Hsia⁴ Ch'ing¹, 大掌戎 Ta⁴ Chang³ Jung², and 大司戎 Ta⁴ Ssu¹ Jung². It was reorganized as the 陸軍部 Lu⁴ Chün¹ Pu⁴ (*see* Nos. 417 and 420).

936A. 練兵處 Lien⁴ Ping¹ Ch'u⁴, Commission for Army Reorganization; established in 1903 (*see* No. 416); amalgamated in 1906 with the 陸軍部 Lu⁴ Chün¹ Pu⁴, Ministry of War (*see* Nos. 417 and 420). It consisted of three Departments: 1. 軍政司 Chün¹ Chêng⁴ Ssu¹, Department of Military Administration, 2. 軍令司 Chün¹ Ling⁴ Ssu¹, Department of Military Direction, and 3 軍學司 Chün¹ Hsüeh² Ssu¹, Department of Military Education (*see* No. 430A).

936B. 太僕寺 T'ai⁴ P'u² Ssu⁴, Court of the Imperial Stud; literary designation, 冏臺 Chiung³ T'ai² (*see* No. 417); superintended the Imperial droves, for which vast pasturages are allotted in various districts of South-eastern Mongolia—at Dolon-nor, the sources of the Liao River, etc. Its personnel was: 1. Two 太僕寺正卿 T'ai⁴ P'u² Ssu⁴ Chêng⁴ Ch'ing¹, Director of the Court of the Imperial Stud; literary designation, 大司僕 Ta⁴ Ssu¹ P'u², 冏卿 Chiung³ Ch'ing¹, 大冏伯 Ta⁴ Chiung³ Po², and 司僕寺卿 Ssu¹ P'u² Ssu⁴ Ch'ing¹; 3B, and 2. Two 太僕寺少卿 T'ai⁴ P'u² Ssu⁴ Shao⁴ Ch'ing¹,

[488]

Sub-Directors of the Court of the Imperial Stud; literary designation, 少司僕 Shao⁴ Ssu¹ P'u²; 4A.

The Court of the Imperial Stud was amalgamated with the 陸軍部 Lu⁴ Chün¹ P'u⁴, Ministry of War (*see* Nos. 417 and 420), *i.e.* with the Department of the Military Stud (*see* No. 433A), in 1906.

937. 刑部 Hsing² Pu⁴, Ministry (Board) of Punishments (*see* No. 438). Reorganized in 1906 as the 法部 Fa⁴ Pu⁴, Ministry of Justice (*see* No. 440).

Other designations of the Ministry of Punishments were 秋曹 Ch'iu¹ Ts'ao², 司寇 Ssu¹ K'ou⁴, 憲曹 Hsien⁴ Ts'ao², 憲部 Hsien⁴ Pu⁴, and 西臺 Hsi¹ T'ai². Its President was called 秋卿 Ch'iu¹ Ch'ing¹, 司憲 Ssu¹ Hsien⁴, 大秉憲 Ta⁴ Ping³ Hsien⁴, and 大秋臺 Ta⁴ Ch'iu¹ T'ai².

937A. 大理寺 Ta⁴ Li³ Ssu⁴, Court of Judicature and Revision (*see* No. 215); reorganized in 1906 as the 大理院 Ta⁴ Li³ Yüan⁴, Supreme Court of Justice (*see* No 215A).

The Court of Judicature and Revision was also called 雲司 Yün² Ssu¹, and 棘寺 Chi⁴ Ssu⁴. Its President was called 廷尉 T'ing² Yü⁴, 大廷尉 Ta⁴ T'ing² Yü⁴, 司刑卿 Ssu¹ Hsing² Ch'ing¹, 棘卿 Chi⁴ Ch'ing¹, 大棘 Ta⁴ Chi⁴, 秋卿 Ch'iu¹ Ch'ing¹, and 大司允 Ta⁴ Ssu¹ Yün³, while the Vice-President was styled 粲平 Ts'an¹ P'ing², and 廷尉少卿 T'ing² Yü⁴ Shao⁴ Ch'ing¹.

938. 商部 Shang¹ Pu⁴, Ministry (Board) of Trade; established in 1903 (*see* Nos. 461 and 461A); amalgamated in 1906 with the 農工商部 Nung² Kung¹ Shang¹ Pu⁴, Ministry of Agriculture, Industry and Commerce (*see* No. 462), *i.e.* with the Department of Commerce (*see* No. 465).

939. 工部 Kung¹ Pu⁴, Ministry (Board) of Works (*see* Nos. 460 and 460A). Amalgamated in 1906 with the 農工商部 Nung² Kung¹ Shang¹ Pu⁴, Ministry of Agriculture, Industry

**940
to
943**

and Commerce (*see* No. 462), *i.e.* with the Department of Industry (*see* No. 464).

The Ministry of Works was also styled 冬曹 Tung¹ Ts'ao², 司空 Ssu¹ K'ung¹, 起部 Ch'i³ Pu⁴, 起曹 Ch'i³ Ts'ao², while its President was called 冬官 Tung¹ Kuan¹, 冬卿 Tung¹ Ch'ing¹, and 大司平 Ta⁴ Ssu¹ P'ing².

940. 理藩院 Li³ Fan² Yüan², Court of Colonial Affairs (*see* No. 491); reorganized in 1906 as the 理藩部 Li³ Fan² Pu⁴, Ministry of Dependencies (*see* No. 491A).

The Court of Colonial Affairs was also known as 同文寺 T'ung² Wên² Ssu⁴, and 司賓寺 Ssu¹ Pin¹ Ssu⁴; its President was called 典客 Tien³ K'o⁴, 同文寺卿 T'ung² Wên² Ssu⁴ Ch'ing¹, and 司賓寺卿 Ssu¹ Pin¹ Ssu⁴ Ch'ing¹, and its Vice-President 同文寺少卿 T'ung² Wên² Ssu⁴ Shao⁴ Ch'ing¹, and 司賓寺少卿 Ssu¹ Pin¹ Ssu⁴ Shao⁴ Ch'ing¹.

941. 學務處 Hsüeh² Wu⁴ Ch'u⁴, Committee of Educational Affairs; established in 1903 (*see* No. 574); reorganized in 1906 as the 學部 Hsüeh² Pu⁴, Ministry of Education (*see* No. 395).

942. 鑾儀衞 Luan² I² Wei⁴, The Imperial Equipage Department (*see* No. 109); transformed in 1909 into the 鑾輿衞 Luan² Yü² Wei⁴ (*see* Decree of 13th April, 1909).

HONORARY TITLES.

943. The following honorary titles are bestowed (加恩賞加 . . . 銜 Chia¹ Ên¹ Shang³ Chia¹ . . . Hsien²) on officials, either during their lifetime or after their death, for distinguished service rendered the State: 1. 太師 T'ai⁴ Shih¹, Grand Preceptor; 1A, 2. 太傅 T'ai⁴ Fu⁴, Grand Tutor; 1A, 3. 太保 T'ai⁴ Pao³, Grand Guardian; 1A, 4. 少師 Shao⁴ Shih¹, Junior Preceptor; 1B, 5. 少傅 Shao⁴ Fu⁴, Junior Tutor; 1B, and 6. 少保 Shao⁴ Pao³, Junior Guardian; 1B.

These correspond to the titles of the six highest Ministers of State of olden times, designated under the general names of 三公 San¹ Kung¹, and 三孤 San¹ Ku¹.

To the above-mentioned there may be added six similar titles, referring to the Heir Apparent (*see* No. 12), which are, much more often, conferred for eminent service : 1. 太子太師 T'ai⁴ Tzu³ T'ai⁴ Shih¹, Grand Preceptor of the Heir Apparent ; 1B, 2. 太子太傅 T'ai⁴ Tzu³ T'ai⁴ Fu⁴, Grand Tutor of the Heir Apparent ; 1B, 3. 太子太保 T'ai⁴ Tzu³ T'ai⁴ Pao³, Grand Guardian of the Heir Apparent ; 1B, 4. 太子少師 T'ai⁴ Tzu³ Shao⁴ Shih¹, Junior Preceptor of the Heir Apparent ; 2A, 5. 太子少傅 T'ai⁴ Tzu³ Shao⁴ Fu⁴, Junior Tutor of the Heir Apparent ; 2A, and 6: 太子少保 T'ai⁴ Tzu³ Shao⁴ Pao³, Junior Guardian of the Heir Apparent ; 2A. The last-mentioned is often granted to officials holding office and it entitles them to be addressed as 宮保 Kung¹ Pao³, this phrase being added to their family name (for instance, in the case of 袁世凱 Yüan² Shih⁴-k'ai³, 袁宮保 Yüan² Kung¹ Pao³).

As regards Europeans, the title of Junior Guardian of the Heir Apparent has been bestowed upon Sir Robert Hart (赫宮保 Ho⁴ Kung¹ Pao³), the Inspector General of the Chinese Imperial Maritime Customs.

In the Peking Gazette there may often be noticed Decrees bestowing on this or that official one of the titles mentioned on the occasion of the 60th anniversary of their attainment of a degree (鄉舉之年適周花甲 Hsiang¹ Chü³ Chih¹ Nien² Shih⁴ Chou¹ Hua⁴ Chia³), for instance, 銘安 Ming² An¹, ex-Tartar General of Kirin, was granted the honorary title of Junior Guardian of the Heir Apparent (*see* Decree of the 25th February, 1908).

As has been stated, honorary titles are also bestowed on officials after their death. The late Grand Secretary 戴鴻慈 Tai⁴ Hung²-tz'u² was invested, after his death, with the title of

944   Junior Guardian of the Heir Apparent (*see* Decree of the 27tl February, 1910)

HEREDITARY RANKS AND TITLES OF HONOUR;
POSTHUMOUS TITLES.

944.　爵廳 Chüeh² Yin⁴, or 世爵 Shih⁴ Chüeh², Hereditary Ranks; arranged in nine grades: 1.　公 Kung¹, Duke, 2.　侯 Hou², Marquis, 3.　伯 Po², Earl, 4.　子 Tzu³, Viscount, 5.　男 Nan², Baron, 6.　輕車都尉 Ch'ing¹ Ch'ê¹ Tu² Yü⁴, 7.　騎都尉 Ch'i² Tu¹ Yü⁴, 8.　雲騎尉 Yün² Ch'i² Yü⁴, and 9.　恩騎尉 Ên¹ Ch'i² Yü⁴.　There are three classes (等 Têng³) of each of the first five ranks.

The three senior ranks, called 超品 Ch'ao¹ P'in³, "Eminent Ranks," are qualified by laudatory epithets (so-called 嘉名 Chia¹ Ming²), for instance, the Earl 李鴻章 Li³ Hung²-chang¹, and the Marquis 曾紀澤 Chêng¹ Chi⁴-tsê², are styled, respectively, 肅毅伯 Su¹ I⁴ Po², and 毅勇侯 I⁴ (Ni⁴) Yung³ Hou², etc.

All the ranks mentioned, the ninth excepted, are heritable within certain limits (世襲 Shih⁴ Hsi²)—for a specified number of generations, ranging from 26 for a 公 Kung¹ of the first class to one for a 雲騎尉 Yün² Ch'i² Yü⁴—or heritable forever (世襲罔替 Shih⁴ Hsi² Wang³ T'i⁴)

Among the Manchus the cases of "perpetual inheritance" of titles (colloquially called 輩輩 Pei⁴ Pei⁴) are very frequent. Possessors of such titles (for instance, that of 公 Kung¹) are distinguished as: 1.　宗室公 Tsung¹ Shih⁴ Kung¹ (*see* No. 39), 2.　覺羅公 Chüeh¹ Lo² Kung¹ (*see* No. 40), and 3.　八旗公 Pa¹ Ch'i² Kung¹ (*see* No. 718).

Among the Chinese there are also found cases of "perpetual inheritance" (Dukes, for instance, being designated 民公 Min²

Kung¹) but these, especially with reference to the titles of 公 **944A**
Kung¹, and 公 Hou² (*see* Nos. 914A and 944B), are rather rare.

Those holding junior titles—commencing with the sixth
often attain the privilege of annexing (兼 Chien¹) to their titles
those of one degree higher.

Any of the titles above-mentioned may be conferred
posthumously (晉贈 Chin⁴ Tsêng⁴, or 追贈 Chui¹ Tsêng⁴) for
distinguished service rendered the State.

944A. Among the Chinese, the posterity of Confucius
alone have the right of "perpetual inheritance" of the Princely
title 衍聖公 Yên³ Shêng⁴ Kung¹, Sacred Prince (1A). This
was bestowed in 1055 A.D., by the Emperor 仁宗 Jên²
Tsung¹, of the 宋 Sung⁴ Dynasty, on 孔宗愿 K'ung³
Tsung¹-yüan⁴, the 47th in line of descent from Confucius. It
carries with it an allowance of 360 taels a year, issued from the
public treasury Also, under the present Dynasty, a piece of
land has been granted, "for eternal possession," to the posterity
of Confucius which, being free of all taxes and dues, brings in a
good profit. Those residing on this land are also exempt from
all taxes and dues.

The holder of the title under consideration is responsible for
the maintenance in good order of the grave of Confucius, situated
in 曲阜縣 Ch'ü¹ Fu⁴ Hsien⁴, Shantung province.

The second son of the Yên Shêng Kung bears the title (also
heritable forever) of 五經博士 Wu³ Ching¹ Po² Shih⁴, Doctor
of the Classics ; 8A. His duties consist in offering sacrifices to
the grandson of Confucius, 子思 Tzu³ Ssu¹.

The title of 五經博士 Wu³ Ching¹ Po² Shih⁴, or simply
博士 Po² Shih⁴ (literary designation, 大翰博 Ta⁴ Han⁴ Po²),
is also transmitted to the eldest, in a direct line, of the
descendants of the following famous men of antiquity :
1. 周公 Chou¹ Kung¹, 2. 顏淵 Yen² Yüan¹, 3. 曾子輿
Tsêng¹ Tzu³-yü², 4. 閔子騫 Min³ Tzu³-ch'ien¹, 5. 仲季路

944B to 944D

Chung⁴ Chi⁴-lu⁴, 6. 有子有 Yu³ Tzu³-yu³, 7. 端木子貢 Tuan¹ Mu⁴ Tzu³ Kung⁴, 8. 卜子夏 Pu³ Tzu³-hsia⁴, 9. 言子游 Yen² Tzu³-yu², 10. 冉伯牛 Jan³ Po²-niu², 11. 冉仲弓 Jan³ Chung⁴-kung¹, 12. 顓孫子張 Chuan¹ Sun¹ Tzu³ Chang¹, 13. 孟子 Mêng⁴ Tzu³, 14. 伏生 Fu² Shêng¹, 15. 韓愈 Han⁴ Yü⁴, 16. 周敦頤 Chou¹ Tun¹-i², 17. 邵雍 Shao⁴ Yung¹, 18. 程顥 Ch'êng² Hao⁴, 19. 程頤 Ch'êng² I², 20. 張載 Chang¹ Tsai³, 21. 朱熹 Chu¹ Hsi³, and 22. 關羽 Kuan¹ Yü³.

944B. The descendants of one of the relatives of the last Emperor of the Ming Dynasty (1368-1644), 崇禎 Ch'ung² Chên¹ (1628-1644), bear the title, "heritable forever," of 朱侯 Chu¹ Hou², Marquis Chu, and the descendants of 施琅 Shih¹ Lang², a native of Fukien province who distinguished himself in the struggle against 鄭成功 Chêng⁴ Ch'êng²-kung¹, Coxinga, the Chinese pirate chief, and rendered great service to the Government in the conquest of Formosa (1621-1696), also bear the title, "of perpetual inheritance," of 施侯 Shih¹ Hou², Marquis Shih.

944C. 正一嗣教眞人 Chêng⁴ I¹·Ssu⁴ Chiao⁴ Chên¹ Jên², Descendant of the Founder of Taoism; 3A. This title is borne by the eldest (in a direct line) of the descendants of the founder of Taoism, 張道陵 Chang¹ Tao⁴-ling², who lived in the 1st century, and was conferred during the time of the 明 Ming² Dynasty on 張正常 Chang¹ Chêng⁴-ch'ang², the 39th in line of descent (see No. 573B).

944D. 恩廕 Ên¹ Yin⁴, "Bestowing the Emperor's Favours on Posterity." Thus are designated those cases in which the titles mentioned in No. 944 are conferred, not upon meritorious public servants themselves but upon their sons, grandsons, younger brothers or nephews. Their bestowal after the death of an official who has lost his life whilst engaged in the public service is designated as 難廕 Nan⁴ Yin⁴ (compare also No. 958)

[494]

944E. Regulations sanctioned by the Emperor on the 22nd September, 1910, define rewards and honours to be bestowed on those who fall in battle, or succumb from wounds received, and on those wounded in action. The table annexed to these regulations provides for three classes of rewards for those who are killed, or wounded, and a fourth for the wounded alone. These rewards are graded as follows : 1. The titles of 騎都尉 Ch'i[2] Tu[1] Yü[4], 雲騎尉 Yün[2] Ch'i[2] Yü[4], and 恩騎尉 Ên[1] Ch'i[2] Yü[4] (see No. 944 ; of perpetual, or qualified, inheritance), 2. The rank of 監生 Chien[4] Shêng[1] (see No. 959), of the seventh, eighth and ninth grades, 3. A yearly pension (恩撫金 Ên[1] Fu[3] Chin[1]) of from 12 to 1,200 taels, and 4. A reward (恩邺金 Ên[1] Hsü[4] Chin[1]), bestowed but once, of from 35 to 2,000 taels.

945. 封贈 Fêng[1] Tsêng[4], Titles of Honour ; conferred for services rendered, because of merit, or by Imperial bounty on the occasion of great rejoicing (through the medium of 恩詔 Ên[1] Chao[4], "Gracious Proclamations.") These may be conferred (授 Shou[4]) upon officials themselves or (封 Fêng[1]) upon their wives, or granted as posthumous distinctions (贈 Tsêng[4]) upon their deceased progenitors. The patents by which these titles are conferred are designated 誥命 Kao[4] Ming[4], for all ranks from the first to the fifth inclusive, and 勅命 Ch'ih[4] Ming[4], for all inferior to these.

Titles of honour are divided into nine ranks, each of which, in turn, is divided into two classes : 1. 光祿大夫 Kuang[1] Lu[4] Ta[4] Fu[1] ; 1A, and 榮祿大夫 Yung[2] Lu[4] Ta[4] Fu[1] ; 1B, 2. 資政大夫 Tzu[1] Chêng[4] Ta[4] Fu[1] ; 2A, and 通奉大夫 T'ung[1] Fêng[4] Ta[4] Fu[2]; 2B, 3. 通議大夫 T'ung[1] I[4] Ta[4] Fu[1]; 3A, and 中議大夫 Chung[1] I[4] Ta[4] Fu[?]; 3B, 4. 中憲大夫 Chung[1] Hsien[4] Ta[4] Fu[1]; 4A, and 朝議大夫 Ch'ao[2] I[4] Ta[4] Fu[1] ; 4B, 5. 奉政大夫 Fêng[4] Chêng[4] Ta[4] Fu[1]; 5A, and 奉直大夫 Fêng[4] Chih[2] Ta[4] Fu[1]; 5B, 6. 承德耶 Ch'êng[1] Tê[2] Lang[2]; 6A,

944L
to
945

946 and 儒林郎 Ju² Lin² Lang²; 6B, 7. 文林郎 Wên² Lin² Lang²; 7A, and 徵仕郎 Chêng¹ Shih⁴ Lang²; 7B, 8. 脩職郎 Hsiu¹ Chih² Lang²; 8A, and 脩職佐郎 Hsiu¹ Chih² Tso³ Lang²; 8B, and 9. 登仕郎 Têng¹ Shih⁴ Lang²; 9A, and 登仕佐郎 Têng¹ Shih⁴ Tso³ Lang²; 9B.

Officials of the class of 吏員 Li⁴ Yüan², *i.e.* those who have entered the public service from the ranks of 書辦 Shu¹ Pan⁴, may attain the following titles of honour: 宣德郎 Hsüan¹ Tê² Lang²; 6A, and 宣議郎 Hsüan¹ I⁴ Lang²; 7A (compare No. 962).

Titles of honour conferred upon the wives of officials are also divided into nine ranks: 1. 一品夫人 I¹ P'in³ Fu¹ Jên², 2. 二品夫人 Êrh⁴ P'in³ Fu¹ Jên², 3. 淑人 Shu² Jên², 4. 恭人 Kung¹ Jên², 5. 宜人 I² Jên², 6. 安人 An¹ Jên², 7. 孺人 Ju² Jên², 8. 八品孺人 Pa¹ P'in³ Ju² Jên², and 9. 九品孺人 Chiu³ P'in³ Ju² Jên².

Upon military officials there are conferred nine ranks of titles of honour, each rank being of two classes: 1. 建威將軍 Chien⁴ Wei¹ Chiang¹ Chün¹; 1A, and 振威將軍 Chên⁴ Wei¹ Chiang¹ Chün¹; 1B, 2. 武顯將軍 Wu³ Hsien³ Chiang¹ Chün¹; 2A, and 武功將軍 Wu³ Kung¹ Chiang¹ Chün¹; 2B, 3. 武義都尉 Wu³ I⁴ Tu¹ Yü⁴, 3A, and 武翼都尉 Wu³ I⁴ Tu¹ Yü⁴; 3B, 4. 昭武都尉 Chao¹ Wu³ Tu¹ Yü⁴; 4A, and 宣武都尉 Hsüan¹ Wu³ Tu¹ Yü⁴; 4B, 5. 武德騎尉 Wu³ Tê² Ch'i² Yü⁴; 5A, and 武德佐騎尉 Wu³ Tê² Tso³ Ch'i² Yü⁴; 5B, 6. 武略騎尉 Wu³ Lüeh⁴ Ch'i² Yü⁴; 6A, and 武略佐騎尉 Wu³ Lüeh⁴ Tso³ Ch'i² Yü⁴; 6B, 7. 武信騎尉 Wu³ Hsin⁴ Ch'i² Yü⁴; 7A, and 武信佐騎尉 Wu³ Hsin⁴ Tso³ Ch'i² Yü⁴; 7B, 8. 奮武騎尉 Fên⁴ Wu³ Hsiao¹ Yü⁴; 8A, and 奮武佐騎尉 Fên⁴ Wu³ Tso³ Hsiao¹ Yü⁴; 8B, and 9. 脩武騎尉 Hsiu¹ Wu³ Hsiao¹ Yü⁴; 9A, and 脩武佐騎尉 Hsiu¹ Wu³ Tso³ Hsiao¹ Yü⁴; 9B.

946. 謚號 Shih⁴ Hao, Posthumous Laudatory Epithets. These are conferred (加恩予謚 Chia¹ Ên¹ Yü² Shih⁴)

posthumously, by Decree, upon. very worthy officials and are indicative of the activity for which bestowed or the praiseworthy character of the one honoured, for instance, 文忠 Wên² Chung¹, 文襄 Wên² Hsiang⁴, 文正 Wên² Chêng⁴, 文敏 Wên² Min³, 文貞 Wên² Chên¹, 文勤 Wên² Ch'in², 文誠 Wên² Ch'êng², 文定 Wên² Ting⁴, 文和 Wên² Ho², 文端 Wên² Tuan¹, 文恭 Wên² Kung¹, 忠烈 Chung¹ Lieh⁴, 忠定 Chung¹ Ting⁴, 忠毅 Chung¹ I⁴ (Ni⁴), 武畧 Wu³ Lüeh⁴, 武忠 Wu³ Chung¹, etc.

To the foregoing epithets the character 公 Kung¹ is usually added (not, however, in this case meaning Duke; compare No. 944). Thus, the full posthumous laudatory epithet of 李鴻章 Li Hung-chang is 文忠公 Wên² Chung¹ Kung¹.

In Decrees bestowing posthumous laudatory epithets on deceased functionaries it is frequently commanded that sacrifices be offered in their memory (入祀 Ju⁴ Ssu⁴) in the 賢良祠 Hsien² Liang² Tz'u² (see No. 572).

DISTINCTIONS FOR MERIT.

947. 行袿 Hsing² Kua⁴, or (the more generally known) 黃馬袿 Huang² Ma³ Kua⁴, Yellow Riding Jacket, and 帶膝貂袿 Tai⁴ Su⁴ Tiao¹ Kua⁴, Jacket with Sable Tails. These ar the two rewards for the greatest merit; the first is often conferred (賞穿 Shang³ Ch'uan¹) for military services.

948. 紫韁 Tzu³ Chiang¹, and 黃韁 Huang² Chiang¹, Purple Bridle Reins, and Yellow Bridle Reins.

The privilege of employing purple or yellow bridle reins, appertaining to Princes (see No. 27A), is bestowed (賞用 Shang³ Yung⁴) upon distinguished officials.

949. 紫禁城內騎馬 Tzu³ Chin⁴ Ch'êng² Nei⁴ Ch'i² Ma³ (also 賞朝馬 Shang³ Ch'ao² Ma³), and 乘座二人肩輿 Ch'êng² Tso⁴ 'Erh⁴ Jên² Chien¹ Yü², Riding on Horseback or in a Sedan-chair within the precincts of the Imperial City. This is

32

950 to 951   an honorary distinction conferred upon old officials who are very frequently summoned to Audiences.

A similar distinction is the 杏黃轎 Hsing⁴ Huang² Chiao⁴, Apricot-yellow Sedan-chair.

950. 翎枝 Ling² Chih¹, The Feather, or Plume ; of two kinds, namely, 孔雀翎 K'ung³ Ch'üeh⁴ (Ch'iao³) Ling², The Peacock Feather (see No. 950ᴀ), and 藍翎 Lan² Ling², The Blue Plume (see No. 950ʙ).

950ᴀ. 孔雀翎 K'ung³ Ch'üeh⁴ (Ch'iao³) Ling², The Peacock Feather (see No. 950). This decoration is arranged in the following three classes : 1. 三眼花翎 San¹ Yen³ Hua¹ Ling², The Three-eyed Peacock Feather ; conferred only on Imperia princes of the first six degrees (see No. 27ᴀ) or very distinguished officials, not unusually for signal military achievements, 2. 雙眼花翎 Shuang¹ Yen³ Hua¹ Ling², The Double-eyed Peacock Feather, and 3. 單眼花翎 Tan¹ Yen³ Hua¹ Ling², The Single-eyed Peacock Feather (commonly called 花翎 Hua¹ Ling²) ; conferred as an ordinary form of reward for public service (compare the expression 賞戴花翎 Shang³ Tai⁴ Hua¹ Ling²), and often obtained by purchase.

950ʙ. 藍翎 Lan² Ling², The Blue Plume (see No. 950 ; colloquially termed 老鴰翎 Lao³ Kua¹ Ling², or The Crow Feather). This distinction is attributed to the rank and file of the Imperial Guards (see No. 99) and is conferred, as a reward for services rendered, upon officials below the sixth rank.

951. 巴圖魯 Pa¹ T'u² Lu³, A representation of the Manchu word " B'at'uru," and of the Mongol word "Baghadur," meaning " Brave " ; conferred solely for active service in the field and qualified by laudatory epithets, for instance, 毅勇巴圖魯 I⁴ (Ni⁴) Yung³ Pa¹ T'u² Lu³ (compare No. 944). This distinction carries with it the right to wear the Peacock Feather

[498]

(*see* No. 950A) should the recipient not already have attained this privilege.

952. 功牌 Kung¹ P'ai², The Soldier's Medal; an oblong thin plate of silver having the character 賞 Shang³, "Reward," embossed upon it; bestowed on meritorious soldiers at reviews and inspections.

952 to 963

DECORATIONS.

953. 雙龍寶星 Shuang¹ Lung² Pao³ Hsing¹, The Order of the Double Dragon. Until lately this was the sole Order found in China, being instituted in response to a Memorial from the Office of Foreign Affairs, dated the 16th October, 1881. The original purpose was to create a distinction which might be bestowed upon the Ministers of Foreign Powers a Peking, Sir Thomas Wade being designated as the first intended recipient. Its scope was, however, enlarged to include foreigners of all classes who distinguish themselves and, because of this, it became necessary to arrange the Order in 等 Têng³, Divisions, and the latter in 第 Ti⁴, Classes.

Dependent upon the official status of the person to be honoured, the Order of the Double Dragon is conferred according to the following schedule :

First Division :

1st Class : Reigning Sovereigns,

2nd Class : Heirs Apparent and members of Royal Families.

3rd Class : Ministers of State and Ambassadors.

Second Division :

1st Class : Ministers Plenipotentiary.

2nd Class : Ministers Resident, Chargés d'Affaires and the Inspector General of Customs.

3rd Class : First Secretaries of Embassies and Legations, Generals, Consuls-General and Heads of Educational Establishments.

953ᴀ Third Division :

1st Class : Second Secretaries of Embassies and Legations, onsuls, Attachés, Colonels, Professors, etc.,

2nd Class : Vice-Consuls, Commanders in the Navy, Lieutenant-Colonels, etc.

3rd Class : Consular Interpreters, Majors, Captains, etc.

Fourth Division : Soldiers and Sailors of the rank and file.

Fifth Division : Artisans, Tradespeople, etc.

Lately there has been noticed a tendency to confer Orders of the Double Dragon of a degree higher than that prescribed by the regulations (for instance, it has become customary to confer upon Ministers Plenipotentiary at Peking the 3rd Class of the First Division).

Since 1908 the Government has been conferring the Order of the Double Dragon upon Chinese officials ; 唐 紹 怡 T‘ang² Shao⁴-i² (*see* No. 925), the Extraordinary Ambassador to the United States of America, was the first Chinese thus honoured. It is now conferred upon : the higher officials of the Ministry of Foreign Affairs, Chinese Ministers abroad, officials deputed for special missions abroad, the higher officials of the Ministry of War, the General Staff and the Army, the Naval Council, the Commission for the Reorganization of the Navy and the higher officers of the New Palace Guard (among these there are many Princes of the Blood who receive the Order of the Double Dragon of the First Division, 2nd Class, for instance, 載 洵 Tsai³ Hsün¹, 載 濤 Tsai³ T‘ao¹, 毓 朗 Yü⁴ Lang⁵, and 載 搜 Tsai³ Fu³).

953ᴀ. In consequence of a Memorial from 貝 勒 載 濤 Pei¹ Lê⁴ Tsai³ T‘ao¹, Prince of the Third Degree, Tsai T‘ao, and others, in which it was requested that Imperial instructions be issued for the drawing up of regulations for Chinese Decorations (勳 章 Hsün¹ Chang¹), a Decree was issued on the 2nd April, 1909, charging the Ministries of Foreign Affairs and of

War, and the Committee of Ministers, to investigate this question.

On the 20th March, 1911, the establishments mentioned, in accordance with the Imperial instructions, presented their reply, with an enclosure in which was elaborated a scheme for the bestowal of New Chinese Orders (頒 給 勳 章 辦 法 Pan[1] Chi[3] Hsün[1] Chang[1] Pan[4] Fa[4]). The recommendations of this reply received Imperial sanction the same day. Accordingly, there have now been instituted in China the following Orders :

1. Special Order for Reigning Sovereigns (皇 上 佩 章 Huang[2] Shang[4] P'ei[4] Chang[1]), namely, 大 寶 章 Ta[4] Pao[3] Chang[1], Order of the Great Treasure (the Imperial Throne), with the ribbon of light yellow colour (帶 綬 Tai[4] Shou[4]).

2. Two Orders for members of Royal Families (皇 族 勳 章 Huang[2] Tsu[2] Hsün[1] Chang[1]), namely, the 黃 龍 勳 章 Huang[2] Lung[2] Hsün[1] Chang[1], Order of the Yellow Dragon, and the 赤 龍 勳 章 Ch'ih[4] Lung[2] Hsün[1] Chang[1], Order of the Red Dragon.

3. Two Orders for zealous service (臣 工 勳 章 Ch'ên[2] Kung[1] Hsün[1] Chang[1]), namely, the 青 龍 勳 章 Ch'ing[1] Lung[2] Hsün[1] Chang[1], Order of the Blue Dragon, and the 黑 龍 章 勳 Hei[1] Lung[2] Hsün[1] Chang[1], Order of the Black Dragon. These two are divided into eight 等 Têng[3], Classes, each.

The Order of the Yellow Dragon is bestowed upon Princes of the Blood alone, for merit shown.

The Order of the Red Dragon if bestowed upon Princes of the Second and Third Degrees and, for very eminent merit and by a special Edict, upon Princes of the Fourth and Fifth Degrees or officials of the first rank.

The First Class of the Order of the Blue Dragon is conferred upon Princes of the Fourth and Fifth Degrees and, for special merit, upon officials of the first rank.

The First Class of the Order of the Black Dragon is bestowed upon Princes of the Fourth and Fifth Degrees and upon officials of the first rank. Also, it may be granted, for special merit and as an act of Imperial favour, to officials of the second rank.

The Second Class of the Order of the Blue Dragon is bestowed upon officials of the second rank, for special merit.

The Second Class of the Order of the Black Dragon is intended for officials of the second rank but, for special merit shown, may be conferred upon officials of the Third rank, as an act of Imperial grace.

The Third Class of the Order of the Blue Dragon is given, for distinguished service, to officials of the third rank.

The Third Class of the Order of the Black Dragon is bestowed upon officials of the third rank and, should the Throne be memorialized with regard to their eminent merit, upon substantive officials of the fourth rank.

The Fourth Class of the Order of the Blue Dragon is granted to officials of the fourth rank, for special merit.

The Fourth Class of the Order of the Black Dragon is conferred upon officials of the fourth rank and, should their merit be brought to the Emperor's notice in a special Memorial, upon officials holding substantive posts of the fifth and sixth ranks.

The Fifth Class of the Order of the Blue Dragon is bestowed, for special merit, upon officials of the fifth rank.

The Fifth Class of the Order of the Black Dragon is destined for officials of the fifth rank but may, also, be given to officials holding substantive posts of the sixth and seventh ranks, provided they are brought to the Imperial notice, because of superior merit, in a special Memorial.

The Sixth Class of the Order of the Blue Dragon is conferred upon officials of the sixth rank, because of special merit.

The Sixth Class of the Order of the Black Dragon is intended for officials of the sixth rank but may be bestowed upon officials holding substantive posts of the seventh and eighth ranks, should their pre-eminent ability be brought to the Imperial notice by a special Memorial.

The Seventh Class of the Order of the Blue Dragon is bestowed upon officials of the seventh rank, for merit shown.

The Seventh Class of the Order of the Black Dragon is destined for bestowal upon officials of the seventh rank and upon officials holding substantive posts of the eighth and ninth ranks, whose marked worthiness is brought to the Emperor's notice by special Memorials.

The Eighth Class of the Order of the Blue Dragon is conferred upon officials of the eighth and ninth ranks, because of special merit.

The Eighth Class of the Order of the Black Dragon is bestowed upon officials holding posts lower than the eighth and ninth ranks in Civil, Marine and Military Establishments. Also, it may be conferred upon persons, not in the Government Service, whose efforts have aided the spread of education, or whose initiative has served to develop industries, and upon those of the most lowly birth, whose worthy character calls for recognition.

As regards foreigners, officials and others, the regulations regarding the new Orders provide that they may be bestowed upon such persons, the grade being determined by the status of the individual honoured.

Everything in connection with the bestowal of Chinese Decorations is to be attended to by a special office, the 勳 章 局 Hsün[1] Chang[1] Chü[2], Office of Decorations. This office is to be under the supervision of the Committee of Ministers; at present it is at the Ministry of Foreign Affairs.

[503]

954 to 957

In addition to the foregoing, the Ministries of War and the Navy have been commanded to arrange for a special Order to be bestowed upon officers and men of the Army and Navy whose courage and self-sacrifice in action prove instrumental in attaining victory. The said Ministries are to present a detailed report of what they recommend, for Imperial sanction.

THE GOVERNMENT SERVICE.

954. 仕進 Shih[4] Chin[4] (also 仕途 Shih[4] T'u[2]), The Government Service. The privilege of 出身 Ch'u[1] Shên[1], "advancement," or entry into the public service, is open to those belonging to the following (*see* Nos. 955 to 962) eight categories:

955. 進士 Chin[4] Shih[4] (literary designation, 甲榜 Chia[3] Pang[3], and 兩榜 Liang[3] Pang[3]), Metropolitan Graduate (Doctor); those having attained the third, or highest, literary degree (*see* No. 629c).

956. 舉人 Chü[3] Jên[2] (literary designation, 鄉進士 Hsiang[1] Chin[4] Shih[4], 乙榜 I[4] Pang[3], and 登賢書 Têng[1] Hsien[2] Shu[1]), Provincial Graduate (Bachelor of Arts); those who have attained the second literary degree (*see* No. 629B).

956A. 科甲出身 K'o[1] Chia[3] Ch'u[1] Shên[1] (compare No. 628), This is the general designation of the two higher classes of Graduates—Metropolitan Graduates (*see* No. 955) and Provincial Graduates (*see* No. 956), who enter the public service.

957. 貢生 Kung[4] Shêng[1], Senior Licentiate (literary designation, 明經 Ming[2] Ching[1]). In this category are Senior Licentiates of the 1st, 2nd and 3rd Classes (*see* No. 629A).

Senior Licentiates are divided into two groups: 恩賜貢生 Ên[1] Tz'u[4] Kung[4] Shêng[1], Licentiates by Examination at the Pi Yung Hall (*see* No. 412; where the Emperor discusses the Classics, 臨雍頒論 Lin[2] Yung[1] Pan[1] Lun[2]), and 2. 恩補貢生

958
to
959

Ên¹ Pu³ Kung⁴ Shêng¹, Licentiates by Imperial Favour (granted the degree of Licentiate by Imperial favour in a jubilee year, after 20, or more, years' tenure of the grade of Salaried Licentiate; *see* No. 629A).

To this category also belong those who have obtained the degree of Senior Licentiate by purchase, namely: 1. 廩貢生 Lin³ Kung⁴ Shêng¹ (from the ranks of Salaried Licentiates), 2. 增貢生 Tsêng¹ Kung⁴ Shêng¹ (from the ranks of Supplementary Licentiates), 3. 附貢生 Fu⁴ Kung⁴ Shêng¹ (from the ranks of Accessory Licentiates), and 4. 例貢生 Li⁴ Kung⁴ Shêng¹ (from the ranks of Collegians of the Imperial Academy of Learning; compare No. 959).

958. 廕生 Yin⁴ Shêng¹, Honorary Licentiate. This is granted on the occasion of national rejoicing (through the medium of an 恩詔 Ên¹ Chao⁴, "Gracious Proclamation," or is bestowed in consideration of services rendered by a progenitor of the person honoured. Accordingly, Honorary Licentiates are distinguished as 恩蔭生 Ên¹ Yin⁴ Shêng¹, or 難蔭生 Nan⁴ Yin⁴ Shêng¹ (for details *see* No. 944c).

The Yin Shêng are arranged in 品 P'in³, Grades (four in all, corresponding to the fifth to the eighth official ranks), each of which is sub-divided into four 等 Têng³, Classes, which distinguish the type of service: 1. 侍衛 Shih⁴ Wei⁴ (*see* No. 99), 2. 文職 Wên² Chih², 3. 外用 Wai⁴ Yung⁴, and 4. 旗員 Ch'i² Yüan².

958A. To start an official career possessed of one of the above-mentioned four titles (*see* Nos. 955 to 958) is designated 正途 Chêng⁴ T'u², "Proper Path."

959. 監生 Chien⁴ Shêng¹ (literary designation, 太學生 T'ai⁴ Hsüeh² Shêng¹, and 上舍 Shang⁴ Shê⁴), Collegian of the Imperial Academy of Learning (國子監 Kuo² Tzu³ Chien⁴; *see* No. 412). These are differentiated as belonging to six categories: 1. 恩賜監生 Ên¹ Tz'u⁴ Chien⁴ Shêng¹ (compare

960 to 962

No. 957); the descendants of well-known persons; granted this title by the Emperor at the Pi Yung Hall, 2. 恩取監生 Ên¹ Ch'ü³ Chien⁴ Shêng¹; these receive their degree after a special examination (compare No. 628), 3. 恩廕監生 Ên¹ Yin⁴ Chien⁴ Shêng¹ (compare No. 958); conferred on occasions of rejoicing upon one of the sons of : A. Civil Court Officials of not lower than the fourth rank, B. Civil Provincial Officials of not lower than the third rank, and C. Military Officials (Court and provincial) of not lower than the third rank, 4. 難廕監生 Nan⁴ Yin⁴ Chien⁴ Shêng¹ (compare No. 958); bestowed upon one of the sons of officials who lose their lives while at sea or during a campaign, 5. 優監生 Yu¹ Chien⁴ Shêng¹; thus are styled Licentiates of the 1st Class (*see* No. 629A) and Military Licentiates (武生 Wu³ Shêng¹; compare No. 629D) chosen by lot by the Provincial Commissioner of Education, and 6. 例監生 Li⁴ Chien⁴ Shêng¹; those obtaining their degree by purchase, four classes in all: A. 廩監生 Lin³ Chien⁴ Shêng¹ (from the ranks of Salaried Licentiates), B. 增監生 Tsêng¹ Chien⁴ Shêng¹ (from the ranks of Supplementary Licentiates of the 2nd Class), C. 附監生 Fu⁴ Chien⁴ Shêng¹ (from the ranks of Licentiates of the 1st Class), and D. 監生 Chien⁴ Shêng¹ (from the ranks of 俊秀 Chün⁴ Hsiu⁴, or 民生 Min² Shêng¹; *see* No. 629); compare No. 957.

960. 生員 Shêng¹ Yüan², (literary designation, 茂才 Mao⁴ Ts'ai², 博士弟子員 Po² Shih⁴ Ti⁴ Tzu³ Yüan², and 弟子員 Ti⁴ Tzu³ Yüan²), Licentiate ; those who have attained the third, or lowest, literary degree (*see* No. 629A).

961. 官學生 Kuan¹ Hsüeh² Shêng¹, Pupil of the Banner Schools ; those who have completed the course of study of one of the Government Banner Schools (*see* Nos. 87 and 717).

962. 吏 Li⁴, Government Clerk (from the ranks of Writers ; compare No. 945).

962ᴀ. Those entering public life belonging to one of the four categories mentioned (*see* Nos. 959 to 962) are said to have obtained employment through the system of 保 舉 Pao³ Chü³, "Recommendation" (Influence).

963. 捐 輸 Chüan¹ Shu¹, Obtaining rank and office by purchase. This system, resorted to on a small scale since the days of the Ming Dynasty, owes its enormous increase to the necessities imposed on the Government by the first war with Great Britain, and by the T'ai P'ing Rebellion, a few years later. A Decree of the 13th December, 1850, finally sanctioned this system.

964. 孝 廉 方 正 Hsiao⁴ Lien² Fang¹ Chêng⁴, "Filial, Disinterested, Straightforward and Upright." This honorary title is bestowed by Imperial bounty, through the medium of a "Gracious Proclamation," upon persons recommended by the local authorities for their extensive capacity and irreproachable moral character, giving them the right to join the public service somewhat similarly to 舉 人 Chü³ Jên² (*see* No. 956). At the same time they are awarded the 六 品 頂 戴 Liu⁴ P'in³ Ting³ Tai⁴ (button of the sixth rank: *see* No. 966). After an Imperial audience they receive appointments corresponding to their rank.

965. The existing system regarding official posts in China classifies all civil and military offices under nine degrees of rank, 品 P'in³. Each rank is sub-divided into two 級 Chi², Classes, *i.e.* 正 Cheng⁴, Principal (designated in this book by the letter ᴀ placed after the numeral indicating the rank of the post), and 從 Tsung⁴, Second (designated in this volume by the letter ʙ). Mention must also be made of a large class, embracing the lowest posts, which is styled 未 入 流 Wei⁴ Ju⁴ Liu², Unclassed.

As regards exterior distinctions, for each of the ranks there is a button worn on the head dress (頂 戴 Ting³ Tai⁴, or 頂 子 Ting³ Tzu³; *see* No. 966), embroidered plaques for the

966 official dresses (for civil officials depicting birds and for military officials depicting animals; *see* Nos. 967 and 968), called 補子 Pu³ Tzu³, or 補服 Pu³ Fu², and, for the first five ranks, a rosary (朝珠 Ch'ao² Chu¹).

966. 頂戴 Ting³ Tai⁴, Buttons (*see* No. 965).

The Buttons of the various ranks are distinguished as follows:

1st Rank: 紅寶石 Hung² Pao³ Shih², Ruby (in daily life officials entitled to this button usually wear one of coral),

2nd Rank: 珊瑚頂 Shan¹ Hu² Ting³, Red Coral,

3rd Rank: 藍寶石 Lan² Pao³ Shih², Transparent Blue (the sapphire),

4th Rank; 青金石 Ch'ing¹ Chin¹ Shih², Dead Blue (azure coloured),

5th Rank: 水晶頂 Shui³ Ching¹ Ting³, Crystal (of transparent white colour),

6th Rank: 硨磲頂 Ch'ê¹ Ch'ü¹ Ting³, Opaque White (milk colour; made of adularia—fluor-spar);

7th Rank: 素金頂 Su⁴ Chin¹ Ting³, Golden;

8th Rank: 鏤金頂 Lou² Chin¹ Ting³, Gilded;

9th Rank: 鏤銀頂 Lou² Yin² Ting³, Silvered.

The Button of the 1st Rank (頭品頂戴 T'ou² P'in³ Ting³ Tai⁴) is often bestowed upon meritorious officials irrespective of their 職 Chih², Rank, or 任 Jên⁴, Post.

Princes of the Blood of the first eight degrees (*see* Nos. 16 to 23), as well as persons bearing the hereditary titles of 公 Kung¹, 侯 Hou², and 伯 Po² (*see* No. 944), wear the Ruby Button (no class being defined—出品 Ch'u¹ P'in³).

Imperial Clansmen (*see* No. 39) wear the Button of the fourth rank.

Buttons of the lower ranks are often bestowed in recognition of contributions for public needs and are often sold outright.

967. 文官補子 Wên² Kuan¹ Pu³ Tzu³, Plaques of embroidery sewn on the breast and back of official dress of civil officials (*see* No. 965). These are differentiated as follows :

1st Rank : 仙鶴 Hsien¹ Hao², Crane (white) ;
2nd Rank : 錦雞 Chin³ Chi¹, Golden Pheasant ;
3rd Rank : 孔雀 K'ung³ Ch'üeh⁴ (Ch'iao³), Peacock ;
4th Rank : 雲鴈 Yün² Yen⁴, Wild Goose ;
5th Rank : 白鷴 Pai² Hsien², Silver Pheasant ;
6th Rank : 鷺鷥 Lu⁴ Ssu¹, Egret ;
7th Rank : 鸂鶒 Ch'i¹ Chih⁴, Mandarin Duck ;
8th Rank : 鵪鶉 An¹ Ch'un¹, Quail ;
9th Rank : 練雀 Lien⁴ Ch'üeh⁴ (Ch'iao³), White-tailed Jay.

Unclassed Rank : 黃鸝 Huang² Li², Oriole.

Officials holding substantive posts wear the insignia corresponding to the rank of the post ; those holding supernumerary or unclassed posts wear the insignia of their personal rank.

968. 武官補子 Wu³ Kuan¹ Pu³ Tzu³, Plaques of embroidery sewn on the breast and back of official dress of military officials (*see* No. 965). These are distinguished as follows :

1st Rank : 麒麟 Ch'i² Lin², Unicorn ;
2nd Rank : 獅子 Shih¹ Tzu³, Lion ;
3rd Rank : 豹 P'ao⁴, Leopard ;
4th Rank : 虎 Hu³, Tiger ;
5th Rank : 熊 Hsiung², Black Bear ;
6th Rank : 彪 Piao¹, Tiger-cat, or 羆 P'i², Spotted Bear ;
7th Rank ; 彪 Piao¹, Tiger-cat ;
8th Rank : 海馬 Hai³ Ma³, Seal ;
9th Rank : 犀牛 Hsi¹ Niu², Rhinoceros.

The foregoing distinctions do not concern the so-called " New Troops," for whom there are special uniforms modelled on those found in foreign armies.

For particulars as to the eventual abolition of all differentiation between civil and military officials *see* No. 657.

969. Princes of the Blood of the first two degrees (*see* Nos. 16 and 17) wear four plaques, 補子 Pu³ Tzu³ (*see* No. 965), embroidered with a dragon (龍 Lung²) having five claws.

Princes of the Blood of the next six degrees, as well as persons bearing the hereditary titles of 公 Kung¹, 侯 Hou², and 伯 Po² (*see* No. 944), wear two plaques, 補子 Pu³ Tzu³, embroidered with a dragon (蟒 Mang³) having four claws.

Nobles of the Imperial Lineage, of the 9th to 12th degrees (*see* Nos. 24 to 27), wear embroidered plaques similar to those of military officials of the first four ranks (*see* No. 968).

Imperial Clansmen (*see* No. 39) employ plaques similar to those of military officials of the fourth rank (*see* No. 968).

970. Those who have obtained the right of entering the public service, thanks to their possession of one of the titles spoken of in Nos. 955 to 962, must first seek presentation at an Imperial Audience (引見 Yin³ Chien⁴). As for the rest, those enrolled for posts of not higher than the fourth rank are, in some cases, not received by the Emperor, but by specially deputed officials (so-called 驗放大臣 Yen⁴ Fang⁴ Ta⁴ Ch'ên²; *see* No. 927).

After reception in a major or minor Audience, the various posts are distributed by lot and the candidates are despatched to the provinces which fortune has decreed, where they are enrolled in the list of " Expectants " (候補班 Hou⁴ Pu³ Pan¹) for an indefinite (sometimes very considerable) period, during which they may be charged with various missions, under the designation of 委員 Wei³ Yüan², Deputies.

From the "expectant" stage the candidates at length emerge (補授 Pu³ Shou⁴) to substantive service (實缺 Shih² Ch'üeh¹), a year of probation (試用 Shih⁴ Yung⁴) being, however, obligatory to all ranks below that of Taotai.

971
to
976

971. Expectants (*see* No. 970) bear various designations, for instance, 侯選 Hou⁴ Hsüan³ (or 侯補 Hou⁴ Pu³), Candidate, 儘先補用 Chin³ Hsien¹ Pu³ Yung⁴, First Candidate, 遇缺即 補 Yü⁴ Chʻüeh² Chi² Pu³, Candidate for the First Vacancy, etc.

972. There are three types of salary received by officials : 1. 俸銀 Fêng⁴ Yin², Salary received by all officials of the Empire (officials at Court and in the provinces), 2. 養廉銀 Yang³ Lien² Yin², " Money Nourishing Honesty "; received only by provincial officials, and 3. 俸米 Fêng⁴ Mi³, Salary in Rice; received only by Court officials.

973. Although 品 Pʻin³, Ranks, are divided into 級 Chi², Classes (*see* No. 965), when meting out punishment for so-called 私罪 Ssu¹ Tsui⁴ (private offences) the former alone are taken into consideration when degradation (降級 Chiang⁴ Chi²) is ordered, being called 實級 Shih² Chi². Thus, an official being condemned to forfeiture of four steps in rank, should he be originally of the 5ᴀ rank, becomes of the 9ᴀ, not 7ᴀ, rank.

The suspension of salary and lowering of rank, as punishment for 公罪 Kung¹ Tsui⁴, " crimes committed while on duty," may be changed to the forfeiture of 加級 Chia¹ Chi², or 紀錄 Chi⁴ Lu⁴ (*see* No. 974).

974. 加級 Chia¹ Chi², Additional Grades (also 虛級 Hsü¹ Chi², Empty Grades), and 紀錄 Chi⁴ Lu⁴, Honourable Records, are of two kinds, namely, 軍功 Chün¹ Kung¹, for military merits, and 尋常 Hsün² Chʻang², ordinary. The latter are often granted in " Gracious Proclamations."

975. 降級留任 Chiang⁴ Chi² Liu² Jên⁴, Lowering of Rank but Detention in Office (to lose rank but retain office). Rehabilitation takes place after three years' irreproachable conduct.

976. 革職留任 Ko² Chih² Liu² Jên⁴, Deprivation of Rank but Detention in Office. Rehabilitation takes place (開名

977 to 980

原官 K'ai¹ Fu⁴ Yüan² Kuan¹) after four years' irreproachable behavior.

977. Officials holding substantive posts (so-called 身列仕版 Shen¹ Lieh⁴ Shih⁴ Pan³, and 現食俸祿 Hsieh⁴ Shih² Fêng⁴ Lu⁴) may obtain by zealous service, or by certain monetary offerings, 加銜 Chia¹ Hsien², Nominal Rank. Thus a 知府 Chih¹ Fu³, Prefect, may obtain by purchase the rank of 鹽運使 Yen² Yün⁴ Shih³, Salt Controller, and thus have the privilege of wearing the button of the secondary class of the third rank.

978. Those who contribute funds to the Government, or distinguish themselves by useful public actions, may be granted 虛銜 Hsü¹ Hsien², Brevet Rank, entitling them to wear the button of the rank concerned (頂戴榮身 Ting³ Tai⁴ Jung² Shên¹).

979. Conforming to the old regulations, regarding mourning, officials who lost one of their parents were forced to retire for the observance of mourning (離任終制 Li² Jên² Chung¹ Chih⁴) for a period of 27 months, should they be of Chinese origin. Manchu Officials, under similar conditions, retired for mourning for 100 days (穿孝百日 Ch'uan¹ Hsiao⁴ Po² Jih⁴).

By Imperial Edict of the 25th March, 1909, issued in reply to a Memorial from the Ministry of Rites, it has been commanded that in future all officials, Manchu or Chinese (滿漢服制 Man³ Han⁴ Fu² Chih⁴) are to vacate office on the death of a parent and enter into mourning for a period of 27 months. An exception is made for officials holding very important and responsible posts; with special Imperial sanction they enter into mourning for 100 days only, on the expiry of which they return to their duties under the designation of 署理 Shu⁴ Li³, Acting.

980. With few exceptions, persons bound together by ties of relationship may not hold office in the same province. The junior must vacate office (廻避 Hui² Pi⁴), being customarily

transferred to an equivalent post in the adjoining province ruled by the same Governor-General.

981. It is the duty of the higher provincial authorities to scrutinize the doings of their subordinates. In virtue of this, reports are periodically submitted to the Emperor with regard to the latter (甄別屬員 Chên[1] Pieh[2] Shu[3] Yüan[2]), rewards being recommended for the worthy and punishments for the others (分別獎懲 Fên[1] Pieh[2] Chiang[3] Ch'êng[3]).

982. The surveillance over the actions of the higher metropolitan and provincial authorities appertains to the Censors (*see* Nos. 210 and 213) who, should any irregularities, or defects in general, be detected, present Memorials of impeachment (奏叅 Tsou[4] Ts'an[1], or 叅劾 Ts'an[1] Hô[2]). The Emperor then deputes high officials to investigate the case (查辦 Ch'a[2] Pan[4]).

Should it be proven that the indictment was without sufficient foundation, it is left without further discussion (無庸置議 Wu[2] Yung[1] Chih[4] I[4], or 無庸再議 Wu[2] Yung[1] Tsai[4] I[4]), the Censor concerned being sometimes reprimanded by the Emperor (傳旨申斥 Ch'uan[2] Chih[3] Shên[1] Ch'ih[4]) or, in very exceptional cases, ordered to return to his original post for service (回原衙門行走 Hui[2] Yüan[2] Ya[2] Mên[2] Hsing[2] Tsou[3]).

Should the impeachment, however, be found to be correct, the guilty official is handed over to the Ministry of Civil Appointments (交部議處 Chiao[1] Pu[4] I[4] Ch'u[4], or 交部處分 Chiao[1] Pu[4] Ch'u[3] Fên[1]) for the definition of a penalty, which may be more severe than those mentioned in Nos. 975 and 976, possibly including summary dismissal from office (即行革職 Chi[2] Hsing[2] Ko[2] Chih[2]).

983. Since the accession of the Throne by the T'ai Ch'ing Dynasty the Manchu officials have gradually developed a custom of styling themselves, in Memorials to the Emperor, as 奴才 Nu[2] Ts'ai[2], Slaves, the Chinese continuing the old title 臣 of Ch'ên[2], Ministers.

A Decree of the 10th March, 1910, commands that hereafter all officials, civil and military, in the Capital and in the

33

984 provinces, Manchu or Chinese, refer to themselves uniformly as 臣 Ch'ên², Ministers.

984. All persons in authority in China, from the Emperor to the lowest officials, employ their own special seals. These are variously designated, dependent on the functionary to whom appropriated, namely: 1. 寶 Pao³ (formerly 璽 Hsi³), Seals used by the Emperor, Empress, Heir Apparent, Imperial Concubines of the first and second ranks and Princes of the first degree, 2. 印 Yin⁴, Seals of Imperial Concubines of the third rank, Princes of the second degree, Ministries and other High Government Establishments at the Capital and some provincial officials, 3. 關防 Kuan¹ Fang², Seals employed by Governors-General, Governors and the majority of provincial officials, 4. 圖記 T'u² Chi⁴, Seals of the Manchu General-in-Chief of Ili and Colonels of provincial garrisons, 5. 條記 T'iao² Chi⁴, Seals of petty provincial officials (of the eighth rank), and 6. 鈐記 Ch'ien¹ Chi⁴, Seals of petty provincial officials (of the ninth and unclassed ranks).

The duty of casting seals rests, as has been seen above (No. 386), with the Office of Seal-casting, attached to the Ministry of Rites.

The dye-stuff used in sealing documents is of three colours: 1. 紫色 Tzu³ Sê⁴, Violet (employed by the Ministries and Higher Government Establishments at the Capital and by Governors-General), 2. 紅色 Hung² Sê⁴, Red (used by the remaining civil officials and by all military officials), and 3. 藍色 Lan² Sê⁴, Blue (used during mourning—27 days for an Emperor and 13 days for an Empress).

Yearly, on the 19th–21st of the 12th Moon, there is performed the 封印 Fêng¹ Yin⁴, "Closing the Seals." These are opened again only on the 19th–21st of the 1st Moon following (開印 K'ai¹ Yin⁴). During the period during which the seals are "closed" all despatches are written on blanks that have been previously sealed (豫用空白 Yü⁴ Yung⁴ K'ung⁴ Pai², or 遵用空白 Tsun¹ Yung⁴ K'ung⁴ Pai²).

SUPPLEMENT.

SUPPLEMENT.

No. 1.   The Emperor is also designated 天王 T'ien[1] Wang[2], 元后 Yüan[2] Hou[4], and 至尊 Chih[4] Tsun[1].

No. 2.   The Empress is also designated 帝匹 Ti[4] P'i[3], and 天下母 T'ien[1] Hsia[4] Mu[3].

No. 11.   Female attendants of the Emperor are also called 宮女 Kung[1] Nü[3].

No. 12.   The Heir Apparent may be styled 東儲 Tung[1] Ch'u[3].

No. 55.   Eunuchs are also styled 大長秋 Ta[4] Ch'ang[2] Ch'iu[1].

No. 56.   Other designations of the Imperial Clan Court are 宗正寺 Tsung[1] Chêng[4] Ssu[4] and 玉牒所 Yü[4] Tieh[2] So[3].

No. 57.   The Presiding Controller of the Imperial Clan Court is also styled 宗伯 Tsung[1] Po[2].

Nos. 58 and 59.   Assistant Controllers of the Imperial Clan Court are also designated 宗正少卿 Tsung[1] Chêng[4] Shao[4] Ch'ing[1] and 大司宗 Ta[4] Ssu[1] Tsung[1].

No. 62.   Another designation of the Vice-Director of the Imperial Clan Court is 宗丞 Tsung[1] Ch'êng[2].

No. 75.   The Imperial Household is also designated 太府寺 T'ai[4] Fu[3] Ssu[4] and 殿中監 Tien[4] Chung[1] Chien[4].

No. 88.   Another designation of the Director of the Palace Stud is 飛龍使 Fei[1] Lung[2] Shih[3].

No. 89.   The Director of the Imperial Armoury is also styled 武庫令 Wu[3] K'u[4] Ling[4].

No. 90.   Another designation of the Imperial Gardens and Hunting Parks is 上林苑 Shang[4] Lin[2] Yüan[4].   The Director

[517]

is also called 宮苑總監 Kung¹ Yüan⁴ Tsung³ Chien⁴ and 上林監 Shang⁴ Lin² Chien⁴.

No. 97. At the head of the Imperial Household Bondservants, making up the three Superior Banners, there is a 三旗包衣統領 San¹ Ch'i² Pao¹ I¹ T'ung³ Ling³; 3A.

No. 99. The Senior Bodyguards are also called 爪士 Chao³ Shih⁴ and 羽林郎 Yü³ Lin² Lang².

Nos. 102 and 102A. In consequence of a Memorial from Prince A Mo Lin Kuei, and others, re the necessity of reorganizing the Household Division of the Banners and the Imperial Guards, an Edict of the 29th November, 1910, appointed Princes A Mo Lin Kuei and Tsai Jun as 管理 Kuan³ Li³, Controllers-General, for the revision of the regulations of the Household Division of the Banners and those of the Imperial Guards. The work of reorganizing these bodies is invested in the Vigilance Office (*see* No. 102). For the protection and patrolling of the Inner Palace, the Ministers of the Imperial Household and the Commandants of the divisions on duty are to continue, as usual, to exercise authority by turns.

No. 105A. The Chancery for the Publication of Imperial Edicts was abolished by a Decree of the 23rd June, 1911, and its functions transferred to the 承宣廳 Ch'éng² Hsüan¹ T'ing¹, Chancery of the Cabinet.

No. 108. 憲政籌備處 Hsien⁴ Chêng⁴ Ch'ou² Pei⁴ Ch'u⁴, Office of Constitutional Reforms (*see* Supplement No. 160); established at the Imperial Household in accordance with a Memorial emanating thence of the 28th March, 1909.

This office has a staff made up of a 總辦 Tsung³ Pan⁴, Chief, 12 協理司員 Hsieh² Li³ Ssu¹ Yüan², Assistants (also 顧問 Ku , Wên⁴, Advisers to the Committee for Drawing up Regulations for Constitutional Government; *see* No. 159B), and 12 Secretaries (from the ranks of 堂主事 T'ang² Chu³ Shih⁴; *see* No. 76).

統 計 處 T'ung³ Chi⁴ Ch'u⁴, Statistical Bureaux (*see* No. 162). In addition to the Imperial Household, found at the Palace Stud (*see* No. 88), the Imperial Armoury (*see* No. 89), the Bureau of Imperial Gardens and Hunting Parks (*see* No. 90), the Buddhist Chapel (*see* No. 104B) and the Summer Palace of the Emperor (*see* No. 104E).

No. 109. The literary designation of the Imperial Equipage Department is 典 掌 儀 衞 Tien³ Chang³ I² Wei⁴.

No. 127. 議 院 I⁴ Yüan⁴, Parliament (commonly styled 國 會 Kuo² Hui⁴). An Edict of the Emperor Kuang Hsü decreed the opening of this assembly in 1917. In consequence of the insistence of, and repeated requests from, the population, however, the date of its opening has been advanced to 1913 by an Imperial Decree of the 4th November, 1910. Regulations for the Parliament and electoral laws are to be promulgated one year previous to the opening.

In connection with the advancement of the date of convening a Parliament, the Scheme of State Laws and the Programme of Constitutional Reforms have been subjected to revision, the most important measures (organization of new Courts of Justice, Self-government, introduction of a new Civil and Criminal Code, institution of a State Budget, reorganization of the Customs and Tribute Systems, the taking of the Census, reform of the Bannermen, the promulgation of laws regarding Parliament and the election of its members, the reorganization of Government Establishments and the organization of : A. 內 閣 Nei⁴ Ko², the Cabinet, B. 弼 德 院 Pi⁴ Tê² Yüan⁴, the Privy Council, C. 行 政 審 判 院 Hsing² Chêng⁴ Shên³ P'an⁴ Yüan⁴, Courts of Administrative Justice, and D. 審 計 院 Shên³ Chi⁴ Yüan⁴, the Audit Department) are to be completed by 1913.

Nos. 128 to 129C. By an Imperial Decree of the 8th May, 1911, the Council of State has been abolished and the 繙 書 房 Fan¹ Shu¹ Fang², Translation Bureau, attached to it, has, by

Edict of the 23rd June, 1911, been removed to the National
Academy (*see* Nos. 191 to 205A).

Nos. 130 to 140. The Grand Secretariat has been
abolished (by an Imperial Decree of the 8th May, 1911), and the
four Grand Secretaries (*see* No. 131) and the two Assistant
Grand Secretaries (*see* No. 132) have been commanded to take
places in the National Academy (*see* No. 191) conforming to
their seniority.

No. 131. Grand Secretaries are also designated 百揆
Po² K'uei², 大柱國 Ta⁴ Chu⁴ Kuo², 大柱石 Ta⁴ Chu⁴ Shih²,
大元輔 Ta⁴ Yüan² Fu³, and 大元宰 Ta⁴ Yüan² Tsai³.

No. 132. Another designation of Assistant Grand Secretaries is 亞相 Ya³ Hsiang⁴.

No. 137. Other designations of Secretaries of the Grand
Secretariat are 內翰 Nei⁴ Han⁴, 內史 Nei⁴ Shih³, 紫微郎
Tzu³ Wei¹ Lang², 大掌翰 Ta⁴ Chang³ Han⁴, and 大內史 Ta⁴
Nei⁴ Shih³.

Nos. 137A and 137B. The Imperial Patent Office was
also styled 西掖 Hsi¹ I⁴, and 紫微閣 Tzu³ Wei¹ Ko². It was
abolished by an Imperial Edict of the 23rd June, 1911, and.its
functions transferred to the 制誥局 Chih⁴ Kao⁴ Chü², Bureau
of Imperial Rewards.

No. 138. The Office for copying the Emperor's endorsements of documents was abolished by an Imperial Decree of the
23rd June, 1911, and its functions transferred to the 承宣廳
Ch'êng² Hsüan¹ T'ing¹, Chancery of the Cabinet.

Nos. 141 to 149. An Imperial Decree of the 8th May,
1911, abolished the Committee of Ministers.

Nos. 128 to 149. The Cabinet. 內閣 Nei⁴ Ko², the
Cabinet (also 責任內閣 Tsê² Jen⁴ Nei⁴ Ko²); established by an
Imperial Edict of the 8th May, 1911, which, at the same time,
sanctioned the 內閣官制 Nei⁴ Ko² Kuan¹ Chih⁴, Regulations
regarding the Cabinet (19 articles), and the 內閣辦事暫行

章程 Nei⁴ Ko² Pan⁴ Shih⁴ Chan⁴ Hsing² Chang¹ Ch'êng²,
Provisional Rules for Cabinet Procedure, both of which were
framed by the Committee for Drawing up Regulations for
Constitutional Government.

The Cabinet is made up of 國務大臣 Kuo² Wu⁴ Ta⁴
Ch'ên², Members of the Cabinet, who are the Emperor's nearest
assistants in the government of the Empire. In addition to the
丨閣總理大臣 Nei⁴ Ko² Tsung³ Li³ Ta⁴ Ch'ên², President of
he Cabinet, and one or two 內閣協理大臣 Nei⁴ Ko² Hsieh²
Li³ Ta⁴ Ch'ên², Vice-Presidents of the Cabinet, appointed by
special Imperial Edicts, the Cabinet Members are as follows:
1. 外務大臣 Wai⁴ Wu⁴ Ta⁴ Ch'ên², Minister of Foreign
Affairs, 2. 民政大臣 Min² Cheng⁴ Ta⁴ Ch'ên², Minister of
the Interior, 3. 度支大臣 Tu⁴ Chih¹ Ta⁴ Ch'ên², Minister of
Finance, 4. 學務大臣 Hsüeh² Wu⁴ Ta⁴ Ch'ên², Minister of
Education, 5. 陸軍大臣 Lu⁴ Chün¹ Ta⁴ Ch'ên², Minister of
War, 6. 海軍大臣 Hai³ Chün¹ Ta⁴ Ch'ên², Minister of the
Navy, 7. 司法大臣 Ssu¹ Fa² Ta⁴ Ch'ên², Minister of Justice,
8. 農工商大臣 Nung² Kung¹ Shang¹ Ta⁴ Ch'ên², Minister
of Agriculture, Industry and Commerce, 9. 郵傳大臣 Yu²
Ch'uan² Ta⁴ Ch'ên², Minister of Posts and Communications
and 10. 理藩大臣 Li³ Fan² Ta⁴ Ch'ên², Minister of
Dependencies.

The President of the Cabinet takes precedence of all other
members and, in carrying out the Emperor's wishes, decides
political questions, supervises the administration of the government and encourages the various branches of governmental
activity to mutual assistance. Should he perceive that any
order or decision given by a Minister, or Ministers, meets with
difficulty in its execution, he may rescind the same, reporting
the matter to the Emperor for final action.

Among other duties, the President of the Cabinet guides
the actions of the high provincial authorities and officials

governing dependencies. He may, with the Emperor's sanction, issue regulations referring to questions subjected to his competence or concerning affairs specially delegated to his authority. Personal access to the Throne, when occasion demands, is also granted him.

All Memorials bearing on matters of a general State character are submitted to the Emperor in the name of the entire Cabinet; those referring to the affairs of a particular Ministry are submitted by the President of the Cabinet and the head of the Ministry concerned.

Other officials, outside the Cabinet, may submit reports to the Emperor—in certain instances they are bound by law to express their opinions to the Emperor—but these must pass through the hands of the Cabinet.

All Edicts concerning branches of the State legislation, the Higher Government, State policy and measures of general importance are signed (署 名 Shu⁴ Ming²) by the President of the Cabinet and the Cabinet Members. Edicts referring to questions affecting a certain Ministry, or Ministries, are signed by the President of the Cabinet and the Minister, or Ministers, concerned.

The following is a schedule of questions coming within the scope of the Cabinet:

1. Codes of laws, official systems, Edicts and Imperial commands.

2. Estimates and the Budget.

3. Extraordinary expenditure.

4. Treaties and important diplomatic negotiations.

5. The promotion or degradation of officials holding posts to which appointment is made by Imperial Edict.

6. Disputes between Ministries with regard to authority.

7. Matters referred to the Cabinet by Edicts and requests and petitions from the people, submitted through the National Assembly.

[522]

8. Important administrative affairs of the various Ministries.

9. Affairs which by law must be transmitted to the Cabinet.

10. Matters which the President of the Cabinet or the Minister of the Ministry concerned consider should be discussed by the Cabinet.

Affairs brought before the Cabinet are decided by the opinion of a majority.

Questions relating to th Army or Navy, except when Imperial Edict commands their discussion by the Cabinet, are to be placed before the Emperor by the Minister of War or Minister of the Navy, direct. The latter will, however, report his action to the President of the Cabinet.

When questions of great importance are being considered, by special Imperial Edict there may be appointed 特任國務大臣 T'ê⁴ Jên⁴ Kuo² Wu⁴ Ta⁴ Ch'ên², Special Members of the Cabinet. These, however, are not classed as belonging to the Cabinet.

The Cabinet meets at the 政事堂 Chêng⁴ Shih⁴ T'ang², Cabinet Hall.

An Imperial Decree of the 23rd June, 1911, sanctioned the 內閣屬官官制 Nei⁴ Ko² Shu³ Kuan¹ Kuan¹ Chih⁴, Regulations regarding Subordinate Officials of the Cabinet, and the 內閣法制院官制 Nei⁴ Ko² Fa⁴ Chih⁴ Yüan⁴ Kuan¹ Chih⁴, Regulations regarding the Legislative Board of the Cabinet, which had been submitted by the Cabinet.

To the Cabinet there are attached: 1. A 閣丞 Ko² Ch'êng², Councillor, who, under the direction of the President of the Cabinet, supervises the various bureaux attached to the Cabinet, 2. A 廳長 T'ing¹ Chang³, Chief of the Chancery, 3. 局長 Chü² Chang³, Directors of the various Bureaux and Manager of the Bureau of Printing and Casting (see infra), 4. 副廳長

Fu⁴ T'ing¹ Chang³, Deputy Chief of the Chancery, 5. 副局長 Fu⁴ Chü² Chang³, Deputy Directors of the various Bureaux and Sub-Manager of the Bureau of Printing and Casting, 6. 僉事 Ch'ien¹ Shih⁴, Secretaries, 7. 印鑄局藝師 Yin⁴ Chu⁴ Chü² I⁴ Shih¹, Chief Engineer of the Bureau of Printing and Casting, 8. 印鑄局藝士 Yin⁴ Chu⁴ Chü² I⁴ Shih⁴, Engineers of the Bureau of Printing and Casting, and 9. 錄事 Lu⁴ Shih⁴, Writers.

Of the officials mentioned above, Nos. 1 to 5 are appointed by the Emperor, Nos. 6 and 7 are appointed by the Emperor on the recommendation of the Cabinet, while Nos. 8 and 9 are appointed by their superiors.

At the Cabinet there are found: 1. 承宣廳 Ch'êng² Hsüan¹ T'ing¹, the Chancery, which controls all matters in connection with the promulgation of Imperial Decrees, Rescripts, commands and instructions, files Imperial Decrees and Rescripts, receives and transmits Memorials or documents intended for Cabinet discussion, seals documents with the Imperial seal or Cabinet seal, has the custody of these seals, etc., 2. 制誥局 Chih⁴ Kao⁴ Chü², the Bureau of Imperial Rewards, which deals with the compilation of honorary titles, posthumous names and posthumous titles for reigning Emperors, frames Imperial Rescripts in connection with the bestowal of hereditary titles and posts, Chinese Orders, etc., 3. 叙官局 Hsü⁴ Kuan¹ Chü², the Bureau of Official Appointments, which is in charge of everything in connection with the appointment of officials in Peking and in the provinces, scrutinizes the records of officials, recommends promotions and transfers, arranges salaries, proposes punishments for guilty civil officials, etc., 4. 統計局 T'ung³ Chi⁴ Chü², the Central Bureau of Statistics, which compiles statistics with reference to all branches of the Government, published yearly statistical reports, exchanges statistical information with Foreign Powers, etc., and 5. 印鑄局 Yin⁴ Chu⁴ Chü², the Bureau of Printing and Casting, which is in charge of the printing of official gazettes, legal codes, regulations and all types of government publications, casts seals, stamps, etc.

Under the direct guidance of the President of the Cabinet the 法制院 Fa⁴ Chih⁴ Yüan⁴, Legislative Board of the Cabinet, attends to the following: 1. The drafting of laws and Government instructions, 2. The examination of draft laws proposed by the various Ministries and the reporting on same, and 3. The interpretation of laws and Government commands now in force.

The Legislative Board is composed of the following: 1. 院使 Yüan⁴ Shih³, President, 2. 副使 Fu⁴ Shih³, Vice-President, and 3. 參議 Ts'an¹ I⁴, Councillors, appointed by the Emperor, 4. 參事 Ts'an¹ Shih⁴, Secretaries, and 5. 僉事 Ch'ien¹ Shih⁴, Assistant Secretaries, appointed by the Throne on the recommendation of the Board, and 6. 錄事 Lu⁴ Shih⁴, Writers, appointed by the Board.

Until the essential laws shall have been promulgated, under the supervision of the Legislative Board there will be placed all affairs which, by the Scheme of Measures Preparatory to the Introduction of Constitutional Government, sanctioned by the Throne, were within the competence of the Committee for Drawing up Regulations for Constitutional Government (now abolished; *see* Supplement Nos. 150–163D).

The 弼德院 Pi⁴ Tê² Yüan⁴, Privy Council, (also 樞密院 Shu¹ Mi⁴ Yüan⁴), to which the Emperor turns for advice on various affairs of government, was called into being by an Imperial Decree of the 8th May, 1911, the same Decree sanctioning the 弼德院官制 Pi⁴ Tê² Yüan⁴ Kuan¹ Chih⁴, Regulations regarding the Privy Council, which were framed by the Committee for Drawing up Regulations for Constitutional Government, in conjunction with the Committee of Ministers.

The Privy Council consists of: A. One 院長 Yüan⁴ Chang³, President, B. One 副院長 Fu⁴ Yüan⁴ Chang³,

Vice-President, and C. 32 顧問大臣 Ku⁴ Wen⁴ Ta⁴ Ch'ên²,
Members of the Privy Council. Only eminent officials, with
special qualifications as regards political affairs, are made
members of the Privy Council.

Cabinet Ministers, the Presiding Controller of the Imperial
Clan Court and Ministers of the Household may, with the
Emperor's sanction, be appointed to the Privy Council.

Attached to the Privy Council there are ten 參議官 Ts'an¹
I⁴ Kuan¹, Councillors.

To the Privy Council are referred:

1. Questions which according to the Statutes of the
Imperial Family (皇室大典 Huang² Shih⁴ Ta⁴ Tien³) are to
be considered by the Privy Council.

2. The investigation and interpretation of constitutional
laws (憲法 Hsien⁴ Fa⁴), as well as laws and commands attendant
thereon.

3. Until the promulgation of essential constitutional laws,
all matters enumerated in the "General Principles of Constitutional Laws (憲法大綱 Hsien⁴ Fa⁴ Ta⁴ Kang¹), Part I:
Prerogatives of the Sovereign (君上大權 Chün¹ Shang⁴ Ta⁴
Ch'üan²), paragraphs 8, 11 and 12.

4. Treaties and diplomatic negotiations.

5. The revision of regulations referring to itself.

At the Privy Council there is a 秘書廳 Pi⁴ Shu¹ T'ing¹,
Secretariat, for dealing with correspondence, accounting, drawing
up of reports of council meetings and managing affairs generally.
The general supervision of this establishment is in the hands of
a 秘書長 Pi⁴ Shu¹ Chang³, Chief Secretary, to whom there are
attached a number of 秘書官 Pi⁴ Shu¹ Kuan¹, Secretaries.

Nos. 150 to 151. By Imperial Edict of the 8th May,
1911, the Presidents and Vice-Presidents of the Cabinet were
placed at the head of the Committee for Drawing up Regulations
for Constitutional Government, as 憲政編查館大臣 Hsien⁴

Chêng⁴ Pien¹ Ch'a² Kuan³ Ta⁺ Ch'ên², Presidents of the Committee for Drawing up Regulations for Constitutional Government (now abolished; *see* below Nos. 150–163D).

Nos. 150 to 163D. The Committee for Drawing up Regulations for Constitutional Government was abolished by an Imperial Decree of the 23rd June, 1911, and its functions transferred to the 法制院 Fa⁴ Chih⁴ Yüan⁴, Legislative Board of the Cabinet.

No. 155. In the text the post of 總務處幫總辦 Tsung³ Wu⁴ Ch'u⁴ Pang¹ Tsung³ Pan⁴, Senior Assistant Chief of the Chancery, has been omitted.

No. 160. Conforming to a Memorial from the Committee for Drawing up Regulations for Constitutional Government, sanctioned by the Emperor on the 30th January, 1910, there have been established, at the Ministries and principal Government Establishments at the Capital, as well as at the Governors-General's and Governors' Yamen, Constitutional Reforms Offices, 憲政籌備處 Hsien⁴ Cheng⁴ Ch'ou² Pei⁴ Ch'u⁴, which have been commanded to twice a year present reports, to the Investigation Department of the Committee for Drawing up Regulations for Constitutional Government, concerning the progress of reforms.

No. 165A. On a Memorial from the National Assembly, sanctioned by the Emperor on the 14th November, 1910, the temporary administrative personnel of the National Assembly, having arranged for the convening of members of that body, has been abolished.

No. 167B. 速記學堂 Su² Chi⁴ Hsüeh² T'ang², School of Stenography (*see* No. 621A); organized at the National Assembly (*see* a Memorial from the Assembly dated the 4th February, 1910, enclosing regulations in 19 articles) with the object of training 速記生 Su² Chi⁴ Shêng¹, Stenographers, for service at the National Assembly, Provincial Assemblies (*see* No.

168) and at popular establishments in general. There are accepted for this school those who have, at least, completed the course of a Middle School (*see* No. 580), or a school of similar rating. The enrollment is 100—12 scholars chosen by the Assembly and 88 students from the provinces, *i.e.* four from each province. The course of study extends over two trimesters.

The subjects of instruction at the School of Stenography are 速 記 術 Su² Chi⁴ Shu¹, Stenography, Chinese Language (官 話 Kuan¹ Hua⁴), Chinese Literature (國 文 Kuo² Wên²) and the general principles of law. Its administrative personnel includes: 1. A 堂 長 T'ang² Chang³, Director (compare No. 635B), 2. A 教 務 員 Chiao⁴ Wu⁴ Yüan², Preceptor (compare No. 636), 3. A 庶 務 員 Shu⁴ Wu⁴ Yüan², Steward (*see* No. 641), and 4. 教 員 Chiao⁴ Yüan², Teachers (not exceeding 5 ; *see* No. 637). All the posts mentioned, with the exception of that of Teacher, are held by officials of the Secretariat of the Assembly (*see* No. 167B).

On completion of the course of the School of Stenography a number of the students are retained for service at the Assembly, as Stenographers, while the rest disperse for similar service in the provinces.

Nos. 184 to 184C. The text of these should read as follows : 184. *The General Staff of the Army.*

In an Edict of the 6th November, 1906, commanding the reorganization of the Ministry of War, it was directed that, as no General Staff of the Army (General Staff Office ; *see* No. 184B) was in being, all matters appertaining to such an institution were to be attended to, temporarily, by the 軍 諮 處 Chün¹ Tzu¹ Ch'u⁴, General Staff Council, attached to the Ministry of War (compare Nos. 184A, 417 and 418).

By an Imperial Edict of the 15th July, 1909, the General Staff Council was made independent of the Ministry of War under the designation following.

184A. 軍諮處 *Chün¹ Tzu¹ Ch'u⁴*.

軍 諮 處 Chün¹ Tzu¹ Ch'u⁴, General Staff of the Army, or General Staff Office. This is an independent establishment, which assists the Emperor, as Commander-in-Chief of the Army and Navy, headed by two 管 理 軍 諮 處 事 務 Kuan³ Li³ Chün¹ Tzu¹ Ch'u⁴ Shih⁴ Wu⁴, Chiefs of the General Staff of the Army.

184B. 軍諮府 *Chün¹ Tzu¹ Fu³*.

By an Imperial Edict, dated the 8th May, 1911, the General Staff of the Army was reorganized into the 軍 諮 府 Chün¹ Tzu¹ Fu³, General Staff Headquarters, under which have been placed :

1. The Military Academy (*see* No. 712) and, prior to the establishment of this institution, the 陸 軍 預 備 大 學 堂 Lu⁴ Chün¹ Yü⁴ Pei⁴ Ta⁴ Hsüeh² T'ang², The Military Preparatory Academy (previous to 1911 styled the Military Staff Officers College at Paotingfu; *see* No. 712A), 2. Schools for Military Draftsmen (*see* No. 715D), 3. Military Attachés at Legations abroad (*see* No. 329), Line Officers of the Army and Navy, etc.

Until the personnel of the General Staff Headquarters has been definitely fixed (軍 諮 府 官 制 Chün¹ Tzu¹ Fu³ Kuan¹ Chih⁴), it will be administered by a provisional staff, sanctioned by the Emperor on the 22nd September, 1909.

184C. 軍諮大臣 *Chün¹ Tzu¹ Ta⁴ Ch'ên²*.

At the head of the provisional staff of the General Staff Headquarters there are two 軍 諮 大 臣 Chün¹ Tzu¹ Ta⁴ Ch'ên² To them there are subordinated : Compare text.

No. 185. At present naval affairs are under the supervision of the Ministry of the Navy (*see* Supplement Nos. 420 to 437 ; particularly No. 434), which was called into existence by an Imperial Decree of the 3rd November, 1910, and which is a development of the Commission for the Reorganization of the Navy.

No. 185A. As proposed by the Presidents of the Commission for the Reorganization of the Navy, to that body there were attached 籌辦海軍事務處顧問官 Ch'ou² Pan⁴ Hai³ Chün¹ Shih⁴ Wu⁴ Ch'u⁴ Ku⁴ Wên⁴ Kuan¹, Naval Advisers (compare No. 184K), an Imperial Edict of the 19th February, 1910, designating 嚴復 Yen² Fu⁴, 伍光健 Wu³ Kuang¹-chien⁴, 魏瀚 Wei⁴ Han⁴ and 鄭清濂 Chêng⁴ Ch'ing¹-lien², to act as such.

No. 186. On the recommendation of a Reader of the Grand Secretariat, 延昌 Yen² Ch'ang¹, there have been established posts for 諮議官 Tzu¹ I⁴ Kuan¹, Advisers, to the Commission for the Revision of the Banner Organization (*see* a Memorial from the Commission, sanctioned by the Emperor on the 27th January, 1910).

No. 191. Literary designations of the National Academy are 木天 Mu⁴ T'ien¹, 鸞坡 Luan² P'o¹, 蘭臺 Lan² T'ai², 麟臺 Lin² T'ai², 芸臺 Yün² T'ai², 玉堂 Yü⁴ T'ang², and 秘閣 Pi⁴ Ko²

No. 192. Literary designations of the Chancellor of the National Academy are 大著作 Ta⁴ Cho⁵ Tso⁴, 判文林館事 P'an⁴ Wên² Lin³ Kuan³ Shih⁴, 內相 Nei⁴ Hsiang⁴, and 太史令 T'ai⁴ Shih³ Ling⁴.

Nos. 193c to 200c. Literary designations of the personnel of the National Academy (so-called 翰林 Han⁴ Lin²) are 太史 T'ai⁴ Shih³, 內翰 Nei⁴ Han⁴, 詞林 Tz'u² Lin², 翰苑 Han⁴ Yüan⁴, 大太史 Ta⁴ T'ai⁴ Shih³, and 大詞翰 Ta⁴ Tz'u² Han⁴.

No. 206. Other designations of the Censorate are 柏府 Po² Fu³, 蘭臺寺 Lan² T'ai² Ssu⁴, 南寺 Nan² Ssu⁴, 南臺 Nan² T'ai², and 柏臺 Po² T'ai².

No. 207A. Other designations of the senior President of the Censorate are 烏臺 Wu¹ T'ai², 掌憲 Chang³ Hsien⁴, 大都憲 Ta⁴ Tu¹ Hsien⁴, and 大司憲 Ta⁴ Ssu¹ Hsien⁴.

No. 210B. Other designations of the Metropolitan Censor are 黃門 Huang² Mên² and 東臺 T'ung¹ T'ai².

No. 213. Other designations of the Provincial Censor are 西臺 Hsi¹ T'ai², 柱石 Chu⁴ Shih², and 大司憲 Ta⁴ Ssu¹ Hsien⁴.

No. 215A. The new regulations regarding Judicial Establishments (section 5th, articles 33 to 45 ; *see* No. 758) define the Supreme Court of Justice as the highest Judicial Establishment of the Empire, being subordinated to the Ministry of Justice only as regards administration. Accordingly, its decisions are not submitted to the latter for approval. Also, the Supreme Court of Justice has functions similar to the Russian Senate as regards interpretation of laws.

For particulars as to the 大理分院 Ta⁴ Li³ Fên¹ Yüan⁴, Branches of the Supreme Court of Justice, *see* No. 759B.

Nos. 218 and 218A. The 刑科 Hsing² K'o¹ has been changed to the 刑事科 Hsing² Shih⁴ K'o¹.

At the head of the various Sections there are 庭長 T'ing² Chang³, Section Chiefs, who hold this position in addition to that of Director, or Secretary, of a Department.

Nos. 219 and 219A. The 民科 Min² K'o¹ has been changed to the 民事科 Min² Shih⁴ K'o¹.

At the head of the various Sections there are 庭長 T'ing² Chang³ (compare Supplement Nos. 218 and 218A).

No. 221. 審判研究所 Shên³ P'an⁴ Yen² Chiu¹ So³, Courses in Jurisprudence (compare No. 758B), for officials of the Supreme Court of Justice; functioning since 1909.

The lectures given in these Courses are under the direction of officials of the Court who are well-versed in the Provisional Criminal Code (*see* a Memorial from the Supreme Court of Justice, dated the 2nd February, 1910).

No. 222. For particulars as to the 總檢察分廳 Tsung³ Chien³ Ch'a² Fên¹ T'ing¹, Branch Attorney-Generals' Offices, *see* No. 763A.

[531]

No. 223. Literary designations of the Imperial Board of Astronomy are 太史監 T'ai⁴ Shih³ Chien⁴, 渾儀監 Hun⁴ I² Chien⁴, 司天監 Ssu¹ T'ien¹ Chien⁴, and 司天臺 Ssu¹ T'ien¹ T'ai².

No. 225. Literary designations of the Director of the Imperial Board of Astronomy are 太史令 T'ai⁴ Shih³ Ling⁴, 日官 Jih⁴ Kuan¹, and 大司天 Ta⁴ Ssu¹ T'ien¹.

Nos. 226 and 227. Literary designations of the Vice-Directors of the Imperial Board of Astronomy are 太史少令 T'ai⁴ Shih³ Shao⁴ Ling⁴ and 太史丞 T'ai⁴ Shih³ Ch'êng².

No. 233. Conforming to replies from the Committee of Ministers, dated the 22nd January and the 4th February, 1910, to a Memorial submitted on the 29th December, 1909, by 繼祿 Chi⁴ Lu⁴, a reform of the Imperial Medical Department (literary designation, 尚藥監 Shang⁴ Yao⁴ Chien⁴) was effected, the ranks of the Commissioner, and other officials, being raised (*see* Nos. 235 to 236 and 238 to 240).

No. 235. The post of Commissioner of the Imperial Medical Department (literary designation, 太醫令 T'ai⁴ I¹ Ling⁴) has been raised from 5A to 4A.

Nos. 236 and 236A. The posts of Senior and Junior Vice-Commissioners of the Imperial Medical Department (literary designations, 尚藥局丞 Shang⁴ Yao⁴ Chü² Ch'êng², and 太醫丞 T'ai⁴ I¹ Ch'êng²) have been raised from 6A to 5A.

No. 238. The post of Imperial Physician (13 in all; literary designation, 侍醫 Shih⁴ I¹), has been raised from 7A to 6A

Nos. 239 and 239A. The posts of Secretaries (literary designation, 太醫正 T'ai⁴ I¹ Chêng⁴) of the eighth rank (13 in all), and of the ninth rank (13 in all), have been raised respectively to 7A and 8A.

No. 240. The post of Physician (literary designation, 尚藥局司藥 Shang⁴ Yao⁴ Chü² Ssu¹ Yao⁴) has been classed 9A.

At the Imperial Medical Department there are : 醫員 I[1] Yüan[2] (literary designation, 尚藥局醫佐 Shang[4] Yao[4] Chü[2] I[1] Tso[3]) Assistant Physicians, and 醫生 I[1] Shêng[1], Medical Assistants, Physicians are arranged according to nine 科 K'o[1], Specialities :

1. 大方脈科 Ta[4] Fang[1] Mo[4] K'o[1], Diseases of Adults, 2. 小方脈痘疹科 Hsiao[3] Fang[1] Mo[4] Tou[4] Chên[3] K'o[1], Diseases of Children, and Smallpox, 3. 傷寒科 Shang[1] Han[2] K'o[1], Fevers, 4. 婦人科 Fu[4] Jên[2] K'o[1], Diseases of Females, 5. 瘡瘍科 Ch'uang[:] Yang[2] K'o[1], Cutaneous Diseases, 6. 鍼灸科 Chên[1] Chih[4] K'o[1], Rheumatic Diseases, 7. 眼科 Yen[3] K'o[1], Ophthalmic Diseases, 8. 口齒咽喉科 K'ou[3] Ch'ih[3] Yen[1] Hou[2] K'o[1], Dental and Throat Diseases, and 9. 正骨科 Chêng[4] Ku[3] K'o[1], Surgery (literally "setting bones.")

No. 242. The second of the Superintendents of the Board of Customs Control is also designated 稅務處會辦大臣 Shui[4] Wu[4] Ch'u[4] Hui[4] Pan[4] Ta[4] Ch'ên[2].

No. 273. The organization of a modern Postal System in China was begun in the period 1896–1898, during which a series of Imperial Edicts were promulgated with reference to the opening of Postal Establishments of a new type throughout the Empire, to be styled 大清郵政 Ta[4] Ch'ing[1] Yu[2] Chêng[4], or Chinese Imperial Post Offices. The Office of Foreign Affairs received Imperial commands to entrust the general control of Postal affairs to the Inspector General of Customs, Sir Robert Hart (赫德 Ho[4] Tê[2]), as 總郵政司 Tsung[3] Yu[2] Chêng[4] Ssu[1], Inspector General of Posts. The latter, in turn, appointed Mr. Th. Piry (帛黎 Po[4] Li[2]), Commissioner of Customs, with the title of 郵政總辦 Yu[2] Chêng[4] Tsung[3] Pan[4], Postal Secretary, to supervise the organization of a Postal System for the Empire and there are now more than 600 Post Offices and 4,200, or more, Postal Sub-Offices.

The question of the transfer of the Postal System to the control of the Ministry of Posts and Communications was first raised, by the Committee for Drawing up Regulations for Constitutional Government, when general regulations defining the functions of the several State Offices were being framed (行政綱目 Hsing[4] Chêng[4] Kang[1] Mu[4]). Further, the said Committee, in the autumn of 1909, when submitting its report concerning preparatory measures to be accomplished by provincial Government Offices during the nine years preceding the granting of a constitution, expressed the opinion that "the Postal System should remain under the control of the Imperial Maritime Customs only so long as there was no special Ministry for its administration, and until the Chinese populace became acquainted with its utility; now, there being a Ministry of Posts and Communications in existence, it should be handed over to the supervision of this Ministry." This report received Imperial sanction, and, in the list of measures to be carried out by the Ministry of Posts and Communications during the period already spoken of, submitted to the Emperor on the 4th October, 1910, there appeared a provision for the transfer of the Postal System as recommended.

The Ministry of Posts and Communications definitely assumed control of the Postal System on the 28th May, 1911, by virtue of an Imperial Decree of the 26th May, promulgated in reply to a Memorial from the President of the Ministry concerned, 盛宣懷 Shêng[4] Hsüan[1]-huai[2] (for further details see Supplement Nos. 479 and 479A).

A detailed scheme concerning the reform of Postal Establishments appeared in the Peking Gazette of the 17th October, 1910.

No. 278. Other designations of the President of a Ministry are 中臺 Chung[1] T'ai[2], 都臺 Tu[1] T'ai[2], and 大常伯 Ta[4] Ch'ang[2] Po[2].

No. 279. Other designations of the Senior Vice-President of a Ministry are 亞卿 Ya[3] Ch'ing[1] and 少常伯 Shao[4] Ch'ang[2] Po[2].

No. 312. By regulations framed by the Ministry of Foreign Affairs, in June, 1909, certain changes have been effected with regard to the official rank of Chinese officials abroad (*see* Nos. 317 to 320 and 322 to 323), namely :

No. 317. The rank of a Consul-General is now 4B.

No. 318. The rank of a Second Councillor is now 4B.

No. 319. The rank of a First Interpreter is now 5A.

No. 320. The rank of a Consul is now 5A.

No. 322. The rank of a Third Councillor is now 5A.

No. 323. The rank of a Second Interpreter is now 5B.

No. 324. The rank of a Vice-Consul is now 5B.

No. 325. The rank of a First Secretary is now 5B.

No. 326. The rank of a Third Interpreter is now 6B.

No. 327. The rank of a Second Secretary is now 6B.

No. 328. The rank of a Third Secretary is now 7B.

No. 332. There is now a Consulate-General at 巴那瑪 Pa¹ Na⁴ Ma¹, Panama (*see* a Memorial from the Ministry of Foreign Affairs, dated the 16th January, 1910).

In accordance with the terms of a Consular Convention (領 事 條 約 Ling³ Shih⁴ T'iao² Yüeh¹) concluded between China and the Netherlands (signed at Peking on the 8th May, 1911), the Ministry of Foreign Affairs submitted a Memorial to the Throne, the same being sanctioned on the 21st July, 1911, concerning the establishment, in the Dutch Indies (和 蘭 東 印 度 屬 地 Ho² Lan² Tung¹ Yin⁴ Tu⁴ Shu³ Ti⁴), of the following Consulates in the islands of the Sunda Archipelago (巽 他 羣 島 Hsün⁴ T'a¹ Ch'ün² Tao³) :

A. A Consulate-General at 巴 達 維 亞 Pa¹ Ta². Wei² Ya³, Batavia, in the island of 爪 哇 島 Chua³ Wa¹ Tao³, Java, with a Consular District (管 轄 區 域 Kuan³ Hsia² Ch'ü¹ Yü⁴) including the island of Java to the East of 三 寶 隴 San¹ Pao³ Lung², all Dutch Borneo (婆 羅 洲 和 屬 全 境 P'o² Lo² Chou¹ Ho² Shu³ Ch'üan² Ching⁴), the island of Billiton (萬 里 洞 全 島

Wan⁴ Li³ Tung⁴ Ch'üan² Tao³), as well as adjacent small islands.

This Consulate-General will be administered by a Consul-General, one Second Interpreter and one Second Secretary.

B. A Consulate at 泗水 Ssu⁴ Shui³, Sourabaya, Java, with a Consular District including the island of Java to the West of 三寶瓏 San¹ Pao³ Lung², the Dutch Celebes (西里伯和屬全境 Hsi¹ Li³ Po² Ho⁵ Shu³ Ch'üan² Ching⁴), Madura Island (馬渡拉 Ma³ Tu⁴ Laⁱ), the island of Karimon Java (峇釐龍目 K'a¹ Li² Lung² Mu⁴) and adjacent small islands.

This Consulate will have a personnel made up of a Consul, one Third Interpreter and one Third Secretary.

C. A Consulate at 巴東 Pa¹ Tung¹, Padang, in the island of 蘇門答臘 Su¹ Mên² Ta¹ La⁴, Sumatra, with a Consular District including Sumatra, the island of 邦加 Pang¹ Chia¹, Banka and adjacent small islands.

The personnel of this Consulate will include a Consul, one Third Interpreter and one Third Secretary.

Nos. 333 to 338. The Ministry of Civil Appointments was abolished by an Imperial Edict of the 23rd June, 1911, its functions being transferred to the 敘官局 Hsü⁴ Kuan¹ Chü², Bureau of Official Appointments.

No. 333A. Other designations of the President of the Ministry of Civil Appointments are 天官 T'ien¹ Kuan¹, 冢宰 Chung³ Tsai³, and 大銓衡 Ta⁴ Ch'üan² Hêng².

Nos. 335 to 338. 憲政籌備處 Hsien⁴ Chêng⁴ Ch'ou² Pei⁴ Ch'u⁴, Office of Constitutional Reforms (*see* Supplement No. 160); established at the Ministry of Civil Appointments (on a Memorial from this Ministry, dated the 12th March, 1910), to replace the 憲政研究所 Hsien⁴ Chêng⁴ Yen² Chiu¹ So³. At the head of this office there was a 總辦 Tsung³ Pan⁴, Chief, who had subordinated to him: 會辦 Hui⁴ Pan⁴, Senior Assistants, 幫辦 Pang⁴ Pan⁴, Junior Assistants, etc. It is composed of four 科 K'o¹, Sections, namely, 1. 叙官科 Hsü⁴ Kuan¹ K'o¹, Section of Personnel, 2. 考績科 K'ao³ Chi¹ K'o¹, Sec⁺ion for Investigation of Merits, 3. 調查科 Tiao⁴ Ch'a² K'o , Intelligence Section, and 4. 編制科 Pien¹ Chih⁴ K'o¹, Revising Section.

學治館 Hsüeh² Chih⁴ Kuan³, Instruction Office at the Ministry of Civil Appointments (for preparing officials for service at this Ministry); directed by a 總辦 Tsung³ Pan⁴, Chief.

No. 344. 圖志館 T'u² Chih⁴ Kuan³, Commission for Preparing a Descriptive Work of the Empire; established at the Ministry of the Interior, in accordance with a Memorial from this Ministry, dated the 13th March, 1910.

This Commission is composed of officials of the Ministry of the Interior and will compile its 一統新志 I¹ T'ung³ Hsin¹ Chih⁴, New Complete Statistical Description of the Chinese Empire, from detailed documents supplied by the provinces.

憲政籌備處 Hsien⁴ Chêng⁴ Ch'ou² Pei⁴ Ch'u⁴, Office of Constitutional Reforms; established at the Ministry of the Interior in accordance with a Memorial emanating thence, dated the 2nd April, 1910.

No. 368A. 造紙廠 Tsao⁴ Chih³ Ch'ang³, Government Paper Mill; operated under regulations framed by the Ministry of Finance and sanctioned by the Emperor on the 27th January, 1911. It is under the supervision of the Ministry of Finance and has been established for the production of all kinds of Government books, and papers and forms for the numerous Government Establishments.

At the head of the Paper Mill there is a 總辦 Tsung³ Pan⁴, Superintendent. He is assisted by: 1. A 幫辦 Pang¹ Pan⁴, Senior Assistant Superintendent, and 2. A 坐辦 Tso⁴ Pan⁴, Junior Assistant Superintendent.

For the management of the Paper Mill there are five Sections : 1. 營運科 Ying² Yün⁴ K'o¹, Section of Transport and Supplies (in charge of the provision of materials and their transport), 2. 監造科 Chien⁴ Tsao⁴ K'o¹, Section of Operation (supervises the execution of orders), 3. 文案科 Wên² An¹ K'o¹, Chancery, 4. 收支科 Shou¹ Chih¹ K'o¹, Section of Finance, and 5. 庶務科 Shu⁴ Wu⁴ K'o¹, Section of General Affairs. Each of these Sections is directed by a 科長 K'o-Chang³, Section Chief, and is divided into Sub-sections (所 So³).

No. 369A. As recommended in a Memorial from the Controller-General of the Salt Gabelle (sanctioned by the Emperor on the 25th February, 1910), there have been established posts for the following officials at the Office of the Controller-General of the Salt Gabelle : 1. One 提調 T'i² Tiao⁴, Proctor, 2. Two 幫提調 Pang¹ T'i² Tiao⁴, Assistant Proctors, 3. One 秘書官 Pi⁴ Shu¹ Kuan¹, Senior Secretary, and 4. Nine 雜事官 Ts'an¹ Shih⁴ Kuan¹, Secretaries.

The Office of the Controller-General of the Salt Gabelle is made up of eight 廳 T'ing¹, Sections : 1. 鹽務總廳 Yen² Wu⁴ Tsung³ T'ing¹, Chief Section of Salt Affairs ; supervising the framing of rules and regulations regarding the salt administration, the most important correspondence and the personnel of the office, 2. 奉直鹽務廳 Fêng⁴ Chih² Yen² Wu⁴ T'ing¹, Section for Salt Affairs of Fengtien and Chihli (and of Kirin, Heilungchiang, Honan, the territory of the Ch'akhars, Jehol and Sui-yüan-ch'êng), 3. 潞東鹽務廳 Lu⁴ Tung¹ Yen² Wu⁴ T'ing¹, Section for Salt Affairs of Shantung and Shansi (and of Shensi, Kansu, Honan, Anhui and Kiangsu), 4. 兩淮鹽務廳 Liang³ Huai² Yen² Wu⁴ T'ing¹, Section for Salt Affairs of Kiangsu and Kiangsi (and of Hupeh, Hunan, the Western part of Anhui and Honan), 5. 兩淅鹽務廳 Liang³ Chê⁴ Yen² Wu⁴ T'ing¹, Section for Salt Affairs of Chekiang (and of Kiangsu, Anhui and Kiangsi), 6. 閩粵鹽務廳 Min³

Yüeh⁴ Yen² Wu⁴ T'ing¹, Section for Salt Affairs of Fukien and Kuangtung (and of Kiangsi, Kuangsi, Hunan and Kueichow), 7. 川滇鹽務廳 Ch'uan¹ Tien¹ Yen² Wu⁴ T'ing¹, Section for Salt Affairs of Szechwan and Yünnan (and of Hupeh, Hunan and Kueichow),. and 8. 庶務廳 Shu⁴ Wu⁴ T'ing¹, Section of General Affairs ; receiving and despatching correspondence, sealing documents, keeping the accounts, etc.

The Chief Section of Salt Affairs is directed by a Proctor and his assistants. To them there are attached: a Senior Secretary (supervising the most important correspondence), two Secretaries, two 坐辦 Tso⁴ Pan⁴, Assistant Secretaries, and an indefinite number of 委員 Wei³ Yüan², Deputies (of the first, second and third ranks, 等 Têng³).

A Secretary is at the head of each of the remaining seven Sections. He has one Assistant Secretary and an indefinite number of Deputies (of the three ranks mentioned) under his orders.

At the Section of General Affairs there has been inaugurated a 譯電所 I⁴ Tien⁴ So³, Sub-Section for the Ciphering of Telegrams, and a 繕寫房 Shan⁴ Hsieh³ Fang², Copying Sub-Section, manned by 書記官 Shu¹ Chi⁴ Kuan¹, Clerks, and 書記生 Shu¹ Chi⁴ Shêng¹, Writers.

There is found at the Office of the Controller-General of the Salt Gabelle an indefinite number of 諮議官 Tzu¹ I⁴ Kuan¹, Advisers. A 會議所 Hui⁴ I⁴ So³, Council, composed of the Proctor, as 議長 I⁴ Chang³, President, and Assistant Proctors, Senior Secretary, Secretaries and Advisers, as 會議員 Hui⁴ I⁴ Yüan², Members of the Council, has also been organized at this office.

No. 373. 幣制局 Pi⁴ Chih⁴ Chü², Currency Office ; established in accordance with a Memorial from the Ministry of Finance, sanctioned by the Emperor on the 20th September, 1910, to replace the Commission for the Study of the Currency

System, 幣制調查局 Pi⁴ Chih⁴ Tiao⁴ Ch'a² Chü², abolished by the same Memorial. The main object of this office is to keep a control over the mints and banks, with regard to issue of the new type of currency, and to supervise the gradual transition to a new currency system. The Minister of Finance is at the head of the office and exerts his authority therein through the Currency Department (*see* No. 356). An Imperial Edict of the 13th day of the 7th moon appointed 盛宣懷 Shêng Hsüan-huai as 帮辦 Pang¹ Pan⁴, to assist the Minister.

At the Currency Office there are: 1. One 提調 T'i² Tiao⁴, Proctor, and 2. Two 帮提調 Pang⁴ T'i² Tiao⁴, Assistant Proctors. The Proctor and Assistant Proctors are in charge of the four 股 Ku³, Sections · A. 調查股 Tiao⁴ Ch'a² Ku³, Intelligence Section; charged with the study of the currency question in China and Europe and the completion of all business left unfinished by the Commission for the Study of the Currency System, B. 籌辦股 Ch'ou² Pan⁴ Ku³, Section of Organization; superintends the introduction of the new currency, provides funds for minting purposes, fixes the currency reserve, checks the quantity of coins minted, arranges for the exchange of old coins for the new currency and manages the correspondence regarding currency matters generally, C. 稽核股 Chi² Ho² Ku³, Section of Supervision; superintends minting operations, purchases silver for coining purposes, arranges for the re-minting of old currency, defines standard and weight of coins, controls the issue of new coins for circulation through banks or other institutions, the issue of bank-notes and the revenue derived from the same, supervises the printing of bank-notes, etc., and B. 編譯股 Pien¹ I⁴ Ku³, Compiling and Translating Section; compiles and translates works appertaining to currency questions, on its own initiative or at the request of the three foregoing Sections.

At the head of each Section there is a 總辦 Tsung³ Pan⁴, who has subordinated to him: A. 幫辦 Pang¹ Pan⁴, Assistants, and B. 委員 Wei³ Yüan², Deputies.

For superintending affairs of economy there is a 庶務處 Shu⁴ Wu⁴ Ch'u⁴, Section of Economical Affairs, at the Currency Office.

No. 376. Other designations of the Ministry of Rites are 祠部 Tz'u² Pu⁴, 儀部 I² Pu⁴, and 大宗 Ta⁴ Tsung¹, and, of its President, 春官 Ch'un¹ Kuan¹, 春卿 Ch'un¹ Ch'ing¹, 大秩宗 Ta⁴ Chih⁴ Tsung¹, and 大典禮 Ta⁴ Tien³ Li³.

Nos. 376-394. 典禮院 Tien³ Li³ Yüan⁴, Court of Rites; established by an Imperial Decree of the 20th July, 1911, to replace the Ministry of Rites, abolished by the same Decree. At the same time Imperial sanction of the 典禮院官制 Tien³ Li³ Yüan⁴ Kuan¹ Chih⁴, Regulations for the Court of Rites, drawn up by the Cabinet of Ministers, in 24 articles, was also signified.

To the Court of Rites have been transferred all functions of the Cabinet of Ministers and the old Ministry of Rites, as regards ritual observances, and under its control has been placed the Music Office (*see* No. 388) and the Office of Sacred Music (*see* No. 390), which were formerly under the supervision of the Board of Music (*see* No. 387).

The casting of seals (*see* No. 386) has been placed under the control of the Bureau of Printing and Casting attached to the Cabinet of Ministers.

The issue of the calendar, control over rites and ceremonies performed by the populace, sacrifices at temples in the provinces and exercises of divination performed in these temples is now the duty of the Ministry of the Interior. Ceremonies enacted in schools and sacrifices in the temple of Confucius are controlled by the Ministry of Education.

[541]

The issue of supplies and allowances to vassal Princes and to Lamas is now invested in the Ministry of Dependencies.

The Court of Rites is responsible for the performance of rites and musical ceremonies at Imperial Temples and Altars and at the Imperial Mausolea, as well as for the construction and safeguarding of buildings of this type. It is composed of a 總務廳 Tsung³ Wu⁴ T'ing¹, Chancery of General Affairs, and four Offices, *i.e.* 1. 禮制署 Li³ Chih⁴ Shu⁴, Office of Ceremonies, 2. 祠祭署 Tz'u² Chi⁴ Shu⁴, Office of Sacrifices, 3. 奉常署 Fêng⁴ Ch'ang² Shu⁴, Office of Sacrificial Worship, and 4. 精膳署 Ching¹ Shan⁴ Shu⁴, Banqueting Office.

The staff of the Court of Rites includes: A. One 掌院大學士 Chang³ Yüan⁴ Ta⁴ Hsüeh² Shih⁴, Chancellor, B. One 副掌院學士 Fu⁴ Chang³ Yüan⁴ Hsüeh² Shih⁴, Sub-Chancellor, C. Eight 學士 Hsüeh² Shih⁴, Senior Members of the Court, D. Eight 直學士 Chih² Hsüeh² Shih⁴, Junior Members of the Court, E. One 廳長 T'ing¹ Chang³, Chief of the Chancery, F. Four 署長 Shu⁴ Chang³, Office Chiefs, G. 僉事 Ch'ien¹ Shih⁴, Secretaries, of the 1st, 2nd and 3rd (等 Têng³) Classes, performing duty in the Chancery and the four Offices, H. 簿正 Pu⁴ Chêng⁴, Overseers, performing duty at the Chancery, I. 典簿 Tien³ Pu⁴, Assistant Overseers, performing duty at the Chancery, J. 司庫 Ssu¹ K'u⁴, Inspectors, attached to the Chancery, K. 贊禮郞 Tsan⁴ Li³ Lang², Ceremonial Ushers, attached to the Office of Sacrificial Worship, L. 讀祝官 Tu² Chu⁴ Kuan¹, Reciters of Prayers, attached to the Office of Sacrificial Worship, M. 鳴贊 Ming² Tsan⁴, Heralds, attached to the Office of Ceremonies, N. 序班 Hsü⁴ Pan¹, Ushers, attached to the Office of Ceremonies, O. 庫使 K'u⁴ Shih³, Assistant Inspectors, attached to the Chancery, and P. 錄事 Lu⁴ Shih⁴, Writers.

Of the officials mentioned above, A and B are selected and appointed by the Emperor himself (特簡 T'ê⁴ Chien³), C to

E are appointed by the Emperor (簡任 Chien³ Jên⁴), F to M are appointed on the strength of Memorials to the Emperor (奏任 Tsou⁴ Jên⁴), while N to P are appointed by the Chancellor (委任 Wei³ Jên⁴).

Nos. 398 to 402. 憲政籌備處 Hsien⁴ Chêng⁴ Ch'ou² Pei⁴ Ch'u⁴, Office of Constitutional Reforms (*see* Supplement No. 160); established at the Ministry of Education, in accordance with a Memorial emanating thence, dated the 25th March, 1910, to replace the 憲政研究所 Hsien⁴ Chêng⁴ Yen² Chiu¹ So³, of that Ministry.

No. 412A. The literary designation of the Libationer and Tutor is 大掌教 Ta⁴ Chang³ Chiao⁴; of the Preceptor, 大典敎 Ta⁴ Tien³ Chiao⁴, and 大傳經 Ta⁴ Ch'uan² Ching¹; of the Doctor, 算學博士 Suan⁴ Hsüeh² Po² Shih⁴ (also 國子監 算學助敎廳 Kuo² Tzu³ Chien⁴ Suan⁴ Hsüeh² Chu⁴ Chiao⁴ T'ing¹).

Nos. 420 to 437. The text of these should be as follows:

No. 420. 陸軍部 Lu⁴ Chün¹ Pu⁴, Ministry (Board) of War, or Ministry (Board) of Land Forces. This Ministry is now the administrative head of all the land forces of the Empire, directs Military Schools, is in charge of ordnance stores and arsenals, etc. The Ministry, established in 1906, was substantially reorganized by an Imperial Edict of the 4th December, 1910, and now, in accordance with the provisional regulations regarding the Ministry of War, sanctioned by the Emperor on the 4th December, 1910, is under the following direction:

No. 420A. At the head of the Ministry of War there are: a 陸軍大臣 Lu⁴ Chün¹ Ta⁴ Ch'ên², Minister of War, and a 陸軍 副大臣 Lu⁴ Chün¹ Fu⁴ Ta⁴ Ch'ên², Assistant Minister of War.

Note. The posts of President (*see* No. 278), Vice-President (*see* Nos. 279 to 280), Senior and Junior Councillor (*see* Nos. 281 to 282) and Senior and Junior Secretary (*see* Nos. 283 to 284), instituted in 1906, have been abolished.

No. 420B. 管理陸軍部事務 Kuan³ Li³ Lu⁴ Chün¹ Pu⁴ Shih⁴ Wu⁴, Controller of the Ministry of War (*see* No. 276).

No. 421. To the Minister of War and his Assistant (*see* Supplement, No. 420A) there are attached: 1. 參事官 Ts‘an¹ Shih⁴ Kuan¹, Secretaries, 2. 檢察官 Chien³ Ch‘a² Kuan¹, Inspector of Military Affairs, and 3. 調查官 Tiao⁴ Ch‘a² Kuan¹, Intelligence Officers (stationed in the provinces to supply necessary information and reports to the Minister).

No. 422. 承政司 Ch‘êng² Chêng⁴ Ssu¹, Chancery; attends to the most important affairs, controls the finances, correspondence, personnel, etc. This is composed of four 科 K‘o¹, Sections, namely, 1. 秘書科 Pi⁴ Shu¹ K‘o¹, Section of Confidential Affairs, 2. 典章科 Tien³ Chang¹ K‘o¹, Section of Army Regulations, 3. 庶務科 Shu⁴ Wu⁴ K‘o¹, Section of General Affairs, and 4. 收支科 Shou¹ Chih¹ K‘o¹, Section of Finance.

No. 423. 軍衡司 Chün¹ Hêng² Ssu¹, Department of Selection; supervises the appointment and transfer of military officials. This has four Sections: 1. 考績科 K‘ao³ Chi¹ K‘o¹, Section for the Investigation of Merits, 2. 任官科 Jên⁴ Kuan¹ K‘o¹, Section of Distribution of Posts, 3. 賞賚科 Shang³ Lai⁴ K‘o¹, Section of Rewards, and 4. 旗務科 Ch‘i² Wu⁴ K‘o¹, Section of Banner Affairs.

No. 424. 軍實司 Chün¹ Shih² Ssu¹, Department of Arms Supply; having two Sections: 1. 製造科 Chih⁴ Tsao⁴ K‘o¹, Section of Manufacture, and 2. 保儲科 Pao³ Ch‘u K‘o¹, Section of Storage.

No. 425. 軍制司 Chün¹ Chih⁴ Ssu¹, Army Inspection Department (further *see* No. 428).

Previous to their being handed over to the Ministry of Posts and Communications, all questions in connection with the Military Posts, formerly under the supervision of the Department of Military Posts (now abolished), are to be attended to by the Army Inspection Department.

No. 426. 軍 需 司 Chün[1] Hsü[1] Ssu[1], Commissariat Department (further *see* No. 429).

No. 427. 軍 醫 司 Chün[1] I[1] Ssu[1], Army Medical and Sanitary Department; consisting of two Sections: 1. 衛 生 科 Wei[4] Shêng[1] K'o[1], Sanitary Section, and 2. 醫 務 科 I[1] Wu[4] K'o[1], Medical Section.

No. 428. 軍 法 司 Chün[1] Fa[4] Ssu[1], Department of Military Law (further *see* No. 432).

No. 429. 軍 牧 司 Chün[1] Mu[4] Ssu[1], Department of the Military Stud (further *see* No. 433). This Department is now in charge of all veterinary affairs formerly under the supervision of the Army Medical and Sanitary Department (*see* Supplement No. 427).

No. 430. 軍 學 處 Chün[1] Hsüeh[2] Ch'u[4], Bureau of Military Education. This is provisionally under the supervision of the Ministry of War but there is a suggestion to make it an independent office under the designation 軍 學 院 Chün[1] Hsüeh[2] Yüan[4], Department of Military Education. Its personnel will be determined later.

No. 431. 審 計 處 Shên[3] Chi[4] Ch'u[4], Office of Control.

To this office there have been transferred all affairs formerly under the supervision of the 財 政 處 Ts'ai[2] Chêng[4] Ch'u[4], Office of Finance, and the 統 計 處 T'ung[3] Chi[4] Ch'u[4], Statistical Bureau, both of which have been abolished. Also, the auditing of accounts and bills has been transferred to its supervision from the Department of Military Posts (*see* Supplement No. 432B), the Department of Arms Supply (*see* Supplement No. 424) and the Commissariat Department (*see* Supplement No. 426).

The Office of Control has two Sections: 1. 綜 察 科 Tsung[1] Ch'a[2] K'o[1], General Revising Section, and 2. 核 銷 科 Ho[2] Hsiao[1] K'o[1], Auditing Section.

No. 432. Each Department of the Ministry of War, as a rule, furnishes employment for : a 司長 Ssu¹ Chang³, Controller, a 司事官 Ssu¹ Shih⁴ Kuan¹, Department Secretary, 科長 K'o¹ Chang³, Section Chiefs (one to each Section), 科員 K'o¹ Yüan², Secretaries (of the first, second and third ranks); and 錄事 Lu⁴ Shih⁴, Writers (in an indefinite number).

No. 432A. The personnel of various Departments and Offices differs from that mentioned above (No. 432) in the following respects :

1. At the Chancery of the Ministry of War (*see* Supplement No. 422) there are a number of 譯員 I⁴ Yüan², Interpreters.

2. The Department of Military Law (*see* Supplement No. 428), having no Sections, furnishes employment for 司法官 Ssu¹ Fa⁴ Kuan¹, Officers of Justice (of the first, second and third ranks), who take the place of Section Chiefs and Secretaries (*see* Supplement No. 432).

3. At the Department of Arms Supply (*see* Supplement No. 424) and at the Army Inspection Department (*see* Supplement No. 425) there are found 繪圖員 Hui⁴ T'u² Yüan², Draughtsmen, 藝師 I⁴ Shih¹, Chief Engineers, and 藝士 I⁴ Shih⁴, Engineers.

4. In place of the customary 司長 Ssu¹ Chang³, at the head of the Office of Control there is a 計長 Chi⁴ Chang³.

No. 432B. The Department of Military Posts (軍乘司 Chün¹ Ch'êng² Ssu¹), the Discipline Department (軍計司 Chün¹ Chi⁴ Ssu¹) and the Department of Military Education (軍學司 Chün¹ Hsüeh² Ssu¹), organized in accordance with regulations framed in 1906, have been abolished. In place of last-mentioned there has been inaugurated a " Bureau of Military Education " (*see* Supplement No. 430).

No. 433. Under the authority of the Ministry of War are:

1. The Military Forces of China :

A. Lu Chün, Regular Troops, and

B. Hsün Fang Tui, Reserves (*see* Nos. 655 to 707).

2. Military Schools (*see* Nos. 708 to 717B).

3. Banner Troops (*see* Nos. 718 to 748).

4. Old Chinese Troops (*see* Nos. 749 to 753).

5. Office of the Government Stud (*see* No. 755).

THE MINISTRY OF THE NAVY.

No. 434. Idem. No. 185.

No. 435. The Ministry of the Navy was called into being by an Imperial Edict of the 4th December, 1910, and its personnel includes the following officials.

1. 海軍大臣 Hai³ Chün¹ Ta⁴ Ch'ên², Ministry of the Navy,

2. 海軍副大臣 Hai³ Chün¹ Fu⁴ Ta⁴ Ch'ên², Assistant Minister of the Navy,

3. 參謀官 Ts'an¹ Mou² Kuan¹, Councillors,

4. 參事官 Ts'an¹ Shih⁴ Kuan¹, Secretaries, and

5. 秘書官 Pi⁴ Shu¹ Kuan¹, Junior Secretaries.

No. 436. The Ministry of War is divided into Departments as follows :

No. 436A. 軍制司 Chün¹ Chih⁴ Ssu¹, Department of Naval Administration ; composed of five Sections : 1. 制度科 Chih⁴ Tu⁴ K'o¹, Section of Naval Codes and Regulations, 2. 考核科 K'ao³ Ho² K'o¹, Revising Section, 3. 器械科 Ch'i⁴ Hsieh⁴ K'o¹, Arms Section, 4. 駕駛科 Chia⁴ Shih³ K'o¹, Section of Navigation, and 5. 輪機科 Lun² Chi¹ K'o¹, Section of Marine Engineering.

No. 436B. 軍政司 Chün¹ Chêng⁴ Ssu¹, Construction Department ; having two Sections : 1. 製造科 Chih⁴ Tsao⁴ K'o¹, Section of Manufacture, and 2. 建築科 Chien⁴ Chu² K'o¹, Building Section.

[547]

No. 436c. 軍學司 Chün¹ Hsüeh² Ssu¹, Department of Naval Education; with five Sections: 1. 教育科 Chiao⁴ Yü⁴ K'o¹, Section of Instruction,· 2. 訓練科 Hsün⁴ Lien⁴ K'o¹, Section of Training, 3. 謀略科 Mou² Lüeh⁴ K'o¹, Section of Strategy, 4. 調查科 Tiao⁴ Ch'a² K'o¹, Intelligence Section, and 5. 編譯科 Pien¹ I⁴ K'o¹, Translation Section.

No. 436D. 軍樞司 Chün¹ Shu¹ Ssu¹, Department of Important Affairs (Chancery); composed of three Sections: 1. 奏咨科 Tsou⁴ Tzu¹ K'o¹, Section of Memorials and Correspondence, 2. 典章科 Tien³ Chang¹ K'o¹, Section of Naval Regulations, and 3. 承發科 Ch'eng² Fa¹ K'o¹, Transmission Section.

No. 436E. 軍儲司 Chün¹ Ch'u³ Ssu¹, Department of Economical Affairs; having three Sections: 1. 收支科 Shou¹ Chih¹ K'o¹, Section of Finance, 2. 儲備科 Ch'u³ Pei⁴ K'o¹, Section of Economy, and 3. 庶務科 Shu⁴ Wu⁴ K'o¹, Section of General Affairs.

No. 436F. 軍防司 Chün¹ Fang² Ssu¹, Department of Defense; consisting of two Sections: 1. 偵測科 Chêng¹ Ts'ê⁴ K'o¹, Intelligence Section, and 2. 銓衡科 Ch'üan² Hêng² K'o¹, Section of Appointments.

No. 436G. 軍法司 Chün¹ Fa⁴ Ssu¹, Department of Naval Law; having no Sections.

No. 436H. 軍醫司 Chün¹ I¹ Ssu¹, Naval Medical and Sanitary Department; of two Sections: 1. 醫務科 I¹ Wu⁴ K'o¹, Medical Section, and 2. 衛生科 Wei⁴ Shêng¹ K'o¹, Sanitary Section.

No. 436I. 主計處 Chu³ Chi⁴ Ch'u⁴, Accounts Office; having two Sections: 1. 會計科 Hui⁴ Chi⁴ K'o¹, Accounts Section, and 2. 統計科 T'ung³ Chi⁴ K'o¹, Statistical Section.

No. 436J. Each Department of the Ministry of the Navy, with a few exceptions, has the following staff: One 司長 Ssu¹ Chang³, Department Controller, one 司副 Ssu¹ Fu⁴, Assistant

Department Controller, 科長 K'o¹ Chang², Section Chiefs (one for each Section), 科員 K'o¹ Yüan², Secretaries, and 錄事 Lu Shih⁴, Writers.

No. 436ᴋ. The personnel of various Departments and Offices differs from that shown above (*see* No. 436ᴊ) as shown below :

1. At the Construction Department (*see* Supplement No. 436ʙ) there are 藝師 I⁴ Shih¹, Chief Engineers, and 藝士 I⁴ Shih⁴, Engineers.

2. The Department of Naval Law (*see* Supplement No. 436ɢ) having no Sections, 司法官 Ssu¹ Fa⁴ Kuan¹, Officers of Justice, take the place of Section Chiefs and Secretaries.

3. At the Accounts Office (*see* Supplement No. 436ɪ) the 計長 Chi⁴ Chang², Office Chief, and 副計長 Fu⁴ Chi⁴ Chang², Assistant Office Chief, take the place of a Controller and an Assistant Controller.

No. 437. Idem. No. 185ᴘ.

Nos. 424 to 434. 憲政籌備處 Hsien⁴ Chêng⁴ Ch'ou² Pei⁴ Ch'u⁴, Office of Constitutional Reforms (*see* Supplement No. 160) ; established at the Ministry of War (*see* an Imperial Decree of the 27th February, 1910, promulgated in reply to a Memorial from the Ministry of the same date).

No. 440. According to the rules for new Judicial Establishments (*see* No. 758), the functions of the Ministry of Justice are now of a purely administrative character, namely, the appointment of officials to the judicial service, the appointment and transfer of judicial officials, the definition of the competence of Judicial Establishments (in territorial respect), the framing of regulations, codes, rules, etc. Furthermore, the Ministry of Justice no longer passes final judgment on death sentences imposed by the Supreme Court of Justice (*see* No. 205ᴀ ; also compare Supplement No. 215ᴀ).

No. 458. 憲政籌備處 Hsien⁴ Chêng⁴ Ch'ou² Pei⁴ Ch'u⁴, Office of Constitutional Reforms (*see* Supplement No. 160); established at the Ministry of Justice, as proposed in a Memorial from the Ministry dated the 27th February, 1910, to replace the 編查處 Pien¹ Ch'a² Ch'u⁴, Compiling Office, organized at that Ministry in 1907. The Senior Councillor of the Ministry is at the head of this office and his staff is the same as that of the former Compiling Office, namely, one 提調 T'i² Tiao⁴, Proctor, one 總纂 Tsung³ Tsuan³, Chief Reviser, six 纂脩 Tsuan³ Hsiu¹, Proof-readers, one 庶務員 Shu⁴ Wu⁴ Yüan², Steward, and five 行走 Hsing² Tsou³, Attachés.

Nos. 463 to 466. 憲政籌備處 Hsien⁴ Chêng⁴ Ch'ou² Pei⁴ Ch'u⁴, Office of Constitutional Reforms (*see* Supplement No. 160); established at the Ministry of Agriculture, Industry and Commerce, as recommended in a Memorial emanating thence, dated the 18th March, 1910, to replace the 憲政研究所 Hsien⁴ Chêng⁴ Yen² Chiu¹ So³, instituted in October, 1907.

No. 464A. 化分礦質局 Hua⁴ Fên¹ Kung³ Chih⁴ Chü², Chemical Laboratory for Analysis of Mining Products; organized in accordance with regulations drawn up by the Ministry of Agriculture, Industry and Commerce, sanctioned by the Emperor on the 23rd January, 1911, at the Offices of Industrial Taotais (*see* No. 839A) or Mining Committees (*see* No. 775). At these Laboratories there may be organized 礦質研究所 Kung³ Chih⁴ Yen² Chiu¹ So³, Courses in Mining, and 礦質陳列館 Kung³ Chih⁴ Ch'ên² Lieh⁴ Kuan³, Museums of Mining Products.

The personnel of a Laboratory for the Analysis of Mining Products includes: 1. 局長 Chü² Chang³, Director of the Laboratory (a post held by the Industrial Taotai or the President of the Mining Committee), 2. One 總理 Ching¹ Li³, Chemist, 3. 技師 Chi⁴ Shih¹, Assistant Chemists (1 or 2), and 4. 書記 Shu¹ Chi⁴, Clerk.

Nos. 476 to 480. 憲政籌備處 Hsien⁴ Chêng⁴ Ch'ou² Pei⁴ Ch'u⁴, Office of Constitutional Reforms (*see* Supplement, No. 160), instituted at the Ministry of Posts and Communications, on a Memorial from the Ministry dated the 28th March, 1910.

No. 479. The text should read as follows :

郵政司 Yu² Chêng⁴ Ssu¹, Department of Posts ; superintending all postal affairs of the Empire (since the 28th May, 1911, when the postal administration was transferred to the Ministry of Posts and Communications ; *see* Supplement No. 273), the improvement of postal communications, the sale of money orders and stamps and the transmission of parcels. It is composed of four K'o¹, Sections : 1. 綜譯科 Tsung¹ I⁴ K'o¹, Translation Section, 2. 經業科 Ching¹ Yeh⁴ K'o¹, Section of Operation, 3. 通阜科 T'ung¹ Fu² K'o¹, Section of Finance, and 4. 建聚科 Chien⁴ Ho² K'o¹, Construction Section. These, in turn, are divided into eight 股 Ku³, Sub-Sections.

No. 479A. 郵政總局 Yu² Chêng⁴ Tsung³ Chü², Directorate General of Posts ; directed by a 局長 Chü² Chang³, Director-General of Posts, who has subordinated to him a 總辦 Tsung³ Pan⁴, Postmaster-General, and a 會辦 Hui⁴ Pan⁴ Associate Postmaster-General ; established in accordance with a Memorial from the Minister of Posts and Communications, 盛宣懷 Shêng⁴ Hsüan¹-huai², sanctioned by the Emperor on the 26th May, 1911, (*see* Supplement No. 273).

No. 523B. As proposed in a Memorial from the Ministry of the Interior, sanctioned by the Throne on the 18th December, 1910, at Peking there has been founded a 民政部高等巡警學堂 Min² Chêng⁴ Pu⁴ Kao¹ Têng³ Hsün² Ching³ Hsüeh² T'ang², Higher Police School of the Ministry of the Interior. This school is arranged so as to supply A. A 正科 Chêng⁴ K'o¹, Complete Course (extending over three years), and B. A 專科 Chuan¹ K'o¹, Special Course (of one year and a half), as well as lower Police Courses. There are yearly enrolled 80 men (10 from the Capital and 70 from the provinces) for the Complete Course, which supplies instruction in administration, policing, prison management, English and Japanese.

At the head of the Higher Police School of the Ministry of the Interior there is a 總辦 Tsung³ Pan⁴, Curator, to whom there are subordinated a 監督 Chien¹ Tu¹, Director, a 提調 T'i² Tiao⁴, Inspector, 教習 Chao⁴ Hsi², Teachers, etc.

No. 551B. 國庫 Kuo² K'u⁴, The Government Treasury.

This has been organized in accordance with regulations framed by the National Assembly, sanctioned by the Emperor on the 27th January, 1911, with the object of combining all Government funds, receiving all revenues, making all payments on Government account, safe-keeping Government moneys and the transaction of money operations generally.

The Minister of Finance is at the head of the Treasury as 總管大臣 Tsung³ Kuan³ Ta⁴ Ch'ên², Superintendent. In the provinces a general control (監督 Chien¹ Tu¹) over the Government Treasury is invested in the Lieutenant-Governor, or Financial Commissioner. Examinations of the Government Treasury are made by specially deputed officials or by the High Authorities of the provinces. Later, when the organization of the 審計院 Shên³ Chi⁴ Yüan⁴, Audit Department, shall have been completed, examinations will be made by that establishment.

The Government Treasury is organized as follows :

總庫 Tsung³ K'u⁴, Central Treasury ; situated at the Capital and supervising Branch Treasuries and Treasury Sections in the provinces. At its head there are a 正總理 Chêng⁴ Tsung³ Li³, Superintendent (a post associated with that of Governor of the Ta Ch'ing Government Bank), and a 副總理 Fu⁴ Tsung³ Li³, Assistant Superintendent (a post associated with that of Deputy Governor of the Ta Ch'ing Government Bank).

分庫 Fên¹ K'u⁴, Branch Treasuries; found at provincial capitals. To these there are subordinated Treasury Sections (*see* below). Each Branch Treasury is under the direction of a 經理 Ching¹ Li³, Manager (a post associated with that of Superintendent of the Ta Ch'ing Government Bank).

支庫 Chih¹ K'u⁴, Treasury Sections; found at cities of importance. Each Treasury Section is under the direction of a 協理 Hsieh² Li³, Manager (a post associated with that of Superintendent of the Ta Ch'ing Government Bank).

At various places, as the judgment of the Ta Ch'ing Government Bank Administration suggests, there are established 派辦處 P'ai⁴ Pan⁴ Ch'u⁴, or 代理處 Tai⁴ Li³ Ch'u⁴, Agencies of the Treasury, for the employment of surplus Government funds.

No. 555. In Kiangsu, Anhui, Shantung, Honan, Shansi, Chekiang and Fukien, as recommended in a Memorial from the Ministry of Finance, dated the 24th March, 1910, the Offices for the Collection of Excise on Native Opium, as well as various 分卡 Fên¹ Ch'ia⁴, Barriers, have been abolished. At Shanghai, in place of an abolished Barrier there has been established a 查驗緝私局 Ch'a² Yen⁴ Chi⁴ Ssu¹ Chü², Office for the Prevention of Opium Smuggling, and, in Shantung, the collection of excise on Native Opium has been transferred to the 籌欵局 Ch'ou² K'uan³ Chü², Office for Providing Government Funds (compare Supplement Nos. 825 to 826).

No. 573A. 僧錄司 Sêng¹ Lu⁴ Ssu¹ (literary designation, 大禪宗 Ta⁴ Ch'an² Tsung¹), Superior of the Buddhist Priesthood at Peking; 6A; two in all.

僧綱司副都綱 Sêng¹ Kang¹ Ssu¹ Fu⁴ Tu¹ Kang¹, Assistant Superior of the Buddhist Priesthood in a prefecture; of unclassed rank.

In the district of 衡山縣 Hêng² Shan¹ Hsien⁴, Hunan province, the Superior is styled 僧綱司 Sêng¹ Kang¹ Ssu¹.

No. 573B. 道錄司 Tao⁴ Lu⁴ Ssu¹ (literary designation, 大鞏籙 Ta⁴ Chang³ Lu⁴), Superior of the Taoist Priesthood at Peking; 6A; two in all.

道紀司副都紀 Tao⁴ Chi⁴ Ssu¹ Fu⁴ Tu¹ Chi⁴, Assistant Superior of the Taoist Priesthood in a prefecture; of unclassed rank.

In the district of 衡山縣 Hêng² Shan¹ Hsien⁴ (*see* above, No. 573A) the Superior is styled 道紀司 Tao⁴ Chi⁴ Ssu¹.

No. 577. In 1909 Primary Schools of the Junior Grade were reformed so as to provide three courses of study, namely, Full Course (of five years, 初等小學堂完全科 Ch'u¹ Têng³ Hsiao³ Hsüeh² T'ang² Wan² Ch'üan² K'o¹), and Abridged Courses (of four years, 四年級小學堂簡易科 Ssu⁴ Nien² Chi² Hsiao⁴ Hsüeh² T'ang² Chien³ I⁴ K'o¹, and of three years, 三年級小學堂簡易科 San¹ Nien² Chi² Hsiao³ Hsüeh² T'ang² Chien³ I⁴ K'o¹).

The Ministry of Education soon became convinced of the inutility of this system and, by a Memorial, sanctioned by the Emperor on the 30th December, 1910, there was introduced a uniform course of four years duration, with four to five hours of instruction daily, for all Primary Schools of Junior Grade throughout the Empire. The subjects of instruction are ethics, classics, Chinese language, arithmetic, history, geography, natural sciences, drawing, callisthenics, handicrafts, singing, principles of agriculture and principles of commerce—the last four are optional.

No. 584. 北洋大學堂 Pei³ Yang² Ta⁴ Hsüeh² T'ang², Peiyang University; established in 1902 on the initiative of Yüan Shih-k'ai, a Preparatory Course (豫科 Yü⁴ K'o¹), of three years, being first organized. In 1906 the first class was graduated from the Preparatory Course and advanced to the 本科 Pên³ K'o¹, Specializing Course.

A reform of the curriculum was effected in 1908, the "Regulations of Instruction" being altered to provide for increased terms of study, instruction in additional subjects and an enlarged staff of teachers. At present there are three Departments: A. 土木工科 T'u³ Mu⁴ Kung¹ K'o¹, Engineering Department (supplying two courses), B. 採鑛及冶金科 Ts'ai³ Kung³ Chi² Yeh³ Chin¹ K'o¹, Department of Mining and Metallurgy (supplying two courses) and C. 法律科 Fa⁴ Lü⁴ K'o¹, Department of Law (supplying one course).

The final examinations of the first class to be graduated are scheduled for the latter half of 1910 and the first half of 1911.

Graduation from the Peiyang University carries with it the attainment of various ranks and privileges, as provided in the University Regulations.

No. 620. By a Memorial from the Ministry of Education, sanctioned by the Throne on the 5th March, 1910, Schools for Training Teachers for Professional Schools have been made equal, as regards status and privileges (獎勵 Chiang³ Li⁴), to Higher Normal Schools (*see* No. 618B), and, like the latter, are to supply a course of study of four years.

These schools are to be organized so as to supply two 科 K'o¹, Courses of Study, namely, A. 完全科 Wan² Ch'üan² K'o¹, Complete Course, and B. 簡易科 Chien³ I⁴ K'o¹, Abridged Course. Those who complete the Abridged Course are to rank with graduates of Lower Normal Schools (*see* No. 618A).

In the Memorial mentioned, the provinces were commanded: 1. To establish, within two years from date, at least one "School for Training Teachers for Professional Schools," supplying the "Complete Course," and B. To found, in the very near future, like schools supplying "Abridged Courses."

Nos. 621 to 621B. 機器學堂 Chi¹ Ch'i⁴ Hsüeh² T'ang², School of Engineering; established in September, 1905, in

Szechwan province, at the 機器局 Chi[1] Ch'i[4] Chü[2], Arsenal, with an enrollment of 30 students—later increased to 50 (*see* a report from 趙爾巽 Chao[4] Êrh[3]-hsün[4], dated the 26th March, 1910).

高等醫學堂 Kao[1] Têng[3] I[1] Hsüeh[2] T'ang[2], Higher Medical School. This has been founded at the city of Hangchow, in Chekiang province, in accordance with a Memorial from the Governor, Tsêng Yün, sanctioned by the Throne on the 12th January, 1911.

No. 623. 法政學堂 Fa[4] Chêng[4] Hsüeh[2] T'ang[2], College of Law and Administration; established at Peking in accordance with a Memorial from the Ministry of Education, dated 1907, for the purpose of preparing students for a judicial or administrative career. As recommended in a Memorial from the same Ministry, sanctioned by the Emperor on the 20th September, 1910, this College has been reorganized and it now serves as a model for similar institutions in the provinces.

As at present constituted, the College of Law and Administration has two Sections, namely: 1. 正科 Chêng[4] K'o[1], Specializing Section, supplying three Courses, *i.e.* A. 政治門 Chêng[4] Chih[4] Mên[2], Course in Administration, B. 法律門 Fa[4] Lü[4] Mên[2], Course in Law, and C. 經濟門 Ching[1] Chi[2] Mên[2], Course in Finance and Political Economy, of three years each, and 2. 別科 Pieh[2] K'o[1], Special Section, of three years.

For the Specializing Section there are yearly accepted pupils who have completed the course of a Middle School: for the Special Section there are accepted as pupils officials or scholars possessing a literary degree not higher than that of 舉人 Chü[3] Jên[2], and aged not more than 25 years.

At the head of the College of Law and Administration there is a Director (*see* No. 635). He has a staff composed of a Preceptor (*see* No. 636), Professors (*see* No. 637; in an indefinite number), Tutors (*see* No. 640), a Steward (*see* No. 641), a 庶務員 Shu⁴ Wu⁴ Yüan², Assistant Steward, Secretaɪ (*see* No. 642), Accountants (*see* No. 643) and Clerks of Works (*see* No. 644).

No. 629c. The literary designations of the first Metropolitan Graduate (Doctor) are 第一人 Ti⁴ I¹ Jên², 大魁 Ta⁴ K'uei², and 殿元 Tien⁴ Yüan².

No. 652. The text should read as follows:

管理日本遊學生監督處 Kuan³ Li³ Jih⁴ Pên³ Yu² Hsüeh² Shêng¹ Chien¹ Tu¹ Ch'u⁴, Inspectorate of Chinese Students in Japan, at the Chinese Legation in Tokyo; reorganized in accordance with a Memorial from the Ministry of Education, sanctioned by the Throne on the 20th March, 1910.

The supreme control and general supervision over this establishment is invested in the Chinese Minister to Japan, but the direct management of the affairs is carried on by a 監督 Chien¹ Tu¹, Controller, appointed on the recommendation of the Chinese Minister and the Ministry of Education, who is assisted by seven 學務委員 Hsüeh² Wu⁴ Wei³ Yüan², Deputies for Educational Affairs, dealing with correspondence, accounts and current affairs, and four 書記生 Shu¹ Chi⁴ Shêng¹, Clerks.

For furnishing instruction in the Japanese language to those who desire to join one of the "five higher schools" in Japan (the number of students yearly sent to these schools has been fixed at 165 by an agreement between the Chinese and Japanese Governments) there have been instituted at Peking, as recommended in a Memorial from the Ministry of Education, sanctioned by the Emperor on the 26th January, 1911, 游學日本高等五校預科 Yu² Hsüeh² Jih⁴ Pên³ Kao¹ Têng³ Wu³ Hsiao⁴ Yü⁴ K'o¹, Preparatory Courses for Students to the Five Higher Schools in Japan, extending over from one to two years. For attending these there are yearly accepted persons unacquainted with the Japanese language who have graduated from Middle Schools.

No. 652A. At the head of the Office for the Selection of Students for America there is a 總辦 Tsung³ P'an⁴, Chief, to whom there are attached two 會辦 Hui⁴ P'an⁴, Assistants (*see* a Memorial from the Ministry of Foreign Affairs, dated the 11th March, 1910).

No. 652E. On their return to Peking, students who have been studying military sciences abroad are called upon to undergo examination. Those who successfully complete this examination receive literary degrees (for instance that of 舉人 Chü³ Jên²), qualified by the branch of military science which they have studied (as 工兵科 Kung¹ Ping¹ K'o¹, Engineering ; 步兵科 Pu⁴ Ping¹ K'o¹, Infantry ; 礮兵科 P'ao⁴ Ping¹ K'o¹, Artillery), and are appointed as lieutenants or sub-lieutenants (*see* No. 658) according to the rating attained in the examination.

No. 702. 軍法會審 Chün¹ Fa⁴ Hui⁴ Shên³, Courts-Martial ; organized in accordance with regulations sanctioned by the Throne on the 20th day of the 9th moon of the 2nd year of Hsün T'ung which, aiming at despatch and simplicity, provide that these be courts from which there is no appeal (instead of the Civil Court organization of three grades).

Courts-Martial are found at Corps, Divisions and Independent Brigades and, further, there are : 1. The 高等軍法會審 Kao¹ Têng³ Chün¹ Fa⁴ Hui⁴ Shên³, Supreme Court-Martial (at the Ministry of War), and 2. The 臨時軍法會審 Lin² Shih² Chün¹ Fa⁴ Hui⁴ Shên³, Courts-Martial Extraordinary (convened in cases of necessity at separate military detachments smaller than a Corps, Division or Brigade).

The personnel of ordinary Courts-Martial is drawn from the officers of the military body interested ; the personnel of the Supreme Court-Martial is drawn from the Department of Military Law of the Ministry of War.

A Court-Martial is composed of :

1. 審判長 Shên³ P'an⁴ Chang³, President of the Court (of the rank of Lieutenant-Colonel, or higher, in dependence on the rank of the accused),

2. 司法官 Ssu¹ Fa⁴ Kuan¹, Officers of Justice (drawn from the ranks of Officers of the military body concerned),

3. 審判官 Shên³ P'an⁴ Kuan¹, Members of the Court (of the rank of Lieutenant, or higher, in dependence on the rank of the accused),

4. 錄事 Lu⁴ Shih⁴, Writers, and

5. 陸軍檢察官 Lu⁴ Chün¹ Chien³ Ch'a² Kuan¹, Prosecutors. Also, there are 陸軍警察隊 Lu⁴ Chün¹ Ching³ Ch'a² Tui⁴, Squads of Military Police.

No. 715D. At the School for Military Draftsmen in Peking there is a 模範班 Mo² Fan⁴ Pan⁴, Model Section, where students from the various provinces are taught, with the object of disseminating the sciences of surveying and drafting. The final examinations of the first class to be graduated from this school took place, after a course of one year and seven months study, in 1910, and the most capable of the students received the degree of Bachelor of Arts (舉人 Chü³ Jên²) and the rank of sub-lieutenant ; the less successful received the degree of Senior Licentiate of the 1st Class (see No. 629A).

No. 749. Battalions (營 Ying²) of the Army of the Green Standard have various designations : 1. 中營 Chung¹ Ying², Middle (Central), 2. 左營 Tso³ Ying², Left (Eastern), 3. 右營 Yu⁴ Ying², Right (Western), 4. 前營 Ch'ien² Ying², Van (Southern), 5. 後營 Hou⁴ Ying², Rear (Northern), and 6. 城守營 Ch'êng² Shou³ Ying², Garrison.

No. 750. The literary designation of the Provincial Commander-in-Chief is 大元侯 Ta⁴ Yüan² Hou².

No. 751. Literary designations of a Brigade General are 總鎮 Tsung³ Chên⁴, and 大總侯 Ta⁴ Tsung³ Hou².

No. 752. Literary designations of a Colonel are 協鎭 Hsieh² Chên⁴, and 協 戎 Hsieh² Jung².

No. 752A to 752F. Literary designations of a Lieutenant Colonel are 大 參 戎 Ta⁴ Ts'an¹ Jung², and 大 分 麾 Ta⁴ Fên¹ Hui¹; of a Major, 大 遊 戎 Ta⁴ Yu² Jung², and 大 分 麾 Ta⁴ Fên¹ Hui¹; of a Captain, 大 都 閫 Ta⁴ Tu¹ K'un³, and 都 戎 Tu¹ Jung²; of a 1st Lieutenant, 牙 將 Ya² Chiang¹, and 大 守 侯 Ta⁴ Shou³ Hou²; of a 2nd Lieutenant, 大 戎 伯 Ta⁴ Jung² Po², and 大 長 侯 Ta⁴ Chang³ Hou²; of a Sub-Lieutenant, 把 戎 Pa² Jung².

No. 753. In the Disciplined Forces (練 軍 Lien⁴ Chün¹) a 營 Ying², Battalion, divided into four 哨 Shao⁴, Companies, of 84 men each, was considered as the principal unit. Companies, in turn, were each divided into eight 隊 Tui⁴, Platoons, of 10 (in some Companies 12) 散 勇 San³ Yung³, Privates.

Platoons were commanded by 什 長 Shih² Chang³, Sergeants (23 to a Battalion) and Companies by 哨 官 Shao⁴ Kuan¹, Company Commanders (of the rank of 1st Lieutenant, 2nd Lieutenant, or Sub-Lieutenant; four to a Battalion; (see Nos. 752D to 752F), assisted by 哨 長 Shao⁴ Chang³, Assistant Company Commanders (of the rank of Sub-Lieutenant, Ensign, or Colour-Sergeant; four to a Battalion; see Nos. 752F to 752H). A Battalion was commanded by a 營 官 Ying² Kuan¹, also 管 帶 Kuan³ Tai⁴, Battalion Commander, to whom there was attached a 幫 帶 Pang¹ Tai⁴, Assistant Commander (of the rank of Colonel, Lieutenant-Colonel, or Major; see Nos. 752 to 752B).

To the Commander of a Battalion there were attached 60 親 兵 Ch'in¹ Ping¹, Convoys, divided into six 隊 Tui⁴, Platoons, each headed by a 親 兵 什 長 Ch'in¹ Ping¹ Shih² Chang³, Sergeant of Convoys (one of these bore the designation of 藍 旗 Lan² Ch'i², and performed duty as Adjutant to the Commander).

To each Company Commander there were attached five 護 勇 Hu⁴ Yung³, Guards.

Battalion Commanders, and their assistants, Company Commanders, and their assistants, as well as Platoon Commanders, were allowed one 伙 夫 Huo³ Fu¹, Cook, each (42 to a Battalion).

At the head of a detachment made up of several Battalions there was a 統 領 T'ung³ Ling³, Commander of a Detachment (of the rank of 提 督 T'i² Tu¹, or 總 兵 Tsung³ Ping¹; see Nos. 750 to 751), and in command of a number of Detachments there was a 總 統 Tsung³ T'ung³, styled 兵 部 尚 書 Ping¹ Pu⁴ Shang⁴ Shu¹, Minister of War.

No. 754. In connection with the successful extension of the net of postal establishments of the European type throughout the Empire (see Supplement No. 273), the Ministry of Posts and Communications submitted a Memorial recommending the gradual abolition of the Military Post Stations and their replacement by the new Post Offices. For the carrying out of this scheme it was proposed that the Military Post Stations be placed under the general supervision of the Ministry of Posts and Communications and that their direction in the provinces be invested in the hands of the Industrial Taotais (on the abolition of the post of Provincial Judge ; see No. 830 ; compare No. 839).

Although the Ministry of War considered the proposed abolition of the Military Post Stations to be premature, nevertheless, it agreed to hand over all affairs in connection with these Post Stations, as well as the Couriers Office and Depôt of Military Horses, to the Ministry of Posts and Communications, in January, 1911.

No. 756. 統 制 巡 洋 長 江 艦 隊 T'ung³ Chih⁴ Hsün² Yang² Ch'ang² Chiang¹ Hsien³ Tui⁴, Commander-in-Chief of the Ocean and Long River (Yangtsze River) Naval Squadrons. On the 6th December, 1910, the well-known Admiral Sah Chên-ping was appointed to this post.

[561]

No. 758F.   For the examination of those who wish to serve in Judicial Establishments (**法 官** Fa⁴ Kuan¹) there is an Examining Board composed of the following :

1.   **監 臨 官** Chien¹ Lin² Kuan¹, President of the Examining Board (appointed from the ranks of the higher officials of the Ministry of Justice),

2.   **考 官** K'ao³ Kuan¹, Examiners (appointed from the ranks of officials well versed in jurisprudence, in an indefinite number ; on the first Examining Board convened there were four),

3.   **襄 校 官** Hsiang¹ Chiao⁴ Kuan¹, Assistant Examiners (appointed from the ranks of professors of judicial sciences ; on the first Examining Board convened, which examined about 3,000 candidates—there were 16),

4.   **監 試 御 史** Chien¹ Shih⁴ Yü⁴ Shih³, Censors for the Detection of Malpractices on the part of the Examining Board (appointed from the ranks of officials of the Censorate ; there were four for the first Examining Board—two for duty without the examination hall, **外 場**, and two for duty within the examination hall, **內 場**, and

5.   **執 事 官** Chih² Shih⁴ Kuan¹, Officials attached to the Examining Board, *i.e.*

A.   **提 調 官** T'i² Tiao⁴ Kuan¹, Proctors (2),

B.   **收 掌 官** Shou¹ Chang³ Kuan¹, Collectors of Examination Papers, and

C.   **彌 封 官** Mi² Fêng¹ Kuan¹, Sealers of Examination Papers (2).

For particulars as to the duties of these officials *see* No. 6521.

No. 771.   **工 會** Kung¹ Hui⁴, Crafts Associations (regulations regarding these Associations were drawn up by the Ministry of Agriculture, Industry and Commerce and sanctioned by the Throne on the 23rd January, 1911).

[562]

Crafts Associations have been instituted with the object of studying all varieties of handicrafts, guiding and improving them and, by introducing new methods, increasing their efficiency.

At provincial capitals there are found 總會 Tsung³ Hui⁴, Central Crafts Associations; other cities have 分會 Fên¹ Hui⁴, Branch Associations. The former are directed by a 總理 Tsung³ Li³, Chairman, and a 協理 Hsieh² Li³, Vice-Chairman, while the latter are under the guidance of a 總理 Tsung³ Li³, Chairman.

No. 793. Literary designations of the Prefect of the Metropolitan Prefecture and the Governor of Peking (京府 Ching¹ Fu³) are 京尹 Ching¹ Yin³, 京兆尹 Ching¹ Chao⁴ Yin³, 大畿牧 Ta⁴ Chi¹ Mu⁴, 大保釐 Ta⁴ Pao³ Li³, and 大邦伯 Ta⁴ Pang¹ Po², and, of the Vice-Governor, 少京兆 Shao⁴ Ching¹ Chao⁴, 京少尹 Ching¹ Shao⁴ Yin³, 大貳侯 Ta⁴ Êrh⁴ Hou², and 大貳牧 Ta⁴ Êrh⁴ Mu⁴.

No. 796A. Another designation of the Censors of the Five Districts (Cities) is 巡城御史 Hsün² Ch'êng² Yü⁴ Shih³ (literary designation, 巡使 Hsün² Shih³, and 大直指 Ta⁴ Chih² Chih³).

To the Police Magistrate (literary designation, 市令 Shih⁴ Ling⁴, and 大司城 Ta⁴ Ssu¹ Ch'êng²) and to the Assistant Police Magistrate (literary designation, 市丞 Shih⁴ Ch'êng²), as well as to the Police Master and Jail Warden (literary designation, 京城游徼 Ching¹ Ch'êng² Yu² Chiao³), there were attached assistants styled, respectively, 揀發正指揮 Chien³ Fa¹ Chêng⁴ Chih³ Hui¹, 揀發副指揮 Chien³ Fa¹ Fu⁴ Chih³ Hui¹, and 揀發吏目 Chien³ Fa¹ Li⁴ Mu⁴.

No. 797. Literary designations of the General Commandant of the Gendarmerie are 金吾 Chin¹ Wu² and 式道侯 Shih⁴ Tao⁴ Hou².

No. 800. With a view to meeting urgent calls for the maintenance of order, the General Commandant of the Gendarmerie, Prince Yü Lang, has organized a 兩翼游緝隊 Liang³ I⁴ Yu² Chi² Tui⁴, Detachment of Fleet Police. At the same time there was also organized a 馬步游緝公所 Ma³ Pu⁴ Yu² Chi² Kung¹ So³, Office of Mounted and Pedestrian Fleet Police, directed by the Chief of the Fleet Police.

The Fleet Police numbers 1,800 men.

No. 804. The text should read as follows :

巡撫 Hsün² Fu³, Governor ; one for the provinces of Kirin (residing at Kirin) and Heilungchiang (residing at Tsitsihar). With reference to the Banner Forces this official has the authority of a 副都統 Fu⁴ Tu¹ T'ung³, Manchu Brigadier-General (compare Nos. 745, 745I and 821).

The post of Governor of Fengtien was abolished by Imperial Decree of the 26th April, 1910.

No. 805. As recommended in a Memorial from the Governor-General, 趙爾巽 Chao Êrh-hsün, dated the 20th June, 1911, there has been established at the Yamen (公署 Kung¹ Shu⁴) of the Governor-General of Manchuria a 東三省文牘總核處 Tung¹ San¹ Shêng³ Wên² Tu³ Tsung³ Ho² Ch'u⁴, (Provisional) Committee for the Study of Current Correspondence Regarding Manchurian Affairs, and a 審計處 Shên³ Chi⁴ Ch'u⁴, Audit Office (charged with accounting for, and auditing, all expenditure made in Manchuria). At the same time the Head Office of Mongolian Affairs, previously independent (see Nos. 812A and 901), was annexed, to the Yamen of the Governor-General of Manchuria.

No. 808. Conforming to a Memorial from the Governor-General of Manchuria, 趙爾巽 Chao Êrh-hsün, dated the 20th June, 1911, the previously independent 倉務局 Ts'ang¹ Wu⁴ Chü², Bureau of Government Stores, has been abolished and its functions transferred to the Bureau of Finance.

No. 812A. The Head Office of Mongolian Affairs has been abolished (*see* a Memorial from the Governor-General of Manchuria, 趙 爾 巽 Chao Êrh-hsün, dated the 20th June, 1911: compare Nos. 805 and 901).

No. 818. By virtue of an Imperial Edict of the 26th September, 1910, there has been placed at the head of the Salt Administration of Manchuria a 鹽 運 使 Yen² Yün⁴ Shih³, Salt Controller (*see* No. 835), charged with the reorganization of this administration.

Until the reorganization of the Salt Administration of Manchuria has been completed, the 鹽 務 總 局 Yen² Wu⁴ Tsung³ Chü², Head Office of Salt Affairs, established in 1906 as recommended in a Memorial from the Military Governor, Chao Êrh-hsün, will function as usual.

No. 820. Since the reorganization of the Ministry of War (in 1910; *see* Supplement No. 420), the Governors-General are styled 都 察 院 右 都 御 史 Tu¹ Ch'a² Yüan⁴ Yu⁴ Tu¹ Yü⁴ Shih³, Junior President of the Censorate (*see* No. 207B), alone.

No. 821. Since the reorganization of the Ministry of War (in 1910; *see* Supplement No. 420), the Governors are styled 都 察 院 副 都 御 史 Tu¹ Ch'a² Yüan⁴ Fu⁴ Tu¹ Yü⁴ Shih³, Vice-President of the Censorate (*see* No. 209), alone.

Nos. 825 to 826. 財 政 總 匯 處 Ts'ai² Chêng⁴ Tsung³ Hui⁴ Ch'u⁴, Central Financial Bureaux. The establishment of such institutions throughout the provinces was decreed by Imperial Edict of the 24th May, 1909, with a view to curtailing expenses in connection with the maintenance of various financial establishments in the provinces and the subordination of all finances to the Lieutenant-Governor.

The first Financial Bureau to be established was that at Tientsin (*see* a Memorial from the Chihli Governor-General, 陳 夔 龍 Ch'ên² K'uei²-lung², dated the 24th March, 1910), headed by the Lieutenant-Governor (*see* No. 825) as 總 辦 Tsung³

Pan⁴, Chief, and the Salt Controller (*see* No. 835) as 幫總辦 Pang¹ Tsung³ Pan⁴, Assistant. It consists of four 股 Ku³, Sections: 1. 海防糧餉股 Hai³ Fang² Liang² Hsiang³ Ku³, Section for Issue of Rations and Pay of Troops of the Coast Defence, 2. 淮軍糧餉股 Huai² Chün¹ Liang² Hsiang³ Ku³, Section for the Issue of Rations and Pay of the "Huai Chün" Troops, 3. 練軍糧餉股 Lien⁴ Chün¹ Liang² Hsiang³ Ku³, Section for the Issue of Rations and Pay of the "Lien Chün" Troops, and 4. 籌款股 Ch'ou² K'uan³ Ku³, Section for the Provision of Government Funds (among other duties this Section controls the collection of stamp-duties).

Each Section of the Tientsin Financial Bureau is headed by a 坐辦 Tso⁴ Pan⁴, Section Chief, and a 幫坐辦 Pang¹ Tso⁴ Pan⁴, Assistant Section Chief.

With the inauguration of the Financial Bureau at Tientsin the following were abolished: 1. 海防支應局 Hai³ Fang² Chih¹ Ying⁴ Chü², Treasury of the Maritime Defence (at Tientsin; compare No. 859), 2. 淮軍銀錢所 Huai² Chün¹ Yin² Ch'ien² So³, Office for the Issue of Pay to the "Huai Chün" Troops (at Tientsin), 3. 籌款局 Ch'ou² K'uan³ Chü², Office for the Provision of Government Funds (at Paotingfu; supervising the collection of excise on wine and opium), 4. 練餉局 Lien⁴ Hsiang³ Chü². Office for the Issue of Pay to the "Lien Chün" Troops (at Paotingfu), and 5. 印花稅局 Yin⁴ Hua¹ Shui⁴ Chü², Office for the Collection of Stamp-duties (at Paotingfu; established in April, 1908).

In accordance with the terms of the Imperial Edict mentioned (of 24th May, 1909), and for the purpose therein stated, in all provinces there are now found 財政公所 Ts'ai² Chêng⁴ Kung¹ So³, Financial Offices, under the direction of the Lieutenant-Governors, controlling all financial affairs with the exception of Salt, Grain and Customs revenues, which are under the administration of their respective Taotais.

Although these Offices are everywhere under the control of the Lieutenant-Governor, their organization is not uniform throughout the Empire. In the majority, however, there are six Sections: 1. 總務科 Tsung³ Wu⁴ K'o¹, Section of General Affairs (found in Hunan, Kiangsi and Chekiang), 2. 田賦科 T'ien² Fu⁴ K'o¹, Section of Land Taxes (in Hunan, Kiangsi and Chekiang), 3. 制用科 Chih⁴ Yung⁴ K'o¹, Section of Expenditure (found in Hunan and Kiangsi), 4. 會計科 Hui⁴ Chi⁴ K'o¹, Audit Section (found in Hunan and Kiangsi), 5. 稅務科 Shui⁴ Wu⁴ K'o¹, Section of Customs Duties (in Kiangsi; in Hunan, 筦榷科 Kuan³ Ch'üeh⁴ K'o¹, Section of Excise; in Chekiang, 釐稅科 Li² Shui⁴ K'o¹, Section of Likin), and 6. 行政科 Hsing⁴ Chêng⁴ K'o¹, Section of Administration (in Hunan), etc. These Sections may be further sub-divided into Sub-sections (for instance, in Hunan, there are 16 Sub-sections).

At the head of each Section there is a 科長 K'o¹ Chang³, Section Chief, to whom there are subordinated 科員 K'o¹ Yüan², Secretaries, and 書記 Shu¹ Chi⁴, Clerks (for instance, in Hunan and Kiangsi).

No. 829B. As regards educational affairs in the counties, spreading public instruction, establishment of schools and libraries, etc., these are invested in the hands of auxiliary branches of town and county self-government institutions, the 鄉學連合會 Hsiang¹ Hsüeh² Lien² Ho² Hui⁴, Village (Town) Educational Associations, which, in accordance with regulations sanctioned by the Throne on the 2nd December, 1910, are established at places far from important centres, or where there is a dearth of funds.

No. 832. The text should read as follows:

交涉使 Chiao¹ Shê⁴ Shih³, Commissioner for Foreign Affairs; 3A; charged with dealing with questions arising with foreigners in the province concerned. This official holds a position intermediate between that of Lieutenant-Governor (*see* No. 825) and Commissioner of Education (*see* No. 827). He is directly subordinated to the Governor-General (*see* No. 820) or Governor (*see* No. 821) of the province to which he is accredited and, at the same time, is also subject to the control of the Ministry of Foreign Affairs.

Commissioners of Foreign Affairs are appointed from the ranks of those who have seen service at the Ministry of Foreign Affairs, or who have held substantive diplomatic posts in the provinces (ranking not lower than that of Taotai—*see* No. 838), and they are found in Manchuria (*see* No. 806), Yünnan (post established in August, 1908), Chekiang (post established in April, 1910), Chihli, Kiangsu, Hupeh, Kuangtung and Fukien (these latter were appointed on the 18th August, 1910).

In the provinces of Anhui, Kiangsi, Hunan and Kuangsi the supervision of affairs in which foreigners are interested is invested in the hands of the Commissioners of Foreign Affairs of the provinces under the jurisdiction of the same Governors-General, *i.e.* those of Kiangsu, Hupeh and Kuangtung.

The provinces of Heilungchiang, Shantung, Shansi, Honan, Kansu, Hsinchiang, Szechwan and Kueichow as yet have no Commissioners of Foreign Affairs.

Regulations regarding the Commissioner of Foreign Affairs (交涉使章程 Chiao¹ Shê⁴ Shih³ Chang¹ Ch'êng²), framed by the Ministry of Foreign Affairs on the 19th July, 1910, in reply to a Memorial from the Committee of Ministers, were sanctioned by the Throne by Imperial Edict of the 18th August, 1910.

At the cities where Commissioners of Foreign Affairs reside there are found 交涉公所 Chiao¹ Shê⁴ Kung¹ So³, Offices of Foreign Affairs. These are organized into two Sections: 1. 秘書科 Pi⁴ Shu¹ K'o¹, Section of Confidential Correspondence, and 2. 繙譯科 Fan¹ I⁴ K'o¹, Translation Section. These Sections are administered by 委員 Wei³ Yüan², subordinated to the Commissioner of Foreign Affairs concerned, numbering, in some provinces, seven to eight for each Section, in others, four to five, as the volume of affairs seems to demand, and 書記生 Shu¹ Chi⁴ Shêng¹, Clerks, of a number sufficient to attend to the business of the Section concerned.

In provinces where the post of Commissioner of Foreign Affairs has not been established, Heilungchiang excepted, duties appertaining to this official are invested in the 洋務局 Yang² Wu⁴ Chü², Office of Foreign Affairs (see No. 859), attached to the Governor-General's (or Governor's) Yamen. In Heilung-chiang there is a 交涉總局 Chiao¹ Shê⁴ Tsung³ Chü² (see No. 806A) for similar duties.

No. 835. There are also the 四川鹽運使 Ssu¹ Ch'uan¹ Yen² Yün⁴ Shih³, Szechwan Salt Controller, residing at Ch'engtu Fu (this post was established by Imperial Decree of the 26th September, 1910, to replace that of 鹽茶道 Yen² Ch'a² Tao⁴, abolished; see No. 841), and the 東三省鹽運使 Tung¹ San¹ Shêng³ Yen² Yün⁴ Shih³, Salt Controller of Manchuria (see Supplement No. 818).

No. 835c. 兩廣鹽政公所 Liang³ Kuang³ Yen² Chêng⁴ Kung¹ So³, Salt Bureau of Kuangtung and Kuangsi; established at Canton on a Memorial from the Office of the Controller-General of the Salt Gabelle, sanctioned by the Emperor on the 2nd November, 1910. This is directly subordinated to the Office mentioned, and to the Ministry of Finance, and is charged with the reorganization of the Salt Administration of Kuangtung and Kuangsi.

At the head of the Salt Bureau of Kuangtung and Kuangsi there is a 正監督 Chêng⁴ Chien¹ Tu¹, Chief, who has subordinated to him two 副監督 Fu⁴ Chien¹ Tu¹, Assistants,

[569]

and various other officials. His duties differ from those of the Salt Controller in that he is in charge of the reorganization and framing of regulations with regard to the Salt Administration of the provinces concerned, while the latter exercises a general supervision, as do other Salt Controllers.

No. 838. As regards authority, the Industrial and Police Taotais are provincial Commissioners rather than ordinary Taotais.

No. 841. The post of 四川鹽法道 Ssŭ[1] Ch'uan[1] Yen[2] Ch'a[2] Tao[4], Salt and Tea Taotai of Szechwan, was abolished by Imperial Edict of the 26th September, 1910, salt affairs being transferred to the newly-appointed Salt Controller (see Supplement No. 835) and tea affairs to the local Industrial Taotai.

No. 843. As recommended in a Memorial from the Liang Kiang Governor-General, dated the 28th December, 1910, the direct supervision of the 堤工局 T'i[2] Kung[1] Chü[2], Office of Conservation of the Grand Canal, has been transferred to the 淮 陽海道 Huai[2] Yang[2] Hai[3] Tao[4], Huai-yang-hai Taotai.

No. 859. On a Memorial from the Governor-General, dated the 26th March, 1910, the following offices in the province of Chihli have been abolished: the 直隸賑撫局 Chih[2] Li[4] Chên[4] Fu[3] Chü[2], Chihli Relief Committee (organized in 1891), the 直隸水利局 Chih[2] Li[1] Shui[3] Li[2] Chü[2], Chihli Irrigation Office (established in 1907), and the 北洋建造局 Pei[5] Yang[2] Chien[4] Tsao[1] Chü[2], Peiyang Construction Office.

In Szechwan the 官報書局 Kuan[1] Pao[4] Shu[1] Chü[2], Government Newspaper Office, has been reorganized as the 官 印刷局 Kuan[1] Yin[4] Shua[1] Chü[2], Government Printing Office, on a Memorial from the Governor-General, 趙爾巽 Chao Êrh-hsün, dated the 26th March, 1910.

No. 880. At the Chancery of the Assistant Military-Governor, P'u Jun, as proposed in a Memorial from this official, sanctioned by the Throne on the 16th November, 1910, there has been established a 憲政籌備處 Hsien⁴ Chêng⁴ Ch'ou² Pei⁴ Ch'u⁴, Office of Constitutional Reforms.

No. 901. The Head Office of Mongolian Affairs has been abolished in accordance with a Memorial from the Governor-General, 趙爾巽 Chao Êrh-hsün, dated the 20th June, 1911, (compare Supplement Nos. 805 and 812A).

No. 907. The text should read as follows :

駐藏大臣 Chu⁴ Tsang⁴ Ta⁴ Ch'ên², Imperial Resident of Tibet (this post was established in 1709) ; residing in Anterior, or Eastern, Tibet ; appointed from the ranks of higher Chinese officials and under the control of the Ministry of Dependencies (see No. 491A). Among other functions, this official acts as a medium of communication between the Chinese Government and the Court of Nepal, which is known in Chinese as 廓爾喀 Kuo² Êrh³ K'a¹, 白布 Pai² Pu⁴, or 巴布 Pa¹ Pu⁴, i.e. Parbuttiya. He is assisted by a staff of 夷情章京 I² Ch'ing² Chang¹ Ching¹, Secretaries for Native Affairs.

The Imperial Resident of Tibet is invested with the supreme command of both the Chinese garrison troops and the native soldiery (番兵 Fan¹ Ping¹) and, through the 噶廈 Ka¹ Hsia⁴, Council Chamber (see No. 910), controls the entire Tibetan civil administration.

Previous to 1911, to the Imperial Resident there were attached a 帮辦大臣 Pang¹ Pan⁴ Ta⁴ Ch'ên², Assistant Resident (this post was established in 1727 ; residing until 1909 in Ulterior, or Western, Tibet, since then in Anterior, or Eastern, Tibet), and a 參贊 Ts'an¹ Tsan⁴, Councillor, charged with the supervision of the three marts open to foreign trade (this post was instituted in 1909 and the Councillor resided in Ulterior, or Western, Tibet ; see No. 909).

As proposed in a Memorial from the Committee of Ministers, dated the 17th March, 1911, in reply to a report from the Imperial Resident 聯豫 Lien Yü, dated the 29th January, 1911, the post of Assistant Resident has been abolished and replaced by that of 左參贊 Tso³ Ts'an¹ Tsan⁴, Senior Councillor, who is to reside in Anterior Tibet and, under the guidance of the Imperial Resident, will supervise the whole of Tibet.

At the same time the designation of the existing Councillor (*see* above) was changed to 右參贊 Yu⁴ Ts'an¹ Tsan⁴, Junior Councillor, his functions remaining unchanged.

ALPHABETICAL INDEX OF CHINESE CHARACTERS

ALPHABETICAL INDEX OF CHINESE CHARACTERS.

(The numerals refer to paragraphs; when preceded by S, to paragraphs in the Supplement. Those in heavy type denote the paragraphs in which the character or expression is explained in most detail. A Stroke, thus |, indicates repetition of the character above).

Chao⁴

照 磨 794, 826, 830A, 850, 853
| 廳 826

Ch'ao¹

超 品 944
| 等 幫 辦 267
| 等 總 巡 263

Ch'ao²

朝 議 大 夫 945
| 考 629c
| 珠 965

Chê²

哲 里 木 盟 885
| 布 尊 丹 巴 胡 圖 克 圖 875; 916A

Ch'ê¹

車 駕 司 415A, 425A, 433A
| 臣 汗 部 870

Chên¹

甄 錄 652c
| 別 屬 員 981
鍼 灸 科 S. 240

Chên³

診 治 科 514

Chên⁴

賑 1
賑 撫 局 S. 859
振 威 將 軍 945
鎮 103D, 525B, 656B, c
| 監 701
| 臺 751
| 議 事 會 525B
| 國 27A
| 國 公 20, 22, 873
| 國 將 軍 24
| 標 749, 751
| 董 事 會 525B

Ch'ên²

臣 983
陳 列 館 774B
| 列 所 771, 771A

Chêng

徵 兵 總 署 656
| 仕 郎 945
偵 測 科 S. 436F

Chêng³

整 宣 尉 125
| 儀 尉 125

Chêng⁴

正 573B
| 齋 857
| 詹 事 929
| 場 考 試 672c
| 教 習 577B, 578, 63
| 教 員 709, 711A, 712
| 監 造 司 庫 94A
| 監 造 94
| 監 理 官 539
| 監 督 185M, 543, 551A, 551, 711A, S. 835c
| 執 法 官 672
| 指 揮 796A
| 卿 216A, 933, 934, 935, 936B
| 軍 醫 官 675, 677
| 軍 械 官 668
| 軍 需 官 673
| 軍 校 658
| 學 長 711A
| 黃 旗 718
| 紅 旗 718
| 一 嗣 教 真 人 573B, 944c
| 乙 真 人 573B
| 醫 官 713A
| 議 員 823A
| 考 官 629B
| 科 622, 623, 627A, 850, S.523B, 623
| 科 員 154c, 160A

[vii]

教育科 400, 407, 430, 430A, 700B, S. 436c
｜ 育分會 829B
｜ 育會 829, 829B
｜ 育總會 829B
｜ 育研究所 410
｜ 諭 618A, **957**, 860
校對 190, 205A, 393
｜ 對科 158
窖廠 460A

Chieh[1]

街道廳 796A

Chieh[2]

捷報處 425B

Chieh[4]

解元 629B
戒煙局 188A
｜ 煙社會 188B

Chien[1]

兼按察使銜 830B
｜ 河工事務 820D
｜ 會辦鹽政大臣銜 835B
｜ 管關海關稅事務 833B
｜ 管巡撫事 820C, 821A
｜ 管河道 820D
｜ 管順天府府尹事務 793.
｜ 理官房租庫事務 82
｜ 理工程處事務 95
｜ 理菜宮事務 104D
｜ 理錢法堂事務 366A, 460A
｜ 理昇平署事務 79B
｜ 理御船處事務 93
｜ 理御書處事務 94A
｜ 理御藥房事務 92
｜ 攝銀庫事務 77
｜ 攝六庫事務 77
｜ 攝織染局務司官 96
｜ 首領廳事 237
｜ 提督 750A
｜ 總管內務府大臣 751A

兼都察院右都御史 820
｜ 尹 793A
監 See also Chien[4]
｜ 察御史 213
｜ 長 702
｜ 塲官 652I
｜ 製官 835A
｜ 製同知 835A
｜ 副 702
｜ 修 189
｜ 修總裁 190
｜ 學 619
｜ 學官 646
｜ 學會議所 593B
｜ 學員 646
｜ 國攝政王 126
｜ 理 550B
｜ 理官 539, 546
｜ 臨官 652I, S. 758F
｜ 丞 546A, 792
｜ 試御史 652I, S. 758F
｜ 守信礦官 801A
｜ 司 838, 844
｜ 造 94
｜ 造司庫 94A
｜ 卒 702
｜ 督 103C, 172, 185M, O, 189, 425B, 460A,
498, 514, 522, 525A, 526, 529, 530,
543, 551A, 558, 561, 561A, B, 565,
566, 567, 568, 619, 627A, 633, 634,
635, 652, 652A, 653, 654, 654A,
709, 712, 754, 773, 786, 829A, 833,
S. 551B, 652.
｜ 督處 652
｜ 印委員 778
｜ 獄 701, **776**B
｜ 獄學堂 523A, 766B
｜ 獄學裏科 623A
｜ 獄傳習所 766B

Chien[3]

揀發正指揮 S. 796A
｜ 發副指揮 S. 796A

二
二

Ch'ing¹

青龍勳章 953A
｜ 色 特 啟 勒 圖 盟 876A
｜ 島 特 別 高 等 專 門 學 堂 653
｜ 豫 科 535
滿 軍 通 判 849A
｜ 軍 同 知 849
｜ 漪 園 90
｜ 理 財 政 局 536
｜ 理 財 政 處 374, 534
｜ 書 521, 696, 697, 712
｜ 道 股 504B
｜ 音 850
輕 車 都 尉 944

Ch'ing²

擎 蓋 司 119

Ch'ing⁴

慶 親 王 27A
｜ 豐 司 83

Chio¹˙²˙⁴ (Chüeh)

覺 羅 40, 759, 914
｜ 羅 公 944

Chio² (Chüeh)

爵 廳 944

Chiu³

九 門 提 督 797
｜ 品 孺 人 915
｜ 品 吏 目 239A
｜ 品 銖 事 481, 766
｜ 品 繙 譯 官 309
｜ 品 奉 祀 官 413A

Chiu⁴

廄 長 88
｜ 副 88

Ch'iu¹

秋 獮 937, 937A
｜ 官 438
｜ 官 正 229
｜ 曹 937

Chiung³

閌 卿 936B
｜ 臺 936B

Cho¹

卓 尼 財 912, 914B
｜ 尼 爾 喇 嘛 914B
｜ 索 圖 盟 885

Chou¹

州 795, **846**, 856B
｜ 貳 守 851A
｜ 牧 851
｜ 判 598, **851A**, 855A
｜ 別 駕 851A
｜ 司 馬 851A
｜ 同 598, **851A**, 855A
周 易 學 門 585
｜ 禮 學 門 585

Ch'ou¹

抽 查 履 歷 委 員 781

Ch'ou²

仇 香 857
籌 賑 處 859
｜ 械 科 185G
｜ 設 海 軍 基 礎 大 臣 185
｜ 欵 局 S. 555, 825 to 826
｜ 欵 股 S. 825 to 826
｜ 辦 處 173, 527, 758A, B,
｜ 備 科 698
｜ 備 憲 政 考 核 處 822A
｜ 備 憲 政 督 催 處 822A
｜ 辦 海 軍 大 臣 185A, 756
｜ 辦 海 軍 事 務 處 185. S. 185A
｜ 辦 股 S 373

Ch'u³

主 政 292
｜ 計 長 756
｜ 計 處 S. 4361
｜ 計 官 756
｜ 計 員 851B

Ch'uan²

船 廠 757 B
| 政 司 185H, 476
| 政 同 知 849
| 渠 757
| 塢 757c
傳 旨 申 斥 982
| 習 所 618A, 758c 766B, 788
| 臚 629c

Chuang¹

莊 頭 處 78A
| 親 王 41

Chuang⁴

壯 勇 753
狀 元 629c

Ch'uang¹

瘡 瘍 科 S. 240

Chui¹

追 贈 944

Ch'ui¹

吹 手 850

Ch'ui²

垂 簾 訓 政 126c
| 簾 聽 政 126c

Ch'un¹

春 卿 S. 376
| 秋 三 傳 學 門 585
| 秋 左 傳 學 門 585
| 坊 中 允 929
| 坊 庶 子 929
| 坊 贊 善 929
| 官 S. 376
| 官 正 229

Ch'un²

醇 親 王 27A, 126

Chung¹

中 廠 366B
| 丞 821
| 將 659A
| 初 兩 等 工 業 學 堂 605
| 舉 629B
| 軍 752, J, 800, 824
| 軍 官 663
| 傳 55
| 翰 137
| 憲 大 夫 945
| 學 787
| 學 教 員 618B
| 學 辦 事 官 618B, 635c
| 學 堂 580, 708, **710**, 716
| 護 929
| 譯 912
| 職 大 夫 945
| 官 正 229
| 國 文 學 門 587
| 國 史 學 門 587
| 國 紅 十 字 總 會 437A
| 國 紅 十 字 分 會 437A
| 宮 2
| 士 658
| 書 137, 137A, D83, 618B, 625
| 書 行 省 819A
| 書 科 **137A**, 583, 618B
| 書 科 中 書 **137A**, 583, 618E
| 審 書 819A
| 所 120
| 祀 572
| 臺 S. 278
| 堂 131, 132
| 等 教 育 科 400, 407
| 等 科 568, 786
| 等 工 業 學 堂 607
| 等 班 717A
| 等 農 業 學 堂 602
| 等 商 船 學 堂 615
| 等 商 業 學 堂 611
| 等 實 業 學 堂 598, 617A
| 佐 659A

[xvii]

繙譯科 S. 832
　｜書房 S. 128 to 129c
旛纛司 120

Fan²

藩臬爾司 830c
　｜司 825
　｜臺 825

Fan⁴

飯銀處 497

Fang¹

方丈 573A
　｜客館 139
　｜伯 825
　｜音學堂 621, 626
　｜言肄習所 626A
坊官 796A

Fang²

防疫股 504B
　｜守尉 746
　｜禦 97K, 746, 748

Fei¹

妃 8
飛龍使 S. 88

Fen¹

分卡 S. 555
　｜教習官 514
　｜局局役 520
　｜區城勸局 761
　｜防通判 849A
　｜防同知 849
　｜府 849
　｜行 792
　｜巡兵備道 816, 844
　｜巡道 830B, 836, 838, 841, **844**
　｜會 772, S. 771
　｜科大學 584

分庫 S. 551B
　｜館 331
　｜管佐領 726
　｜類科 618B
　｜判所官 514
　｜別獎戀 981
　｜守道 844
　｜司 835A, 857
　｜倉 818
　｜纂 404A, 625A

Fen⁴

奮武驍尉 945
　｜武佐驍尉 945

Feng¹

封贈 945
　｜印 984

Feng⁴

奉常寺 933
　｜常寺卿 933
　｜常大夫 933
　｜常署 S. 376 to 394
　｜政大夫 945
　｜宸苑 90, 654
　｜宸苑卿 90
　｜直大夫 945
　｜直鹽務廳 S. 369A
　｜國 27A
　｜國將軍 26
　｜祀
　｜祀官 413A, 572, 860
　｜恩 27A
　｜恩將軍 27
　｜恩鎮國公 20, 873
　｜恩輔國公 21, 873
俸餉股 422A
　｜米 972
　｜搶房 493
　｜銀 972

Ha¹

Hai³

Hsiao¹

滑 防 隊 513
鎗 算 科 425
驍 騎 97B, E, 718, **730**, 746, 748
　| 騎 校 **727**, 746, 748, 874
　| 騎 營 97B, 718
　| 騎 參 領 722, 737

Hsiao³

小 京 官 **299**, 713, 766
　| 軍 機 129B
　| 九 處 743A
　| 方 脈 痘 疹 科 S. 240
　| 學 576
　| 學 教 員 618A, B
　| 學 教 育 科 400, 407
　| 學 簡 易 科 577
　| 學 辦 事 官 618A, B, 635C
　| 學 補 習 科 618B
　| 學 師 範 講 習 所 618A
　| 學 堂 **576**, 577A, 578, 579, 708, 709,
　　　　717A, B.
　| 學 堂 堂 長 619
　| 學 堂 完 全 科 577

Hsiao⁴

孝 廉 629B, 964
　| 廉 方 正 964
校 長 577B, 835A
　| 閱 大 臣 682
　| 閱 員 684, 685, 686, 687, 688, 689,
　　　　690, 691
　| 兵 科 700

Hsieh²

協 656B, D, **672**
　| 鎮 S. 752
　| 軍 校 **658**, 716
　| 辦 礮 912

Hsieh² (continued)

協 修 94, 177A, 180, 190, 393
　| 戎 S. 752
　| 揆 132
　| 理 221, 411, 547, 770A, 771A, 772,
　　　　774, 775, 783, 792, 811A, 874,
　　　　S. 108, 551C, 771
　| 理 關 防 事 務 85
　| 理 司 員 S. 108
　| 理 台 吉 874
　| 理 資 政 院 事 務 165A
　| 理 欽 天 監 天 文 算 學 事 務 232
　| 理 事 務 雲 麾 使 114
　| 領 670, 746
　| 領 官 670
　| 律 郎 389, 391
　| 標 749, 752
　| 辦 大 學 士 132
　| 台 752
　| 參 領 658
　| 都 統 658
　| 尉 799

Hsieh⁴

挈 壺 正 231

Hsien¹

先 鋒 官 696
　| 鋒 舢 板 707

Hsien²

咸 安 宮 官 學 87A
閒 散 863A, 732A, 874
　| 散 喇 嘛 918
　| 散 台 吉 863

Hsien³

洗 馬 929

Hsien⁴

現 食 俸 祿 977

巡 兵 521
| 捕 778, 800, 824
| 捕 中 營 800
| 捕 南 營 800
| 捕 北 營 800
| 捕 五 營 797, 800
| 捕 五 營 步 軍 統 領 800
| 捕 (東) 左 營 800
| 捕 (西) 右 營 800
| 使 S. 796A
| 視 鹽 政 御 史 835B
| 司 857
| 鹽 司 272
| 艇 弁 269
| 關 直 指 835B
| 關 御 史 835B
辭 常 576, 974
| 常 小 學 堂 576
勳 舊 726

Hsün⁴

況 749, 752F
訓 科 857
| 練 科 430A, 700B, S. 436C
| 練 近 畿 陸 軍 各 鎮 軍 官 695A
| 練 處 103A
| 部 618A, 658, 794, 850, 851A, 853,
855A, 857, 860
| 衙 857
馴 象 司 118
| 象 所 122

Hu¹

呼 畢 勒 罕 914A, 916
| 圖 克 圖 875, 916, 916A, 917

Hu³

虎 槍 739
| 槍 長 739
| 槍 副 長 739
| 槍 營 738, 739

Hu⁴

戶 籍 科 342A
| 籍 股 504D
| 部 349, 932
| 部 造 幣 總 廠 551
| 部 銀 行 542
鵠 房 80
護 局 夫 779, 780, 781
| 軍 734, 741, 742
| 軍 校 734, 741, 742
| 軍 官 663
| 軍 參 領 734, 741
| 軍 統 領 734, 742
| 軍 營 97A, D, 733, 734, 734A, 741,
741A, 742
| 路 巡 營 784
| 目 665, 669, 674, 677, 702, 706B, C
| 兵 665, 669, 672, 674, 677, 702, 704,
705, 706A, B, C, 812A
| 兵 長 696
| 衛 45, 97E, 812A
| 衛 股 504D
| 衛 馬 隊 812A
| 衛 營 97E
| 勇 520, S. 753

Hua¹

花 翎 99, 950A
| 翎 侍 衛 99

Hua²

譁 商 地 方 商 會 774
| 商 賽 會 773
| 商 商 會 774

Hua⁴

化 分 碳 質 局 S. 464A
| 分 碳 質 所 464A
| 學 科 771
| 學 門 589
| 身 914

K'an¹

看護人 437A
｜守 514, 766B
｜守長 514, 766B
｜守所 221, 766B, 767
｜守所長 221, 767
｜守所協理 221
｜守所官 221, 767
堪布 915B

K'an³

刊印所 654A

K'ang²

扛轎 850

Kao¹

高等教育會議所 409
｜等檢察廳 758C, 762, **763**
｜等檢察分廳 764A
｜等專門學堂 653
｜等軍法會審 S. 702
｜等小學堂 576. **577A**, 578, 717A,
｜等學堂 **583**, 592A, 621, 627, 717A
｜等巡警學堂 522, 621A
｜等醫學堂 S. 621 to 621B
｜等科 568, 766B, 786
｜等工業學堂 608
｜等農學堂 ｝
｜等農務學堂 ｝603, 770B
｜等農業學堂 ｝
｜等班 653, 788
｜等商船學堂 616
｜等商業學堂 612
｜等審判廳 758, 759
｜等審判分廳 759A, 760B
｜等實業學堂 598, 598C, 787
膏伙 629A

Kao⁴

誥命 945

K'ao³

考查政治館 150
｜察政治大臣 920
｜察海軍大臣 923
｜察憲政大臣 920A
｜察股 805A
｜察陸軍大臣 923A
｜察財政 922. 922A
｜察財政大臣 922
｜績科 426, S. 335 to 338, 123, 436A
｜核處 822A
｜核專科 160, 822A
｜官 629B, S. 758F
｜功 520
｜功科 426A, 698
｜工官 185H
｜工局 487
｜工處 514
｜工司 306
｜功司 336
｜試 628, 652C
｜驗處 771A

K'en³

墾務局 777, 782
｜務分局 777
｜務科 816A
｜務大臣 778, 809
｜**務總局** 777, 782

Ko²

戈戟司 122
革輅管理 124
｜職留任 976
格致科 589, 652E
｜致科大學 589
閣 104A
｜丞 S. 128 to 149
｜學 133
｜老 131

Kua⁴

掛號分局 776A

Kuan¹

官 長 707
｜ 制 大 臣 819A
｜ 錢 局 549
｜ 房 租 82
｜ 學 87, 87A, B, C. 717. 961
｜ 學 生 961
｜ 醫 院 517, 859
｜ 報 局 158, 859
｜ 報 書 局 S. 859
｜ 書 局 859
｜ 聽 799
｜ 聽 簿 記 374A
｜ 鹽 採 逿 局 818
｜ 銀 號 549
｜ 印 刷 局 S. 859
｜ 運 總 局 818
關 卡 909
｜ 防 85, 984
｜ 防 事 務 處 ｜ 85
｜ 防 衙 門 ｜
｜ 稅 學 門 592
｜ 大 使 850, 851A
｜ 督 842
觀 察 838, 844
｜ 象 台 166

Kuan³

管 旗 章 京 874
｜ 旗 副 章 京 874
｜ 駕 副 269
｜ 駕 二 副 269
｜ 駕 官 269
｜ 駕 三 副 269
｜ 織 染 局 大 臣 96
｜ 卷 書 記 163C
｜ 河 同 知 849
｜ 轄 番 役 81

管 學 大 臣 574
｜ 課 官 640
｜ 庫 司 事 709, 711A
｜ 股 委 員 163B
｜ 理 124, 654A, S. 102 to 102A
｜ 理 欽 天 監 事 務 224
｜ 理 欽 天 監 天 文 算 學 事 務 232
｜ 理 清 漪 園 等 事 處 務 90
｜ 理 傳 習 所 788
｜ 理 軍 諮 處 事 務 184C, S. 184A
｜ 理 奉 宸 苑 事 務 90
｜ 理 漢 文 文 案 稅 務 司 258
｜ 理 河 道 258
｜ 理 咸 安 宮 官 學 事 務 87A
｜ 理 憲 政 編 查 事 務 151
｜ 理 學 部 事 務 276, 395A
｜ 理 日 本 遊 學 生 監 督 處 652, S. 652
｜ 理 國 子 監 大 臣 412A
｜ 理 工 程 處 事 務 95
｜ 理 陸 軍 貴 胄 學 堂 事 務 713A
｜ 理 陸 軍 部 事 務 276, 421, S. 420B
｜ 理 某 宮 事 務 104D
｜ 理 上 駟 院 事 務 88
｜ 理 太 醫 院 事 務 234
｜ 理 造 辦 處 事 務 86
｜ 理 武 備 院 事 務 89
｜ 理 武 英 殿 修 書 處 事 務 94
｜ 理 燒 造 磁 瓦 官 571
｜ 理 御 藥 房 事 務 92
｜ 理 樂 部 事 務 387A
｜ 理 銀 庫 事 務 72
｜ 理 御 茶 膳 房 事 房 91
｜ 理 御 船 處 事 務 93
｜ 理 御 鳥 槍 處 事 務 93A
｜ 理 御 書 處 事 務 94A
｜ 理 員 167B, 172, 652
｜ 理 圓 明 園 暢 春 園 事 務 90
｜ 輪 正 269
｜ 輪 副 269
｜ 糧 通 判 849A
｜ 馬 正 委 員 711A
｜ 馬 副 委 員 711A

[XXXV]

Liao⁴

料估所 460A

Lien²

廉 856
| 訪 830
| 俸司 358
| 捕 857

Lien⁴

練軍 753, S. 753
| 軍糧餉股 S. 825 to 826
| 習所 703
| 習營 756
| 餉局 S. 825 to 826
| 兵處 416, **936A**

Lin²

林學科 603
| 學門 590
| 業科 601, 602
遴材科 424
臨朝 176C
| 時考試 631
| 時代理公使 331
| 時軍法會審 S. 702
| 雍頌諭 957
麟趾 S. 191

Lin³

廩監生 959
| 貢生 957
| 膳生 629A
| 生 577C, 629A, 631

Ling²

陵寢 569
| 寢祭祀供應官 571A
| 寢駐防 571, 743B
| 寢防禦 571, 743B
| 寢副總管 571

陵寢翼長 571
| 寢管理燒造磚瓦官 571A
| 寢司工匠 571A
| 寢總管 571
翎枝 950
靈盞耶 230

Ling³

領閣事 104B
| 班 129B, 790
| 班章京上行走 129B
| 辦 162B, 493, 790
| 辦處 493, 879
| 催 96, 97E, 729, **746**, 748, 799, **874**
| 隊大臣 865
| 事 320, 332
| 事府 332
| 事館 332
| 事署 332
| 事官 320, 332
| 侍衛府 98
| 侍衛內大臣 98
| 選 834

Ling⁴

令 856
| 長 856
| 尹 856

Liu²

留館 201

Liu⁴

六局 850
| 科 210B
| 品庫掌 86, 89
| 品司庫 77
| 品贊禮官 382B
| 品讀祝官 382B
| 品苑丞 90
| 部 274
| 色 850

Pan⁴

牛 日 小 學 科 618B
｜ 日 學 堂 579
｜ 箇 佐 領 726A
辦 事 處 171
｜ 事 官 425B, 618A, B, 623, 635C
｜ 事 司 員 882
｜ 事 室 654A
｜ 事 大 臣 879A, 880, 905
｜ 事 員 525B

P'an⁴

判 文 林 領 事 S. 192

Pang¹

戥 掌 印 308
｜ 掌 印 上 行 走 308
｜ 主 稿 308
｜ 主 稿 上 行 走 308
｜ 領 班 129B
｜ 領 班 率 京 上 行 走 129B
｜ 辦 102, 160A, 162B, 246, 267, 493,
535, 697, 700, 779, 780, 781, 783,
805A, 811A, S. 335 to 338, 368A.
373
｜ 辦 翼 尉 799
｜ 辦 稅 務 大 臣 243
｜ 辦 大 臣 879A, 907, S. 907
｜ 辦 土 藥 統 稅 事 務 大 臣 554
｜ 辦 延 吉 邊 務 大 臣 817
｜ 帶 S. 753
｜ 提 調 145, 245, 310, 393, 535, 697,
S. 369A, 373
｜ 坐 辦 S. 826, 826
｜ 總 辦 147, 783, S. 155, 825 to 826
｜ 總 書 記 163C
｜ 統 官 706A

Pang³

榜 眼 629C

Pao (Po)¹

包 衣 47, 97, 737
｜ 衣 參 領 48
｜ 衣 佐 領 49
｜ 衣 統 領 S. 97

Pao³

保 安 科 343A
｜ 儲 科 427, S. 424
｜ 舉 962A
｜ 惠 司 461A
｜ 姆 575
｜ 存 會 654
寶 984
｜ 星 953
｜ 泉 局 366
｜ 源 局 460A

Pao⁴

豹 尾 班 侍 衞 99
報 房 435C

P'ao⁴

礮 匠 680
｜ 驍 騎 737, 716
｜ 領 催 746
｜ 兵 科 428, 686, 716, S. 652E
｜ 兵 科 校 閱 員 686
｜ 手 850
｜ 手 首 領 269
｜ 隊 656A, F, 659, 670, 714
｜ 隊 科 430
｜ 隊 專 門 學 堂 714
｜ 隊 協 領 官 670

Pei¹

貝 勒 18, 27A, 863, 873
｜ 子 19, 27A. 873

Pei³

北 廠 366B
| 監 457. 766
| 京 儲 蓄 銀 行 548
| 路 79C
| 路 捕 盗 廳 同 知 795D
| 營 800
| 洋 將 弁 學 堂 711B
| 洋 醫 學 堂 715A
| 洋 大 臣 476, 789. **820B**
| 洋 大 學 堂 S. 584

Pei⁴

備 查 壇 廟 大 臣 106
| 補 兵 680

P'ei²

陪 祀 冠 軍 使 115·
| 審 官 812A

P'ei⁴

配 戍 科 425.

Pen³

本 科 252, 602, 603, 607, 611, 612,
　　615, 618C, 623A, 627, 787.
　　S. 584
| 房 138

P'eng²

棚 656B, F, 706

Pi³

比 877A
| 阿 哈 拉 克 齊 877A
| 部 438
筆 帖 式 70, 76, 104D, 123, 201A. 202,
　　203, 204, 210, 212A. B, 229,
　　230, 231, **293**, 295, 713. 754.
　　798
| 政 293

Pi⁴

弼 德 院 S. 127
陛 下 1
畢 都 里 雅 諾 爾 盟 872A
| 業 考 試 631
秘 書 長 167B, S. 128 to 149
| 閣 S. 191
| 書 科 422, S. 422, 832
| 書 官 167B, 755, 756
| 書 官 補 756
| 書 廊 199
| 書 廳 167B. S. 128 to 149
| 書 員 805, 822, S. 369A
幣 制 局 S. 373
| 制 調 查 局 373, S. 373

P'i¹

批 本 處 138
| 驗 大 使 835A
| 驗 所 大 使 835A

P'i²

皮 庫 77
| 匠 680

Piao¹

標 656B, E

P'iao⁴

票 簽 處 138
| 莊 550A

Pieh²⁽⁴⁾

別 駕 849A, 851A
| 科 568, 617, 623, 627, S. 623

Pien¹

編 案 處 180
| 查 處 458, S. 458
| 查 館 150A, 151
| 輯 410, 488
| 輯 科 158, 541

梳頭管理 124
樞密院 S. 128 to 149

Shu²

淑人 945

Shu³

署 see also Shu⁴
| 正 384B, 389, 391
| 丞 389, 391
| 名 129, S. 128 to 149
| 州 855
| 屬 廳 854

Shu⁴

庶常館 201
| 吉士 201, 593c, 629c
| 子 929
| 務長 641, 771A
| 務處 155, 163D, 181, 514, S. 373
| 務科 167B, 399, 411, 422, 541, 652,
    755, 766B, 787, 811A, S. 368A,
    422, 436E
| 務官 652I, see 庶務員
| 務所 769
| 務司 306, 466. 480
| 務提調 522, 641
| 務廳 S. 369A
| 務總辦 181
| 務委員 163D, 252, 523. 641
| 務員 103B, 310, 374A, 409, 410,
    525A, B, 526, 578, 618A, 641,
    S. 167B, 458, 623
署 see also Shu³
| 長 S. 376 to 394
| 前鋒校 738
| 親軍校 100
| 副稅務司 267
| 護軍參領 741
| 理 979
| 理三等總巡 268
| 理頭等總巡 268

醫班領 99
| 稅務司 267

Shua¹

刷印匠 712
| 印手 103c

Shuai⁴

帥 820, 821

Shuang¹

雙龍寶星 953
| 龍嵌十字記章 437A
| 眼花翎 950

Shui³

水產學校 602A
| 產科 599
| 產業科 602
| 利局 S. 859
| 利通判 849A
| 利同知 849
| 陸師提督 750B
| 部 460
| 師 749, **756**
| 師巡船管帶官 805A
| 師巡防隊 707
| 師學堂 757, 757A
| 師提督 750B. 756B
| 師營 747, 756c
| 手首領 269

Shui⁴

稅課分司大使 850
| 課司大使 850, 855A
| 課司 354
| 關 909
| 務處 241, S. 242
| 務處會辦大臣 S. 242
| 務專科 568
| 務學堂 252, 621A

[li]

Tao⁴

道 213, 815, **838**, 838A
｜ 正 573B
｜ 紀 573B
｜ 紀司 S. 573B
｜ 紀司道紀 573B
｜ 紀司副都紀 S. 573B
｜ 敎 573
｜ 會 573B
｜ 錄司 573B, S. 573B
｜ 臺 **838**, 844
｜ 員 658
稻田塲 90A

Tê² (4).

得木奇 918
德國文學門 587
｜ 木齊 918
｜ 文科 625

T'ê¹

特別高等專門學堂 653
｜ 任國務大臣 S.. 128 to 149

Têng¹

登賢書 956
｜ 仕郞 945
｜ 仕佐郞 945
燈船執事人 272
｜ 船主 272
｜ 船大副 272
｜ 塔處 272

Ti³

邸 13

Ti⁴

地質學門 589
｜ 鄕 932

地方檢察廳 762, 764
｜ 方檢察分廳 765A
｜ 方官 525B, 856B
｜ 方看守所 766B
｜ 方商會 774
｜ 方審判廳 758, 760
｜ 方審判分廳 760A, 761A
｜ 方自治 **525**, 525A, 526
｜ 官 349
｜ 會 932
弟子員 960
帝匹 S. 2
第一人 S. 629C
｜ 一科 177
｜ 一股 247
｜ 一班 711A
｜ 一廳 184F
｜ 一庭 218A, 219A
｜ 二科 178
｜ 二股 248
｜ 二班 711A
｜ 二廳 184F
｜ 二庭 218A, 219A
｜ 三股 249
｜ 三廳 184F
｜ 三庭 218A
｜ 四股 250
｜ 四廳 184F
｜ 四庭 218A
｜ 五廳 184F
｜ 巴 906, 912
遞事官 149
｜ 事員 103B

T'i²

提舉 835A
｜ 舉閣事 104B
｜ 法司使 ⎫ 758A, 810, 830, 830B, **831**,
｜ 法使 ⎬ 839
｜ 法司 810, 826A, **831**A
｜ 刑按察使司 830

殿 試 628, 629c
| 元 S. 629c
電 政 局 790
| 政 司 478, 790
| 氣 專 門 學 堂 785A
| 氣 學 門 591
| 氣 化 學 科 608
| 氣 科 607, 608
| 信 隊 103D
| 話 局 791
| 話 分 局 791
| 話 總 局 791
| 報 局 790

T'ien¹

天 津 銀 錢 總 廠 551
| 下 母 S. 2
| 官 S. 333A
| 曹 333
| 子 1
| 王 S. 1
| 文 科 230
| 文 算 學 232
| 文 臺 經 理 官 593

T'ien²

田 賦 科 S. 825 to 826
| 賦 司 352

Ting¹

丁 憂 979

Ting³

頂 戴 964, 965, 966
| 戴 榮 身 978
| 子 965

Ting⁴

定 埠 913
| 邊 參 贊 大 臣 879
| 邊 左 副 將 軍 879

T'ing¹

聽 講 員 622
| 事 780, 781
廳 795, **846**, S. 369A
| 長 184G, 760, S. 128 to 149
| 丞 759, 760

T'ing²

廷 則 216
| 試 652c
| 尉 937A
| 尉 少 卿 937A
庭 218A, 219A
| 長 759, 760, S. 218, 218A, 219, 2

To¹

多 羅 貝 勒 18, 873
| 羅 格 格 35
| 羅 郡 王 17, 873
| 羅 額 駙 15

T'ou²

投 票 監 察 員 172
| 票 管 理 員 172
頭 品 頂 戴 966
| 等 差 官 778
| 等 鈴 子 手 268
| 等 出 使 大 臣 313
| 等 幫 辦 267
| 等 參 贊 316
| 等 總 巡 268
| 等 通 譯 官 319
| 等 驗 貨 268

Tsa²

雜 務 委 員 251, 712
| 務 官 644
| 務 員 644

Ts'un²

存古學堂 621B, 627A

Tsung¹

宗正 58, 59
｜ 正寺 S. 56
｜ 正少卿 S. 58, 59
｜ 丞 S. 62
｜ 卿 57
｜ 學 717
｜ 人 60, 61
｜ 人府 56
｜ 令 57
｜ 女 35A
｜ 伯 933, S. 57
｜ 師 827A
｜ 室 39, 215A, 218A, 219A, 759, 944
｜ 室公 944
｜ 室覺羅八旗 717
｜ 室覺羅八旗高等學堂 583B, 717A
｜ 室侍衛 99
椶毯管理 124
綜察科 S. 431
｜ 課科 S. 479

Tsung³

總查 778
｜ 鎮 S. 751
｜ 承 93A
｜ 稽查 653
｜ 稽察守衛事宜大臣 102
｜ 教習 252, 712
｜ 教習官 252, 514
｜ 監督 525A, 529, 633

總檢察廳 222, 762
｜ 檢察廳廳丞 222
｜ 檢察分廳 763A, S. 222
｜ 執法官 672
｜ 局差役 520
｜ 局護勇 520
｜ 局書識 520
｜ 軍械官 668
｜ 軍需官 673
｜ 軍醫官 675
｜ 核 153, 162A, 535
｜ 核官 535, 755
｜ 核官制大臣 819A
｜ 核委員 780
｜ 核員 153, 535
｜ 憲 207
｜ 行 792
｜ 巡 268
｜ 巡官 520
｜ 會 772, S. 771
｜ 匯處 796C, S. 825 to 826
｜ 議事會 525A
｜ 戎 751
｜ 督奏摺 493
｜ 堪布 917
｜ 庫 S. 551B
｜ 管 87A, 97E, 570, 571, 748, 755, 801A, 877A, 873
｜ 管官學事務 87A
｜ 管理處 792
｜ 管六庫事務 77
｜ 管內務府大臣 76
｜ 管收掌 766
｜ 大臣 S. 551B
｜ 管太監衛宮殿監督領侍 50
｜ 管太監衛宮殿監副侍 52
｜ 管太監衛宮殿監正侍 51
｜ 管電政 790
｜ 工程司 783

Tsung⁴

Ts'ung²

Tu¹

都察院 206
｜察院副都御史 S. 821
｜察院右都御史 S. 820
｜轉 835
｜轉運使 834
｜戎 S. 752A to F
｜闈 752c
｜老爺 213
｜事 211, 212B, 826
｜事司 451
｜事廳 211, 826
｜水司 460A
｜水監 820D
｜司 752c, 800
｜蠢 S. 278
｜典簿 220
｜統 **719**, 719A, 755, 897, 898
｜尉 945
｜虞司 80
｜御史 207
｜迴 835
督撫 821B
｜撫司道 837
｜撫衙門幕職 822
｜學局 407
｜學使者 827A
｜理水利通判 849A
｜糧道 836
｜糧通判 849A
｜練處近畿一帶各鎮大臣 695A
｜練處 656, 695
｜練公所 695
｜練大臣 695A
｜辦 188, 695, 754, 783, 812A, 818
｜辦吉林邊務大臣 817
｜辦川滇邊務大臣 845A
｜辦訓練近畿陸軍各鎮大臣 695A
｜辦墾務大臣 778, 899
｜辦邊務大臣 817, 845A

督辦稅務大臣 242
｜辦大臣 242, 369, 553, 778, 817, 818, 899
｜辦鹽政大臣 369
｜辦鹽政處 369A
｜辦鹽務大臣 818
｜辦土藥統稅事務大臣 553
｜標 **749**, 752J, 824
｜捕同知 849
｜操 521
｜催處 822A
｜催所 493
｜隊官 661

Tu²

獨任推事 760, 761
｜立協 672
讀祝官 79, 382B, S. 376 to 394

Tu⁴

度支科 402, 796c, 822
｜支部 274, **346**B, 932, 932A
｜支部簿記講習所 374A
｜支司 808
｜支司使 808
｜支大臣 S. 128 to 149

T'u²

圖記 984
｜志館 S. 344
｜畫館 485, **654**, 654A
｜稿繪靈科 607, 608
｜伯特國王 906
｜書處 **157**
｜書科 828
｜書館經理官 593
｜宝 167B

T'u³

土州 861
｜府 861

通官 392
| 判 583, 625, 658, 713, 794, **849A**, 850A, 852, 854, 882, 892
| 商各關 267
| 商口岸 253
| 商大臣 820B
| 事 778, 779, 781
| 守 849A
| 贊官 413A

T'ung²

同知 795A, to D, **849**, 849A, 850A, 852, 853A, 854, 861A, 894
| 進士出身 593C, 629C, 631
| 轉 835A
| 文館 311, 930A
| 文寺 940
| 文寺卿 940
| 文寺少卿 940
童生 629
銅元局 859

T'ung³

統計局 154B, S. 128 to 129
| 計處 161, **162**, 347, 364, 385, 454, 470, 489, 796B, S. 108, 431, 436I
| 計科 163B, 429
| 計股 504A
| 制巡洋長江艦隊 S. 756
| 制官 661
| 捐局 859
| 領 { 661, 706, 707, 734, 735, 742,
| 領官 { 797, S. 97, 753
| 稅分卡 S. 555
| 稅分局 555
| 稅總局 552

Tzu¹

資政院 **164**, 165A, 167
| 政院議員 167

資政院幫辦事務 165A
| 政院參議 165A
| 奉大夫 945
諮議局 168
| 議局籌辦處 173
| 議官 182, **302**, 405, **423A**, 535, S. 186, 369A
| 議廳 805
| 議員 159B, 652
輜重兵科 428, 716
| 重隊 656A, 659
| 重隊科 430
| 兵科校閱員 688

Tzu³

子 944
紫韁 948
| 禁城內騎馬 949
| 色 984
| 薇閣 S. 137A
| 薇郎 S. 137

Tzu⁴

自治 **525**, 525A, B, 526, 527, **527A**
| 治監督 525A, B, 526
| 治職員 525A, B, 526
| 治籌辦處 527
| 治行政 526
| 治總監督 525A
| 治委員 526
| 治研究所 518, 527A

Tz'u²

祠祭司 376A, 381
| 祭署 S. 376 to 394
| 部 S. 376
詞林 S. 193C to 200C
| 部 376
磁庫 77

Tz'u⁴

次等 658
刺史 851, 855

Yin²

銀 錢 所 S. 825 to 826
｜ 錢 總 廠 551
｜ 鑄 局 S. 128 to 149
｜ 鑄 局 藝 師 ⎱ S. 128 to 149
｜ 鑄 局 藝 士 ⎰
｜ 行 542, 542A, **550A**, 792
｜ 行 及 保 險 學 門 592
｜ 行 講 習 所 568
｜ 行 學 堂 548
｜ 號 549, 550A
｜ 庫 71, 72, 77, 497
｜ 糧 莊 頭 處 78A
｜ 臺 928
｜ 元 局 859

Yin³

引 見 970

Yin⁴

印 984
｜ 務 泰 領 721
｜ 務 章 京 724
｜ 務 處 497
｜ 花 稅 局 S. 825 to 826
｜ 刷 科 158
｜ 刷 局 368, S. 859
｜ 刷 員 103B
廕 生 958

Ying¹

英 國 文 學 門 587
｜ 文 科 627
應 用 化 學 科 608
｜ 用 化 學 門 591
廳 房 80

Ying²

營 103D, **656**C, F. 703, 706, 707, 749,
752B, S. 749, 753
｜ 官 S. 753

營 轄 司 345, 460A
｜ 造 處 82
｜ 造 司 82
｜ 總 737, 741, 753
｜ 務 處 706D, 805A, 824, 824A
｜ 務 刑 名 822
｜ 業 科 343A
｜ 業 股 504D
｜ 運 科 S. 368A

Yu¹

優 級 師 範 科 592B
｜ 級 師 範 選 科 618C
｜ 級 師 範 學 堂 618, 618B
｜ 監 生 959
｜ 貢 582A, 631
｜ 貢 生 628, 629A
｜ 廩 生 582A, 631
｜ 等 652E, 716

Yu²

遊 擊 752B, 800
｜ 緝 公 所 ⎱ S. 800
｜ 緝 隊 ⎰
｜ 脚 僧 道 850
｜ 徼 S. 796A
｜ 方 僧 道 850
｜ 府 752B
｜ 學 生 監 督 652, 652B
｜ 學 生 監 督 處 652
｜ 學 日 本 高 等 五 校 預 科 S. 652
｜ 戎 752B
｜ 美 學 務 處 652A
｜ 美 肄 業 館 652A
郵 政 分 局 273
｜ 政 副 總 辦 273
｜ 政 司 479, S. 479
｜ 政 總 局 850
｜ 政 總 辦 273, S. 273
｜ 傳 科 822, 839A
｜ 傳 部 274, 472

院 長 S. 128 to 149
| 判 236, 236A
| 使 235, S. 128 to 149
| 簹 575

Yüeh⁴

粵 海 關 部 833A
| 桂 科 535
樂 兵 679
| 部 387
| 生 389
閲 卷 大 臣 629c
| 報 所 486A
| 書 室 654A

Yün²

芸 臺 S. 191
雲 騎 尉 944, 944E
| 麾 使 114, 123, 125
| 司 937A

Yun⁴

運 籌 科 699B
| 籌 司 1851
| 副 835A
| 庫 大 使 835A
| 判 835A
| 輸 科 699
| 司 835
| 同 835A

SOURCES OF INFORMATION.

Baranoff (Captain of Cavalry of the Zaamur District) : " Barga and Khalkha " : " Researches in Manchuria and Mongolia "; second volume, " Mongolia." Harbin, 1905.

By the same author : " Dictionary of Mongolian Expressions " (11th volume of " Researches in Manchuria and Mongolia.") Harbin, 1907.

A. A. Batorsky : " Short Military, Statistical and Descriptive Treatise on Mongolia "; Parts I and II (originally published in the " Magazine of Geographical, Topographical and Statistical Researches in Asia," Nos. 37 and 48); edition issued by the Instruction Committee of the General Staff. St. Petersburg, 1889 and 1891.

V. V. Hagelstrom, (Student-interpreter of the Imperial Russian Legation, Peking): " Confucianism in 1906–1907 : The Descendant of Confucius, K'ung Ling-i." St. Petersburg, 1909.

By the same author : " A Short Description of the Judicial Establishments of China " (published in the " Chinese Good News " of the 28th May, 1909, issues Nos. 7 and 8).

John Zakharow (teacher of Manchu at the Imperial University of St. Petersburg): " Complete Manchu-Russian Dictionary." St. Petersburg, 1875.

The Monk Iakhinf (Bichurine): Civil and Moral Aspect of China." St. Petersburg, 1848.

By the same author : " Description of Peking " (translated from the Chinese). Peking, 1906.

A manuscript: " Sketch of the Political Organization of China."

A. von Landesen and P. Shkurkine (active members of the " Society of Russian Orientalists ") : " Reference Book of China "; volume I, " Section of General Information." Harbin, 1909.

Stephan Lipovtzev : " Institutes of the Chinese Colonial Office " (translated from the Manchu); two volumes. St. Petersburg, 1828.

Z. Matussovsky : " Geographical Review of the Chinese Empire." St. Petersburg, 1888.

Archimandrite Palladium (late Chief of the Russian Ecclesiastical Mission at Peking) and P. S. Popoff (Senior Interpreter of the Imperial Russian Legation at Peking) : "Chinese-Russian Dictionary "; two volumes. Peking, 1888.

A. Pozdneef : "Mongolia and the Mongols. Results of a Journey to Mongolia, 1892–1893." Volume I ; Diary and Itinerary, 1892. St. Petersburg, 1896. Volume II ; Diary and Itinerary, 1893. St. Petersburg, 1898.

D. Pokotiloff : " Ou T'ai and its Past " (Memoirs of the Imperial Russian Geographical Society, section of General Geography, 22nd volume, No. 2). St. Petersburg, 1893.

Polumordvinoff (Captain of Cavalry) : " The Chinese Army Organization " (" Researches in Manchuria, Mongolia and China," issue No. 21). Harbin, 1908.

By the same author : " The Chinese Army : Military Administration and Organization " (" Researches in Manchuria, Mongolia and China "; issue No. 22). Harbin, 1908.

By the same author : " The Chinese Army ; Troops of the Hsün-fang-tui Category ; Military Equipment" ("Researches in Manchuria, Mongolia and China "; issue No. 26). Harbin, 1908.

P. S. Popoff : " The Central Government Organization of China and Branches of the Administration." St. Petersburg, 1903. Supplement, 1909.

Colonel Putiata: " Armed Forces of China and the Principles of Military Science as Interpreted by the Ancients " (" Magazine of Geographical, Topographical and Statistical Researches in Asia "; issue No. 39). St. Petersburg, 1889.

By the same author : " China " (" Magazine of Geographical, Topographical and Statistical Researches in Asia "; issue No. 59). St. Petersburg, 1895.

A. Spitzyne: " Administrative Organization of Manchuria " (article in the " Messenger of Asia "; No. 2, October, 1909).

V. N. von Sharenberg-Shorlemer (First Lieutenant) : " Short Dictionary of Military and Naval Words and Expressions of Contemporaneous Chinese." Peking, 1910.

大 清 光 緒 新 法 令 Ta⁴ Ch'ing¹ Kuang¹ Hsü⁴ Hsin¹ Fa⁴ Ling⁴ : Collection of New Laws and Commands Issued during the Reign of the Emperor Kuang Hsu (during the Period 1901–1908). 20 册 Ts'ê⁴, volumes. Edition issued by the 商 務 印 書 館 Shang¹ Wu⁴ Yin⁴ Shu¹ Kuan³, Shanghai, 1908.

大 清 宣 統 新 法 令 Ta⁴ Ch'ing¹ Hsüan¹ T'ung³ Hsin¹ Fa⁴ Ling⁴ : Collection of New Laws and Commands Issued during the Reign of Hsüan T'ung (during the period 1909–1911). 27 册 Ts'ê⁴, volumes (in course of issue). Edition issued by the 商 務 印 書 館 Shang¹ Wu⁴ Yin⁴ Shu¹ Kuan³, Shanghai, 1909–1911.

康 南 海 官 制 議 K'ang¹ Nan² Hai³ Kuan¹ Chih⁴ I⁴ : Discussion of Ranks, by K'ang Yu-wei. Edition issued by the 廣 智 書 局 Kuang³ Chih⁴ Shu¹ Chü², Shanghai, 1906.

清 國 新 政 法 Ch'ing¹ Kuo² Hsin¹ Chêng⁴ Fa⁴ : Administrative Organization of the Chinese Empire ; second edition. Issued by the 廣 智 書 局 Kuang³ Chih⁴ Shu¹ Chü², Shanghai, 1906.

清國新改治組織通表 Ch'ing[1] Kuo[2] Hsin[1] Kai[3] Chih[4] Tsu[3] Chih[4] T'ung[1] Piao[3] : Table of New Political Organizations of China. Compiled in a form indicated by 胡維德 Hu[2] Wei[2]-tê[2], Chinese Minister to Tokyo, 1909.

欽定大清會典 Ch'in[1] Ting[4] Ta[4] Ch'ing[1] Hui[4] Tien[3] : Collected Institutes of the Ta Ch'ing Dynasty (approved by the Emperor).

欽定經商新律十種 Ch'in[1] Ting[4] Ching[1] Shang[1] Hsin[1] Lü[4] Shih[2] Chung[3] : New Commercial Laws Sanctioned by the Emperor, in 10 Categories. Edition issued by the 北新譯書局 Pei[3] Hsin[1] I[4] Shu[1] Chü[2], Peking, 1906.

欽定巡警新章 Ch'in[1] Ting[4] Hsün[2] Ching[3] Hsin[1] Chang[1] : New Police Regulations Sanctioned by the Emperor. Two 册 Ts'ê[4], volumes.

欽定章程類纂 Ch'in[1] Ting[4] Chang[1] Ch'êng[2] Lei[4] Tsuan[3] : Collection of Rules and Regulations Sanctioned by the Emperor. Five 册 Ts'ê[4], volumes. Edition issued by the 北新譯書局 Pei[3] Hsin[1] I[4] Shu[1] Chü[2], Peking, 1908.

職官一覽表 Chih[2] Kuan[1] I[1] Lan[3] Piao[3] : Table of Officials. A periodical publication issued by the 作新社分局 Tso[4] Hsin[1] Shê[4] Fên[1] Chü[2]. Nos. 6 to 13. Peking, 1909–1911.

支那政府組織 Chih[1] Na[4] Chêng[4] Fu[3] Tsu[3] Chih[4] : The Government Organization of China. Edition issued by the 北支那每日新聞社 Pei[3] Chih[1] Na[4] Mei[3] Jih[4] Hsin[1] Wên[2] Shê[4], Tientsin, 1904.

中國大官一覽表 Chung[1] Kuo[2] Ta[4] Kuan[1] I[1] Lan[2] Piao[3] : Table of the Higher Officials of China. A periodical publication formerly issued by the 作新社分局 Tso[4] Hsin[1] She[4] Fên[1] Chü[2]. Nos. 1 to 5. Peking, 1909.

中國地理學教科書 Chung[1] Kuo[2] Ti[4] Li[3] Hsüeh[2] Chiao[4] K'o[1] Shu[1] : Manual of the Geography of the Chinese Empire, by 屠寄 T'u[2] Chi[4]. Third edition. Issued by the 商務印書館 Shang[1] Wu[4] Yin[4] Shu[1] Kuan[3], Shanghai, 1906.

[lxxvii]

中國鐵路指南 Chung[1] Kuo[2] T'ieh[3] Lu[4] Chih[3] Nan[2]: Chinese Railway Handbook. Edition issued by the 廣智書局 Kuang[3] Chih[4] Shu[1] Chü[2], Shanghai, 1905.

政治官報 Chêng[4] Chih[4] Kuan[1] Pao[4]: The Peking Gazette, Peking, 1907–1910.

Ball, J. Dyer: "Things Chinese or Notes connected with China." Fourth Edition. Shanghai, 1903.

Betz, Dr.: "Die Provinzialbehörden" (cf. infra Hauer).

Giles, Herbert A. (H.B.M's. Consul at Ningpo): "A Chinese-English Dictionary." London, 1892.

By the same author: "A Glossary of Reference on Subjects connected with the Far East. Third Edition. Shanghai, 1900.

Gory, Jules (Chinese Customs): "Notes on the Chinese Government Bank." Peking, 1908.

De Groot, J. J. M. (*Ph. D.*): "The Religious System of China, Its Ancient Forms, Evolution, History and Present Aspect. Manners, Customs and Social Institutions connected therewith." Volume III (Book 1, Disposal of the Dead: Part III, The Grave). Leide, 1897.

Hauer, Dr.: "Pekinger Zentralreigierung" (Mittheilungen des Seminars für Orientalischen Sprachen an der Königlichen Friedrich-Wilhelms-Universität zu Berlin. Jahrgang XII. Erste Abtheilung: Ostasiatische Studien. Berlin, 1909).

Hoang, P. Pierre: "Exposé du Commerce public du Sel." Chang-hai, 1898. (Variétés Sinologiques No. 15).

By the same author: "Mélanges sur l'Administration," Chang-hai, 1902. (Variétés Sinologiques No. 21).

Jernigan, T. R. (Ex-Consul-General of the United States of America at Shanghai, China): "China's Business Methods and Policy." Shanghai, 1904.

[lxxviii]

Kennelly: " M. Richard's Comprehensive Geography of the Chinese Empire and Dependencies (Translated into English, revised and enlarged by——). Shanghai, 1908.

Mayers, William Frederick: "The Chinese Government." A Manual of Chinese Titles categorically arranged and explained, with an appendix. Third Edition (revised by G. Playfair). Shanghai, 1896.

Mayers, S. F. (Assistant Chinese Secretary, H.B.M's. Legation, Peking): " List of the Higher Metropolitan and Provincial Authorities of China." (Compiled by the Chinese Secretaries H.B.M's. Legation, Peking). Shanghai, 1908.

Morse, Hosea Ballou (A. B., Harvard; Member R. A. S., England; Commissioner of Customs and Statistical Secretary, I. G. of Customs, China): " The Trade and Administration of the Chinese Empire." Shanghai, 1908.

Okamoto: " A Chinese Pronunciation Dictionary in Peking Dialect." Fifth Edition. Tokyo, 1907.

Parker, E. H.: "China. Her History, Diplomacy and Commerce from the Earliest Times to the Present Day." Second Edition. London, 1901.

Piry, A. Theophile : " Manuel de Langue Mandarine ou Recueil Idéologique en Chinois, Francais et Anglais des termes, locutions et idiotismes de la Langue Mandarine du Nord (Texte Anglais par M. Ch. H. Oliver, M.A.). Shanghai, 1895.

Williams, S. Wells : " The Middle Kingdom. A Survey of the Geography, Government, Literature, Social Life, Arts and History of the Chinese Empire and its Inhabitants." Revised edition. In two volumes. New York, 1904.

EXTRACTS FROM CRITICISMS OF THE RUSSIAN EDITION OF "THE PRESENT DAY POLITICAL ORGANIZATION OF CHINA."

(*Translation.*)

It is with great pleasure we note, and heartily welcome, the appearance of this creditable work, produced by the combined effort of H. S. Brunnert and V. V. Hagelstrom, former students of the Department of Oriental Languages of St. Petersburg University, with the active and intelligent assistance of the Chinese Secretary of the Imperial Russian Legation at Peking.

We venture to say with confidence that in the list of works of this kind, enumerated by the authors in their "Sources of Information," the present volume, in the abundance, variety and up-to-dateness of the information supplied, has no equal; and its modest title by no means describes its contents in full.

The book gives more than the "Present Day Political Organization of China;" it discusses other, not less interesting, institutions of China now in the process of reformation, for instance, education, military forces, banks, railways, telegraphs and telephones, colonization, judicial establishments, etc.

Our attention was particularly attracted to the comparatively large portion concerning education, in which is found much valuable and detailed information as to the present system of education in China in general and, in particular, the types and management of present day schools—elementary, primary, middle, higher, normal, professional and special, universities and schools for females. At the same time there is much information concerning educational schemes, educational administration and the teaching staff.

When considering new establishments the authors do not confine themselves to the mere enumeration of their functions and those of their sections; exact dates of the Imperial Decrees calling the institutions concerned into existence are given and, in many cases, these Decrees are quoted, either in part or in toto. When reviewing reformed establishments they invariably add historical comments.

The translation of the Chinese designations of the numerous institutions, posts and ranks into Russian, to correspond to our nomenclature—no light task— has been exceedingly well done.

In conclusion, I venture to express my opinion that this work, being the best reference book on the Present Political Organization of China, will prove a necessity in reading books concerning government establishments which China, in consequence of the reform movement, has been lately so enriched and, also, will be found indispensable in the examination of government and private records and documents.—P. S. I'OPOFF, *Professor of Chinese at St. Petersburg University, sometime Chinese Secretary of H. I. R. M's. Legation, Peking.*

Nous connaissions jusqu'ici très imparfaitement l'organisation politique de la Chine. Quelques services qu'aient rendus le "Chinese Government" de Mayers et les "Mélanges sur l'Administration" du P. Hoang, aucun de ces deux ouvrages n'etait suffisamment détaillé, et d'ailleurs l'un et l'autre sont antérieurs à la plupart des réformes qui ont transformé les rouages du gouvernement chinois. Aussi ne pouvons-nous qu'accueillir avec le plus vif empressement le volumineux ouvrage dans lequel MM. Brunnert et Hagelstrom, sous le contrôle de M.

Kolessoff, out étudié avec un soin extrême l'organisation politique contemporaine ; toutes les innovations y ont été indiquées ; pour beaucoup d'entre elles on a noté la date exacte où elles ont été promulguées et on a cité le texte du décret qui les a instituées ; il y a là une foule de renseignements que, dès maintenant, on aurait de la peine à retrouver et que plus tard l'historien recueillera précieusement. Nous souhaitons très vivement que cet ouvrage soit traduit en une langue accessible à un plus grand nombre de lecteurs que le russe ; d'autre part nous voudrions y voir ajouter l'indication des mots mandchous qui entrent dans la composition d'un assez grand nombre de titres et qui sont simplement transcris en chinois.—*T'oung Pao*. Décembre 1910, No. 5.

. . . . Only a sinologue of high standing would be justified in criticising the work of Messrs. Brunnert and Hagelstrom ; whereas even the tyro to whom transliterations of ideographs are but meaningless sounds can see at a glance that in this Russian publication the authors and compilers have successfully accomplished an almost colossal task of profound and tireless erudition. Their work appears to be in the most literal sense an exhaustive one of reference in which all the essential data in any way connected with Chinese metropolitan and provincial executive and administrative institutions may be ascertained at a glance. The volume consists of four sections, with appendices, an index, a key to the Chinese readings, a list of authorities, and errata. The first section deals with the Emperor and Imperial House, the metropolitan governmental institutions other than Ministries. The second comprises the Ministries, police, banks, mints, Customs, temples, education, census, libraries, military and naval matters. The third treats of the Metropolitan Province and Manchuria, and the provincial administration and colonial possessions of China ; while the fourth deals with such subjects as officials despatched on special missions, institutions reformed or abolished, honourable ranks, hereditary and honourable titles, posthumous ranks and titles, rewards, orders, etc.

It is a pity that a work of such comprehensive scope must remain a sealed book to the majority of English readers, who would otherwise, at a juncture like the present, be eager to avail themselves of the most up-to-date information regarding the Chinese movement in the direction of constitutional reform. Thus in the first section are described the new Chinese Parliament to be opened in 1913, the Imperial Council, the Imperial Chancellery, the Committee of Ministers, the Constitutional Reforms Commission, the Constitutional Chamber and Provincial Advisory Committees, the Commission on Legislative Reforms, the Anti-Opium Commission, the General Staff, the Committee on Fleet Re-organization and the Chief Naval Administration ; and in the second part will be found much valuable material concerning the old-style and modern Chinese armies, the Chinese fleet, Courts and prisons, agriculture, railways, telegraphs and telephones. The intrinsic usefulness of all this classified matter to the specialist is enhanced by the fact that in every instance the authors have been careful to furnish the Chinese terminology with a Russian transliteration.

Before taking leave of a really monumental piece of work which may justly be said to represent the last word on the subject, we cannot do better than translate some extracts from the strikingly modest yet illuminating preface . . . . *Japan Chronicle*, 10th October, 1910.

For Product Safety Concerns and Information please contact our EU
representative GPSR@taylorandfrancis.com
Taylor & Francis Verlag GmbH, Kaufingerstraße 24, 80331 München, Germany

9 780415 515207